Canadian
Law Dictionary

Seventh Edition

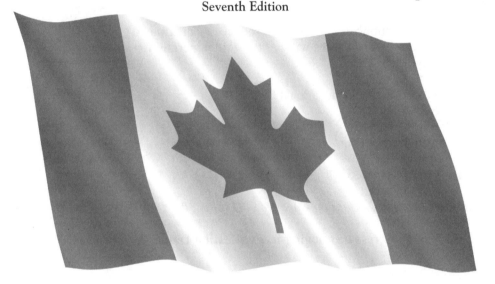

Steve Coughlan, Ph.D., LL.B
Professor, Schulich School of Law
Dalhousie University

Contributing Authors

John A. Yogis, Q.C., LL.B, LL.M
Former Professor of Law
Dalhousie University

Catherine Cotter, LL.B, MLIS
Reference Librarian
Gerard V. LaForest Library
University of New Brunswic

BARRON'S

Published by Barron's Educational Series, Inc.
750 Third Avenue
New York, NY 10017
www.barronseduc.com

ISBN: 978-1-4380-0151-7

Library of Congress Catalog Card No. 2013005330

Library of Congress Cataloging-in-Publication Data

Yogis, John A., 1940–
   Canadian law dictionary / Steve Coughlan, Ph.D., LL.B, LL.M Professor,
Schulich School of Law, Dalhousie University; John Yogis, Q.C., LL.B,
LL.M former Professor of Law, Dalhousie University; Catherine Cotter,
LL.B, MLIS Reference/Instruction Librarian, Gerard V. Laforest, Law
Library University of New Brunswick. — Seventh Edition.
     pages cm
   Includes bibliographical references and index.
   ISBN 978-1-4380-0151-7
  1. Law—Canada—Dictionaries. I. Coughlan, Steve, 1957–
II. Cotter, Catherine (Catherine Anne) III. Title.
   KE183.Y63   2013
   349.71′03—dc23   2013005330

9 8 7 6 5 4 3

Contents

Preface
to the Seventh Edition

When I was a first-year law student thirty years ago, I had the good fortune to be taught legal research and writing by John Yogis. Indeed, I worked for him as his research assistant the following summer, when among his projects was the first edition of this dictionary. John was an effective teacher, a helpful supervisor, and a good colleague when I eventually joined the faculty at Dalhousie, and so it is a special pleasure to have been invited to take over this project now that he has decided to let it pass into other hands.

Quite apart from all the work John and his later co-author Catherine Cotter put into the first six editions, I am grateful to many people for their contributions to this seventh edition. I must single out my extremely capable research assistant, Alex Gorlewski, who not only undertook the thankless task (other than these thanks, of course) of finding new cases and more recent editions of texts to include in existing definitions, but along the way found the time to suggest and draft dozens of new definitions and make many other useful suggestions for changes. In addition, I want to thank the Schulich Academic Excellence Fund and the Dean of the Schulich School of Law, Kim Brooks, for providing the funding to hire Alex. Further, many of my colleagues cheerfully tolerated me showing up unannounced at their door seeking advice on the nuances of particular words in their fields of expertise. My sincere thanks go to Bruce Archibald, Sarah Bradley, Elaine Craig, Rob Currie, Diana Ginn, Philip Girard, Michael Hadskis, Lorraine Lafferty, Jennifer Llewellyn, Geoff Loomer, Constance MacIntosh, Graham Reynolds, Len Rotman, Phil Saunders, Jonathan Shapiro, Sheila Wildeman, and Faye Woodman. I am also grateful to the following individuals for their contributions: Mark Lewis and David Michels in the law library; my assistant, Michelle Kirkwood; and two anonymous reviewers who suggested new dictionary entries. Sandy Beeman in particular, as well as Martin LaPlante and Peter O'Brien offered valuable assistance on Latin pronunciation. Finally, I am appreciative of my wife, Dale Darling (herself a former research assistant to John Yogis) for all her support.

This seventh edition contains over six hundred new definitions, as well as changes throughout the work that reflect the latest developments in the law. New definitions have focused particularly on the areas of Aboriginal justice, the *Canadian Charter of Rights and Freedoms*, criminal law, evidence, intellectual property, international law, and police powers, but updates have been made with relation to many other areas of law as well.

Key to Effective Use
of This Dictionary

Alphabetization: The reader should note carefully that all entries have been alphabetized letter by letter rather than word by word. Thus *ab initio,* for example, is located between *abeyance* and *aboriginal rights,* rather than at the beginning of the listings. In the same manner, *actionable* appears before, not after, *action ex delicto.*

Brackets: Material in brackets [thus] represents an alternate expression for (or another form of) the preceding word or phrase. For example, **"MAIL BOX RULE [POSTAL ACCEPTANCE RULE]"** indicates that "postal acceptance rule" is another term sometimes used for the "mail box rule," while "ABROGATE [ABROGATION]" includes a form the reader is likely to encounter.

Cross References: **Boldface type** has been used within the text of the definitions and at the end of them to call attention to terms that are defined in the dictionary as separate entries and that should be understood and, if necessary, referred to specifically, in order to understand the word whose definition has been sought in the first instance.

Terms emphasized in this manner include many that appear in the dictionary but in a different form or as a different part of speech. For example, although the term "alienate" may appear in boldface in the text of a definition, it will not be found as a separate entry, since it is expected that the reader can readily draw the meaning of that term from the definition given for the word "alienation"; likewise, the reader coming across the word "estop" printed in boldface should not despair upon discovering that it is not in fact an entry here, but should instead refer to the term "estoppel."

Also, the reader must not assume that the appearance of a word in regular type precludes the possibility of its having been included as a separate entry, for by no means has every such word been printed in boldface in every definition. Terms emphasized in this manner include primarily those an understanding of which was thought to be essential or very helpful in the reader's quest for adequate comprehension. Many terms that represent very basic and frequently used concepts, such as "property," "possession" and "crime," are often printed in regular type. Furthermore, boldface is used to emphasize a word only the first time that word appears in a particular definition.

Gender: Every attempt has been made to use gender neutral terms throughout this book. However, where quotations from other sources do not use gender-neutral language, that has not been changed.

Sources: Many entries in this dictionary refer to statutes or judicial decisions. Canadian statutes and judicial decisions are freely available at *www.canlii.org.*

Subentries: Words printed in SMALL CAPITALS include:
(1) those whose significance as legal concepts was not deemed sufficiently substantial to warrant their inclusion in the dictionary as separate entries, though some explanation or illumination was thought desirable, and
(2) those which, though important, are most logically and coherently defined in the context of related or broader terms.
Words emphasized in this manner either have been separately and individually defined in the manner of "subcategories" or have been defined or illustrated, implicitly or explicitly, within the text of the definition of the main entry.

Pronunciation Guide

The purpose in providing this pronunciation guide is *not* to indicate the "correct" mode of pronouncing the various terms; rather, the goal has been to afford the user a guide to an acceptable pronunciation of them, based largely on widespread legal usage and the author's personal preferences.

The phonetic symbols used here were drawn from what the author perceives as a commonly recognised and understood "system." The following guide should be of some assistance in interpreting them

ă as in *a*t

ā as in *a*pe

â as in f*a*re

ä as in *a*rmy

ȧ as in *a*rrive

aủ as in o*u*t

ĕ as in *e*gg

ē as in *e*vil

ê as in *ea*rn

ĭ as in *i*ll

ī as in *i*ce

ŏ as in *o*x

ō as in *o*pen

ô as on *o*rgy

ŭ as in *u*p

ū as in r*u*de

û as in *u*rge

A

ABANDONMENT The surrender of interests, rights or property by one person to another. It includes both the intention to abandon and the actual physical act of relinquishment. One abandons a **contract** when one knows or believes the contract to be incomplete and fails to complete it—e.g., where the owner abandons a construction contract by repudiating it and the contractor accepts the **repudiation**, thereby terminating the contract. *Taylor v. Foran and Ontario Loan and Debenture Co.* (1931), 44 B.C.L.R. 529 (Co.Ct.). The fact that no work has been done on a project does not necessarily mean that there has been abandonment. Cessation of work is not necessarily abandonment of work. *Dieleman Planer Co. Ltd. v. Elizabeth Townhouses Ltd.*, [1972] 4 W.W.R. 236 (B.C.Co.Ct.) [1975] 2 S.C.R. 449. Similarly, a union can abandon its collective bargaining rights against an employer, but more than mere inactivity is needed. *United Brotherhood of Carpenters and Joiners of America, Local 1985 v. Graham Construction and Engineering Ltd.*, 2008 SKCA 67.

One can abandon or desert a child *Criminal Code*, R.S.C. 1985, c. C–46, s. 218. *R. v. Hudon*, [1965] R.L. 203 (Que.S.C.). Abandoning a child under the age of ten is a **hybrid offence** and can result in a prison term under the *Criminal Code*, R.S.C. 1985, c. C–46, s. 218. *R. v. A.D.H.*, 2011 SKCA 6.

A defence of abandonment may be used to disprove common intent in s. 21(2) of the *Criminal Code*. It has two elements: "The first is that there is a change of heart or an abandonment of the common purpose. Secondly, the change of heart or abandonment of common intention, where it is practical to do so, must be communicated in a timely manner." *R. v. S.R.B.*, 2009 ABCA 45.

A person can abandon a privacy interest in something, with the result that any investigation of that thing will not constitute a search or seizure. "The question is whether the claimant to s. 8 protection has acted in relation to the subject matter of his privacy claim in such a manner as to lead a reasonable and independent observer to conclude that his continued assertion of a privacy interest is unreasonable in the totality of the circumstances." *R. v. Patrick,* 2009 SCC 17.

An application for a **trade-mark** can be deemed to be abandoned where the Registrar concludes the applicant is in default in the prosecution of an application filed under the Act. *Trade-marks Act*, R.S.C., 1985, c. T–13, s. 36.

ABATABLE NUISANCE A **nuisance** that can be removed or rendered harmless, and whose continuation is not authorized under law.

ABATEMENT A reduction or rebate. For example, in **real property**, the purchase price of a plot of land may be abated because of a defect in **title**. See *Sokoloff v. 5 Rosehill Avenue Developments Inc.* (1998), 21 R.P.R. (3d) 176 (Ont.Gen. Div.). An ABATEMENT OF TAXES is a tax rebate or decrease. An ABATEMENT OF A LEGACY is the reduction or extinction of a **legacy** to a **beneficiary** by payment of debts owed by the **decedent's estate**. Also when assets do not satisfy a debt, a proportionate deduction of the balance due may be made. The ABATEMENT OF AN ACTION signifies its death.

ABDUCTION The **criminal** or **tortious** act of taking another person by **fraud**, persuasion or violence. The *Criminal Code*, R.S.C. 1985, c. C–46 limits abduction to the taking of young persons, as opposed to **kidnapping** or hostage-taking: see ss. 279–286. The consent of a young person is not a **defence** to a charge of abduction, because the offence is one against the rights of the parents, not the child. *R. v. Chartrand*, [1994] 2 S.C.R. 864.

ABET To encourage another in the commission of an **offence**. Abetting "includes encouraging, instigating, promoting or procuring the **crime** to be committed." *R. v. Greyeyes,* [1997] 2 S.C.R. 825. By s. 21(1)(c) of the

Criminal Code, R.S.C. 1985, c. C–46, a person who abets another in the commission of an offence is a party to that offence. "Mere presence at the scene of a crime is not sufficient to ground culpability. Something more is needed." *R. v. Dunlop and Sylvester,* [1979] 2 S.C.R. 881. See also **aid and abet**.

ABEYANCE Generally denotes an undetermined or incomplete state of affairs. In British law, an inheritance that has no present owner is in abeyance. In property, when a **freehold estate** is not vested in a presently existing person, it is in abeyance. Common law holds that there must always be a **tenant** of the freehold.

AB INITIO (*ăb ĭn-ĭ′-shē-ō*) Lat.: from the beginning. Most commonly used in referring to the time when a **contract**, **statute**, marriage, or **deed** becomes legally valid; e.g., an unlawful marriage is void ab initio, from the outset.

ABORIGINAL PEOPLES [OF CANADA] Includes the Indian, Inuit and Métis peoples of Canada. *Constitution Act, 1982,* Part II, Rights of the Aboriginal Peoples of Canada, s. 35(2). See **aboriginal rights**.

ABORIGINAL RIGHTS "[I]n order to be an aboriginal right, an activity must be an element of a practice, custom, or tradition integral to the distinctive culture of the aboriginal group claiming the right." *R. v. Van der Peet,* [1996] 2 S.C.R. 507. Different aboriginal groups have different rights, but such rights can include aboriginal land title and the right to hunt, fish, or log. See *R. v. Guerin* (1984), 13 D.L.R. (4th) 321 (S.C.C.); *Simon v. The Queen,* [1985] 2 S.C.R. 387; *R. v. Marshall,* [1999] 3 S.C.R. 533, *R. v. Powley,* 2003 SCC 43. Aboriginal rights existed at common law, but now are constitutionally protected in s. 25 of the **Canadian Charter of Rights and Freedoms**. Section 35(1) of the *Constitution Act, 1982* recognises and affirms the existing aboriginal and **treaty** rights of aboriginal peoples. See *R. v. Sparrow* (1990), 70 D.L.R. (4th) 385. See **extinguishment**.

ABORIGINAL RIGHTS (LANDS) "[T]hose lands on which only specific aboriginal rights exist (e.g., right to hunt for food, social and ceremonial purposes) because the occupation and use by the particular group of aboriginal people is too limited and, as a result, does not meet the criteria for the recognition, at **common law**, of aboriginal title." *R. v. Van der Peet,* [1996] 9 W.W.R. 1 at 50 (S.C.C.).

ABORIGINAL TITLE "Aboriginal title is the aspect of aboriginal rights related specifically to aboriginal claims to land; it is the way in which the common law recognizes aboriginal land rights." *R. v. Van der Peet,* [1996] 2 S.C.R. 507. It is a unique bundle of **property** rights associated with land exclusively occupied by an aboriginal community before the assertion of British sovereignty. Aboriginal title can only be sold to the **Crown** and "is held communally by the members of an Aboriginal nation." The right to exclusive occupation and use is conferred by aboriginal title and is not limited to integral traditional practices, but "the use to which the land is put must be consistent with the nature of the group's historic attachment to that land." For example, aboriginal title normally includes mineral rights and lands which can be mined, although it may not be a customary practice. However, if the land was historically a place of ceremonial significance, then mining this area may violate the restriction on its use. B. Ziff, *Principles of Property Law* 197–98 (5th ed. 2010). See *Delgamuukw v. British Columbia,* [1997] 3 S.C.R. 1010.

ABORTION Until 1988, abortion, or procuring a miscarriage of a female, was an **indictable offence** under s. 287 of the *Criminal Code,* R.S.C. 1985, c. C–46. The Supreme Court ruled in *Morgentaler, Smoling, and Scott v. The Queen* (1988), 37 C.C.C. (3d) 449 that this provision violated a woman's right to security of the person, as guaranteed by s. 7 of the **Canadian Charter of Rights and Freedoms**.

See also s. 288 (supplying noxious things with knowledge of the intention to use them for procuring a miscarriage).

ABRIDGMENT A condensation or digest—e.g., the *Canadian Abridgment*, which, **inter alia**, contains digests of reported decisions of the **Supreme Court of Canada**, the **Federal Court**, and the **courts** of the common-law provinces and of Quebec.

ABROGATE [ABROGATION] To annul, revoke or repeal. In law, abrogation is the annulment of a former law by legislative power, by constitutional authority or by usage. Section 2 of the **Canadian Bill of Rights**, 1960, c. 44, reprinted R.S.C. 1985, App. III, states that unless expressly declared otherwise, Acts of the Canadian **Parliament** will be construed so as not to abrogate the provisions of the *Bill.* See *R. v. Drybones*, [1970] S.C.R. 282; but compare *Attorney-General of Canada v. Lavell & Bedard,* [1974] S.C.R. 1349. See also the **Canadian Charter of Rights and Freedoms**, ss. 21, 22, 25, 29, contained in the *Constitution Act, 1982.* Compare **derogate**.

ABSCOND To travel secretly out of the **jurisdiction** of the courts, or to hide in order to avoid a legal process. One must intend to be willfully and permanently absent rather than temporarily absent with intention of returning. *Williams v. Sanford* (1911), 10 E.L.R. 151 (N.S.Co.Ct.). "One who absconds from a particular place not only leaves it but leaves it with the purpose of frustrating or rending more difficult, by his absence, the effective application to him of the laws current in the jurisdiction whence he absconds." *Carolus v. Minister of National Revenue* (1976), 76 DTC 6359 (F.C.T.D.) Some jurisdictions do not require clandestine departure. An ABSCONDING DEBTOR is one who remains out of the jurisdiction with the intent to defeat or delay his **creditors**. Various jurisdictions have defined the absconding **debtor** by **statute**, e.g., the *Absconding Debtors Act,* R.S.N.B. 2011, c. 100. In **criminal law**, abscond means to voluntarily be absent from a trial in order to prevent its continuation. Where an **accused** absconds during a criminal trial, s. 475 of the *Criminal Code* R.S.C. 1985, c. C–46 permits the trial to continue. In that context the term "imports that the accused has voluntarily absented himself from his trial for the purpose of impeding or frustrating the trial, or with the intention of avoiding its consequences." *R. v. Garofoli* (1988), 41 C.C.C. (3d) 97, 64 C.R. (3d) 193 (Ont.C.A.), aff'd [1990] 2 S.C.R. 1421.

ABSOLUTE DISCHARGE A direction of the court in which a person who has either pleaded guilty or been found guilty of an offence is deemed not to have been convicted.

An absolute discharge is only available in situations where (1) there is no minimum penalty for the offence; (2) the **offence** is not punishable by imprisonment for fourteen years or life; (3) the **Court** considers an absolute discharge to be in the best interests of the **accused** and not contrary to the public interest. *Criminal Code*, R.S.C. 1985, c. C–46, s. 730.

ABSOLUTE LIABILITY The imposition of liability without fault. Absolute liability offences are a type of **regulatory offence** in which liability is based on proof that the **accused** committed the prohibited act. Unlike **strict liability** offences, absolute liability offences do not afford the **accused** the defence of due diligence or **mistake of fact**. Because of the possible harshness of holding people absolutely accountable, the courts will only interpret a regulatory offence as being one of absolute liability if there is a clear indication that the legislature intended it to be an absolute liability offence. An absolute liability offence that has imprisonment as a sanction violates s. 7 of the *Charter.* See *Ref. Re Section 94(2) of the Motor Vehicle Act (B.C.),* [1985] 2 S.C.R. 486; *R. v. Wholesale Travel Group Inc.,* [1991] 3 S.C.R. 154. All regulatory offences are **prima facie** strict liability offences until proven otherwise. To determine if the offence is one of absolute liability, the court will look at the (1) overall regulatory pattern; (2) subject matter; (3) importance of penalties (fines and/or imprisonment); and (4) precision of the language used. *R. v. Sault Ste. Marie* (1978), 40 C.C.C. (2d) 353 (S.C.C.).

ABSOLUTE PRIVILEGE See **libel**; **privilege**.

ABSQUE HOC (*äb'-skwā hŏk*) Lat.: without this; if it had not been for this. A technical phrase used in pleading at common law by way of special **traverse**. It presents the negative portion of a plea.

ABSTRACT OF TITLE A chronological summary of all recorded instruments and events that entitle a person to **property**. It is a history of the **title** containing reference to conveyances, **grants**, **wills**, and **transfers**, including all the **encumbrances** to which the property is subject (**liens**, **judgments**, **restrictive covenants**, rights of way), and whether the latter have been released. It is designed to allow the purchaser to determine that there is clear and good title. See **chain of title**.

ABSURDITY PRINCIPLE A principle of **statutory interpretation** applied in the case of an ambiguous provision, allowing a **court** to infer that the **legislature** did not intend absurd results. "Where a provision is open to two or more interpretations, the absurdity principle may be employed to reject interpretations which lead to negative consequences, as such consequences are presumed to have been unintended by the legislature." *Ontario v. Canadian Pacific Ltd.*, [1995] 2 S.C.R. 1031. Absurdity is a factor to consider in the interpretation of ambiguous statutory provisions but is not itself an independent rule. *R. v. McIntosh*, [1995] 1 S.C.R. 686.

ABUSE OF DISCRETION A legal appellate technique for reviewing the exercise of **discretion** by lower courts and **administrative tribunals**; a rationale to overturn determinations that are unreasonable, arbitrary, or inconsistent with the facts and circumstances before a court.

The *"abuse of discretion"* standard of review is also used in administrative settings. Thus, where a board has misused discretionary power, the misuse may be corrected by a reviewing court.

The Crown **Prosecutor** has broad discretion whether to prosecute, and it is very difficult to prove abuse of discretion. See *R.v. Nixon*, 2011 SCC 34.

ABUSE OF PATENT Refusing to **licence** the use of a patented article or doing so under unfairly prejudicial conditions. See *Patent Act*, RSC 1985, c P–4, s. 65(2).

ABUSE OF PROCESS A use of the criminal or civil process for a purpose other than that intended by law. In a civil action it is an abuse of process to allow a party to re-litigate a position that it has already advanced and lost. *Freedman v. Reemark Sterling I Ltd.*, (2003) 62 O.R. (3d) 743 (Ont. C.A.). "[I]t is an abuse of process to invoke the criminal law in order to advance private rights." *R. v. Miles of Music* (1989), 74 O.R. (2d) 518 (C.A.). The tort of abuse of process has four elements: (1) the plaintiff is a party to a legal process initiated by the defendant; (2) the legal process was initiated for the predominant purpose of furthering some indirect, collateral, and improper objective; (3) the defendant took or made a definite act or threat in furtherance of the improper purpose; and (4) some measure of special damage has resulted. *Harris v. GlaxoSmithKline Inc.*, 2010 ONCA 872. In criminal law, the **common law** doctrine of abuse of process has been merged with s. 7 of the *Charter* to provide a remedy against prosecutorial misconduct. There are two categories of abuse of process in that context: "(1) prosecutorial conduct affecting the fairness of the trial; and (2) prosecutorial conduct that 'contravenes fundamental notions of justice and thus undermines the integrity of the judicial process.'" *R. v. Nixon*, 2011 SCC 34.

ABUT [ABUTTING] To adjoin; to cease at point of contact; to empty onto. *Catkey Construction (Toronto) Ltd. v. Bankes,* [1971] 1 O.R. 205 at 206 (C.A.) defined an abutting owner as "an owner, the front, rear or side of whose property is contiguous to *a side of* a highway [in this case] which is stopped up, but does not mean or include an owner whose property is contiguous to either terminus of such a highway."

In its primary meaning, abutting implies a closer proximity than does the term *adjacent,* and whether adjacent is to be interpreted as lying near to or actually adjoining depends on the facts of each situation.

Abutting **property** is **real property** that borders on another property.

ACCELERATION The hastening of the time for the vesting and enjoyment of an **estate** or other property right that would otherwise have occurred at a later time. This term applies to **personalty** as well as **realty**. It is associated with gifts devised by **will**, to the vesting of a **remainder** due to the premature termination of a **preceding estate**, and with clauses commonly found in **mortgage** agreements (see **acceleration clause**), stipulating that an entire debt may be deemed due upon the default of a single instalment, or other duty of the borrower.

ACCELERATION CLAUSE A provision in a **contract** or document that, upon the occurrence of a certain event, a party's expected interest in the subject **property** will become prematurely **vested**. Such a clause is often found in instalment contracts and can cause an entire debt to become due upon failure to pay an instalment as agreed.

Such clauses are common and are generally enforceable, subject to statutory exceptions such as the *Residential Tenancy Act,* S.B.C. 2002, c. 78, s. 22, which renders acceleration clauses void and unenforceable.

ACCEPTANCE 1. In contracts, acceptance to create a binding **contract** is the assent to an **offer** by words or conduct on the part of the person to whom the offer is made. Acceptance must be unequivocal and can be by way of oral or written statement as well as by conduct. "Whether or not there has been acceptance depends upon whether the offeree has so conducted himself that a reasonable man would believe that he has accepted, or is accepting, the offer in question, at least as long as the offeror has acted on such belief." *Samek v. Black Tusk Energy Inc.*, 2000 ABQB 684, quoting Fridman, *The Law of Contract in Canada* (6th ed. 2011) 47. Acceptance may also be governed by **statutes**, as, e.g., the *Sale of Goods Act,* R.S.O. 1990, c. S. 1, s. 34.

2. In **property** law, it is an element essential to completion of a gift **inter vivos** and a **donatio mortis causa**. The property must be accepted by the recipient as a gift; however, a valid gift may be made without the **donee's** knowledge, subject to his right to repudiate it upon learning of the transfer. *Horne v. Huston,* [1919] 16 O.W.N. 173 (H.C.). There is a presumption of acceptance of a gift subject to the donee's right of refusal. *Benquesus v. Canada* [2006] 3 C.T.C. 2191 (Tax Ct.).

3. Acceptance by a bank of a cheque or other **negotiable instrument** is a formal procedure whereby the bank promises to pay the payee named on the **cheque**. Acceptance is the drawee's [bank's] signed engagement to honour the **draft** [negotiable instrument] as presented. It must be written on the draft and may consist of the **drawee's** signature alone. It becomes operative when completed by **delivery** or, notification. *Bills of Exchange Act* R.S.C. 1985, c. B–4, s. 2.

4. A **solicitor** may choose to accept service of a **pleading** or court document on behalf of a client.

ACCESS In **family law**, the right of a parent or other person who does not have **custody** to visit with a child.

ACCESSION 1. A doctrine intended primarily "to resolve disputes in which two or more **chattels** become attached, such as when A's paint is applied to B's car…. In relation to the more conventional situation of the fusion of two chattels, the title of one of the chattels is subsumed in the other…the law appears to prescribe that an accession is made to the 'principal' or dominant chattel, which has been taken to mean the item that has the greatest (market) value. However, doubts have been raised as to whether monetary worth should be the exclusive criterion." B. Ziff, *Principles of Property Law* 123–24 (5th ed. 2010). Compare **confusion of goods**.

2. A method for states to become parties to a **treaty** for which they did not take part in its original negotiation phase. Accession has the same legal effect as **ratification** at international law. P. Malanczuk, *Akehurst's Modern Introduction to International Law* 133 (7th ed. 1997).

ACCESSORY *Particeps criminis quasi accedens ad culpam* [as though assenting to the offence]. An accessory performs acts that facilitate others in the commission or attempted commission of a criminal **offence** or in avoiding apprehension for **crime**. Compare **accomplice**; **aid and abet**; **conspirator**.
ACCESSORY AFTER THE FACT As defined by s. 23(1) of the *Criminal Code, R.S.C.* 1985, c. C–46, "one who, knowing that a person has been a party to the offence, receives, comforts or assists that person for the purpose of enabling that person to escape."
A person can be convicted of being an accessory after the fact even if the person assisted cannot be convicted: see s. 23.1 of the *Criminal Code*. This rule applies even if the person assisted has been acquitted. *R. v. Shalaan* (1997), 159 N.S.R. (2d) 285 (C.A.). See also ss. 240, 463, 469 of the *Criminal Code*.

ACCESSORY BEFORE THE FACT At common law, one who counseled, procured, or commanded another to commit a crime. The *Criminal Code* has replaced the common law distinctions with s. 21. *R. v. Hibbert*, [1995] 2 S.C.R. 973. Under s. 21, the issue is whether the accused **aided or abetted**, or had a **common intention** with the person who committed an offence. See also s. 22, making it an offence to **counsel** another person to commit an offence.

ACCESS TO JUSTICE The ability of individuals to make use of the courts and other aspects of the legal system. Access to justice concerns focus on access by low- and middle-income earners, particularly with regard to **civil law** and **family law** matters. See **legal aid**.

ACCOMMODATION ENDORSEMENT The co-signing of an instrument without **consideration**, solely for the benefit of the holder, creating a liability on the cosigner should the other (accommodated) party fail to pay. In England, this is an ACCOMMODATION BILL. See **endorsement**.

ACCOMMODATION PARTY The *Bills of Exchange Act,* R.S.C. 1985, c. B–4, s. 54(l), defines an accommodation party to a bill as a person "who has signed a bill as **drawer**, acceptor or endorser, without receiving value therefor and for the purpose of lending his name to some other party." The party is gratuitously obligating himself to guarantee the debt of the accommodated party. The accommodation party has a right of recourse against the principal. *Dartmouth Community Credit Union Ltd. v. Smith & Hefler* (1977), 24 N.S.R. (2d) 541 (S.C.).
"A name is lent for the purpose of this concept if it is used to support or aid the obtaining of credit by the person to whom it is 'lent.' This necessarily implies that the latter person is himself obligated to the principal creditor in respect of the debt in question. It then follows that the accommodation party will in such circumstances become the **surety** for or guarantor of the person accommodated." *Bank of Montreal v. Kilpatrick* (1976), 18 N.S.R. (2d) 173 at 177 (S.C.A.D.).

ACCOMPLICE One who is involved in the commission of an offence in some manner. "Accomplice" is not a term of art in criminal law. **Secondary liability** depends on whether the person is a **party to the crime** for having **aided**, **abetted**, had a **common intention**, or **counseled** the offence. The fact that a witness was an accomplice has no automatic significance with regard to the treatment of that witness's testimony: "There is no special category for 'accomplices.' An accomplice is to be treated like any other witness testifying at a criminal trial and the judge's conduct, if he chooses to give his opinion, is governed by the general rules." *R. v. Vetrovec*, [1982] 1 S.C.R. 811.

Compare **accessory**; **aid and abet**; **conspirator**.

ACCORD AND SATISFACTION An agreement whereby one party agrees to accept a **consideration** to extinguish another's liability, usually less than what could be claimable under the contractual or other liability of such other party. "Accord and satisfaction is the purchase of a release from an obligation arising under **contract** or **tort** by means of any valuable **consideration**, not being the actual performance of the obligation itself. The accord is the agreement by which the obligation is discharged. The satisfaction is the consideration which makes the agreement operative." *British Russian Gazette & Trade Outlook Ltd. v. Associated Newspapers*, [1933] 2 K.B. 616 at 643–44; in *Bow Valley Husky (Bermuda) Ltd. v. Saint John Shipbuilding Ltd.*, [1997] 3 S.C.R. 1210.

See also *Somers v. Liberty School District*, [1928] 2 D.L.R. 334 (Alta. Dist.Ct.); *Re Cohen & Sweigman, ex parte Gelman,* [1925] 4 D.L.R. 359 (Ont.S.C.).

ACCOUNT 1. A registry of debts, credits and charges or a detailed statement of a series of receipts, credits and disbursements of money that has taken place between two or more persons. **2.** Any account with a bank, including a checking, interest or savings account.

In **equity**, the principal tool for awarding money is the ACTION OF ACCOUNT, as in an action for **breach of trust**, where the **trustee** has lost the **trust funds**. The action originally lay against certain persons who had received money or **property** belonging to another under circumstances that made them liable to give the owner an accounting, such as **guardians** and **bailiffs**. Their obligation was not to restore the exact thing received, but to make an accounting for its equivalent, or the profit derived from it.

In property law, where one TENANT IN COMMON (see **tenancy**) receives all the profits, he or she shall account for this in proportionate share to the other cotenants. See *Sproule v. Clements,* [1927] 2 W.W.R. 825 at 833–34 (B.C.C.A.).

ACCRETION The adding on or adhering of something to **property**; a means by which a property owner gains ownership of something additional. **1.** It usually refers to a gradual addition of sediment to the shore by the action of water; it is created by operation of natural causes. It is gradual and imperceptible, whereas **avulsion** is the sudden and perceptible loss or addition to land by the action of water. See, e.g., *Chuckry v. The Queen,* [1973] S.C.R. 694.

2. In the law of **succession**, accretion is said to take place when a **co-heir** or co-legatee dies before the property **vests**, or rejects the **inheritance** or **legacy**, or omits to comply with a **condition**, or becomes incapable of taking. The result is that the other heirs or legatees can share in that part. Where no contrary intention is shown by **will**, property that falls into the hands of the **executor** after the death of the **testator** is not distributable under the will unless such property is an accretion to the property disposed of by the will. *Re Jardine; Re Carey; Royal Trust Co. v. Jardine* (1955), 17 W.W.R. (N.S.) 197 (Alta. S.C.A.D.); *Royal Trust Co. & McMurray v. Crawford* (1956), 1 D.L.R. (2nd) 225 (S.C.C.).

3. In situations involving a **trust**, the term refers to any addition to the principal or to income that results from an extraordinary occurrence, that is, an occurrence that is forseeable but that rarely happens.

See **alluvion**; **avulsion**; **reliction**.

ACCRUE To accumulate; to come into existence as an enforceable claim. The time that a **cause of action** accrues determines how long a plaintiff may wait to initiate an **action** under the appropriate **statute of limitations**.

ACCUMULATION An increase by repeated additions; profit accruing on the sale of principal **assets**, or the increase derived from their investment, or both. The adding of interest or income of a fund to **principal** pursuant to provisions of a **will** or deed. The practice of the **executor** or **trustee** of amassing rents, dividends, and other incomes and treating them as **capital**, investing it and making new capital so that he is said to accumulate the fund; the capital and procured income constitute accumulations.

ACCUSATION A **charge** against a person or corporation. In its broadest sense it includes **indictment**, information, and any other form in which a charge of an **offence** can be made against an individual. It is a formal charge of having committed a criminal offence, made against a person in accordance with established legal procedure and laid before a magistrate.

It is a criminal offence to conspire to falsely accuse someone of an offence that person did not commit. (*Id.,* s. 465(1)(*b*)).

ACCUSE To directly and formally institute legal **proceedings** against a person, charging that he has committed an offence recognized by law, i.e., to **prosecute**; "threaten to accuse" means "threaten to prosecute." *R. v. Maloney* (1934), 40 R. de Jur. 351 (Que.Sess.Ct.).

ACCUSED A person against whom a criminal **proceeding** is initiated; the one who in a legal manner is held to answer for an offence at any stage of the proceedings, or against whom a complaint in any lawful manner is made, charging an offence, including all proceedings from the order of **arrest** to final execution. Generally, the person against whom a criminal proceeding is initiated is called the accused if one proceeds by **indictment**. If one proceeds by **summary conviction**, that person is referred to as the **defendant**. This reflects the **felony/misdemeanour** dichotomy in England.

ACKNOWLEDGEMENT [also ACKNOW-LEDGMENT] An admission, declaration, affirmation, or confession. It may refer to a formal declaration made before an authorized official, by a person who executed an instrument, that it is his free act and deed.

A written promise recognising a debt and an obligation to pay that entitles the **creditor** to bring an action within the limitation period from the date of the acknowledgement. See, e.g., *The Limitation of Actions Act,* R.S.N.S. 1989, c. 258, ss. 6, 8, 17.

A COELO USQUE AD CENTRUM (*ä sē'-lō us'-kwä äd sĕn'-trūm*) Lat.: from the sky to the centre of the earth. An outdated **property** maxim that marked the boundaries of land ownership. It has been modified by statute, for example, to allow for the flight patterns of aircraft over land or to permit the intrusion of power poles or lines into the airspace of property owners. See *Didow v. Alberta Power Ltd.,* [1988] 5 W.W.R. 606 (Alta.C.A.); *Hydro and Electric Energy Act,* R.S.A. 2000, c. H–16, subs. 37(3). See **cujus est solum ejus est usque ad coelum et usque ad inferos**.

ACQUIESCENCE An assent to an **infringement** of rights, by express or implied conduct, by which the right to equitable **relief** is usually lost. It takes place when a person, with full knowledge of his own rights and of acts that infringe them, has, by his conduct, led the persons responsible for the infringement to believe that he has waived or abandoned his rights.

To acquiesce connotes an element of knowledge on the part of the principal. There must be concurrence of the principal's will to act or a tacit concurrence. See *Udell v. M. N. R.,* [1969] C.T.C. 704 at 713 (Ex.Ct.).

ACQUIT To set free or judicially discharge from an **accusation** of suspicion of guilt. An individual is acquitted either when a **verdict** of not guilty has been rendered at the close of **trial** or on **appeal**.

ACQUITTAL 1. Broadly, the release or discharge of an acquitted individual, without further prosecution for the same act or transaction. See **double jeopardy**. **2.** In **contract**, the release from an obligation, liability, or engagement.

ACT A decree proclaiming the law in an area, passed by a competent legislative body, that may proclaim new law, alter or modify existing law, or repeal previously existing law. See **statute**.

ACTA The *Anti-Counterfeiting Trade Agreement*, a **treaty** intended to create an international regime for targeting **counterfeit** goods, generic medicines, and **copyright** infringement on the

Internet. Canada became a signatory to ACTA in October 2011, but as of May 2013 the treaty had not yet been ratified by enough countries to be in force.

ACTIO (*ak'-tē-ō*) Lat.: performance, activity; also, **proceedings**, lawsuit, **process**, **action**, permission for a **suit**.

ACTIO NON (*ak'-tē-ō nŏn*) Lat.: not an action. In **pleading**, a **nonfeasance**. See **nonsuit**.

ACTION [AT LAW] A judicial **proceeding** whereby one party (the **plaintiff** or the Crown) **prosecutes** another for a wrong or injury done, for damage caused, or for protection of a right or prevention of a wrong. A proceeding by which one party seeks in a court of justice to enforce some right or to restrain the commission of some wrong by another party. It includes both civil and criminal proceedings. *Dorosh v. Bentwood Chair & Table Mfg. Co.,* [1939] 3 D.L.R. 344 (Man.C.A.).

An action is the **common law** mode of obtaining redress for a wrong done or a duty not performed. *Frontenac County v. Kingston* (1871), 30 U.C.Q.B. 584 (Ont.O.B.).

An action or suit does not come to a conclusion when a trial judge renders his decision; as long as a right of appeal exists, the matter has not been finally determined. *Hampton Lumber Mills Ltd. v. Joy Logging Ltd.,* [1977] 2 W.W.R. 289 (B.C.S.C.).

ACTIONABLE Giving rise to a **cause of action**; thus, it refers to wrongful conduct that may form the basis of a civil **action**, as in ACTIONABLE NEGLIGENCE, which is the **breach** or non-performance of a **legal duty** through neglect or carelessness, resulting in damage to another. Describes an action that is afforded a **remedy** by law or **equity**.

ACTION EX DELICTO (*ĕks dĕ-lĭk'-tō*) Lat.: arising out of wrongs. A **cause of action** that arises out of fault, misconduct or **misfeance**, and through violation of a **duty**. It is essentially a **tort** action.

ACTION IN PERSONAM An action in which the plaintiff claims that the defen-

dant ought to give or do something good for the plaintiff.

An action **in personam** is brought "for the specific recovery of goods and **chattels**, or for damages or other redress for **breach of contract** or other injuries, of whatever description, the specific recovery of lands, tenements, and hereditaments only excepted...." *McConnell v. McGee* (1917), 37 D.L.R. 486 at 489 (Ont.S.C.A.D.). See **in personam**; **jurisdiction**.

ACTION IN REM An action in which the plaintiff claims that the thing in dispute is against all other persons.

An action **in rem** is "brought for the *specific* recovery of lands, tenements and hereditaments." *McConnell v. McGee* (1917), 37 D.L.R. 486 at 489 (Ont.S.C.A.D.).

It is a proceeding to determine the status of the thing itself. *Fry v. Botsford & McQuillan* (1902), 9 B.C.R. 234 (C.A.).

An action in rem is a proceeding to determine the disposition of an item under the court's control. Consequently, a judgment in rem exists where the court adjudicates upon the **title** or the right to **possession** of the **property** within its control. See *Warehouse Security Finance Co. Ltd. v. Oscar Niemi Ltd.,* [1944] 3 D.L.R. 568 (B.C.C.A.). See **in rem**; **jurisdiction**.

ACTION ON THE CASE An action started by a **writ** permitted as a result of the *Statute of Westminster II, 1285*. The **statute** contained a provision that a new kind of writ might be granted to a plaintiff in every case where his claim, though not exactly covered by an existing writ, was based upon circumstances like those that would have entitled him to a writ. An action started by one of these new writs was called an action on the case; the commonest type came to be the action of TRESPASS ON THE CASE (see **trespass**), where a plaintiff was unable to prove direct injury (or **trespass**) by the defendant but could show that harm resulted to him indirectly by some act that was like a trespass, e.g., the defendant's **negligence**.

ACTIONS [ACTIO] MIXTA "[A] mixed action is one partaking of the nature of real and personal actions, that is, one in which some **real property** is demanded, as well as personal **damages** for a wrong sustained." *McConnell v. McGee* (1917), 37 D.L.R. 486 at 489 (Ont.S.C.A.D.).

ACT OF GOD A manifestation of the forces of nature that are unpredictable and impossible to foresee; a result of the direct, immediate and exclusive operation of the forces of nature, uncontrolled or uninfluenced by the power of man and without human intervention, of such a character that it could not have been prevented or avoided by prudence or foresight. Examples are tempests, lightning, earthquakes, and a sudden illness or death of a person. *R. v. Syncrude Canada Ltd.* (2010) 30 Alta. L.R. (5th) 97 (Prov.Ct.)

ACTUAL DAMAGES See **damages**.

ACTUAL NOTICE See **notice**.

ACTUAL POSSESSION See **possession**.

ACTUAL VALUE See **market value**.

ACTUARY One who computes various insurance and property costs; especially, one who calculates the cost of life insurance risks and insurance premiums.

ACTUS REUS (*äk'-tŭs rā'-ŭs*) Lat.: loosely, the criminal act; more properly, the guilty act or deed of **crime**. Also referred to as the "external elements." Every criminal **offence** has two elements, the physical actus reus and the mental **mens rea**. The actus reus is the actual conduct of the **accused** that falls within the definition of the act proscribed coupled with any required circumstances; for example, the offence of causing a false alarm of fire requires that the accused cause an alarm of fire and also that the alarm is false. In Canada, all criminal offences are statutory (see *Criminal Code,* R.S.C. 1985, c. C–46, s. 9), and the statutory definition of the proscribed act or conduct, as construed by the courts, defines the actus reus. In order to constitute a criminal offence, the required mens rea, or intent to commit the offence, must be present concurrently. (For example, the actus reus of **murder** is **homicide**; the mens rea is the

intent—either willful or reckless—that the person die as a consequence of the act.)

Although mens rea is generally required, there are offences of **strict liability** and **absolute liability** for which one may be convicted on the strength of the actus reus alone. For offences of **strict liability**, the doing of the prohibited act **prima facie** imports the offence, leaving the burden on the accused to prove the defence of reasonable care or **due diligence**. As for **absolute liability**, there is no **mens rea**–related defence open to the accused. See *R. v. City of Sault Ste. Marie* (1978), 21 N.R. 295 (S.C.C.), where the city was held liable for polluting a river when unknown to the municipality a contractor disposed of collected waste into the water supply.

ADDITUR See **remittitur**.

ADEMPTION Removal or extinction. "[A] rule of the law of wills whereby a specific bequest 'adeems,' or fails, if at the testator's death the specified property is not found among his or her assets—either because the testator has parted with it, or because the property has 'ceased to conform to the description of it in the will,' or because the property has been wholly or partially destroyed. (J. MacKenzie, ed., Feeney's Canadian Law of Wills (4th ed., looseleaf, 2000) at s. 15.2.). *Wood Estate v. Arlotti-Wood*, 2004 BCCA 556. In some jurisdictions the common law rule has been limited by statute; see, e.g., *Substitute Decisions Act, 1992*, S.O. 1992, c. 30, s. 36(1). See *Diocesan Synod of Fredericton v. Perrett & New Brunswick Protestant Orphans Home*, [1955] S.C.R. 498.

ADHESION The process of an **Indian Band** becoming signatory to a **treaty** or other binding obligation that has already been concluded with another band or bands, such as the **numbered treaties**.

ADHESION CONTRACT Usually a contract in standard form prepared by one party and submitted to the other on a take-it-or-leave-it basis. It implies an inequality in bargaining power, resulting in the strict construction of or special rules concerning such contracts by the courts. See e.g., *Civil Code of Quebec.* L.R.Q.C.C–1991, arts 1435–37.

AD HOC (*ăd hŏk*) Lat.: for this; for this particular purpose. An ad hoc committee is one commissioned for a special purpose.

AD IDEM (*ăd áydĕm*) Lat.: at one. See **consensus ad idem**.

ADJECTIVE LAW [PROCEDURAL LAW] See **substantive law**.

ADJOINING Neighbouring, near, and sometimes adjacent. See *Dann v. Pitt* (1849), 6 N.B.R. 385 (S.C.). Adjoining, as applied to parcels of land, does not necessarily imply that the parcels are to be in physical contact with each other; houses in a row, with a house between two others, are all said to be adjoining. See *McKenzie v. Miniota Municipal School District,* [1931] 2 W.W.R. 105 (Man.K.B.). The word *adjoining* has been given a wide, liberal construction in the determination of whether land is adjoining another property. See *Huson v. The Township of South Norwich* (1892), 21 S.C.R. 669. Every owner of land is entitled to receive from the adjoining land such support [lateral physical pressure] for his land as is sufficient while it is in its natural state. See *Lotus Ltd. v. British Soda Co. Ltd.,* [1972] Ch. 123.

ADJOURN [ADJOURNMENT] To put off or delay to another time or place. **Parliament** and the provincial **legislatures** may be adjourned; or, in the discretion of the judge, a **court** may be adjourned. The term is also used in connection with public and company meetings. An adjournment may be a mere suspension of the original meeting or sitting. If the adjournment is final, it is said to be **sine die**.

ADJUDICATION "A deliberated judicial decision [which] has been come to after a hearing at which both sides ... at least had an opportunity of being heard." *Stewart v. Braun & Patterson,* [1924] 2 W.W.R. 1103 at 1107 (Man.K.B.). The determination of a **controversy** and pronouncement of **judgment** based on **evidence** presented; implies a final judgment of the court or other body

deciding the matter. Compare **disposition**.

ADJUDICATIVE FACTS "[T]he where, when, and why of what the accused is alleged to have done." *R. v. Spence,* 2005 SCC 71.

ADJUSTER One who makes a determination of the amount of an insurance claim and then makes an agreement with the insured as to a settlement.

AD MEDIUM FILUM AQUAE (*ăd mē'-dē-ŭm fē'-lŭm ä'kwē*) Lat.: to the centre line of the water. A common law rule that the owner of land abutting a stream or a non-tidal river owns the bed of the river to the centre. The rule has not been consistently adopted across Canada: see *R. v. Nikal,* [1996] 1 S.C.R. 1013.

ADMINISTRATIVE LAW Those rules of law that concern the exercise of the powers and privileges of the **executive** branch of government. More specifically, administrative law is concerned with the actions and decisions pursuant to the powers given to the executive by **Parliament** or the provincial **legislatures**. Nearly every modern **statute** delegates to the **Governor-in-Council** (or the **Lieutenant-Governor-in-Council** of a province) or to a minister of the **Crown** the power to make **regulations** to secure desired legislative ends.

Administrative law is also a body of law which governs **tribunals**, statutory bodies, boards, or commissions which have been set up to administrate various legislative schemes and to make decisions outside the framework of the ordinary courts. Administrative law is particularly concerned with the rules that exist to control **administrative tribunals**, bodies, boards, or commissions and administrative action in its broadest sense.

ADMINISTRATIVE NOTICE The ability of an **administrative tribunal** to recognize certain facts as true despite the absence of evidence proving them. See **judicial notice**.

ADMINISTRATIVE OFFENCE See **regulatory offence**.

ADMINISTRATIVE TRIBUNALS A large number of special courts or bodies outside the ordinary judicial framework, generally set up under federal or provincial **statutes** to decide matters that may arise in the administration of some particular area of government: e.g., boards dealing with immigration, labour relations, workmen's compensation, public utilities, liquor control, rent review, etc. The required procedures for such tribunals vary greatly. The tribunals are sometimes said to perform a QUASI-JUDICIAL function (see **quasi**). There may or may not be statutory provision for appeal from the decisions of these bodies. However, the tribunals may be subject to the control of the **superior courts** if there has been a serious irregularity in their **proceedings** or failure to abide by the principles of **natural justice**. Some jurisdictions—for example, Ontario—have specific enactments to control the exercise of power by such bodies. See *Statutory Powers Procedure Act,* R.S.O. 1990, c. S. 22. See chart, **Appendix I**.

ADMINISTRATOR   [ADMINISTRATRIX] One who is appointed to handle the affairs of a person who has died **intestate**; one who manages the **estate** of a person who has left no **executor**. The administrator derives authority from the **Surrogate Court** (or, in some jurisdictions, the **Probate** Court).

An administrator is empowered to carry out duties and functions by documents known as LETTERS OF ADMINISTRATION, which are conclusive evidence of the **intestacy** of the deceased; the person in whose name they are granted has the incontestable right to the administration of the estate. See *Doyle v. Diamond Flint Glass Co.* (1904), 8 O.L.R. 499 (Div.Ct.).

ADMIRALTY AND MARITIME JURISDICTION Expansive **jurisdiction** over all actions related to events occurring at sea; extends to all transactions relating to sea commerce and navigation, to damages and injuries upon the sea and all maritime **contracts**, and **torts**. See *Federal Courts Act,* R.S.C. 1985, c. F-7, s. 22.

Admiralty and maritime jurisdiction is the "jurisdiction to hear an action under any statute of the **Parliament** of Canada in relation to 'any matter coming within the class of subject of navigation and shipping.' *Robert Simpson Montreal Ltd. v. Hamburg-Amerika Linie Norddeutscher,* [1973] F.C. 1356 at 1361–62 (C.A.).

ADMISSIBLE EVIDENCE Evidence that may be received by a trial court to aid the **fact finder** (judge or jury) in deciding the merits of the **controversy**. Each jurisdiction has established rules of evidence to determine questions of admissibility. "The organizing principles of the law of evidence may be simply stated. All relevant evidence is admissible, subject to a discretion to exclude matters that may unduly prejudice, mislead, or confuse the trier of fact, take up too much time, or that should otherwise be excluded on clear grounds of law or policy. Questions of relevancy and exclusion are, of course, matters for the trial judge, but over the years many specific exclusionary rules have been developed for the guidance of the trial judge, so much so that the law of evidence may superficially appear to consist simply of a series of exceptions to the rules of admissibility, with exceptions to the exceptions, and their sub-exceptions." *R. v. Corbett,* [1988] 1 S.C.R. 670.

ADMISSIONS 1. In criminal law, a statement by the accused that certain facts are true. "The distinction between an admission and a confession is apposite here. Under the rules of evidence, statements made by an accused are admissions by an opposing party and, as such, fall into an exception to the hearsay rule. They are admissible for the truth of their contents. When statements are made by an accused to ordinary persons, such as friends or family members, they are presumptively admissible without the necessity of a *voir dire*. It is only where the accused makes a statement to a '**person in authority**' that the Crown bears the onus of proving the voluntariness of the statement as a prerequisite to its admission." *R. v. S.G.T.* 2010 SCC 20. **2.** In civil procedure, a pretrial **discovery** device by which one party asks another for a positive affirmation or denial of a **material** fact or **allegation** at issue. Also, a party may request another to admit the truth of any relevant fact or the authenticity of any relevant document.

ADOPTION 1. By court order, a person of the **age of majority** may adopt a child born of another so that the child becomes the child of the adopting parent and the adopting parent becomes the parent of the adopted child. See *Children and Family Services Act,* S.N.S. 1990, c. 5, ss. 67–87. *Child and Family Services Act,* R.S.O. 1990, c. C.11, ss. 136–177.

2. In **contract**, the term is used to suggest the continued acceptance of a contract as binding on both parties, although the circumstances might entitle the injured party to repudiate it.

3. The formal acceptance and making effective of a proposal, finding, resolution or amendment.

ADOPTION BY REFERENCE The adoption of either rules of **substantive law** or rules of **procedure** in force in another jurisdiction; a technique used by legislative bodies, where it is desired to enact the same laws as in another jurisdiction. See *Attorney-General for Ontario v. Scott,* [1956] S.C.R. 137. There can be no enlargement of the legislative authority of the adopting body, only a borrowing of provisions that are within its legislative competence and were enacted for its own purposes. But neither **Parliament** nor a provincial **legislature** is capable of delegating to the other or of receiving from the other any of the powers to make laws conferred upon it by the *Constitution Act, 1867.* See *Coughlin v. Ontario Highway Transport Board,* [1968] S.C.R. 569. *Reference Re Securities Act*, 2011 SCC 66.

AD TESTIFICANDUM (*ăd tĕs-tĭ-fĭ-căn'-dŭm*) Lat.: for testifying. A person sought ad testificandum is sought to appear as a **witness**. See **subpoena** [SUBPOENA AD TESTIFICANDUM].

ADULTERATION Adding to or extracting or omitting from a food or drug a prescribed substance. See *Food and Drugs Act,* R.S.C. 1985, c. F–27, s. 30.

ADULTERY Voluntary sexual intercourse between persons of the opposite sex, one of whom is married to a third party. *Orford v. Orford* (1921), 49 O.L.R. 15 (Ont. S.C.). Recent cases have established that adultery can occur between two persons of the same gender: "In the modern understanding of marriage, the wrong for which the petitioner seeks redress is something akin to violation of the marital bond. Viewed from this perspective, the heterosexual nature of the sexual acts is not determinative. Intimate sexual activity outside of marriage may represent a violation of the marital bond and be devastating to the spouse and the marital bond regardless of the specific nature of the sexual act performed." *S.E.P. v. D.D.P.* (2005), 259 D.L.R. (4th) 358 at para. 48 (B.C.S.C.). See also *Thebeau v. Thebeau* (2006), 302 N.B.R. (2d) 190 (Q.B.). This area of law is still evolving with the advent of the *Civil Marriage Act,* S.C. 2005, c. 33. Under the *Divorce Act,* R.S.C. 1985, c. 3 (2nd Supp.), s. 8(2)(b)(i), adultery is one of the three grounds for determining if there has been a breakdown of the marriage, which must be established in order to obtain a **divorce**.

AD VALOREM (*ăd vȧ-lô-rĕm*) Lat.: according to value. Designates an assessment of taxes against **property** at a certain rate upon its value.

AD VALOREM TAX See **tax**.

ADVANCE To move forward in position, time or place. (1) To pay money before it is due. See *Williams Manufacturing Co. v. Michener* (1908), 13 O.W.R. 46 (S.C.). (2) To furnish credit, to loan **capital** in aid of a projected enterprise, payment beforehand or in anticipation of payment or security of future reimbursement—hence a loan. See *Diebel v. Stratford Improvement Co.* (1916), 37 O.L.R. 492 (S.C.).

ADVANCE COSTS Costs that are paid to a litigant prior to the completion of the action, in order to permit the action to proceed. Special rules surround the payment of advance costs, which are sometimes available in **family law**, corporate, **trust**, or public interest litigation. In the latter context: "[a] litigant must convince the court that three absolute requirements are met...

1. The party seeking interim costs genuinely cannot afford to pay for the litigation, and no other realistic option exists for bringing the issues to trial—in short, the litigation would be unable to proceed if the order were not made.

2. The claim to be adjudicated is *prima facie* meritorious; that is, the claim is at least of sufficient merit that it is contrary to the interests of justice for the opportunity to pursue the case to be forfeited just because the litigant lacks financial means.

3. The issues raised transcend the individual interests of the particular litigant, are of public importance, and have not been resolved in previous cases.

In analysing these requirements, the court must decide, with a view to all the circumstances, whether the case is sufficiently special that it would be contrary to the interests of justice to deny the advance costs application, or whether it should consider other methods to facilitate the hearing of the case." *Little Sisters Book and Art Emporium v. Canada (Commissioner of Customs and Revenue)*, 2007 SCC 2. See **costs**.

ADVANCE CARE DIRECTIVE See **living will**.

ADVANCEMENT "Advancement is a gift during the transferor's lifetime to a transferee who, by marriage or parent-child relationship, is financially dependent on the transferor...In the context of the parent-child relationship, the term has also been used because 'the father was under a moral duty to advance his children in the world.'" *Pecore v. Pecore*, 2007 SCC 17. An advancement can give rise to either a presumption of advancement or a presumption of **resulting trust**. A gratuitous transfer is generally presumed to create a resulting trust, and so normally where a transfer is made for no consideration, the onus is on the transferee to demonstrate that it was intended to be a gift. The presumption of advancement, in contrast, places the onus on the person challenging the transfer to rebut the presumption that it was a gift. Historically the presumption of advancement applied to transfers

by a husband to his wife or by a father to his child. In *Pecore v. Pecore*, the Supreme Court of Canada concluded that the presumption applies equally to transfers made by a mother to her children. However, that same decision also ruled that the presumption applies only to transfers made to minor children, not to either independent or dependent adult children. Some statutes also consider how to deal with advancements: see, e.g., *Intestate Succession Act*, R.S.N.S. 1989, c. 236, s. 13(3); *Estates Administration Act*, R.S.O. 1990, c. E.22, s. 25.

ADVERSARY The opponent or **litigant** in a legal controversy or litigation. See **adverse party**; **adversary proceeding**.

ADVERSARY PROCEEDING A **proceeding** involving a real **controversy** contested by two opposing **parties**.

ADVERSARY SYSTEM A system for trying disputes that works on the assumption that harnessing the self-interest of opposing parties is the best method of guaranteeing that all relevant evidence comes to light. The adversary system incorporates a passive and neutral arbiter, party presentation of evidence, and formal rules of admissibility. "Courts function as impartial arbiters within an adversary system. They depend on the parties to present the evidence and relevant arguments fully and skillfully. '[C]oncrete adverseness' sharpens the debate of the issues and the parties' personal stake in the outcome helps ensure that the arguments are presented thoroughly and diligently." *Canada (Attorney General) v. Downtown Eastside Sex Workers United Against Violence Society*, 2012 SCC 45. The Canadian judicial system, like most **common law** jurisdictions, operates on an adversarial model, which is generally contrasted with the inquisitorial system, which is typical in Europe and other countries. "There are two types of judicial systems, and they ensure that the full case is placed before the judge in two different ways. In inquisitorial systems, as in continental Europe, the judge takes charge of the gathering of evidence in an independent and impartial way. By contrast, an adversarial system, which is the norm in Canada, relies on the parties—who are entitled to **disclosure** of the case to meet, and to full participation in open proceedings—to produce the relevant evidence." *Charkaoui v. Canada (Citizenship and Immigration)*, 2007 SCC 9.

ADVERSE EFFECT DISCRIMINATION See **discrimination**.

ADVERSE INTEREST An interest contrary to and inconsistent with that of some other person.

ADVERSE POSSESSION A method of acquiring complete **title** to land as against all others, including the owner who holds the registered title (see **registry acts**), through certain acts over an uninterrupted period of time, as prescribed by statute. The occupation must be "open, actual, exclusive, continuous and notorious... to give possessory title." Consequently, "isolated acts of **trespass** committed from time to time" do not constitute adverse possession. *Re Colling* (1975), 11 N.B.R. (2d) 516 (S.C.). The purpose of the requirements is to give notice that HOSTILE [adverse] possession had begun. *Spicer v. Bowater Mersey Paper Co.* (2004), 237 D.L.R. (4th) 453 (N.S.C.A.). In some jurisdictions the doctrine has been governed by statute. See *Real Property Limitations Act*, R.S.O. 1990, c. L. 15, s. 4. See **notorious possession**.

ADVERSE WITNESS See **witness**.

ADVISORY OPINION A formal opinion by a **judge**, **court**, or law officer upon a **question of law** submitted by a legislative body or a government official, but not actually presented in a concrete case at law. Such opinion, while of considerable persuasive value, has no binding force as law. Compare **declaratory judgment**; **reference case**.

ADVOCATE A person professionally conducting and presenting a **case** in **court**; in Canada, a **barrister and solicitor**; a lawyer.

ADVOCACY 1. The art of persuasion. **2.** In practice, the active espousal of a legal cause and the pleading of the legal rights (or cause) of another in **court**. "When acting as an advocate, the lawyer must treat the court or tribunal with courtesy and respect and must represent the client resolutely, honourably and within the limits of the law." *Canadian Bar Association (C.B.A.)*

Code of Professional Conduct (1974, as am. 1987, 1996, 2006, 2009).

AFFIDAVIT A written statement in the name of a person known as the **deponent** who signs and swears to its veracity; a written statement made or taken under oath before an officer of the court or a **notary public** or other person who has been duly authorized to certify the statement.

AFFILIATION The act of being allied with another person or group; an association that is less than membership in a certain group.

In **family law**, affiliation refers to a procedure where a woman issues a complaint against a man who may be the father of a child born out of wedlock. The complaint is based on the fact that the child has been left without support. The mother must be able to produce corroborative evidence to prove the alleged paternity, such as evidence of continuous sexual liaisons between the parties; e.g., *Barath v. Bacsek* (1975), 25 R.F.L. 218 (Ont.Div.Ct.). See *McLeod v. Hill* (1975), 23 R.F.L. 309 (Sask.Prov.Ct.), concerning facial resemblance between child and alleged father.

An AFFILIATION ORDER may be a declaration of paternity or a maintenance order or both; it varies from **jurisdiction** to jurisdiction in Canada. *Works v. Holt* (1976), 22 R.F.L. 1 (Ont.Prov.Ct.).

AFFINITY A relationship created by **marriage**. The doctrine of affinity grew out of the idea that marriage makes partners to a marriage one entity. One partner has the same relation, by affinity, to the other partner's blood relations, and vice versa. Affinity is a bar to marriage within prohibited degrees. *Re Schepull and Bekeschus and Provincial Secretary,* [1954] 2 D.L.R. 5 (Ont.H.C.). SECONDARY AFFINITIES are the relationships that subsist between the husband's and the wife's relations. COLLATERAL AFFINITY is the relationship between the husband and the relations of his wife's relations. See **consanguinity**.

AFFIRM 1. To approve, confirm, ratify; refers to the assertion of an **appellate court** that the **judgment** of the court below is correct and should stand. Compare **reversal**.

2. To attest to, as in an affirmation of faith or fidelity.

AFFIRMATION See **solemn affirmation**.

AFFIRMATIVE ACTION The use of laws, programs, or activities to remedy the negative consequences caused by **discrimination** (e.g., based on sex, race, etc.) against disadvantaged groups or individuals. Although most commonly applied to employment (see, e.g., *Employment Equity Act,* S.C. 1995, c. 44), the term may be applied to any positive measure whose purpose is to reduce discrimination (e.g., paternity support legislation (*Shewchuck v. Ricard* (1986), 20 C.R.R. 364 (B.C.S.C.)).

Affirmative action policies are protected by the **Canadian Charter of Rights and Freedoms**, s. 6(4) under mobility rights and s. 15(2), under equality rights, and by the *Canadian Human Rights Act,* R.S.C. 1985, c. H–6, s. 16, as well as several provincial human rights codes. See *Action Travail des Femmes v. Canadian National Railway Co.,* [1987] 1 S.C.R. 1114; *Human Rights Act,* R.S.N.S. 1989, c. 214, s. 6(i). If an ameliorative measure falls under s. 15(2) of the *Charter*, then it is by definition not **discrimination**, infringing the equality rights guarantee in s. 15(1). *R. v. Kapp*, 2008 SCC 41.

AFFIRMATIVE DEFENCE In a statement of **defence**, a plea, which the defendant has the burden of establishing at trial, which admits the truth of material facts stated in the plaintiff's statement of claim, but destroys the legal effect of these admissions by pleading "further facts which, if true, avoid the legal consequences argued for by the plaintiff…" G. Watson et al., *Civil Litigation* 410 (5th ed. 1999). See **burden of proof**.

AFFIX To attach to or add to; to annex, as to affix a **chattel** to **realty**; e.g., to attach a chandelier to the ceiling is to affix it to the **real property**. A tree is affixed to the land.

AFFRAY The act of fighting in a public place or a place to which the public has access.

A FORTIORI (*ä för-shē-ô'-rē*) Lat.: from stronger reasoning. Refers to a logical inference that, because a certain conclusion or fact is true, a second included conclusion must also be true. For example, A is not guilty of **theft**; then, a fortiori, he is not guilty of **robbery**.

AFTER-THE-FACT CONDUCT See **post-offence conduct**.

AGAINST THE [MANIFEST] [WEIGHT OF THE] EVIDENCE An evidentiary standard permitting the **trial court**, after **verdict**, to order a new trial, where the verdict, though based on legally sufficient evidence, appears in the view of the trial court judge to be unsupported by the substantial, credible evidence. It is a PERVERSE FINDING by a jury in favour of one party when the evidence at trial would appear to strongly support the case of the other. Compare **directed verdict**; **judgment n.o.v.** See *Johnson v. Laing*, 2004 BCCA 364.

AGE OF MAJORITY Full legal age; adulthood; the age when a child acquires the right to vote and to bind himself to contracts, and the age when support payment may be terminated by parents. Historically, the age of majority was twenty-one, and this common-law notion was adopted by many Canadian provinces. In Canada, since 1970, the age of majority has been reduced to eighteen years in six jurisdictions and to nineteen in seven jurisdictions. For example, *Age of Majority Act,* R.S.N.S. 1989, c. 4.

AGENCY The relationship that exists between two persons when one, called the **agent**, is considered in law to represent the other, called the **principal**, in such a way as to be able to affect the principal's legal position, in respect of strangers to the relationship, by the making of contracts and the disposition of property. Agency is a consensual and **fiduciary** relationship between the parties. See *Chender v. Lewaskewicz* (2007), 37 B.L.R. (4th) 161 (N.S. C.A.) and *4414790 Manitoba Ltd. v. Nelson* (2003), [2004] 2 W.W.R. 552 (Man. Q.B.). See also **apparent authority**; **respondeat superior; scope of employment**. Compare **partnership**.

AGENT One who, by mutual consent, acts for the benefit of another; one authorized by a party to act on that party's behalf. Compare **servant**; **contractor** [INDEPENDENT CONTRACTOR].

AGGRAVATED ASSAULT A form of **assault** that is more heinous than common assault and that provides for a more severe penalty upon conviction. Sections 268 and 273 of the *Criminal Code,* R.S.C. 1985, c. C–46, deal with aggravated assault. See *R. v. Stenning,* [1970] S.C.R. 631. "The 'aggravation' in aggravated assault...comes from the consequences." *R. v. Williams,* [2003] 2 S.C.R. 134.

AGGRAVATED DAMAGES See **damages**.

AGGRAVATING CIRCUMSTANCES Factors that tend to make an **offence** more serious and can be taken into account to increase the sentence, which would otherwise be imposed on the offender. See *Criminal Code,* R.S.C. 1985, c. C–46, s. 718.2: "A court that imposes a sentence shall also take into consideration the following principles: (*a*) a sentence should be increased or reduced to account for any relevant aggravating or **mitigating circumstances** relating to the offence or the offender, and, without limiting the generality of the foregoing, (i) evidence that the offence was motivated by bias, prejudice, or hate based on race, national or ethnic origin, language, colour, religion, sex, age, mental or physical disability, sexual orientation, or any other similar factor, (ii) evidence that the offender, in committing the offence, abused the offender's **spouse** or common-law partner, (ii.1) evidence that the offender, in committing the offence, abused a person under the age of eighteen years, (iii) evidence that the offender, in committing the offence, abused a position of trust or authority in relation to the victim, (iv) evidence that the offence was committed for the benefit of, at the direction of, or in association with a **criminal organization**, or (v) evidence that the offence was a **terrorism** offence shall be deemed to be aggravating circumstances."

AGGRIEVED PARTY/PERSONS [or PERSONS AGGRIEVED] 1. One who has been injured or has suffered a loss; **2.** the statutory meaning when discussing the right of the aggrieved party to appeal an **order**, **conviction**, **judgment** or determination. "[T]he words 'person aggrieved' do not really mean a man who is disappointed of a benefit which he might have received if some other order had been made. A 'person aggrieved' must be a man who has suffered a legal grievance, a man against whom a decision has been pronounced which has wrongfully deprived him of something, or wrongfully refused him something, or wrongfully affected his title to something." *Ex parte Sidebotham* (1880), 14 Ch.D. 458 at 465, cited and followed in *Re Workmen's Compensation Bd.* (1976), 14 N.S.R. (2d) 693 at 700 (S.C.A.D.); *Halifax Atlantic Invest. Ltd. v. City of Halifax* (1978), 28 N.S.R. (2d) 193 at 214 (S.C.A.D.).

AGREEMENT See **contract**.

AGRICULTURAL LAND RESERVE Under the *Agricultural Land Commission Act,* S.B.C. 2002, c. 36, land that is designated for use as agricultural land: without special permission, no portion of an agricultural land reserve may be used for no-farming purposes.

AID AND ABET To actively or intentionally assist another individual in the commission or attempted commission of a **crime**. To abet is to encourage or instigate a crime to be committed, whereas to aid means to assist without necessarily encouraging the actor or **principal**. "While it is common to speak of aiding and abetting together, the two concepts are distinct, and liability can flow from either one. Broadly speaking, '[t]o aid under s. 21(1)(*b*) means to assist or help the actor...To abet within the meaning of s. 21(1)(*c*) includes encouraging, instigating, promoting, or procuring the crime to be committed.'" *R. v. Briscoe,* 2010 SCC 13. See *Criminal Code,* R.S.C. 1985, c. C–46, ss. 21–22, 463–466. See also **abet**. Compare **accessory**; **accomplice**; **conspirator**.

AIR OF REALITY The test for determining whether a **defence** should be put to the jury or considered by a trial judge in a **criminal** trial. There is an air of reality to a defence if there is evidence that could support each of the elements of that defence. In determining whether there is an air of reality, the trial judge considers the totality of the evidence and assumes the evidence relied upon by the accused to be true. It is an **error of law on the face of the record** to fail to consider a defence for which there is an air of reality, or to consider one for which there is not. See *R. v. Cinous*, 2002 SCC 29.

ALEATORY Uncertain; risky, involving an element of chance.

ALEATORY CONTRACT An agreement, the performance of which by one party depends upon the occurrence of a **contingent** event. An ALEATORY PROMISE is one, the performance of which is by its own terms subject to the happening of an uncertain and fortuitous event or upon some fact the existence or part occurrence of which is also uncertain and undetermined. Examples of such **contracts** include life and fire insurance contracts. Such agreements are enforceable notwithstanding an uncertainty of terms at the time of the making so long as the risk undertaken clearly appears. A contract where performance is contingent upon the outcome of a bet, however, is a gambling contract and is generally unenforceable by statute or as a matter of public policy.

ALIAS 1. Otherwise known as. **2.** A fictitious name used to disguise one's true identity.

ALIBI A provable account of an individual's whereabouts at the time of the commission of a **crime**, which would make it impossible or impracticable to place him or her at the scene of the crime. An alibi therefore negates the physical possibility that the suspected individual could have committed the crime. A fabricated or concocted alibi designed to deceive can be used as positive evidence of guilt. See *R. v. Baltovich* (2004), 191 C.C.C. (3d) 289, 26 C.R. (6th) 298 (Ont. C.A.).

ALIEN A person born in a foreign country, who owes allegiance to that country; one not a **citizen** of the country in which he or she lives. The term "alien"

has been dropped from statutory use in Canada, although the term "enemy alien" is still present in the *Criminal Code* R.S.C. 1985, c. C–46, and the term "aliens" is used in the **Constitution Act, 1867**, s. 91(25).

ALIENABLE Capable of being transferred. See **alienation**.

ALIENATION In the law of **real property**, the voluntary and absolute transfer of **title** and **possession** of real property from one person to another. The law recognizes the power to alienate property as one of the essential ingredients of **fee simple** ownership, and therefore unreasonable restraints on alienation are generally prohibited as contrary to public policy. See, e.g., **Rule Against Perpetuities**.

ALIENATION OF AFFECTION A **tort** that establishes a cause of action for one spouse to sue a third party for **damages** for misconduct that enticed away the marital partner and in that way alienated the affections of the one **spouse** for the other.

The interference or **enticement** may be (but not necessarily) **adultery** (a tort called **criminal conversation**). *Kungl v. Schiefer*, [1962] S.C.R. 443, held that no separate action lay in Ontario for alienation of affection, but alienation was merely in support of the claim for **damages** in an enticement action. The Court has subsequently characterized *Kungl* as saying that the tort does not exist in Canada: *Frame v. Smith*, [1987] 2 S.C.R. 99.

ALIMONY "[T]he word alimony is properly and usually used in reference to financial support payments where the marriage tie still subsists as in the case of judicial separation or in reference to payments for the wife's support pending the hearing of a divorce petition. The word maintenance is the proper term to be used in reference to payments subsequent to the divorce decree." *Black v. Hubenet* (1951), 2 W.W.R. (N.S.) 694 at 695 (B.C.S.C.).

Actions for alimony separate from another action are unknown at **common law**; the right to take action for alimony alone is derived from provincial **legisla-**

tion, e.g., *Family Law Act,* R.S.O. 1990, c. F. 3. The term "alimony" has largely been replaced by the phrase "spousal support." See e.g., *Miglin v. Miglin,* 2003 SCC 24 or *Divorce Act,* R.S.C. 1985, c. 3 (2nd Supp.), s. 15.2.

ALIQUOT (*ä'-lē-kwō*) Lat.: some; so many. An even part of the whole; one part contained in a whole that is evenly divisible without leaving a **remainder**, as in real **property**. See, e.g., *Re Pinewood Aggregates Ltd. & Director of Titles,* [1964] 1 O.R. 83 at 85–87 (H.C.).

ALIUNDE (*äl-ē-ŭn'-dē*) Lat.: from another source. EVIDENCE ALIUNDE refers to evidence from an outside source.

ALL AND SINGULAR All without exception. A comprehensive term often employed in conveyances, **wills**, and the like that includes the whole and also each of the separate items.

ALLEGATION In **pleading**, an assertion of fact; a statement of the issue that the contributing party is prepared to prove.

ALLOCUTION The requirement at **common law** that, upon the **verdict** of conviction, the trial judge address the **accused** asking him or her to show legal cause why the sentence of conviction should not be pronounced. The modern allocution does not ask the **accused** why **sentence** ought not be imposed but rather asks whether the offender, if present, has anything to say. *Criminal Code,* R.S.C. 1985, c. C–46, s. 726. See **mitigating circumstances**.

ALLODIAL Owned freely without obligation to one with superior right; not subject to the restriction on **alienation** that existed with feudal **tenures**; free of any superior rights vested in another, such as a lord. No person can now have such an absolute property, since the highest estate is in **fee simple**.

ALLOPHONE A person whose first language is not an **official language**.

ALLOTMENT The act of assigning a share. In corporate law, "the acceptance by resolution of the board of directors of the application for shares (in a company)." H. Sutherland, *Fraser's Handbook on Canadian Company Law* 110 (8th ed. 1994).

"Allotment is generally neither more nor less than the acceptance by the company of the offer to take shares." *Imperial Bank of Canada v. Dennis* (1926), 59 O.L.R. 20 at 23 (S.C.A.D.).

ALLUREMENT [DOCTRINE OF] The doctrine of allurement applies "where an occupier has reason, because of the nature of the property or some artificial attraction thereon, to anticipate the presence of children (usually trespassing children) whose vulnerability, immaturity, and want of judgment are such that they will not likely discover or appreciate the risks of injury which they may encounter. The doctrine cannot be invoked in the case of teenagers, who are required to conform to the reasonable person standard." *McErlean v. Sarel et al.* (1987), 61 O.R. (2d) 396 (C.A.).

ALLUVION Deposits of sedimentary material (earth, sand, gravel, etc.) that have accumulated gradually and imperceptibly along the bank of a river, lake, or sea. Alluvion is the result of **accretion** and becomes part of the property on which it settles or becomes attached, if it occurs "by small and imperceptible degrees." *Chuckry v. Manitoba (Minister of Public Works)* (1972), 27 D.L.R. (3d) 164 (S.C.C.), quoted in *Bryan's Transfer Ltd. v. Trail (City)* (2010), 296 B.C.A.C. 207 (B.C.C.A.). See also **avulsion**; **reliction**.

ALTER EGO TRUST See **trust**.

ALTERNATIVE DISPUTE RESOLUTION Processes that deal with legal disputes and problems outside of the civil court system. The aim of alternative dispute resolution is to achieve efficient and effective resolutions with a process that is less expensive than the traditional **civil action** route. The processes include **mediation**, negotiation, **arbitration**, and **med-arb**.

ALTERNATIVE PLEADING Or "pleading in the alternative" as, e.g., in a **statement of defence**. In raising an **affirmative defence**, the defendant will "admit the relevant allegation made by the plaintiff, but then set forth further facts which, if true, avoid the legal consequences argued for by the plaintiff." This plea can be combined with a **traverse** where the defendant denies the plaintiff's allegations placing "the facts denied in issue and the plaintiff then has the burden of proving those facts to the satisfaction of the court at trial." G. Watson et al., *Civil Litigation* 410 (5th ed. 1999). For example "a defendant may first deny that a contract was made and then go on to plead in the alternative that if there was a contract as alleged, it was subsequently terminated by further agreement." *Id.*

ALTERUM NON LAEDERE (*äl' tĕr-ŭm nōn lā'dĕ rĕ*) Lat.: to hurt nobody by word or deed. This term describes the underlying principle of **tort** law. "The law of torts exists for the purpose of preventing men from hurting one another, whether in respect of property, their persons, their reputations, or anything else which is theirs." R. Heuston & R. Buckley, *Salmond & Heuston on the Law of Torts* 33 (21st ed. 1996).

AMALGAMATION See **merger**.

AMBIGUITY A double or doubtful meaning. In the case of a written instrument, such as a **will**, a PATENT AMBIGUITY is one that is apparent on the face of the document and a LATENT AMBIGUITY is one that becomes apparent only in the light of surrounding circumstances. See, e.g., *In re Smalley,* [1929] 2 Ch. 112 C.A.

AMELIORATING WASTE See **waste**.

AMEND To change, to improve upon. A **legislature** amends an established law by passing a **statute** (AMENDMENT) that continues the law in changed form. One amends an already existing **pleading** by an addition or a subtraction.

AMICUS CURIAE (*ä-mē'-kŭs kyū'-rē-ī*) Lat.: friend of the **court**. One who gives information to the court on some matter of law that is in doubt. "Historically... there were three situations in which the appointment was made: (1) where there is a matter of public interest in

which the court invites the Attorney General or some other capable individual to intervene; (2) to prevent an injustice; for example, to make submissions on points of law that may have been overlooked; and (3) to represent the unrepresented...There has been a trend, however, toward permitting *amicus* to take on greater duties." I. Carter, "A Complicated Friendship: The Evolving Role of *Amicus Curiae*" (2008) 54 C.R. (6th) 89.

AMNESTY An act of oblivion for past acts, granted by a government to persons accused of crimes generally of a political nature, e.g., **treason**, **sedition**, desertion. Legally, amnesty differs from **pardon** in that pardon implies guilt, whereas amnesty does not. Amnesty is the abolition and forgetfulness of the offence.

AMORTIZATION The gradual **extinguishment** of a debt; "the system of repayment of a debt by instalments of principal and interest at the same time, in order to extinguish the debt within a fixed period....The payments are equal in amount and are applied in payment of the accrued interest and a portion of the principal." *Price v. Green,* [1951] 4 D.L.R. 596 at 599–600 (Man.C.A.).

ANALOGOUS GROUND A basis upon which an equality rights claim can be brought under the **Canadian Charter of Rights and Freedoms** other than one of the grounds listed in section 15(1). "A ground or grounds will not be considered analogous under s. 15(1) unless it can be shown that differential treatment premised on the ground or grounds has the potential to bring into play human dignity." *Law v. Canada,* [1999] 1 S.C.R. 497. See **enumerated ground**.

ANCIENT LIGHTS The right to light; windows through which the access of light has been enjoyed otherwise than by consent or permission for twenty years and upwards. The right to light has been abolished by statute in some Canadian provinces. See *Limitation of Actions Act,* R.S.N.S. 1989, c. 258, s. 33.

ANCILLARY POWERS DOCTRINE A method of creating new police powers at **com-**

mon law. The ancillary powers doctrine is based on a two-part test formulated in the English case of *R. v. Waterfield*, [1963] 3 All E.R. 659. Under that test, proposed police powers must fall "within the general scope of [a police] duty imposed by statute or recognised at common law" and must involve a justified "use of powers associated with the duty." See, e.g., *R. v. Dedman*, [1985] 2 S.C.R. 2; *R. v. Mann*, 2004 SCC 52.

ANCILLARY RELIEF Incidental relief, such as an **injunction** where **damages** are the main remedy asked for.

***ANDREWS v. PARTINGTON*, RULE IN** A rule of **construction** in **class gifts** for closing the group of potential recipients where the gift would otherwise violate **the rule against perpetuities**. According to the rule in *Andrews v. Partington*, if one of the members of the class is able to meet the requirements of the gift when the instrument takes effect, the class of recipients would close to include only those who were alive at that time. *Andrews v. Partington* (1791) 3 Bro. C.C. 401, 29 E.R. 610, [1775–1802] All E.R. Rep. 209.

ANIMALS See **ferae naturae**.

ANIMO (*ăn'-ĭ-mō*) Lat.: with the **intention**; purposefully.
ANIMO REVERTENDI The intention to return.
ANIMO REVOCANDI The intention to **revoke**.
ANIMO TESTANDI The intention to make a **will**.

ANIMUS POSSIDENDI (*ă'-nĭ-mŭs pŏ'-sĭ-dĕn-dī*) Lat.: the intention to possess **property**. *Animus possidendi* is one of the elements required to establish a possessory interest in property. *Langille v. Schwisberg* (2010), 4 R.P.R. (5th) 263 (Ont. S.C.J.).

ANNS TEST The basis of the test used in **tort** law for determining the existence of a common-law duty of care in a given situation. The test was established by Lord Wilberforce in *Anns v. Merton London Borough Council*, [1978] A.C. 728 (H.L.) and consists of two parts. First, it must be determined if there is a sufficient range of proximity or "neighborhood" between the **plaintiff** and the **defendant**, such that a **reasonable person** would have foreseen that the defendant's actions would have caused harm or injury to the plaintiff. Second, if there is a duty of care, it must be determined if there are any policy considerations that would limit the scope of that duty. "This two-step *Anns* formulation...was used for nearly two decades, but it has now been substantially reworked by the Supreme Court of Canada." A. Linden & B. Feldthusen, *Canadian Tort Law* (9th ed. 2011) 290. See **neighbor principle**.

ANNUITANT One who receives the benefits of an **annuity**.

ANNUITY A fixed sum payable periodically, subject to the limitations imposed by the **grantor**. "Ordinarily an annuity is thought of as a series of annual payments which a person has purchased or arranged for with a sum of money or other assets of a capital nature." *W. M. O'Connor v. Minister of National Revenue*, [1943] 4 D.L.R. 160 at 167 (Ex.Ct.).

ANNUL To make void; to dissolve what once existed, as to annul the bonds of matrimony. A **marriage** that is annulled by an ACTION FOR ANNULMENT [to have the marriage declared NULL AND VOID— "declaration of **nullity**"] is void **ab initio**, as compared to a marriage that is dissolved by a decree of **divorce**; divorce only terminates the marriage from that point forward and does not affect the former validity of the marriage. See, e.g., *R. v. R.* (1976), 18 N.S.R. (2d) 662 (S.C.A.D.).

ANSWER In pleading, a **defence** on the facts (presented in a **proceeding**). The term also applies more broadly to the **statement of defence**, in which the **accused** or **defendant** "can invoke every means in fact and law to meet the **charge** [or defeat the action]." *R. v. Romer* (1914), 23 C.C.C. 235 (Police Ct., Montreal).

ANTICIPATORY BREACH [OF CONTRACT] A **breach** committed before the actual time of required **performance**.

It occurs when one party by words or conduct refuses to perform or disables himself from so doing. The terms **renunciation** and repudiation are also used when a party who has partly performed the **contract** refuses by words or conduct to further perform it. See *O'Connell v. McBeth* (2006), 410 A.R. 312 (Alta. Prov. Ct.), and *Brealta Energy Inc. v. First Capital Management Ltd.* (2011), 87 B.L.R. (4th) 287 (Alta Q.B.). "An anticipatory breach occurs when a party, by express language or conduct, or as a matter of implication from what that party has said or done, repudiates his or her contractual obligations before they fall due. The authorities indicate that in order for an anticipatory breach to occur there must be: (1) conduct that amounts to a total rejection of the obligations of the contract, and (2) a lack of justification of such conduct." *Summach v. Allen*, 2003 BCCA 176. When there has been an anticipatory breach, the **aggrieved party** may (1) treat the contract as at an end for all purposes except that of bringing an action on it for the breach committed by the other in renouncing, or (2) treat it as at an end and sue on a **quantum meruit** for a reasonable reward for service by the aggrieved party under the contract, or (3) treat the contract as still operative, wait for the time of performance, and then hold the other party responsible for all the consequences of non-performance. See *Frost v. Knight* (1872), L.R. 7 Ex. 111 at 112.

ANTI-SLAPP LEGISLATION Laws designed to prevent **strategic lawsuits against public participation**. See, e.g., *Code of Civil Procedure*, R.S.Q., c. C–25, art. 54.1 to 54.6.

ANTITRUST LAWS See **combines legislation**.

ANTON PILLER ORDER A court order that "authorizes a private party to insist on entrance to the premises of its opponent to conduct a surprise search, the purpose of which is to seize and preserve evidence to further its claim in a private dispute." *Celanese Canada Inc. v. Murray Demolition Corp.*, 2006 SCC 36. It is "a thoroughly 'draconian' measure equiva-

lent to a private search warrant reserved for 'exceptional circumstances'...where 'unscrupulous defendants' may, if forewarned, make 'relevant evidence disappear.'" *British Columbia (Attorney General) v. Malik*, 2011 SCC 18. "There are four essential conditions for the making of an *Anton Piller* order. First, the plaintiff must demonstrate a strong *prima facie* case. Second, the damage to the plaintiff of the defendant's alleged misconduct, potential or actual, must be very serious. Third, there must be convincing evidence that the defendant has in [his or her] possession incriminating documents or things, and fourthly, it must be shown that there is a real possibility that the defendant may destroy such material before the discovery process can do its work." *Celanese Canada*.

A POSTERIORI (*ä pŏs-tĕr-ē-ô'-rē*) Lat.: from the latter. From the most recent point of view. Relates to factual knowledge that can be known only from experience. The term relates to the means by which a concept or proposition is known or validated. It is distinguished from **a priori** reasoning, in which a proposition is known or validated solely through logical necessity, rather than actual experience or observation.

APPARENT AUTHORITY Ostensible authority; a doctrine involving the accountability of a **principal** for the acts of his **agent**: "Where a person, by words or conduct, represents or permits it to be represented that another person has authority to act on his behalf, he is bound by the acts of such other person with respect to anyone dealing with him as an agent on the faith of any such representation, to the same extent as if such other person had the authority that he was represented to have, even though he had no actual authority." F. M. B. Reynolds, *Bowstead & Reynolds on Agency* 364 (19th ed. 2010). Principle cited and followed in *Cowe and Ritzhaupt v. United Contractors Ltd. and United Contractors (Moncton) Ltd.* (1975), 13 N.B.R. (2d) 573 at 577 (S.C.). See also *Clermont v. Mid-West Steel Products Ltd.* (1965), 51 D.L.R. (2d) 340 (Sask.Q.B.).

APPEAL An application for judicial review by a **superior court** of an inferior court's decision. The judicial system in all Canadian **jurisdictions** provides for a right of appeal in almost all cases. See *Clark v. Chutorian; Clark v. Orloff,* [1955] 2 D.L.R. 472 (Man.C.A.). In the provinces the appeal from the trial decision will be to the **Court of Appeal**.

Most appeals deal with errors of law, such as incorrect instruction by the trial judge to the jury, misapplication of the law to the facts, or admitting of **evidence** that is challenged as inadmissible on appeal.

Appeals are argued on the basis of trial transcripts, which form the basis of the APPEAL BOOK, containing the written record of evidence given by witnesses at trial, **affidavits**, the decision and any other pertinent documents or exhibits. The **appellant**, or party who initiates the appeal, files a **factum** containing a statement of facts and an outline of the legal points on which the case is based. The **respondent** files a similar document. The time period allowed before the right to appeal is lost is set out in the various procedure rules in the provinces.

Further appeals from the provincial courts are to the **Supreme Court of Canada**, the court of final appeal for both civil and criminal matters. Appeals to the Supreme Court are heard only with the Court's permission. Also there are automatic rights to appeal (1) in criminal cases where an acquittal has been set aside and a conviction has been entered, or where there has been a dissenting judgment on a point of law and (2) (prior to abolition) in capital murder convictions. In civil cases, appeals are heard only if leave is given on a matter of public importance, or on an important issue of law or mixed fact and law. See *Supreme Court Act,* R.S.C. 1985, c. S–26, ss. 35–43. See also **appellate court**.

APPEAL, COURT OF See **appellate court**.

APPEARANCE 1. The coming into court by a **party summoned** in an **action**, either personally or through a lawyer. **2.** The voluntary submitting of oneself to the **jurisdiction** of the court.

APPEARANCE GRATIS An appearance entered before service of summons. A defendant, being aware that **proceedings** have been instituted, can enter such an appearance. This is a substantive right of the defendant to expedite proceedings, since the service of summons is for the benefit of the defendant, and he or she can waive that right. *Otto v. Massel* (1973), 2 O.R. (2d) 706 (H.C.).

APPEARANCE "UNDER PROTEST" See, *e.g., Nelson v. Payne* (1968), 64 W.W.R. (N.S.) 175 (B.C.S.C.). An appearance of specific application: "a person served as a partner in a firm, who denies that he was a partner or liable as such, may enter an appearance under protest." *Id.*

COMPULSORY APPEARANCE An appearance in court by one who has been validly served process and so is compelled to appear.

CONDITIONAL APPEARANCE Appearing in a court for the sole purpose of disputing the jurisdiction of that court. A person making a conditional appearance does not **attorn** to the jurisdiction of the court. *Trylinski-Branson v. Branson,* 2010 ABCA 322. It is not possible to make a conditional appearance only to challenge a procedural defect in service. *R. v. Sinopec Shanghai Engineering Co.,* 2011 ABCA 331.

APPEARANCE NOTICE According to the *Criminal Code,* R.S.C. 1985, c. C–46, ss. 493–529, a peace officer can compel the appearance of an **accused** before a justice to answer a **charge** (if the officer does not arrest immediately) by serving the accused with an appearance notice. See especially ss. 496 and 501 (issuance of an appearance notice and contents of an appearance notice). See, e.g., *R. v. Burton* (1977), 35 C.C.C. (2d) 292 (B.C.Prov.Ct.). The notice sets out the name of the accused, the substance of the charge, and the time and place the accused must attend court to answer the charge.

APPELLANT The party who appeals a decision; the party who brings the proceeding to a reviewing or **appellate court**. Compare **respondent**.

APPELLATE COURT A court having **jurisdiction** to review the law as applied to a prior determination of the same case. In most instances a **superior court** first decides a lawsuit, with review then available in one or more appellate courts. In Canada, appeals may be heard by the supreme courts, the provincial courts of appeal, and the **Supreme Court of Canada**.

The powers of the appellate court are very broad, ranging from the right to **affirm**, vary, or **reverse** a decision of a lower court. The most important limitation regards the findings of fact by the trial court, which cannot be the basis of an appeal, notwithstanding that the appeal court would have come to a different finding. It is possible, in some circumstances, for a trial judge's shortcomings in the treatment of evidence to amount to an error of law. *R. v. J.M.H.*, 2011 SCC 45. See **Courts of Appeal**. See also **appeal**.

APPELLATE JURISDICTION See **appeal**; **appellate court**.

APPLICATION FOR PARTICULARS See **bill of particulars**.

APPOINTED DAY A day fixed for the coming into force of a statute.

APPOINTMENT, POWER OF See **power of appointment**.

APPORTION To divide fairly or according to the parties' respective interests—proportionately, but not necessarily equally (as in apportionment legislation respecting **joint tortfeasors**, e.g., *Tortfeasors Act*, R.S.N.S. 1989, c. 471).

APPRAISE To estimate the value; to put in writing the worth of property.

APPRECIATE 1. To incrementally increase in value. Compare **depreciation**. **2.** To be aware of the value or worth of a thing or person. **3.** In criminal law, as part of the mental disorder test, the word is used to signify the **accused's** subjective understanding of the wrongfulness of his conduct: Appreciate "imports an additional requirement to mere knowledge of the physical quality of the act. The requirement, unique to Canada, is that of perception, an ability to perceive the consequences, impact, and results of a physical act." *R. v. Cooper*, [1980] 1 S.C.R. 1149.

APPREHEND To arrest or seize a person; "'apprehension' means the seizure or taking hold of a man .... It means the taking hold of him and detaining him with a view to his ultimate surrender." *R. v. Commercial Brokerage Co. Ltd.*, [1922] 3 W.W.R. 508 (Alta.S.C.).

APPROPRIATE "[T]o exercise dominion over **property** to the extent and for the purpose of making it subserve to one's own proper use and pleasure." *Re Levy*, [1924], 26 O.W.N. 300 at 301 (Wk.Ct.).

"To set apart for or assign to a particular purpose, person, or use, to the exclusion of others," *Re Somerville* (1926), 31 O.W.N. 289 at 290 (H.C.).

Compare **conversion**; **misapplication of property**.

APPROPRIATION OF PERSONALITY See **misappropriation of personality**.

APPROVAL, SALE ON Sale of a **chattel** with the buyer's reserved right to return the goods if not satisfied with them. A buyer who does not return them within a reasonable period will be deemed to have accepted them. The **property** in the goods does not pass until the buyer has accepted or has been deemed to accept the goods. *Sale of Goods Act*, R.S.O. 1990, C. S-1, s. 19, r. 4.

The acceptance may be by words or conduct or "any act which is consistent only with his being purchaser." See *Kirkham v. Attenborough*, [1897] 1 Q.B. 201. Or the acceptance may be by keeping the goods beyond a reasonable time. *Massh v. Hughes-Hallett* (1900), 16 T.L.R. 376 (Q.B.).

APPURTENANT Attached to something else; annexed to, or inseparably connected with. See *R. v. Bear* (1968), 63 W.W.R. (N.S.) 754 at 757 (Sask.Dist. Ct.).

In the law of **real property**, the term refers especially to a burden (e.g., an **easement** or **covenant)** that is attached to a piece of land and benefits or restricts the owner of such land in his use and enjoyment thereof.

À PRENDRE (*ä prän'-dr'*) Fr.: to take, seize. In property law, a PROFIT À PRENDRE is the right to enter on the land of another to take some profit of the soil that is capable of ownership, such as minerals, soil, or trees, for the use of the owner of the right. It is an **incorporeal hereditament** and may be held as a **right in gross**. See *Chain Lakes Logging Corp. v. Abitibi-Price Inc.* (2005), 245 Nfld. & P.E.I.R. 147 (Nfld. & Lab. C.A.) and *Eckdhal v. Long* (2012), 394 Sask.R. 163 (Sask. Q.B.).

A profit à prendre may be created by **statute**, **grant**, reservation, or **prescription**, and is to be distinguished from an **easement**.

A PRIORI (*ä prē-ô'-rē*) Lat.: from the preceding; from the first. To reason a priori is to reason with the historical knowledge of certain proven facts, so that certain factual situations that follow in time must follow the reasoning of those truths; e.g., if *X* is true, then it may be deduced that certain subsequent facts will necessarily follow.

ARBITER A referee, umpire; one appointed informally to decide a controversy, according to the law, although the decision maker is not a judicial officer.

ARBITRARINESS A **principle of fundamental justice** under s. 7 of the **Canadian Charter of Rights and Freedoms** requiring the effect of a law to be related to its purpose. "The jurisprudence on arbitrariness is not entirely settled. In *Chaoulli*, three justices . . . preferred an approach that asked whether a limit was "necessary" to further the state objective (paras. 131-32). Conversely, three other justices . . . preferred to avoid the language of necessity and instead approved of the prior articulation of arbitrariness as where "[a] deprivation of a right . . . bears no relation to, or is inconsistent with, the state interest that lies behind the legislation" (para. 232)." *Canada (Attorney General) v. PHS Community Services Society*, 2011 SCC 44.

ARBITRARY "A discretion is arbitrary if there are no criteria, express or implied,

which govern its exercise." *R. v. Hufsky*, [1988] 1 S.C.R. 621.

ARBITRATION The settling of a dispute by an **arbitrator**; where arbitrators cannot agree they may appoint an umpire. The decision of an arbitrator is known as an AWARD. See **collective bargaining**, **mediation** and **med-arb**.

ARBITRATOR An impartial person, chosen by the parties to resolve a dispute between them, who is vested with the power to make a final determination concerning the issue(s) in controversy. Historically, an arbitrator was said to be bound only by his or her own discretion, and not restricted by the rules of law or equity. This distinction between an **arbiter** and an arbitrator appears not to be used in the modern context, and the powers and duties of an arbitrator may be just as regulated by law. In Canadian law, the term appears to be used more often in the formal, legal context. It is often synonymous with **umpire** or **referee**. Provision for **arbitration** is made in many provincial statutes. See, e.g., *Arbitration Act, 1991*, S.O. 1991, c. 17. See also *Labour Relations Act, 1995*, S.O. 1995, c. 1, Sch. A, s. 48.

ARCTIC CLAUSE See **UNCLOS III**.

ARGUENDO (*är-gyū-ĕn'-dō*) Lat.: in the course of his argument; for the sake of argument. For example, "Let us assume arguendo that *X* is true." A person arguing in this fashion is not being inconsistent by later arguing that *X* is not true.

ARGUMENT Persuasion by giving reasons; a connected series of statements intended to establish or subvert a position and to induce belief. Often refers specially to an oral argument in appellate **advocacy**.

ARM'S LENGTH, AT A phrase to describe a relationship between two parties who are unrelated or strangers; thus each owes no special obligation to the other party. The term is commonly applied in areas of taxation, corporate law, and **contracts**, describing parties who carry out a particular transaction, each acting in self-interest.

ARRAIGN To call a person in custody to answer the **charge** under which an **indictment** has been handed down. See **arraignment**.

ARRAIGNMENT In criminal procedure, "the calling of the **accused** to the **bar** of that court to plead to the charge made against him ... the clerk of the court will call the accused by name to appear before the presiding judge. He will then read the charges set out in the indictment or information to the accused and ask him to plead to each count." R. Salhany, *Canadian Criminal Procedure* c. 6 at 49–50 (6th ed. 1994). The accused is also put to an election, to have a trial by judge alone or by jury, where the choice is open. See *Criminal Code,* R.S.C. 1985, c. C–46, ss. 562, 606, and especially 801. See also *R. v. Fraser & Louie* (1971). 17 C.R.N.S. 164 (B.C.C.A.); *R v. Smith* (1972), 7 C.C.C. (2d) 174 (Ont.C.A.).

ARRANGEMENT A plan for a settlement, a satisfaction, or an extension of the time of payment of debts. *Inex Pharmaceuticals Corp. (Re)*, 2006 BCCA 265. See generally *Companies' Creditors Arrangement Act*, R.S.C., 1985, c. C–36.

ARRAY See **jury panel**.

ARREARS That which is unpaid, though due to be paid. A person IN ARREARS is behind in payment. "[S]omething which is behind in payment, or which remains unpaid, as, for instance, arrears of rent, meaning rent not paid at the time agreed upon by the tenant. It means a duty and a default." *Corbett v. Taylor* (1864), 23 U.C.Q.B. 454 at 455.

ARREST 1. To deprive an alleged or suspected offender of liberty by legal authority, by "the actual seizure or touching of [the] person's body with a view to his detention. The mere pronouncing of words of arrest is not an arrest, unless the person sought to be arrested submits to the process and goes with the arresting officer. Arrest may be made either with or without a **warrant**." 10 *Halsbury's Laws of England* 342 (3d ed.), cited and followed in *R. v. Whitfield* (1970), 9 C.R.N.S. 59 at

60 (S.C.C.). See also *Criminal Code,* R.S.C. 1985, c. C–46, ss. 494–495.

Section 10 of the **Canadian Charter of Rights and Freedoms** provides for rights on arrest or **detention** including the right to counsel (see *R. v. Brydges* (1990), 74 C.R. (3d) 129 (S.C.C.)) and the right to be informed promptly of the reasons. See **Canadian Charter of Rights and Freedoms—Legal rights**. **2.** Under a warrant, to seize an item against which there is an **in rem** claim. For example, under the *Federal Courts Rules*, SOR/98-106, s. 481, a person can have a warrant issued to have the sheriff arrest a ship and take control of it.

ARREST OF JUDGMENT The court's withholding of **judgment** because of some technical error apparent from the face of the **record**.

ARSON An **indictable offence** of willfully setting fire to personal (see **personalty**) or **real property**. See *Criminal Code,* R.S.C. 1985, c. C–46, ss. 433–436; *R. v. Jorgenson* (1954), 111 C.C.C. 30 (B.C.C.A.).

ARTICLES OF CLERKSHIP [ARTICLING] Serving a period of apprenticeship (articling) prior to admission to the practice of law. The bar societies in the common law provinces of Canada require a period (normally eight to twelve months, depending upon the jurisdiction) in which the ARTICLED CLERK works in a law office under the supervision of a qualified practitioner with a certain number of years of experience at the bar. In recent years, all or part of the articling period may be served other than with a private law firm, e.g., by working in certain federal or provincial government departments, or by working as a clerk to a judge of the **Supreme Court of Canada**, to a **Federal Court** judge or to a Supreme Court judge in certain **provincial courts**.

ARTICLES OF INCORPORATION In Canada, a memorandum of association. See **association, memorandum of**.

ARTIFICE A fraud or a cunning device used to accomplish some evil; usually implies craftiness or deceitfulness. See

R. v. Leger (1975), 28 C.C.C. (2d) 480 (Ont.Co.Ct.); *Moufarrège v. Deputy Minister of Revenue of Quebec*, [2004] Q.J.N. 3783.

ARTIFICIAL PERSON A legal entity, not a human being, recognized as a person in law to whom legal rights and duties may attach—e.g., a body corporate. See **corporation**.

ASSAULT In criminal law, the intentional application of force to the person of another without that person's consent, or the attempt or threat by act or gesture to apply force to another, if the other believes one has the apparent, present ability to do so. See *Criminal Code,* R.S.C. 1985, c. C–46, ss. 264.1– 278. "There must be a threatening act or gesture and no mere words can amount to an assault." *R. v. Byrne,* (N.S.) 63 W.W.R. 385 at 387 (B.C.C.A.).

What is referred to in criminal law as an assault is, if force is actually applied, in the law of **torts** called **battery**. The intentional tort of assault "is the intentional creation of the apprehension of imminent harmful or offensive contact." A. Linden & B. Feldthusen, *Canadian Tort Law,* 46 (9th ed. 2011).

In tort law no physical injury need be proved to establish an assault. An assault being both a personal tort and a criminal offence, it may be the basis for a civil **action** and/or a criminal **prosecution**.

AGGRAVATED ASSAULT Any of a variety of serious assaults or particularly reprehensible behaviour calling for a more severe punishment. The *Criminal Code,* R.S.C. 1985, c. C–46, ss. 266, 267, makes a distinction between common assault and assault causing bodily harm, with the latter being one example of aggravated assault. Common assault is an offence punishable on summary **conviction**, whereas assault causing bodily harm is an **indictable** offence carrying a maximum five-year imprisonment. See **sexual assault**.

ASSEMBLY, FREEDOM OF [ASSEMBLY, FREEDOM OF PEACEFUL] See **freedom of assembly**.

ASSEMBLY, UNLAWFUL See **unlawful assembly**.

ASSENT Consent; agreement. See **royal assent**.

ASSESS To determine the value of something; to fix the value of **property** upon which a tax will be imposed.

ASSETS Anything of value; any interest in **real property** or **personal property** that can be **appropriated** for the payment of debts.

ASSIGN To transfer one's interest in **property**, **contract**, or other rights to another. See **assignment of a contract**.

ASSIGNMENT The act whereby one transfers to another an **interest** in a right or **property**. See *Norwich Union Life Insurance Ltd. v. Low Profile Fashions Ltd.*, [1992] 1 E.G.L.R. 86 (C.A.). See **PPSA**.

ASSIGNMENT OF A CONTRACT Generally, the **common law** did not recognize assignments of debts or other contractual rights, although the **Courts of Equity** did assist the assignee by compelling the assignor to bring an **action** or to allow his name to be used as nominal **plaintiff** in an action brought by the assignee. With passage of the English *Supreme Court of Judicature Act, 1873,* specific provision was made for assignment, subject to certain formalities such as writing and notice. Some Canadian jurisdictions have adopted the English provisions. See, e.g., *Conveyancing and Law of Property Act,* R.S.O. 1990, c. C. 34, s. 53(1); *Judicature Act,* R.S.N.S. 1989, c. 240, s. 43(5).

For more detailed treatment see, e.g., G.H.L. Fridman, *The Law of Contract in Canada* (6th ed. 2011), c. 17.

ASSIGNMENT FOR BENEFIT OF CREDITORS A transfer by a **debtor** of property to an assignee in **trust** to apply that which is transferred to the debts of the ASSIGNOR (debtor). See *Bankruptcy and Insolvency Act,* R.S.C. 1985, C. B–3, ss. 42, 49.

ASSIGNMENT OF A LEASE A transfer of the **lessee's** entire interest in the **lease**. When there exists an express **covenant** in the original lease to pay rent, the assignor (the original **tenant**) remains secondarily liable to the **landlord** after an assignment. Compare **sublease**; **subtenant**. See *Norwich Union Life Insurance Ltd. v. Law Profile Fashions Ltd.*, [1992] 1 E.G.L.R. 86 (C.A.).

ASSIGNS All those who take from or under the ASSIGNOR, whether by **conveyance**, **devise**, **descent**, or **operation of law**.

ASSISTANCE, WRIT OF An obsolete writ used by the English Court of Chancery to enforce an order for possession of land. In Canada, "after a number of constitutional challenges, writs of assistance were abolished." R. Salhany, *Canadian Criminal Procedure* c. 3 at 68 (6th ed. 1994). See e.g., *R. v. Noble* (1984), 14 D.L.R. (4th) 216 (Ont. C.A.), where provisions for searches under the *Narcotic Control Act,* R.S.C. 1970, c. N–1, and the *Food and Drugs Act,* R.S.C. 1970, c. F–27, authorized by writs of assistance were found to violate s. 8 of the **Charter of Rights and Freedoms** and be of **no force and effect**.

ASSIZE [or ASSISE] **1.** An ancient **writ** issued from a court of assize to the **sheriff** for the recovery of property; **2.** the actions of the special court that issued the writ. See **Court of Assize and Nisi Prius**. **3.** Assizes may also refer to the sittings of a court, e.g., the sittings of judges on circuit to the major cities or towns of a province.

ASSOCIATION, ARTICLES OF Regulations, prescribed by statute, concerning the internal management of a company. See, e.g., *Companies Act,* R.S.N.S. 1989, c. 81, ss. 20–23 and Sched. 1, Table A.

ASSOCIATION, MEMORANDUM OF The document, prescribed by statute, regulating the **incorporation** of a company. Generally, the memorandum must state the name of the company, its objectives and the number of shares the company proposes to issue. See, e.g., *Companies Act,* R.S.N.S. 1989, c. 81, ss. 9–19.

ASSUMPSIT (*à-sŭmp'-sĭt*) Lat.: he promised; he undertook. In the old **forms of**

action, an ACTION OF ASSUMPSIT lay whenever the defendant had promised to do something or not to do something, and then breached the **undertaking**. It was a method for the enforcement of contracts not under **seal** and came to cover the whole sphere of simple contracts. In the historical sense, assumpsit is the foundation of our modern law of simple contract. Compare **trespass** [TRESPASS ON THE CASE].

ASSUMPTION OF THE RISK In the law of **torts**, an **affirmative defence** used by the **defendant** to a negligence suit in which it is claimed that **plaintiff** had knowledge of a situation obviously dangerous to him- or herself and yet, impliedly or expressly, assented voluntarily to expose him- or herself to the hazard created by the defendant, who is thereby relieved of legal responsibility for resulting injury. "If people consent to run the risk of injury…they are 'co-authors' of the harm inflicted upon themselves." A. Linden & B. Feldthusen, *Canadian Tort Law*, 518 (9th ed. 2011). See also **volenti non fit injuria**.

Assumption of risk is based fundamentally on consent, whereas CONTRIBUTORY NEGLIGENCE (see **negligence**) arises when the plaintiff fails to exercise **due care**. See *Lagasse v. Rural Municipality of Richot,* [1973] 4 W.W.R. 181 (Man.Q.B.).

ASSURED See **insured**.

ASYLUM 1. A shelter for the unfortunate or afflicted, e.g., for the insane, the crippled, the poor, etc. **2.** A POLITICAL ASYLUM is a state that accepts a citizen of another state as a shelter from prosecution by that other state.

AT BAR A term meaning before the **court**. See **bar**.

ATTACHE A person in the foreign service attached to an embassy or consulate; a diplomat.

ATTACHMENT A **proceeding** in law by which a defendant's **property** is seized and held in legal custody on application by the plaintiff, to be applied against a claim on which the plaintiff seeks a **judgment** against the defendant, e.g., in an action for a debt. See, e.g., *Creditors' Relief Act,* S.O. 2010, c. 16. See also **garnishment**; **replevin**.

ATTAINDER See **bill of attainder**.

ATTEMPT An overt act, beyond mere preparation, moving directly toward the actual commission of a criminal **offence**. "When the preparation to commit a crime is in fact fully complete and ended, the next step done by the **accused** for the purpose and with the intention of committing a specific crime constitutes an **actus reus** sufficient in law to establish a criminal attempt to commit that crime." *R. v. Cline* (1956), 115 C.C.C. 18 at 29 (Ont.C.A.). See *Criminal Code,* R.S.C. 1985, c. C–46, s. 24, which establishes attempt as a separate and complete offence in itself. See also *United States v. Dynar,* [1997] 2 S.C.R. 462. *The Criminal Code* also establishes sanctions for attempts of specific crimes: see, e.g., s. 239 [attempted murder] See E. Meehan & J.H. Currie, *The Law of Criminal Attempt* (2nd ed. 2000).

IMPOSSIBLE ATTEMPT An attempt that occurs when the accused's intended offence was impossible to complete in the circumstances. Traditionally, a distinction was drawn between "factually impossible" attempts and "legally impossible" attempts. See, e.g., *Anderton v. Ryan,* [1985] 1 A.C. 560 (H.L.). A factually impossible attempt was thought to occur when the accused's intended offence was impossible to commit because of circumstances unknown to him or her at the time he or she acted (for example, attempting to commit murder with an unloaded firearm). A legally impossible attempt was thought to occur when an accused did everything he or she intended to do in order to commit an offence, but failed to do so (for example, taking possession of stolen property that is not, in fact, stolen). Historically, a "preponderance of… case law and legal opinion" in common law countries held that factually impossible attempts were criminally punishable, while legally impossible attempts were not. E. Meehan & J.H. Currie, *The Law of Criminal Attempt*

201 (2nd ed. 2000). In Canada, however, the distinction between factual impossibility and legal impossibility has been rejected by the Supreme Court, rendering all attempts, whether "impossible" or not, culpable under s. 24 of the *Criminal Code. United States of America v. Dynar,* [1997] 2 S.C.R. 462.

ATTEST To affirm as true; to sign one's name as a **witness** to the **execution** of a document; to bear witness to. See *Ridley v. McGregor & Canadian Bank of Commerce,* [1934] 2 D.L.R. 399 (Ont.C.A.).

ATTORN To submit to. To attorn to the jurisdiction of a court is to be bound by its decision. A party can attorn to the jurisdiction of a court without explicitly doing so by participating in a suit on the merits. *Hnatiuk v. Assured Developments Ltd.,* 2012 ABCA 97. Some rules of court provide for actions that a defendant can take without attorning to the jurisdiction of that court. See *Federal Courts Rules,* SOR 98–106, s. 208.

ATTORNEY, POWER OF See **power of attorney**.

ATTORNEY-GENERAL [OF CANADA OR OF A PROVINCE] The chief law officer of the Crown; the minister in the **Cabinet** responsible for the public prosecution of criminal offenders and for advising the government with respect to legal matters. The Attorney-General is a member of Parliament or of a provincial legislature, appointed to the position by the **Crown** on the advice of the Prime Minister or the Premier of a province.

ATTRACTIVE NUISANCE See **allurement [doctrine of]**.

AUDI ALTERAM PARTEM (*aŭ'-dē ŏl'-têr-ŭm pär'-tĕm*) Lat.: hear the other side. "The audi alteram partem rule, which is a component of the principles of natural justice and of procedural fairness, requires that a person who is a party to proceedings before a tribunal be informed of the proceedings and provided with an opportunity to be heard by the tribunal." *Telecommunications Workers Union v. Canada (Radio-tele-*

vision and Telecommunications Commission), [1995] 2 S.C.R. 781.

AUDITOR 1. A public officer charged by law with the duty of examining and approving the payment of public funds; **2.** An accountant who performs a similar function for private parties.

AUTHORIZATION In the **Criminal Code**, a **warrant** allowing for the interception of private communications: *Criminal Code*, R.S.C. 1985, c. C–46, s. 183. Also, a specific power included in another warrant: for example, a warrant to **arrest** a person might contain an authorization to enter a dwelling house in order to do so: *Criminal Code*, s. 529.

AUTOMATISM A disassociative state; "a term used to describe unconscious, involuntary behaviour, the state of a person who, though capable of action is not conscious of what he is doing. It means an unconscious voluntary act where the mind does not go with what is being done." *R. v. K.* (1971), 3 C.C.C. (2d) 84 (Ont.C.A.) as quoted in *R. v. Rabey*, [1980] 2 S.C.R. 513 at 518.

Criminal law distinguishes between mental disorder automatism and non–mental disorder automatism. The former leads to a finding that the accused was **not criminally responsible by reason of mental disorder**, while the latter leads to an acquittal. The two are distinguished by considering a number of factors, including whether the automatism was caused by something internal to the accused as opposed to something external. The second major consideration is whether there is a risk of continuing danger, assessed by looking at the psychiatric history of the patient and the likelihood the triggering event will reoccur. *R. v. Stone*, [1999] 2 S.C.R. 290. See also *R. v. Parks* (1992), 140 N.R.161 (S.C.C.).

AUTREFOIS ACQUIT/CONVICT (*ō'-tr'-fwä ä'-kē/kōn-vĭk'*) Fr.: formerly acquitted or convicted. See **double jeopardy**.

AVERMENT A positive statement or **allegation** of facts in a pleading as opposed to an argumentative one or one based on inference.

AVOIDANCE Measures taken to reduce the tax owing. Some tax avoidances are acceptable, but others are prohibited by particular rules in the *Income Tax Act* RSC 1985, c 1 (5th Supp) or by the **GAAR**. See **avoidance transaction**; **evasion**.

AVOIDANCE TRANSACTION Under the *Income Tax Act*, RSC 1985, c 1 (5th Supp), a transaction that results in a tax benefit and is not undertaken primarily for a *bona fide* non-tax purpose.

AVULSION An abrupt change in the course of a river or stream, resulting in the sudden loss of part of the land from one **riparian** landowner to another. The sudden and perceptible nature of this change distinguishes avulsion from **accretion**. This distinction is important, for when the change is abrupt, the property in the part separated remains in the original owner, instead of becoming part of the other owner's land, which occurs with gradual accretion. Compare **reliction**. See also **alluvion**.

B

BAD DEBT An uncollectable **debt** that may be written off as a business expense. Such classification is important in tax law. See *McCool v. The Queen*, 2005 TCC 357.

BAD FAITH An act undertaken to mislead another party or to neglect the fulfillment of some obligation, not through an honest mistake. Bad faith, or MALA FIDE, is generally used in relation to **fraud**. Bad faith on the part of the police can be a factor in deciding whether **evidence** should be excluded as a **remedy** for a breach of a right under the **Canadian Charter of Rights and Freedoms**.

BAD TITLE Title that is legally insufficient to **convey** property to the purchaser; title that is not **marketable**; one that a purchaser is not compelled to accept; a radically defective title. A defect in title as opposed to a defect in quality. *Scott v. Alvarez*, [1895] 2 Ch. 603 (C.A.).

BAIL The popular term for what is referred to in the *Criminal Code*, R.S.C. 1985, c. C–46 as **judicial interim release**. The word "bail" is sometimes used in describing the overall process (a "bail hearing"), the general fact of release (being "out on bail"), or a deposit of money made to secure release ("cash bail," which is the exception rather than the rule for judicial interim release). None of these uses reflect the language of the *Criminal Code*, which does not use the term "bail" in any provision. However, s. 11(e) of the **Canadian Charter of Rights and Freedoms** guarantees everyone charged with an offence the right "not to be denied reasonable bail without just cause." The Supreme Court of Canada has held, in considering that section, that "'bail' should be read as a reference to judicial interim release in general and not as a reference to any particular form of interim release." *R. v. Pearson*, [1992] 3 S.C.R. 665.

BAIL BOND An agreement whereby a **surety** submits to the **jurisdiction** of a court and agrees to the **execution** of a **judgment** against him or her as a means of securing the release of property that has been **arrested** because of an **in rem** action. The judgment only becomes enforceable against the surety if any eventual settlement or judgment is not paid by the **debtor**. The term is also sometimes used to describe the document upon which a person who has been arrested is released, but that usage does not reflect any statutory language in the **Criminal Code**.

BAILEE One to whom the **property** involved in a **bailment** is delivered; the party who holds the goods of another for a specific purpose pursuant to an agreement between the parties; the person to whom possession of goods is entrusted by the owner, but with no intention of transferring ownership.

A bailee acquires a special interest or property in the goods. He or she is bound to take care of the goods bailed and is liable for **negligence** in relation to the bailed goods. The degree of negligence (gross, slight, or ordinary) for which he or she is liable varies with the type of bailment. The bailee's negligence is presumed, and he or she must rebut this presumption on a balance of probabilities. See *Gobeil v. Elliot* (1996), 150 Sask. R. 285 (Sask. Q.B.). See B. Ziff, *Principles of Property Law* 313–33 (5th ed. 2010).

BAILIFF A court attendant; a person to whom some authority, **guardianship**, or **jurisdiction** is entrusted. A person employed by the **sheriff** to serve **writs** and to make arrests and executions of court orders. The bailiff is bound annually to the sheriff by a bond with **sureties** for the proper execution of the office and is therefore called a BOUND BAILIFF.

BAILMENT The delivery of **personal property** or **chattels** from the **bailor** (one who delivers goods) to the **bailee** (one who receives goods) in **trust**, with a special purpose, to benefit either or both of the parties. The purpose of the trust conforms to an express or implied **contract**. The elements of lawful **possession** and the duty to account for the article as the property of another are important aspects of bailment. See *McLennan v. Charlottetown Flying Services* (1979) 65 A.P.R. 72 (P.E.I.S.C.).

ACTUAL BAILMENT One established by an actual or constructive delivery of **property** to the **bailee** or his **agents**.

CONSTRUCTIVE BAILMENT One that arises when the person having **possession** holds it under such circumstances that the law imposes an obligation to deliver to another, even where such person did not come into **possession** voluntarily, and thus no bailment was voluntarily established. *Munn v. Wakelin* (1944), 17 M.P.R. 447 (P.E.I.S.C.). A primary example is that of the finder who, although possessing goods without the knowledge or consent of the owner, is deemed to owe a duty of reasonable care and a duty not to convert the **chattel**.

GRATUITOUS BAILMENT One in which the care and custody of **bailor's** property is accepted without **consideration** by the **bailee**. In this type of bailment, the bailee is liable for the loss of the bailed property only if the loss results from the bailee's gross **negligence**. *Chiaravalloti v. Leading Edge Auto Collision*, 2012 ONSC 4554; *Canada (Attorney General) v. Canadian Sturgeon Conservation Center Ltd.*, 2005 NBQB 287.

INVOLUNTARY BAILMENT One that arises whenever the goods of one person have by accident become lodged on another's land or person. If the person upon whose land the **personal property** is located should refuse to deliver the goods to their owner upon demand or to permit their removal, the bailee might be liable for **conversion** of that property. *McCutcheon v. Lightfoot*, [1929] 1 W.W.R. 694 (Man.C.A.), affirmed [1930] S.C.R. 108.

BAILOR The party who bails or delivers goods, **chattels**, or **personal property** to another in a contract or **bailment**. The bailor need not be the owner of the

property involved. *Reichardt v. Shard* (1914), 31 T.L.R. 24 (C.A.).

BAIT 1. To set one animal against another that is confined in such a manner that it cannot get away. Anyone encouraging, or assisting at the fighting or baiting of animals is guilty of an offence. *Criminal Code,* R.S.C. 1985, c. C–46, s. 445(1)(b). **2.** Food that is left to lure an animal. Some statutes make it an offence to use bait for hunting wildlife in certain circumstances. See, e.g., *Wildlife Act*, R.S.Y. 2002, c. 229; *Wildlife Act*, R.S.N.W.T. 1988, c. W–4.

BAIT AND SWITCH Advertising "at a bargain price a product that the person does not supply in reasonable quantities having regard to the nature of the market in which the person carries on business, the nature and size of the person's business, and the nature of the advertisement." *Competition Act*, R.S.C. 1985, c. C–34, s. 74.04. Bait and switch is reviewable conduct under the *Competition Act,* which could lead to a penalty being imposed.

BALANCE OF PROBABILITIES A standard of proof requiring the person who has the **burden of proof** to demonstrate that a fact or facts are more likely than not. Also referred to as the civil standard.

BANC [EN] See **en banc**.

BANCO [IN] Lat.: literally, a seat or bench. See **en banc**.

BAND A body of **Indians** for whose use and benefit in common, lands vested in the Crown have been set apart as a reserve. *Indian Act*, R.S.C. 1985, c. I–5, s. 2(1).

BAND COUNCIL [INDIAN] Created under the *Indian Act*, R.S.C. 1985, c. I–5, s. 74, a "federal board" within the meaning of s. 2(1) of the *Federal Court Act*, R.S.C. 1985, c. F–7. It has the power to enact by-laws for the band and consists of one chief and one councillor for every one hundred members of the band.

BANKRUPTCY Insolvency, i.e., the inability of a **debtor** to pay his or her **debts** as they become due; the legal process by which assets of the debtor are liquidated to pay off **creditors**. Historically, bankruptcy proceedings could only be brought against traders and were directed solely to preventing fraudulent traders from escaping their creditors. Currently, a bankrupt as defined under the *Bankruptcy and Insolvency Act,* R.S.C. 1985, c. B–3, s. 2, includes anyone who has made an **assignment** or against whom a receiving order has been made—in other words, a person who has the legal status of being bankrupt and has consequently been declared unable to meet his debts and **liabilities**. Bankruptcy proceedings are judicial or quasi-judicial and are for the purpose of distributing the bankrupt's property among the creditors and relieving the bankrupt of the unpaid balance of the liabilities. A bankrupt may decide alternatively to make voluntary arrangements with the creditors.

BANNS OF MARRIAGE The formal public announcement by a religious authority of an intended **marriage**. In some provinces and territories, the publication of banns is deemed to be a legally valid alternative to obtaining a marriage license. See, e.g., *Marriage Act*, R.S.O. 1990, c. M.3; *Marriage Act*, R.S.M. 1987, c. M50; *Marriage Act*, R.S.N.W.T. 1988, c. M–4.

BAR 1. A previous **judgment** is a bar to another action by the same parties on the same set of facts. When a judgment becomes absolute, it can no longer be questioned, and hence no further action may be taken between the same parties regarding the same matter. This may also be termed ESTOPPEL BY DEED (see **estoppel**). *Tencer v. Rockroy Construction (Hamilton) Ltd.* (1976), 15 O.R. (2d) 526 (Co.Ct.). See also **res judicata**; **double jeopardy**.

2. If an **action** is not brought within the time set out by **statute**, it is barred by the *Statute of Limitations* (or a similar act, depending on the **jurisdiction**), which is to say that the action can no longer be brought. This is sometimes termed an ABSOLUTE BAR; there may also be a PRESUMPTIVE BAR that arises from a lapse of time otherwise than under statute. *O'Dell v. Hastie* (1968), 63 W.W.R. (N.S.) 632 (Sask.Q.B.).

3. Technically, the bar is the barrier that separates the general public from the space occupied by the judges, the counsel and the parties to the case. In England, outer-barristers stand behind the bar with the public while the other persons dealing with the case stand within the bar, including the solicitors. Thus, counsel appear AT THE BAR to argue a case, and the CASE AT BAR is the case now before the court.

4. The members of the legal profession, the lawyers, are collectively known as MEMBERS OF THE BAR and are CALLED TO THE BAR when they have been accepted into the profession.

5. All persons who are not members of a legislative body and who wish to address the members of that body or who are summoned to it appear AT THE BAR (the outer boundary of the House) for that purpose.

6. Formerly, A PLEA AT BAR was a type of plea that showed a substantial defence to the action.

BAR ADMISSION The process by which a person is admitted to practice law in a particular jurisdiction. The requirements are set by the relevant **law societies** and vary from province to province, but generally require a period of apprenticeship known as **articles of clerkship (articling)** as well as supplementary courses and examinations. Once the requirements have been met in full, the person is admitted as a MEMBER OF THE BAR in the relevant jurisdiction.

BAR ASSOCIATION In Canada the term generally refers to an independent organization of lawyers at the national, provincial, or local level that represents the common interests of the legal profession, or a segment of its members, and which may advocate or promote the organization's interests to the profession's governing bodies, various levels of government, the business community, and the general public; e.g., the Ontario Bar Association, the Ontario Trial Lawyers Association, etc. See **Canadian Bar Association**. It is vital to distinguish the vast array of "associations" from the governing bodies of the legal profession in each province and territory. See **Law Society, disbarment**.

BARGAIN An **agreement** between two or more persons, intended to be enforceable at law. Bargain and **contract** express the same legal concept. The term also suggests negotiation over the terms of an agreement.

BARGAIN AND SALE Generally applies to land and refers to a **contract** for the sale of any estate or interest in **real property** or **chattels** followed later by payment of the agreed purchase price. The phrase is also applied to transfers of **personalty** where there is an **executory** agreement of sale followed by a completed sale. However, bargain and sale as a method of **conveyancing** has now become obsolete. Compare **quitclaim deed**; **warranty deed**.

BARGAINING AGENT A trade union (or council of trade unions as in Newfoundland) that acts on behalf of employees (1) in **collective bargaining** or (2) as a party to a collective agreement with an employer.

BARGAINING IN GOOD FAITH See **good faith bargaining**.

BARGAINING UNIT A group of employees to which a collective agreement applies or which has been certified as appropriate for **collective bargaining**. See, e.g., *Canada Labour Code*, R.S.C. 1985, c. L-2, s. 3(1).

BARRISTER AND SOLICITOR A lawyer; a person called to the bar by the law society of a particular province. In Canada, a lawyer is both barrister and solicitor, whereas in England, there is a distinction: The barrister does the actual court work, presenting and arguing the case in court, but does not prepare the case from the start; the solicitor's function is to assemble the legal materials, do the research and compile the legal precedents. A solicitor also is employed to perform a wide variety of legal work, such as the preparation of documents like **wills** and **mortgages**, **conveyancing**, company work and advising on tax matters.

BASTARD An illegitimate child; a child born out of lawful wedlock. The common-law rules relating to illegiti-macy have been modified by **statute** in Canada, but the **legislation** is not uniform. In Ontario, the status of a child as a bastard has been abolished, and a child's status is independent of whether the child is born within or outside marriage. *Children's Law Reform Act,* R.S.O. 1990, c. C. 12, s. 1

BATTERY "An unprivileged and unconsented to invasion of one's bodily security." *Reibl v. Hughes* (1980), 114 D.L.R. (3d) 1 (S.C.C.). In **tort** law, in order for there to be a battery, there must be actual, unconsented-to physical contact, although there need not be any injury done. If the contact is offensive, even though harmless, it entitles the plaintiff to an award of NOMINAL DAMAGES (see **damages**). See generally *Malette v. Shulman* (1990), 67 D.L.R. (4th) 321 (Ont. CA).

There is no crime of battery in Canada per se. However, the statutory definition of **assault** in the *Criminal Code* recognizes, but obviates, the common-law distinction between assault and battery. *Criminal Code,* R.S.C. 1985, c. C–46, s. 265.

A battery may thus, in effect, result in both tortious and **criminal** liability. See **assault**.

BAWDY HOUSE A place that is **kept** or occupied, or is resorted to by one or more persons, for the purpose of **prostitution** or the practice of acts of **indecency**. *Criminal Code,* R.S.C. 1985, c. C–46, s. 197.

BEARER INSTRUMENT A cheque, note, or draft made payable to the bearer so that anyone who presents the instrument is paid the amount shown on its face.

The *Bills of Exchange Act,* R.S.C. 1985, c. B–4, s. 2, defines the bearer as the person in possession of a bill or note that is payable to the bearer.

BENCH 1. The court; the judges composing the court collectively. **2.** The place where the judge sits (as in APPROACH THE BENCH).

BENCHER A member of the governing body of certain provincial law societies (e.g., the Benchers of the Law Society of Upper Canada), either elected or appointed, **ex officio**. They are responsible for regulation of the profession, including admission to the bar, discipline, and disbarring. See, e.g., the *Law Society Act,* R.S.O. 1990, c. L. 8, ss. 10–25.

BENCH WARRANT A court order empowering the proper legal authorities to arrest a person: most commonly used to compel one's attendance before the court to **answer** a **charge** of **contempt** when, for example, one has failed to answer to a **summons**, to appear as a **witness** after being subpoenaed or to appear for trial after being released on bail. See *Criminal Code,* R.S.C. 1985, c. C–46, ss. 704, 705.

BENEFICIAL INTEREST See **interest**.

BENEFICIALLY ENTITLED Having a **beneficial interest** in property.

BENEFICIAL OWNER A person who is not in law the owner of property but in **equity** is entitled to it. "The beneficial owner of property has been described as 'the real owner of property even though it is in someone else's name.'" *Csak v. Aumon* (1990), 69 D.L.R. (4th) 567 (Ont. H.C.J.), at p. 570. *Pecore v. Pecore*, 2007 SCC 17. See **beneficial use**.

BENEFICIAL USE With respect to property, such right to its enjoyment as exists where the legal **title** is in one person while the right to such use or interest is in another. A person who has beneficial use does not hold legal title of property. Legal title is held in **trust** by another. See **beneficial interest**; **mortgage**; **trust**; **use**.

BENEFICIARY In general, the person receiving or designated to receive a benefit or advantage. **1.** The person having the beneficial enjoyment of property rather than the legal possession—for example, the person for the benefit of whom a **trust** is created, or, in other words, the CESTUI QUE TRUST [see **trust**] in a trust relationship; **2.** the third party who is designated as the receiver of benefits from a **contract**; **3.** the person named in an **insurance** policy as the one to receive any benefits accruing

under it; **4.** the person named in a **will** to receive property under the will.

INCIDENTAL BENEFICIARY A person who may incidentally benefit from the creation of a trust. Such a person has no actual interest in the trust and cannot enforce any right to incidental benefit.

BEQUEATH To make a gift of **personalty** by means of a **will**. Strictly, it signifies a gift of **personal property**, which distinguishes it from a **devise**, which is a gift of **real property**. A DISPOSITION is the generic name encompassing both a bequest of personalty and a devise of realty.

BEQUEST A **gift** or disposition of **personalty** contained in a **will**. A **devise** ordinarily passes **real property**, and a bequest, personal property. Compare **legacy**.

CONDITIONAL BEQUEST One that will take effect or continue only if a certain event occurs or fails to occur.

EXECUTORY BEQUEST A bequest of **personalty** or money that does not take effect until the happening of a possible or certain future event upon which it is thus said to be contingent.

RESIDUARY BEQUEST A bequest consisting of that which is left in an **estate** after payment of **debts** and general legacies and other specific gifts. *Higgins v. Dawson,* [1902] A.C. 1 (H.L.)

SPECIFIC BEQUEST A bequest of particular items of a testator's estate or all property of a certain class or kind. *Shepheard. v. Beetham,* [1877], 6 Ch.D. 597.

BEST EVIDENCE RULE A rule of evidence law requiring that the most persuasive **evidence** available be used to prove the terms of a writing. "The best evidence rule, or perhaps better stated, 'the original documents' rule, as it exists today, is confined to cases where a party has the original document and could produce it but does not. The party may satisfy the court that the original is lost, destroyed, or is otherwise in the possession of another and cannot be attained." D. Paciocco and L. Stuesser, *The Law of Evidence* 467 (6th ed. 2011).

BESTIALITY Human sexual intercourse with an animal. Anyone who commits bestiality is guilty of a **hybrid offence**. *Criminal Code,* R.S.C. 1985, c. C–46, s. 160. See also *R. v. Triller* (1980), 55 C.C.C. (2d) 411 (B.C.Co.Ct.).

BEST INTERESTS OF THE CHILD A central consideration in legal decision-making involving children. In **custody** decisions, it involves "...[d]eciding what, objectively, appears most likely in the circumstances to be conducive to the kind of environment in which a particular child has the best opportunity for receiving the needed care and attention. Because there are stages to childhood, what is in a child's best interest may vary from childhood to childhood." *MacGyver v. Richards* (1995), 123 D.L.R. (4th) 562 at 570 (Ont.C.A.). In the context of considering whether a child should be removed from the custody of his or her parents, some statutes have articulated factors to be taken into account, such as the mental, emotional, and physical health of the child; the views and preferences of the child, where they can be determined; and the child's cultural and religious heritage. See, e.g., *Family Services Act,* SNB 1980, c F-2.2. The criterion is also made a consideration in other statutes, including the *Immigration and Refugee Protection Act,* S.C. 2001, c. 27; the *Youth Criminal Justice Act,* S.C. 2002, c. 1; and the *Divorce Act,* R.S.C. 1985, c. 3 (2nd Supp.). Although the best interests of the child is an important consideration in many contexts, it is not a **principle of fundamental justice**. *Canadian Foundation for Children, Youth, and the Law v. Canada (Attorney General)*, 2004 SCC 4.

BETTERMENT A term in property law used to describe any acts or efforts that enhance the value of **real property**; improvements.

BEYOND A REASONABLE DOUBT See **reasonable doubt**.

BFOR See **bona fide occupational requirement**.

BIAS A lack of impartiality; the basing of a decision on preconceived ideas and beliefs rather than on the facts; describes a person who is not neutral. It is bias to act from partiality or prejudice. "Four classes of potential juror prejudice have been identified—interest, specific, generic, and conformity ... Interest prejudice arises when jurors may have a direct stake in the trial due to their relationship to the defendant, the victim, witnesses, or outcome. Specific prejudice involves attitudes and beliefs about the particular case that may render the juror incapable of deciding guilt or innocence with an impartial mind. These attitudes and beliefs may arise from personal knowledge of the case, publicity through mass media, or public discussion and rumour in the community. Generic prejudice, the class of prejudice at issue on this appeal, arises from stereotypical attitudes about the defendant, victims, witnesses, or the nature of the crime itself. Bias against a racial or ethnic group or against persons charged with sex abuse are examples of generic prejudice. Finally, conformity prejudice arises when the case is of significant interest to the community, causing a juror to perceive that there is strong community feeling about a case coupled with an expectation as to the outcome." *R. v. Williams*, [1998] 1 S.C.R. 1128. See **reasonable apprehension of bias**. Contrast **impartiality**.

BID An offer by an intending purchaser to buy goods or services at a stated price, or an offer by an intended seller to sell goods or services for a stated price. In the context of building contracts, contractors usually solicit bids based on building specifications from several subcontractors in order to complete the project. Governmental units may be required by law to construct highways and buildings and to buy goods and services in accordance with a procedure wherein competitive bids are solicited by advertisement from the public, with the lowest competent bid winning the contract. See **tender**.

BID BOND A conditional bond given to the bidder to guarantee his or her entry into the contract. If the bidder is unsuccessful, the bond is returned to the bidder. However, the bond can be forfeited if the bidder is successful and yet refuses to perform the contract.

BIGAMY Under s. 290(1) of the *Criminal Code,* R.S.C. 1985, c. C–46, everyone commits bigamy who, in Canada, is already married and marries another person, or knowing that another person is married, marries that person, or on the same day or simultaneously goes through a form of marriage with more than one person. Also under s. 290(1), everyone commits bigamy who, being a Canadian citizen resident in Canada, leaves Canada intending to do any of the above and in fact does any of the above outside Canada. *R. v. Howard,* [1966] 3 C.C.C. (N.S.) 91 (B.C.Co.Ct.)

Section 290(2) of the Code lists four sets of circumstances, any one of which, if met, would mean bigamy had not been committed. These sets of circumstances are that (*a*) the person "in good faith and on reasonable grounds" believes his or her spouse is dead, (*b*) the spouse of the person has been continuously absent for seven years immediately preceding the time of the marriage, unless he or she knew the spouse was alive at any time during these seven years, (*c*) the person has been divorced from the bond of the first marriage, and (*d*) the former marriage has been declared void by a court of competent jurisdiction. Section 291(1) states that everyone who commits bigamy is guilty of an **indictable offence** and is liable to imprisonment for five years. A bigamous marriage is **void**.

BILATERAL CONTRACT See **contract**.

BILL A proposition or statement reduced to writing. **1.** In commercial law, an account of goods sold, services rendered and work done, or a written statement of the terms of contract or specification of the items of a transaction; a charge or invoice.

2. In **legislation**, a document submitted to **Parliament** or a provincial **legislature** for its consideration and/or enactment. If approved, it becomes law in the form of a **statute**.

PRIVATE BILL A **bill** that applies only to an individual or a corporation (corporate individual). For example, a bill to incorporate a specific company. *Private bills* are generally introduced in the **Senate** rather than the **House of Commons**.

PUBLIC BILL A bill that is general in nature and applies to all persons in a given jurisdiction. Public bills are introduced in the House of Commons and can be one of two types: (1) GOVERNMENT BILLS—bills introduced by the government of the day which deal with the implementation of government policy (e.g., *Copyright Modernization Act*, S.C. 2012, c. 20.); (2) PRIVATE MEMBERS BILLS—Bills introduced by individual Members of Parliament, including opposition and third party members, which are completely separate from government policy. Most Private Members Bills do not make it beyond first reading unless they are supported as part of government policy.

BILL OF ATTAINDER An abolished bill that declared persons charged with certain crimes—e.g., treason—to be *attainted,* involving the forfeiture of land, the **confiscation** of property, and the **corruption of blood**. Any traces of attainder have been removed from Canadian law by the *Criminal Code,* first enacted in 1892.

BILL OF COST An account of a lawyer's charges and **disbursements** incurred in the conduct of the client's business. The lawyer is obliged to deliver a statement of account to the client in order to give the client an opportunity of taxing it, i.e., having it examined by an appointed official or taxing master and possibly reduced. See **costs**.

BILL OF EXCEPTIONS A writing setting out the objections to rulings made or instructions given by a trial judge. By Ord. LVIII, r. 1 of the English *Supreme Court of Judicature Act, 1875,* bills of exception were abolished.

BILL OF EXCHANGE As defined in the *Bills of Exchange Act,* R.S.C. 1985, C. B–4, s. 16(1), a bill of exchange is an unconditional order in writing, addressed by one person to another, signed by the person giving it, requiring the person to whom it is addressed to pay, on demand or at a fixed or determinable future time, a sum certain in money to or to the order of a specified person, or to bearer. It is assignable, at common law, by mere endorsement. Many names may possibly be attached to one bill as endorsers, and each of them is liable to be sued upon the bill, if it is not paid in due time. The person who makes or draws the bill is called the DRAWER; the person to whom it is addressed is, before acceptance, the DRAWEE, and, after acceptance, the ACCEPTOR; the person in whose favour it is drawn is the PAYEE; if he endorses the bill to another, he is called the ENDORSER, and the person to whom it is thus assigned, or negotiated, is the ENDORSEE, or HOLDER. See **bearer instrument**; **draft**; **negotiable instrument**.

BILL OF LADING A written acknowledgement of receipt of goods. It represents the **contract** of carriage and serves as evidence of the conditions of carriage agreed upon between the two parties, and it is a document of title to the goods described therein. *Can. Gen. Electric Co. Ltd.. v. Les Armateurs du St.-Laurent Inc.*, [1977] 1 F.C. 215. An important function served by a bill of lading is to express the conditions under which the carrier seeks to limit the **liability** that would otherwise be imposed on it under common law.

BILL OF PARTICULARS A bill served on an opposing party to enable the party asking for the particulars to know what **claim**, **defence**, or other matter stated in pleadings must be met at **trial**, to save unnecessary expense and to avoid parties from being taken by surprise. *Spedding v. Fitzpatrick* (1888), 38 Ch.D. 410. The rules of civil procedure entitle an opposing party to apply for further and better particulars or facts of any matter stated in a **pleading**. Particulars narrow the generality of the propositions contained in the statement of material facts, thereby further limiting and defining the issues to be tried. Particulars also determine the scope of discovery and govern the admission of evidence at the trial. *Bruce. v. Odhanu Press Ltd.,* [1936] 1 K.B. 697 (C.A.).

In criminal law, an **accused** who is unable to prepare a defence properly because the **charge** does not contain sufficient information may submit to the court a DEMAND FOR PARTICULARS. The court may order the prosecutor at its discretion to furnish the accused or **counsel** with the particulars requested. *Criminal Code,* R.S.C. 1985, c. C-46, s. 587.

BILL OF RIGHTS A declaration delivered by the English Lords and Commons to the Prince and Princess of Orange in 1689 and afterwards enacted in Parliament when they became king and queen (1 W. & M., c. 2). It set forth that King James, by the assistance of evil counsellors, endeavoured to subvert the laws of the kingdom by, **inter alia**, levying money for the use of the Crown without consent of Parliament, by violent prosecutions, by excessive bail and by the infliction of cruel punishments—all of which were declared to be illegal. The Act of Parliament recognises all the rights and liberties asserted to be "the true, ancient, indisputable rights of the people of this kingdom."

The Bill of Rights is recognised as a landmark in the struggle of the individual and Parliament for control of the **executive**. It is also regarded as one of the fundamental traditions of government and constitutional law that Canada inherited from England. See, e.g., *R. v. Hess No. 2*, [1949] 4 D.L.R. 199 (B.C.C.A.) at 208–09: "[T]he purported powers...to deny an acquitted person bail, to obstruct and delay his application therefore, and to detain him in custody for an offence of which the Court has acquitted him and when there is no offence charged against him are all contrary to the written constitution of the United Kingdom, as reflected in Magna Carta (1215), the Petition of Right (1628), the Bill of Right (1689) and the Act of Settlement (1700–1701)." See **Canadian Bill of Rights**, a statute passed by the federal government in 1960.

BILL OF SALE A written agreement under which **title** to personal **chattels** is transferred; in a more technical sense, a document evidencing a **contract** of the sale of goods that may be required to be registered under the various provincial *Bill of Sale* and *Personal Property Security* statutes. In certain cases, a bill of sale must be registered; otherwise the sale may be treated as **void** as regards third parties, e.g., the creditors of the seller, as well as subsequent buyers and mortgagees in good faith. See, e.g., *Personal Property Security Act*, S.N.S. 1995–96, c. 13.

BIND Something that obligates or constrains the bound individual. A bind places one under legal duties and obligations. One can bind oneself as in a **contract** or one can be bound by a **judgment**.

BINDER A **contract** for temporary insurance; a written memorandum of the most important items of a preliminary contract, one that covers the insured and the **underwriter** on risk for the period while the insurance proposal is being considered and until a policy is either granted or refused. Also termed a COVER NOTE. *Rainer v. Primerica Life Insurance Co. of Canada*, 2002 ABCA 50. See also B. Billingsley, *General Principles of Canadian Insurance Law* 69–71 (2008).

BINDING As used in a statute, commonly means obligatory. At common law, a superior court's decision on a point of law is binding on an inferior court.

BINDING AGREEMENT A conclusive agreement.

BINDING ARBITRATION A process providing for final settlement of differences between the parties to a **collective agreement** concerning its interpretation, application, administration, or an alleged contravention. Binding arbitration can arise from the terms of the collective agreement or by **statute**. See, e.g., *Canada Labour Code*, RSC 1985, c L–2, s. 57.

BINDING INSTRUCTION An instruction that directs the jury how to determine an issue in the case if the condition stated in that instruction is shown to exist. See **directed verdict**.

BIND OVER The power exercisable by a magistrate, on facts established to his or her satisfaction, to order anyone to enter into a **recognizance** to keep the peace. *Regina v. White, Ex parte Chohan*, [1969] 1 C.C.C. 19 at 22 (B.C.S.C.).

BLACK LETTER LAW A term referring to well-established legal rules that are undisputed in an area of law. The term originates from the practice of printing legal rules in textbooks in a dark print, followed by general comments and explanatory text in a lighter print. S.M. Waddams, *Introduction to the Study of Law* 25–26 (6th ed. 2004).

BLASPHEMY At **common law**, the **misdemeanour** of reviling or ridiculing the established religion (Christianity) and the existence of God; *Gathercole's Case* (1838), 2 Lewin 237; 168 E.R. 1140. Under s. 296 of the *Criminal Code*, R.S.C. 1985, c. C–46, everyone who publishes a blasphemous libel is guilty of an **indictable offence** and is liable to imprisonment for two years. However, arguments upon a religious subject that are expressed in good faith and in decent language are allowable, and no one can be convicted of an offence for arguing in this manner. See s. 296(3). See also *John William Gott* (1922), 16 Cr.App.R. 87: *Rex v. Rahard* (1935), 65 C.C.C. 344 (Que.Ct. of Sess.).

BLOOD, CORRUPTION OF See **corruption of blood**; **bill of attainder**.

BLUE LAW A law prohibiting commercial activity on Sundays. Where such laws are motivated purely by religious purposes, they are **unconstitutional** under s. 2(a) of the **Canadian Charter of Rights and Freedoms**. *R. v. Big M Drug Mart Ltd.*, [1985] 1 S.C.R. 295. Laws prohibiting commercial activity on Sundays for secular purposes, however, are constitutional. *R. v. Edwards Books and Art Ltd.*, [1986] 2 S.C.R. 713.

BLUE SKY LAWS Legislation imposing strict standards beyond mere disclosure on issues of securities. Under blue sky laws, the administrator of securities has the responsibility to decide whether it is fair for the public to be allowed to buy questionable securities; disclosure is not enough. See D. Johnston

& K. Rockwell, *Canadian Securities Regulation* 21 (4th ed. 2006).

BODILY HARM "Any hurt or injury to a person that interferes with the health or comfort of the person and that is more than merely transient or trifling in nature." *Criminal Code*, R.S.C. 1985, c. C–46, s.2.

BOILERPLATE Generic or standardized wording used with little or no attention to the particular context. The term can be attached to language used in many circumstances, including judges' instructions to a **jury** or reasons for **judgment**, or in an application for a **warrant**.

BONA (*bō'-na*) Lat.: good, virtuous. Also, goods and **chattels**; property moveable and immoveable (civil law).

BONA FIDE (*bō'-na fīd*) Lat.: in or with **good faith**; without fraud or deceit.

BONA FIDE OCCUPATIONAL REQUIREMENT (BFOR) In human rights legislation, a refusal, expulsion, suspension, or preference deemed *not* to be discrimination if the employer has established that the characteristic (e.g., height, weight) is necessary for the safe and adequate performance of a job. "[A] rule or standard must accommodate individual differences to the point of undue hardship if it is to be found reasonably necessary. Unless no further accommodation is possible without imposing undue hardship, the standard is not a BFOR in its existing form and the *prima facie* case of discrimination stands." *British Columbia (Public Service Employee Relations Commission) v. BCGSEU*, [1999] 3 S.C.R. 3. See **duty to accommodate**; **undue hardship**.

BONA FIDE PURCHASER One who in **good faith** acquires legal **title** to **property** by paying valuable **consideration** and has no notice of third party claims. *Burns v. Young* (1900), 46 N.S.R. 199 (S.C.); *Stubbert. v. Scott & Temple*, [1931] 1 W.W.R. 598 (B.C.S.C.).
BONA FIDE PURCHASE One made in **good faith** for valuable **consideration** and without notice of a competing claim. The plea of a purchase of a legal estate for value without notice is an absolute defence against the claims of any prior equitable owner. *iTrade Finance Inc. v. Bank of Montreal*, [2011] 2 S.C.R. 360.

BONA VACANTIA (*bō'nă věkăn'shă*) Lat.: ownerless goods. At common-law, when the owner of personal property dies without heir or next of kin, his or her property becomes vested in the Crown as "bona vacantia." B. Ziff, *Principles of Property Law* 313–33 (5th ed. 2010).

BOND A written **instrument** whereby a person makes a promise to another. Usually a bond binds the person making it as well as his or her **heirs**, **executors**, and **administrators**, and in the case of a **corporation** its **successors**. The term is also used to refer to instruments of indebtedness issued by governments (such as Canada Savings Bonds) and **companies** to secure repayment of money borrowed by them. This obligation can be represented by detachable coupons for current interest. Typically a bond issued by a **corporation** is for a longer term than a **debenture**.

BONDSMAN Formerly, a person who posted a bail bond in order to secure the release of an arrested person. Under the current bail provisions the nearest equivalent is a **surety**.

BOYCOTT To refrain by concerted effort from commercial dealing with someone; the refusal by a person or group to work for, purchase from, or handle the products of an employer. Boycotting is not necessarily illegal. *Ken Miller & Associates Bakery Distributors Ltd. v. Bakery & Confectionery Workers International Union, Local 468 and Kemmis*, [1971] 5 W.W.R. 460 (B.C.S.C.); *Slade & Stewart Ltd. v. Retail, Wholesale & Department Store Union Local 580* (1969), 69 W.W.R. (N.S.) 374 (B.C.S.C.).

BREACH 1. The failure of **performance** by a **party** of some contracted-for or agreed-upon act; **2.** The invasion of a right as in a breach of a DUTY OF CARE (see **duty**) in **negligence** law. A breach of a contractual or other right converts it into a right to obtain a remedy for the breach, generally a right of **action**.

See **anticipatory breach**; **fundamental breach**; **material breach**. **3**. A violation of a person's rights under the **Canadian Charter of Rights and Freedoms**.

BREACH OF CONTRACT A wrongful non-performance of any contractual duty that results in the entitlement of the innocent party to maintain an action for **damages**. In certain instances the innocent party has the right to treat the contract as **discharged**. See S.M. Waddams, *The Law of Contracts* (6th ed. 2010), c. 16. See **anticipatory breach**; **material breach**.

BREACH OF DUTY Failure to perform a duty owed to another or to society; e.g., the violation by a **trustee** of any duty he or she owes, in a capacity as trustee, to the **beneficiary**.

BREACH OF PROMISE Often used as short form of breach of the promise of marriage. Breach of promise to marry gives rise to a right of action for damages at common law. A promise to marry need not be in writing nor need it be evidenced by writing. Either the man or the woman may sue for the breach. *LeBlanc v. Wetmore,* [1944] 2 D.L.R. 130 (N.B.S.C.A.D.); *Lakusta v. Jones* (1997), 56 Alta. L.R. (3d) 214 (Alta. Q.B.).

BREACH OF THE PEACE Violent action that threatens to disturb the public peace. "A breach of the peace does not include any and all conduct which right-thinking members of the community would regard as offensive, disturbing, or even vaguely threatening. A breach of the peace contemplates an act or actions which result in actual or threatened harm to someone." *Brown v. Durham (Regional Municipality) Police Force* (1998), 131 C.C.C. (3d) 1, 21 C.R. (5th) 1 (Ont. C.A.). Breach of the peace is not itself an **offence**, but an **arrest** to prevent the continuance or renewal of a breach of the peace can be made. *Criminal Code,* R.S.C. 1985, c. C–46, ss. 30–31. Those provisions require that a breach of the peace has already occurred, but there is also a **common law** power to arrest for an apprehended breach of the peace. *Hayes v. Canada (Royal Canadian Mounted Police)* (1985), 18 C.C.C. (3d) 254, 44 C.R. (3d) 316 (B.C.C.A.). See also **disturbance of the peace**.

BREACH OF TRUST A violation by a **trustee** of a **duty** that **equity** lays upon him or her, in disregard of either the terms of the **trust** or the rules of equity. This would include acts done by a trustee in contravention of fiduciary duties, or in excess of them, or by way of neglect or omission of them. The concurrence or acquiescence of co-trustees is also a breach of trust. However, a mere error of judgment does not constitute a breach of trust. *Dover v. Denne* (1902), 3 O.L.R. 664 (C.A.); *Brown v. Brown,* [1932] 2 D.L.R. 819 (Ont.C.A.). For the applicable statute governing trusts, one should see the *Trustee Act* (or equivalent) in the appropriate jurisdiction.

BREACH OF WARRANTY A **warranty** is a **guarantee** and is breached when the thing so guaranteed is deficient according to the terms of the warranty. A warranty in contract law must be distinguished from a **condition**. A warranty is a provision that is subsidiary or collateral to the main purpose of the contract. In distinguishing between a condition and a warranty, see *Hong Kong Fir Shipping Co. Ltd. v. Kawasaki Kisen Kaisha Ltd.,* [1962] 2 Q.B. 26 at 70 (C.A.), where it was held that obligations could not satisfactorily be classified without taking into account the "nature of the event to which the breach gives rise." Breach of warranty entitles the innocent party only to **damages**, whereas breach of condition entitles a person to treat the contract as at an end.

In the sale of goods, a warranty is defined by statute in the appropriate provincial *Sale of Goods Act:* e.g., in s. 2(O) of the Nova Scotia statute (R.S.N.S. 1989, c. 408) warranty is defined as "an agreement with reference to goods which are the subject of a contract of sale, but collateral to the main purpose of such contract, the breach of which gives rise to a claim for damages, but not a right to reject the goods and treat the contract as repudiated." *Bezanson v. Kaintz* (1967), 61 D.L.R. (2d) 410 (N.S.S.C.).

BREAKING A CLOSE [BREACH OF CLOSE] The **common-law trespass** of unlawful entering upon the land of another. See **quare clausum fregit**.

BREAKING AND ENTERING See **burglary**.

BREATHALYZER (BREATH ANALYSIS INSTRUMENT) "[A]n instrument... designed to receive and make an analysis of a sample of the breath of a person in order to measure the concentration of alcohol in the blood of that person." SI/85–201, *Canada Gazette,* Part II, 27/11/85, p. 4692. See also *Criminal Code,* R.S.C. 1985, c. C–46, s. 254.

BREVE Lat.: a **writ**.

BRIBERY At common law, bribery is the receiving or offering of any undue reward by or to any person in a public office in order to influence behaviour in office and induce that person to act contrary to the known rules of honesty and integrity. *Rex v. Hogg* (1914), 19 D.L.R. 113 (Sask.S.C.). Bribery is now a statutory **offence**. See *Criminal Code,* R.S.C. 1985, c. C–46, ss. 119–125, 139, and 426.

BRIEF A written argument concentrating upon legal points and authorities, which is used by the lawyer to convey to the court (trial or appellate) the essential facts of his or her client's case, a statement of the questions of law involved, the law he or she would have applied and the application he or she desires made of it by the court; it is submitted in connection with an application, motion, trial, or appeal. Compare **memorandum**.

A brief is often referred to as a **factum** in Canadian law. It includes a concise statement of facts, a list of issues, arguments, order or relief sought, and appendices containing a list of case citations, statutes, and regulations. See, e.g., *Nova Scotia Civil Procedure Rules,* 40, 90. 32–33.

BRITISH NORTH AMERICA [B.N.A.] ACT, 1867 [CONSTITUTION ACT, 1867] The principal document of the Canadian constitution until the enactment of the *Constitution Act, 1982.* The Act, a statute of the British Parliament, in its preamble proclaimed the desire of the four founding provinces (Nova Scotia, New Brunswick, Quebec, and Ontario) to be "federally united into one Dominion" with a constitution "similar in principle to that of the United Kingdom." In the key sections 91 and 92, legislative powers were divided between the Federal Parliament and the provincial legislatures. See **constitution, division of powers**; See Appendix III.

BROADCAST To transmit programs by radio waves or other means of telecommunication for reception by the public by means of broadcasting-receiving apparatus, other than a transmission made solely for performance or display in a public place: *Broadcasting Act,* SC 1991, c 11, s. 2.

BROADCASTING UNDERTAKING An entity that **broadcasts** programs and has some measure of control over the content, as opposed to merely providing the mode of transmission. See *Reference re Broadcasting Act,* 2012 SCC 4.

BROKER A person who, for a commission or a fee brings parties together and assists in negotiating contracts between them for the purchase and sale of goods, stocks, shares, or policies of insurance. Under the *Canada Business Corporations Act,* R.S.C. 1985, c. C–44, s. 63, a broker gives to his or her customer, to the issuer of securities, and to a purchaser certain **warranties** as provided for in the section. Compare **jobber**.

BRUTUM FULMEN (*brū'-tŭm fŭl'-měn*) Lat.: inert thunder. An empty threat or charge. Sometimes used to refer to a **void judgment**, which in legal effect is no judgment.

BUBBLE ZONE The popular term for an area within which various acts of protest are prohibited, most commonly used in the context of facilities performing abortion services. See *Access to Abortion Services Act,* R.S.B.C. 1996, c. 1.

BUGGERY Also termed **sodomy**. The provision that previously made buggery an indictable offence (*Criminal Code,* R.S.C. 1985, c. C–46, s. 156) was repealed in 1985. Under the provision of s. 159, anal intercourse is an indictable offence, punishable for a term not exceeding 10 years, or on summary conviction, unless engaged in, in private, between spouses, or two consenting persons, each of whom is eighteen years or older. Various courts have found the provision to violate the guarantee of **equality rights** in the **Canadian Charter of Rights and Freedoms** because it sets a different age of consent for same-sex sexual activity than for opposite-sex sexual activity or because it is limited to activity including two people. *R. v. C.M.* (1995), 23 OR (3d) 629 (C.A.); *R. v. Roth*, 2002 ABQB 145.

BUMPING A term used in labour law to describe a system for determining layoffs based on seniority: "[A] procedure by which the employee with the greatest seniority who is about to be laid off is allowed to invoke his or her seniority rights so as to displace (bump) a more junior employee from a job unaffected by the layoff. If there are no limitations in the agreement, a chain process is set off in which each displaced employee is permitted, in turn, to exercise his or her seniority rights against some other more junior employee." Brown and Beatty, *Canadian Labour Arbitration* 6–27 (5th ed. 2012).

BURDEN OF PROOF [ONUS PROBANDI] The duty or onus to prove one's case, or to provide evidence with regard to some fact in issue. In **civil law** a **plaintiff** has the obligation to prove his or her case on a **balance of probabilities**. In **criminal** law the onus is on the **Crown prosecutor** to prove every element of the **offence**, subject to any statutory **reverse onus**. The terms "legal burden" and "evidentiary burden" are often used to describe different types of burdens. Both the plaintiff in a civil matter and the Crown prosecutor in a criminal matter are spoken of as having the legal burden, in the sense that, as a matter of law that party will not succeed if he or she does not meet the burden imposed. The legal burden on a plaintiff is balance of probabilities, and on the Crown beyond a reasonable doubt. An evidentiary burden is the obligation to provide enough evidence to raise an issue concerning some fact, and to show that it arises for consideration, but the evidentiary burden does not require the party to prove the particular fact. The **air of reality** test is an instance of an evidentiary burden in this sense. However, "legal burden" and "evidentiary burden" are also used in a slightly different way when referring to the obligations sometimes imposed on an accused in a criminal trial. See **reverse onus**. See D. Paciocco and L. Stuesser, *The Law of Evidence*, 534–35 (6th ed. 2011).

BURGLARY [BREAKING AND ENTERING] At common law, "the breaking and entering of the dwelling house of another, in the night time, with the intent to commit a felony therein whether or not the felony is committed." 3 Coke Inst. 63, 4 Bl. Comm. 224.

In the *Criminal Code,* R.S.C. 1985, c. C–46, the term BREAK AND ENTER is used. The Code has extended break and enter offences to include some that do not amount to burglaries at common law. The offence now extends to structures other than dwelling houses, and there is no distinction between breaking and entering by day or by night. See *id.,* ss. 348–351; *Regina v. Govedarov, Popovic & Askov* (1974), 3 O.R. (2d) 23 (C.A.).

BUSINESS ASSETS "[R]eal or personal property primarily used or held for or in connection with a commercial, business, investment or other income-producing or profit-producing purpose, but does not include money in an account with a chartered bank, savings office, loan company, credit union, trust company or similar institution where the account is ordinarily used for shelter or transportation or for household, educational, recreational, social or aesthetic purposes." *Matrimonial Property Act*, R.S.N.S. 1989, c. 275, s. 2. However, the matrimonial property legislation in most jurisdictions allows a spouse to apply for a share in the business assets of the other spouse in situations where he or she has made some form of contribution to the acquisition and/or operation of the business asset. *Id.*, s. 18.

BUSINESS RECORDS EXCEPTION See **hearsay rule**.

"BUT FOR" TEST A test for factual causation in tort law. It is a hypothetical exercise comparing what happened in the real world to what would have happened "but for" the defendant's actions and, if the result is the same, then causation is not made out. *Barnett v. Chelsea & Kensington Hospital,* [1968] 3 All ER 1068 (QBD). See **cause in fact**.

BY-LAWS 1. Rules and regulations pertaining to corporations; **2.** A form of subordinate legislation made by some authority subordinate to a **legislature** for the purposes of regulation, administration, or control—e.g., the by-laws of a municipal government.

BY OPERATION OF LAW See **operation of law**.

BY THE ENTIRETY See **tenancy** [TENANCY BY THE ENTIRETY].

CABINET Section 11 of the **Constitution Act, 1867** provides that "there shall be a Council to aid and advise in the Government of Canada." This council, known as the Cabinet, is composed of Ministers of the **Crown**, who serve as confidential advisers to the Sovereign and meet, on the instance of the Prime Minister, to advise the Sovereign collectively on policy. Since the powers of the Crown are, with rare exceptions, exercised on the advice and responsibility of ministers—either individually or as the Cabinet—the Cabinet is the centre of the **executive** government. Its functions are not, however, confined to executive acts. As a body that leads the majority party in the House of Commons, it is able to act as a ruling committee controlling the business of the House of Commons. Nearly all **legislation** passed through **Parliament** originates with the Cabinet. Thus the Cabinet formulates and introduces the legislation that represents the policy of the ruling party in the House of Commons, and also shapes and supervises the execution of the acts that are governed by the principles laid down in legislation. The Cabinet also has extensive lawmaking powers. Statutes frequently delegate the power to make rules and regulations, in furtherance of the legislative purpose, to the Governor-General, a government minister, etc.; in reality, these regulations are usually made or approved by the Cabinet. The term "Cabinet" is equally applicable to the body that represents the leadership of the majority party in a provincial legislature. See **executive council**; **governor in council**; **lieutenant governor in council**.

CADIT QUAESTIO (*kéydĕt kwést(i)yow*) Lat.: the question falls; the matter at issue before the court allows for no further argument.

CALL In corporate law, a term that applies to partially paid **shares**. It is a demand by a **corporation** on a **shareholder** to pay any outstanding amount owing proportionate to his or her share of **stock**. However, shares are nearly always issued as fully paid and non-assessable, so that the partly paid share has fallen into disuse. Also, the *Canada Business Corporations Act,* R.S.C. 1985, c. C–44, s. 2(1), defines call as "an option transferable by delivery to demand delivery of a specified number or amount of securities at a fixed price within a specified time but does not include an option or right to acquire **securities** of the corporation that granted the option or right to acquire...."

CALUMNY Slander, defamation; false or **malicious prosecution** or accusation. Formerly used in **civil law** to indicate unjust prosecution or defence of a suit.

CANADA ACT See **constitution**.

CANADA GAZETTE The official gazette of Canada, authorized by the *Statutory Instruments Act,* R.S.C. 1985, c. S–22, s. 10. *The Canada Gazette* is published in three parts:
Part I: all items required by federal statute or regulation to be published in the *Canada Gazette;*
Part II: **regulations** and other statutory instruments and documents;
Part III: PUBLIC ACTS OF PARLIAMENT and their enactment regulations.

CANADIAN BAR ASSOCIATION (CBA) The CBA describes itself as "the essential ally and advocate of all members of the legal profession; it is the voice for all members of the profession and its primary purpose is to serve its members; it is the premier provider of personal and professional development and support to all members of the legal profession; it promotes fair justice systems, facilitates effective law reform, promotes equality in the legal profession and is devoted to the elimination of discrimination; the CBA is a leading edge organization committed to enhancing the professional and commercial interests of a diverse membership and to protecting the independence of the judiciary and the Bar."

The mandate of the Canadian Bar Association is to:
- "Improve the administration of justice;
- Improve and promote the knowledge, skills, ethical standards and well-being of members of the legal profession;
- Represent the legal profession on a national and international level;
- Promote the interests of the members of the CBA; and
- Promote equality in the profession."

The Canadian Bar Association is also affiliated with international associations, including the Commonwealth Law Association, International Bar Association and the Union internationale des avocat(e)s. Membership in these groups provides the Association with input on recent developments in the legal profession on a broad scale. See The Information Service of the Canadian Bar Association at *http:// www.cba.org.*

CANADIAN BILL OF RIGHTS An Act for the recognition and protection of human rights and fundamental freedoms, passed by the federal **Parliament** in 1960 S.C. 1960, c. 44, reprinted R.S.C. 1985, App. III. However, this legislation was enacted as a federal statute, rather than entrenched—by amendment of the **British North America Act**—in the **constitution**; hence, the *Canadian Bill of Rights* can be directly amended or repealed by Parliament and is limited in its application to federal laws. See **Canadian Charter of Rights and Freedoms**.

CANADIAN CHARTER OF RIGHTS AND FREEDOMS Part I of the *Constitution Act, 1982.* A bill of rights that is entrenched as part of the Constitution, and can therefore be altered only by constitutional amendment; this gives it more force than the **Canadian Bill of Rights**; S.C. 1960, c. 44, reprinted R.S.C. 1985, App. III, which has only the force of a statute.

The Constitution Act, 1982 was an appendix to the *Canada Act, 1982* (U.K.), c. 11. The *Act* was passed by the British Parliament as its final legislative act for Canada. The *Charter* came into force on April 17, 1982 (with the exception of s. 15, which came into force April 17, 1985 as provided by s. 32(2) of the *Charter*), and operates prospectively from that day.

The *Charter* reiterates the fundamental freedoms (freedom of religion, expression, assembly, and association) and legal rights (the rights of life, liberty, and security of the person) set out in the **Canadian Bill of Rights**, but includes additional rights.

The major provisions of the *Charter* are:

GUARANTEE OF RIGHTS AND FREEDOMS s. 1
See **Oakes test**

FUNDAMENTAL FREEDOMS s. 2
Freedom of conscience and religion (*R. v. Big M Drug Mart Ltd.,* [1985] 1 S.C.R. 295); freedom of thought, opinion, and expression (includes freedom of the press and other media of communication) (*Irwin Toy Ltd v. Quebec,* [1989] 1 S.C.R. 927); freedom of peaceful assembly (*R. v. Collins* (1982), 31 C.R. (3d) 283 (Ont. Co. Ct.)), freedom of association. *Health Services and Support-Facilities Subsector Bargaining Assn v. British Columbia,* 2007 SCC 27.

DEMOCRATIC RIGHTS ss. 3–5
The right to vote in the election of the members of the Canadian House of Commons and of a provincial legislative assembly (s. 3) (*Sauvé v. Canada,* 2002 SCC 68); the right to stand for office in either of these institutions; the requirement that no House of Commons and no legislative assembly continue for longer than five years, except in extraordinary circumstances (s. 4); the requirement that there be annual sitting of Parliament and each legislature (s. 5);

MOBILTY RIGHTS s. 6
The right of every citizen of Canada to enter, remain in, and leave Canada; the right of every citizen of Canada, or any person having the status of a permanent resident, to move and take up residence in any province, and to pursue the gaining of a livelihood in any province (*Black v. Law Society of Alberta* (1989), 93 N.R. 266 (S.C.C.));

LEGAL RIGHTS SS. 7–14

The right to life, liberty, and security of the person (s. 7) (*R. v. Malmo–Levine*, 2003 74); protection against unreasonable **search and seizure** (s. 8) (*Hunter v. Southam Inc.*, [1984] 2 S.C. R. 145) or arbitrary detention or imprisonment (s. 9) (*R. v. Grant*, 2009 SCC 32); on arrest or detention, the right to be informed without unreasonable delay of the charge (*R. v. Evans* (1991), 63 C.C.C. (3d) 289 (S.C.C.)), the right to legal **counsel** (*Clarkson v. The Queen*, [1986] 1 S.C.R. 383), and the right to have the validity of the detention determined by *habeas corpus* (s. 10) (*Olson v. The Queen*, [1989] 1 S.C.R. 296); on being charged with an offence, the rights in proceedings in criminal and penal matters include the right to the **presumption of innocence** (*R. v. Oakes*, [1986] 1 S.C.R. 103), and the right not to be denied **bail** without just cause (s. 11) (*R. v. Hall*, 2002 SCC 64; the right not to be subjected to any **cruel and unusual punishment** (s. 12) (*R. v. Wiles*, 2005 SCC 84); protection against self-incrimination (s. 13) (*R. v. Henry*, 2005 SCC 76); and the right to an interpreter when a party or witness to a proceeding (s. 14) (*R. v. Petrovic* (1984), 10 D.L.R. (4th) 697 (Ont. C.A.)).

EQUALITY RIGHTS S. 15

The guarantee of equality to every individual before and under the law, and the right to equal protection and benefit of the law without **discrimination**. See also **equality**. *Withler v. Canada (Attorney-General)*, 2011 SCC 12. Section 15(2) states that s. 15(1) does not preclude any progam that has as its object the amelioration of conditions of disadvantaged persons or groups. See **affirmative action**.

OFFICIAL LANGUAGES OF CANADA SS. 16–22

Includes official language provisions for Canada and New Brunswick.

MINORITY LANGUAGE EDUCATIONAL RIGHTS S. 23

Lavoie v. Nova Scotia (Attorney-General) (1988), 50 D.L.R. (4th) 405 (N.S.S.C.);

ENFORCEMENT (INCLUDING EXCLUSION OF EVIDENCE) S. 24

R. v. Grant, 2009 SCC 32.

PROTECTION OF ABORIGINAL RIGHTS AND FREEDOMS S. 25

(See also *Constitution Act 1982*, Part II, Rights of the Aboriginal Peoples of Canada, s. 35);

PRESERVATION OF MULTICULTURAL HERITAGE S. 27

R. v. Keegstra, [1990] 3 S.C.R. 697.

GUARANTEE OF EQUAL RIGHTS AND FREEDOMS TO MALE AND FEMALE PERSONS S. 28

Re Shewchuk and Ricard (1986), 28 D.L.R. (4th) 429 (B.C.C.A.).

PROTECTION OF DENOMINATIONAL, SEPARATE, AND DISSENTIENT SCHOOLS S. 29

Reference re s. 79(3), (4) and (7) of the Public Schools Act (Manitoba), [1990] 2 W.W.R. 289 (Man. C.A.).

APPLICATION OF CHARTER S. 32

RWDSU v. Dolphin Delivery, [1986] 2 S.C.R. 573; *McKinney et al. v. University of Guelph et al.*, [1990] 3 S.C.R.; *Eldridge v. British Columbia (A.G.)*, [1997] 3 S.C.R. 624.

Notwithstanding Clause – s.33

See **override**

For the full text of the *Charter*, see **Appendix II**.

CANADIAN CITIZEN A person accorded the status of citizen under s. 3 of the *Citizenship Act*, R.S.C. 1985, c. C–29. The precise definition is complex, but, in general, it refers to a person who was born in Canada (other than the child of diplomatic or other personnel of a foreign country who are resident in Canada); a person born outside Canada to parents, at least one of whom was a Canadian citizen (for one generation); a child adopted by a Canadian citizen and granted citizenship; or an adult who, having been a permanent resident for the necessary time, applies for and is granted citizenship. See H.M. Kindred et al., *International Law, Chiefly as Interpreted and Applied in Canada* 495–498 (7th ed. 2006).

CANADIAN ENCYCLOPEDIC DIGEST A Canadian legal encyclopedia containing entries on many aspects of Canadian law, consisting of more than 30 loose-leaf volumes.

CANADIAN HUMAN RIGHTS ACT Federal antidiscrimination legislation. The *Canadian Human Rights Act,* R.S.C. 1985, c. H–6, prohibits discrimination (e.g., based on sex, religion, marital status, etc.) in areas including the provision of goods, services, facilities, accommodations, and employment. See **human rights [legislation]**.

CANON 1. A rule of ecclesiastical law, primarily concerning the clergy, but also at times embracing lay members of a congregation. **2.** A rule of **construction**; one of an aggregate of rules indicating the proper way to construe **statutes** and **regulations. 3.** An ecclesiastical dignitary. *Randolph v. Milman* (1868), 4 L.R.C.P. 107. *Middleton et ux. v. Croft* (1737), 2 Strange 1056; 93 E.R. 1030 (K.B.). **4.** A professional canon is a rule or standard of conduct adopted by a professional group to guide or discipline the professional conduct of its members; e.g., the canons contained in the *Code of Judicial Conduct.*

CAPITAL Broadly, all the money and other property of a **corporation** or other enterprise used in transacting its business; each investment. A corporation's **legal liability** is ordinarily limited by its capital.

CAPITAL COST ALLOWANCE In calculating the taxable income of a taxpayer, a deduction allowed for depreciation on many tangible fixed assets and some intangible fixed assets. See V. Krishna, *Income Tax Law* 238–49 (2nd ed. 2012). Also see *Income Tax Act,* R.S.C. 1985, c. 1 (5th Supp.) and *Income Tax Regulations,* C.R.C., c. 945, Sch. II, Part XI.

CAPITAL EXPENDITURE Expenditure from which benefits may be expected over a relatively long period; expenditure made for the improvement or betterment of a capital asset. *Minister of National Revenue v. Dominion Natural Gas Co. Ltd.,* [1941] S.C.R. 19.

CAPITAL GAIN "Unforeseen increases in the real value of a man's existing property not directly attributable to his efforts, intelligence, capital or risk-taking" (as distinct from income). Seltzer, *The Nature of Tax Treatment of Capital Gains and Losses,* as quoted in *Wood v. M.N.R.,* [1967] C.T.C. 66 at 74. However, for taxation purposes certain proportions of capital gains are treated as income. See *Income Tax Act,* R.S.C. 1985, c. 1 (5th Supp.).

CAPITAL PROPERTY The assets of an individual or corporation that are not consumed with use. See further V. Krishna, *Income Tax Law* 266–75 (2nd ed. 2012).

FIXED CAPITAL "That which a company retains, in the shape of assets upon which the subscribed capital has been expended, and which assets either themselves produce income, independent of any further action by the company, or being retained by the company are made use of to produce income or gain profits." *Ammonia Soda Co. v. Chamberlain,* [1918] 1 Ch. 266 at 286. On the other hand, CIRCULATING CAPITAL "is a portion of the subscribed capital of the company intended to be used by being temporarily parted with and circulated in business in the form of money, goods or other assets, and which, or the proceeds of which, are intended to return to the company with an increment, and are intended to be used again and again, and to always return with some accretion." *Id.,* at 286–87.

NOMINAL or AUTHORIZED CAPITAL is the number of **shares** or the aggregate **par** value that the company is authorized to issue. SUBSCRIBED CAPITAL is the number of shares taken or agreed to be taken by subscribers. ISSUED CAPITAL is the number of shares issued and allotted. PAID-UP CAPITAL is the amount paid up by subscribers, whether for all or part of issued or subscribed capital. See *Canada Business Corporations Act,* R.S.C. 1985, c. C–44.

WORKING CAPITAL is the amount required by a corporation to actually carry on its business.

UNCALLED CAPITAL is the amount that has not yet been called for payment.

CAPITAL OFFENCE A criminal **offence** punishable by death. The following were formerly capital offences under the *Criminal Code,* R.S.C. 1970, c. C–34: **treason, piracy** involving **murder** or attempted murder or an act endangering life, and capital murder.

In 1976 the *Criminal Code,* S.C. 1974–75–76, c. 105, s. 21 abolished **capital punishment**, and all capital offences became punishable by life imprisonment.

CAPITAL PUNISHMENT The punishment of death for commission of a **capital offence**. Capital punishment was abolished in 1976 under the *Criminal Code,* S.C. 1974–75–76, c. 105, s. 21.

For the specific legislative provisions dealing with capital punishment, see *Criminal Code,* R.S.C. 1970, c. C–34, ss. 669–681.

CAPTION 1. The heading of a legal document, containing the names of the **parties**, the court, index or **docket** number of the case, etc. **2.** The act of seizing, which, together with ASPORTATION (the act of carrying away), was a necessary element of common-law **larceny**.

CARTEL A group of independent industrial corporations, usually operating on an international scale, that agree to restrict trade to their mutual benefit. See **monopoly**; **oligopoly**.

CASE An **action, cause, suit** or controversy at **law** or in **equity**; a **trial**; the **evidence** and argument on behalf of the parties. Also, an abbreviation of **trespass on the case**. See *Letang v. Cooper*, [1965] 1 Q.B. 232 (C.A.). A judicial proceeding for the determination of a disagreement between two or more parties.

CASE AT BAR See **bar**.

CASE DISMISSED See **dismiss**.

CASE LAW See **common law**.

CASE METHOD An approach to legal education whereby law is taught with reference to actual judicial decisions, rather than through theoretical summaries of legal rules and principles. The case method is the prevailing pedagogical method used by North American law schools. See S. Waddams, *Introduction to the Study of Law* 21–22 (6th ed. 2010).

CASE OF FIRST IMPRESSION See **first impression**.

CASE, ON THE See **trespass** [TRESPASS ON THE CASE].

CASE OR CONTROVERSY See **controversy**.

CASE REPORTER An ongoing publication that prints judicial or administrative decisions, occasionally with accompanying annotations or commentary. The many case reporters now published in Canada typically focus on specific areas of law (e.g., *Criminal Reports, Business Law Reports*), jurisdictions or geographical regions (e.g., *Nova Scotia Reports, Western Weekly Reports*), or levels of court (e.g., *Supreme Court Reports, Ontario Appeal Cases*). They also differ in status, ranging from official reporters published by the Queen's Printer, semi-official reporters published by provincial law societies, and unofficial reporters printed by various commercial publishers.

CASH VALUE See **market value**.

CAUSA (*kâw'-zà*) Lat.: cause.

"BUT FOR" CAUSE A basic part of the rule of recovery for negligence. "The plaintiff must show on a balance of probabilities that 'but for' the defendant's negligent act, the injury would not have occurred. Inherent in the phrase 'but for' is the requirement that the defendant's negligence was necessary to bring about the injury—in other words, that the injury would not have occurred without the defendant's negligence. This is a factual inquiry." *Clements v. Clements*, 2012 SCC 32.

CAUSA CAUSANS (*kâw'-zà kâw'-zănz*) Lat.: the immediate cause; the last link in the chain of causation. Must be distinguished from CAUSA SINE QUA NON (following), which refers to a preceding link but for which the causa causans could not have become operative.

CAUSA PROXIMA (*prŏk'-sĭ-mà*) Lat.: proximate cause, most closely related cause; used to indicate legal cause. That which is sufficiently related to the result as to justify imposing liability on the actor who produces the cause, or likewise, to relieve from liability the actor who produces a less closely related cause. See **cause** [PROXIMATE CAUSE].

CAUSA SINE QUA NON (*sē'-nā kwä nŏn*) Lat.: a cause without which it would not have occurred. See CAUSA CAUSANS.

CAUSE 1. That which effects a result; **2.** A **suit**, matter pending or **action**; **3.** A motive or reason. In law, *cause* is not a constant and agreed-upon term.

CAUSE IN FACT (factual causation) Whether something is a *cause in fact* depends on whether "the relation between the defendant's **breach of duty** [in negligence law] and the plaintiff's injury is one of cause and effect in accordance with 'scientific' or 'objective' notions of physical sequence. If such a causal relation does not exist, that puts an end to the plaintiff's case: to impose liability for loss to which the defendant's conduct has not *in fact* contributed would be incompatible with the principle of individual responsibility on which the law of torts has been traditionally based." See also A. Linden and B. Feldthusen, *Canadian Tort Law* 120–32 (9th ed. 2011). In **criminal** law, factual causation is usually settled by the "but for" test but does not ask merely whether the accused is the medical or mechanical cause of the result. *R. v. Maybin*, 2012 SCC 24.

DIRECT CAUSE The active, efficient cause that sets in motion a train of events that brings about a result without the intervention of any other independent source. Often used interchangeably with PROXIMATE CAUSE, *Straathof v. Kamphius*, 2005 ABPC 340.

ESSENTIAL, SUBSTANTIAL, AND INTEGRAL CAUSE The factual causation test in cases of first-degree murder. The requirement is much higher than that of a not-insignificant cause, which applies to other offences. The test "requires that the accused play a very active role—usually a physical role—

in the killing." *R. v. Harbottle*, [1993] 3 S.C.R. 306.

INTERVENING CAUSE (*NOVUS ACTUS INTERVENIENS*) A cause that arises after that of the defendant or accused, which is so overwhelming as to render the earlier cause merely a part of the background. Where an intervening cause is found to arise, it will absolve the defendant or accused of responsibility. No single test exists for determining whether a later action is or is not an intervening cause. Whether the later action was reasonably foreseeable and whether it was the action of an independent agent can be relevant considerations, but the ultimate question remains whether the original action is still a not-insignificant cause. *R. v. Maybin*, 2012 SCC 24.

LEGAL CAUSE In criminal law, a further requirement that must be met beyond factual causation before an accused can be held legally responsible for a result. "Legal causation...is a narrowing concept that funnels a wider range of factual causes into those that are sufficiently connected to a harm to warrant legal responsibility." Also referred to as imputable causation, it asks whether the accused *ought* to be found responsible for the result. *R. v. Maybin*, 2012 SCC 24.

NOT-INSIGNIFICANT CAUSE The test in criminal law for determining whether the accused has met the test for factual causation of the prohibited result in cases other than first-degree murder. The accused's actions must have been a contributing cause that is not insignificant. The terms "significant," "more than trivial," and "beyond *de minimis*" are all meant to convey the same degree of causation, but the Supreme Court of Canada has recommended avoiding the Latin phrase in order to be clearer to juries. *R. v. Nette*, 2001 SCC 78.

PROXIMATE CAUSE That which in natural and continuous sequence, unbroken by any new independent cause, produces an event, or without which the injury would not have occurred. In criminal and **tort** law, the defendant's **liability** is generally limited to results proximately caused by his or her conduct or omission. That the defendant's negligence has been established as a causal factor for the injury does not necessarily suffice for legal liability. See further A. Linden and B. Feldthusen, *Canadian Tort Law* (9th ed. 2011).

CAUSE OF ACTION A claim in law and fact sufficient to demand judicial attention; the composite of facts necessary to give rise to the enforcement of a right. A RIGHT OF ACTION is the legal right to sue; a cause of action is the set of facts that give rise to a right of action. Should a cause of action not be disclosed in the documentation, the case will be **dismissed**.

The violation of any legal right committed knowingly constitutes **prima facie** a cause of action. *Sleuter v. Scott* (1914), 6 W.W.R. 451 (B.C.S.C.). Also see *Read v. Brown* (1888), 22 Q.B.D. 128 (C.A.).

CAVEAT (*kā'-vē-ăt*) Lat.: let him beware. In general, a warning for caution. It is a notice to some officer or judge to make an entry in order that a certain step in **proceedings** will not be taken without prior notice to the individual (CAVEATOR) who lodges the caveat. An example of a caveat would be a notice in writing that no **grant** is to be sealed in the estate of the deceased named (in the case of a **will)** without notice to the caveator. The main object of a caveat in this case is to enable a person who is considering opposing a grant to obtain evidence or legal advice on the matter. *Re McDevitt,* [1913] 5 O.W.N. 333 (S.C.); *Grace v. Kuebler & Brunner* (1917), 56 S.C.R. 1.

CAVEAT EMPTOR (*kā'-vē-ăt ĕmp'-tôr*) Lat.: let the buyer beware. The rule of law that a purchaser buys at his or her own risk. In the areas of commercial and consumer law, the provincial legislatures have modified this harsh principle. Consumers now have certain rights respecting the purchase of goods—for example, warranties and conditions of fitness, merchantability (except where goods are bought expressly "as is"). *Public Utilities Commission for City of Waterloo v. Burroughs Business*

Machines Ltd., [1973] 2 O.R. 472 (H.C.J.); *Venus Electric Ltd. v. Brevel Products Ltd.* (1978), 19 O.R. (2d) 417 (C.A.).

CERTIFICATE OF DEPOSIT A bank's acknowledgement of receipt of money, with an engagement to repay it, establishing a debtor-creditor relationship between bank and depositor. The writing may or may not be a **negotiable instrument**, depending on whether it meets the requirements of negotiability. See *Bills of Exchange Act,* R.S.C. 1985, c. B–4.

CERTIFICATION In accordance with the appropriate provincial and federal legislation, a board may certify a trade union as a bargaining agent of employees or a unit and give the union full bargaining rights. The basis of certification by the board is that the **trade union** has the support of the majority of the employees in the unit. See, e.g., *Canada Labour Code,* R.S.C. 1995, c. L–2.

CERTIFICATION MARK A mark used to distinguish wares or services that are of a defined standard with respect to quality, working conditions for production, persons involved in production, or area within which the wares were produced or the services performed. *Trade-marks Act,* RSC 1985, c T–13, s. 2.

CERTIORARI (*sêr'-shē-ô-rä'-rē*) A means of achieving judical review; a **common-law writ** issued from a superior court to one of inferior **jurisdiction**, inquiring into the validity of the proceedings of the latter. The writ is issued in either **civil** or **criminal** proceedings and it is commonly used for the purpose of **quashing** orders, alleged to be erroneous, of courts of summary jurisdiction. The writ is used to determine whether there have been any irregularities in the proceedings of the inferior **tribunal**. *R. v. Titchmarsh* (1914) 32 O.L.R. 569 (S.C.A.D.). Many provinces have codified judicial review procedure. See *Judicial Review Procedure Act,* R.S.O. 1990, c. J. 1.

CESSION yielding or giving up; the act of one party **assigning** his or her property rights to another.

CESTUI QUE (*sĕ'-tĭ kŭ*) See **trust**.

CESTUI QUE USE (*sĕ'-tĭ kŭ yúwz*) The person for whom a use was designed to benefit. Legal title was vested in one person to hold for the benefit of another (*cestui que use*). He or she holds the equitable right to the property. See **use**.

CESTUI QUE VIE (*sĕ'-tĭ kŭ vē*) The person whose life marks the duration for which another holds an **estate** or an interest in **real property**. See also **life estate; per [pur] autre vie**.

CETERIS PARIBUS (*sĕ'-têr-ēs par-ĕ-būs*) Lat.: other things being equal.

CHAIN OF TITLE The successive **conveyances** of a certain property, commencing with the Crown **grant** or other original source, each being a perfect conveyance of the **title** down to and including the conveyance to the present holder. The recorded chain of title consists only of the documents affecting title that are recorded in a manner that makes the fact of their existence readily available to a **bona fide purchaser**. In Canada, there are two major systems for recording land documents. The first is the REGISTRY SYSTEM, in which the instruments concerning land are registered in the appropriate registry office in grantor/grantee indices from which one can trace the title to land. This system is governed by statute in each province. See e.g., *Registry Act,* R.S.O. 1990, c. R. 20.

See **registry [of deeds]**. This system is slowly being supplanted by the LAND TITLES SYSTEM (or Torrens system, as it is known in some countries). A main distinction between land titles and registration is that under land titles the Government in effect guarantees the accuracy of the title as shown on the record. See e.g., *Land Titles Act,* R.S.O. 1990, c. L–5; *Land Titles Act,* R.S.A. 2000, c. L–4. See **abstract of title; clear title; registry acts; title search; warranty deed**.

CHALLENGE Generally, the right to take exception to the **jurors** selected for a **civil** or **criminal** action. A challenge may be made by either party in a civil action. In criminal actions challenges may be made on the part of either the **Crown** or the **accused**.

CHALLENGE TO THE ARRAY An exception taken to the panel of jurors collectively on the grounds of partiality, fraud or willful misconduct on the part of the sheriff or his deputies by whom the jurors were returned.

CHALLENGE FOR CAUSE The prosecutor and the accused are entitled to challenge the selection of an individual potential juror on a number of bases, the most important of which is that the juror "is not indifferent between the Queen and the accused." See *Criminal Code*, R.S.C. 1985, c. C–46, s. 389. See **peremptory challenge**.

CHAMPERTY See **maintenance**.

CHANCELLOR 1. In early English law, the name of the King's minister who would dispense justice in the King's name by extraordinary equitable relief (see **relief**) where the remedy at law was inadequate to do substantial justice. **2.** Later, the name given to the chief judge of the Court of **Chancery**, i.e., the court of equity. In Canada and England, the courts of equity and law have been fused by the **judicature acts** of the provinces.

CHANCERY The jurisprudence that is exercised in a **court of equity**, originally by the **chancellor**; synonymous with **equity**, or equitable jurisdiction. See *In re K. (Infant),* [1965] A.C. 201 (H.L.).

Equitable jurisdiction also existed in many of the provinces. In Ontario, a Court of Chancery was created in 1837. A judge known as the Vice-Chancellor exercised judicial powers over matters such as fraud, deceit, partnership, lunacy, trust, account, and guardianship. The Court of Chancery came to an end in 1881.

CHARACTER EVIDENCE Evidence with regard to a person's disposition: "a compendious summary of a person's past actions, good and bad." Bryant et al., *The Law of Evidence in Canada* (3d ed., 2009), §10.1. In **civil** cases, character evidence can be led if it is directly **relevant** to a fact in issue, e.g., evidence of a person's prior incompetence could be relevant in defending against a **wrongful dismissal** action.

In **criminal** cases, an **accused** is allowed to enter evidence of good character to support a line of reasoning that he or she was not the type of person to have committed an offence. An accused can also lead evidence of a victim's reputation for violence (to support, e.g., an argument that the victim rather than the accused was at fault for an altercation) or of a co-accused's character (to support the inference that the co-accused is more likely to be the guilty party). Evidence concerning previous bad behaviour or a discreditable disposition on the part of the accused cannot be led by the Crown where its only purpose or effect will be to stigmatize the accused as a bad person. However, where the accused leads good character evidence or otherwise puts his or her character in issue, the Crown can lead bad character evidence in reply. In addition, evidence of prior bad acts is admissible when it is proffered to prove some particular point in issue, such as identity. See *R. v. Handy*, 2002 SCC 56. See **similar act evidence**.

CHARGE 1. In criminal law, the underlying substantive offence contained in an **accusation** or **indictment**.

2. In trial practice, an address delivered by the court to the **jury** at the close of the **case**, instructing the jury as to the principles of law they are required to apply in reaching a decision. Evidence concerning the character of the **complainant** in a **sexual assault** case is regulated by the *Criminal Code*, R.S.C. 1985, c. C–46, ss. 276ff, and evidence that the complainant has engaged in sexual activity "is not admissible to support an inference that, by reason of the sexual nature of that activity, the complainant (a) is more likely to have consented to the sexual activity that forms the subject-matter of the charge; or (b) is less worthy of belief."

The matters to be discussed in a charge to the jury include: instruction on the relevant legal issues, in particular the charges faced by the accused; the theories of each side; a review of the salient facts that support the theories and case of each side; a review of the evidence

relating to the law; a direction informing the jury that it is for them to make the factual determinations; instruction about the burden of proof and presumption of innocence; the possible verdicts open to the jury; and the requirements of unanimity for reaching a verdict. "The cardinal rule is that it is the general sense that the words used must have conveyed, in all probability, to the mind of the jury that matters, and not whether a particular formula was recited by the judge. The particular words used, or the sequence followed, is a matter within the discretion of the trial judge and will depend on the particular circumstances of the case." *R. v. Daley*, 2007 SCC 53.

3. In property law, a charge is an **encumbrance**, **lien**, or claim, a burden on the land. As such, it is a form of security for the satisfaction of a debt or performance of an obligation.

4. In its broadest sense, it means simply to entrust with, by way of responsibility, duty, etc. *F. C. Richert Co. v. Larkin* [1928] 3 W.W.R. 305 (Alta.S.C.A.D.); *Dominion Creosoting Co. v. T. R. Nickerson Co.* (1917), 55 S.C.R. 303.

CHARITABLE PURPOSES At common law, a purpose that falls into one of four categories: "(1) the relief of poverty; (2) the advancement of education; (3) the advancement of religion and (4) certain other purposes beneficial to the community, not falling under any of the preceding heads." *A.Y.S.A. Amateur Youth Soccer Association v. Canada (Revenue Agency)*, 2007 SCC 42. The last category is intended to allow incremental change in the law to reflect changing social attitudes. The common law definition is used for purposes of the *Income Tax Act*, R.S.C. 1985, c. 1, (5th Supp). Some provincial statutes offer broader definitions of charitable purpose. See, e.g., *Charitable Fund-raising Business Act*, S.S. 2002, c. C–6.2, s. 2: "a philanthropic, benevolent, educational, health, humane, religious, cultural, artistic, athletic, conservation, or recreational purpose."

CHARLOTTETOWN ACCORD, THE A proposal for amending the **Constitution** of Canada, agreed to by the **Prime**

Minister, all ten provincial premiers, and representatives from territorial and **aboriginal** groups on August 28, 1992. The Accord was presented to the Canadian people and was defeated on October 26, 1992 by means of two referenda, one held in Quebec and the other held in the rest of the country. Nationally the vote was 50.4% against the Accord, and it was also defeated in six of the ten provinces and one of the two territories. Quebec had a 56.7% "no" vote.

The Charlottetown Accord would have had several effects. It would have affected the **division of powers** by transferring authority over some matters to the provincial governments, limiting the federal power of **disallowance**, and imposing controls on the federal spending power by guaranteeing federal funding for some provincial programs. It also included a process for moving toward **Aboriginal** self-government, as well as for reform of the **Senate** to provide for the possibility of elected senators and to apportion seats by province and to Aboriginal peoples. Quebec was to be guaranteed a minimum of 25% of seats in the **House of Commons**, and some matters before the Senate would require a "double majority," i.e., a majority of all senators and a majority of all francophone senators. In addition, the Accord proposed the creation of a "social charter" aimed at promoting objectives such as health care, welfare, education, environmental protection, and collective bargaining.

CHARTER 1. A document issued that establishes a corporate entity; the governing instrument of a company that, among other things, contains the company name and purposes, its **capital**, and the number of **shares** into which that capital is divided. See **association**, **memorandum of**.

2. In earlier law, the term referred to a grant from the Sovereign guaranteeing to the person or persons therein named certain rights, privileges, and powers.

The Magna Carta, or Great Charter, granted by King John to the English barons in 1215, established the basis for English constitutional government. *Miller v. Thompson* (1866), 16 U.C.C.P.

513. In common usage, the **Canadian Charter of Rights and Freedoms** contained in the *Constitution Act, 1982*. See **Appendix II**.

CHARTER REMEDY See **remedy**.

CHATTEL In general, any property less than **freehold**. A CHATTEL PERSONAL is any tangible, moveable thing. CHATTELS REAL are interests in land less than freehold—for example, **leasehold**. *Davidson v. Reynolds* (1865), 16 U.C.C.P. 140. *Re Estate of Isabella McMillan* (1902) 4 O.L.R. 415 (in chambers). See **personal property**.

CHATTEL MORTGAGE See **mortgage**; **PPSA**.

CHEQUE The *Bills of Exchange Act*, R.S.C. 1985, c. B–4, ss. 165(l), defines a cheque as a **bill of exchange** (see s. 16(1) drawn on a bank and payable on demand. *McLellan v. McLellan* (1911), 25 O.L.R. 214 (Div.Ct.); *Northern Bank v. Yuen* (1909), 11 W.L.R. 698.

CERTIFIED CHEQUE A cheque containing a certification that the drawer of the cheque has sufficient funds to cover payment of the cheque. It indicates that the bank will retain a sufficient amount of the drawer's funds to cover payment of the cheque on demand.

CHILD IN NEED OF PROTECTION The standard under much child welfare legislation that can trigger investigation by the state and potential intervention, including the removal of the child from the home. Typical criteria include that the child is likely to be physically harmed or neglected. See, e.g., *Child and Family Services Act*, C.C.S.M. c. C80, s. 17, or *Child and Family Services Act*, S.S. 1989–90, c. C–7.2, s. 11.

CHILD OF THE MARRIAGE Under the *Divorce Act*, RSC 1985, c. 3 (2nd Supp), s. 2, a child of two spouses or former spouses who is under the age of majority and who has not withdrawn from their charge, or is the age of majority or over and under their charge but unable, by reason of illness, disability, or other cause, to withdraw from their charge or to obtain the necessaries of life. The Act makes clear that "a child of two spouses or former spouses" includes step-parents ("(a) any child for whom they both stand in the place of parents; and (b) any child of whom one is the parent and for whom the other stands in the place of a parent"). A central significance of the definition is whether one parent will continue to be required to pay maintenance to the custodial parent for that child. The "other cause" for being unable to withdraw from the parents' charge can include attending a post-secondary institution, being unable to find employment, or being involved in sporting activity. See *Ethier v. Skrudland*, 2011 SKCA 17.

CHILD PORNOGRAPHY Generally, a pornographic representation of a person under eighteen years of age or, if explicit sexual activity is shown, a person who is depicted as being under that age. Where the representation is visual, child pornography includes anything that depicts "a sexual organ or the anal region" of the person, or that depicts him or her "engaged in explicit sexual activity." Where the representation is written or auditory, it includes anything that depicts a person under eighteen years of age engaged in sexual activity that would constitute an offence under the *Criminal Code*, or that counsels such an offence. *Criminal Code*, R.S.C. 1985, c. C–46, s. 163.1(1). See further *R. v. Sharpe*, 2001 SCC 2. The presence of child pornography constitutes part of the **actus reus** of numerous criminal offences. See, e.g., *Criminal Code*, R.S.C. 1985, c. C–46, ss. 163.1(2), 163.1(4).

CHILD SUPPORT See **maintenance**.

CHILD SUPPORT GUIDELINES Rules created under s. 26.1 of the *Divorce Act*, R.S.C. 1985, c. 3 (2nd Supp), setting out the amount to be paid as support for a **child of the marriage** after a **divorce** in most provinces. The guidelines take the form of tables and allow the calculation of support based on the number of children, province of residence, and paying parent's income.

CHOICE OF FORUM CLAUSE In a **contract**, a clause indicating in which **jurisdiction** any disputes will be determined. The choice of forum is not required to also be the **choice of law**, though frequently the

two will go together. Whether to enforce a choice of forum clause is discretionary, but unless there is a strong cause for a domestic court to exercise jurisdiction in preference to that in the choice of forum clause, the parties will be held to their bargain. *Z.I. Pompey Industrie v. ECU-Line N.V.*, 2003 SCC 27. See **forum non conveniens**; **conflict of laws**.

CHOICE OF LAW The decision over what law will govern a legal dispute where, because of the facts surrounding it, the law of more than one jurisdiction could apply. A dispute could be governed by the law of one jurisdiction even though the courts of another jurisdiction hear the matter.

CHOICE OF LAW CLAUSE In a **contract**, a clause indicating which **jurisdiction's** laws will apply to the contract, and in particular to the resolution of any disputes that arise. The applicable law will not necessarily be that of the forum in which the dispute is litigated. See **choice of forum clause**; **forum non conveniens**; **conflict of laws**.

CHOSE (*shōz*) Fr.: thing. A thing either presently possessed [CHOSE IN POSSESSION] or claimed [CHOSE IN ACTION].
CHOSE IN ACTION "A chose in action ... is an **incorporeal right** to something not in one's possession and, accordingly, it is not possible for the debtor to have possession of it." *Re Attorney-General for Ontario and Royal Bank of Canada,* [1970] 2 O.R. 467 at 470 (C.A.). The right to recover money **(debt)** or **damages** in a legal action; merely a right to sue. It becomes a CHOSE IN POSSESSION only upon successful completion of a lawsuit. *Re Dominion Coal Co. Ltd.* (1974), 9 N.S.R. (2d) 312 (S.C.A.D.).
CHOSE IN POSSESSION As opposed to a chose in action, a thing actually possessed (or possessable).

C.I.F. Cost, insurance, and freight; also written c.f.i. In a **contract** of sale, it means that the cost of the goods, the insurance thereon, and the freight to the destination are included in the contract price. The seller's responsibilities in this sort of contract are the following: "firstly to ship at the port of shipment goods of the description contained in the contract; secondly to procure a contract of affreightment, under which the goods will be delivered at the destination contemplated by the contract; thirdly to arrange for an insurance upon the terms current in the trade which will be available for the benefit of the buyer; fourthly, to make out an invoice ... and finally to tender these documents to the buyer so that he may know what freight he has to pay and obtain delivery of the goods, if they arrive, or recover for their loss if they are lost on the voyage." *Schmidt v. Wilson & Canham Ltd.* (1920), 47 O.L.R. 194 (H.C.).

CIRCUIT COURT In Canada, refers to the practice of the superior court of the province travelling to various points in the province for sitting.

CIRCUMSTANTIAL EVIDENCE Indirect evidence; secondary facts by which a principal fact may be rationally inferred. Sometimes a fact in **issue** cannot be proved by direct evidence and must be established by proof of other facts. If sufficient other facts are proved, the court may from the circumstances infer that the fact in issue exists or does not exist. In this case proof is made by the circumstantial evidence. For a judicial consideration of circumstantial evidence, see *The King v. Edward Cook* (1914), 48 N.S.R. 150 (S.C.).

In **criminal** cases, the rule in *Hodge's Case*, (1838) 2 Lewin 227; 168 E.R. 1136 (Crown) had often been relied on in the past: it states that in a criminal case based on circumstantial evidence, the circumstances must be consistent with the conclusion that the act was committed by the accused and inconsistent with any other conclusion. The status of the rule is in some doubt today. It is frequently referred to as a "so-called rule," and one current view is that the rule in *Hodge's Case* is "simply one device to ensure that the doctrine of proof beyond a reasonable doubt is fairly applied to the facts": *R. v. Pelech*, 2012 ABCA 134. However, the rule has not been explicitly rejected.

CITATION 1. A reference to a source of legal authority, e.g., a citation to a statute or case. See further the Key to Effective Use of This Dictionary for examples of such citations. **2. A writ** that may be issued calling upon a person who is not a party to an **action** or **proceeding** to appear before the court. Compare **subpoena**.

NEUTRAL CITATION A type of case citation that includes only a case's name, year, level of court, and sequential number. It is "neutral" in the sense that it does not refer to any specific **case reporter**.

PARALLEL CITATION A secondary citation to a case following an initial citation. Cases are often printed in more than one **case reporter**, and citations to multiple reporters may be included "as a courtesy to the reader, who may have access to only one of the... reporters listed in the citation." T. Tjaden, *Legal Research and Writing* 24 (3rd ed. 2010).

CITIZEN Refers to a **Canadian Citizen**.

CITIZEN'S ARREST An arrest without warrant by any person other than a peace officer in situations where someone is found committing an indictable offence or where a person reasonably believes that someone has committed a crime and is in the process of escaping from lawful authority. A property owner can arrest any person that he or she finds committing an offence on or against his or her property. After such an arrest the alleged offender must be delivered immediately into the custody of a peace officer. *Criminal Code*, R.S.C. 1985, c. C–46, s. 494. See *R. v. Asante-Mensah*, 2003 SCC 38.

CIVIL 1. The branch of law that pertains to suits other than criminal practice and is concerned with the rights and duties of persons in **contract, tort**, etc.; **2.** civil law as opposed to **common law**.

CIVIL ACTION An action to protect a private, **civil** right or to compel a civil remedy in a dispute between private parties, is distinguished from a criminal **prosecution**.

CIVIL CODE In a **civil law** jurisdiction, a statute governing all **private law** matters. The *Civil Code of Québec*, L.R.Q., c C–1991, contains provisions dealing with the relationships among people, such as privacy rights, responsibility for injuries caused to others, family law, and so on. It also sets out the rules governing the relationships between people and property, such as sales contracts, leasing, and so on.

CIVIL CONTEMPT See **contempt of court**.

CIVIL LAW 1. Roman law embodied in the *Justinian Code* (*Codex Justinianeus*) and presently prevailing in most western European states and in Louisiana in the United States. The **private law** of the province of Quebec is governed by two major civil codes: the *Civil Code* of the province of Quebec and the *Code of Civil Procedure*. The former is an exhaustive code containing rules and principles governing virtually all areas of **substantive law**. The latter contains approximately 950 articles and sets out the rules of civil procedure for Quebec. **2.** The part of the law concerned with non-criminal matters. **3.** The body of laws prescribed by the supreme power of the state, as distinguished from **natural law**.

CIVIL LIABILITY Amenability to **civil action**, as distinguished from criminal action; liability relating to actions seeking private remedies or the enforcement of personal rights, based on **contract**, **tort**, etc.

CIVIL LIBERTIES See **civil rights**.

CIVIL MARRIAGE ACT, S.C. 2005, c. 33. Under this Act, two persons of the same sex can be legally married in Canada. Section 2 states that "[m]arriage, for civil purposes, is the lawful union of two persons to the exclusion of all others." See also **marriage**, **Reference re Same Sex Marriage**.

CIVIL PROCEDURE Refers to the rules and regulations surrounding the process of civil litigation. See Rules of Civil Procedure for each province.

CIVIL RIGHTS From the Latin *civilis;* a citizen as distinguished from a barbarian. In general, civil rights mean the rights that are the outgrowth of civilization, that the needs of civil as distinguished from barbaric communities, and that are given, defined, and circumscribed by such positive laws, enacted by such communities, as are necessary to the maintenance of organized government. *Hill v. Hill,* [1929] 2 W.W.R. 41 at 47 (Alta.S.C.A.D.).

Section 92(13) of the *Constitution Act, 1867,* confers upon the provincial legislature the power to make laws in relation to "property and civil rights in the province." A distinction is to be drawn here between civil rights and civil liberties as understood in a Canadian context: the former, as employed in the *Constitution Act, 1867,* refers to those proprietary, contractual, and tortious rights between individuals in society, while the latter refers to those democratic rights and freedoms that govern the relationship between the individual and the institutions—whether social, political, or economic—of society. P. Hogg, *Constitutional Law of Canada* 21–3–4 (5th ed. 2007). Historically, civil liberties in Canada were accorded no direct constitutional protection. The passage in 1960 of the **Canadian Bill of Rights** did not alter this situation, for, as a federal statute, the *Canadian Bill of Rights* could be amended or repealed by Parliament and was limited in its application to federal laws. Consequently, civil liberties were deemed to "exist when there is an absence of legal rules: whatever is not forbidden is a civil liberty." *Id.* However, a direct constitutional safeguard for Canadian civil liberties was effected by the passage of the *Constitution Act, 1982,* for that legislation, **inter alia**, entrenched the **Canadian Charter of Rights and Freedoms** in the constitution. See **Human Rights**.

CIVIL STANDARD See **balance of probabilities**.

CIVITAS (*sĭ'-vĭ-täs*) Lat.: the citizenry; the community. In Roman Law, any body of people living under the same laws; a state, commonwealth, community.

CLAIM 1. The assertion of a right to money or **property**. **2.** The aggregate of operative facts giving rise to a right enforceable in the courts. A claim must show the existence of a right, an injury, and a **prayer** for **damages**. One who makes a claim is the CLAIMANT.

CLARITY ACT A statute passed by **Parliament** in 2000 to respond to the decision of the **Supreme Court** in *Reference re Secession of Quebec*, [1998] 2 S.C.R. 217, dealing with the legality of Quebec's potential unilateral separation from Canada. The legislation outlines two minimum conditions under which the federal government would be prepared to negotiate with a province about secession. First, the **House of Commons** would have to decide that the question that the province "intends to submit to its voters in a **referendum** relating to the proposed secession" is sufficiently clear. Second, the House of Commons would have to decide that the result of the referendum indicates "a clear expression of a will by a clear majority of the population of that province that the province cease to be part of Canada." The legislation also recognizes that the secession of any province would require a constitutional amendment, and would therefore involve negotiations with every other province and the federal government. *An Act to give effect to the requirement for clarity as set out in the opinion of the Supreme Court of Canada in the Quebec Secession Reference*, S.C. 2000, c. 26. See P.J. Monahan, *Constitutional Law* 222–28 (3rd ed. 2010).

CLASS ACTION A lawsuit brought by representative member(s) of a large group of persons on behalf of all members of the group. The number of persons represented must be so numerous that it is not practicable to join them as plaintiffs. The class must be ascertainable, the members must share a common interest in the issues of law and fact raised by the plaintiff(s) and the action must satisfy other special requirements applicable to class actions before the trial court will specifically certify the **action** to be one maintainable as a class action.

For the procedures to be taken in the case of a class action, see L.S. Abrams and K.P. McGuinness, *Canadian Civil Procedure Law* 532–79 (2nd ed. 2010). See also *Shaw v. Real Estate Board of Greater Vancouver* (1973), 36 D.L.R. (3d) 250 (B.C.C.A.); *Farnham v. Fingold*, [1973] 2 O.R. 132 (C.A.); *Ontario Rules of Civil Procedure*, R.R.O. 1990, Reg. 194 r. 12.

CLASS GIFT A gift to a group made up of individuals who share some type of common characteristic rather than to a specific individual. See **Andrews v. Partington**, **[rule in]**; **rule against perpetuities**.

CLEAN HANDS The concept in **equity** that claimants who seek equitable **relief** must not themselves have indulged in any impropriety in relation to the transaction in which relief is sought. A party with "unclean hands" cannot ask a court of conscience [the equity court] to come to his or her aid. *Klemkowich v. Klemkowich* (1954), 14 W.W.R. (N.S.) 418 (Man.O.B.).

CLEAR DAY A period of time not including the days on which the events in question occurred. For example, if a **tenant** is to be given seven clear days notice to surrender possession of a property, the notice must be given early enough that there are seven days, not counting the day upon which the notice is given or the day of surrender.

CLEAR TITLE Also termed **good title**. A clear or good **title** is one that is free from any **encumbrance**, obstruction, burden, or limitation that presents a doubtful or even a reasonable question of law or fact. *Canadian Northern Ry. v. Peterson*, [1914], 6 W.W.R. 1194 (Sask.S.C.D.). See **marketable title**.

CLEMENCY See **pardon**.

CLERICAL ERROR An immediately correctable mistake resulting from the copying or transmission of legal documents. As distinguished from a **judicial error**, a clerical error is known by the character of the error and is not dependent on who makes the error, be it clerk or judge. See also **rectification**.

CLOSE 1. An ancient term referring to an enclosure, whether surrounded by a visible or an invisible boundary. **2.** Land rightfully owned by a party, the **trespass** upon which is **actionable** at law. See **breaking a close**. **3.** To terminate or complete—for example, to close an account, a **bargain**, an **estate**.

CO-CONSPIRATOR'S EXCEPTION An exception to the **hearsay rule**. "Statements made by a person engaged in an unlawful conspiracy are receivable as admissions as against all those acting in concert if the declarations were made while the conspiracy was ongoing and were made towards the accomplishment of the common object." *R. v. Mapara*, 2005 SCC 23, quoting Sopinka et al., *The Law of Evidence in Canada* (2nd ed., p. 303, 1999). The **trier of fact** must be satisfied beyond a reasonable doubt that a conspiracy existed, and there must be independent evidence, directly admissible against the accused, which establishes on a balance of probabilities that the accused was a member of the conspiracy.

CODE A systematic compilation of the laws of one particular jurisdiction or of one area of law—for example, the *Human Rights Code,* R.S.O. 1990, c. H. 19. Codification is more prevalent in American jurisdictions; however, a notable exception is the **civil law** of Quebec encompassed in the Civil Code. See also **criminal code**.

CODICIL A supplement to a **will** or an addition made by the **testator** and annexed to and to be taken as part of a testament. A reference to the will carries with it a reference to that which is merely a supplement to it, and the mere fact that the testator describes the will only to its original date is not sufficient to exclude the inference that the will referred to is the will as modified by the codicils. *Re Hunter* (1911), 24 O.L.R. 5 (Div.Ct.).

COERCION The use of physical or moral force in an attempt to interfere with the exercise of free choice. *Hodges v. Webb,*

[1920] 2 Ch. 70. See **duress**; **undue influence**.

COGENT Appealing forcibly to the mind; convincing. The word *cogent* is frequently used to describe the quality of a particular legal argument.

COGNIZABLE Within the **jurisdiction** of the court. An interest is cognizable in a court of law when that court has power to **adjudicate** the interest in controversy. See **justiciability**.

COHABIT To live together in a **conjugal relationship**; generally applied only to persons who are **common-law partners**.

COHABITATION AGREEMENT An agreement whereby unmarried individuals determine their respective rights and obligations while they cohabit or after they cease to do so, including ownership in or division of property, support obligations, some matters relating to children, and so on. See e.g., *Family Law Act*, R.S.N.L. 1990 c. F–2, s. 63; *Family Law Act*; S.N.W.T. 1997, c.18, s. 4.

CO-HEIR One who inherits property jointly with another or others, either by **will** or upon **intestacy**.

CO-INSURANCE A plan of **insurance** wherein the **insurer** provides **indemnity** for only a certain percentage of the insured's loss. The plan reflects the division of risk between insurer and **insured**. This division is dependent on the relative amount of the policy and the actual value of the property insured. *Eckhardt v. Lancashire Insurance Co.* (1900), 27 O.A.R. 373 at 382–83 (C.A.), affirmed by 31 S.C.R. 72.

COLLATERAL 1. Situated at the side; parallel or additional. Usually does not mean secondary or auxiliary unless specifically implied by the context. *The Royal Bank of Canada v. Slack,* [1958] O.R. 262 (C.A.). **2.** In commercial transactions, collateral security "is any property which is **assigned** or pledged to secure the performance of an obligation and as additional thereto, and which upon the performance of the obligation is to be surrendered or discharged." *Id.,* at 273 (C.A.). To obtain credit, it is sometimes necessary to offer some collateral, i.e., to place within the legal control of the lender some property that in the event of a default may be sold and applied to the amount owing.

COLLATERAL CONTRACT A **contract** that is additional to another contract, as "a contract the consideration for which is the making of some other contract....It is collateral to the main contract, but each has an independent existence, and they do not differ in respect of their possessing to the full the character and status of a contract." *Heilbut, Symons & Co. v. Buckleton,* [1913] A.C. 30 at 47 (H.L.).

COLLATERAL WARRANTY A **warranty** collateral to the main contract.

COLLATERAL ATTACK [RULE AGAINST]

An attack on an order or judgment that is made in a proceeding other than one specifically aimed at the reversal, variation, or nullification of the order or judgment. A judicially created rule holds that such attacks are not permitted. "The fundamental policy behind the rule against collateral attack is to "maintain the **rule of law** and to preserve the repute of the administration of justice... The idea is that if a party could avoid the consequences of an order issued against it by going to another forum, this would undermine the integrity of the justice system. Consequently, the doctrine is intended to prevent a party from circumventing the effect of a decision rendered against it." *Garland v. Consumers' Gas Co.,* 2004 SCC 25.

COLLATERAL ESTOPPEL

The doctrine that recognizes that the determination of facts **litigated** between two **parties** in a **proceeding** is binding on those parties in all future proceedings against each other. In a subsequent **action** between the parties on a different **claim**, the judgment is conclusive as to the **issues** raised in the subsequent action, if these issues were actually litigated and determined in the prior action. See **estoppel**. See also **bar**; **res judicata**.

COLLECTIVE AGREEMENT See **collective bargaining agreement**.

COLLECTIVE BARGAINING In general, negotiating with a view to the conclusion of a collective agreement, or the renewal or revision of an existing collective agreement. See the appropriate federal or provincial labour **legislation**. *Otis Elevator Co. Ltd. v. Int'l Union of Elevator Constructors, Local No. 82,* [1973] 4 W.W.R. 355 (B.C.C.A.).

COLLECTIVE BARGAINING AGREEMENT Also termed "collective agreement." An agreement between an employer and a **trade union** setting forth terms and conditions of employment. *Otis Elevator Co. Ltd. v. Int'l Union of Elevator Constructors, Local No. 82,* [1973] 4 W.W.R. 355 (B.C.C.A.).

COLLOQUIUM An old term in **pleading**. Words in a **declaration** or complaint of **libel** under **common-law** pleadings, which purport to connect the libelous words with the **plaintiff** by setting forth extrinsic facts showing that they applied to him or her and were so intended by the **defendant**.

COLLUSION 1. The making of an agreement with another for the purposes of perpetrating a **fraud**, or engaging in illegal activity, or in legal activity while having an illegal end in mind. Compare **conspiracy. 2.** In the context of divorce law, the *Divorce Act,* R.S.C. 1985, c. 3, (2nd Supp.), s. 11(4) defines collusion as "...an agreement or conspiracy to which an applicant for a divorce is either directly or indirectly a party for the purpose of subverting the administration of justice, and includes any agreement, understanding, or arrangement to fabricate or suppress evidence or to deceive the court, but does not include an agreement to the extent that it provides for separation between the parties, financial support, division of property or the custody of any child of the marriage."

Under s. 11(l)(*a*) of the Act, it is the duty of the court to satisfy itself that there has been no collusion when an application for divorce is made, and to dismiss the application if there has been collusion.

COLLUSIVE ACTION An impermissible **action** maintained by non-**adversary parties** to determine a hypothetical point of law or to produce a desired legal **precedent**. Because such a suit does not contain an actual **controversy**, it will not be entertained by a court. Compare **declaratory judgment**.

COLOUR Semblance; disguise. Often used to designate the hiding of a set of facts behind a deceptive, but technically proper, legal theory.

COLOURABLE Presenting an appearance that does not correspond with reality, or an appearance intended to conceal or deceive. *Etherington v. Wilson* (1875), 1 Ch.D. 160. Legislation is said to be colourable for **division of powers** purposes when it is made to look as though it deals with a matter within the enacting level of government's **jurisdiction** when, in fact, it does not. "The doctrine of colourability applies where a legislature purports to exercise its power in relation to a matter within its jurisdiction but, in fact, is directing its legislative effort to a matter outside its jurisdiction." *Consortium Developments (Clearwater) Ltd. v. Sarnia (City)*, [1998] 3 S.C.R. 3. Colourable legislation will be **ultra vires**. However, a finding of colourability has overtones of deliberate deception and is not necessary for a law to be declared *ultra vires*.

COLOUR OF LAW Mere semblance of a legal right. An action done under colour of law is one done with the apparent authority of law but actually in contravention of law.

COLOUR OF RIGHT "The term...generally, although not exclusively, refers to a situation where there is an assertion of a proprietary or possessory right to the thing which is the subject matter of the [alleged offence]. One who is honestly asserting what he believes to be an honest claim cannot be said to act 'without colour of right,' even though it may be unfounded in law or fact.... The term 'colour of right' is also used to denote an honest belief in a state of facts which if it actually existed would at law justify or excuse the act done.... The term when used in the latter sense

is merely a particular application of the doctrine of mistake of fact." *Regina v. DeMarco* (1973), 22 C.R. (N.S.) 258 at 260 (Ont.C.A.). In the former of those two senses, colour of right is an exception to the rule that ignorance of the law is no excuse (**ignorantia legis non excusat**). See **mistake** [MISTAKE OF FACT]. See also *Criminal Code,* R.S.C. 1985, c. C–46, s. 429(2). See also *R. v. Dorosh*, 2003 SKCA 134.

COLOUR OF TITLE Something lending the appearance of **title**, when in reality there is no title at all; said of an **instrument** that, on its face, professes to pass title and that one relies on as passing title, but that fails to do so, either because title is lacking in the person conveying or because the **conveyance** itself is defective. Thus, one possessing a forged or false **deed** has mere colour of title. Colour of title is sometimes an element of **adverse possession**. A person is said to hold under colour of title when he occupies land in the belief that he or she has legal title to the land but in fact does not. There are numerous ways in which such a mistake as to title may arise. The most common is where a deed is improperly executed or registered. A party does *not* hold under colour of title when he or she believes he or she has been given permission to occupy the land and in fact has not. See *Walker v. Russell,* [1966] 1 O.R. 197 (H.C.); *Wood v. LeBlanc* (1904), 34 S.C.R. 627; *Harris v. Mudie* (1882), 7 O.A.R. 414 (C.A.).

COMBINES [LEGISLATION] In Canada, most restraint of trade offences are dealt with under the *Competition Act,* R.S.C. 1985. c. C–34. This Act attempts to prevent monopolies or illegal trade practices, such as resale price maintenance, misleading advertising, conspiracy to prevent competition, etc., making each an offence under the Act. Proceedings are undertaken in either the criminal courts or the Federal Court, and the court may impose as a penalty a fine or imprisonment or both. See *Criminal Code,* R.S.C. 1985, c. C–46, ss. 466–467. In the United States, legislation designed to prevent monopolies by insuring freedom of competition are termed antitrust laws.

COMITY [COMITAS] Courtesy; compatibility; respect. The informal and non-mandatory courtesy sometimes referred to as a set of rules to which the courts of one **jurisdiction** often defer in determining questions where the laws or interests of another jurisdiction are involved. *C.N.R. v. Lewis,* [1930] 4 D.L.R. 537 (Ex.Ct.) "Comity refers to informal acts performed and rules observed by states in their mutual relations out of politeness, convenience, and goodwill, rather than strict legal obligation...Comity means that when one state looks to another for help in criminal matters, it must respect the way in which the other state chooses to provide the assistance within its borders. That deference ends where clear violations of international law and fundamental human rights begin." *R. v. Hape,* 2007 SCC 26.

COMMENT The statement made by a judge or counsel concerning the defendant, such a statement not being based on fact, but rather on **alleged** facts. It should be noted that a judge may comment on the weight of the evidence and the credibility of witnesses provided that the **jury** understands it is their province to decide such questions. By s. 4(6) of the *Canada Evidence Act,* R.S.C. 1985, c. C–5, "the failure of the person charged or of the wife or husband of such person, to testify shall not be made the subject of comment by the judge, or by counsel for the prosecution."Also, a prosecutor may not comment on the refusal to testify of a defendant in a criminal proceeding, and the court may not instruct a jury that such silence is evidence of guilt. *R. v. Diggs* (1987), 77 N.S.R. (2d) 432 (N.S.C.A.); *R. v. Biladeau,* 2008 ONCA 833.

COMMERCIAL EXPRESSION Expression aimed at an economic purpose, such as advertising and commercial signage. Commercial expression is protected under Canada's constitutional guarantee of **freedom of expression** in s. 2(b) of the **Canadian Charter of Rights and Freedoms**. *Irwin Toy Ltd. v. Québec (Attorney-General),* [1989] 1 S.C.R.

927; *Canada (Attorney-General) v. JTI–Macdonald Corp.,* 2007 SCC 30.

COMMERCIAL PAPER A negotiable **instrument**; i.e., a writing **endorsed** by the **maker** or **drawee**, containing an unconditional promise or order to pay a certain sum on demand or at a specified time, made payable to order or to bearer. The term comprehends **bills of exchange, cheques,** notes, and **certificates of deposit**. In common, untechnical usage, it also may be used to refer to **bills of sale** (chattel mortgages) and **conditional sales contracts**. See also **bearer instrument; mortgage** [CHATTEL MORTGAGE].

COMMISSION EVIDENCE Evidence that is ordered by a court to be taken in front of a person authorised to receive that evidence (the commissioner) and that is to be taken in the same manner as if the witness were testifying in court. Commission evidence is commonly used when the witness is out of the jurisdiction or is too ill to attend court. See, e.g., *The Court of Queen's Bench Act,* C.C.S.M. c. C280, s. 70; *Criminal Code,* R.S.C. 1985, c. C–46, s. 709.

COMMISSION OF INQUIRY An *ad hoc* body established by a government to investigate some particular incident or issue. The precise task performed by any particular commission of inquiry will depend upon the terms of reference that established it. "A commission of inquiry is neither a criminal trial nor a civil action for the determination of liability. It cannot establish either criminal culpability or civil responsibility for damages. Rather, an inquiry is an investigation into an issue, event, or series of events. The findings of a commissioner relating to that investigation are simply findings of fact and statements of opinion reached by the commissioner at the end of the inquiry. They are unconnected to normal legal criteria. They are based upon and flow from a procedure that is not bound by the evidentiary or procedural rules of a courtroom. There are no legal consequences attached to the determinations of a commissioner. They are not enforceable and do not bind courts considering the same subject matter." *Canada (Attorney-Gen-*

eral) *v. Canada* (*Commission of Inquiry on the Blood System*), [1997] 3 S.C.R. 440. Under the *Inquiries Act*, R.S.C. 1985, c. I–11, a Royal Commission can be established to investigate "any matter connected with the good government of Canada or the conduct of any part of the public business thereof." Similar legislation exists in the provinces; see, e.g., *Public Inquiries Act*, R.S.A. 2000, c. P–39, or *Public Inquiries Act, 2006*, S.N.L. 2006, c. P–38.1.

Notable public inquiries include the 1970 Royal Commission on the Status of Women; the 1977 Mackenzie Valley Pipeline Inquiry; the 1989 Royal Commission on the Donald Marshall, Jr., Prosecution (which inquired into the wrongful conviction of Donald Marshall, Jr., as well as to issues of systemic racism in the justice system); the 1996 Royal Commission on Aboriginal Peoples, the 1997 Somalia Commission of Inquiry (which inquired into Canadian participation in the United Nations peacekeeping mission in Somalia in 1992–93); and the 2006 Commission of Inquiry into the Sponsorship Program and Advertising Activities (which investigated allegations of misuse of public funds).

COMMITTEE 1. "[A]n individual or a body to which others have committed or delegated a particular duty, or have taken on themselves to perform it in the expectation of their act being confirmed by the body they profess to represent or act for." *Reynell v. Lewis* (1846), 153 E.R. 959 at 959 (Ex.). **2.** Frequently used to refer to a person to whom the **custody** of another or the **estate** of an insane person has been committed.

COMMODITY "Something produced for use or **sale**, all things, which have prices and are offered for sale, everything moveable which is bought and sold, anything moveable that is the subject of trade and commerce..." *Underwriters' Survey Bureau Ltd. v. Massie & Renwick Ltd.,* [1937] Ex.C.R. 15 at 21; varied without reference to this point, [1937] S.C.R. 265.

COMMON BAWDY HOUSE Refers to a place that is (a) kept or occupied, or (b) resorted to by one or more persons for the purpose of **prostitution** or the practice of acts of indecency. Everyone who keeps a common bawdy house is guilty of an **indictable offence** and liable to imprisonment for a term not exceeding two years. *Criminal Code*, R.S.C. 1985, c. C–46, s. 210. See **keeper**.

COMMON BETTING HOUSE Refers to a place that is opened, kept, or used for the purpose of (a) enabling, encouraging, or assisting persons who resort thereto to bet between themselves or with the keeper, or (b) enabling any person to receive, record, register, transmit, or pay bets or to announce the results of betting. Everyone who keeps a common betting house is guilty of an indictable offence and liable to imprisonment for a term not exceeding two years. *Criminal Code*, R.S.C. 1985, c. C–46, s. 201 (1). See **keeper**.

COMMON GAMING HOUSE Refers to a place that is (a) kept for gain to which persons resort for the purpose of playing games, or (b) kept or used for the purpose of playing games (i) in which a bank is kept by one or more but not all of the players, (ii) in which all or any portion of the bets on or proceeds from a game is paid directly or indirectly to the keeper of the place, (iii) in which, directly or indirectly, a fee is charged to or paid by the players for the privilege of playing or participating in a game or using gaming equipment, or (iv) in which the chances of winning are not equally favourable to all persons who play the game, including the person, if any, who conducts the game; **disorderly house** means a **common bawdy house**, a **common betting house**, or a **common gaming house**; **game** means a game of chance or mixed chance and skill. *Criminal Code*, R.S.C. 1985, c. C–46, s. 201(1). See **keeper**.

COMMON INTENTION A person who has an intention in common with another person to commit an offence is guilty of any other offences that other person commits, if he or she knew or ought to have known that the other offence was a probable consequence. *Criminal Code*, R.S.C. 1985, c. C–46, s. 21(2). A common intention does not require that the person desires to commit the initial crime. *R. v. Hibbert*, [1995] 2 S.C.R. 973.

COMMON LAW The system of **jurisprudence**, which originated in England and was later applied in Canada, that is based on judicial **precedent** rather than legislative enactments; it is to be contrasted with **civil law** (the descendant of Roman law prevalent in other Western countries and in Quebec) and **equity** (the body of rules administered by the Court of Chancery). Common law depends for its authority upon the recognition given by the courts to principles, customs, and rules of conduct previously existing among the people. It is now recorded in the law reports that embody the decisions of the judges, together with the reasons they assigned for their decisions. *The King v. Mason* (1918), 39 D.L.R. 54 (Que. Police Mag. Ct.).

COMMON-LAW PARTNER A term used by the federal government and some provincial **legislatures** (e.g., Manitoba and Nova Scotia) to extend benefits and obligations to partners who live together in a **conjugal relationship** without being married. This applies to both opposite-sex and same-sex partners. See **spouse**.

COMMON-LAW SPOUSE See **spouse**.

COMMON MISTAKE See **mistake** [MUTUAL MISTAKE].

COMMON NUISANCE See **nuisance**.

COMMON PROPERTY See **property**.

COMMONS 1. Land set aside for public use, e.g., public parks. 2. The untitled class of Great Britain, represented in Parliament by the House of Commons. 3. As a carry-over from the British parliamentary system, the term **House of Commons** is also applied to the main Canadian federal legislative body (i.e., the federal **legislature**).

COMMUTATION Substitution; change. 1. The change to a lesser penalty from a greater one, such as life imprisonment instead of death, or a shorter term instead of a longer one. The Governor-General in Council has the power of clemency, which includes the broad power in his or her discretion to commute a sentence. See **pardon** and **reprieve**. 2. The **conversion** of the right to receive a variable or periodic payment into the right to receive a fixed or gross payment.

COMPANY Broadly, any group of people voluntarily united for performing jointly any activity, business, or commercial enterprise. The terms *company* and *corporation* are today often used interchangeably. "The word 'company' has no strictly technical meaning. It involves...two ideas...first that the association is of persons so numerous as not to be aptly described as a firm; and secondly, that the consent of all the other members is not required to the transfer of a member's interest." *In re Stanley, Tennant v. Stanley,* [1906] 1 Ch. 131 at 134. Historically, the term has been employed to cover a wide range of organizations, including **corporations**, **joint stock companies**, **partnerships**, etc., and usually implies an enterprise for purposes of gain. In the modern context, a company is usually regarded as a business entity incorporated under the *Companies* or *Corporations Acts* of the provincial and federal jurisdictions.
HOLDING COMPANY See **holding company**.
JOINT STOCK COMPANY See **joint stock company**.

COMPELLABLE Subject to being required to testify at a **trial**. An accused person is **competent** to testify at his or her own trial but is not compellable by the Crown. Similarly, the spouse of an accused is not compellable by the Crown, other than for some particular offences. *Canada Evidence Act*, RSC 1985, c. C–5, s. 4.

COMPENSATION Remuneration for work done; indemnification for injury sustained; that which constitutes, or is regarded as, an equivalent or recompense; that which compensates for loss or privation. Often used with reference to the expropriation of property for public use; a FAIR COMPENSATION is just both to the owner of the property taken and to the public. See also **damages**.

COMPETENT Capable of doing a certain thing; having the capacity to understand and to act reasonably. Competent **evidence** is relevant to the issues being **litigated**; a competent court has proper **jurisdiction** over the person or property at issue. An individual is competent to make a **will** if he or she is "of sound mind, memory and understanding." "When a will is contested on the ground of mental incapacity, the propounder must prove the testator understood what he or she was doing: that the testator understood the 'nature and quality of the act.' The testator must be able to comprehend and recollect what property he or she possessed, the persons that ordinarily might be expected to benefit, the extent of what is being given to each beneficiary and, finally the nature of the claims of others who are being excluded." James MacKenzie, *Feeney's Canadian Law of Wills: Testamentary Capacity,* c.2 at para. 2.6 (4th ed. 2000). See *De Araujo v. Neto,* [2001] B.C.J. No. 1314 (S.C.); *Russell v. Fraser* (1980), 118 D.L.R. (3d) 733 (B.C.C.A.)

As a general rule, any person is a competent witness, but there are exceptions. At **common law** a spouse was not a competent witness to give evidence for or against his or her spouse in a **criminal** matter. This rule has been amended by statute to make a spouse competent to testify for his or her spouse, and against his or her spouse with regard to some offences, primarily assaults and sexual offences. See *Canada Evidence Act,* RSC 1985, c. C–5, s. 4. Issues of competence can also arise for witnesses with mental deficiencies and for children under the age of 14, though the incompetence of any such witness must be established. *Canada Evidence Act,* ss 16, 16.1. The fact that a witness is competent does not mean that that witness is **compellable**.

COMPLAINANT 1. Generally, the person who initiates the complaint in an **action** or **proceeding. 2.** The person against whom it is alleged that the offence was committed.

COMPLAINT 1. A statement of fact, being the initiating step in a civil proceeding. **2.** An **allegation** against a person. **3.** A statement made to a third party by a person against whom a sexual offence has been committed. The fact of making a complaint and the complaint itself, although admissible, do not constitute corroboration of the act complained of. *R. v. Ball* (1957), 117 C.C.C. 366 (B.C.C.A.).

COMPOS MENTIS (*kŏm'-pōs mĕn'-tĭs*) Lat.: mentally competent. Compare **non compos mentis**.

COMPOUNDING A FELONY See **compounding an offence**.

COMPOUNDING AN OFFENCE 1. At common law, to agree not to report or to prosecute an offence in exchange for compensation. Section 141 of the *Criminal Code,* R.S.C. 1985, c. C–46 makes it an offence to compound an indictable offence. **2.** In casual use, to make an offence worse through some aggravating factor, e.g., by, after stealing a vehicle, driving it in a dangerous manner.

COMPREHENSIVE CLAIMS Agreements negotiated in areas of the country where neither **Aboriginal rights** nor **Aboriginal title** are yet covered by **treaty**. Comprehensive claims agreements normally cover land ownership, hunting and fishing rights, participation in land, and resource management. Measures to promote economic development, Aboriginal culture, or Aboriginal self-government can also be included.

COMPULSION See **duress**.

COMPULSORY APPEARANCE See **appearance; appearance notice**.

COMPULSORY JOINDER See **joinder**.

COMPUTER FORENSICS See **digital forensics**.

CONCERTED ACTION [CONCERT OF ACTION] 1. Action done in pursuance of some scheme, which has been planned and agreed upon between the parties acting together. Thus, in criminal law, concerted action is found only where there has been a **conspiracy** to commit an illegal act, i.e., all must share the criminal intent of the actual perpetrator. **2.** The term also applies to **joint tortfeasors** where there is tort liability for conspiracy. *Southam Co. Ltd. v. Gouthro*, [1948] 1 W.W.R. 593 (B.C.S.C.).

CONCLUSION OF FACT A conclusion reached solely through use of facts and natural reasoning, without resort to rules of law; inferences from evidentiary facts. See **question of fact**.

CONCLUSION OF LAW A conclusion reached through application of rules of law. In a case where one can arrive at the ultimate conclusion only by applying a rule of law, the result reached embodies a conclusion of law rather than fact. See **question of law**.

CONCLUSIVE PRESUMPTION See **presumption**.

CONCUR To agree. A concurring opinion states agreement with the conclusion of the majority but may give different reasons why such a conclusion is reached. An opinion "concurring in the result only" is one that implies no agreement with the reasoning of the prevailing opinion but fails to state reasons of its own. Compare **dissent**. See **opinion**.

CONCURRENT Running together; in conjunction with; existing together. In criminal law, the words *concurrent and consecutive* are generally used to indicate the intentions of the Court with respect to **sentencing**. When adapted to **judgments** in criminal cases, the opposite of concurrent is *consecutive* and *accumulative:* If sentences are not concurrent, they are consecutive and they accumulate. "Although the discretion whether to order the sentences to be served concurrently or consecutively rests with the trial judge, the general practice of the court in the past has been to order concurrent sentences where the offences are committed together within a short period of time and are in reality one transaction. Here the court should approach the problem by setting one over-all sentence rather than passing a multiplicity of short consecutive sentences adding up to a substantial sentence. On the other hand, if the offences are totally unrelated and took place at separate times and places, the court will consider imposing consecutive sentences." R. Salhany, *Canadian Criminal Procedure* c. 8 at 30 (6th ed. 1994). See *Criminal Code,* R.S.C. 1985, c. C–46, s. 718.3(4). See also *Regina v. Chisholm* (1965), 4 C.C.C. (N.S.) 289 (Ont.C.A.); *Regina v. Courtney,* [1956], 115 C.C.C. 260 (B.C.C.A.).

CONCURRENT CONDITION See **condition**.

CONCURRENT JURISDICTION See **jurisdiction**.

CONCURRING OPINION See **opinion**.

CONDEMN 1. To declare to be wrong; to convict of guilt; to sentence judicially. **2.** To pronounce unfit for use—e.g., an unsafe building. **3.** To declare forfeited or taken for public use—e.g., the adjudging of a captured vessel to be a lawful prize. See also **confiscate**.

CONDITION A term of a **contract** that goes so directly to the root of the contract or is so essential to its nature that, if the circumstances are, or become, inconsistent with the condition, all **executory** obligations under the contract may be treated as discharged by a party who is not in **default**. See S.M. Waddams, *The Law of Contracts* 584–86 (6th ed. 2010). See **warranty**.

A condition may be EXPRESS or IMPLIED. Whether a particular term is to be implied depends, as a rule, solely upon the intention of the parties, as gathered from all the circumstances "with the object of giving to the transaction such efficacy as both parties must have intended that at all events it should have." *The Moorcock* (1889), 14 P.D. 64 at 68 (C.A.), quoted in *Zeitler v. Zeitler Estate,* 2010 BCCA 216.

CONCURRENT CONDITION A condition precedent that exists when the obligation of each party to a contract, consisting of mutual promises, is conditional upon performance by the other.

CONDITION PRECEDENT A condition, express or implied, that the contract shall not bind one or both of the parties until or unless some event has happened.

CONDITION SUBSEQUENT A condition, express or implied, that, upon the occurrence of some event after the contract has become binding, it shall cease to be binding, or that one party or both parties shall have the right to avoid it.

CONDITIONAL Dependent upon the happening or non-happening of the **condition**; implies a type of **encumbrance**.

CONDITIONAL BEQUEST See **bequest**.

CONDITIONAL DISCHARGE See **discharge**.

CONDITIONAL FEE [ESTATE] A **fee simple** [complete ownership of **real property**] that is limited in that it must eventually pass from the **donee** to certain **heirs** or the **issue** [children] of the donee **[heirs of the body]**. Should the designated heir fail to be in existence at the time of the death of the donee, the property **reverts** [goes back] to the donor or his or her **estate**. However, the entire estate rests with the donee until his or her death, the donor having the mere **possibility of a reverter**. Such a reverter may be released to the donee, thereby converting the estate from a fee simple conditional to a fee simple absolute. See also **determinable fee**; **life estate**.

CONDITIONAL SALES CONTRACT A **contract** for the sale of goods or land under which the purchase price is payable by installments and the property in the goods or land is to remain in the seller until the installments are paid. See **PPSA**.

CONDITIONAL SENTENCE "A disposition in which the accused is found guilty and sentenced to imprisonment, but serves the sentence in the community so long as he or she successfully fulfils conditions." Kent Roach, *Criminal Law*, 518 (5th ed. 2012). See *Criminal Code*, R.S.C. 1985, c. C–46, s. 742.1. *R. v. Proulx*, [2000] 1 S.C.R. 61. A conditional sentence of imprisonment is popularly referred to as "house arrest."

CONDITION PRECEDENT An event or **condition** [express or **implied**] that must happen or be performed before an **estate** can **vest** or be enlarged, or before a **contract** is performed.

CONDITION SUBSEQUENT In property law, a condition or an event that causes the grantee's estate to be subject to termination by the grantor after the estate has been bestowed. If the condition is breached or the event occurs, the grantor has the option of using a right of re-entry to reclaim the estate. See *Tilbury West Public School Bd. v. Hastie*, [1966] 2 O.R. 20. See **condition**.

CONDOMINIUM A type of ownership of individual units, generally in a multi-unit development or project—e.g., an apartment condominium. The owner will normally receive a deed upon purchase describing the scope of his or her ownership and the interest he or she possesses as **tenant in common** with other owners, such as hallways, elevators, gardens, etc. See, e.g., *Condominium Act, 1998,* S.O. 1998, c. 19. R.S.N.S. 1989, c. 85. A condominium is distinguished from a **cooperative** form of occupancy when the **title** to the unit **premises** is not in the individual occupant, but in another entity such as a **corporation**.

CONDONATION "Condonation of a matrimonial offence means the forgiveness of the offence with a full knowledge of the circumstances followed by a reinstatement of the offending party to his or her former position." C. Davies, *Family Law in Canada* 417–18 (4th ed. 1984).

Section 11(1)(c) of the *Divorce Act,* R.S.C. 1985, c. 3 (2nd Supp.), provides that "where a divorce is sought in circumstances described in paragraph 8(2)(b) [adultery, or physical or mental cruelty] to satisfy itself that there has been no condonation or **connivance** on the part of the spouse bringing the proceeding, and to dismiss the application for a divorce if that spouse has condoned or connived at the act or conduct complained of unless, in the opinion of the court, the public interest would be better served by granting the divorce."

CONFEDERATION A term that describes a political association comprised of a loose association of states in which the central government is subordinate to the governments of the member states. However, the term confederation is an accepted name for the Canadian union of provinces, despite the fact that "In

Canada, the union of provinces... established a central government...[which] was independent of the provinces and coordinate with them. Indeed, to the extent that the provinces and the central government are not coordinate, it is the provinces who are subordinate." P.W. Hogg, *Constitutional Law of Canada* 5–5 (5th ed. 2007). Compare **federalism**. See **British North America Act**.

CONFESSION A statement made by an **accused** to a **person in authority**. A confession is a form of **admission** that is distinguished by the "person in authority" requirement: to be **admissible evidence**, it must be proven **beyond a reasonable doubt** that the statement was made **voluntarily**. "[T]here are several factors to consider in determining whether there is a reasonable doubt as to the voluntariness of a statement made to a person in authority, including the making of threats or promises, oppression, the operating mind doctrine, and police trickery." *R. v. Spencer*, 2007 SCC 11. The traditional **common law** rule was that a confession was not voluntary if it was motivated by fear of prejudice or hope of advantage held out by a person in authority. *Ibrahim v. The King*, [1914] A.C. 599. The law today holds that not every offer of an inducement to an accused automatically renders a statement involuntary: "While a *quid pro quo* is an important factor in establishing the existence of a threat or promise, it is the strength of the inducement, having regard to the particular individual and his or her circumstances, that is to be considered in the overall contextual analysis into the voluntariness of the accused's statement." *Spencer*.

CONFESSION AND AVOIDANCE A pleading by which a **party** admits the **allegations** against him or her, either expressly or by implication, but which presents new matter that avoids the effect of the failure to deny those allegations. Thus a **litigant** "confesses" rather than denies the allegation, but his or her presentation of new matter acts to "avoid" a **judgment** against him or her. See G. Watson et al., *Civil Litigation* 410 (5th ed. 1999). See **defence**. Compare **denial**.

CONFIDENTIALITY The obligation to keep information secret and not to disclose it. A lawyer's duty of confidentiality to a client is broader than **solicitor-client privilege** and "applies without regard to the nature or source of the information or to the fact that others may share the knowledge." *CBA Code of Professional Conduct* (2009), ch. IV.

CONFISCATE To take private property without just **compensation**; to transfer property from a private use to a public use. See also **condemn**.

CONFLICT OF INTEREST Having a duty that cannot be entirely discharged without some disharmony with the person's own interests or with another duty owed by that person. "A public office holder is in a conflict of interest when he or she exercises an official power, duty, or function that provides an opportunity to further his or her private interests or those of his or her relatives or friends or to improperly further another person's private interests." *Conflict of Interest Act*, S.C. 2006, c. 9, s. 4. A lawyer is in a conflict of interest if he or she represents two clients whose interests are not consonant with one another. See *Macdonald Estate v. Martin*, [1990] 3 S.C.R. 1235; *R. v. Neil*, 2002 SCC 70. See **duty of loyalty**.

CONFLICT OF LAWS The body of law by which the court where the **action** is maintained determines or chooses which law to apply where a diversity exists between the applicable law of that court's state [the **forum** state] and the applicable law of another **jurisdiction** connected with the controversy. The considerations comprising that decision formerly rested on simple and traditional rules such as LEX LOCI CONTRACTUS (law of the place where a contract is made) and LEX LOCI DELICTI (law of the place where the wrong is committed) in tort. More modern doctrine focuses on an interest analysis that very often arrives at the same choice but includes, along with the traditional considerations of place of contracting and place of the wrong, the public policy of the forum and, in general, which jurisdiction maintains the most significant relationship or contacts with the subject matter of the controversy. The interest analysis is referred to as CENTER OF GRAVITY or CONTACTS APPROACH. J. Walker, *Canadian Conflict of Laws* (6th ed. 2005); S.G.A. Pitel and N.S. Rafferty, *Conflict of Laws* (2010). See also **comity**; **forum non conveniens**.

CONFUSION OF GOODS The mixing together of **personal property** belonging to two or more owners to the point when the property of any of them no longer can be identified except as part of a mass of like goods. Compare **accession**.

CONGLOMERATE A group of **corporations** engaged in unrelated businesses and controlled by a single corporate entity.

CONJUGAL RELATIONSHIP A defining characteristic of two people who are considered **spouses**. Whether a relationship is conjugal is assessed by the presence of shared shelter, sexual and personal behaviour, services, social activities, economic support and children, and the societal perception of the couple. These elements may be present in varying degrees, and not all are necessary for the relationship to be found to be conjugal. Same-sex couples can qualify as spouses under this definition. *M. v. H.*, [1999] 2 S.C.R. 3.

CONJUGAL RIGHTS The rights of married persons, which include the enjoyment of association, sympathy, confidence, domestic happiness, the comforts of dwelling together in the same habitation, eating meals at the same table and profiting by the joint property rights, as well as the intimacies of domestic relations. See **consortium**. See also **spouse**.

CONNIVANCE "Connivance means that the adultery of one spouse has been caused by or has been knowingly, willfully, or recklessly permitted by the other as an accessory. It is the essence of connivance that it precedes the event, and generally, the material event is the inception of the adultery, and not its repetition." C. Davies, *Family Law in Canada* 426–27 (4th ed. 1984).

Maddock v. Maddock, [1958] O.R. 810 (C.A.).

Section 11(1)(*c*) of the *Divorce Act*, R.S.C. 1985, c. 3 (2nd Supp.) provides that "where a divorce is sought in circumstances described in paragraph 8(2) (*b*) [adultery, or physical or mental cruelty] to satisfy itself that there has been no **condonation** or connivance on the part of the spouse bringing the proceeding and to dismiss the application for a divorce if that spouse has condoned or connived at the act or conduct complained of unless, in the opinion of the court, the public interest would be better satisfied by granting the divorce."

Compare **collusion**.

CONSANGUINITY Relationship by blood; it is a requirement of a valid marriage in Canada that the parties must not be within prohibited degrees of consanguinity or **affinity** (relationship by marriage). The *Marriage (Prohibited Degrees) Act*, S.C. 1990, c. 46, s. 2(2) prohibits marriage between persons related "lineally, or as brother or sister or half-brother or half-sister, including by adoption." Under s. 3(2) of the *Act*, such marriages are void.

Archbishop Parker's Table of 1563, printed in the Book of Common Prayer of the Church of England, lists the degrees of prohibited relationship for male and female persons (17 each). The table speciifies that the prohibited degrees are "by the whole or the half blood, and whether legitimate or illegitimate."

CONSCIOUSNESS OF GUILT See **post-offence conduct**.

CONSECUTIVE SENTENCE A sentence that is to be served following the completion of another sentence. See **concurrent**.

CONSENSUS AD IDEM (*kän-sĕn'-sŭs äd ē'-dĕm*) Lat.: agreement as to the same thing. Of the same mind; similar in all essential matters. A binding contract requires consensus ad idem [mutual agreement on the same subject matter] by both parties—i.e., a meeting of the minds.

CONSENT A deliberate and free act of the mind; an act of reason accompanied by deliberation. Thus an instrument such as a **will** may be invalidated if consent is obtained by fraud or **undue influence**. In **tort** law, the phrase informed consent is sometimes used with respect to the requirement that a patient be apprised of the nature and risks of a medical procedure before the physician can validly claim exemption from liability for **battery** or from responsibility for medical complications.

In **criminal** law, true consent of the complainant to the activity that forms the substance of the charge is a **defence** to the charge, if the consent is not consent to death (*Criminal Code* s.14), not excluded by the nature of the offence, freely given, and informed. Other examples where consent is no defence include s. 286 (abduction of a child) and an assault that intentionally causes "serious or non-trivial bodily harm…in the course of a fistfight or brawl." *R. v. Jobidon* (1991), 66 C.C.C. (3d) 454 at 494 (S.C.C.).

Consent is a central issue in sexual assault. Section 273.1(2) of the *Criminal Code* outlines situations where no consent can be obtained to negate liability for the act of sexual assault. In *R. v. Ewanchuk*, the court rejected implied consent through conduct as a defence that negates the **actus reus** of sexual assault and held consent is to be determined from "the complainant's subjective internal state" (1999), 131 C.C.C. (3d) 481 (S.C.C.). The accused may argue as a defence he or she did not have the requisite **mens rea** for the act of sexual assault, and "honestly but mistakenly (and not necessarily reasonably)…believed that the defendant was consenting to the sexual act." *R. v. Seaboyer* (1992), 66 C.C.C. (3d) 321 at 393 (S.C.C.). However, s. 273.2 specifies that belief in consent might not be a defence, requiring the accused to take reasonable steps to discover whether the victim in fact consented. See also Kent Roach, *Criminal Law*, 454–451 (5th ed. 2012).

CONSEQUENTIAL DAMAGES See **damages**.

CONSERVATION EASEMENT A voluntary agreement entered into by a landowner and some other party whereby the landowner grants to that party an easement over the land with the goal of preserving ecologically sensitive land—the habitat of rare or endangered plant or animal species; places of archaeological, palaeontological, historical, or cultural significance; or protecting similar interests. A conservation easement runs with the land in the event that the land is sold. It may be terminated by agreement, or in some cases by court order. See, e.g., *Conservation Easements Act*, RSNB 2011, c. 130, or *Conservation Easements Act*, SNS 2001, c. 28.

CONSERVATOR Temporary court-appointed guardian or custodian of **property**.

CONSIDERATIO CURIAE (*kŭn-sĭd'-êr-ā-shē-ō kyū'-rē-ī*) Lat.: judgment of the court.

CONSIDERATION Something of value given in return for a performance or a promise of performance by another, for the purpose of forming a **contract**; one element of a contract that is generally required to make a promise binding and to make the agreement of the parties enforceable as a contract. To find consideration, there must be a performance or a return promise that has been bargained for by the parties. Restatement, *Contracts* 2d s. 75 (as adopted and promulgated May 1979). Consideration represents the element of bargaining, to indicate that each party agrees to surrender something in return for what it is to receive. It is consideration that distinguishes a contract from a mere **gift**.

"A valuable consideration may consist either in some right, interest, profit or benefit occurring to the one party or in some forbearance, detriment, loss or responsibility given, suffered or undertaken by the other." *Currie v. Misa* (1875), L.R. 10 Ex. 153 at 162.

"The essence of a valid, binding contract is the idea of a 'bargain' between the parties. A contract consists of an exchange of promises, acts, or acts and promises, as a result of which each side receives something from the other…

If there is no consideration, there is no contract; and if there is no contract, there is nothing upon or from which to found or create liability." G.H.L. Fridman, *The Law of Contract in Canada* 82 (6th ed. 2011).

Courts have used the word *consideration* with many different meanings. It is often used merely to express the legal conclusion that a promise is enforceable. Historically, its primary meaning may have been that the conditions were met under which an action of **assumpsit** [an early form of contract action] would lie. It was also used as the equivalent of the **quid pro quo** required in an action of **debt**. A **seal**, it has been said, imports a consideration, although the law was clear that no element of bargain was necessary to enforcement of a promise under seal. On the other hand, consideration has sometimes been used to refer to almost any reason asserted for enforcing a promise, even though the reason was insufficient [as in] promises in consideration of love and affection, illegal consideration, past consideration, and consideration furnished by reliance on a gratuitous promise where in fact there has been no consideration at all.

The phrase SUFFICIENT CONSIDERATION is used by some courts to express the legal conclusion that one requirement for an enforceable bargain has been met. This is redundant and misleading, however, since any performance or return promise that has been bargained for and received is legally sufficient to satisfy the consideration element of a contract. The law will not in general inquire into the adequacy of "consideration," and hence the term does not add anything of substance to the word *consideration.* So long as the bargained-for promise is not illusory or the performance a sham pretext, a sufficient exchange will have taken place to justify the enforcement of the agreement so far as consideration is at issue.

The performance may be any lawful act done for the benefit of the other contracting party or a third person and may include an act of forbearance. A MORAL CONSIDERATION will not generally qualify as consideration so as to render the promise enforceable.

FAILURE OF CONSIDERATION refers to the circumstances in which consideration was bargained for but either has become worthless, has ceased to exist or has not been performed as promised. Failure of consideration may be partial or total and is often used interchangeably with WANT OF CONSIDERATION.

CONSIGNMENT 1. The act of consigning; the act of sending off goods to an **agent** for **sale. 2.** Goods sent or delivered to an **agent** for **sale**. See **PPSA**.

CONSOLIDATION See **merger**.

CONSORTIUM The **conjugal** fellowship of spouses, and the right of each spouse to the company, cooperation and aid of the other. Where a person willfully interferes with this relation, depriving one spouse of the consortium of the other, he or she may be liable in **damages**. Loss of consortium can figure in an award of damages in a **tort** action for injury or wrongful death of a spouse. See, e.g., *Best v. Samuel Fox & Co.,* [1952] A.C. 716 (H.L.). In some Canadian jurisdictions, purposeful interference with consortium may also give rise to an action for **alienation of affection**. Some provinces have replaced the common law rules around loss of consortium with a statutory scheme. See, e.g., *Tort-feasors Act*, RSA 2000, c. T–5, s. 2.1. See also **conjugal rights**.

CONSPIRACY An **inchoate** offence that attaches liability to the agreement to commit a crime. "The word 'conspire' derives from two Latin words, 'con' and 'spirare,' meaning 'to breathe together.' To conspire is to agree. The essence of criminal conspiracy is proof of agreement. On a charge of conspiracy, the agreement itself is the gist of the offence...The **actus reus** is the fact of agreement...The agreement reached by the co-conspirators may contemplate a number of acts or offences. Any number of persons may be privy to it. Additional persons may join the ongoing scheme, while others may drop out. So long as there is a continuing overall, dominant plan, there may be changes in methods of operation, personnel, or victims, without bringing the conspiracy to an end. The important inquiry is not as to the acts done in pursuance of the agreement, but whether there was, in fact, a common agreement to which the acts are referable and to which all of the alleged offenders were privy." *Papalia v. R.*, [1979] 2 S.C.R. 256. There is no offence of attempted conspiracy in Canadian law. *R. v. Déry*, 2006 SCC 53.

Conspiracy to injure another person's interests can also be a tort, even if the behaviour of each individual concerned would not itself be unlawful. "I am of the opinion that whereas the law of tort does not permit an action against an individual defendant who has caused injury to the plaintiff, the law of tort does recognize a claim against them in combination as the tort of conspiracy if:

(1) whether the means used by the defendants are lawful or unlawful, the predominant purpose of the defendants' conduct is to cause injury to the plaintiff; or,

(2) where the conduct of the defendants is unlawful, the conduct is directed toward the plaintiff (alone or together with others), and the defendants should know in the circumstances that injury to the plaintiff is likely to and does result.

In situation (2) it is not necessary that the predominant purpose of the defendants' conduct be to cause injury to the plaintiff, but, in the prevailing circumstances, it must be a constructive intent derived from the fact that the defendants should have known that injury to the plaintiff would ensue. In both situations, however, there must be actual damage suffered by the plaintiff." *Canada Cement LaFarge Ltd. v. British Columbia Lightweight Aggregate Ltd.*, [1983] 1 S.C.R. 452.

CONSPIRATOR One involved in a **conspiracy**. There must be at least two conspirators in order for there to be a conspiracy. However, provided it is proven at trial that at least two people conspired, it is possible for just one person to be convicted.

CONSTITUTION The construct of rules, regulations and laws—either written or unwritten—that establishes and orders the political, governmental, and legal structure of the state. A constitution defines the state's mode of political organization (e.g., republic, monarchy, oligarchy), establishes the state's principal institutions (e.g., legislative, executive, and judicial), regulates the functions of the various departments of the state apparatus and governs the relationship between the individual and the state. P.W. Hogg, *Constitutional Law of Canada* 1–1–2 (5th ed. 2007).

In Canada, the central constitutional document is the **British North America Act** of 1867 (as of 1982, renamed *Constitution Act, 1867*). This act united the three colonies of Nova Scotia, New Brunswick and Canada (Ontario and Quebec) as the Dominion of Canada, and provided for the admission of other British North American colonies and territories into the Dominion. But the *Constitution Act, 1867* was not a declaration of Canadian independence; rather, it established Canada as an internally self-governing subordinate within the British imperial system. As such, the *Constitution Act, 1867* is not and was never intended to be a definitive constitutional document: for example, it does not mention such entrenched features of the Canadian political structure as the office of the Prime Minister, the federal Cabinet or the party system. Thus, the *Constitution Act, 1867* is "only part of our whole working Constitution," the rest of which has been added by imperial amendment, by federal legislation, by custom, by the judgments of the courts and by joint federal provincial agreements. E. Forsey, *How Canadians Govern Themselves* 10 (7th ed. 2010).

The *Constitution Act, 1867,* contained no provision for its own amendment, for, as an act of the British Parliament, the amending process of the *Constitution Act, 1867* was vested in that legislative body. To remedy this situation, the Canadian House of Commons and the Senate approved, in December of 1981, a Joint Address to the Crown requesting the patriation—i.e., the transfer of the amending process to the Canadian Parliament of the Canadian constitution. Following this request, the British Parliament enacted the CANADA ACT, which ended British legislative powers over Canada. Parliament simultaneously passed the *Constitution Act, 1982,* which incorporated the following new provisions into the Canadian Constitution: an indigenous amending procedure, a Charter of Rights and Freedoms, an affirmation of the existing rights of native peoples, an entrenchment of the principle of equalization and a delineation of provincial powers over resources. E. Forsey, *The Constitution and You* 10 (1982). See **division of powers**.

CONSTITUTION ACTS, 1867–1982 See **British North America Act, 1867**; see **constitution**.

CONSTITUTIONAL CONVENTIONS Those rules, values, and principles—either written or unwritten—based on custom or precedent but lacking direct constitutional authority, which "regulate the working of the various parts of the constitution, their relations to one another, and to the subject." Holdsworth, *The Conventions of the Eighteenth Century Constitution,* 17 Iowa L. Rev. 161 at 162 (1932). Constitutional conventions govern the exercise of legal powers accorded by the **constitution** to the various offices, institutions, and branches (bodies) of the political structure some conventions have the effect of transferring effective power from one political office to another, while other conventions limit an apparently broad legal power or even prescribe that a legal power shall not be exercised at all. P. W. Hogg, *Constitutional Law of Canada* 1–22.1 (5th ed. 2007). For example, the Queen, or her representative (in Canada, the Governor-General or the Lieutenant-Governor) is empowered to veto any bill in Parliament or a provincial legislature, but by constitutional convention consent cannot be refused (this veto power cannot be exercised). This situation dramatizes the relationship between **law** and convention; for here is a constitutional law creating wide **discretionary** powers, which is limited and neutralized by a countervailing constitutional convention. *Reference Re Amendment of the Constitution of Canada* (1981), 125 D.L.R. (3d) 1 (S.C.C.). See also *Gallant v. The King* (1949), 2 D.L.R. 425; (1949), 23 M.P.R. 48 (P.E.I.S.C.).

However, constitutional conventions derive their authority from neither judicial nor statutory sources, but rather from the institutions of government themselves. Hence a convention is legally unenforceable; for, in the breach of convention, no illegality has been committed. *Reference Re Amendment of the Constitution of Canada* (1981), 125 D.L.R. (3d) 1 (S.C.C.). Thus, the remedy for the breach of convention is political rather than legal in nature.

CONSTITUTIONAL EXEMPTION The term "constitutional exemption" is used in two ways. First, it refers to the exemption of a person from the application of a statute, while the statute "remains valid for all other purposes." R.J. Sharpe & K. Roach, *The Canadian Charter of Rights and Freedoms* 410 (4th ed. 2012). For example, a convicted **offender** given a constitutional exemption from a mandatory minimum sentence when it would constitute **cruel and unusual punishment** under s. 12 of the *Canadian Charter of Rights and Freedoms* would receive a sentence lower than the minimum, but the mandatory minimum would remain in the law. The availability of this kind of constitutional exemption was rejected by the Supreme Court in *R. v. Ferguson,* 2008 SCC 6. Second, when a **court** grants a **declaration of invalidity** striking down a statute as a **remedy** for a breach of the *Charter,* it sometimes suspends that declaration of invalidity so that the law will continue to have force for some short time in order to allow **Parliament** or the **legislature** to draft a new law. In those circumstances, the successful litigant is sometimes given a constitutional exemption, in the sense that the suspension of the declaration of invalidity does not apply to that litigant, and so the law is, for that time, invalid only for him or her.

CONSTRUCTION The giving of an interpretation to something that is less than totally clear—e.g., to determine the construction of a **statute** or **constitution** is to determine the meaning of an ambiguous part of it; the act of construing. See also **strict construction**.

CONSTRUCTIVE Not actual but accepted in law as a substitute for whatever is otherwise required. Thus, anything the law finds to exist constructively will be treated by the law as though it were actually so. If an object is not in a person's actual **possession** but he or she intentionally and knowingly has dominion and control over it, the law will treat it as though it were in his or her actual possession by finding a constructive possession. The same is true in many other contexts.

CONSTRUCTIVE DELIVERY See **delivery**.

CONSTRUCTIVE DISMISSAL A term used to describe "a change in an employee's job responsibilities and/or benefits so significant that, viewed objectively, the employer would be deemed to have radically altered the nature of the employee's service contract. If such occurs, the employee is justified in resigning his or her position and maintaining an action for damages as if actually dismissed without cause." *Winsor v. Canada Trust Co.* (1993), 49 C.C.E.L. 235 at 237 (Nfld.C.A.).

CONSTRUCTIVE FRAUD See **fraud**.

CONSTRUCTIVE MURDER [FELONY MURDER] A form of murder that did not require proof of an intent to kill. Constructive murder has been struck down as a violation of s. 7 of the **Canadian Charter of Rights and Freedoms**. At common law, the felony murder rule provided that any death caused while committing a felony was murder, whether the death was intended or not. More limited forms of that rule were adopted in the *Criminal Code* but have been struck down and are inconsistent with the **principle of fundamental justice** that an offence of high stigma or high punishment must have **subjective** fault. *R. v. Vaillancourt*, [1987] 2 S.C.R. 636; *R. v. Martineau*, [1990] 2 S.C.R. 633.

CONSTRUCTIVE NOTICE See **notice**.

CONSTRUCTIVE POSSESSION See **possession**.

CONSTRUCTIVE TRUST See **trust**.

CONSUMER PROTECTION Legislative provisions aimed particularly at the rights of consumers in commercial transactions. Some federal legislation plays this role, such as the prohibitions on false advertising or on pyramid sales schemes in the *Competition Act*, RSC 1985, c. C–34. Many provinces have legislation that also prohibits or regulates certain practices, such as negative option selling (in which a vendor provides a service and requires the consumer to indicate that he or she does not wish to receive it) or contracts for advance payment of services (such as at a health or fitness club). See, e.g., *Consumer Protection Act*, R.S.N.S. 1989, c. 92.

CONSUMMATION The first act of sexual intercourse between spouses after **marriage**. At common law, inability to consummate at the time of the marriage renders it voidable, and it can be annulled by either party. The cause of a spouse's inability to consummate is immaterial and could be either physical or mental in nature, so long as it "[renders] sexual intercourse impracticable." *Halsbury's Laws of Canada*, "Family" 137 (2010). See also S.R. Fodden, *Family Law* 13–15 (1999); M.J. Mossman, *Families and the Law: Cases and Commentary* 95–103 (2012).

CONTEMPT OF COURT "Any act done or writing published calculated to bring a Court or a judge of the Court into contempt, or to lower his authority, is a contempt of Court...Further, any act done or writing published calculated to obstruct or interfere with the due course of justice or the lawful process of the Courts is a contempt of Court." *R. v. Gray*, [1900] 2 Q.B. 36. Contempt is divided into criminal contempt and civil contempt. Criminal contempt is preserved by s. 9 of the *Criminal Code*, R.S.C. 1985, c. C–46, and is the only remaining **common law** crime in Canada. It consists of "public defiance that 'transcends the limits of any dispute between particular litigants and constitutes an affront to the administration of justice as a whole'... The gravamen of the offence is rather the open, continuous, and flagrant violation of a court order without regard for the effect that may have on the respect accorded to edicts of the court." *U.N.A. v. Alberta (Attorney General)*, [1992] 1 S.C.R. 901. Civil contempt similarly requires a breach of a court order but does not require the element of public defiance of a court order. "A three-pronged test is required. First, the order that was breached must state clearly and unequivocally what should and should not be done. Second, the party who disobeys the order must do so deliberately and wilfully. Third, the evidence must show contempt beyond a reasonable doubt. Any doubt must clearly be resolved in favour of the person or entity alleged to have breached the order." *Prescott-Russell Services for Children and Adults v. G.(N.)* (2006), 82 O.R. (3d) 686 (Ont. C.A.).

CONTEMPT IN THE FACE OF THE COURT [CONTEMPT EX FACIE] Behaviour that disrupts court proceedings themselves, generally occurring in the courtroom itself, though picketing outside a courthouse in order to dissuade persons from entering is also contempt in the face of the court. Courts have the power to punish contempt in the face of the court "so as to maintain the dignity and authority of the judge and to ensure a fair trial." *R. v. Arradi*, 2003 SCC 23.

CONTEMPT NOT IN THE FACE OF THE COURT [CONTEMPT EX FACIE] Behaviour that threatens the **rule of law** but that does not occur in the courtroom itself, such as disobedience to a court order or reporting on a matter that is **sub judice** in a manner that is likely to affect the mind of the trier of fact and therefore create a real risk of prejudice. *Manitoba (A.G.) v. Groupe Quebecor Inc.*, [1987] 5 W.W.R. 270 (Man. C.A.).

CONTIGUOUS Near to or in close proximity to.

CONTIGUOUS ZONE See **UNCLOS III**.

CONTINENTAL SHELF See **UNCLOS III**.

CONTINGENCY Something related to a possible future and uncertain event. See **lawyer's fees**.

CONTINGENT ESTATE An **interest** in land that might or might not begin in the future, depending upon the occurrence of a specific but uncertain event or depending on the determination or existence of the person(s) to whom the estate is limited. Thus, if property is granted "to A for life and then to the heirs of B," there is a contingent estate (a contingent **remainder)** in the heirs of B, which will **vest** [become certain] at the death of A unless B is without heirs. If B is without heirs, the estate **reverts** [goes back] to the original grantor. Because a contingent estate was regarded as a mere possibility or expectancy, it was not ALIENABLE INTER VIVOS [transferable during one's lifetime] at common law. Contingent remainders were made alienable in England in 1845 and are freely alienable today in the majority of common-law jurisdictions. C. Moynihan, *Introduction to the Law of Real Property* 139–40 (2d ed. 1988). See also B. Ziff, *Principles of Property Law* 245–47 (5th ed. 2010). Compare **conditional fee**; **determinable fee**. See also **condition**; **future interest**; **vested**.

CONTINUANCE An adjournment or postponement to a specified subsequent date of the proceedings in an **action**.

CONTRA (*kän'-trà*) Lat.: against, in opposition to, contrary to; the reverse of; in violation of; in answer to, in reply to; in defiance of. Thus, "the Court's most recent decision is contra an established line of **precedent**."

CONTRA BONOS MORES (*kän'-trà bō'nōs mô'-rāz*) Lat.: against good morals. Refers to conduct that offends the average conscience and commonly accepted standards. See **public policy**.

CONTRACT "A contract is a legally recognized agreement between two or more persons, giving rise to obligations that may be enforced in the courts. By such an agreement the parties not only restrict their present or future freedom to act, by the limitations imposed upon themselves by the agreement, they are creating a...set of legal rules...binding as regards themselves and only themselves." G.H.L. Fridman, *The Law of Contract in Canada* 6 (6th ed. 2011).

The persons entering into a contract are called the **parties** to the contract: he or she who makes a promise is the PROMISOR; he or she to whom a promise is made is the PROMISEE. If both parties promise mutually to perform or not to perform different acts, the contract is called a BILATERAL CONTRACT. If only one party makes a promise (the other party merely performing or not performing some act), it is known as a UNILATERAL CONTRACT.

A contract may be under **seal** (a formal contract or **deed**) or simple (an informal contract). A simple contract may be made orally or in writing. However, in order to be enforceable, a simple contract may be required by the various **statutes of fraud** to be evidenced in writing that is signed by the party to be **charged**. The three essential elements of a simple contract are often said to be **offer**, **acceptance**, and **consideration**. In addition, the parties must have the capacity to contract, an intention to create legal relations, and a legal purpose, and the terms of the contract must be sufficiently certain.

See **quasi** [QUASI-CONTRACT]. See also **breach of contract**; **privity**.

CONTRACTING IN "[A] situation where non-bargaining unit personnel are brought into the workplace to work alongside bargaining unit employees, performing the same work as those employees, under the same supervision, and utilising the same materials and equipment provided by the employer; the way in which the bargaining unit and non-bargaining unit employees work is 'virtually indistinguishable.'" *Hydro Ottawa Limited v. International Brotherhood of Electrical Workers (Local 636)*, 2007 ONCA 292.

CONTRACTING OUT "[A] situation where 'an integral function or a whole operation of the business of the employer is assigned to an independent contractor'; the work is often done off site and, where done at the same location as the bargaining unit employees, usually involves work of a different nature even though it is bargaining unit work; the independent contractor controls the work, and the employer has 'effect-ively abdicated' the work to the outside contractor." *Hydro Ottawa Limited v. International Brotherhood of Electrical Workers (Local 636)*, 2007 ONCA 292.

CONTRACT OF ADHESION See **adhesion contract**.

CONTRACTOR 1. One who is party to a **contract**. **2.** One who contracts to do work for another. In tort law, "an INDEPENDENT CONTRACTOR is one who is his own master...engaged to do certain work, but to exercise his own discretion as to the mode and time of doing it—he is bound by his contract, but not by his employer's orders." R. Heuston & R. Buckley, *Salmond & Heuston on the Law of Torts* 449 (21st ed. 1996). A GENERAL BUILDING CONTRACTOR is one who contracts directly with the owner of the property upon which the construction occurs, as distinguished from a **subcontractor**, who would deal only with one of the general contractors.

CONTRACTUAL BREACH See **breach of contract**.

CONTRACT UNDER SEAL A **contract** that is signed and has the **seal** of the signer attached. The term **deed** is also applied to an instrument under seal. A sealed contract is sometimes called a FORMAL CONTRACT as distinguished from a contract without a seal, or SIMPLE CONTRACT. At common law, a contract under seal did not require **consideration**, and this was the principal distinction between it and the simple contract. See further G.H.L. Fridman, *The Law of Contract in Canada* 116–118 (6th ed. 2011). The formal requirement of delivery may be by actually handing over the instrument to the other party or to someone on his or her behalf, or by doing any act or using words showing an intention to treat the instrument as a presently binding deed. *Xenos v. Wickham* (1867), L.R. 2 H.L. 296 at 312. See **sealed instrument**.

CONTRA PACEM (*kän'-trà pā'-sĕm*) Lat.: against the peace. This phrase was used in the Latin forms of **indictments** and also in **actions** for **trespass** to signify that the alleged offence was committed against the public peace.

CONTRA PROFERENTEM RULE (*kŏn'-trŭ prŏ'-fĕr-ĕn-tŭm*) Lat.: Against the profferor. The general rule that where there is ambiguity in the wording of a contract, the contract should be interpreted against the interests of the party who set the terms of the contract (i.e., the promissor); "This interpretation will therefore favour the party who did not draft the term, presumably because that party is not responsible for the ambiguity therein and should not be made to suffer for it. This rule endeavours to encourage the drafter to be as clear as possible when crafting an agreement upon which the parties will rely." *Coupar v. Velletta & Co.*, 2010 BCSC 483. See also G.H.L. Fridman, *The Law of Contract in Canada* 455–58 (6th ed. 2011). Quoted in G.H.L. Fridman, *The Law of Contract in Canada* 455 (6th ed. 2011).

CONTRIBUTION A right to demand that a person jointly responsible with someone else for an injury to another person contribute to the one required to compensate the victim; the equal sharing of a common burden. In the law of **torts**, a right of contribution exists, if at all, generally by statutes although some courts have upheld the right of contribution upon the broad equitable principle that persons who are equals in the duty of bearing a common burden may be compelled by their associates to bear their share of that burden. The duty generally involves an equal sharing of the loss, but in some **jurisdictions** it may be apportioned among the **joint tortfeasors** according to their degrees of relative fault. Compare **indemnity**.

CONTRIBUTORY NEGLIGENCE See **negligence**.

CONTROLLED SUBSTANCE A chemical compound whose production, sale, possession, and disposal is regulated or prohibited under the *Controlled Drugs and Substances Act*, S.C. 1996, c. 19.

CONTROVERSY A dispute that occurs when there are adversaries on a particular **issue**; an **allegation** on one side and a **denial** on the other. It is distinguished from an opinion advising what the law would be upon a hypothetical state of facts. Compare **advisory opinion**; **reference case**. See also **justiciable**; **standing**.

CONTUMACY Wilful disobedience to the **summons** or orders of a court; signifies overt defiance of authority. Contumacious conduct may result in a finding of **contempt of court**.

CONVENTION REFUGEE A Convention refugee is a person who, by reason of a well-founded fear of persecution for reasons of race, religion, nationality, membership in a particular social group, or political opinion,
(a) is outside each of his or her countries of nationality and is unable or, by reason of that fear, unwilling to avail himself or herself of the protection of each of those countries; or
(b) not having a country of nationality, is outside the country of his or her former habitual residence and is unable or, by reason of that fear, unwilling to return to that country.
Immigration and Refugee Protection Act, S.C. 2001, c. 27, s. 96. See also **refugee**; **person in need of protection**.

CONVERSION The **tortious** deprivation of another's property without his authorization. "[A]n act, or complex series of acts, of wilful interference, without lawful justification, with any chattel in a manner inconsistent with the right of another, whereby that other is deprived of the use and possession of it. Two elements are combined in such interference: (1) a dealing with the chattel in a manner inconsistent with the right of the person entitled to it, and (2) an intention in so doing to deny that person's right or to assert a right that is in fact inconsistent with such right." R.F.V. Heuston & R.A. Buckley, *Salmond & Heuston on the Law of Torts* 97–98 (21st ed. 1996).

CONVEY In the law of **real property**, to transfer property from one to another; broadly, the transfer of property or the **title** to property from one person to another by means of a written **instrument** and other formalities. Compare **alienation**. See also **grant**.

CONVEYANCE An instrument that transfers property from one person to another; "includes an **assignment**, appointment (see **power of appointment**), **lease**, **settlement** and other assurance, made by **deed**, on a **sale**, **mortgage**, **demise**, or settlement of any **property** or on any other dealing with or for any property, and **'convey'** has a meaning corresponding with that of conveyance." *Conveyancing and Law of Property Act*, R.S.O. 1990, c. C. 34, s. 1(1). See similar provincial statutes.

CONVICT 1. One who has been determined by the court to be guilty of the crime charged. **2.** To determine such guilt. One is convicted upon a valid plea of guilty or a verdict of guilty and judgment of conviction entered thereupon.

CONVICTION An adjudication of **guilt**.

CO-OPERATIVE A form of concurrent ownership of housing in which members have a shared right of use and governance but enter into occupancy agreements to have the right to live in a specific unit. In an equity co-op, "members contribute financially to the enterprise in order (i) to defray costs associated with the premises (repairs, mortgage payments, and so forth) and (usually) (ii) to augment the value of their investment." B. Ziff, J. deBeer, D. Harris and M. McCallum, *A Property Law Reader* (2d ed. 2008).

CO-OPERATIVE ASSOCIATION A union of individuals—commonly, labourers, farmers or small capitalists—formed for the pursuit in common of some productive enterprise, the profits being shared in proportion to the capital or labour contributed by each.

Organizing a company as, and calling it, a co-operative is not sufficient in law; it is the actual nature of its activities that governs its designation. So where an association holds profits other than on account for its member-producers, it is not a co-operative. See *Montreal Milk Producers' Co-op Agricultural As'sn v. M.N.R.*, [1958] Ex.C.R. 19.

CO-ORDINATE JURISDICTION See **jurisdiction** [CONCURRENT JURISDICTION].

COPARCENERS Persons who, by virtue of **descent**, have become concurrent owners. See **parcener**; **co-heir**; **joint tenancy**, **tenancy** [TENANCY IN COMMON].

COPYLEFT A form of **licence** intended to allow an item of **intellectual property** to be easily distributed and modified. A person receiving the work could be entitled to, for example, copy it, modify it, or distribute it, on the condition that any such copies or modifications are distributed on the same basis.

COPYRIGHT The protection by **statute** of the works of authors and artists giving them the exclusive right to "publish" their works and to determine who may so publish. The *Copyright Act,* R.S.C. 1985, c. C–42, s. 6, as amended by S.C. 1993, c. 44, s. 58, provides that copyright subsists for the life of the author, the remainder of the calendar year in which the author dies, plus fifty years after the end of that calendar year. There is no copyright in ideas or information; only the expression of the idea is protected. See *CCH Canadian Ltd. v. Law Society of Upper Canada*, [2004] 1 S.C.R. 339. Copyright exists in literary, dramatic, musical, and artistic works and such other works as provided in the *Copyright Act.* Compare **plagiarism**. The *Copyright Act* also gives the author certain moral rights, such as the right to the integrity of his or her work. See *Snow v. Eaton Centre Ltd.* (1982), 70 C.P.R. (2d) 105 (Ont. H.C.).

CORAM NOBIS, WRIT OF See **writ of coram nobis**.

CORBETT APPLICATION An application to a trial judge to exclude all or part of an **accused's** prior criminal record, where the **probative** value of that record is outweighed by its **prejudicial effect**. See *R. v. Corbett*, [1988] 1 S.C.R. 670. A decision on a *Corbett* application should normally be made no later than the close of the Crown's case, so that the accused knows its result before deciding whether to testify. *R. v. Underwood*, [1998] 1 S.C.R. 77.

CO-RESPONDENT A person cited in **divorce** proceedings who is alleged to have had an extra-marital relationship with the defendant **spouse**.

COROLLARY RELIEF See **maintenance**.

CORONER A judicial officer who investigates the cause and circumstances of a suspicious death that occurs within that **jurisdiction** and makes a finding in a coroner's **inquest**. See also **post mortem**. Coroners' courts were once recognized as **courts of record**, but this is no longer the case in Canada. *Faber v. The Queen*, [1976] 2 S.C.R. 9. See also *Coroners Act*, R.S.O. 1990, c. C.37, s. 2; *Coroners Act, 1999*, S.S. 1999, c. 38.01, s. 23.

CORONER'S WARRANT Refers to an authorization by the coroner directing that a person alleged by the coroner's inquisition to have committed **murder** or **manslaughter** be taken before a justice or entered into a **recognizance** to appear before a justice. Coroner's warrants were once provided for under the *Criminal Code*, R.S.C. 1985, c. C–46, s. 529, but have been repealed (S.C. 1994, c. 44, s. 52).

CORPORAL PUNISHMENT Punishment inflicted upon the body (such as whipping, which was abolished in Canada in 1972). The term may or may not include imprisonment.

CORPORATE CRIME A term used to describe crimes committed by **corporations** through acts or omissions of their individual employees. Also referred to as "white collar crime." See *Canadian Dredge and Dock Co. Ltd. et al. v. R.* (1985), 45 C.R. (3d) 289 (S.C.C.). Special rules govern when a corporation can be found guilty of an offence as a **party**. See *Criminal Code*, R.S.C. 1985, c. C–46, ss. 22.1, 22.2.

CORPORATION An association of **shareholders** created under law and regarded as an **artificial person** by the courts and thus "treated like any other independent person with its rights and liabilities appropriate to itself, and...the motives of those who took part in the promotion of the company are absolutely irrelevant in discussing what those rights and liabilities are." *Salomon v. Salomon & Co.*, [1897] A.C. 22 at 30 (H.L.). A corporation has the capacity of taking, holding and conveying **property**, suing and being sued, and exercising such other powers as may be conferred on it by law, just as a **natural person**.

A corporation's **liability** is normally limited to its assets; thus **shareholders** are protected against personal liability in connection with the affairs of the corporation. (But see **piercing the corporate veil**.) The corporation is taxed at special corporate tax rates, and shareholders must pay an additional tax upon **dividends** or other profits from the corporation. Corporations are subject to regulation by the province of incorporation (see, e.g., *Corporations Act*, R.S.O. 1990, c. C. 38) and by the **jurisdictions** in which they carry on business. The federal government has the power of incorporation of companies with objects "other than provincial." *Citizens Insurance Co. of Canada v. Parsons* (1881–82), 7 A.C. 96 at 116 (P.C.). See further J.A. VanDuzer, *The Law of Partnerships and Corporations* 90–145 (3rd ed. 2009).

CORPOREAL HEREDITAMENT See **hereditaments**.

CORPUS DELICTI (*kôr'-pŭs dĕ-lĭk'-tī*) Lat.: body of the crime. The ingredients of the offence. In a murder trial, the discovery of the body affords the best evidence of the fact of death, and the term *corpus delicti* has popularly come to mean the dead body. *R. v. McNicholl*, [1917] 2 I.R. 557 (Cr.Ca.R.). If it is not possible to find the body, the accused may still be convicted if the fact of death is proved by **circumstantial evidence**. *R. v. Huculak* (1963), 2 C.C.C. (N.S.) 1 (S.C.C.).

Corpus delicti applies to every crime.

CORPUS JURIS (*kôr'-pŭs jūr'-ĭs*) Lat.: body of law. The term is sometimes used to refer to the entire body of law of a jurisdiction.

CORROBORATION Evidence that confirms or supports a witness's testimony.

CORRUPTION OF BLOOD Incapacity to **inherit** or pass **property**, usually because of attainder, such as for **treason**. (See **bill of attainder**.) According to this feudal doctrine, which was abolished in England in 1870, the blood of the attainted person was deemed to be corrupt, so that he or she could not transmit an estate to his or her heirs nor could they take by **descent**.

COST OF COMPLETION In a **breach of contract** situation, a measure of **damages** representing the total amount of additional expense, over and above the **contract** price, that the injured party would have to incur in order to obtain a substituted **performance** that would place him or her in the same position he or she would have been in if the contract had not been breached; often used as a measure of damages for breaches of construction contracts. Compare **diminution in value**; **damages**; **specific performance**.

COSTS A court order requiring one person to pay legal costs incurred by another person. A trial judge or other court officer has some discretion over the amount of an award of costs, but the amount is also structured by legislation. See, e.g., *Court of Queen's Bench Rules*, Reg. 553/88 Tariff A, issued under *The Court Of Queen's Bench Act*, C.C.S.M. c. C280. A costs award of this sort will not provide for full recovery of the money spent by the successful applicant; these are referred to as "party and party" costs. It is possible for full recovery to be provided for through an order for **solicitor-client costs**. An award of costs will also usually allow recovery for **disbursements**.

Most commonly the losing party is ordered to pay the costs of the successful party, but in some circumstances other awards are possible. For example, if a **defendant** has offered to settle on terms as favourable as those the **plaintiff** succeeded in obtaining at trial, the successful plaintiff can be liable for the defendant's costs. *Court of Queen's Bench Rules*, s. 49.10(2). Where a lawyer for a party has caused costs to be incurred unreasonably, costs might be awarded against that lawyer person-

ally. *Court of Queen's Bench Rules*, s. 57.07(1). The exact rules on costs vary from province to province. See **advance costs**.

COSTS IN ANY EVENT OF THE CAUSE See **costs in the cause**.

COSTS IN THE CAUSE An order indicating that the **costs** involved in an **interlocutory** application will be determined by the costs order regarding the ultimate result. In contrast, a party receiving an order for "costs in any event of the cause" is entitled to receive costs associated with the interlocutory application no matter what the ultimate result in the action.

CO-TENANCY Possession of a unit of property by two or more persons. The term does not refer to an **estate** but rather to a relationship between persons as to their **holding** of property. It encompasses both tenancy in common and **joint tenancy** [and, thus, tenancy by the entirety as well]. See **tenancy**.

COUNSEL 1. A person retained by a client to plead his or her cause in a court of law; a barrister; an advocate. See **barrister and solicitor**. **2.** The advice given in respect to the matters or things that barristers and solicitors are authorized by law to do or perform.

COUNSELLING Encouraging or inducing another person to commit a crime, while intending or being aware of the unjustified risk that the crime is likely to be committed. *R. v. Hamilton*, 2005 SCC 47. Counsel includes procure, solicit, or incite. *Criminal Code*, R.S.C. 1985, c. C-46, s. 22(3).

COUNT A distinct statement of a **plaintiff's cause of action**. In **indictments**, a count, like a charge, is an allegation of a distinct offence. A complaint or indictment may contain one or more counts. There is no restriction under the *Criminal Code*, R.S.C. 1985, c. C-46, as to the number of counts that may be included in a single indictment. Section 591(1) provides that any number of counts for any number of **indictable offences** may be joined in the same indictment; but where they are so joined, each count may be treated as a separate indictment (s. 591(2)). However, where the offence charged is **murder**, no count charging any other offence may be included in the same indictment unless the offence other than murder arises out of the same transaction as the count that charges murder, or the accused consents to the joinder of the counts (s.589). Nevertheless, this does not preclude two counts of murder in the same indictment although it is not generally considered desirable. *Re Rina v. Haase* (1963) 2 C.C.C. (N.S.) 56 (B.C.C.A.), affirmed [1965] 2 C.C.C. (N.S.) 123 (S.C.C.).

COUNTERCLAIM A counter-demand made by **defendant** in his or her favor against the **plaintiff**. It is not a mere **answer** or **denial** of plaintiff's **allegations**, but rather asserts an independent **cause of action** the purpose of which is to oppose or deduct from plaintiff's claim. "Today a **defendant** can assert any claim against the **plaintiff** by counterclaim, subject only to the power of the court to exclude the defendant's claim where it cannot be conveniently dealt with in the plaintiff's action." L.S. Abrams and K.P. McGuinness, *Canadian Civil Procedure Law* 783–84 (2nd ed. 2010). The counterclaim is pleaded separately as part of the statement of defence, and the defendant may counterclaim against the plaintiff in respect of any cause of action, whenever and however arising. See **setoff**.

COUNTERFEIT An imitation of something made without lawful authority and with a view to defraud by passing the false copy as genuine or original; e.g., counterfeit coins, paper money, bonds, deeds, shares. See *Criminal Code,* R.S.C. 1985, c. C–46, ss. 376, 458.

COUNTER OFFER A rejection of the original offer by the offeree and the creation of a new offer. "Whenever the offeree adds anything to the simple words of acceptance the question arises whether the addition amounts to a departure from the terms of the offer. If so, the offeree has not assented to the offeror's terms. The reply is at most a counter offer and a further communication of assent will be required from the offeror." S.M.

Waddams, *The Law of Contracts* 46 (6th ed. 2010). See **offer**.

COUNTY COURT A federally appointed court that heard intermediate civil cases and most serious criminal cases—in particular, **indictable offences** by election, appeals of **summary conviction offences**, appeals from small claims courts and family courts, and cases involving permanent wardship or adoption. County courts are now abolished in all of the provinces of Canada, with Nova Scotia being the last to do so in 1993.

COURSE OF EMPLOYMENT See **scope of employment**.

COURT A government body responsible for the public administration of justice that is under the control of one or more judges.

COURT-MARTIAL A court for the trial of a member of Her Majesty's Forces upon a charge of having committed any service offence. A service offence is defined in the *National Defence Act,* R.S.C. 1985, c. N–5, s. 2(1), as "an offence under this Act, the **Criminal Code**, or any other Act of Parliament, committed by a person while subject to the Code of Service Discipline." The Act provides for various kinds of court-martial: general courts-martial, disciplinary courts-martial, standing courts-martial, special general courts-martial. See *National Defence Act,* R.S.C. 1985, c. N–5, ss. 165–196.1; 230; 234–237; 245. The right to appeal is provided in s. 230; appeals may be heard by a court-martial appeal court (s. 234(1)) and the Supreme Court of Canada (s. 245(1)).

COURT-MARTIAL APPEAL COURT See **Military Courts**.

COURT OF APPEAL The highest level of court with jurisdiction in each province and territory. The judges of a court of appeal are appointed by the federal government and have jurisdiction over all matters that can be adjudicated by lower courts in that jurisdiction. The exact number of judges on the court of appeal varies from jurisdiction to jurisdiction.

See **Appendix I, Outline of Canada's Court System**.

COURT OF ASSIZE AND NISI PRIUS In English law, a court "composed of two or more commissioners, who [were] twice in every year sent by the king's special commission all around the kingdom to try by jury cases under their jurisdiction." See 3 Bl.Comm. *58, *59.

COURT OF EQUITY Historically, a court having **jurisdiction** where an adequate remedy was not available in the courts of **common law**. A court of equity would be one that applied the system of law developed by the English Court of **Chancery**. Courts guided primarily by equitable doctrine are said to be courts of equity. Courts of equity had their own principles (e.g., the **clean hands** doctrine) and their own unique remedies (e.g., **injunction**, **specific performance**). In England the courts of law and equity were merged by the *Judicature Act,* modelled on the English *Judicature Acts of 1873–75,* and the equity court as a distinct tribunal was abolished. Some Canadian jurisdictions also had a separate court of equity. In Nova Scotia, e.g., the courts of law and equity were merged in 1884 by a *Judicature Act* modelled on the English Acts.

COURT OF QUEEN'S [KING'S] BENCH See **queen's [king's] bench**.

COURT OF RECORD A phrase used to refer to a court, the records of which are maintained and preserved, and which may punish for **contempt of court**.

COURT OF STAR CHAMBER See **star chamber**.

COVENANT 1. To enter into a formal agreement; to **bind** oneself in **contract**; to make a stipulation. **2.** An agreement or promise to do or not to do a particular thing; a promise incidental to a **deed** or contract, either express or implied; an agreement, convention, or promise of two or more parties, by written **deed** signed and delivered, by whichever of the parties pledges himself or herself to the other that something is either done or shall be done or stipulates for the truth of certain facts.

Covenants for **title** are frequently termed *real* covenants. Examples of such covenants are that the vendor is **seised in fee**; has power to **convey**; for **quiet enjoyment** by the purchaser, his or her **heirs** and **as signs**; that the land shall be held free from **encumbrance**; and for further assurance (which obligates the **covenanter** to perform whatever acts are reasonably demanded by the **covenantee** for the purpose of perfecting or "assuming" the title). All covenants for the benefit of the **estate run with the land,** as he or she who has the one is subject to the other; they bind those who come in by act of law (as personal representatives) and those who come in by act of the parties. See **restrictive covenant**. See also *Galbraith v. Madawaska Club Ltd.,* [1961] S.C.R. 639.

COVENANTEE One who receives the **covenant**, or for whom it is made.

COVENANTOR One who makes a **covenant**.

COVERTURE At **common law**, a married woman's legal condition; "under the cover," influence and protection of her husband. In effect, the **real property** of which the woman was **seised** at the time of marriage, or afterwards, **vested** in both husband and wife during coverture, in right of the wife, and the husband was entitled to the profits therefrom and had sole control and management. As to personal property (see **personalty),** at common law the husband became absolute owner of his wife's personal **chattels**. The disabilities of coverture in respect of property were eliminated by the English *Married Women's Property Act,* 1882, and equivalent statutes in the Canadian provinces. See **marital unity; Married Women's Property Acts**.

CREATIVE COMMONS LICENCE A licence for the use of digital works that allows the free distribution of copyrighted work while retaining some copyright protections, for example, by requiring attribution, preventing modification, or limiting use of the work to non-commercial purposes.

CREDIBILITY An assessment of the veracity of a **witness** and how worthy his or her testimony is of belief. Credibility is distinct from **reliability**, and "a credible witness may give unreliable evidence." *R. v. H.C.*, 2009 ONCA 56. See *R. v. H.P.S.*, 2012 ONCA 117.

CREDIT That which is extended to a buyer or borrower on the seller or lender's belief that what is given will be repaid. The term can be applied to unlimited types of transactions. In accounting, a credit is money owing and due to one, and is considered an asset. The word is also used with respect to one's reputation or business standing in a given community. For example, a person who has a healthy, profitable business and who has always repaid debts in the past will be considered a good "credit risk" by a prospective lender.

CREDITOR One to whom money is owed by the **debtor**; one to whom an obligation exists. In a strict legal sense, a creditor is one who voluntarily gives **credit** to another for money or other property; in a more general sense, he or she is one who has a legal right to demand and recover from another a sum of money.

CREDITOR'S BILL [SUIT] A **proceeding** in **equity** in which a **judgment creditor** (a creditor who has secured **judgment** against a **debtor** and whose **claim** has not been satisfied) attempts to gain a discovery, accounting, and deliverance of **property** owed to him or her by the **judgment debtor**, which property cannot be reached by **execution** (seizure and forced sale) at law; commonly referred to as **discovery** in aid of execution.

CRIME 1. An **offence** that makes behaviour unlawful because it is inherently wrongful and morally blameworthy. Common law crime has been abolished in Canada, with the single exception of criminal contempt of court, and so crimes must be created by statute. *Criminal Code*, R.S.C. 1985, c. C–46, s. 9. Most crimes are contained in the *Criminal Code,* but some are in other federal statutes, such as the *Controlled Drugs and Substances Act*, S.C. 1996, c. 19. **2.** A law that falls within the jurisdiction of the federal **Parliament** under s. 91(27) of the **Constitution Act, 1867**. To qualify as a crime for **division of power** purposes, "it must possess three prerequisites: a valid criminal law purpose backed by a prohibition and a penalty (*Reference re Firearms Act (Can.)*, [2000] 1 S.C.R. 783, 2000 SCC 31, at para. 27). The criminal power extends to those laws that are designed to promote public peace, safety, order, health, or other legitimate public purpose." *R. v. Demers*, 2004 SCC 46. The fact that a law is **intra vires** as criminal law under s. 91(27) does not determine whether it is a crime in the sense that it is inherently wrongful; an **offence** can be a crime for division of powers purposes but nonetheless be a **regulatory offence**. See, e.g., the *Competition Act*, R.S.C., 1985, c. C–34. Because crime is within the jurisdiction of Parliament, provinces can only create regulatory offences. An attempt by a province to create a prohibition and penalty with a criminal law purpose will be **ultra vires**. See, e.g., *R. v. Morgentaler*, [1993] 3 S.C.R. 463. Similarly, a law passed by Parliament that purports to be an exercise of the criminal law power but that is aimed at a purpose in provincial jurisdiction will be *ultra vires*. See *Reference re Firearms Act (Can.)*, 2000 SCC 31.

CRIME AGAINST NATURE Sexual deviations that were considered crimes at **common law** and have been carried over by statute into the **Criminal Code**; includes **sodomy**, **bestiality**, and **buggery**.

CRIME COMICS Obscene material prohibited under s. 163(7) of the *Criminal Code,* R.S.C. 1985, c. C–46; "magazine, periodical or book that exclusively or substantially comprises matter depicting pictorially (a) the commission of crimes, real or fictious, or (b) events connected with the commission of crimes."

CRIMEN FALSI (*krī'-mĕn fäl'-sē*) Lat.: a **crime** of **deceit**. At **common law**, a *crimen falsi* was a crime containing the elements of falsehood and fraud. Examples of *crimen falsi* include **forgery** and **perjury**.

CRIMES AGAINST HUMANITY Initially, a concept at international law that some offences were so clearly contrary to fundamental rules of human behaviour that they could be treated as criminal even if to do so violated the **nulla poena sine lege** ("no punishment without a law") principle. The **Rome Statute** now defines "crimes against humanity" as any of a number of acts (including murder, enslavement, torture, rape, apartheid, or persecution of an identifiable group) when committed as part of a widespread or systematic attack directed against any civilian population. The definition at **customary international law** is similar but not identical.

CRIMINAL 1. An adjective denoting an act done with malicious intent. See **malice**; **malice aforethought**. **2.** One who has been convicted of a violation of the criminal law. After the criminal has satisfied whatever sanction has been imposed and is released, he or she is called an EX-OFFENDER. A person who re-offends after having been judicially dealt with for one offence is called a **recidivist**.

CRIMINAL CODE A federal **statute**, first enacted in 1892 (currently R.S.C. 1985, c. C–46), which substantially embodies the criminal law of Canada. It is amended, usually more than once in each session of Parliament, to take account of necessary changes and innovations in the criminal law. The *Criminal Code* is not, however, a complete delimitation of the criminal law of Canada and has no privileged status other than as a statute. See **crime**.

CRIMINAL CONTEMPT See **contempt of court**.

CRIMINAL CONVERSATION An action for **damages** in **tort** brought by one spouse against a third party and based on an act of **adultery**. The tort has generally been abolished by statute, either before the coming into force of the **equality** provision in s. 15 of the **Canadian Charter of Rights and Freedoms** (*Family Law Reform Act*, R.S.O. 1980, c. 152, s. 69) or as a result of it (*Charter Compliance Act*, S.N.B. 1985, c. 41, s. 4(6)). "[T]he sexism of the quasi-proprietary right of the husband in the wife, which underlies these archaic causes of action, is a blatant contradiction of the provisions of *The Canadian Charter of Rights and Freedoms* touching upon freedom of association and equality. Accordingly, I think that the *Charter* now is a defence to any such action at common law, whether brought by the husband or wife." *Davenport v. Miller* (1990), 70 D.L.R. (4th) 181 (N.B. Q.B.).

CRIMINAL LAW See **crime**.

CRIMINAL LIBEL The *Criminal Code*, R.S.C. 1985, c. C–46 offence of defamatory libel. A defamatory libel is published matter that is likely to injure the reputation of any person by exposing that person to hatred, contempt, or ridicule, or that is designed to insult the person of or concerning whom it is published. Although it is not a requirement, in practice a charge for this offence tends only to be laid when the person allegedly defamed is associated with the justice system, such as a police officer, prison guard, or judge. The maximum penalty under s. 300 of the *Code* for publishing a defamatory libel that the person knows to be false (sometimes called "aggravated defamatory libel") is five years imprisonment, and that offence does not violate the *Charter*. See *R. v. Lucas*, [1998] 1 S.C.R. 439. There is lower court authority holding that the offence under s. 301 of the *Code* of publishing a defamatory libel that one does not know to be false does violate the *Charter*. See, e.g., *R. v. Prior*, 2008 NLTD 80.

CRIMINAL HARASSMENT The offence under the *Criminal Code*, R.S.C. 1985, c. C–46, s. 264 of engaging in conduct that causes another person to reasonably fear for his or her own safety or the safety of anyone known to him or her. The forms of conduct that are prohibited if they have this result are "(a) repeatedly following from place to place the other person or anyone known to them; (b) repeatedly communicating with, either directly or indirectly, the other person or anyone known to them; (c) besetting or watching the dwelling house, or place where the other person, or anyone known to them, resides, works, carries on business, or happens to be; or (d) engaging in threatening conduct directed at the other person or any member of their family." Criminal harassment is popularly referred to as stalking. "[A] single incident of threatening conduct can found a conviction for criminal harassment if, in the circumstances, 'the consequence is that the complainant is being harassed... while being in a harassed state involves a sense of being subject to ongoing torment, a single incident in the right context can surely cause this feeling.'" *R. v. O'Connor*, 2008 ONCA 206, quoting *R. v. Kosikar* (1999), 138 C.C.C. (3d) 217.

CRIMINAL NEGLIGENCE See **negligence**.

CRIMINAL ORGANIZATION Under the *Criminal Code*, R.S.C. 1985, c. C–46, a group that is composed of three or more persons in or outside Canada and that has as one of its main purposes or main activities the facilitation or commission of one or more serious offences that, if committed, would likely result in the direct or indirect receipt of a material benefit, including a financial benefit, by the group or by any of the persons who constitute the group. The *Criminal Code* also states that the term does not include a group of persons that forms randomly for the immediate commission of a single offence. Although no particular structure is required, some form of structure and degree of continuity are required to meet the definition. *R. v. Venneri*, 2012 SCC 33.

CRITICAL LEGAL THEORY "[A] theory of jurisprudence…that is essentially an amalgamation of traditional legal realism and modern cynicism. Whereas a realist will identify extra-legal factors that impact upon the judicial decision-making process, the critical legal theorist will go much farther. He will identify what he believes are dysfunctional aspects of the legal system, having regard to the underlying purposes, values and assumptions that serve as the underpinning of the legal system. Moreover, he will challenge those same purposes, values and assumptions in terms of their contemporary relevance,

their rationale and, indeed, their validity." G. Gall, *The Canadian Legal System* 17 (4th ed. 1995).

CROSSCLAIM A lawsuit commenced by one **defendant** against another defendant within the same pre-existing **action**. See, e.g., *Nova Scotia Civil Procedure Rules*, Rule 4.09. Compare **counterclaim**.

CROSS-EXAMINATION Questioning of a witness in a **trial** by the lawyer for the party who did not call him or her, after examination of the **witness** by the lawyer for the party calling him or her, which is known as the EXAMINATION-IN-CHIEF. The main purposes of cross-examination are to test the veracity of the witness and to obtain answers that assist the case of the cross-examining party.

CROWN A term frequently used when speaking of the Sovereign, or the rights, duties and prerogatives belonging to him or her. However, the royal prerogative powers are for the most part exercised by the Government in the name of the Queen. In practice, "the Crown" means "the Government of the day and its various departments." The phrase covers "all the departments of State and the official activities of all servants and agents of the State." G. Borrie, *Public Law* 57–58 (2d ed. 1970).

CROWN PROSECUTOR A **counsel** appointed by the **Attorney-General**, under the provisions of provincial statutes, to take charge of and conduct, on behalf of the **Crown**, the **prosecution** of criminals. Sometimes referred to as a Crown attorney or simply "the Crown." See also P.W. Hogg, *Constitutional Law of Canada* (5th ed. 2007), c. 10. See **prosecutor**.

CROWN ELECTION The decision of a **Crown prosecutor**, in the case of a **hybrid offence**, as to whether to proceed by way of indictment or by way of summary conviction proceedings.

CRUEL AND UNUSUAL PUNISHMENT Section 12 of the **Canadian Charter of Rights and Freedoms** provides that "everyone has the right not to be subjected to any cruel and unusual treatment or punishment." There has been no judicial ruling that clearly defines the limits of such punishment, but the Supreme Court of Canada has considered the gravity of the offence, the personal characteristics of the offender, and the particular characteristics of the case when evaluating the treatment and its effects. See *R. v. Smith*, [1987] 1 S.C.R. 1045; *R. v. Ferguson*, 2008 SCC 6.

The *Canadian Bill of Rights*, S.C. 1960, c. 44, reprinted R.S.C. 1985, App. III; s. 2(b) provides similar protection. Under this provision, the Court stated that the punishment would have to be so excessive as to outrage standards of decency. *Miller and Cockriell v. The Queen*, [1977] 2 S.C.R. 680.

CRUELTY TO ANIMALS A **hybrid offence** under s. 445.1 of the *Criminal Code*, R.S.C. 1985, c. C–46. In general, the offence involves wilfully causing or "being the owner" and wilfully permitting to be caused "unnecessary pain, suffering, or injury to an animal... or bird." Numerous specific activities also fall under the offence, including wilfully administering a "poisonous or injurious substance" to an animal or bird in captivity, or aiding or assisting in "the fighting or baiting of animals or birds." See *R. v. Menard* (1978), 43 C.C.C. (2d) 458 (Que. C.A.).

CRUMBLING SKULL DOCTRINE [RULE] A general rule in **tort** law that if **plaintiff** with a deteriorating condition suffers an injury which accelerates the process of that deterioration, he or she is compensated on the basis of his or her whole post-accident condition, but only for the amount of aggravation caused by the defendant's actions. Contrast with **thin skull rule**.

CUJUS EST SOLUM EJUS EST USQUE AD COELUM ET USQUE AD INFEROS (*kū-yŭs ĕst sō-lŭm ă-yus ĕst ūś-kwā ăd sē'-lŭm ĕt ūś-kwā ăd ĭń-fâr-ŏs*) Lat.:"Whoever owns the soil, owns all the way up to the heavens and down to the depths of the earth." A former principle of property law now subject to many exceptions and of limited validity, but retaining some relevance. See *R. v. Patrick*, [2009] 1 S.C.R. 579. See **a coelo usque ad centrum**.

CULPABLE Deserving of moral blame or punishment; "criminal." Implies, in addition to intention, recklessness as well as an indifference or disregard for the consequences that might ensue from an act, as in "culpable" **homicide**. See, e.g., *Criminal Code*, R.S.C. 1985, c. C–46, ss. 222, 229–230. See also **constructive murder**.

CUMULATIVE DIVIDEND See **dividend**.

CURATIVE PROVISO A provision allowing an **accused** person's **appeal** against conviction to be dismissed despite an error at the trial if "no substantial wrong or miscarriage of justice has occurred." *Criminal Code*, R.S.C. 1985, c. C–46, s. 686(1)(b)(iii). Also sometimes referred to as "harmless error," the standard for showing that the curative proviso should be applied is deliberately very high. *R. v. Sarrazin*, 2011 SCC 54. An error can only be found to be harmless on one of two bases: that it was "so trivial that it could not have caused any prejudice to the accused and thus could not have affected the verdict," or if "the case against the accused was so overwhelming that a reasonable and properly instructed jury would inevitably have convicted." *R. v. Van*, 2009 SCC 22.

CURIA REGIS (*kyū'-rē-à rā'-gĭs*) Lat.: the King's Court.

CURTESY The husband's right, at **common law**, upon the death of his wife, to a **life estate** in all the **estates** of **inheritance** in land that his wife possessed during their marriage; "a life estate to which the husband was entitled in all lands of which his wife was **seised** in **fee simple** or in **fee tail** at any time during the marriage, provided that there was **issue** born alive capable of inheriting the estate. On the birth of such qualified issue the husband's **tenancy** by the marital right was enlarged to an estate for his own life...Although...the husband's estate for his life was called 'curtesy initiate' prior to his wife's death and 'curtesy consummate' after her death, he had a present life estate in both situations and there was no substantial difference between the two types of curtesy." C. Moynihan, *Introduction to the Law of Real Property* 48–9 (2d ed. 1988). The right of curtesy has been abolished in Canada. See B. Ziff, *Principles of Property Law* 190 (5th ed. 2010). Compare **dower**.

CURTILAGE At **common law**, the land around the **dwelling house**; a piece of ground within the common enclosure belonging to a dwelling house, and enjoyed with it, for its more convenient occupation.

CUSTODY 1. As applied to property, it is not **ownership**, but a keeping, guarding, care, watching, inspection, preservation, or security of a thing, which carries with it the idea of the thing being within the immediate personal care and control of the person to whose custody it is subjected. 2. As applied to persons, it is such restraint and physical control over the person as to insure his presence at any **hearing**, or the actual imprisonment resulting from a criminal **conviction**. 3. The legal **guardianship** of children. "The custodial parent is responsible for the care and upbringing of the child, including decisions concerning the education, religion, health, and well-being of the child." *Young v. Young*, [1993] 4 S.C.R. 3. Custody is often at issue between parents in **divorce** or **separation** proceedings, though other adults may also seek custody where they have a pre-existing "family or social relationship with the child." S.R. Fodden, *Family Law* 184 (1999). Custody orders may be granted under either s. 16 of the *Divorce Act*, R.S.C. 1985, c. 3 (2nd Supp.), or under relevant provincial legislation, depending on whether the child's parents are seeking a divorce or separation.

INCIDENTS OF CUSTODY "[T]he various aspects of care or decision-making subsumed within the exercise of custody. In ordinary circumstances, the 'incidents of custody' subject to contention include choice of school, religious education, and extra-curricular activities." *Halsbury's Laws of Canada*, "Infants and Children" 213 (2009).

JOINT CUSTODY A custody arrangement whereby divorced or separated parents share varying degrees of physical and legal control of their children. See, e.g., *Warcop v. Warcop* (2009), 66 R.F.L. (6th) 438 (Ont. S.C.J.).

SOLE CUSTODY A custody arrangement granting one parent exclusive authority to care for his or her children and to make fundamental decisions affecting their lives. The parent without sole custody will usually still enjoy a right of access, meaning a right to spend designated time with the children without the legal rights granted to the custodial parent. See, e.g., *Izyuk v. Bilousov*, 2011 ONSC 6451.

SPLIT CUSTODY A relatively uncommon custody arrangement that involves awarding exclusive physical and legal control of at least one of multiple children to each parent. See, e.g., *Funk v. Funk*, 2004 BCSC 1800.

CUSTOM An unwritten law established by long usage. In England after the Norman Conquest, the judges recognized certain Anglo-Saxon laws and customs as appropriate for general application throughout the realm, and thus these became part of the **common law**. Some special and local customs remained and will be recognized even today if certain difficulties of proof and reasonableness are satisfied. For example, to be recognized as law, the custom must have existed "before legal memory" (before 1189, the first year of the reign of Richard I). The party alleging the custom must prove it, but in practice the courts raise a presumption in his favour if he or she can prove the custom as far back as living memory. See *Mercer v. Denne*, [1905] 2 Ch. 538 (C.A.).

CUSTOMARY INTERNATIONAL LAW A set of international legal norms that are binding upon states and are derived from the behaviour of states rather than from explicit agreements. There are two requirements for finding a customary international law obligation: "(1) that there is a state practice that is general (though not necessarily universal) and uniform; and (2) that the state practice is accompanied by a belief on the part

of states that the practice is obligatory."
See **opinio juris**.

CUSTOM OF THE TRADE Refers to the standards or practices usually adhered to in a particular industry or trade. In negligence law, evidence of compliance with custom is relevant but not necessarily decisive in determining a defendant's liability. *Cavanagh v. Ulster Weaving Co. Ltd.*, [1959] 2 All E.R. 745 (H.L.); *Waldick v. Malcolm,* [1991] 2 S.C.R. 456.

Inter *Neuzen v. Korn* (1995), 127 D.L.R. (4th) (S.C.C.), the plaintiff was infected with HIV after being artificially inseminated by the defendant doctor. In recruiting semen donors the defendant adhered to standard screening process in place in Canada at that time. The Supreme Court of Canada held that custom or "standard practice" (reasonable screening methods) can be negligent if it is "'fraught with such obvious risks' such that anyone is capable of finding it negligent, without the necessity of judging matters requiring diagnostic or clinical expertise....*" Id.*

CUSTOMS Duties charged on commodities upon their importation into or exportation out of a country. *Attorney-General for B.C. v. MacDonald Murphy Lumber Co.,* [1930] 1 W.W.R. 830 at 834 (P.C.). The power to legislate with respect to customs matters is exercised by the federal Parliament. See, e.g., *Customs Act,* R.S.C. 1985 c. 1 (2nd Supp.); *Customs Tariff,* S.C. 1997, c. 36. See **excise**.

CYBERCRIME A criminal offence in which a computer network or electronic information is the object of the crime, or is a tool used to commit the crime. Cybercrimes include illegal access to or destruction of electronic data, misuse of computer systems, or use of computer networks to commit fraud or distribute child pornography. See *Convention on Cybercrime*, 23 November 2001, 2296 U.N.T.S. 167. See **phishing**.

CY-PRÈS (*sī'-prĕ*) Fr.: so near, as near. In the law of **trusts** and **wills**, the principle that **equity** will, when a charity bequest is illegal or later becomes impossible or impracticable of fulfillment, substitute another charitable object that is believed to approach the original purpose of the **testator** or **settlor** as closely as possible. The courts will exercise this power, however, only when the purpose for which the fund was established cannot be carried out and diversion of the income to some other purpose can be found to fall within the general intent of the donor expressed in the **instrument** establishing the trust.

D

DAGENAIS/MENTUCK TEST The test governing all **discretionary** actions by a trial **judge** that limit **freedom of expression** by the press during a judicial proceeding. Because a **publication ban** or similar order conflicts with the **open court principle**, the limit must be justified in order not to violate the guarantee on freedom of expression in the **Canadian Charter of Rights and Freedoms**. The test has two parts: (a) the order is necessary in order to prevent a serious risk to the proper administration of justice because reasonably alternative measures will not prevent the risk; and (b) the salutary effects of the order outweigh the deleterious effects on the rights and interests of the parties and the public, including the effects on the right to free expression, the right of the accused to a fair and public trial, and the efficacy of the administration of justice. *Vancouver Sun (Re)*, 2004 SCC 43.

DAMAGES Monetary **compensation** the law awards to one who has suffered damage, loss, or injury by the wrong of another; recompense for a legal wrong such as **breach of contract** or a **tortious** act. See, e.g., *Moore v. Kyba*, 2012 BCCA 361. It is one of several forms of relief that can be obtained from the court. Compare **specific performance**.

ACTUAL DAMAGES Losses that can readily be proven to have been sustained, and for which the injured party should be compensated as a matter of right.

AGGRAVATED DAMAGES See EXEMPLARY [PUNITIVE] DAMAGES following.

CONSEQUENTIAL [SPECIAL] DAMAGES A loss or injury that is indirect or mediate. In contract law, consequential damages are recoverable if it was reasonably foreseeable at the time of contract that the injury or loss was probable if the contract were broken. *Hadley v. Baxendate* (1854), 9 Ex. 341; 156 E.R. 145. They are damages that follow because of knowl-

edge of special conditions imputed to the defaulting party and increase the standard of liability. Thus they are synonymous with SPECIAL DAMAGES (see following).

DOUBLE [TREBLE] DAMAGES Twice [or three times] the amount of damages that a court or jury would normally find a party entitled to, which is recoverable by an injured party for certain kinds of injuries pursuant to a statute authorizing the double [or treble] recovery. These damages are intended in certain instances as a punishment for improper behaviour.

EXEMPLARY [PUNITIVE] DAMAGES "Punitive damages are awarded against a defendant in exceptional cases for 'malicious, oppressive, and high-handed" misconduct that "offends the court's sense of decency.' *Hill v. Church of Scientology of Toronto*, [1995] 2 S.C.R. 1130, at para. 196. The test thus limits the award to misconduct that represents a marked departure from ordinary standards of decent behaviour. Because their objective is to punish the defendant rather than compensate a plaintiff (whose just compensation will already have been assessed), punitive damages straddle the frontier between civil law (compensation) and criminal law (**punishment**)." *Whiten v. Pilot Insurance Co.*, 2002 SCC 18.

EXPECTATION DAMAGES A measure of the money **damages** available to the **plaintiff** in an action for **breach of contract**, based on the value of the benefit he or she would have received from the contract if the **defendant** had not breached but had completed **performance** as agreed. The amount is generally computed on the basis of the monetary value of the contract to the plaintiff, based on full performance thereof minus whatever costs the plaintiff was able to avoid by not performing his own part of the contract. When the buyer breaches the expectation damages will ordinarily be the contract price, less costs saved; when the seller breaches, the buyer's expectation damages will be measured by the fair **market value** of the promised performance at the time and place of promised tender [delivery]. Compare **cost of completion**; **diminution in value**; **specific performance**.

GENERAL DAMAGES Those that the law will presume to be the direct natural or probable consequence of the act complained of, as in negligence claims for personal injuries. For example, where the element of continuance of health, employment, or disposition to work enters into the computation, the damages are general and include bodily pain and suffering and personal inconvenience. *Wersh v. Wersh and Wersh,* [1945] 1 W.W.R. 609 (Man.C.A.). Compare SPECIAL DAMAGES (see following).

INCIDENTAL DAMAGES Damages that include losses reasonably incident to, or conduct giving rise to, a claim for ACTUAL DAMAGES. A buyer's incidental damages would include expenses reasonably incurred in inspection, receipt, transportation, and care and custody of goods rightfully rejected. A seller's incidental damages would include any commercially reasonable charges, expenses or commissions incurred in stopping delivery, in the transportation, care and custody of goods after the buyer's **breach**, in connection with return or resale of the goods.

LIQUIDATED DAMAGES The genuine, reasonable, pre-estimate of the damages, agreed upon in advance by parties to a contract, that will be paid in the event of a **breach**. "Where such agreement is made and the parties are bound thereby, the result is that, regardless of the amount of the actual loss, the defaulting party's **liability** to pay damages is limited to the amount agreed upon, and the **aggrieved party** may not recover more than that amount." *Mitchell v. Paddington Homes Ltd.* (1977), 3 B.C.L.R. 330 at 332 (S.C.). Contrasted with unliquidated damages, which is a sum of money not agreed upon in advance between the parties but awarded by a **court**. Compare **penalty**.

NOMINAL DAMAGES The amount (usually, a trivial sum) paid to the plaintiff who has "proved the infraction of a legal right, but has failed to prove

what damage, if any, was caused thereby. Nevertheless [the defendant] has been guilty of breaches of the agreement, and these breaches entitle [the plaintiff] to nominal damages." *Hudson's Bay Oil & Gas Co. Ltd. v. Dynamic Petroleums Ltd.* (1958), 26 W.W.R. (N.S.) 504 (Alta.S.C.).

SPECIAL DAMAGES Such damages as are capable of exact computation. *Gruden v. McLean,* [1972] 1 O.R. 860 at 861 (C.A.).

DAMNUM ABSQUE INJURIA (*däm'-nŭm äb'-skwā ĭn-jū-rē'-ä*) Lat.: loss without **injury**. The gist of this maxim is that if there is loss or damage without a legally recognized injury, the law provides no **cause of action** and consequently no legal remedy. See, e.g., *Brown v. Douglas,* 2011 BCCA 521. Compare **injuria absque damno**.

DANGEROUS OFFENDER A person subject to indefinite detention in a penitentiary because of the nature of his or her criminal activity, under s. 753 of the *Criminal Code*, R.S.C. 1985, c. C–46. A person can only be declared a dangerous offender after an evaluation ordered following a conviction of a serious personal injury offence, which includes sexual offences or offences involving violence and carrying a potential sentence of ten years or more. To be declared a dangerous offender, it must be shown that the accused has a pattern of violent or aggressive behaviour, has displayed such a brutal nature that he or she "is unlikely to be inhibited by normal standards of behavioural restraint," or has shown a failure to control his or her sexual impulses and a likelihood of causing injury, pain, or other evil to other persons through failure in the future to control his or her sexual impulses. In some cases, a person might be subject to an order for something less than indeterminate detention if a lesser measure will adequately protect the public. See **long-term offender**; **habitual criminal**.

DANGEROUS [DEADLY] WEAPON See **offensive weapon**.

DAY IN COURT A time when a person who is a party to a lawsuit has been duly cited to appear before the court and be heard. See also **appearance**; **due process of law**.

DEBAUCH "[T]he verb 'debauch,' as defined in ordinary dictionaries, means entice, lead astray, vitiate or corrupt. When used as a legal term it has more signification, *viz.,* to seduce and violate a woman." *Guiry v. Wheeler,* [1952] O.W.N. 657 at 659 (H.C.).

DE BENE ESSE (*dě bě'-ně ěs'-sě*) Lat.: conditionally; provisionally. "To do a thing de bene esse signifies allowing or accepting certain evidence for the present until more fully examined, *valeat quantum vatere potest.* It is regarded as an additional examination to be utilized if necessary only in the event that witnesses cannot be examined later in the action in the regular way. This evidence therefore was taken 'for what it was worth.'" *C. T. Gogstad & Co. v. The S.S. "Camosun"* (1941), 56 B.C.R. 156 at 157 (Admiralty).

DEBENTURE "...a debenture is a **contract** evidencing or acknowledging a debt which might, or might not have charging provisions relating to the **grantor's** property. That is, the terms of the debenture are to be negotiated between the parties as in any contract." *Re Selmas-Cromie Ltd.; Gardner v. M/S Apparel Ltd.* (1976), 21 C.B.R. (N.S.) 10 at 21 (B.C.S.C.). Typically "debenture" today refers to an **instrument** evidencing a loan made to a **corporation** and secured by a **security interest**. A debenture is a type of **bond**. See *Halsbury's Laws of Canada*, "Business Corporations I" 525–27 (1st ed. 2008); P. Davies, *Gower and Davies' Principles of Modern Company Law* 1135–53 (8th ed. 2008). See **bond**.

DEBT "[A] sum payable in respect of a liquidated money demand, recoverable by an action." *Diewold v. Diewold,* [1941] 1 D.L.R. 561 (S.C.C.). "[T]hat which is owed or due; anything, as money, goods or service, which one person is under obligation to pay or render another." *Secretary of State of Canada v. Neitzke* (1921), 62 S.C.R. 262. See **bankruptcy**; **creditor**; **insolvency**.

DEBTOR One who has the obligation of paying a **debt**; one who owes a debt. "The relation of debtor and **creditor** arises whenever one person, by contract or law, is liable and bound to pay another an amount of money certain or uncertain, as between a bank and its customer." *The Royal Bank of Canada v. Slack,* [1958] O.R. 262 at 276 (C.A.).

DECEASED One who has died; in property, the alternate term DECEDENT is generally used. In criminal law, "the deceased" refers to the victim of a **homicide**.

DECEDENT See **deceased**.

DECEIT The **tort** of **fraudulent** representation. "To succeed in the common-law action of deceit the plaintiff must show actual fraud, that is, an intention to deceive or that the statements complained of were made recklessly without regard for their truth or falsity." *McCusker v. O'Day,* [1975] W.W.D. 86 (B.C.C.A.). "Every person must be held responsible for the consequences of a false representation made by him to another, upon which a third person acts, and, so acting, is injured or damnified— provided it appear that such false representation was made with the intent that it should be acted upon by such third person in the manner that occasions the injury or loss...." *Barry v. Croskey* (1861), 2 Johns & Hem. 1 at 23–4, 70 E.R. 945 at 955, cited and followed in *Cherewick v. Moore,* [1955] 2 D.L.R. 492 at 494 (B.C.S.C.).

DECISION A conclusion; a determination; a formal **judgment**. A decision presupposes an existing dispute between two or more parties and involves presentation of the case by the **parties** to the dispute, ascertainment of facts by means of **evidence** adduced by the parties, submission of legal arguments, and the decision itself, which disposes of the matter by a finding on disputed facts and an application of the law of the land to the facts so found including, where necessary, ruling on any disputed **questions of law**.

DECISION ON THE MERITS See **on the merits**.

DECISION TREE Written instructions for a **jury** setting out the decisions they must make and the order in which they must make them. *R. v. Foti*, 2002 MBCA 122.

DECLARANT The person reported to have made a statement that is sought to be admitted as **hearsay**.

DECLARATION See **complaint**.

DECLARATION OF INVALIDITY An order by a court that a rule or **statute** has no force or effect. A declaration of invalidity is available as a **remedy** when a law violates the **division of powers** in ss. 91 and 92 of the **Constitution Act, 1867**, or when it is inconsistent with a guarantee in the **Canadian Charter of Rights and Freedoms**. A law that has been declared to be invalid might continue to appear in the statute even though it is unenforceable, because only an **Act** of **Parliament** or a **legislature** can change the text of the statute. For example, the prohibition on **abortion** in the *Criminal Code*, R.S.C. 1985, c. C–46, s. 287 continues to appear in the statute even though it was declared invalid by the Supreme Court in 1998. *R. v. Morgentaler*, [1988] 1 S.C.R. 30.

DECLARATION OF TRUST An acknowledgment by a person that he or she holds **property** in **trust** for another. It may be implied from conduct. *Edell v. Sitzer* (2001), 55 O.R. (3d) 198 (Ont. S.C.J.).

DECLARATORY JUDGMENT A **judgment** of the court granting relief to an applicant, in the form of a **declaration** stating "the legal position concerning a matter in dispute, so that the remedy… is not in itself an order of the court and is thus non-coercive. Applicants do, however, frequently apply for an injunction as well as a declaration, so that the relief obtained is, so far as the injunction is concerned, enforceable." H. Hanbury, R. Maudsley, & J. Martin, *Hanbury and Maudsley Modern Equity* 153 (11th ed. 1981). See, e.g., the *Courts of Justice Act*, R.S.O. 1990, c. C. 43, s. 97, or corresponding provincial Supreme Court rules. In some cases, such as an action for **defamation**, a plaintiff might be primarily interested in a declaratory judgement because it "is

as valuable to its reputation as any pecuniary award." *Éditions Écosociété Inc. v. Banro Corp.*, 2012 SCC 18. Compare **advisory opinion**.

DECLARATORY POWER The power of the federal government under s. 92(10)(c) of the **Constitution Act, 1867** to assume jurisdiction over a local work (a matter within provincial jurisdiction) within federal jurisdiction by declaring it to be "for the general advantage of Canada." P.W. Hogg, *Constitutional Law of Canada* 22–15–16 (5th ed. 2007). Most declarations relate to transportation and communication, but they are not limited to these areas. See *Ont. Hydro v. Ont.*, [1993] 3 S.C.R. 327. The 1992 **Charlottetown Accord** would have made this power subject to the approval of the province involved, and although the Accord was unsuccessful, the government has made declarations sparingly since then. *Id.*

DECLARATORY STATUTE One that merely declares the existing law without proposing any additions or changes, for the purpose of resolving conflicts or doubts concerning a particular point of the **common law** or the meaning of a **statute**.

DECREE A law; a **judgment** or order of the court. Under a previous version of the *Divorce Act*, parties were initially granted a decree nisi, or conditional decree of divorce, three months after which it was possible to apply for a decree absolute, which actually dissolved the marriage. Under the *Divorce Act*, R.S.C. 1985, c. 3 (2nd Supp.), that terminology is no longer used, and a divorce takes effect 31 days after the day on which the judgment granting the divorce was rendered, barring special circumstances or an appeal.

DECRIMINALIZE Broadly, the withdrawing of an offence from the *Criminal Code*, R.S.C. 1985, c. C–46, so that it is no longer a crime. The term is sometimes used to mean that the behaviour in question is now entirely legal but often carries the implication that it has been made the subject of a **regulatory offence** or is dealt with by the law in some other fashion.

DEDICATION A **conveyance** of land by a private owner in the nature of a **gift** or **grant**, and an **acceptance** of that land by or on behalf of the public; "the setting apart of land for the public use," such as streets acquired by a town through a dedication to the public of the property comprising the streets (*Van Campenhout v. Government of Saskatchewan* (1959), 30 W.W.R. (N.S.) 485 (Sask.C.A.)

DEED An **instrument** in writing that **conveys** an **interest** in land from the **grantor** to the **grantee**; an instrument used to effect a transfer of **realty**. Its main function is to pass **title** to land. See **bargain and sale**; **quitclaim deed**; **specialty**; **warranty** [WARRANTY DEED]. See also **inter vivos**.

DEED OF TRUST A transfer of legal **title** to property from the **settlor** to the **trustee**, for the purpose of placing the legal title with the trustee as **security** for the **performance** of certain obligations, monetary or otherwise. Compare **mortgage**.

DEEMED A fact that is, by law, to be taken to be true. In some cases, the deemed fact is meant to be irrebuttably established. For example, an offence committed on an aircraft in flight that eventually lands in Canada is deemed to have been committed in Canada. *Criminal Code*, R.S.C. 1985, s. C–46, s. 7(1). On other occasions, the deemed fact is initially presumed, but that presumption can be rebutted. See, e.g., the *Survivorship Act*, S.N.B. 1991, c. S–20, s. 4(2): "Unless a contrary intention appears in a written agreement to which both spouses are parties, marital property shall be deemed, for the purposes of this Act, to have been held by them in common in equal shares."

DE FACTO (*dē fäk'-tō*) Lat.: in fact; by virtue of the deed or accomplishment; in reality; actually. Used to qualify many legal terms—e.g., DE FACTO CORPORATION: one that has inadvertently failed to comply with all the provisions of the laws relating to the creation of a **corporation** but has made a good faith effort to do so and has in good faith exercised the franchise of a corpora-

tion. Alternatively, police might not use words of arrest while taking someone into custody, but their actions might constitute a DE FACTO ARREST. *R. v. Latimer*, [1997] 1 S.C.R. 217. Compare **de jure**.

DE FACTO EXPROPRIATION The taking of land by government, in fact, without the use of formal procedures of expropriation and without a change in legal title. Extensive regulation of land, even if it dramatically limits the use of that property or lowers its value, is not sufficient. "Both the extinguishment of virtually all incidents of ownership and an acquisition of land by the expropriating authority must be proved." *Mariner Real Estate Ltd. v. Nova Scotia (Attorney General)* (1999), 178 NSR (2d) 294 (N.S. C.A.).

DE FACTO POSSESSION Actual physical possession.

DE FACTO SPOUSE See **spouse**.

DEFALCATION The failure of one entrusted with money to pay it when it is due to another. Similar to misappropriation and **embezzlement** but wider in scope because it does not necessarily imply any criminal **fraud** and might rest on extreme recklessness. For examples involving fraud, see, e.g., *Criminal Code*, R.S.C. 1985, c. C–46, ss. 330–332. See also **misapplication of property**.

DEFAMATION The publication of anything that is injurious to the good name or reputation of another or tends to bring him or her into disrepute. "A defamatory **libel** is matter published, without lawful justification or excuse, that is likely to injure the reputation of any person by exposing him to hatred, contempt or ridicule, or that is designed to insult the person of or concerning whom it is published." *Criminal Code*, R.S.C. 1985, c. C–46, s. 298(1). See also ss. 299–317. An oral defamation is a **slander**. A **tort** action under libel, slander, or defamation may be brought to recover **damages**.

DEFAULT Failure to discharge a duty, to one's own disadvantage; an omission to do that which ought to have been done by one of the parties. See *Alsip v. Robinson* (1911), 18 W.L.R. 39 (Man.T.D.).

The term is most often used to describe the occurrence of an event that cuts short the rights or remedies of one of the parties to an agreement or a legal dispute. It is often used in the context of **mortgages** to describe the failure of the MORTGAGOR (see **mortgage**) to pay **installments** when due and in the context of judicial **proceedings** to describe the failure of one of the parties to take the procedural steps necessary to prevent entry of a **judgment** against him (called a DEFAULT JUDGMENT or judgment by default).

DEFAULT JUDGMENT See **judgment** [DEFAULT JUDGMENT].

DEFEASANCE An **instrument** that, in effect, negates the effectiveness of a **deed** or **will**; a **collateral** deed that defeats the force of another deed upon the performance of certain conditions.

DEFEASIBLE Subject to **revocation** if certain **conditions** are not met; capable of being avoided or annulled or liable to such avoidance or annulment. Used in context of estates in **real property**.

DEFECTIVE 1. Wanting as to an essential; incomplete, deficient, faulty. For example, an **indictment** that fails to specify some essential element of the **charge** might be defective. See *Criminal Code*, R.S.C. 1985, c. C–46, s. 601. **2.** Not reasonably safe for a use that can be reasonably anticipated. See, e.g., *McMorran v. Dominion Stores Ltd.* (1977), 74 D.L.R. (3d) 186 (Ont.H.C.). See also **products liability**; **strict liability**; **warranty**.

DEFECTIVE TITLE One that is unmarketable. **1.** With reference to **title** in land, it means that the person making the **conveyance**, claiming to own **good title**, is actually subject to the partial or complete **ownership** of the title by someone else. **2.** As to **negotiable instruments**, the term denotes title obtained through illegal means or means that amount to **fraud**.

DEFENCE A legal argument that defends against a claim, whether by the **Crown**

prosecutor in a **criminal** matter or the **plaintiff** in a **civil** matter. Sometimes the term is limited to refer to substantive defences, which raise countervailing considerations after the behaviour complained of has been proven, such as the defence of **necessity** in criminal matters or a claim of **self-defence** in a **tort** action for **assault**. In some cases, the term is used more broadly to include any basis upon which a person might be found not liable. The defence of **mistake of fact** in criminal matters, for example, does not arise after the offence has been proven, but rather is a way of showing that part of the **mens rea** of the offence is not proven in the first place. Similarly, a limitation period might or might not be classified as a "defence" in a civil action. *144096 Canada Ltd.* (*USA*) *v. Canada* (*Attorney-General*) (2003), 63 O.R. (3d) 172 (Ont. C.A.).

EQUITABLE DEFENCE A defence that is recognized by **courts of equity** acting solely upon inherent rules and principles of **equity**. Examples of such defence include **fraud**, **duress** and illegality. Such defences can now be asserted in courts of law as well. The term also refers to equitable doctrines such as **unclean hands** that may operate to bar a plaintiff from pursuing an equity action and thus constitute equitable defences to such an action.

DEFENCE OF PROPERTY Under the *Criminal Code*, R.S.C. 1985, c. C–46, a defence available to a person in peaceable possession of either **real property** or **personal property**, permitting the use of reasonable force in its protection.

DEFENDANT 1. In **civil proceedings**, the party responding to the claim of the **plaintiff**; the party sued in an **action**. **2.** In **criminal** proceedings when charges are brought by way of **summary conviction**, the **accused**. See also **respondent**.

DEFERRED PAYMENTS Payments extended over a period of time or put off to a future date. Installment payments are usually a series of equal deferred payments made over a course of time.

DEFINED BENEFIT PENSION "A defined benefit pension plan pays its members a fixed pension benefit independent of the financial performance of the "pension fund." The plan does not assign particular assets to an individual employee's account. Participants in a plan do not receive individual statements reflecting investments. Instead, contributions are generally placed into a single pool of pension plan assets. When a pension member retires, the pension plan provides the retiree with a pension annuity, calculated according to a prescribed 'benefit formula' on the date of retirement." *Best v. Best*, [1999] 2 S.C.R. 868. Compare **defined contribution pension**.

DEFINED CONTRIBUTION PENSION "A defined contribution plan consists of an investment account in each employee's name into which the employer (and often the employee) deposits contributions...Over time, a defined contribution pension accrues value just like an investment portfolio. At retirement, a defined contribution account is customarily liquidated and used to purchase a pension annuity to provide the retiree with regular income." *Best v. Best*, [1999] 2 S.C.R. 868. Compare **defined benefit pension**.

DEFRAUD To deprive a person of **property** or **interest**, **estate** or right by fraud, **deceit**, or **artifice**. "To defraud is to deprive by deceit; it is by deceit to induce a man to act to his injury. More tersely it may be put, that to deceive is by falsehood to induce a state of mind; to defraud is by deceit to induce a course of action." *Re London and Globe Finance Corp. Ltd.*, [1903] 1 Ch. 728 at 732, cited in *Scott v. Metropolitan Police Commissioner* (1974), 60 Cr.App.R. 124 at 127, 130 (H.L.), "... to deprive a person dishonestly of something which is his or of something to which he is or would or might but for the perpetration of the fraud, be entitled."

DEI GRATIA (*dā'-ī grā'-shē-ě*) Lat.: by the grace of God.

DE JURE (*dě jū'-rā*) Lat.: by right, by justice; lawful; legitimate. Generally used in contrast to **de facto** in that *de jure* connotes "as a matter of law" whereas *de facto* connotes "as a matter of conduct or practice not founded on law."

DELAY In assessing whether there has been a violation of the right to a trial within a reasonable time under s. 11(b) of the **Canadian Charter of Rights and Freedoms**, "the period from the charge to the end of the trial." *R. v. Morin*, [1992] 1 S.C.R. 771.

DELEGATED LEGISLATION See **legislation**; **subordinate [delegated] legislation**.

DELICTUM (*děliktěm*) Lat.: A **tort**; a fault, wrong or injury.

DELINQUENT 1. In a monetary context, something that has been made payable and is overdue and unpaid; implies a previous opportunity to make payment. See **default**. **2.** With reference to persons, *delinquency* implies carelessness or recklessness. See also **juvenile delinquent**.

DELIVERY A voluntary transfer of **title** or **possession** from one party to another; a legally recognized handing over of one's possessory rights to another. ACTUAL DELIVERY is sometimes very cumbersome or impossible, and in those circumstances the courts may find a CONSTRUCTIVE DELIVERY sufficient where there is no actual delivery, provided that the intention is clearly to transfer title. Thus, "where goods are ponderous and incapable ... of being handed from one to another, there need not be an actual delivery; but it may be done by that which is tantamount, as delivery of the key of a warehouse in which the goods are lodged, or by delivery of some other **indicia** of property." *McLean v. McGhee*, [1920] 2 W.W.R. 394 at 397 (Man.C.A.). Such an action is also called a SYMBOLIC DELIVERY. See **gift**; **livery of seisin**. Compare **bailment**; **conveyance**; **grant**.

DEMAND NOTE A note payable on demand. **1.** A negotiable **instrument** that by its express terms is payable immediately on an agreed-upon date of **maturation**; the **maker** of the note acknowledges his or her **liability** as of the due date. **2.** An instrument payable upon presentation or one in which no time for payment is stated. See *Bills of Exchange Act,* R.S.C. 1985, c. B–4, ss. 176–187.

DEMESNE LANDS Under the old English tenurial system, the land of a lord that was not granted out in tenancy but held back for the lord's own private use.

DE MINIMIS NON CURAT LEX (*dĕ mĭ'-nĭ-mĭs nōn kyū'-ràt lĕks*) Lat.: the law does not concern itself with trifles. Something that is *de minimis* in interest is one that does not rise to a level of sufficient importance to be dealt with judicially. The doctrine applies in **civil** actions and might, for example, be applied when a contracted shipment of several tonnes of grain was short by a few kilograms. It is questionable whether the doctrine applies as a defence in criminal matters. "[T]he Supreme Court of Canada has touched upon, but not resolved, the question whether the *de minimis* principle provides a defence to a criminal charge." *R. v. Kubassek* (2004), 25 C.R. (6th) 340 (Ont. C.A.).

DEMISE A term used to describe the **conveyance** of an **estate** in **real property**. See, e.g., *Evergreen Building Ltd. v. IBI Leaseholds Ltd.*, 2005 BCCA 583; *Newfoundland and Labrador (Mineral Claims Recorder) v. Vinland Resources Ltd.*, 2008 NLCA 12. Most commonly used in a lease as a synonym for "let"—i.e., to grant a lease. *Bowater Power Co. Ltd. v. M.N.R.,* [1971] C.T.C. 818 (F.).

DEMOCRATIC RIGHTS See **Canadian Charter of Rights and Freedoms**.

DEMONSTRABLY JUSTIFIED "[Under s. 1 of the **Canadian Charter of Rights and Freedoms**] the phrase…puts the onus of justifying a limitation on a right or freedom set out in the Charter on the party seeking to limit it." *Hunter v. Southam Inc.*, [1984] 2 S.C.R. 145 at 169.

DEMURRAGE Damages payable to compensate for delay, for example, when a vessel is returned later than the period for which it was chartered, or goods are not unloaded from a vessel or train by the agreed date.

DEMURRER "A demurrer was a form of **pleading** under the old system by which a party objected that his opponent's pleading disclosed no **cause of action** or ground of defence. When a demurrer was pleaded the question raised was forthwith set down for argument and decision, and the **judgment** was given by the full court sitting *in banc*…If he lost the demurrer, he lost the case and the facts were never gone into at all." W. Williston & R. Rolls, *The Law of Civil Procedure* 686 (1970). See rr. 21.01(1), (2) of *Ontario Rules of Civil Procedure,* R.R.O. 1990, Reg. 194. Demurrer has been abolished, and alternative modes of procedure are now used. See, e.g., *Nova Scotia Civil Procedure Rules*, r. 13. See *Stevens v. Moritz* (1913), 14 D.L.R. 699 (Ont.S.C.). Compare **summary judgment**.

DENIAL [or TRAVERSE] A **defence** by denial of an essential **allegation** of fact of the plaintiff's **statement of claim**. In a **statement of defence**, the defendant must admit or deny the plaintiff's allegations of fact; if he or she does not specifically admit them, they are deemed to be denied. See, e.g., *Nova Scotia Civil Procedure Rules* (1998), rr. 14.14–14.17. See **traverse**. Compare **confession and avoidance**.

DE NOVO (*dĕ nō'-vō*) Lat.: new, young, fresh; renewed, revived; a second time. See **hearing** [HEARING DE NOVO]; **trial** [TRIAL DE NOVO].

DENUNCIATION An objective of sentencing under s. 718 of the *Criminal Code,* R.S.C. 1985, c. C–46, requiring that a proper sentence "should … communicate society's condemnation of [an] offender's conduct. In short, a sentence with a denunciatory element represents a symbolic, collective statement that the offender's conduct should be punished for encroaching on society's basic code of values as enshrined within our substantive criminal law." *R. v. C.A.M.,* [1996] 1 S.C.R. 500. Denunciation is related to, but distinct from, **retributive justice,** insofar as the latter "requires that a judicial sentence properly reflect the moral blameworthiness of [a] particular offender" by "attaching negative consequences to undesirable behaviour." *Id.*

DEPARTURE ORDER See **deportation**.

DEPENDENT COVENANT An expression used in contract law "to define the sort of term that, if broken by one party, will excuse the other [from his or her obligations under the contract]... [a] covenant which goes to the whole of consideration." Also referred to as a repudiatory breach. S. M. Waddams, *Law of Contracts* 438 (6th ed. 2010). See **repudiation**; **breach**.

DEPONENT A **witness**; one who gives information concerning some fact or facts known to him or her, under **oath** in a **deposition**.

DEPORTATION Under the *Immigration and Refugee Protection Regulations,* SOR/2002–227, s. 223, there are three types of removal orders which may be issued against a person requiring him or her to leave Canada, viz., departure orders, exclusion orders, and deportation orders.

A departure order is prescribed as a circumstance that relieves a **foreign national** from some of the rigours of obtaining official authorization in order to return to Canada. (*Regulation* s. 224. (1)).

An exclusion order obliges the foreign national to obtain a written authorization under the requirements of the *Immigration and Refugee Protection Act,* S.C. 2001, c. 27, and its Regulations, in order to return to Canada during the one-year period after the exclusion order was enforced. (*Regulation* s. 225.(1)).

A deportation order obliges the foreign national to obtain a written authorization (in compliance with the *Act* and *Regulations*) in order to return to Canada at any time after the deportation order was enforced. (*Regulation* s. 226. (1)).

DEPOSIT 1. In banking, "when a customer pays money into his account in the usual way of business, he sells it to the banker..... In exchange for the money the banker makes an entry of an equal sum in credit in favour of his customer. And it is the entry to the credit of the customer, which, in the technical language of modern banking, is termed a deposit." *Re Alberta Legislation,* [1938] 2 D.L.R. 81 at 99 (S.C.C.)

2. In the sale of goods or real property, sometimes part of the price is prepaid by way of security, when the contract is entered into. "The return of the deposit in case the sale goes off is usually a matter of agreement, but in the absence of a different agreement the deposit is forfeited if the sale goes off through the buyer's default." *Erickson v. Andrew,* [1943] 2 D.L.R. 732 at 736 (Alta.S.C.A.D.).

DEPOSITION A method used in pretrial examination for **discovery**; it consists of a statement of a witness under oath, taken in question-and-answer form as it would be in court, with opportunity given to the adversary to be present and cross-examined, with all this reported and transcribed.

Such statements are the most common form of discovery, and may, if the appropriate conditions are met, be taken of any witness (whether or not a party to the action). See *Nova Scotia Civil Procedure Rules* (1998), r. 18. In Ontario, the "party to an action may examine for discovery any other party adverse in interest ..." *Ontario Rules of Civil Procedure,* R.R.O. 1990, Reg. 194, r. 31.03(1). When taken in the form described, the statement is called an "oral deposition." Depositions may also be taken on written **interrogatories**, where the questions are served to the party in written form, to which a written answer to interrogatories is returned. See, e.g., *Nova Scotia Civil Procedure Rules* (1998), r. 19.

DEPRECIATION Loss in value of assets over a period of time.

DERELICT "A vessel [that] had been **abandoned** and deserted at sea by those who were in charge of it without hope on their part of recovering it and without intention of returning to it." *Davie v. Ship "Young Hustler No. 1"* (1962), 32 D.L.R. (2d) 470 at 474 (Ex.Ct.).

DERELICTION A recession of the waters of the sea, a navigable river or other stream, by which land that had been covered with water is left dry. In such case, if the alteration takes place suddenly and sensibly, the ownership remains according to former bounds; but if it is made gradually and imperceptibly, the derelict or dry land belongs to the **riparian** owner from whose shore or bank the water has receded. The term may also refer to the land itself that is thus left uncovered. In order for contiguous landowners to gain ownership of the newly uncovered land, the withdrawal of the water must appear permanent, not merely seasonal. Compare **accretion**; **avulsion**; **reliction**.

DERIVATIVE ACTION 1. "[A]n action brought in the name or on behalf of a corporation or any of its subsidiaries … by a shareholder or other complainant, to assert or defend rights to which the corporation or its subsidiary is entitled. Proceedings of this kind are termed 'derivative' because … the rights of the plaintiff shareholders (or other potential complainants) derive from the primary corporate right to redress the wrongs against it." *Halsbury's Laws of Canada*, "Business Corporations II" 945 (1st ed. 2008). See **stockholder's derivative action**.
  2. Also used to describe a **cause of action** that is founded on an injury to another, as when a husband sues for loss of **consortium** or services of his wife because of an injury to her by the defendant, or when a father sues for the loss of services of his children.

DEROGATE To detract from; to partially **abrogate** a law. "The 'later in time' principle gives priority to a more recent statute, based on the theory that the legislature is presumed to be aware of the content of existing legislation. If a new enactment is inconsistent with a prior one, therefore, the legislature is presumed to have intended to derogate from the earlier provisions." *Century Services Inc. v. Canada* (*Attorney-General*), 2010 SCC 60.

DESCENT "…the taking of **real estate** by **inheritance**, that is, as heir of the former holder.…'Descent' is used in respect of real estate…of an **intestate**." *Re Stone,* [1925] 1 D.L.R. 60 at 70 (S.C.C.). See, e.g., the *Intestate Succession Act,* R.S.N.S. 1989, c. 236; *Estates Administration Act,* R.S.O. 1990, c. E. 22. Compare **devise**.

DESERTION 1. Continual absence from **cohabitation**, which under a previous version of the *Divorce Act* was relevant to grounds for divorce. It is not a consideration in the new legislation. *Divorce Act*, R.S.C., 1985, c. 3 (2nd Supp.). **2.** Improper absence from one's place of duty with the Canadian Armed Forces with the intention of remaining permanently absent.

DESTRUCTIBILITY A **common-law** rule of **future interests** that "a **contingent remainder** must **vest** at or before the termination of the preceding **life estate** or be destroyed." A. Sinclair, *Introduction to Real Property Law* 97 (3d ed. 1987). "There are at least three ways that this life estate supporting the contingent remainder in freehold could be destroyed other than by natural means, viz., by (a) **forfeiture**; (b) **merger**; and (e) **disclaimer**." *Id.* at 73.

DETAINER [FORCIBLE] See **forcible detainer**.

DETENTION As used in ss. 9 and 10 of the **Canadian Charter of Rights and Freedoms** which guarantees rights "on arrest or detention," detention is restraint of liberty, by police or another agent of the state, other than arrest, where an individual may require the assistance of counsel. *R. v. Therens,* [1985] 1 S.C.R. 613. Detention falls into three categories: physical detention (where police bodily take control of a person), detention by legal compulsion (such as by means of a **breathalyzer** demand, where failure to comply is an offence), and psychological detention (where despite the fact that police have no actual power to compel a person to remain, a reasonable person would feel detained). "Detention under ss. 9 and 10 of the *Charter* refers to a suspension of the individual's liberty interest by a significant physical or psychological restraint. Psychological detention is established either where the individual has a legal obligation to comply with the restrictive request or demand, or a reasonable person would conclude by reason of the state conduct that he or she had no choice but to comply." *R. v. Grant,* 2009 SCC 32.

DETERMINABLE FEE [FEE SIMPLE DETERMINABLE] An **interest** in **property** that may last forever, but that will automatically terminate upon the happening or non-happening of a specified event; e.g., "O grants [Blackacre] to A and his heirs so long as the land is used for church purposes. Using the words 'so long as,' O... grants a fee simple determinable and retains a possibility of reverter. When (if ever) the land is not used as specified, O or O's estate will get the land back and resume the rights of ownership in fee simple absolute." A.M. Sinclair & M.E. McCallum, *An Introduction to Real Property Law* 26–27 (6th ed. 2012).

DETERRENCE The discouraging or impeding of a certain activity. Deterrence is recognized as a goal of sentencing under s. 718 of the *Criminal Code*, R.S.C. 1985, c. C–46. There are two forms of deterrence in the sentencing context: general deterrence and specific deterrence. The objective of general deterrence is to ensure that "potential criminals will not engage in criminal activity because of the example provided by the punishment imposed on the offender." *R. v. B.W.P.*, 2006 SCC 27. Specific deterrence is aimed at deterring the actual offender before the court from future criminal activity. *Id.* Compare **denunciation**; **rehabilitation**; **retributive justice**; **separation**.

DETINUE At **common law**, an **action** for the wrongful detention of **personal property (personalty)**; "A continuing cause of action which accrues at the date of the wrongful refusal to deliver up goods and continues until the delivery up of the goods or judgment in the action for detinue." *General Finance Facilities Ltd. v. Cooks Cars (Romford) Ltd.*, [1963] 2 All E.R. 314, cited in *Schentag v. Gauthier* (1972), 27 D.L.R. (3d) 710 at 712 (Sask.Dist.Ct.). "Detinue is the proper action to bring if the plaintiff wishes to recover possession of his goods, and not merely their value." *Id.* at 713. Compare **conversion**; **detainer [forcible]**; **replevin**; **trover**.

DEVISE A gift of land or an interest in land (**real property**) made by **will**. Compare **bequest**, which is a gift of personal property made by will.

DEVISEE One who is in receipt of a **gift** of **real property** by **will**.

DEVISOR One who makes a **gift** of **real property** by **will** to a **devisee**.

DEVOLVE To pass **property** from one person to another by **operation of law**, without any voluntary act of the previous owner. The **estate** does not devolve from one person to another as the result of some positive act or agreement between them. The word implies a result without the intervention of any voluntary actor.

DIAL-A-DOPE "The term 'dial-a-dope' refers to the sale of drugs arranged by the buyer contacting the seller by way of a cellular telephone. A meet is then arranged, where the drugs are sold." *R. v. Swan*, 2009 BCCA 142.

DIALOGUE THEORY The view that **judicial review** of **unconstitutional** legislation is part of an ongoing interplay, or "dialogue," between the judicial and legislative branches of government, in which neither enjoys an inherent advantage over the other. Under this conception, "[t]he work of the legislature is reviewed by the courts, and the work of the court in its decisions can be reacted to" either by passing new legislation or by using the *Charter's* **notwithstanding clause**. *Vriend v. Alberta*, [1998] 1 S.C.R. 493. Dialogue theory has been invoked by the Supreme Court in a variety of contexts. See, e.g., *R. v. Mills*, [1999] 3 S.C.R. 668; *R. v. Hall*, 2002 SCC 64.

DICTA [DICTUM] See **obiter dictum**.

DIE WITHOUT ISSUE See **failure of issue**.

DIGESTS "[V]olumes containing summaries of decided cases organized by subject matter. They vary in amount of synthesis and commentary they provide. The **Canadian Encyclopedic Digest**, for example, is a general treatise on Canadian Case law with cases cited as footnotes to a continuous text. On the other hand, the *Canadian Abridgement* is a collection of case summaries with no commentary." S. M. Waddams, *Introduction to the Study of Law*, 78 (6th ed. 2004).

DIGITAL FORENSICS The use of advanced techniques to recover and preserve data stored in various digital devices, such as computers and smartphones, for use as evidence in civil or criminal proceedings. See, e.g., *Warman v. National Post Co.*, 2010 ONSC 3670; *R. v. Baxter*, 2009 ONCJ 16.

DIGITAL RECORDING AMMETER See **DRA**.

DILATORY PLEA [PLEA IN ABATEMENT] At common law, a **plea** aimed at avoiding a **judgment** by the court. "Under the common law system ... A plea could be either a dilatory plea or a peremptory plea, also known as a plea in bar. A dilatory plea sought to prevent a final judgment on the merits. It could be made on the grounds that the court had no jurisdiction over the parties or the subject matter, or on a ground that would defeat or defeat the particular action without destroying the right of action itself, such as a plea of wrong **venue**, the personal disability of a party, that the action was premature, that there was another action extant for the same cause, and so forth. On the other hand, a peremptory plea sought to bring about a final judgment on the merits. Such a plea could take the form of a **traverse, confession and avoidance**, or an **estoppel**." *Patym Holdings Ltd. v. Michalakis*, 2005 BCCA 636. In **criminal** matters, a dilatory plea is accomplished by a plea of not guilty. *R. v. Lindsay*, 2011 BCCA 99.

DIMINUTION IN VALUE A measure of **damages** for breach of contract that reflects a decrease, occasioned by the breach, in the value of property with which the **contract** was concerned. In a building contract, it is the difference between the value of the building as constructed and its value had it been constructed in conformance with the contract. There are two general rules with variations where there are damages to **realty** and, in some cases, **personalty** attached to realty. There is the before-and-after value of realty rule, sometimes referred to as the diminution rule. There is also the restoration or replacement rule, which will generally be applied by the court if the injury is temporary and replacement is possible, or if it involves an amount less than that derived from application of the diminution rule.

Compare **cost of completion**; **damages** [EXPECTATION DAMAGES]; **specific performance**.

DIPLOMATIC IMMUNITY Immunity from the jurisdiction of a **state** extended to diplomatic personnel of a foreign state serving within the territory of the first state.

DIPLOMATIC PROTECTION Measures taken by a state to support one of its nationals in a dispute with a foreign **state**. It can include "consular action, negotiation, mediation, judicial and arbitral proceedings, reprisals, retorsion, severance of diplomatic relations, [and] economic pressures." *Khadr v. Canada (Prime Minister)*, 2009 FC 405.

DIRECT CAUSE See **cause**.

DIRECT EVIDENCE **Evidence** that proves a fact without the need for the **trier of fact** to draw an inference. Eyewitness testimony identifying an accused person or a document establishing some fact in question are examples of direct evidence. Direct evidence is normally contrasted with **circumstantial evidence**.

DIRECT INDICTMENT A method by which a **Crown prosecutor** can require an **accused** person to face **trial** despite having been discharged at a **preliminary inquiry** or not having been given a complete preliminary inquiry at all. *Criminal Code*, R.S.C. 1985, c. C–46, s. 577. The section refers to the indictment being preferred, and so it is also sometimes referred to as a "preferred indictment." A direct indictment can only be preferred with the written consent of the **Attorney-General** or an order of the judge of the court in which it is preferred.

DIRECTED VERDICT The verdict returned by a **jury** at the direction of the trial judge, by whose instruction the jury is bound. In **civil proceedings**, either party may receive a directed verdict in its favour if the opposing party fails to present a prima facie case or a necessary defence. In criminal proceedings, while there may be a directed verdict of acquittal (sometimes called a judgment of acquittal), there may be no directed verdict of conviction, as such a procedure would violate a person's rights under s. 11(f) of the **Canadian Charter of Rights and Freedoms**. See *R. v. Krieger*, 2006 SCC 47.

DIRECTOR One who sits on a board of directors of a **company** or **corporation** and who has the legal responsibility of exercising control over the officers and affairs of that company or corporation. "Agents for the company for which they act." *Finnemore v. Underwood Ltd.*, [1930] 3 D.L.R. 939 (Alta.S.C.A.D.).

A director has a **fiduciary duty** to the corporation and its **shareholders** to manage the affairs of the corporation in a manner consistent with their interests. Any **breach** of this fiduciary duty may subject him or her to personal liability to both the shareholders and the corporation. See. e.g., *D'Amore v. McDonald*, [1973] 1 O.R. 845 (H.C.).

DIRECTOR OF PUBLIC PROSECUTIONS [D.P.P.] In England, the D.P.P. under the supervision of the **Attorney-General** has the duty "to institute, undertake and carry on...criminal proceedings and to give...advice and assistance to persons concerned in criminal proceedings as may be prescribed by regulations or may be directed in a special case by the Attorney-General." 27 *Halsbury's Laws of England* (5th ed.) paras. 23, 34.

In Canada, it is traditionally one of the responsibilities of the **Attorney-General** of Canada or of a province to prosecute criminal offences. See S. Coughlan, *Criminal Procedure* 43–46 (2nd ed. 2012).

However, some **jurisdictions** (e.g., Nova Scotia) have attempted by **statute** to insulate prosecution decisions from possible political considerations by establishing an independent Public Prosecution service or division to prosecute criminal cases and some violations of provincial law. The Attorney-General remains the chief law enforcement officer for the province (and is the cabinet minister responsible for the service). The Attorney-General may also issue instructions to the D.P.P. but these must be made public.

DIRECTORY As an adjective, indicating that a particular piece of legislation, typically a procedural provision, is one with which non-compliance is not a fatal error. Contrasted with **mandatory**. "If the authority fails to observe such a condition, is its action **ultra vires?** The answer depends upon whether the condition is held to be mandatory or directory. Non-observance of a mandatory condition is fatal to the validity of the action. But if the condition is held to be merely directory, its non-observance will not matter for this purpose. In other words, it is not every omission or defect that entails the drastic penalty of invalidity." *British Columbia (Attorney-General) v. Canada (Attorney-General); An Act respecting the Vancouver Island Railway (Re)*, [1994] 2 S.C.R. 41, quoting W. Wade, *Administrative Law* (6th ed. 1988). The Supreme Court of Canada has expressed doubt as to whether the distinction is a worthwhile one: "The 'mandatory' and 'directory' labels themselves offer, no magical assistance as one defines the nature of a statutory direction. Rather, the inquiry itself is blatantly result-oriented... The temptation is very great, where the consequences of holding a statute to be imperative are seriously inconvenient, to strain a point in favor of the contention that it is mere directory." *Id.*

DIRECT TAXATION A tax that is demanded from the person who is intended to be ultimately responsible for paying it, such as income tax. Direct taxation is distinguished from indirect taxation, a tax that is demanded of one person with the expectation that the expense will be passed along to others, for example, customs duty paid by an importer that will be recovered from the ultimate purchasers by means of a higher price. Whether a tax is direct or indirect is determined by the general tendencies of the tax and the common understanding concerning it. *Canadian Industrial Gas & Oil Ltd. v. Government of Saskatchewan, et al.*, [1978] 2 S.C.R. 545. Under ss. 91 and 92 of the **Constitution Act, 1867**, the federal government is entitled to use any form of taxation, but the provinces are limited to direct taxation within the province.

DISABILITY "[T]he absence of legal capacity to do certain acts or enjoy certain benefits, such as disability to sue, to enter into contracts, to alienate property etc.... Its other meaning...refers rather to want of physical or mental ability, either native or by reason of intervening cause." *Grini v. Grini* (1969), 68 W.W.R. (N.S.) 591 at 595 (Man K.B.). Any want of legal capacity such as **infancy** or **insanity** renders a person legally **incompetent**.

DISALLOWANCE The power of the federal government, under s. 90 of the **Constitution Act, 1867**, to declare provincial legislation invalid. Although the power exists, it has been argued that it has been abandoned. See *Reference re The Power of the Governor General in Council to Disallow Provincial Legislation and the Power of Reservation of a Lieutenant-Governor of a Province,* [1938] S.C.R. 71; *Reference re Secession of Quebec*, [1998] 2 S.C.R. 217.

DISBAR To deprive a lawyer of the right to practice law by rescinding the certificate to so practice, as a result of illegal or unethical conduct. See, e.g., *Legal Profession Act*, S.N.S. 2004, c. 28, ss. 2(m), 45(4)(a).

DISBURSEMENTS Out-of-pocket expenses actually incurred by a lawyer in the course of representing a client.

DISCHARGE A general word covering the methods by which a legal **duty** is extinguished. The factors bringing about a discharge of contractual obligation include full **performance, rescission, release, annulment, dismissal**, informal written **renunciation**, and contract not to sue.

DISCHARGE OF AN ACCUSED **1.** To release an accused at the end of a preliminary inquiry if, on the whole of the evidence, no sufficient case was made out to put the accused on trial. *Criminal Code*, R.S.C. 1985, c. C–46, s. 548(1)(b). **2.** "Where an accused... pleads guilty to or is found guilty of an offence, other than an offence for which a minimum punishment is prescribed by law or an offence punishable by imprisonment for 14 years or for life, the court... may, if it

considers it to be in the best interests of the accused and not contrary to public interest, instead of convicting the accused, by order direct that the accused be discharged absolutely or upon the conditions prescribed in a probation order." *Criminal Code*, s. 730. See **acquit**.

DISCHARGE OF A BANKRUPT "An order of discharge releases the bankrupt from all claims provable in **bankruptcy**" (*Bankruptcy and Insolvency Act*, R.S.C. 1985, c. B–3, s. 178(2)), except such debts as alimony, maintenance, fines imposed by the court, liability for fraud, embezzlement, or misappropriation; or debts for goods supplied as necessaries for life (s. 178(1)). See, e.g., *Re Mascherin* (1976), 22 C.B.R. (N.S.) 263 (Ont.S.C.).

DISCHARGE OF A CONTRACT The termination of obligations under a contract which can occur in four ways: (1) by performance by both parties of the contractual obligations (see **accord and satisfaction**); (2) by express agreement between the parties to the contract; (3) by frustration of the contract where a subsequent event makes the performance of the contract impossible; and (4) by breach of contract. G.H.L. Fridman, *The Law of Contract in Canada* 555 (6th ed. 2011).

DISCHARGE OF A DEBT Settlement of a **debt**. A debt is discharged and the **debtor** released when the **creditor** has received something, either money or its equivalent, from the debtor that satisfies him. It may consist of **offsetting** mutual demands or of wiping out mutual disputed **claims** by mutual concessions, in which event no money is required to pass from one to the other. See, e.g., *Garcelon v. Eaton,* (1857), 8 N.B.R. 411 (N.B.S.C.). See also **satisfaction**.

Discharge also refers to the termination of one's employment by his or her employer; dismissal.

DISCLAIMER 1. A denial or repudiation of a person's **claim** or right to a thing, though previously that person insisted on that claim or right; **2.** complete renunciation of right to **possess** and of claim of **title**, e.g., renunciation of a gift, devise or bequest. **3.** With regard to a **trade-mark**, a statement by the applicant disclaiming the right to exclusive use of a portion of the trade-mark. *Trade-marks Act*, R.S.C., 1985, c. T–13, s. 35.

DISCLOSURE In **criminal** law, the constitutional obligation on a **Crown prosecutor** to give to an accused person all **relevant** information relating to a prosecution. The obligation arises by virtue of s. 7 of the **Canadian Charter of Rights and Freedoms** and obliges the prosecutor to provide all evidence in its possession, both **inculpatory** and **exculpatory**, and whether the prosecutor intends to use the evidence at trial or not. The right to disclosure does not apply to evidence that is protected by a **privilege**, such as **informer privilege**. *R. v. Stinchcombe*, [1991] 3 S.C.R. 326. See **production**; **McNeil disclosure**.

In **administrative law**, disclosure involves releasing to parties information that the agency or board has about the decision to be made that will affect the interests of the party or parties, as part of the general duty of fairness owed by administrative bodies. See D. Mullan, *Administrative Law* 238–44 (2001).

DISCLOSURE STATEMENT With regard to a **condominium**, a **document** that must be provided to a purchaser providing certain information, such as the existing or proposed by-laws or rules, or the existence of any outstanding **judgments** against the corporation. See, e.g., the *Condominium Act*, 2009, SNL 2009, c. C–29.1, s. 41. The failure to comply with the requirements for a disclosure statement can give rise to a legal **remedy** for the purchaser. See, e.g., *Abdool v. Somerset Place Developments of Georgetown Ltd.* (1992), 10 O.R. (3d) 120 (C.A.).

DISCONTINUANCE 1. In practice, the cessation of **proceedings** in an **action** where the **plaintiff** voluntarily puts an end to it, with or without the leave of the court; judicial leave may be required depending upon each jurisdiction's rules of practice and procedure. See, e.g.,

Nova Scotia Civil Procedure Rules, r. 40. See also **nonsuit**.

2. In real property, "the difference between dispossession and discontinuance of **possession** might be expressed in this way: the one is where a person comes in and drives out the others from possession; the other case is where a person in possession goes out and is followed into possession by other persons." *Rains v. Buxton* (1880), 14 Ch.D. 537 at 539–40, cited and followed in *Rooney v. Petry* (1910), 22 O.L.R. 101 at 103–04 (C.A.).

DISCOUNT A deduction from a specified sum. "To discount a negotiable security [instrument] is…to buy it at a discount; or it may mean, using another sense of the word, to lend money on the security, deducting the interest in advance." *Jones v. Imperial Bank* (1876), 23 Gr. 262 at 270.

DISCOVERABLE In the context of assessing whether a claim is barred by a **statute of limitations**, a matter is discoverable if, by exercising **due diligence**, the **cause of action** would have been clear to the **plaintiff**. See *Canada (Attorney-General) v. Lameman*, 2008 SCC 14.

DISCOVERY A modern pre-trial procedure by which one **party** gains vital information held by the **adverse party** concerning the case; the disclosure by the adverse party of facts, deeds, documents and other such things that are exclusively within his or her knowledge or possession and that are necessary to the other party's defence. See, e.g., *Nova Scotia Civil Procedure Rules*, r. 18 [examination for discovery]. Compare *Magna v. R.* (1978), 40 C.R. (N.S.) 1 (Que.S.C.). See **depositions**; **interrogatories**.

DISCRETE AND INSULAR MINORITIES A term used in the context of human rights cases to describe a social group which has suffered from political, historical or legal disadvantage and is vulnerable to **discrimination**. *R. v. Turpin*, [1989] 1 S.C.R. 1296.

DISCRETION The reasonable exercise of a power or right to act in a judicial capacity. Discretion involves the idea of choice, so that **abuse of discretion** includes more than a difference in judicial opinion between the **trial** and **appellate courts**; in order to constitute an abuse of discretion, the **judgment** must demonstrate a perversity of will, a defiance of good judgment, or bias. "[T]here is no such thing as an absolute and untrammelled 'discretion' [in public regulation], that is that action can be taken on any ground for any reason that can be suggested to the mind of the administrator; no legislative Act can, without express language, be taken to contemplate an unlimited arbitrary power exercisable for any purpose, however capricious or irrelevant, regardless of the nature or purpose of the statute..... 'Discretion' necessarily implies good faith in discharging public duty." *Roncarelli v. Duplessis,* [1959] S.C.R. 121 at 140. See **prosecutorial discretion**.

JUDICIAL DISCRETION The reasonable use of judicial power, i.e., discretion "exercised according to the rules of law." *Jones v. Murray* (1908), 9 W.L.R. 204 at 205 (Sask., in chambers).

LEGAL DISCRETION The use of one of several equally satisfactory provisions of law.

DISCRIMINATION "Discrimination may be described as a distinction, whether intentional or not, but based on grounds relating to personal characteristics of the individual or group, which has the effect of imposing burdens, obligations, or disadvantages on such individual or group not imposed upon others, or which withholds or limits access to opportunities, benefits, and advantages available to other members of society. Distinctions based on personal characteristics attributed to an individual solely on the basis of association with a group will rarely escape the charge of discrimination, while those based on an individual's merits and capacities will rarely be so classed." *Andrews v. Law Society of British Columbia,* [1989] 1 S.C.R. 143 (S.C.C.). See **formal equality**; **substantive equality**.

"[I]n assessing a claim of discrimination, it can be said that where the discriminatory effect is said to be the perpetuation of disadvantage or prejudice, evidence that goes to establishing a claimant's historical position of disadvantage or to demonstrating existing prejudice against the claimant group, as well as the nature of the interest that is affected, will be considered. Where the claim is that a law is based on stereotyped views of the claimant group, the issue will be whether there is correspondence with the claimants' actual characteristics or circumstances." *Withler v. Canada (Attorney-General),* 2011 SCC 12.

Section 15(1) of the *Canadian Charter of Rights and Freedoms* provides for equality before and under the law, and the right to equal protection and benefit of the law without discrimination. See also *Canadian Bill of Rights,* S.C. 1960, c. 44, reprinted R.S.C. 1985, App. III, s. 1, and the *Canadian Human Rights Act,* R.S.C. 1985, c. H–6, s. 2 (purpose), and ss. 3–25 (proscribed discrimination, and discriminatory practices). A claim of discrimination does not necessarily rest on proof of membership in a particular claimant group. "[I]t is a misconception to require the complainant to demonstrate membership in an identifiable group made up of only those suffering the particular manifestation of the discrimination. It is sufficient that the individual experience differential treatment on the basis of an irrelevant personal characteristic that is enumerated in the grounds provided in the Code." *B. v. Ontario (Human Rights Commission),* 2002 SCC 66.

ADVERSE EFFECTS DISCRIMINATION The imposition of "obligations, penalties or restrictive conditions" resulting from a rule or practice that is "neutral" (i.e., non-discriminatory) on its face and applies equally to all, but that in practice has a negative effect on an individual or group because of an immutable characteristic of that individual or group. The concept of adverse effects discrimination was adopted by the Supreme Court of Canada in *Ontario (Human Rights Commission) and O'Malley v.*

Simpson-Sears Ltd., [1985] 2 S.C.R. 536 at 551. However, the Supreme Court found the distinction between adverse and direct discrimination to be problematic and adopted a unified approach to applying **human rights legislation** to the workplace. See *Re Meiorin*, [1999] 3 S.C.R. 3.

DIRECT DISCRIMINATION A practice or rule that on its face discriminates against an individual or group on a prohibited ground of discrimination— for example, an employer who states that he or she will not hire Catholics (religion), persons with visual impairments (disability), or women (sex). See *Ontario Human Rights Commission v. Borough of Etobicoke*, [1982] 1 S.C.R. 202. See also *Central Alberta Dairy Pool v. Alberta (Human Rights Commission)*, [1990] 2 S.C.R. 489.

SYSTEMIC DISCRIMINATION Discrimination in an employment context resulting from "the application of established practices and policies that in effect, have a negative impact upon the hiring and advancement prospects of a particular group. It is compounded by attitudes of managers and coworkers who accept stereotyped visions of the skills and 'proper role' of the affected group, visions which lead to the firmly held conviction that members of that group are incapable of doing a particular job, even when that conclusion is objectively false." *Action Travail des Femmes v. Canadian National Railway Co.*, [1987] 1 S.C.R. 1114 at 1143. See R. Abella, *Report of the Commission on Equality in Employment* (Ottawa: Minister of Supply and Services Canada, 1984).

In the **administrative law** context, the term "discriminate" is sometimes used "in the nonpejorative but most neutral sense of the word" simply to refer to drawing a distinction. If an administrative body is not authorized to draw a particular distinction, then laws or regulations can be "rendered invalid even though the distinction on which they are based is perfectly rational or reasonable in the narrow or political sense, and was conceived and imposed in good

faith, without favouritism or malice." *Montréal v. Arcade Amusements Inc.*, [1985] 1 S.C.R. 368.

DISEASE OF THE MIND See **mental disorder**.

DISHONOUR To refuse to make payment on a **negotiable instrument** when such an instrument is duly presented for payment See *Bills of Exchange Act*, R.S.C. c. B–4, ss. 80–81; 94; 95–107. When a bank, for example, refuses to pay a cheque that has been presented to it for payment, it may do so because there are not adequate funds in the **drawer's** account to "cover" the cheque, or it may do so for other reasons. When such an instrument is dishonoured, for whatever reason, the holder may pursue his or her **remedies** against either the principal party [drawer or **maker**] or any subsequent **endorser**. See *id.*, s. 82.

DISINHERITANCE The act by the **donor** that dissolves the right of a person to **inherit** the **property** to which he or she previously had such a right; the act of terminating another's right to inherit.

DISJUNCTIVE ALLEGATIONS Charges that the **defendant** did one thing or another. Whenever the word *or* would leave the **averment** uncertain as to which of two or more things is meant, it is inadmissible. An **allegation** that charges the commission of a **crime** by one act "or" another is **defective** if it does not sufficiently and clearly inform the defendant of the charge against him or her so that he or she can prepare a **defence**. The same standard is applied to **pleadings** in **civil** cases, where both disjunctive allegations and disjunctive denials generally constitute defective pleadings and are therefore inadmissible. Compare **alternative pleading**; **denial**. See also **negative pregnant**.

DISMISS In a legal context, to remove a case from court; to terminate a case before **trial** or without a complete trial. See **demurrer**. Compare **summary judgment**.

DISMISSAL A cancellation. Dismissal of a motion is a denial of the motion. Dismissal of an **appeal** places the parties in the same condition as if no appeal had been taken or allowed, and is thus a confirmation of the judgment of the lower court. Compare **summary judgment**.

DISMISSAL WITH PREJUDICE Usually an **adjudication** upon the **merits** that operates as a **bar** to future action. See **res judicata**.

DISMISSAL WITHOUT PREJUDICE Usually an indication that the dismissal affects no right or **remedy** of the parties, i.e., is not **on the merits** and does not bar a subsequent **suit** on the same **cause of action**. See **collateral**; **estoppel**; **res judicata**.

DISORDERLY HOUSE Refers to a **common bawdy house**, a **common betting house**, or a **common gaming house**.

DISPARAGEMENT See **bait and switch**.

DISPOSITION 1. The giving up or the relinquishment of anything; often used in reference to a testamentary **proceeding**, e.g., "the disposition of the estate"; **satisfaction** of a debt. See also **bequeath**. **2.** Courts and other decision-makers are said to "dispose" of **cases** by finally determining them, and so a **decision** is sometimes referred to as a disposition.

DISPUTABLE PRESUMPTION See **presumption** [REBUTTABLE PRESUMPTION].

DISSEISIN The act of wrongfully depriving a person of **seisin** of land; the taking possession of land under claim or **colour of title**.

DISSENT To differ in opinion; to disagree; to be of contrary sentiment. The most common usage is in a situation where a judge's **opinion** of the **case** differs from that of the majority of the court and the "dissenting judge" writes a judgment disagreeing with the result. A dissenting opinion should be distinguished from a **concurring opinion** (or minority opinion), in which a judge agrees with the result in the majority judgment but for different reasons. Compare **concur**.

DISSENTING OPINION See **opinion**.

DISSIPATE To dispose of funds or assets foolishly, often with some **intent** to avoid having the assets available at a later date

when they might need to be shared under **matrimonial property** legislation or used to satisfy a **judgment**.

DISSOLUTION OF PARLIAMENT The bringing to a close of a session of Parliament. A dissolution is granted by the **Governor-General**, but he or she will only do so at the advice of the Prime Minister, who has the sole authority to make such a request. A dissolution is generally only requested before a general election. Compare **prorogation**.

DISTRIBUTION The division of property of an **intestate** among the next of kin. See **intestate succession**.

DISTRIBUTION OF POWERS See **division of powers**.

DISTRICT COURT "[A]n inferior court created by statute [which] possesses only that **jurisdiction** expressly conferred by the Act." W. Williston & R. Rolls, *The Law of Civil Procedure* 56–57 (1970). There are no longer any district courts in Canada. R. Salhany, *Canadian Criminal Procedure* c. 1 at 3 (6th ed. 1994).

DISTURBANCE OF THE PEACE "[S]omething more than mere emotional upset. There must be an externally manifested disturbance of the public peace, in the sense of interference with the ordinary and customary use of the premises by the public." *R. v. Lohnes*, [1992] 1 S.C.R. 167.

DIVERS Many, several, sundry; a grouping of unspecified persons, things, acts, etc.

DIVESTITURE A statutory remedy, by virtue of which the court orders an offending party to rid itself of property or assets gained by wrongful conduct. Compare **restitution**.

DIVIDEND "[A] sum of money from the corporate net earnings that is divided and distributed to a class of shareholders." *Metz v. Metz*, 2004 ABQB 528. See J.A. VanDuzer, *The Law of Partnerships and Corporations* 231–35 (3rd ed. 2009).

CUMULATIVE DIVIDEND A dividend with regard to which it is agreed that if at any time it is not paid in full, the difference shall be added to the following payment.

LIQUIDATION DIVIDEND A dividend resulting from **winding up** the affairs of a firm or **corporation**, settling with its **creditors** and **debtors**, and appropriating and distributing to its shareholders a residue proportionate to the profit and loss.

PREFERRED DIVIDEND A dividend paid to one class of stockholders in priority to that to be paid to another class.

STOCK DIVIDEND A dividend paid not in cash, but in stock so that each stockholder obtains a greater absolute number of shares but the same relative number of shares. See *Hosmer v. Royal Trust Co.,* [1953] R.L. 502 (Que.S.C.).

DIVISIBLE CONTRACT See **severable contract**.

DIVISION OF POWERS The allocation of **jurisdiction** over different matters between the **federal** and **provincial** governments under the **Constitution**, specifically in ss. 91 and 92 of the **Constitution Act, 1867**. Some matters, such as authority over the postal service, banking, or criminal law are assigned to the federal government, while others, such as hospitals, local works, and undertakings or the administration of justice in the province are assigned to the provinces. See P. W. Hogg, *Constitutional Law of* Canada, 5–15–17 (5th ed. 2007). See **constitution**; **pith and substance**; **double aspect doctrine**; **federalism**; **incidental effect**; **interjurisdictional immunity**; **intra vires**; **ultra vires**.

DIVORCE The dissolution of a valid marriage. Proceedings commence with the filing of a **petition**, in a prescribed form, which sets out the facts on which the petitioner relies as proof of the grounds for divorce, and which concludes with a request that the marriage be dissolved. See *Divorce Act,* R.S.C. 1985 c. 3 (2nd supp.).

DOCKET 1. A list of cases on a court calendar; **2.** a summary or list of court decisions.

DOCUMENT Any material substance on which the thoughts of people are represented by writing, or any other species of conventional mark or symbol. A photograph of a deceased person is a document subject to production [for the purposes of discovery]. *Fox v. Sleeman* (1897), 17 P.R. 492 at 494 (C.A.).

A tape recording may be regarded as a document for the purposes of discovery and, where relevant to the issues, it is proper on oral examination to require the plaintiff to listen to the tape and answer questions as to the identity of voices. *Mouammar v. Bruner* (1977), 17 O.R. (2d) 526 (S.C.). The term "document" also includes electronically stored information. *R. v. Vu,* 2011 BCCA 536.

DOCTRINE OF WORTHIER TITLE See **worthier title, doctrine of**.

DOMAIN 1. Absolute ownership of land. **2.** Land of which one is absolute owner. See also **eminent domain**; **public domain**.

DOMAIN NAME The unique identifier for an address on the **Internet**. "A domain name has two parts. The first part is the Internet Protocol (IP) number, or the numerical technical layer used to make communication between computers possible. IP numbers are allocated through regional internet registries and are independent of individual users. The second part of the domain name is the distinctive readable address in Uniform Resource Locators (URLs) and is what we usually think of as a domain name. Both parts are functionally necessary. An Internet user wishing to access a web page does so by entering the domain name URL into a browser or software program used for viewing information on the Internet, and the underlying corresponding IP numbers take a person to that web page." *Tucows.com Co. v. Lojas Renner S.A.,* 2011 ONCA 548.

DOMESDAY BOOK A record made in the time of William the Conqueror (1081–1086) consisting of accurate and detailed surveys of the lands in England and the means by which the alleged owners obtained title. See 2 Bl.Comm. (original pagination) 49.

DOMESTIC CONTRACT See **marriage contract**.

DOMESTIC PARTNER (DOMESTIC PARTNERSHIP) A term which principally refers to an individual who is a party to a registered domestic partnership declaration made in accordance with provincial law. It may apply to both opposite-sex and same-sex common-law relationships. For example, in Nova Scotia upon registration of a domestic partnership declaration, domestic partners, as between themselves and with respect to any person, have as of the date of registration the same rights and obligations as a "spouse" under many provincial statutes dealing with a vast array of subjects including **insurance**, **wills**, **intestate succession**, **matrimonial property**, pensions, **workers' compensation**, etc.. See the *Vital Statistics Act*, R.S.N.S. 1989, c. 494 (as am.), Part II Domestic Partners. See **spouse**.

DOMICILE The place of a person's permanent residence, even while he or she is temporarily living elsewhere. "A person has one domicile at any point in their life, no matter what their circumstances or actions. That domicile may change from time to time, but there is always only one domicile for a person. A new domicile 'displaces' an older domicile. The circumstances into which one is born (generally, parental domicile) dictate a person's first domicile, which is known as a 'domicile of origin.' Other domiciles are ones in which a person has chosen to live and are called 'domiciles of choice.'" *David v. Foote Estate*, 2009 ABQB 654. The location of a person's domicile has numerous legal implications. For example, at common law, the essential validity of a **marriage** is dependent on the law of the spouses' domicile. S.G.A. Pitel & N.S. Rafferty, *Conflict of Laws* 386 (2010).

DOMINANT ESTATE [TENEMENT] An estate whose owners are entitled to the **beneficial use** of another's property; **property** retained by an original grantor when a particular tract is subdivided and a portion is **conveyed**, and to which certain rights or benefits are legally owed by the conveyed or **servient estate**. These rights and benefits may be in the nature of an **easement**, so that the owner of the retained land (dominant estate) is said to have a right of easement in the servient estate.

DONATIO (*dō-nä'-shē-ō*) Lat.: a **gift**; donation.

DONATIO MORTIS CAUSA See **gift**.

DONATIVE INTENT Voluntary intent on the part of the **donor** to make a **gift**.

DONEE The recipient of a **gift**, **trust**, power, right, or interest; one who takes without first giving **consideration**. See, e.g., *Wurtele Estate v. M.N.R.,* [1963] C.T.C. 167 at 173 (Ex.Ct.). Compare bailee; **trustee**.

DONOR One who gives or makes a **gift**; a creator of a **trust**; a party conferring a power, e.g., the **grantor** of a **power of appointment**.

DOUBLE ASPECT DOCTRINE In **division of powers** analysis, the acknowledgment that "some matters are, by their very nature, impossible to categorize under a single head of power: they may have both **provincial** and **federal** aspects. Thus, the fact that a matter may, for one purpose and in one aspect, fall within federal **jurisdiction** does not mean that it cannot, for another purpose and in another aspect, fall within provincial competence." *Canadian Western Bank v. Alberta*, 2007 SCC 22. See **pith and substance**.

DOUBLE CRIMINALITY The requirement in **extradition** that the behaviour for which extradition is sought violates the law of both the requesting **state** and the state from which extradition is requested.

DOUBLE JEOPARDY A "general principal of common law that no person is to be placed twice in jeopardy for the same or substantially the same cause. Thus, if prosecuted again, the accused can plead his former **conviction** [AUTREFOIS CONVICT] or **acquittal** [AUTREFOIS ACQUIT] as a complete defence to this second charge.... [T]he former conviction [must have been] entered or acquittal...granted by a court with the proper jurisdiction to do so.... To succeed on the **defence** of **autrefois acquit** or **autrefois convict**, the accused must establish two things: the first is that there was a final verdict on the first charge; the second is that the 'matter' in both charges is the same in whole or in part and the charge before the court is the same, or implicitly included in the earlier charge, either in law or on the evidence presented if it had been legally possible at the time to make the nec-essary amendments." R. Salhany, *Canadian Criminal Procedure* c. 6 at 57–8 (6th ed. 1994). The special pleas autrefois acquit and autrefois convict are based on this principle. See *Criminal Code,* R.S.C. 1985, c. C–46, ss. 607–610. See, e.g., *R. v. Feeley, McDermott & Wright,* [1963] 1 C.C.C. 254 (Ont.C.A.); *R. v. Prince,* [1986] 2 S.C.R. 480. Compare **issue estoppel**; **res judicata, Kienapple principle**.

Section 11(*h*) of the **Canadian Charter of Rights and Freedoms** provides that any person finally acquitted of an offence, has the right not to be tried for it again, and, if found guilty of an offence and punished, not to be tried and punished for it again. *R. v. Wigglesworth,* [1987] 2 S.C.R. 541.

DOWER At **common law**, the right of a wife on surviving her husband to a life **estate** in one-third of the **freehold estates** of **inheritance** of which her deceased husband was solely **seised** at any time during the marriage and which her issue by him might possibly have inherited. 2 Bl.Comm. 131. Dower was the estate that a wife had for her life in certain freehold estates of her deceased husband. Until his death, her right was said to be INCHOATE. *Allan v. Rever* (1902), 4 O.L.R. 309 (K.B.). During the lifetime of her husband, a wife nevertheless had an interest in all his **real property**, and that interest could not be **alienated** or interfered with by the husband without the wife's consent. *Freedman v. Mason* (1956), 4 D.L.R. (2d) 576 (Ont.H.C.) B. Ziff, *Principles of Property Law* 189–90 (5th ed. 2010). However, legislation serves a similar purpose; see, e.g., *Dower Act,* R.S.A. 2000, c. D–15 and *Karafiat v. Webb,* 2012 ABCA 115. Compare

curtesy. Dower has been abrogated or abolished in most Canadian jurisdictions. See **family property**; **homestead legislation**.

DOWRY Money and **personalty** the wife brings to the husband to support the expenses of marriage; a donation to the maintenance and support of the marriage.

DRA A Digital Recording Ammeter. "A DRA is a small electrical meter that measures electrical power flowing into a residence in one-ampere increments. It is installed by the utility company, usually for an average of five days. After this period, a graph is produced by the utility company, showing electricity usage. Because marijuana is typically grown in 12- and 18-hour light cycles, patterns indicating such cyclical, high usage of electricity are often indicative of a marijuana **grow operation** within the home." *R. v. Gomboc,* 2010 SCC 55. The nature of the information gathered by a DRA infringes a person's **reasonable expectation of privacy**. *Id.*

DRAFT 1. An order in writing directing a person other than the **maker** to pay a specified sum of money to a named person; see **bill of exchange**. Drafts may or may not be **negotiable instruments** depending upon whether the elements of negotiability are satisfied. **2.** The preliminary form of a legal document (e.g., the draft of a contract—often called a "rough draft"). **3.** The process of preparing or DRAWING a legal document (e.g., drafting a will) or piece of proposed legislation. **4.** In a military context, the conscription of citizens into the military service.

DRAWEE One to whom a **bill of exchange** or a **cheque** directs a request to pay a certain sum of money specified therein. In the typical chequing account situation, the bank is the drawee, the person writing the cheque is the **maker** or **drawer**, and the person to whom the cheque is written is the PAYEE.

DRAWER A person by whom a **cheque** or **bill of exchange** is drawn.

DRM Digital Rights Management. Technology incorporated by manufacturers and publishers into products to limit the available uses of those products after sale, in order to protect **intellectual property** rights.

DROIT (*drwä*) Fr.: a right. Law; the whole body of the law.

DRUG TREATMENT COURT A specialized court intended to provide an alternative forum for the prosecution of substance abusers accused of non-violent offences linked to their addictions. As with the **mental health court** system, drug treatment courts emphasize therapy for abusers rather than punitive responses to their offences, such as incarceration.

DUCES TECUM See **subpoena** [SUBPOENA DUCES TECUM].

DUE CARE See **duty** [DUTY OF CARE].

DUE DATE The time fixed for payment of a debt, tax, interest, etc.

DUE DILIGENCE The degree of prudence and carefulness that would be exercised by a **reasonable person** in similar circumstances. Due diligence operates as a defence to **strict liability** offences. It allows the accused to prove on a balance of probabilities that he or she exercised reasonable care and was not negligent. *R. v. Sault Ste. Marie* (1978), 40 C.C.C. (2d) 353 (S.C.C.). See also *R. v. Wholesale Travel Group Inc.*, [1991] 3 S.C.R. 154.

DUE PROCESS OF LAW The **Canadian Bill of Rights**, s. 1, provides that the individual has a right not to be deprived of life, liberty, security of the person, or enjoyment of property, except by due process of law. 28 Edw. III, c. 3 (1354) made it clear that no person should be harmed in any way "except" by due process of law. The phrase made its way into American jurisprudence by way of the Fifth Amendment to the United States Constitution.

The Supreme Court of Canada avoided defining the phrase for some time after its enactment. The Alberta Appellate Division in *R. v. Martin* (1961), 35 C.R. 276, felt that "due process of law" meant "the law of the land as applied to all the rights and privileges of every person in Canada when suspected of or charged with a crime [in the case at bar]." In *Curr v. The Queen*, [1972] S.C.R. 889,

the Supreme Court of Canada rejected the notion of "substantive due process" as being implied in the Canadian legislation and said that the main intent of the subsection was to govern procedure. Laskin, J., felt that it was difficult to see what more could be read into s. I(*a*) (from a procedural standpoint) than was already comprehended by ss. 2(*e*) and (*f*)—a "fair hearing in accordance with the principles of fundamental justice and a fair and public hearing by an independent and impartial tribunal."

The phrase was adopted in s. 7 of the **Canadian Charter of Rights and Freedoms**, which guarantees that:

7. Everyone has the right to life, liberty, and security of the person and the right not to be deprived thereof except in accordance with the principles of fundamental justice.

In the context of the *Charter,* the Supreme Court of Canada defined the phrase "**principles of fundamental justice**" to refer to both procedural and substantive matters. Lamer, J., stated "the principles of fundamental justice are to be found in the basic tenets and principles, not only of our judicial process, but also of the other components of our legal system." *Reference re Section 94(2) of the Motor Vehicle Act* (1985), 48 C.R. (3d) 289 at 317 (S.C.C.).

DUPLICITOUS The adjective applied to a **pleading** open to objection for **duplicity**.

DUPLICITY An objection to a **pleading** that has more than one **claim**, **charge**, or **defence** contained in it. "In *R. v. City of Sault Ste. Marie*, [1978] 2 S.C.R. 1299, Dickson J. (as he then was) established the criteria for finding that an Information is defective because of duplicity, namely: '[D]oes the accused know the case he has to meet, or is he prejudiced in the preparation of his defence by ambiguity in the charge?'" *R. v. Katigbak*, 2011 SCC 48. See also **joinder; misjoinder**.

DURABLE POWER OF ATTORNEY See **power of attorney**.

DURABLE POWER OF ATTORNEY FOR HEALTH CARE See **living will; power of attorney**.

DURESS An action by a person that compels another to do what he or she need not otherwise do. It is a **defence** to any act, such as a **crime**, **tort**, or **breach of contract**, that must be voluntary in order to create **liability** in the actor.

In criminal law, duress is a defence to a crime and exists in both a statutory and a common law form. "The defence of duress, in its statutory and common law forms, is largely the same. The two forms share the following common elements:

There must be an explicit or implicit threat of present or future death or bodily harm. This threat can be directed at the accused or a third party.

The accused must reasonably believe that the threat will be carried out.

There is no safe avenue of escape. This element is evaluated on a modified objective standard.

A close temporal connection between the threat and the harm threatened.

Proportionality between the harm threatened and the harm inflicted by the accused. The harm caused by the accused must be equal to or no greater than the harm threatened. This is also evaluated on a modified objective standard.

The accused is not a party to a conspiracy or association whereby the accused is subject to compulsion and actually knew that threats and coercion to commit an offence were a possible result of this criminal activity, conspiracy, or association." *R. v. Ryan*, 2013 SCC 3.

The statutory defence of duress is contained in s. 17 of the *Criminal Code*, R.S.C. 1985, c. C–46 where it is referred to as COMPULSION. The **principal** to an offence is required to rely on the statutory defence of duress, while a **party** will rely on the common law defence. The primary difference between the statutory and common law versions is that "the statutory version of the defence has a lengthy list of exclusions, whereas it is unclear in the Canadian common law of duress whether any offences are excluded." There is some question as to whether the existence of the statutory exclusions might violate the *Charter*, particularly as the defence is based on the notion of **moral involuntariness**, which is a **principle of fundamental justice**. *Id.*

Duress will similarly provide a vitiating factor in contractual relations, provided that the threats are unlawful. Where however, the threat is of a criminal prosecution that would be well-founded, it is not destructive of the contract so long as there is adequate consideration and no agreement to stifle the prosecution. *Bank of Montreal v. Dresler*, 2003 NBQB 17.

DUTY 1. An obligation imposed by law to do or refrain from doing an act. **2.** In **tort** law, a legally sanctioned obligation the **breach** of which results in the **liability** of the person owing the duty. See **due care. 3.** In tax law, a levy or tax on imports and exports.

DUTY OF CARE A concept used in **tort** law to indicate the standard of **legal duty** one owes to others. **Negligence** is the failure to use due care, which is the amount of care that would be taken by a **reasonable person** in the circumstances. See *R. v. Coté* (1974), 51 D.L.R. (3d) 244 at 252 (S.C.C.). "The duty of care...is confined to reasonably foreseeable dangers, the broad general test being...whether a reasonable person should have anticipated that what happened might be a natural result of that act or omission." *University Hospital Bd. v. Lepine*, [1966] S.C.R. 561 at 579. See **neighbor principle**; **Anns test**.

STATUTORY DUTY A duty imposed by statute.

DUTY OF ADDUCING EVIDENCE See **burden of proof**.

DUTY OF CARE Part of the test for whether a person is liable to another for the **tort** of **negligence**. "The test for determining whether a person owes a duty of care involves two questions: (1) Does the relationship between the plaintiff and the defendant disclose sufficient foreseeability and proximity to establish a *prima facie* duty of care; and (2) If so, are there any residual policy considerations that ought to negate or limit that duty of care?" *Hill v. Hamilton-Went-*

worth Regional Police Services Board, 2007 SCC 41. See **pure economic loss**; **standard of care**.

DUTY OF FAIR REPRESENTATION The duty on the part of a union to represent the interests of each of its members in a way that is not arbitrary, discriminatory, or in bad faith. *Canada Labour Code*, R.S.C. 1985, c. L–2, s. 37.

DUTY OF LOYALTY A duty owed by a lawyer to a client, to give that client priority. The duty of loyalty engages other duties, including the duty to avoid **conflicts of interest** (including the lawyer's personal interest, the duty of commitment to the client's cause (also referred to as "zealous representation"), and the duty of candour with the client on matters relevant to the retainer. *R. v. Neil*, 2002 SCC 70.

DUTY TO ACCOMMODATE 1. The duty on an employer, as a part of **equality rights** and **human rights** law, to avoid the discriminatory impact of a policy or practice by accommodating difference, to the point of **undue hardship**. Relevant factors include whether there are alternative approaches which do not have a discriminatory effect, whether it is necessary for all employees to meet a single standard for the employer to accomplish its legitimate purpose, and whether there is a way to accomplish that purpose in a less discriminatory way. See *British Columbia (Public Service Employee Relations Commission) v. BCGSEU*, [1999] 3 S.C.R. 3. The duty also arises in other contexts where equality rights or human rights claims arise, such as in making services available to the public (see *Council of Canadians with Disabilities v. VIA Rail Canada Inc.*, 2007 SCC 15). See **bona fide occupational requirement**. **2.** The duty on a government, while discharging the **duty to consult** with Aboriginal peoples, to make provision for Aboriginal and treaty rights. "Where a strong *prima facie* case exists for the claim, and the consequences of the government's proposed decision may adversely affect it in a significant way, addressing the Aboriginal concerns may require taking steps to avoid irreparable harm or to minimize the effects of

infringement, pending final resolution of the underlying claim." *Haida Nation v. British Columbia (Minister of Forests)*, 2004 SCC 73. The duty to accommodate in the Aboriginal rights context does not require accommodation to the point of undue hardship for the non-Aboriginal population. *Beckman v. Little Salmon/ Carmacks First Nation*, 2010 SCC 53.

DUTY TO CONSULT A duty on the part of governments to consult with Aboriginal groups when making decisions that may adversely impact lands and resources to which Aboriginal peoples lay claim. "[T]he duty to consult arises when: (1) the Crown has knowledge, actual or constructive, of potential Aboriginal claims or rights; (2) the Crown proposes conduct or a decision; and (3) that conduct or decision may have an adverse impact on the Aboriginal claims or rights." *Rio Tinto Alcan Inc. v. Carrier Sekani Tribal Council*, 2010 SCC 43. See *Haida Nation v. British Columbia (Minister of Forests)*, 2004 SCC 73. See **duty to accommodate**.

DWELLING HOUSE One's residence or abode; a structure or apartment used as a home or family unit. A motel unit is a dwelling house. *R. v. Henderson*, [1975] 1 W.W.R. 360 (B.C.Prov.Ct.). In a **conveyance** the term may also refer to the surrounding land reasonably necessary to enjoyment of the building. *Olafson v. Melsted* (1939), 3 W.W.R. 375 (B.C.S.C.)

In criminal law, evidence that a person was in or entered a dwelling house without lawful excuse is **prima facie** evidence that he or she intended to commit an **indictable offence** therein. *Criminal Code*, R.S.C. 1985, c. C–46, s. 349(2). The offence of breaking and entering a dwelling house, intending to commit or committing an indictable offence, is more severely punished than the same offence in relation to other buildings. *Id.*, s. 348.

DYING DECLARATIONS See **hearsay rule**.

DYNAMIC ENTRY See **knock and announce rule**.

EARNEST "[S]omething given by the buyer, at the time of contract, and accepted by the seller as indicating the completion of the agreement. To be earnest it must be given outright, by the buyer to the seller, with no hope or intention of being returned." G.H.L. Fridman, *Sale of Goods in Canada* 44–45 (5th ed. 2004).

EASEMENT An interest one has in the land of another, known as a privilege without a profit; an incorporeal **hereditament**. The owner of the dominant **tenement** has the right to compel the owner of the servient tenement to do or refrain from doing something in respect of the dominant tenement.

The characteristics of an easement are (1) there must be a dominant and a servient tenement, (2) an easement must accommodate the dominant tenement, (3) the dominant and servient owners must be different individuals, and (4) to amount to an easement, the right over land must be capable of definition and not be uncertain. *Re Ellenborough Park*, [1956] Ch. 131 (C.A.).

EASEMENTS OF NECESSITY are those without which enjoyment of the land or building would be impossible.

Easements may be created in a number of ways: first, by express **grant**; secondly, by implied grant usually through the notion that a person cannot **derogate** from his or her grant; thirdly, by **prescription**. See also **public easement**; **conservation easement**.

ECONOMIC LOSS, PURE In tort action for negligence, a loss that is not connected to or the result of damage to person or property, but that is entirely financial in nature. Types recognized by the Supreme Court of Canada include:

NEGLIGENT MISREPRESENTATION An untrue, inaccurate, or misleading statement that was made negligently. To be actionable, there must be a duty between the parties based on foreseeable reasonable reliance, the party suffering the loss must have reasonably relied on the statement, and damages must have resulted. See *Hedley Byrne & Co. Ltd. v. Heller & Partners Ltd.*, [1964] A.C. 465 (H.L.); *Queen v. Cognos Inc.*, [1993] 1 S.C.R. 87; *Hercules Managements Ltd. v. Ernest & Young*, [1997] 2 S.C.R. 165. See **misrepresentation**.

NEGLIGENT PERFORMANCE OF A SERVICE Where a defendant undertakes to perform a service upon which the plaintiff relies, only to fail to do so carefully and economic loss results. *Whittingham v. Crease & Co.* (1978), 88 D.L.R. (3d) 353 [beneficiaries of will suing solicitor]; *Fletcher v. Manitoba Public Insurance Co.*, [1990] 3 S.C.R. 191 [insurance agents].

DEFECTIVE PRODUCTS OR BUILDINGS "Deals with claims to recover the cost of repairing or replacing defective products or structures...against the remote manufacturer or builder with whom the plaintiff is not in **privity** of contract." A. Linden & B. Feldthusen, *Canadian Tort Law* 479 (9th ed. 2011). *Winnipeg Condominium v. Bird Construction Co.*, [1995] 1 S.C.R. 131.

RELATIONAL ECONOMIC LOSS The defendant causes injury to a third party, which causes economic loss to the plaintiff who is usually in a contractual relationship with the injured third party. It applies only in special circumstances where the "(1) claimant has a possessory or proprietary right in damaged property; (2) general average cases; and (3) cases where the relationship between the claimant and property owner constitutes a joint venture." *Bow Valley Husky (Bermuda) Ltd. v. Saint John Shipbuilding Ltd.* (1997), 153 D.L.R. (4th) 385 at 406. See also *Canadian National Railway Co. v. Norsk Pacific Steamship Co.* (1992), 91 D.L.R. (4th) 289.

INDEPENDENT LIABILITY OF STATUTORY PUBLIC AUTHORITIES Where a level of government is negligent in its inspections, and the owner sues the authority for cost of repair. *Rothfield v. Manolakos*, [1989] 2 S.C.R. 1259.

See further A. Linden & B. Feldthusen, *Canadian Tort Law* 659–704 (9th ed. 2011).

EDICT A formal declaration, command or proclamation issued by an officer of the court or a public official.

EEZ Exclusive Economic Zone. See **UNCLOS III**.

EFFECTS Refers to a person's personal property, chattels and goods.

E.G. [EXEMPLI GRATIA] (*ĕg-zĕm'-plē grā'-shē-ă*) Lat.: for example.

EGRESS See **ingress and egress**.

EJECTMENT A mixed action combining real and personal **remedies**. It is real in the sense that it is an action for the recovery of land. *Point v. Dibblee Construction Co. Ltd.* [1934] O.R. 142 (S.C.). It is personal in that it also includes an action for damages for wrongful withholding of land.

Originally the action was applicable only to a **leaseholder** wrongfully dispossessed but was extended by way of legal fiction so that it might be used by one entitled to the **freehold**. Such a fiction necessarily developed because of the extremely complex nature of a real action for the recovery of land by the person entitled to the freehold.

The Common Law Procedure Act, 1852, s. 168, abolished this fiction and made the action of ejectment similar to other actions except that it had no **pleadings**. See also **adverse possession**. Compare **eviction**.

EJUSDEM GENERIS RULE (*ĕ-yūs'-dĕm jĕn'-ĕr-ĭs*) Lat.: of the same class. A rule of **construction** of documents, sometimes known as Lord Tenterden's rule. Where general words follow an enumeration of particular persons or things having a specific meaning, the general words are constructed as being limited to all other persons or articles of a like class or nature. Thus, where s. 92(10)(a) of the **Constitution Act, 1867**, refers to "Lines of Steam or other Ships, Railways, Canals, Telegraphs, and other Works and Undertakings," the "other works and undertakings" are limited to those that physically connect one province to another, as do the things specifically enumerated. *Consolidated Fastfrate Inc. v. Western Canada Council of Teamsters*, 2009 SCC 53.

This rule of interpretation is not universal in its application and must give way to the general intent of the enactment or document under consideration. This is true where the specific words exhaust the category or genus and the general words would be meaningless if governed by the rule of *ejusdem generis.*

Of course, the *ejusdem generis* doctrine does not apply where there is no genus or category to which the subsequent general words could be limited. "[P]aragraph 12 of Schedule II, cited above, includes exemptions for 'snow sheds, tunnels, bridges, [and] dams.' I tried in vain to find a common denominator for these terms in this enumeration, especially for snow sheds." *Montréal (City) v. Montréal Port Authority*, 2008 FCA 278.

ELECTION The exercise of choice by an unrestrained will to take or do one thing or another. The obligation conferred upon a person to choose between two inconsistent or alternative rights or claims.

A person charged with having committed an **indictable offence** may elect to be tried by a provincial court judge, a judge alone, or by judge and jury. See *Criminal Code,* R.S.C. 1985, c. C–46, s. 536(2).

An Act relating to the representation of the people is usually defined as the election of a member to serve in **Parliament** or the provincial assemblies. See *Canada Elections Act,* S.C. 2000, c. 9; *Elections Act,* R.S.N.S. 1989, c. 140.

ELECTION OF REMEDIES A choice of **remedies** permitted by law for the enforcement of a right or the redress of a wrong. Where these remedies are inconsistent, in the sense that pursuit of one implies a negation of the other, a person who has unequivocally elected for one remedy and communicated this election to the other party cannot thereafter have the benefit of a different remedy. Alternative remedies may be pleaded but an election need not be made until the time of **judgment**. As well, if a party by his or her actions manifests an **election**, he or she will thereafter be bound by it. *Tracy (Representative ad litem of) v. Instaloans Financial Solutions Centres (B.C.) Ltd.*, 2010 BCCA 357.

ELECTION UNDER THE WILL By the equitable doctrine of **election**, to take a benefit under a will requires conformity to all provisions of the will and renunciation of every right inconsistent with those provisions. One cannot approbate and reprobate. *Rosborough v. Trustees of St. Andrews Church* (1917), 55 S.C.R. 360. Thus, if a **testator devises** *A*'s property to *B* as well as devising his or her own property to *A*, then *A* is put to an election. He or she can accept the legacy only if he or she gives his or her own property or its value to *B*. Otherwise he or she may reject the **gift** and keep his or her own property.

Similarly, when a testamentary **beneficiary** is left two inconsistent claims to benefits (e.g., a devise or **bequest** under a will and a statutory claim under the *Family Property Act*, C.C.S.M. c. F25 or similar legislation), the beneficiary must choose between the two claims and relinquish one.

ELECTIVE FRANCHISE See **franchise**.

ELECTRONIC COMMERCE The buying, selling, and exchanging of goods, services, and information using electronic media. The law of **contract** will generally apply to electronic commerce transactions, unless specifically amended by statutory authority (for example, consumer protection **legislation**).

ELECTRONIC SIGNATURE "[I]nformation in electronic form that a person has created or adopted in order to sign a document and that is in, attached to, or associated with the document." *Electronic Commerce Act*, S.N.S. 2000, c. 26, s. 2(b). Every Canadian province and territory has enacted electronic commerce legislation that recognizes electronic signatures as functionally equivalent to written signatures in the formation of contracts. See, e.g., *Electronic Commerce Act, 2000*, S.O. 2000, c. 17; *Electronic Transactions Act*, R.S.A. 2000, c. E–5.5; *Electronic Transactions Act*, S.N.W.T. 2011, c. 13.

ELECTRONIC SURVEILLANCE Covertly observing or listening to persons for the purpose of police investigations with the aid of electronic devices like microphones, wiretaps, or cameras. Various forms of electronic surveillance may be authorized by judges under the *Criminal Code*. See, e.g., *Criminal Code*, R.S.C. 1985, c. C–46, s. 186.

ELEGIT Lat.: he has chosen. A **writ** of **execution** exercised by a **creditor** in which he or she is given the debtor's land to hold until such time as the **debt** is satisfied.

EMANCIPATION The process of freeing someone from the control of another; derived from the Roman Law doctrine of emancipation, which was concerned with the act by which a father relinquished control over his child so that the child became **sui juris**. Such a child is sometimes referred to as an EMANCIPATED MINOR.

Emancipation has never been judicially defined with any precision. It occurs where there ceases to be the exceptional influence of parent over child and is a **question of fact** to be decided on the circumstances of every case. *Lancashire Loans Ltd. v. Black*, [1934] 1 K.B. 380 (C.A.).

EMBARRASSING PLEA A pleading that is irrelevant, would involve useless expense, and would prejudice the trial by raising a dispute that is wholly apart from the issues. The irrelevancy must be apparent at first glance. An embarrassing pleading is an abuse of process. See *Patym Holdings Ltd. v. Michalakis*, 2005 BCCA 636.

EMBEZZLEMENT The fraudulent appropriation to the use of a servant or agent of property received by him or her in the name of his or her employer or principal. *Canadian Surety Co. v. Quebec Insurance Agencies Ltd.,* [1936] S.C.R. 281.

There is no crime in the *Criminal Code* known as embezzlement nor was it a crime at common law. It was first made a crime in England by the Statute 21 Hen. VIII, c. 7, which is not in force in Canada. *Canadian Surety Co. v. Doucett* (1936), 10 M.P.R. 403 (N.B.S.C.A.D.). Embezzlement in Canada is included under the definition of **theft**. Compare **defalcation**; **misapplication [misappropriation] of property**.

EMBLEMENTS Crops produced annually through agricultural labour.

EMBRACERY Originally, a **common-law misdemeanour** committed by a person who by any means whatever, except the production of **evidence** and presentation of agreement in open court, attempted to influence a **juror**. The offence exists in Canada through s. 139(3) of the *Criminal Code,* R.S.C. 1985, c. C–46, in essentially its common-law form.

EMINENT DOMAIN The right of the government to take private property for public purposes or for the common good. The doctrine is unknown to the common law, and the term is of American origin. However, it has been given statutory effect in Canada. Compare **public domain**.

EMOLUMENT A profit or advantage; that is, anything by which a person is benefited. Consequently, the term is wider than mere remuneration.

EMPANELLING [IMPANELLING] 1. The process by which **jurors** are selected and sworn in. **2.** The listing of those selected to serve on a particular **jury**. A potential juror is empanelled when called unless either counsel challenges. See *Criminal Code,* R.S.C. 1985, c. C–46, ss. 631-644.

EMPLOYMENT EQUITY Measures taken to achieve equality in the workplace in order to accommodate differences and to prevent employment practices that create unfair or unequal employment opportunities for those protected by **human rights legislation**.

EMPLOYMENT LAW That area of law dealing with the relationship between employers and employees in a non-unionized setting, including reason-able notice or termination, **constructive dismissal**, and other areas. See **labour law**.

EMPTOR Lat.: a buyer or purchaser. See **caveat emptor**.

ENABLING STATUTE A piece of **legislation** granting powers from the legislative branch of government to another public authority, such as an **administrative** body. See, e.g., *Canadian Human Rights Act*, R.S.C. 1985, c. H–6.

ENACTING CLAUSE Generally, the preamble of a **statute**, or the part that identifies the statute as a legislative act and authorizes it as law.

ENACTMENT The process of being enacted; something that has been enacted. Refers to all **statutes** but may equally well be used to describe a particular provision in a statute. Enactment does not mean the same thing as **"Act."** "Act" means the whole Act, whereas a section or part of a section in an Act may be an enactment. Refer to *Interpretation Act,* R.S.C. 1985, c. I–21.

EN BANC (*än bänk*) Fr.: By the full [bench of a] court. In English law, the term usually referred to the sittings of judges of a superior court sitting as a full court, as distinguished from the sittings of individual judges at **nisi prius** or on circuit. In the Canadian context, a supreme court sitting **in banco** [en banc] might refer to three or more judges sitting together on an appeal.

ENCLOSURE Land enclosed by something more than an imaginary boundary line—e.g., a wall, hedge, ditch, fence or other actual obstruction. Compare **close**.

ENCROACH To make gradual inroads on; to trench usurpingly on the property, rights or authority of another; to intrude beyond the natural or conventional limits—for example, a clause in a **trust settlement** that allows the **trustee** to "encroach" upon the **capital** sum in set circumstances.

ENCROACHMENT The unauthorized extension by a person of a right possessed by him or her. The term is usually used in reference to land such as where an owner of land takes in or adds to it other land adjoining or near to it so that it appears that the added land is part of the original holding. Similarly, with regard to **easements**, where the owner of the **dominant tenement** does something in relation to his or her land that places a further burden or restriction on the **servient tenement**, he or she is said to commit an encroachment. *Merner v. D'Hollander*, 2011 BCSC 1733.

ENCUMBRANCE A **claim**, **lien**, or **liability** that is attached to **property**. *Beaument Estate v. M.N.R.,* [1968] C.T.C. 558 (Ex.). In essence, the term means that a legal or equitable **estate** has had a burden or charge placed upon it by the owner or another interested party. See, e.g., *Ontrea Inc. v. British Columbia*, 2009 BCCA 101. *Encumbrance* includes **mortgages** and other voluntary **charges** as well as liens, registered **judgments**, and **lites pendentes**.

ENDORSE Generally, to sign the back of the **document**. It is not essential to the validity of an endorsement of a **bill of exchange** or **promissory note**, however, that the endorsement be on the back of the document; it may equally well be on the face. *Endorse* is equivalent to *sign*.

ENDOWMENT **1.** Properly, this signifies the giving or assigning of **dower** to a woman. **2.** More usually, it pertains to a permanent fund of **property** or money bestowed on a person, charity, or institution, the income from which is used to support the specific purpose for which the endowment was originally set up. For example, an endowment may be bestowed on a college for the support of that institution.

ENDURING POWER OF ATTORNEY See **power of attorney**.

ENFEOFF To create a **feoffment**, which was an early common-law method of **conveying freehold estates**.

ENFEOFFMENT The act of investing with any dignity or possession; also, the **instrument** or **deed** by which a person is invested with **possessions**.

ENFORCEMENT JURISDICTION The ability of a state to give effect to its laws. "Enforcement jurisdiction is the power to use coercive means to ensure that rules are followed, commands are executed, or entitlements are upheld." *R. v. Hape*, 2007 SCC 26. See **prescriptive jurisdiction**.

ENFRANCHISE To set free. Now chiefly used to signify the admittance to political rights and, most importantly, the right to vote at elections.

ENJOIN To command or instruct with authority; to abate, suspend, or restrain. To prohibit or restrain from doing a specific act by way of an **injunction** issued by a court with equitable **jurisdiction**.

ENJOY[MENT] The taking of the benefit of some **right**.

ENTAIL To convert into a **fee tail**. To settle land on a number of persons in **succession** so that it cannot be dealt with by any one possessor as absolute owner of a **fee simple**. Originally, in England a device by which the family estate was maintained within a strict lineal descent and could not be alienated.

Creation of an **estate** tail was accomplished by **conveyance** to a man and "the heirs of his body." These words of limitation gave what was originally known as a fee simple conditional (see **conditional fee**) and later as a fee tail. The **condition** was that, if the line of heirs ceased, the land would revert to the original owner or his estate. The effect was to tie up land indeterminably. Therefore, the judiciary began to view the condition as fulfilled if **issue** were born and the estate became a fee simple absolute. The landowners in 1235 forced the passage of the statute *De Donis Conditionalibus*. Following passage of this enactment, a person who had been granted a fee simple conditional was forbidden from conveying a fee simple absolute. This was enforced by the **reversioner**, who was given certain **remedies**. Thus, the **donee** could not alienate the land; it could only pass to his issue.

Eventually, fictitious proceedings known as FRISE [dispossession by force] and **recoveries** were developed to **bar** estates tail so that the estate of a tenant in tail could be converted into a fee simple absolute against both the donee's issue and the reversioner in tail. By the *Fines and Recoveries Act, 1833,* a tenant in tail was able to bar the entail against his own issue and against the reversioner if he had the consent of the protector of the settlement.

A general entail exists where the gift is to *A* and the "heirs of his body." A specific entail exists where the "heirs of body" must be by a certain wife or some other specific condition. The gift can be further limited by the restriction that the property goes to *A* and the male heirs of his body. If the restriction is to the female heirs, then a female entail is created.

Legislative changes have "led to the demise of the fee tail in Canada; now only (at most) traces remain." B. Ziff, *Principles of Property Law* 174 (5th ed. 2010).

ENTICEMENT The action of enticement developed in the eighteenth century out of the action of **trespass** *per quod consortuim amisit,* which here itself did not apply because of the wife's complicity. The **tort** consists of deliberately inducing a wife to leave her husband with a knowledge of her marital status and with intent to interfere with the spouses' mutual duty to give **consortium**. Originally, a reciprocal action by the wife was not possible. However, developments in some common-law countries have resulted in the wife's being allowed to bring an action for enticement. *Wener v. Davidson* (1970), 15 D.L.R. (3d) 631 (Alta.S.C.). On the other hand, the action has been abolished altogether in England and in South Australia. Enticement has been abolished in British Columbia, Manitoba, Saskatchewan, Ontario, and Newfoundland & Labrador. G.H.L. Fridman, *The Law of Torts in Canada* 693 (3rd ed. 2010). See, e.g., *Family Relations Act,* R.S.B.C. 1996, c. 128, s. 123.

ENTIRETY See **tenancy** [TENANCY THE ENTIRETY].

ENTRAPMENT A common-law **defence** to a criminal charge. "The defence is available when (a) the authorities provide a person with an opportunity to commit an offence without acting on a reasonable suspicion that this person is already engaged in criminal activity or pursuant to a bona fide inquiry; (b) although having such a reasonable suspicion or acting in the course of a bona fide inquiry, they go beyond providing the opportunity and induce the commission of an offence." *R v. Barnes* (1991), 63 C.C.C. (3d) 1 (S.C.C.). See also *R. v. Mack* (1988), 44 C.C.C. (3d) 513 (S.C.C.).

ENTRY, FORCIBLE See **forcible entry**.

ENUMERATED GROUND A basis upon which an equality rights claim can be brought under the **Canadian Charter of Rights and Freedoms**, which is specifically listed in section 15(1): race, national or ethnic origin, colour, religion, sex, age, or mental or physical disability. See **analogous ground**.

ENURE See **inure**.

EN VENTRE SA MERE (*än vän'-tr sà mär*) Fr.: in his mother's womb. A descriptive phrase used to indicate an unborn child. Such a child is capable of receiving property under a will, (*Re Burrows, Cleghorn v. Burrows,* [1895] 2 Ch. 497), and may have a guardian assigned to it.

ENVIRONMENTAL IMPACT ASSESSMENT A mandatory process imposed by both the federal and provincial levels of government by which the changes to the environment likely to be caused by or result from an activity, project, structure or program are predicted and evaluated. See, e.g., the *Clean Environment Act,* R.S.N.B. 1973, c. C–6.

ENVIRONMENTAL LAW Those rules of law aimed at pollution prevention and the protection of the natural environment. Because environmental law is not a discrete area of jurisdiction on its own, federal, provincial, and municipal governments have all enacted **legislation** governing activities that might adversely affect the environment. Sometimes this takes the form of legislation aimed exclusively at those issues, such as the *Canadian Environmental Protection Act, 1999*, S.C. 1999, c. 33. On other occasions, it will be as an aspect of a broader regulatory scheme, such as Part 8 of the *Canada Shipping Act, 2001*, S.C. 2001, c. 26, which makes rules concerning the discharge of materials from ships in Canada's **EEZ**. Provincial legislation includes **statutes** respecting clean air and water, and municipal legislation can deal with matters such as noise pollution or waste disposal.

EQUALITY Equality before and under the law, and the right to equal protection and benefit of the law, without discrimination is guaranteed to every individual in the **Canadian Charter of Rights and Freedoms**, s. 15 (Equality Rights), which came into effect on April 17, 1985. "Equality is not about sameness, and s. 15(1) does not protect a right to identical treatment. Rather, it protects every person's equal right to be free from **discrimination**. Accordingly, in order to establish a violation of s. 15(1), a person 'must show not only that he or she is not receiving equal treatment before and under the law or that the law has a differential impact on him or her in the protection or benefit accorded by law but, in addition, must show that the legislative impact of the law is discriminatory.'" *Withler v. Canada* (*Attorney-General*), 2011 SCC 12. "The central s. 15(1) concern is substantive, not formal, equality. A formal equality analysis based on mirror comparator groups can be detrimental to the analysis. Care must be taken to avoid converting the inquiry into substantive equality into a formalistic and arbitrary search for the 'proper' comparator group. At the end of the day there is only one question: Does the challenged law violate the norm of substantive equality in s. 15(1) of the *Charter*?" *Id.*

EQUALITY RIGHTS See **Canadian Charter of Rights and Freedoms**.

EQUITABLE DEFENCE See **defence**; **equity**.

EQUITABLE ESTATE See **equity**; **estate**.

EQUITABLE ESTOPPEL See **equity**; **estoppel**.

EQUITABLE INTEREST See **equity**; **interest**.

EQUITABLE LIEN See **equity**; **lien**.

EQUITABLE MAXIMS [MAXIMS OF EQUITY] Phrases meant to represent the cornerstones of the law of **equity**. The maxims are expressed differently by different writers. Commonly invoked maxims include: (1) He who comes to equity must do equity. (2) He who comes to equity must come with clean hands. (3) Equity aids the vigilant. (4) Equity acts specifically. (5) Equity acts **in personam**. (6) Equity follows the law. (7) Equity suffers no wrong without a remedy. (8) Equity regards that as done which ought to have been done. (9) Equity regards the substance and intent, not the form. (10) Equity imputes an intent to fulfil an obligation. (11) Equality is equity. (12) Where the equities are equal, the law will prevail. (13) Where the equities are equal, priority of time will prevail.

EQUITABLE RELIEF See **equity**; **relief**.

EQUITABLE SEISIN See **equity**; **seisin**.

EQUITABLE TITLE See **equity**; **title**.

EQUITY Primarily, justice or fairness. In a very broad philosophical sense, equity means to do to all persons as we would have them do unto us. It may be used to mean the discretionary power to do justice in particular cases where strict rules of **common law** would cause hardship. See **equitable maxims**.

In England, this was supplied by exercise of the Chancellor, who was **petitioned** by subjects who could not obtain justice in the common-law courts. Originally, equity mitigated the rigours of the early **common law** courts which were committed to a strict adherence to **writs** and **forms of action**. However, in more modern times equity became excessively rigid and incapable of forming new remedies. Access to equity jurisdiction was denied because wrong writs were used, defeating the notion that equity would afford relief which was unavailable at law.

The common-law and equity courts are now fused and administered through one body by the judicature acts of the various provinces. Where common-law and equitable principles conflict, equity will prevail.

The term *equity* is also used in accounting to denote the net value of the assets of a business, determined by subtracting **liabilities** from **assets**. For incorporated business enterprises, equity is owned by the common and preferred **shareholders**. If the corporation is publicly held, the shares will be traded on a stock exchange or over-the-counter, which together comprise the EQUITY MARKET. In the case of a **partnership**, equity denotes the total net value of **capital** and current accounts.

EQUITABLE INTEREST refers to the **interest** a person is **beneficially entitled** to in property, the legal **title** in which rests with another person, such as a mortgagor's interest in a building that has been **mortgaged** or a **beneficiary's** interest in property held in **trust**.

EQUITY OF REDEMPTION An **estate** in land; the person entitled to redeem is in **equity** the **owner** of the land. Where land is **mortgaged**, the mortgagor instantly acquires a contractual right to redeem on the date set for **redemption**. There is also an equitable right to redeem where the mortgagor has fallen into **default** on the payments of the mortgage. Strictly, the term *equity of redemption* only becomes appropriate after the legal or contractual right has been forfeited, *Garrow v. Baird,* [1931] 1 W.W.R. 129 (Man.K.B.), but generally the **interest** the mortgagor has in mortgaged land is referred to as his or her equity of redemption.

The mortgagor cannot **contract** out of his or her equity of redemption at the time of making the mortgage, but may agree that the mortgage be not redeemed for a reasonable period of time. See *Stephens v. Gulf Oil Canada Ltd.* (1974), 45 D.L.R. (3d) 161 (Ont.H.C.). Also, the equity of redemption may be extinguished by a lapse of time, by **foreclosure** and judicial sale or by a sale under a power of **sale**. Otherwise, the mortgagor, upon payment of the mortgage debt, is entitled to a reconveyance of the legal estate that had been **vested** in the mortgage by virtue of the mortgage.

EQUITY'S DARLING A **bona fide purchaser** for value without notice of a prior legal estate. Such a purchaser was protected in **equity**.

ERGA OMNES (*âr'-gă ŏm-nēz*) Lat.: Towards all. When a statute is struck down, it is invalid *erga omnes*, rather than only invalid with regard to the applicant. A statutory right is a right *erga omnes*, since it is enforceable against all other people. At international law, *erga omnes* obligations are owed to the international community generally, not to a particular state.

ERGO (*ĕr'-gō*) Lat.: therefore; consequently; because.

ERRATUM (*e-'rät-m*) Lat.: error; mistake.

ERRONEOUS Involving a mistake. It signifies a deviation from the requirements of the law. It is to be distinguished from "illegal" in that it does not connote a lack of legal authority.

ERROR OF LAW ON THE FACE OF THE RECORD An error that may be ascertained without recourse to the **evidence** adduced in the **proceedings** but merely on **examination** of the proceedings. For these purposes, the **record** consists of the reasons for the decision or **order** given, the **pleadings** or documents that initiated the proceedings and also, by incorporation, any documents referred to or mentioned in the decision. *R. v. Northumberland Compensation Appeal Tribunal, ex parte Shaw,* [1952] 1 K.B. 338 (C.A.)

Where a decision-maker in judicial proceedings makes such an error, the courts may intervene to set the decision aside. Error of law on the face of the record includes applying the incorrect onus of **proof**, wrongful admission of **evidence**, wrongful refusal to hear evidence or failure to consider a relevant factor when exercising discretion. See, e.g., *R. v. Cunningham,* 2010 SCC 10. Compare **admissible evidence**.

ESCALATOR CLAUSE The part of a **lease** or **contract** that provides for an increase in the contract price upon the determination of certain acts or other factors beyond the parties' control, such as an increase in the cost of labour or of a necessary commodity, or the fixing of maximum prices by a government agency.

ESCHEAT A type of **reversion** wherein **property** reverts to the state as the ultimate proprietor of land; originally a part of the English feudal system. Under escheat, the land reverted to the Crown or lord of the **fee** from when or from whose ancestor or predecessor the **estate** was derived, taking it on the failure, natural or legal, of the **intestate** tenant's family.

Escheat might occur in two ways. First, where a person was outlawed for a **felony** known as *propter delictum tenentis,* such a person became incapable of holding or inheriting land, and it escheated to the lord. The other form of escheat is *propter defictum sanguinis,* which applied where the tenant died without an heir. *Mercer v. Attorney-General of Ont.* (1881), 5 S.C.R. 538.

The following Canadian provinces have retained escheat by statutory enactment: British Columbia, Manitoba, New Brunswick, Nova Scotia, Ontario, Prince Edward Island and Saskatchewan. See **forfeiture**.

ESCROW Originally, a written **instrument** such as a **deed** temporarily deposited with a third party, a stranger to the transaction, by agreement of the parties directly involved. It is to be held by him or her until certain specified conditions are fulfilled and then delivered by him or her to the other party to take effect absolutely. *Terrapin International Ltd. v. Inland Revenue Commissioners,* [1976] 2 All E.R. 461 (Ch.Div.)

Once, for a writing to be an escrow the word *escrow* had to be written on it. Now, a writing is an escrow if the circumstances of delivery are such as to indicate that it is conditional on the performance of prescribed stipulations. If the conditions are not fulfilled, the deed never takes effect.

The term "escrow" is no longer exclusively associated with deeds or written instruments but now is used more generally to refer to money, stocks, or other property "when the property is held by a third person for the benefit of a pledge-holder." *Caisse populaire Desjardins de Val-Brillant v. Blouin,* 2003 SCC 31.

ESTATE A term that signifies the relation between a person and the **property** in which he or she has an **interest** (*Thompson v. Yockney* (1912), 8 D.L.R. 776 (Man.K.B.)) and also the interest itself. More technically, it refers to the degree, nature and extent of an interest or ownership in land. "Estate" is a derivation from the notion that no one can be the absolute owner of land and one can only have a limited estate or interest in it. The Crown is the ultimate proprietor of all land.

Estates were divisible by reference to the potential limit of their duration into **freehold estates** and less than freehold estates.

Freehold estates could be estates of **inheritance**—such as **fee simple**, **fee tail**, or **frankmarriage**—or estates not of inheritance. If the latter, they were created either by the act of the parties or by operation of law. Those created by the act of the parties included estates for life (see **life estate)** and estates **pur autre vie**, whereas those resulting from operation of law included the estate of a tenant in tail after possibility of issue extinct and estates arising through **dower**.

Less than freehold estates could be of either certain duration (estates for years) or uncertain duration (estates at will or at sufferance).

Estates were also distinguishable by their quality, that is, by whether they were absolute, determinable or conditional. An ABSOLUTE ESTATE is one granted without condition or termination, a FEE SIMPLE ABSOLUTE. A DETERMINABLE ESTATE is one that has the potential to continue as though it were absolute but determines on the happening of some event. A CONDITIONAL ESTATE is one liable to be defeated on the fulfilment of some condition. See **conditional fee; determinable fee**.

Estates may be further divided into ESTATES IN POSSESSION, where there is a present right of enjoyment, and ESTATES IN EXPECTANCY, which could not be enjoyed until some future time.

Estate has also come to mean property, particularly where speaking in regard to the estate of a deceased person. Estate has also become a fictitious entity such as where a debt is owing to the estate of a bankrupt individual. The estate represents the individual to whom it originally belonged.

See **preceding estate**.

ESTATE AT SUFFERANCE See **tenancy** [TENANCY AT SUFFERANCE].

ESTATE AT WILL See **tenancy** [TENANCY AT WILL].

ESTATE BY THE ENTIRETY See **tenancy** [TENANCY BY THE ENTIRETY].

ESTATE FOR LIFE See **life estate**.

ESTATE FOR YEARS See **tenancy** [TENANCY FOR YEARS].

ESTATE FROM YEAR TO YEAR [PERIOD TO PERIOD] See **tenancy** [PERIODIC TENANCY].

ESTATE IN COMMON See **tenancy** [TENANCY IN COMMON].

ESTATE PUR AUTRE VIE See **pur autre vie**.

ESTATE TAX See **tax**.

ESTOPPEL Originally known as preclusion; a **bar**; a rule whereby a **party** is precluded in any subsequent **proceedings** from alleging or proving that certain facts are otherwise than they were originally made to appear. "Estoppel is a complex legal notion involving a combination of several essential elements— statement to be acted upon, action on the faith of it, [and] resulting detriment to the actor. Estoppel is often described as a rule of evidence, as indeed it may be so described. But the whole concept is more correctly viewed as a substantive rule of law. The purchaser or other transferee must have acted upon it to his detriment ... It is also true that he cannot be said to rely on the statement if he knew that it was false; he must reasonably believe it to be true and therefore act upon it. Estoppel is different from contract both in its nature and consequences. But the relationship between the parties must also be such that the imputed truth of the statement is a necessary step in the constitution of the cause of action. But the whole case of estoppel fails if the statement is not sufficiently clear and unqualified." *Canada and Dominion Sugar Ltd. v. Canadian National West Indies Steamships Ltd.,* [1947] A.C. 46 at 56 (P.C.). Specific forms of estoppels include:

ESTOPPEL BY DEED An estoppel that arises where a statement of fact is made in a **deed** and verified by **seal**. The rule simply states that one cannot deny the veracity of statements made in his or her deed. *Desoto Resources Ltd. v. Encana Corp.,* 2010 ABQB 448. If on the construction of the deed the statement in contention is that of all the parties, then all are bound. Otherwise, it is only binding on the person making it.

ESTOPPEL BY RECORD Sometimes referred to as **res judicata**. It arises where an issue of fact that had been judicially determined in a final manner by a **tribunal** having **jurisdiction** arises subsequently between the same parties. *Ross v. Canada,* 2003 FC 534. Consequently, the issue must be taken as conclusively determined in the initial proceedings. *Apotex Inc. v. Merck & Co.,* 2004 FC 1038.

ESTOPPEL **in pais** Also known as ESTOPPEL BY CONDUCT. The usual meaning of the word *estoppel:* When one person by his or her conduct leads another to believe that certain facts are true and these are acted upon, then in subsequent **proceedings** this person cannot deny the truth of such facts.

PROMISSORY ESTOPPEL A doctrine derived from a principle of **equity**, *Hughes v. The Directors of the Metropolitan Ry. Co.* (1877), 2 A.C. 439 at 443 (H. L.), which has seen considerable expansion in recent years. It comes into existence where one party by words or conduct gives an assurance to the other party with the intention of affecting the legal relations between them and where the other party acts on the assurance accordingly. The one making the assurance cannot now revert to the previous legal relation but must abide by the qualifications he or she introduced. *Combe v. Combe,* [1951] 2 K.B. 215 at 220 (C.A.).

The doctrine is subject to the limitation that the promisor can resile from his or her promise by giving reasonable notice to allow the promisee the opportunity to regain his or her original position. If such cannot be regained, then the promise is irrevocable *Ajayi v. R. T. Briscoer (Nigeria) Ltd.,* [1964] 3 All E.R. 556 at 559 (P.C.)

PROPRIETARY ESTOPPEL A form of promissory estoppels that arises when "(a) the owner of land (O) induces, encourages, or allows the claimant (C) to believe that he has or will enjoy some right or benefit over O's property; (b) in reliance upon this belief, C acts to his detriment to the knowledge of O; and (c) O then seeks to take unconscionable advantage of C by denying him the right or benefit [that] he expected to receive." *Schwark v. Cutting,* 2010 ONCA 61.

ESTOVERS Generally, any kind of sustenance, but **1.** commonly used in reference to a **tenant's** right to remove wood from the landlord's estate in order to effect repairs. This was the right of any tenant for life or years unless the agreement between the parties specifically provided otherwise. Estovers were also known as BOTES and were sometimes divided into *house-bote* for repairs to the dwelling, *fire-bote* for taking fuel, *plough-bote* for making and repairing agricultural instruments and *hay-bote* for repairing fences.
2. Less frequently, it was used to denote **alimony** for a widow or for a wife separated from her husband and also **maintenance** for an imprisoned felon.

ET AL. (*ĕt äl*) Lat.: and others; abbreviation of *et alii.* Where there are a number of **plaintiffs**, **grantors**, persons addressed, etc., it is common to set out fully the name of the person first mentioned followed by the words *et al.,* thereby including all relevant persons.

ET NON (*ĕt nŏn*) Lat.: and not. This phrase is used primarily in introducing a special **traverse** in **pleading** and thus is called the "inducement to the traverse"; synonymous in use with **absque hoc**, which means "without this."

ET SEQ. (*ĕt sĕk*) Lat.: and the following; an abbreviation of *et sequentes* or *et sequentia.* Usually used to denote a reference to a certain page and the following pages: page 13 *et seq.*

ET UX. (*ĕt ŭks*) Lat.: and wife; abbreviation of *et uxor.* Used in old legal documents such as **wills** and other **instruments** that purport to **grant** or **convey**.

EULA End User License Agreement. Licensing terms imposed by the manufacturer of software on the consumers who ultimately use the product.

EUTHANASIA Also known as mercy killing; the suggested practice of painlessly putting to death those persons suffering from terminal diseases. See *Rodriguez v. British Columbia (A/G),* [1993] 3 S.C.R. 519. See also *Criminal Code,* R.S.C. 1985, c. C–46, ss. 14 and 241.

EVASION To know that **tax** is owing and intend to avoid or to attempt to avoid payment of that tax. Tax evasion is a crime. *R. v. Klundert* (2004), 187 C.C.C. (3d) 417, 23 C.R. (6th) 274 (Ont. C.A.). See **avoidance**; **avoidance transaction**.

EVICTION 1. Dispossession of a **tenant** by his or her **landlord**. A mere **trespass** will not be sufficient to constitute an eviction. Rather the act must be of a grave and permanent character done with the intention of depriving the tenant of enjoyment of the whole of the **demised premises**. **2.** Generally, the recovery of land by operation of law. Compare **ejectment**; **ouster**.

EVIDENCE Any species of proof or probative matter legally presented by the acts of **parties** and through the medium of **witnesses**, **records**, **documents**, **exhibits**, or other concrete objects for the purpose of inducing belief in the minds of the court or jury as to their content. The rules of evidence (see **admissible evidence**) control the presentation of facts before the court. The purpose is to facilitate the introduction of all logically relevant facts without sacrificing any fundamental policy of the law which may be of more importance than the ascertainment of the truth. The admissibility of evidence is partially governed by legislation. See *Canada Evidence Act,* R.S.C. 1985, c. C–5, and provincial evidence statutes. See D. Paciocco & L. Stuesser, *The Law of Evidence* (6th ed. 2011); A.W. Bryant, S.N. Lederman, & M.K. Fuerst, *The Law of Evidence in Canada* (3rd ed. 2009). See **circumstantial evidence**; **hearsay rule**; **presumptive evidence**.

INADMISSIBLE EVIDENCE Generally, evidence that is logically **probative** is admissible unless explicitly disallowed by some specific rule of exclusion—for example, the **hearsay rule**. Inadmissible evidence should not be considered in any form or for any purpose by the jury.

Evidence may also be found to be inadmissable under s. 24(2) of the **Canadian Charter of Rights and Freedoms** where admitting the evidence could bring the administration of justice into disrepute. See *R. v. Grant,* 2009 SCC 32.

EVIDENCE ALIUNDE See **aliunde**.

EVIDENTIAL BURDEN See **burden of proof**.

EXAMINATION-IN-CHIEF See **cross-examine**.

EXCEPTION 1. An objection or challenge taken to an answer contained in the **pleadings**. For example, a **plaintiff** might file an exception to a **defendant's** answer if it were insufficient or scandalous. See **demurrer. 2.** A clause in a **deed** preventing the thing excepted from passing in the **grant**.

EXCESSIVE FORCE In **criminal** law, force that is disproportionate to the injury or harm it is intended to prevent because it is not reasonable in all the circumstances, taking into account the accused's subject-

ive belief as to the nature of the danger or harm but assessing that belief against objective criteria. *R. v. Szczerbaniwicz,* 2010 SCC 15. The question of whether excessive force has been used arises in various contexts, such as **self-defence**, defence of property, or in using force to carry out an **arrest** or some other authorized procedure. Because the use of excessive force in one of these contexts might remove the actor's **justification** for applying force, it can also give rise to liability in **tort**.

EXCHEQUER COURT OF CANADA A former **federal court** established by Parliament under the *Supreme and Exchequer Court Act*, R.S.C. 1875, c. 11. It was given jurisdiction over cases involving matters of federal jurisdiction, such as tax, immigration, admiralty, copyright, trademarks, and various others. The Exchequer Court was replaced by the **Federal Court** of Canada in 1971, which had a modified structure (trial and appeals division) and greater jurisdiction. See *Federal Courts Act*, R.S.C. 1985, c. F–7. P. W. Hogg, *Constitutional Law of Canada*, 7–26–34 (5th ed. 2007).

EXCISE Broadly, any kind of tax that is not directly on property or the rents or incomes of real estate. Usually, though not exclusively, used to indicate a duty imposed on goods manufactured in another country before they reach the consumer. See *Excise Act*, R.S.C. 1985, c. E–14.

EXCLUDED PROPERTY Property owned by one spouse that is exempt from division on the breakdown of a marriage according to the relevant statutory scheme. Examples include property acquired by a spouse by inheritance (*Matrimonial Property Act*, R.S.A. 2000, c. M–8) or an award or settlement of damages in tort (*The Family Property Act*, SS 1997, c. F–6.3).

EXCLUSION OF EVIDENCE The refusal by a court to receive otherwise **admissible evidence**, as a remedy under s. 24(2) of the **Canadian Charter of Rights and Freedoms** for a person whose rights have been violated. The test for exclusion is whether admission of the evidence could bring the administration of justice into disrepute. See *Collins v. The Queen*, [1987] 1 S.C.R. 265. The factors to assess in answering that question are "(1) the seriousness of the *Charter*-infringing state conduct; (admission may send the message the justice system condones serious state misconduct); (2) the impact of the breach on the *Charter*-protected interests of the accused (admission may send the message that individual rights count for little); and (3) society's interest in the adjudication of the case on its merits." *R. v. Grant*, 2009 SCC 32.

EXCLUSION ORDER See **deportation**.

EXCLUSIONARY RULE A rule of law that provides that otherwise **admissible evidence** may not be used in evidence.

EXCLUSIVE ECONOMIC ZONE See **UNCLOS III**.

EXCULPATORY Refers to **evidence** and/or statements that tend to clear, justify or excuse a **defendant** from alleged fault or **guilt**. Compare **incriminate**; **inculpatory**.

EXCUSE A category of **defence** to a **criminal** charge in which the accused is forgiven for his or her behaviour rather than commended for it; compare **justification**. "[A]n 'excuse' concedes the wrongfulness of the action but asserts that the circumstances under which it was done are such that it ought not to be attributed to the actor. The perpetrator who is incapable, owing to a disease of the mind, of appreciating the nature and consequences of his acts; the person who labours under a mistake of fact; the drunkard; the sleepwalker: these are all actors of whose 'criminal' actions we disapprove intensely, but whom, in appropriate circumstances, our law will not punish." *Perka v. The Queen*, [1984] 2 S.C.R. 232.

EX DEBITO JUSTITIAE (*ĕks dē'-bĭ-tō jūs-tĭ'-shē-ī*) Lat.: because of the demands of justice. A **remedy** granted as of right, where the action is proved, as opposed to a discretionary remedy such as **certiorari**.

EXECUTE To complete or carry into effect. **1.** Where a legal **instrument** is involved, to complete all the formalities necessary in order to give validity thereto. Thus, to execute a deed requires that it be signed, sealed and delivered. **2.** To carry into effect or to enforce a judgment of the court. **3.** To put a person to death by authority of the state.

EXECUTED Fully accomplished, leaving nothing to be performed. *Redican v. Nesbitt*, [1924] S.C.R. 135. Compare **executory**.

EXECUTED INTEREST See **interest**.

EXECUTIVE The **Crown** in its administrative aspect; the branch of government that puts laws into execution as distinguished from the legislative branch, which enacts the laws, and the judiciary, which interprets them. Compare **governor in council**; **lieutenant governor in council**.

In the broad sense, the executive consists of the Government departments and their officers under the respective Ministers. The principal executive body is the Cabinet; the Prime Minister is its head.

EXECUTIVE AGREEMENT See **treaty**.

EXECUTIVE COUNCIL The term used to refer to the provincial **cabinet** in many provinces and territories. See, e.g., *Executive Council Act*, R.S.O. 1990, c. E.25; *Executive Council Act*, R.S.P.E.I. 1988, c. E–12; *Legislative Assembly and Executive Council Act*, S.Nu. 2002, c. 5.

EXECUTOR [EXECUTRIX] The person to whom the execution of a **will** is entrusted, that is, the duty to carry out its provisions. Anyone capable of making a will can be an executor; a **corporation** may also be appointed to act as executor. The duties of an executor include seeing that the deceased is buried; proving the will; collecting the **estate** and, if required, converting it into money; and distributing **legacies** and any residue to those entitled. *Re Adamson* (1875), L.R. 3 P. & D. 253. The duties of an executor are more specifically governed by provincial legislation. See, e.g., *The Administration of Estates Act*,

S.S. 1998, c. A–4.1, or the *Probate Act*, R.S.P.E.I. 1988, c. P–21.

It is not essential that the executor be expressly named provided the implication is obvious. Such an executor is known as an "executor according to the tenor," and to constitute an executor of this nature, it must be evident on a reasonable construction of the will that the **testator** intended this person to carry out the duties of an executor. *Re Adamson* (1875), L.R. 3 P. & D. 253.

Compare **administrator [administratrix]**.

EXECUTOR DE SON TORT (*ĕg-zĕk-yū-tôr dĕ sōn tôr*) One who assumes the office of executor, despite the lack of appointment to that position by the deceased or by the court, on the failure of the deceased to make such a selection. *Pickering v. Thompson* (1911), 24 O.L.R. 378 (Div.Ct.). Meddling with the goods of the deceased is sufficient to render one an executor de son tort. An executor *de son tort* "becomes liable to the rightful representatives and other interested persons, to the extent of such assets as he has received less any proper payments he has made." S. Bailey, *The Law of Wills* 294–95 (7th ed. 1973), quoted in *Tsang v. Chen*, 2005 ABQB 772. Compare **trustee** de son tort.

EXECUTORY That which remains to be carried into effect; the opposite of **executed**. For example, an EXECUTORY CONTRACT is one in which some performance remains to be completed. *Redican v. Nesbitt*, [1924] S.C.R. 135.

EXECUTORY BEQUEST See **bequest**.

EXEMPLARY DAMAGES See **damages**.

EXEMPTION CLAUSES A clause inserted into a written contract which serves to absolve the person making the offer of any liability under the contract. "Exemption clauses may be broadly divided into three categories. First, there are clauses which purport to limit or reduce what would otherwise be the defendant's duty, i.e., the substantive obligations to which he would otherwise be subject under the contract, for example, by excluding express or implied terms, by limiting liability to cases of wilful neglect or default, or by binding a buyer of land or goods to accept the property sold subject to 'faults', 'defects', or 'errors of description'. Secondly, there are clauses which purport to exclude or restrict liability which would otherwise attach to a breach of contract, such as the liability to be sued for breach or to be liable in damages, or which take away from the other party the right to treat as repudiated or rescind the agreement. Thirdly, there are clauses which purport to exclude or restrict the duty of the party in default fully to indemnify the other party, for example, by limiting the amount of damages recoverable against him, or by providing a time-limit within which claims must be made." H. G. Beale, ed., 1 *Chitty on Contracts* 910 (30th ed. 2008). See **Himalaya clauses**.

EX GRATIA (*ĕks grä'-shē-à*) Lat.: out of grace; gratuitously. That which is done as a favour rather than as a required task or as of right. Payments made to avoid litigation are often made *ex gratia,* that is, without admission of liability.

EXHIBIT Items of evidence that exist prior to a trial but that are entered into evidence and become part of the record. Exhibits can include documents, physical items, or statements that have been reduced to writing or videotaped. See *Canadian Broadcasting Corp. v. The Queen*, 2011 SCC 3.

EX OFFICIO (*ĕks ō-fĭ'-shĕ-ō*) Lat.: by virtue of his or her office. Powers that are a concomitant of holding a certain office may be exercised without any further instrument conferring such authority. For example, the Lord Mayor of London is *ex officio* a justice of the peace for the City of London.

EXONERATE To declare innocent of any blame or wrong doing; to dismiss any charges or allegations of criminal activity brought against a person.

EX PARTE (*ĕks pär'-tā*) Lat.: on behalf of. **1.** In its precise sense, an *ex parte* application in a judicial proceeding is made by a person who is not a party to the proceeding but who has a sufficient interest entitling him or her to make the application. *Stewart v. Braun Ex parte Patterson*, [1924] 3 D.L.R. 941 (Man.K.B.). **2.** More usually, the term indicates an application made by one party to a proceeding in the absence of the other party. Generally, such an application is only made in cases of emergency where it is not possible to give the adverse party **notice** of the **proceeding**. However, some applications are of necessity made *ex parte*, such as an application for a **search warrant** or an **Anton Piller Order**, because the order sought is one that would be undermined if the other party cannot know in advance.

EXPATRIATION The voluntary surrendering of one's citizenship and all the rights and the privileges that accompany it.

EXPECTANCY Contingency as to **possession** or **enjoyment**. In the law of **property**, **estates** may be either in possession or in expectancy; if an expectancy is created by the parties, it is a **remainder**; if by **operation of law**, it is a **reversion**. See **future interest**; **vested**.

EXPECTATION DAMAGES See **damages**.

EXPERT TESTIMONY [EVIDENCE] See **expert witness**.

EXPERT WITNESS A person possessed of a special skill or knowledge acquired through study or experience that entitles him or her to give an opinion or evidence concerning his or her area of expertise. *R. v. Abbey*, 2009 ONCA 624. The opinion of such an expert is only admissible where the subject in issue before the court is such that competency to form an opinion on it can only be acquired by a course of specific study or by experience. Expert evidence "must be given by a witness who is shown to have acquired special or peculiar knowledge through study or experience in respect of the matters on which he or she undertakes to testify." *R. v. Mohan*, [1994] 2 S.C.R. 9. It is the fact that the subject matter is one requiring expert knowledge that permits the introduction of **opinion evidence**, which is otherwise **inadmissible**. "[O]nly an expert witness can put opinions before the court and, even then,

only when the trial judge would be unable to determine the issue in question properly without expert assistance." *R. v. D.A.I.*, 2012 SCC 5. The *Canada Evidence Act*, R.S.C. 1985, c. C–5, s. 7, allows only five such witnesses to be called by each party unless leave is given to call more.

EX POST FACTO (*ĕks pōst fäk'-tō*) Lat.: after the fact; by a subsequent act. It signifies something done subsequently that affects another thing committed earlier. The most common usage is in regard to a statute that makes punishable an act that when committed was not punishable. Similarly, the term also applies to a statute that imposes a greater punishment for a crime than was possible at the time the crime was committed.

EXPRESSION [FREEDOM OF] In the context of s. 2(*b*) of the **Canadian Charter of Rights and Freedoms**, it covers any activity which "conveys or attempts to convey meaning." "Expression has both a content and a form, and the two can be inextricably connected. Activity is expressive if it attempts to convey meaning. That meaning is its content. Freedom of expression was entrenched in our constitution and is guaranteed in the Quebec Charter so as to ensure that everyone can manifest their thoughts, opinions, beliefs, indeed all expressions of the heart and mind, however distasteful or contrary to the mainstream." *Irwin Toy Ltd. v. Quebec (Attorney General)*, [1989] 1 S.C.R. 927 at 968.

EXPRESSIO UNIUS EST EXCLUSIO ALTERIUS (*ĕks-prĕ-sē-ō ū'-nē-ūs ĕst ĕks-klū'-sē-ō äl-tĕr'-ē-ūs*) Lat.: the express mention of one person or thing is the exclusion of another. For example, an agreement of purchase and **sale** of a home that expressly includes the dining room chandelier will, thereby, implicitly exclude the hall chandelier. The phrase is a maxim for interpreting **statutes** and other written **instruments** but should not be applied without scrutiny of the specific circumstances.

EXPROPRIATION Compulsorily depriving a person of a right of property belonging to him or her; a present manifestation of the **eminent domain** of the

Crown or state. **Compensation** may be promised or paid. See **de facto expropriation**; **regulatory taking**.

EX REL. (*ĕks rĕl*) Lat.: from a narrative or information; abbreviation of *ex relatione*. When a report of a decision is made by one who derives his or her knowledge, not from having been present in court, but indirectly from notes or information disclosed to him or her by a barrister or, occasionally, a solicitor who heard the proceeding, the decision is said to be reported in *ex relatione*.

An action brought to restrain interference with a public right or to compel performance of a public duty must have the Attorney-General as a party unless there is at the same time interference with a private right or special damage is suffered over and above that of the general public. Where the Attorney-General is a necessary party, the action is brought by him or her at the relation (*ex relatione*) of the person seeking either to enforce the public duty or to restrain interference with that right. Compare **relator action**.

EXTENUATING CIRCUMSTANCES Unusual factors related to and tending to contribute to the consummation of an illegal act, but over which the actor had little or no control. These factors therefore reduce the responsibility of the actor and serve to mitigate his or her punishment or his or her payment of **damages**.

EXTERNAL ELEMENTS See **actus reus**.

EXTINGUISHMENT The termination or discharge of an obligation or right. Thus, the obligation to pay a **debt** is extinguished when the debt is in fact paid or when the **creditor** releases the **debtor** from his or her **liability**. Similarly, an easement may be extinguished by express or implied agreement or by **unity** of **possession**—that is, where the dominant and servient **tenements** become united in the same person for an **estate** in **fee simple**.

Extinguishment can also refer to **aboriginal rights** that can be extinguished by legislation or through the consent of **Aboriginal peoples**. See *R. v. Sparrow*, [1990] 1 S.C.R. 1075.

EXTORTION 1. In common law, a **misdemeanour** committed by a holder of public office who by virtue of his or her office wrongfully received from another any money or valuable things. **2.** The inducing of a person to do anything by the use of threats, **accusations**, menaces, or violence without reasonable justification. "Extortion requires the Crown to establish beyond a reasonable doubt (i) that the accused has induced or attempted to induce someone to do something or to cause something to be done; (ii) that the accused has used threats, accusations, menaces, or violence; (iii) that he or she has done so with the intention of obtaining something by the use of threats; and (iv) that either the use of the threats or the making of the demand for the thing sought to be obtained was without reasonable justification or excuse." *R. v. Barros*, 2011 SCC 51. In Canada extortion is an **indictable offence** carrying a maximum penalty of life imprisonment. *Criminal Code*, R.S.C. 1985, c. C–46, s. 346.

EXTRADITION The surrendering by one state, at the request of another, of a person accused of a crime under the laws of the requesting state. It is usually regulated by reciprocal extradition **treaties** between states.

EXTRA HAZARDOUS ACTS "[A]cts commissioned by an employer that are so hazardous in their nature that the law has thought it proper to impose a direct obligation on the employer to see that care is taken." G.H.L. Fridman, *The Law of Torts in Canada* 571–74 (6th ed. 2010).

EXTRAJUDICIAL MEASURES Under the *Youth Criminal Justice Act*, S.C. 2002, c. 1, measures other than judicial proceedings used to deal with a young person alleged to have committed an offence. Such measures include warnings, cautions administered by the police or the **Crown**, referrals to an agency, or extrajudicial sanctions that are part of a program authorized by the provincial **Attorney-General**.

EXTRATERRITORIALITY Legislative action by a government outside its territorial boundary. See **real and substantial connection**; **territorial principle**.

EXTREMIS See **in extremis**.

EXTRINSIC FRAUD See **fraud**.

EX TURPI CAUSA NON ORITUR ACTIO
(*ĕks têr'-pē kŏ'-ză nŏn ôr'-ĭ-têr ăk'-shē-ō*) Lat.: no disgraceful [foul, immoral, obscene] matter can give rise to an **action**. Sometimes known as the illegality **defence**, it was used predominantly in **contract** cases but has recently been adopted in **tort** law. The doctrine is invoked "to maintain the internal consistency of the law...where a given plaintiff genuinely seeks to profit from his or her illegal conduct, or where the claimed compensation would amount to an evasion of criminal sanction." *Hall v. Hebert* (1993), 101 DLR (4th) 129 (S.C.C.). In *Hall*, it was also held that criminal conduct would not wholly deny recovery for personal injury, but would be a factor in **contributory negligence**.

FACINUS QUOS INQUINAT AEQUAT (*fä'-sĭ-nŭs kwōs in'-kwĭ-nät ī'-kwät*) Lat.: villainy and guilt make all those whom they contaminate equal in character.

FACTA SUNT POTENTIORI VERBIS (*fäk'-tä sŭnt pō-tĕn'-tē-ô'-rē vĕr'-bēs*) Lat.: deeds or accomplishments are more powerful than words.

FACT FINDER See **trier of fact**.

FACTO (*fäk'-tō*) Lat.: in fact; by a deed, accomplishment or exploit. See also **de facto**.

FACTOR A type of mercantile **agent** to whom goods or documents of **title** are entrusted for the purpose of being sold. *Stevens v. Biller* (1883), 25 Ch.D. 31. The commission received by the factor for his or her services is known as FACTORAGE. A factor has a **lien** on the goods entrusted to him or her for his or her remuneration. Sales by a factor will bind the **principal** whether they are in derogation of private instructions by the principal or not unless the purchaser has knowledge of such instructions prior to the sale. See also **Factors Act**. Compare **jobber**.

FACTORS ACT A statute, of English origin, which has been adopted in most Canadian provinces, e.g., *Factors Act, R.S.N.S.* 1989, c. 157. The general purpose and effect of such an enactment is to protect **bona fide purchasers** from mercantile **agents (factors)** who may have lost the capacity to dispose of goods that nonetheless remain in their **possession**. Such incapacity may result where the **agency** has been revoked, where the goods have already been sold or where goods have been entrusted for a different purpose. The *Factors Act* protects the bona fide purchaser for value without notice by validating sales to such a person where there appears to be no limit on the factor's power to deal with the goods in his or her possession.

FACTUAL INNOCENCE The state of a person who is accused of a **criminal** offence but who did not, in fact, commit the offence. The term is sometimes used by courts but has no strict meaning, since the criminal justice system only asks whether a person has been proved guilty **beyond a reasonable doubt** or not. See **not guilty**.

FACTUM (*fäk'-tūm*) Lat.: literally, a deed, act, exploit, or accomplishment. Also, the written argument submitted by a lawyer to the court. See **brief**.

FACTUM PROBANDUM (pl.: **FACTA PROBANDA**) (*fäk'-tūm prō'-băn'-dūm; fäk'-tà prō-băn'-dà*) Lat.: in the law of **evidence**, the principal fact, the fact in issue. The fact that must be proved and, therefore, the fact to which evidence is directed.

FACTUM PROBANS (pl.: **FACTA PROBANTIA**) (*fäk'-tūm prō'-bănz; fäk'-tà pro'-băn'-tē-à*) Lat.: a fact given in **evidence** in order to prove the **factum probandum**. Also known as an EVIDENTIARY FACT.

FAILURE OF CONSIDERATION See **consideration**.

FAILURE OF ISSUE A phrase used in a **will** or **deed** to refer to a **condition** that operates in the event no children survive the decedent. An equivalent expression sometimes used is "die without **issue**." The words may fix a condition whereby an estate, instead of being **alienable** and therefore capable of being conveyed to a third person, will, in the event of failure of issue, pass automatically to an alternative designated in the original **instrument**. Unless there was a contrary intention, the common law interpreted this condition as continuing *ad infinitum*.

Such a **construction** was termed INDEFINITE FAILURE OF ISSUE. Thus, if children of the first taker themselves fail to leave children, the estate will still go to the alternative. The first taker has a **fee tail** and the descendants are TENANTS IN TAIL. This common-law presumption has been reversed in all the common-law provinces of Canada (e.g., *Wills Act, R.S.N.S.* 1989, c. 505, s. 28), so that the condition is fulfilled where the first taker has issue surviving at his or her death.

FAIR COMMENT A **defence** to an action for **defamation** in which the **defendant** shows that, although the statements might have been defamatory, they were based on honest belief and were not motivated by malice. The requirements of the defence are that: "(a) the comment must be on a matter of public interest; (b) the comment must be based on fact; (c) the comment, though it can include inferences of fact, must be recognisable as comment; (d) the comment must satisfy the following objective test: could any [person] honestly express that opinion on the proved facts?; (e) even though the comment satisfies the objective test, the defence can be defeated if the plaintiff proves that the defendant was [subjectively] actuated by express malice." The onus is on the defendant to make out the first four elements, but if he or she does so, the onus is on the plaintiff to prove malice. *WIC Radio Ltd. v. Simpson*, 2008 SCC 40.

FAIR DEALING The use, without authorization, of a substantial part of a **copyright**-protected work, provided the dealing is done for one of several listed purposes and is considered fair. In Canada, fair dealing categories include research, private study, criticism, review, some educational uses, and news reporting. See *Copyright Act*, RSC 1985, c. C–42, ss. 29, 29.1, 29.3.

FAIR HEARING [FAIR TRIAL] The obligation of the state to accord fair procedures to a person charged with an offence or appearing in front of an **administrative tribunal**. The right to a fair trial is a **principle of fundamental justice** under s. 7 of the **Canadian Charter of Rights and Freedoms**, and s. 11(d) of the *Charter* guarantees anyone charged with an offence the right to "a fair and public hearing by an independent and impartial tribunal." A right to a fair hearing is also a requirement of **natural justice**. The right to a fair hearing has a number of facets. "It comprises the right to a *hearing*. It requires that the hearing be *before an independent and impartial*

magistrate. It demands a *decision by the magistrate on the facts and the law*. And it entails the *right to know the case put against one*, and the *right to answer that case*. Precisely how these requirements are met will vary with the context. But for s. 7 to be satisfied, each of them must be met in substance." *Charkaoui v. Canada (Citizenship and Immigration)*, 2007 SCC 9. An accused's right to a fair trial also includes the right to **disclosure** of evidence, and if this disclosure is not made, it can mean that no trial will take place at all. *R. v. Ahmad*, 2011 SCC 6. A fair trial also requires that both sides be given an opportunity to present a case.

To give each side the opportunity of adequately presenting its case is also referred to as the principle of **audi alteram partem**. Other elements of a fair hearing often mentioned are the right to reasonable notice of the hearing, the right to counsel, the right to examine witnesses and the right to written reasons for the decision. An attempt to outline the procedures governing tribunals at or following a **hearing** may be embodied in a statute, e.g., *The Statutory Powers Procedure Act*, R.S.O. 1990, c. S. 22.

FAIR MARKET VALUE See **market value**.

FALSE ARREST A **tort** action arising when a person has been **arrested** in the absence of any lawful authority for that arrest. A claim for false arrest can be brought against police officers or in the case of a **citizen's arrest**. See *Chartier v. Att. Gen. (Que.)*, [1979] 2 S.C.R. 474; *Ferri v. Ontario (Attorney-General)*, 2007 ONCA 79. Compare **false imprisonment**.

FALSE IMPRISONMENT "Anyone who intentionally confines another person within fixed boundaries is liable for the tort of false imprisonment." A. Linden & B. Feldthusen, *Canadian Tort Law* 50 (9th ed. 2011). False imprisonment has three elements. The plaintiff "must have been totally deprived of liberty; this deprivation must have been against his or her will; and it must be caused by the defendant." *Kovacs v. Ontario Jockey Club* (1995), 126 D.L.R. (4th)

576 (Ont. C.J.). See *P.L. v. Alberta*, 2011 ABQB 821.

Furthermore, the restraint need only be imprisoned for an appreciable amount of time; therefore, if the restraint is only momentary, the tort will still have been committed. *Bird v. Jones* (1845), 7 Q.B. 742; 115 E.R. 668.

The restraint may be accomplished by the direct application of force or by threat of force. A plaintiff is imprisoned where he or she submits to such threats rather than risk violence. *Bahner v. Marwest Hotel Co.* (1969), 6 D.L.R. (3d) 322, aff'd by (1970), 12 D.L.R. (3d) 646 (B.C.C.A.). Similarly, when a person submits to restraint in order to avoid embarrassment, there is an imprisonment. Finally, it is not necessary that the person confined be aware of the restraint. *C.H.S. v. Alberta* (*Director of Child Welfare*), 2008 ABQB 513. Compare **kidnapping**.

FALSE PRETENCE "[A] representation of a matter of fact either present or past, made by words or otherwise, that is known by the person who makes it to be false and that is made with a fraudulent intent to induce the person to whom it is made to act on it." *Criminal Code, R.S.C. 1985, c. C–46, s. 361(1).

FALSE VERDICT A manifestly unjust verdict; one inconsistent with the evidence. Originally, if a jury gave a false verdict, the party injured by the decision might sue out a writ of attaint either under the common law or by the Statute of 1495, 11 Hen. VII, c. 24, in order to reverse the verdict and at the same time punish the jurors. Such a practice was superseded early in the seventeenth century by the custom of setting aside verdicts and granting new trials.

FALSI CRIMEN See **crimen falsi**.

FAMILY LAW The law governing family relationships. The federal **Parliament** has sole jurisdiction with respect to **marriage**, while provincial **legislatures** may specify formal marriage requirements such as **licenses**, **residency**, and age. The federal Parliament has sole **jurisdiction** in **divorce** matters. However, the provincial power under the **Constitution Act, 1867** over prop-

erty and civil rights has enabled provinces to enact legislation respecting **custody** of children, and spousal support. These matters may be adjudicated prior to divorce by provincially appointed judges sitting in **provincial courts**. The petition for divorce must be filed in a **superior court** before a federally appointed judge whose final orders respecting property, custody, and support take precedence over provincial court orders. Provincial legislatures and provincially appointed judges can regulate many matters relating to children, such as **adoption** and **guardianship**. Several provinces have adopted a **unified family court** regime in which all matters relating to the family are heard by federally appointed judges.

FAMILY PATRIMONY See **family property**.

FAMILY PROPERTY Property that is divisible between spouses upon application by one of the spouses, normally because of the breakdown of the relationship. The division of family property is governed by provincial legislation. See e.g., *Family Property Act*, C.C.S.M. c. F25; *Family Law Act*, R.S.O. 1990, c. F.3; *Matrimonial Property Act*, R.S.A. 2000, c. M–8. The terms "matrimonial property" and "marital property" are used in some corresponding provincial legislation, while the *Civil Code of Québec*, L.R.Q., c. C–1991 uses the term "family patrimony." See **homestead legislation**.

FAMOSUS LIBELLUS (*fā-mō'sŭs lē-bĕl'-ŭs*) Lat.: an infamous **libel**; a **slanderous** or libelous letter, handbill, advertisement, petition, written **accusation** or **indictment**. Its legal usage connotes a libelous writing.

FAULT A failing; a responsibility for failure or wrongdoing.

FAULT ELEMENTS See **mens rea**.

FAVOURED BENEFICIARY One who, in the circumstances of the particular case, has been favoured over others having equal claim to the **testator's** bounty. Confidential relations, accompanied with activity of a favoured beneficiary in the preparation and execution of a will, raises a presumption of **undue influence**.

FEALTY The vassal oath of fidelity between lord and **tenant**; the essential feudal bond. Fealty involved a number of obligations: that the tenant do no bodily harm to his lord; that he do no secret damage to him in his house; that he not injure his lord's reputation; that he render it easy for the lord to do any good and not make it impossible to be done that which was before in his lord's power to do.

Fealty was a seignorial incident and was therefore due on every change of tenancy of the seignory.

See also **homage**.

FEDERAL COURTS Initially created in 1970 and now governed by the *Federal Courts Act*, R.S.C. 1985, c. F–7, courts that are the successor to the former **Exchequer Court of Canada** and the Citizenship Appeal Court, combining their jurisdiction and expanding it. The Federal Court (formerly the Federal Court, Trial Division) consists of a chief and thirty-two other judges, while the Federal Court of Appeal (formerly the Federal Court, Appeal Division) consists of a chief justice and twelve other judges. At least ten Federal Court judges and at least five Federal Court of Appeal judges must have been judges or members of the bar of Quebec.

The jurisdiction of the Federal Courts extends to suits against the **Crown** in right of Canada, **patents** and **trademarks**, **copyright**, **Admiralty** matters, and cases involving appeals from federal boards and **tribunals**. See Chart, **Appendix I**.

FEDERAL COURT OF APPEAL See **Federal Court**.

FEDERAL COURT TRIAL DIVISION See **Federal Court**.

FEDERALISM A system of government wherein governmental power is divided between two or more sovereign, independent authorities. Canada is a federal state with the division of law-making powers between the **Parliament** of Canada and the respective provincial legislatures. The **division of powers** is achieved principally by ss. 91 and 92 of the **Constitution Act, 1867**.

In a true federal state, the central and regional governments are neither superior nor subordinate to one another. Rather, they are coordinate in the sense of being independent and autonomous. That is, neither is capable of altering the form of the other. This is opposed to a unitary state such as England or New Zealand, where local or regional authorities are essential to the proper governing of the state but are clearly subordinate to the central authority in the sense that power delegated to them can be retracted or modified unilaterally. See **Constitution**.

FEE 1. A reward or recompense for services rendered; **2.** frequently used in reference to **real property** to indicate an estate in land that is capable of being **inherited** or **devised**.

"Fee" derives from "feudal" or *feodor*, meaning "land," importing that such land is held by some superior to whom certain **services** are due. Fee, **fee simple**, and fee simple absolute are often used as equivalents. The word *fee* indicates that it is an estate of **inheritance**; the word *simple* signifies that there are no restrictions on the inheritable characteristics of the estate. But a fee may be qualified, such as a **conditional** or **determinable fee**, which could continue forever but would be discontinued upon the happening of a certain event.

FEE SIMPLE An **estate** of virtually infinite duration **conveyed** or **granted** absolutely to a person and his or her heirs forever; also known as FEE SIMPLE ABSOLUTE. There are no conditions, restrictions, or limitations on the holder of such an estate, and the **property** is freely alienable or hereditable.

The holder of the estate is known as the tenant in fee simple (see **tenant**) because, technically, he or she is merely a tenant of the **Crown**, though he or she has the highest and most extensive estate possible. However, to all intents and purposes he or she is the absolute owner.

At **common law**, it was necessary to use the words "to A and his heirs" in order to convey a fee simple. *Re*

Airey (1921), 21 O.W.N. 190 (H.C.). Without the phrase "and his heirs," only a **life estate** was created. At present the presumption is in favour of the conveyance of a fee simple unless there is manifest an intention to create a more limited estate. *Bartrop v. Blackstock* (1957), 10 D.L.R. (2d) 192 (Sask.C.A.). Furthermore, it is no longer necessary in some Canadian jurisdictions to use the word *heirs* to convey a fee simple. It may suffice if the words *in fee simple* are used or other words sufficiently indicative of that intention (e.g., *Conveyancing Act,* R.S.N.S. 1989, c. 97, s. 13). See further A.M. Sinclair & M.E. McCallum, *An Introduction to Real Property Law* 11–13 (6th ed. 2012).

See **words of limitation**. Compare **fee tail**.

FEE SIMPLE CONDITIONAL See **conditional fee**.

FEE SIMPLE DEFEASIBLE See **defeasible**; **fee simple**.

FEE SIMPLE DETERMINABLE See **determinable fee**.

FEE TAIL The estate created by **deed** or **will**, to a person "and the **heirs of his body**." A fee tail establishes a fixed line of inheritable **succession** and cuts off the regular succession of **heirs** at law. It is a limited estate in that **inheritance** is through lineal descent only, which if exclusively through males is called FEE TAIL MALE or if exclusively through females is called FEE TAIL FEMALE. If the family line runs out **(failure of issue)**, the fee **reverts** to the grantor or his successors in **interest**. See **words of limitation**. Fee tail has been abolished by statute throughout Canada. See A.M. Sinclair & M.E. McCallum, *An Introduction to Real Property Law* 13–14 (6th ed. 2012).

FELLOW SERVANT A co-worker; defined for the doctrine of common employment, which relieved an employer of **liability** for **injury** caused to one servant by the **negligence** of a fellow servant. *Priestly v. Fowler* (1857), 3 M. & W. 1; 150 E. R. 1030. Because of the hardship inflicted by the doctrine, it fell into disrepute as social conditions altered and has been abrogated by

statute, e.g., **Worker's Compensation Acts**. *Cooperators Insurance Ass'n v. Kearney* (1965), 48 D.L.R. (2d) 1 (S.C.C.).

FELON One who has been convicted of a **felony**. See **criminal**.

FELONY A generic term employed at **common law** to distinguish certain high crimes from minor offences known as **misdemeanours**. The distinction between felony and misdemeanour does not exist in the *Criminal Code of Canada,* R.S.C. 1985, c. C–46. Instead, serious crimes are those designated as punishable by **indictment** and lesser crimes as those punishable by **summary conviction**. See **indictable offence**.

FEMME COVERT Fr.: a married woman.

FEMME SOLE Fr.: a single woman, widow or divorcee.

FEOFFMENT Originally, the **conveyance** of **freehold** land through public or overt delivery by the owner to the purchaser, including **livery of seisin**, a cumbersome ceremony in which both parties to the transfer (FEOFFOR [owner] and FEOFFEE [purchaser]) entered onto the land and **seisin** was delivered when the feoffor symbolically transferred the land by conveying to the feoffee a twig or piece of sod or by appropriate words and then leaving the feoffee in possession. Gradually, it became the practice to record such a transaction in writing, and this gained statutory force in England by passage of the **Statute of Frauds**, 1677, s. 1. Feoffment came to be known as the **deed** evidencing the transfer of possession of the freehold estate. See further A.M. Sinclair & M.E. McCallum, *An Introduction to Real Property Law* 21–23 (6th ed. 2012).

FERAE NATURAE (*fĕr'-ī nä-tūr'-i*) Lat.: wild beasts of nature. **Animals** are described as *ferae naturae* when they are wild by nature and it is impossible to completely domesticate them: consequently, it requires the continuous exercise of force to subjugate them. *McLean v. Thompson*, 2009 BCPC 415.

A wild animal not tamed or ordinarily kept in captivity cannot be stolen unless it has been sufficiently reduced into possession or is in the course of being reduced into possession. *M.V. "Polar Star" v. Arsenault* (1964), 43 D.L.R. (2d) 354 (P.E.I.S.C.). See also *R. v. Roberts* (1991), 13 W.C.B. (2d) 131 (Ont. C.A.).

FERTILE OCTOGENARIAN A legal fiction created in regard to the **Rule Against Perpetuities**, conclusively presuming that an adult of any age is capable of having children regardless of such physiological facts as menopause, impotence, or surgical removal of reproductive organs. See *Re Fasken* (1959), 19 D.L.R. (2d) 182 (Ont.C.A.). See further A.M. Sinclair & M.E. McCallum, *An Introduction to Real Property Law* 106 (6th ed. 2012).

FETUS [FOETUS] An unborn child after approximately the first six to eight weeks of pregnancy (embryonic stage).

FEUDALISM A system of government and a means of holding property in England and Western Europe that grew out of the chaos of the Dark Ages (the fifth to tenth centuries). Through a ceremony called **homage**, in which mutual duties of support and protection were promised, the vassal in effect gave land to the lord and the lord then had a duty to protect it and the vassal. Though the vassal thenceforth owned no land, he held the land of the lord as a **tenant** and retained a **use** in that land. This method of holding land was very different from the modern landlord-tenant situation. The land that the vassal held was called a feud, fief or feudum. The relationship between the lord and vassal could become more indirect by the process of **subinfeudation**, so that theoretically there could be placed between the lord and the vassal any number of persons at different levels, each serving as a link in the chain of relations between the lord at the top and the least of the vassals. Eventually, the king became the ultimate lord over all, and all land in England was held of him. Only in England was feudalism the sole method of holding land, although it was the general method elsewhere in Western Europe. See further A.M. Sinclair &

M.E. McCallum, *An Introduction to Real Property Law* 2–8 (6th ed. 2012).

FIAT (*fē′ ät*) Lat.: let it be done. A command or decree made by a court or a public official.

FIAT JUSTITIA (*fē′ät jūs-tĭ′-shē-à*) Lat. let justice be done.

FIDUCIARY Relating to or proceeding from trust or confidence. One stands in a fiduciary relationship with regard to another person when he or she has rights and powers he or she must exercise for the benefit of that other person. Consequently, a fiduciary is not allowed to benefit personally in any way from the position he or she holds unless he has the requisite consent. *Boardman v. Phipps,* [1966] 3 All E.R. 721 (H.L.). "A fiduciary duty imposes the highest duty in law on the party holding the duty—the fiduciary—to act altruistically for the sole benefit of the beneficiary, to the fiduciary's own detriment if necessary...a fiduciary duty exists because the fiduciary has assumed a position, and taken on a responsibility, in which the beneficiary's interest is dependent upon the fiduciary's actions." *Ben-Israel v. Vitacare Medical Products Inc.* (1997), 78 C.P.R. (3d) 94 at para. 39 (Ont. Gen. Div.).

The number of circumstances in which a fiduciary relationship exists is indefinite and open-ended. Nonetheless, the following relationships are considered to be fiduciary: **trustee** and **beneficiary**, guardian and ward, **solicitor** and client, **principal** and **agent**, and wherever one reposes confidence in another. The **Federal** government has an obligation to act in a fiduciary capacity toward Aboriginal peoples. *R. v. Sparrow*, [1990] 1 S.C.R. 1075.

FINAL HEARING See **hearing**.

FINAL JUDGMENT See **judgment**.

FINAL ORDER See **order**.

FINDING Any conclusion upon an inquiry of fact made in a judicial proceeding. Findings of fact made by a **jury** or, in the absence of a jury, by a judge sitting alone.

FINE "[A] pecuniary penalty or other sum of money, but does not include restitution." *Criminal Code*, R.S.C. 1985, c. C–46, s. 716.

FIREARM "[A] barrelled weapon from which any shot, bullet or other projectile can be discharged and that is capable of causing serious bodily injury or death to a person, and includes any frame or receiver of such a barrelled weapon and anything that can be adapted for use as a firearm." *Criminal Code*, R.S.C. 1985, c. C–46, s. 2. See also, *id.*, ss. 84–117.15.

FIRST DEGREE MURDER See **murder**.

FIRST DEVISEE The first person who is to receive an **estate devised** by **will**. "Next devisee" refers to those who will receive the **remainder** in tail (see **fee tail)**.

FIRST IMPRESSION First discussion or consideration. **1.** A case that presents to a court a **question of law** never before considered, and consequently one for which there is no **precedent**, is said to be a case of first impression. **2.** In the case of false or misleading advertising, the test is one of first impression: "the one a person has after an initial contact with the entire advertisement, and it relates to both the layout of the advertisement and the meaning of the words used." *Richard v. Time Inc.*, 2012 SCC 8.

FIRST NATIONS A term used to describe **Aboriginal peoples** in Canada other than the Métis and Inuit. Neither the *Indian Act*, RSC 1985, c. I–5, nor the **Canadian Charter of Rights and Freedoms** use the term, but it is reflected in some legislation. See, e.g., the *First Nations Land Management Act*, SC 1999, c. 24, or the *Privacy Act*, RSC 1985, c. P–21, s. 8.

FISCAL Of or pertaining to financial matters—as in FISCAL YEAR, meaning the financial year.

FISHER APPLICATION An application for state funding to pay **counsel** at a higher rate than the normal **legal aid** rate or for some similar expense, on the basis that the accused's fair trial right will otherwise be violated. *R. v. Fisher*, [1997]

S.J. No. 530. There are no specific criteria for a Fisher application, which will succeed only in exceptional cases. See **Rowbotham application**.

FIXED CHARGE See **floating charge**.

FIXTURES Articles of **personalty** that have been annexed to land to such an extent that they are thereafter regarded as part of the **realty** (i.e., PERMANENT). A lighting fixture will not be a fixture in the legal sense if it can be easily removed. Area carpets are not fixtures, but wall-to-wall carpeting may be. Articles attached to the land only by their weight are not considered fixtures unless intent is apparent. However, articles even slightly affixed are considered part of the land in the absence of a contrary intention. In determining whether an article has become a fixture, regard must be had to the degree and object of the annexation, and to the purpose to which the article will be put. That is, whether it is for the better and more effectual use of the land as realty or for the better use of the article as a **chattel**. *La Salle Recreation Ltd. v. Canadian Candex Investments Ltd., Chester, Sigurdson and White Spot No. 12 Ltd.* (1969), 4 D.L.R. (3d) 549 (B.C.C.A.).

Fixtures are divided into two categories: (1) **landlord's** fixtures, or those that belong to the landlord, and (2) **tenant's** fixtures, which can be removed by the tenant. Tenant's fixtures can be further subdivided into **(a)** TRADE FIXTURES, which are articles annexed to land simply for purposes of trade, and **(b)** ORNAMENTAL FIXTURES, which are articles for domestic use or added because of their ornamental value.

FLAG STATE In the context of **maritime law**, the jurisdiction in which a ship is registered. "The registration of ships in Canada entails responsibilities for this country as a flag state at international law." E. Gold, A. Chircop & H. Kindred, *Maritime Law* 176 (2003). See also **UNCLOS III**.

FLIR A Forward-Looking Infra-Red camera, used by police to detect the heat emanating from a building as a method of gaining **reasonable grounds to believe** that premises are being used as a

grow-op in order to obtain a **search warrant**. "FLIR technology records images of thermal energy or heat radiating from a building. Once a baseline is calibrated, cooler areas show up as dark, and warmer areas are lighter. FLIR imaging cannot, at this stage of its development, determine the nature of the source of heat within the building. It cannot distinguish between heat diffused over an external wall that came originally from a sauna or a pottery kiln, or between heat that originated in an overheated toaster or heat from a halide lamp. In short, the FLIR camera cannot 'see' through the external surfaces of a building .... However, the substantial amounts of heat generated by marijuana growing operations must eventually escape from the building. The FLIR camera creates an image of the distribution of escaping heat at a level of detail not discernible by the naked eye. A FLIR image, put together with other information, can help the police get reasonable and probable grounds to believe that a marijuana growing operation is in residence." *R. v. Tessling*, 2004 SCC 67. The use of a FLIR does not infringe on a person's **reasonable expectation of privacy**, and so it can be used without a warrant. *Id.*

FLOATING CHARGE A type of **security interest** in which a loan is secured not by signing over the legal interest in a particular property (a "fixed charge") but by being notionally attached to real property or to personal property that changes in quality or quantity, such as the inventory of a store. This security interest allows the borrower to continue to use the assets subject to the charge in the ordinary course of its business. The assets subject to a floating charge can be sold or replaced with other assets because the interest "floats" over the property without requiring any legal interest in it to be handed over. Upon the occurrence of certain specified events, such as a default on the loan, a floating charge "crystallizes" and becomes like a fixed charge on the then-existing assets of the borrower. Whether a charge is fixed or floating, the order of priority of creditors is determined by the **PPSA**.

"The critical significance of the characterization of an interest as being fixed or floating, of course, is that it describes the extent to which a creditor can be said to have a proprietary interest in the collateral. In particular, during the period in which a charge over inventory is floating, the creditor possesses no legal title to that collateral. For this reason, if a statutory trust or lien attaches during this time, it will attach to the debtor's interest and take priority over a subsequently crystallized floating charge. However, if a security interest can be characterized as a fixed and specific charge, it will take priority over a subsequent statutory lien or charge; in such a case, all that the lien can attach to is the debtor's equity of redemption in the collateral." *Bank of Montreal v. Innovation Credit Union*, 2010 SCC 47, quoting *Royal Bank of Canada v. Sparrow Electric Corp.*, [1997] 1 S.C.R. 411.

FLOTSAM Goods that have fallen from a ship and become separated from it. Compare **jetsam**.

FOIL In an **identification parade**, any person other than one suspected of committing the offence.

FORBEARANCE TO SUE A promise "not to enforce a valid claim" against another party, usually as new **consideration** for the variation of terms in a pre-existing **contract**. "For example, a creditor to whom a sum of money has become due may promise to give the debtor extra time to pay, in return for the debtor's promise to give additional security or to pay higher interest. In such a case, there is good consideration for the debtor's promise." H.G. Beale, ed., 1 *Chitty on Contracts* 280–81 (30th ed. 2008). It is not necessary for the promisor to believe that his or her claim would succeed, but only that the claim was valid in law. *Id*, 283; *Southwest Properties Ltd. v. Radio Atlantic Holdings Ltd.* (1994), 131 N.S.R. (2d) 141 (N.S.S.C.).

FORCE-MAJEURE CLAUSE A clause inserted in a contract "by which one (or both) of the parties is excused from performance of the contract, in whole or in part, or is entitled to suspend performance, upon the happening of a specified event or events beyond his control." The onus is on the party relying on the force majeure clause to prove that non-performance of the contract was due to events beyond his or her control and that there were no measures that he or she could have undertaken to prevent or avoid the extraordinary event or its consequences. H.G. Beale, ed., 1 *Chitty on Contracts* 981–83 (30th ed. 2008). See *Fibrosa Spolka Akcyjna v. Fairbairn Lawson Combe Barbour Ltd.*, [1943] A.C. 32 (H.L.). See **act of god**; **frustration**.

FORCIBLE DETAINER A **hybrid offence** committed by anyone who in **possession** of **real property** detains it without **colour of right** against a person entitled to possession in such a manner as to cause a **breach of the peace** or reasonable apprehension of such. Punishment is up to two years' imprisonment. See *Criminal Code*, R.S.C. 1985, c. C–46, ss. 72, 73.

Compare **tenancy** [TENANCY AT SUFFERANCE].

FORCIBLE ENTRY 1. Entry onto land in the **possession** of another in a manner likely to cause a **breach of the peace** or reasonable apprehension of such; a **hybrid offence** under the *Criminal Code*, R.S.C. 1985, c. C–46, ss. 72, 73. See also **trespass. 2.** An entry by police to execute a warrant that does not comply with the **knock and announce rule**. Also referred to as a dynamic entry or hard entry.

FORECLOSURE Generally, the termination of a right to **property**. When there is a default by the mortgagor in a **mortgage** agreement, the right to foreclosure arises, but only if there is a forfeiture by breach of **condition**. *Sampson v. Pattison* (1842), 1 Hare 533, 66 E.R. 1143 (Ch.). The foreclosure proceeding itself is any proceeding by which the mortgagor's **equity of redemption** is **barred** or **extinguished** beyond the possibility of recall, thus **vesting** the property absolutely in the mortgagee.

FOREIGN NATIONAL means "a person who is not a **Canadian citizen**, or a **permanent resident**, and includes a stateless person." See *Immigration and Refugee Protection Act,* S.C. 2001, c.27, s. 2.(1). A foreign national may acquire the status of a permanent resident, or a **temporary resident**, by fulfilling requirements set out in the *Act,* or regulations made thereunder.

FORESEEABILITY A concept used in various areas of the law to limit the **liability** of a party for the consequences of his or her acts to the consequences that are within the scope of a FORESEEABLE RISK, i.e., a risk whose consequences a person of ordinary prudence would reasonably expect might occur as a result of his or her actions.

In the law of **negligence**, foreseeability of harm plays a number of roles, including being required in order to establish a **duty of care**. In addition, the **defendant** must have been able to foresee the specific harm suffered by the **plaintiff** in order for the plaintiff to establish that the harm is not too remote. *Overseas Tankship (U.K.) Ltd. v. Morts Dock and Engineering Co. Ltd., The Wagon Mound (No. 1)*, [1961] A.C. 388 (P.C.). *Mustapha v. Culligan of Canada*, 2008 SCC 27.

In a contract setting, under the rule in *Hadley v. Baxendale* (1854), 9 Ex. 341, 156 E.R. 145, a party's liability for special or consequential **damage** is limited to the damages arising from the foreseeable consequences of his **breach**. See also *Victoria Laundry (Windsor) Ltd. v. Newman Industries Ltd.*, [1949] 2 K.B. 528 (C.A.).

FORESHORE Land lying between the high water mark and the low water mark. Title to the foreshore normally belongs to the Crown.

FORFEITURE 1. A punishment whereby a person or offender loses all or some of his or her **interests** in his or her **property**. Thus, the **goods** and **chattels** of a criminal were, prior to the English *Forfeiture Act, 1870,* forfeited to the Crown. **2.** In a **lease**, a forfeiture clause reserves to the **lessor** a right of **reentry**, upon which the lease is forfeited. **3. Shares** may be forfeited by resolution of the board of directors of a **corporation** if such power is given in the **Articles of Association**—e.g., where a member fails to pay a **call** properly made on him or her.

FORGERY Defined in the *Criminal Code,* R.S.C. 1985, c. C–46, s. 366(1) as the making of a false document, with knowledge that it is false, intending that it will be acted upon as genuine, to the prejudice of anyone within or without Canada, or with the intent that someone will be induced to do or refrain from doing anything, whether within Canada or not.

FORM A model of a **document** containing the phrases and **words of art** that are needed to make the document technically correct for **procedural** purposes. Forms are used by lawyers in drafting legal documents.

FORMAL EQUALITY To treat all persons in the same way, without regard to differences among those persons. Formal equality is contrasted with **substantive equality**: the latter is the "animating norm of s. 15(1)," the **equality** rights guarantee in the **Canadian Charter of Rights and Freedoms**. *Withler v. Canada (Attorney-General),* 2011 SCC 12.

FORMS OF ACTION Technical categories of personal **actions** developed at **common law**, containing the entire course of legal proceedings particular to those actions. The forms of actions are no longer required, but they continue to affect modern civil procedure and **tort** law.

Forms of action consisted of proceedings for recovery of debts and for recovery of money **damages** resulting from **breach of contract** or injury to one's person, property, or relations. The forms can be classified as (*a*) actions in form *ex cantractu,* including **assumpsit, covenant, debt,** and **account**; and (*b*) actions in form *ex delicto* (i.e., those not based on contracts), including **trespass, trover, case, detinue,** and **replevin**. See L.S. Abrams & K.P. McGuinness, *Canadian Civil Procedure Law* 30–32 (2nd ed. 2010).

"This feature of the common law prevailed for many centuries, and it was in reaction to [the] writ system that much of the present law of civil procedure came about ....Writs permitted a party to obtain relief for a wrong suffered only if he (or far more rarely, she) could bring his claim within the scope of a recognized writ, and utilized the proper form of writ when instituting the claim." *Id* at 30.

FORNICATION Generally, sexual intercourse between two unmarried people of different sexes. If either party is married, the proper term is **adultery**.

In Canada, fornication is not, in itself, an offence, unless it necessarily involves the commission of another offence such as sexual exploitation of a young person sixteen years of age or over, but under the age of eighteen years (see *Criminal Code,* R.S.C. 1985, c. C–46, s. 153); or incest (s. 155).

FORTHWITH Immediately or without delay. In the context of a demand for a breath sample under s. 254(2) of the *Criminal Code,* R.S.C. 1985, c. C–46, the term could, in unusual circumstances, be given a more flexible interpretation and allow for a brief and unavoidable delay. *R. v. Woods,* 2005 SCC 42.

FORUM A court; a place where disputes are settled according to the dictates of law and justice and where **remedies** afforded by law are pursued. The term is also used to indicate the country, state, province, etc., in which **jurisdiction** is exercised. A *forum competens* (or *incompetens*) is a court that has (or has not) the jurisdiction to deal with a matter. See also **venue**.

FORUM NON CONVENIENS (*fôr'-ŭm nŏn kŏn-vē'-nē-ĕns*) Lat.: an inconvenient court. A doctrine under which a court can choose not to hear a matter even though it has jurisdiction to do so. At common law, a court has a residual power to decline to exercise its jurisdiction in order to assure fairness to the parties and the efficient resolution of the dispute. A party asking a court to decline its jurisdiction on this basis must show that there is an alternative forum that is clearly more appropriate. "If a **defendant** raises an issue of *forum non conveniens,* the burden is on him or her to show why the court should decline to exercise its **jurisdiction** and displace the **forum** chosen by the **plaintiff**. The defendant must identify another forum that has an appropriate connection under the **conflicts** rules and that should be allowed to dispose of the action. The defendant must show, using the same analytical approach the court followed to establish the existence of a **real and substantial connection** with the local forum, what connections this alternative forum has with the subject matter of the litigation. Finally, the party asking for a stay on the basis of *forum non conveniens* must demonstrate why the proposed alternative forum should be preferred and considered to be more appropriate." *Club Resorts Ltd. v. Van Breda*, 2012 SCC 17.

In some jurisdictions the common law *forum non conveniens* rules have been replaced by statutory provisions. See, e.g., *Court Jurisdiction and Proceedings Transfer Act*, S.B.C. 2003, c. 28; *The Court Jurisdiction and Proceedings Transfer Act*, S.S. 1997, c. C–41.1; *Court Jurisdiction and Proceedings Transfer Act*, S.N.S. 2003 (2nd Sess.), c. 2. The decision that a court will exercise jurisdiction over a matter does not necessarily settle the **choice of law**.

FORUM SHOPPING A strategic decision by a plaintiff to sue in a jurisdiction in which he or she enjoys the greatest juridical advantage. In the context of defamation referred to as "libel tourism." *Éditions Écosociété Inc. v. Banro Corp.*, 2012 SCC 18. See **real and substantial connection**; **forum non conveniens**.

FOUR UNITIES See **unities**.

FRANCHISE 1. A special privilege that is conferred by the government upon an individual and that does not belong to the citizens of the country generally, of common right. For example, a municipality may grant a franchise to a local bus company giving it sole authority to operate buses in the municipality for a certain number of years. **2.** Also, the right given to a private person or corporations to market another's product within a certain area. Thus, gas stations that sell brand-name gasoline often operate the station through a franchise granted by an oil company.

ELECTIVE FRANCHISE The right of citizens to vote in public elections; sometimes called simply "the franchise."

FRANKMARRIAGE A gift to a prospective bride and groom that was free of services to the donor. When land was given to a woman and her prospective husband "in frankmarriage" by a blood relation, the husband and wife held the land to them and their issue, free of services to the donor, although no words of inheritance or procreation were used in the gift.

FRAUD Intentional deception resulting in actual or potential **injury** to another person. Fraud exists in Canadian law as both a **tort** and as a criminal **offence**.

In the context of tort liability, fraud "is established whenever a person has made a fraudulent statement that intentionally causes another person to rely on it to [his or her] detriment. Most of the cases deal with economic loss arising from fraudulently induced contracts," but the tort "is not restricted to those losses and may extend to property damage and personal injury." P.H. Osborne, *The Law of Torts* 315–16 (4th ed. 2011). In order to establish the tort, the plaintiff "must prove actual damage caused by reliance on" the defendant's "fraudulent misrepresentation." *Id* at 317.

In the criminal context, fraud is an offence under s. 380(1) of the *Criminal Code*, R.S.C., 1985, c. C–46. The offence includes "any deceit, falsehood or other fraudulent means" that "defrauds the public or any person, whether ascertained or not, of any property, money, valuable security or any service." Unlike in the tort law context, the offence may be established without proving that an accused actually caused a loss; it is sufficient that he or she put "the victim's pecuniary interests at risk." *R. v. Théroux*, [1993] 2 S.C.R. 5.

Fraud may also be established as part of the **actus reus** of **sexual assault**. Section 265(3) of the *Criminal Code*, R.S.C., 1985, c. C–46 provides that consent to sexual activity is vitiated where it is procured by means of fraud. Historically, this provision included only fraudulent representations about the "nature and quality" of the accused's act against the victim. *R. v. Clarence* (1888), 22 Q.B.D. 23. In *R. v. Cuerrier*, [1998] 2 S.C.R. 371, however, the Supreme

Court held that a person could commit sexual assault by fraud where the fraud exposed the victim to risk of "serious bodily harm" (for example, by failing to disclose his or her HIV-positive status). The Supreme Court later clarified this requirement in *R. v. Mabior*, 2012 SCC 47. See also **misrepresentation**.

FRAUDULENT See **fraud**.

FRAUDULENT PREFERENCE See **preference**.

FREE AND CLEAR Unencumbered. In property law, one **conveys** land free and clear if he or she transfers a **good title** or **marketable title** unencumbered by any **interest** held by another in the land.

FREEDOM OF ASSEMBLY The right guaranteed in s. 2(c) of the **Canadian Charter of Rights and Freedoms** to assemble peacefully. The right to hold public meetings on the public domain of a city was not a part of the English **common law** and so was not a part of the law of Canada. *Dupond v. City of Montreal et al.*, [1978] 2 S.C.R. 770. Freedom of assembly and association were guaranteed together under s. 1(e) of the **Canadian Bill of Rights**, but under the *Charter* those freedoms have been placed in separate subsections. Very little judicial attention has been given to the *Charter* right of freedom of peaceful assembly. Most typically the *Charter* issue focuses on the collective right of the group to act collectively or on the message that the group is attempting to convey, and so cases tend to discuss the rights to **freedom of association** or **freedom of expression** instead. See, e.g., *British Columbia Teachers' Federation v. British Columbia Public School Employers' Assn.*, 2009 BCCA 39.

FREEDOM OF ASSOCIATION The guarantee in s. 2(d) of the **Canadian Charter of Rights and Freedoms** protecting the right to associate. The right has most frequently been litigated in the context of labour relations, where it has been found that s. 2(d) protects the freedom to establish, belong to, and maintain an association; protects the exercise in association of the constitutional rights and freedoms of individuals, and protects the exercise in association of the lawful rights of individuals. However, the guarantee does not protect an activity solely on the ground that the activity is a foundational or essential purpose of an association. *Professional Institute of the Public Service of Canada v. Northwest Territories (Commissioner)*, [1990] 2 S.C.R. 367. The guarantee also protects the right to collective bargaining. *Health Services and Support—Facilities Subsector Bargaining Assn. v. British Columbia*, 2007 SCC 27. The freedom in s. 2(d) is subject to **reasonable limits in a free and democratic society** under s. 1 of the *Charter*.

FREEDOM OF CONTRACT The ability of parties to agree to the most advantageous bargain between them without interference from the courts. In the eighteenth century there was little restriction placed on this freedom, the philosophy being that persons could pursue their interests in the way they saw fit and that the duty of the law was merely to give effect to the intention of the parties. See, e.g., *Printing and Numerical Registering Co. v. Sampson* (1875), L.R. 19 Eq. 462 (C.A.). This position still finds expression today; see, e.g., *Peachtree II Associates–Dallas, L.P. v. 857486 Ontario Ltd.* (2005), O.R. (3d) 362 (C.A.). However, there are significant areas in the law of **contract** where the courts are disposed to grant relief from contractual arrangements seen to be unreasonable or **unconscionable**. "I take the view that the Courts are not bound to all contracts at face value and enforce contracts without some regard to the surrounding circumstances. I do not think that mere formal consensus is enough. I am of the opinion that the terms of a contract may be declared to be void as being unreasonable where it can be said that in all the circumstances it is unreasonable and unconscionable to bind the parties to their formal bargain." *Davidson v. Three Spruces Realty Ltd.*, [1977] 6 W.W.R. 460 at 476 (B.C.S.C.). Similarly, the courts will frequently strictly construe a **disclaimer** or exemption from liability clause in a contract. See further S. M. Waddams, *The Law *of Contracts* 342–357 (6th ed. 2010). Legislation may also permit interference with a contract where a court finds its terms to be harsh or unconscionable. See, e.g., *Unconscionable Transactions Act,* R.S.A. 2000, c. U–2; *Consumer Protection Act, 2002,* S.O. 2002, c. 30. See **consumer protection**.

FREEDOM OF EXPRESSION The guarantee in s. 2(b) of the **Canadian Charter of Rights and Freedoms** protecting attempts to convey meaning. All communications, no matter what their content, are protected by the guarantee, though the freedom is subject to **reasonable limits in a free and democratic society** under s. 1 of the *Charter.* Freedom of expression can be violated by preventing a person from communicating a message, by requiring a person to do so, or by dictating the language in which communication must take place. Meaning can also be conveyed by actions, and so limits on expressive activity violate freedom of expression, unless that expressive activity takes the form of violence. The guarantee for freedom of expression also has implications for the location of that expression. See *Irwin Toy v. Quebec,* [1989] 1 S.C.R. 927; *Committee for the Commonwealth of Canada v. Canada,* [1991] 1 S.C.R. 139.

FREEDOM OF INFORMATION "Freedom of information legislation ... is designed to give a citizen access to government information.... [It] relates not to personal information but to government information in the nature of 'public business'." G. Gall, *The Canadian Legal System* 573–74 (5th ed. 2004). See *Access to Information Act,* R.S.C. 1985, c. A–1. Compare **privacy**.

FREEDOM OF RELIGION The guarantee in s. 2(a) of the **Canadian Charter of Rights and Freedoms** protecting "the right to entertain such religious beliefs as a person chooses, the right to declare religious beliefs openly and without fear of hindrance or reprisal, and the right to manifest religious belief by worship and practice or by teaching and dissemination." *R. v. Big M Drug Mart Ltd.,* [1985] 1 S.C.R. 295. The freedom in s.

2(d) is subject to **reasonable limits in a free and democratic society** under s. 1 of the *Charter.* See *Syndicat Northcrest v. Amselem,* 2004 SCC 47.

FREEDOMS, FUNDAMENTAL See **Canadian Charter of Rights and Freedoms**.

FREEHOLD An estate in **fee** or a **life estate**.

FREEHOLD ESTATE An **estate** or **interest** in **real property** of infinite duration; a legal right as against all the world. It is an estate of **inheritance** or for life in either a corporeal or an incorporeal **hereditament** existing in or arising from real property of free **tenure**. Estates created under the **common law** could only be **conveyed** by engaging in the **livery of seisin**; upon assuming title by such livery, the **tenant** [or owner] became **seised** to the land and established ownership. Although a charter of **enfeoffment** may have recorded the ceremonious livery of seisin, under the common law, initially, no writing was required to transfer a freehold estate. See further A.M. Sinclair & M.E. McCallum, *An Introduction to Real Property Law* (6th ed. 2012), c. 2.

FRESH PURSUIT 1. In criminal law, a term that refers to the **common-law** right of a police officer to cross jurisdictional lines in order to arrest a **felon**. **2.** The term, as found in s. 494(1)(b)(ii) of the *Criminal Code,* R.S.C. 1985, c. C–46, also refers to the fact that "[a]ny one may arrest without **warrant** . . . a person who, on reasonable grounds, he believes . . . is escaping from and freshly pursued by persons who have lawful authority to arrest that person." See **hot pursuit**.

FRIENDLY SUIT An action brought by agreement between the **parties** in order to obtain a **judgment** that will have a binding effect in circumstances where a mere agreement or settlement will not. For example, the friendly suit is employed when a **claim** in favour of an infant is settled because the infant cannot effectively **release** the claim by a release **contract**, though the entry of a judgment does bind him or her. The friendly suit is usually brought without formal **process**, but the court will demand some kind of proof (often **affidavits** are sufficient) that the settlement is a just and fair one. Suits that are "collusive," that is, those wherein the parties purport to have a controversy but do not, or where they agree to certain facts in order to obtain a certain legal result (as in divorce cases), will be **dismissed**. See **collusion**. Compare **adversary proceeding**; **controversy**; **declaratory judgment**.

FRIEND OF THE COURT See **amicus curiae**.

FRIVOLOUS Clearly insufficient as a matter of law; presenting no debatable question. A case may be dismissed as frivolous where it is clearly unsupported on the facts or is one for which the law provides no **remedy**. It is an action that has no legal basis or merit and is not resasonably purposeful. *Currie v. Halton (Region) Police Services Board* (2003), 233 D.L.R. (4th) 657 (Ont. C.A.)

FRONTIER LANDS Areas within which the right to exploit natural resources such as oil and gas belong to the Crown in right of Canada rather than the Crown in right of the provinces. These include offshore oil and gas rights and oil and gas in the three Territories.

FRUSTRATION The inability to complete or discharge a contract because of circumstances beyond the control of the contracting parties and outside of their contemplation. Prior to 1863, contracts were considered absolute (unless a contrary intention was expressed) so that a person was strictly bound by his contract despite the fact that changed circumstances made performance impossible. In 1803, in *Taylor v. Caldwell* (1863), 122 E.R. 309 (K.B.) [applied, e.g., in *Kerrigan v. Harrison* (1921), 62 S.C.R. 374], the doctrine of frustration was introduced by implying a **condition** that the contract was subject to the continued existence of the subject matter. This was extended to cover the situation where the transaction envisaged by the parties was frustrated. *Jackson v. Union Marine Insurance* Co. *Ltd.* (1874), L.R. 10 C.P. 125 (CP.). It is a question of **construc-**

tion of the contract as to whether a particular event frustrates a contract. Money paid out before discharge of the contract may be recoverable, as in QUASI-CONTRACT (see **quasi**). *Fibrosa Spolka Akcyjna v. Fairbairn Lawson Combe Barbour Ltd.,* [1943] A.C. 32 (H.L.). The doctrine will not be applied where the party seeking to introduce and rely on any such term has personally brought about the event or occurrence that he or she now claims for termination of the contract. See *Dinicola v. Huang & Danczkay Properties* (1996), 29 O.R. (3d) 161 (Ont C.J.).

In spite of the *Fibrosa* decision, the common law did not completely cover the question of the amount recoverable for expenditures incurred before the frustration. As a result, a *Frustrated Contracts Act* was enacted in England in 1943. Similar statutes have been enacted in most Canadian jurisdictions. See, e.g., R.S.O. 1990, c. F. 34.

See **impossibility**.

FUGITIVE One who flees from justice. *Beim v. Goyer* (1965), 57 D.L.R. (2d) 253 (S.C.C.). Under the *Extradition Act,* R.S.C. 1985, c. E–23, s. 2, a fugitive or fugitive criminal is a person in or suspected of being in Canada who is **accused** or **convicted** of an extradition crime committed in a foreign state. This statute was repealed and replaced by the *Extradition Act,* S.C. 1999, c. 18. There is no definition of fugitive in the new Act.

FULL ANSWER AND DEFENCE A right of an **accused** charged with a **crime**, protected as a **principle of fundamental justice** under s. 7 of the **Canadian Charter of Rights and Freedoms**. The right to full answer and defence is linked to the **presumption of innocence**, the right to a fair trial, and the principle against **self-incrimination**, as well as to the right to **disclosure**. The right does not override all other considerations, and so it does not entitle an accused to introduce evidence that is not ordinarily **admissible**, such as **hearsay**, and does not mean that an accused is entitled to disclosure of **privileged** information. See *R. v. Mills*, [1999] 3 S.C.R. 668.

FUNCTUS OFFICIO (*fŭnk'-tŭs ŏf-ĭ'-shē-ō*) Lat.: to have performed one's office. The doctrine that a decision-maker who has rendered a final decision has completed his or her function and has no authority to deal further with the matter. "[T]he principle of *functus officio* exists to allow finality of judgments from courts [that] are subject to appeal... This makes sense: if a court could continually hear applications to vary its decisions, it would assume the function of an appellate court and deny litigants a stable base from which to launch an appeal." *Doucet-Boudreau v. Nova Scotia (Minister of Education)*, 2003 SCC 62.

FUNDAMENTAL BREACH A contractual doctrine that holds that a party is precluded from relying on an exemption clause to excuse him or her from liability for a fundamental breach of contract or the breach of a fundamental term. The Supreme Court has eliminated the doctrine of fundamental breach from Canadian contract law. *Tercon Contractors Ltd. v. British Columbia (Transportation and Highways)*, 2010 SCC 4 (S.C.C.) See G.H.L. Fridman, *The Law of Contract in Canada* 573–85 (6th ed. 2011). See S.M. Waddams, *The Law of Contracts* 447–49 (6th ed. 2010). See also, **breach**; **frustration**.

FUNDAMENTAL FREEDOMS See **Canadian Charter of Rights and Freedoms**.

FUNGIBLE PROPERTY Property in which individual items or amounts are mutually interchangeable. For example, a person buying a DVD player or a blank CD would not normally care which DVD player or CD he or she received. Similarly, a person buying a quantity of fuel oil would accept any portion of the supply equally.

FUTURE INTEREST An **interest** in presently existing **real property** or **personal property** that is limited so as to commence in the future. Future interests are **estates** in expectancy as opposed to estates in **possession** and may be subclassified into two categories, **reversions** and **remainders**. If by **deed** the holder of a **fee simple** grants a particular estate to one person and a subsequent estate to another person, the subsequent estate is known as a remainder since it remains away from the original grantor. Where no subsequent estate is granted, the residue remains with the grantor and is known as a reversion to the grantor on the expiration of the particular estate.

FUTURES Agreements where one person says that he or she will sell a commodity at a certain time in the future for a certain price. The buyer agrees to pay that price, knowing that the person has nothing to deliver at the time, but with the understanding that when the time arrives for **delivery** the buyer is to pay him or her the difference between the **market value** of that commodity and the price agreed upon if the commodity's value declines; if it advances, the seller is to pay the buyer the difference between the agreed-upon price and the market price. Thus, if the price of the commodity rises, the buyer makes a profit and if the price declines, the buyer suffers a loss.

Formerly, such speculative agreements were generally unenforceable in courts of law as being against public policy because they were a form of gambling. Today, futures are traded on commodity futures exchanges. In order to make the transaction legal, the parties must intend to deliver or receive delivery of the commodity, each party being obligated to make delivery or accept delivery of the commodity unless the contract has been **liquidated** by offset on the exchange. If a trader insists on literal satisfaction of his or her contract rights, it must be fulfilled by conveyance of the physical commodity. Thus the fundamental principle underlying all commodity exchanges is that a person who buys or sells a futures contract and does not offset it by a contra-transaction on the exchange must receive the commodity or be called on to deliver it. The fact that most persons who trade on a commodity exchange expect to offset their contracts before the date of delivery or receipt is not a denial of this principle.

G

GAAR General Anti-Avoidance Rule. A rule in the *Income Tax Act*, RSC 1985, c. 1 (5th Supp), s. 245, which provides that if a transaction by a taxpayer results in a tax benefit, it was an **avoidance transaction**, and was abusive. A transaction is abusive if it achieves an outcome the statutory provision was intended to prevent, and defeats the underlying rationale of the provision or circumvents the provision in a manner that frustrates or defeats its object, spirit, or purpose. See *Copthorne Holdings Ltd. v. Canada*, 2011 SCC 63.

GAINFUL EMPLOYMENT [OCCUPATION] Work that is lucrative, remunerative, or based on gain. A person is said to be gainfully employed when he or she receives remuneration from his or her employer in return for the services he or she supplies under the contract of employment.

GAMING The playing of a game of chance and skill for stakes or **wager**, either of money or items of value. "To amount to gaming, the game played must involve the element of wagering— that is to say, each of the players must have a chance of losing as well as of winning." *R. v. Ashton* (1852), 1 E. & B. 286, adopted in *Di Pietro et al. v. The Queen*, [1986] 1 S.C.R. 250. See also *R. v. Pamajewon*, [1996] 2 S.C.R. 821, finding gaming not to be an **Aboriginal right** on the facts of that case. See s. 197, *Criminal Code*, R.S.C. 1985, c. C–46.

GAOL, GAOLER Variant spellings of jail and jailer. Though both forms are correct, recent dictionaries have preferred the *jail/jailer* form.

GARAGEMAN'S LIEN See **lien** [MECHANICS' LIEN].

GARNISH To bring a **garnishment** proceeding or to **attach** wages or other property pursuant to such a proceeding,

In old English law, garnish meant to warn, that is, by giving notice of the proceedings.

GARNISHEE 1. A person who receives notice to retain **custody** of the **assets** of another until he or she receives further notice from the court. The garnishee merely holds the assets until legal **proceedings** determine who is entitled to the property. The term thus signifies one on whom process of **garnishment** has been served.
2. A **debtor** in whose hands a debt has been **attached**, who has been warned not to pay a debt to his or her **creditor** but to a third party who has obtained a **final judgment** against the creditor.

GARNISHMENT A statutory proceeding whereby a person's **property**, money or credits in possession or under control of, or owing by, another are applied to payment of the former's debt to a third person by proper statutory process against **debtor** and garnishee. See, e.g., *Court Order Enforcement Act,* R.S.B.C. 1996, c. 78; a process in which money or goods in the hands of a third person that are owed to a **defendant** are attached by a **plaintiff**: the **garnishee** is warned not to pay over the property to anyone except the plaintiff.

Under the statutory **remedy** the third party is notified to retain something he or she has that belongs to the defendant (debtor), to make disclosure to the court concerning it and to dispose of it as the court shall direct.

See also **attachment**.

GAZETTE The official publication of **Parliament** or a **legislature** containing official government notices such as the **proclamation** of **statutes** or publication of **regulations**. Federal regulations are not normally enforceable until they have been published in the Gazette. *Statutory Instruments Act,* R.S.C., 1985, c. S–22, s. 11(2). See **Canada Gazette**.

GENDER-NEUTRAL LANGUAGE A manner of phrasing that avoids reference to gender in order to be more inclusive. For examples, **statutes** and **judgments** that would once have referred to the "reasonable man" more commonly today refer to the "reasonable person." Although statutes tend now to be drafted in language that avoids reference to gender, the *Interpretation Act*, RSC 1985, c. I–21, s. 33(1) provides that "words importing female persons include male persons and corporations, and words importing male persons include female persons and corporations." Other jurisdictions adopt the same approach. See, e.g., *Interpretation Act*, RSA 2000, c. I–8, s. 26(2). See **sexist language**.

GENERAL CONTRACTOR See **contractor**.

GENERAL DAMAGES See **damages**.

GENERALIA SPECIALIBUS NON DEROGANT (*jĕ'-nêr-ă-lē-ă spĕ'-shē-ăl-ĭ-bŭs nŏn dĕ'-rŭ-gănt*) Lat.: general provisions do not detract from particular ones. "The principle…that where there are provisions in a special act and in a general act on the same subject which are inconsistent, if the special act gives a complete rule on the subject, the expression of the rule acts as an exception of the subject-matter of the rule from the general act." *Ottawa* (*City*) *v. Eastview* (*Municipality*), [1941] S.C.R. 448 at 462. See also *Century Services Inc. v. Canada* (*Attorney-General*), 2010 SCC 60.

GENERAL INTENT See **intent**.

GENERIC A term referring to a group or class of related things, whereas *specific* is limited to a particular, definite or precise thing. In commercial law, where the contract is for a part of a specified whole, generic goods do not become ascertained, and therefore the property does not pass until they have been **appropriated** to the contract.

GENOCIDE Under the *Criminal Code*, R.S.C. 1985, c. C–46, having the intention to destroy in whole or in part any identifiable group, and killing members of that group or deliberately inflicting on the group conditions of life calculated to bring about its physical destruction. Advocating genocide is a **criminal** offence: s. 318.

GENTLEMEN'S AGREEMENT A phrase used to describe an agreement that is not legally enforceable and is binding on the

parties in honour only. S.M. Waddams, *The Law of Contracts* 111–12 (6th ed. 2010).

GEOGRAPHICAL INDICATION A name or sign associated with a particular geographical location that is attached to a product and meant to indicate that the product has particular characteristics or qualities. "Champagne" is an example of a geographical indication, indicating that the grapes from which the product was made were grown in the Champagne region of France.

GERRYMANDER A method of arranging electoral districts in an unnatural manner so that one political party will be capable of electing more representatives than would have been likely under a fair system of division, The practice was originally employed by Ethridge Gerry, from whom the name is derived, and who utilized it in 1812 in Massachusetts in order to gain an unfair electoral advantage.

GIFT A gratuitous, voluntary transfer of **property** from the owner to another. To be valid, the gift must be fully completed, as the courts will not compel a **donor** to perfect his or her gift where the intention is unfulfilled, *McIntyre v. Royal Trust Co.* (1945), 53 Man.R. 353 (C.A.); *Zalys* (*Litigation Guardian of*) *v. Zalys*, 2000 SKQB 301. There are two forms of gifts, **inter vivos** and **mortis causa**:

GIFT INTER VIVOS A gratuitous transfer of **property** from the owner to another person, with the full intention of each that the thing given shall not be returned but shall be retained by the donee as his or her own. There are but three modes by which such a gift can be made: (1) by deed or instrument in writing; (2) by **delivery** to the **donee**, in cases where the subject matter admits of **delivery**; and (3) by declaration of trust in favour of the donee. In all these modes, a present **transfer**, or the equivalent of a transfer, is required, *McIntyre v. Royal Trust Co.*, [1945] 2 W.W.R. 364 at 367–68 (Man.K.B.).

GIFT MORTIS CAUSA [DONATIO MORTIS CAUSA] A gift made in contemplation of impending death. Besides being in contemplation (not expectation) of death, the donor must die while he or she is suffering from the condition that prompted the contemplation. *Thompson v. Meehan*, [1958] O.R. 357 (C.A.). There must be an intention that, should the donor survive the condition, the gift will be **revocable**. *Armstrong v. Hachey Estate* (2000), 232 N.B.R. (2d) 110 (N.B. Q.B.). The courts have taken different positions on whether the condition must be one that, when measured objectively, would inspire a contemplation of death in the reasonable person, or whether "subjective belief of danger should suffice, with the absence of a substantial basis for that fear merely affording evidence as to whether or not that belief was reasonably held." B. Ziff, *Principles of Property Law* 164 (5th ed. 2010). See also *Danicki v. Danicki*, [1995] O.J. No. 3995 (Ont. C.J.). Finally, "in every case, like a gift **inter vivos**, delivery of the property ... is essential. Because the gift is revocable, the courts generally have been less stringent about the delivery requirements for a valid *donatio mortis causa* when the other requirements are met." T.G. Feeney & J. Mackenzie, *Feeney's Canadian Law of Wills* 1.67 (4th ed. 2000).

GIFT OVER An **estate** created upon the expiration of a **preceding estate**—e.g., a gift over to *C* is established when in default of the exercise of a **power of appointment** by *B*, the **donor** *A* has provided that *C* take in default, rather than have the property that is the subject matter of the power **revert** to *A*'s estate.

GNU GENERAL PUBLIC LICENSE A software licence permitting the free redistribution of a work and any modified versions thereof, provided such redistribution is made on the same licence. See **copyleft**.

GOLDEN RULE One of the primary rules of **statutory interpretation** which holds that, "[i]n construing wills and indeed statutes and all written instruments the grammatical and ordinary sense of the words is to be adhered to, unless that would lead to some absurdity, or some repugnancy or inconsistency with the rest of the instrument; in which case the grammatical and ordinary sense of the words may be modified, so as to avoid that absurdity in inconsistency but no farther." *Grey v. Pearson,* (1857) 6 H.L. Cas. 61 at 106.

GOOD CAUSE Substantial or legally sufficient reason for doing something. The concept arises in many contexts. For example, **costs** are usually awarded to the successful party unless there is good cause not to. A lawyer has an ethical duty not to withdraw services from a client except for good cause. Termination of employment without good cause will be a **wrongful dismissal**.

GOOD FAITH A standard implying absence of intent to take advantage of or **defraud** another party; absence of **ulterior** motive.

To act in good faith, one must act openly, fairly and honestly, and the existence of **negligence** is irrelevant. In property law, a good faith purchaser is a person without knowledge of any alleged defect in **title** or any **encumbrance** on the property that would put a reasonably prudent man on notice. See **bona fide**; **bona fide purchaser**. Good faith is a consideration in deciding about **exclusion of evidence** as a **remedy** for a breach or a right under the **Canadian Charter of Rights and Freedoms**. There is some ambiguity about its usage in that context. One prevailing view is that "the absence of good faith does not equate to the existence of bad faith and that the absence of bad faith does not equate to the presence of good faith ... there can be a middle ground where neither mitigating good faith nor aggravating bad faith is found." *R. v. Stanton*, 2010 BCCA 208. Other courts have found that the absence of bad faith amounts to good faith.

GOOD FAITH BARGAINING In labour law, the obligation on the part of a **trade union** and management to make genuine efforts to negotiate an agreement: it "is not limited to a mere right to make representations to one's employer, but requires the employer to engage in a process of consideration and discussion to have them considered by the employer." *Ontario (Attorney-General) v. Fraser,* 2011 SCC 20. See **hard bargaining**; **unfair labour practice**.

GOODS All **chattels** personal, other than things in action and money. In effect, therefore, all things in **possession**, save money used as currency of the realm. FUTURE GOODS are those to be manufactured or acquired by the seller following the making of the **contract** of sale. SPECIFIC GOODS are those identified and agreed upon at the time a contract of sale is made.

GOOD SAMARITAN LEGISLATION Statutes intended to protect would-be rescuers (e.g. at an accident scene) from liability, in the case that their efforts lead to further injury or damage, e.g. *Emergency Medical Aid Act,* R.S.A. 2000, c. E–7, s. 2. See also *Horsley v. MacLaren,* [1970] 2 O.R. 487 (C.A.). In some jurisdictions, rescuers cannot be found liable unless they are **grossly negligent**. *Volunteer Services Act,* R.S.N.S 1989, c. 497, s. 3.

GOOD TITLE A **title** free from present **litigation**, defects, or doubts concerning its validity or merchantability. In a property **conveyance**, if the **vendor** shows that he or she has the title that he or she is bound to convey, then he or she is said to have good title, The term is frequently employed in place of **marketable title** or clear title.

GOODWILL "[A] broad concept that refers to the benefit and advantage of the good name, reputation and connection of a business. It is the attractive force that brings in customers." G. H. L. Fridman, *The Law of Torts in Canada,* 793–95 (6th ed. 2010).

GOVERNMENT LIABILITY Initially, the maxim "the King could do not wrong" was the basis of government immunity, and the only way a suit could be brought against the government was by asking their permission with a petition of right. In tort law, the passing of the Crown Liability Acts in the middle of the 20th century made the Crown responsible for torts committed by its servants, but

determining when there was a duty of care on the part of the government was complex. In *Just v. British Columbia,* [1990] 1 W.W.R. 385, at 406 (S.C.C.) the Supreme Court held that "[t]rue policy decisions should be exempt from tortious claims so that governments are not restricted in making decisions based on social, political or economic factors. However, the implementation of those decisions may well be subject to claims in tort." See also *Crown Liability and Proceedings Act,* R.S.C. 1985, c. C–50. See further, A. Linden & B. Feldthusen, *Canadian Tort Law* 659–704 (9th ed. 2011).

GOVERNOR GENERAL OF CANADA The Head of State in Canada; the personal representative of the Queen. He or she holds in all essential respects the same position in relation to the administration of public affairs in Canada as is held by the Queen in Great Britain. The position of Governor General and the powers given to him or her are created and contained in the **Constitution Act, 1867**. Although the powers of the Governor General are mainly formal, he/she performs such important functions as the proroguing and dissolution of **Parliament**. The Prime Minister and the **Cabinet** receive their power from him or her, and no federal **bill** can become **law** without the Governor General's assent. The provincial counterpart of the Governor General is the **Lieutenant Governor**. See further P.W. Hogg, *Constitutional Law of Canada,* 9-24–9-41 (5th ed. 2007).

GOVERNOR IN COUNCIL The federal **Cabinet**. The Cabinet of a provincial government is referred to as the **Lieutenant Governor in Council**.

GRACE PERIOD A period following the date or time when a particular duty that should have been performed will be permitted to be done **without prejudice**. Such days of grace are often given on insurance policies.

GRAFT The fraudulent obtaining of public money by the corruption of public officials; a dishonest transaction in relation to public or official acts; also commonly used to designate an advantage that one person by reason of his or her peculiar position or superior influence or trust acquires from another.

GRANDFATHERING To allow old rules to continue to apply to those already subject to them, while establishing new rules for the future. "Such a provision is purely a grandfathering clause. It protected existing contracts already validly entered into by municipalities. It did not purport to grant an authority to make such agreements with developers in the future when the very purpose and effect of the repeal was to deny them such powers." *Pacific National Investments Ltd. v. Victoria (City)*, 2000 SCC 64.

GRAND JURY See **jury** [GRAND JURY].

GRANT 1. To agree or consent to; to allow, as in granting a request. **2.** The allocation of rights to a particular person generally for a particular purpose. A common-law **conveyance**. **3.** The **transfer** of **ownership** of **property** as distinguished from the **delivery** of transfer of the property itself. A conveyance is a **deed** of grant. **4.** The **gift** of money out of public funds by virtue of the authority of government to a private or commercial interest because it is deemed to be beneficial to the pubic interest. *G.T.E. Sylvania Canada Ltd. v. The Queen,* [1974] C.T.C. 408 (F.C.T.D.).

GRANTEE A person to whom a **grant** is made. See **chain of title**.

GRANTOR A person who gives a **grant**. See **chain of title**.

GRANT TEST The test used to determine, under s. 24(2) of the **Canadian Charter of Rights and Freedoms**, whether evidence obtained in violation of a protected right should be excluded. In *R. v. Grant,* 2009 SCC 32, the Supreme Court decided that three considerations should be taken into account in making the decision: (1) the seriousness of the *Charter*-infringing state conduct, (2) the impact of the breach on the *Charter*-protected interests of the accused, and (3) society's interest in the adjudication of the case on its merits.

GRATIS (*gră'-tĭs*) Lat.: free; given or performed without reward.

GRATIS DICTUM (*gră'-tĭs dĭk'-tŭm*) Lat.: Mere assertion.

GRATUITOUS BAILMENT See **bailment**.

GRATUITOUS PROMISE A promise by which a person states an intention to do or refrain from doing something without requiring any **consideration** in return. Such a promise is generally not enforceable except when made under **seal**. See *Uhrich v. Ewen*, 2002 SKQB 496; *River Wind Ventures Ltd. v. British Columbia*, 2009 BCSC 589, rev'd by 2011 BCCA 79.

GRAVAMEN The **grievance** particularly complained of. The material part, substance or essence of a **complaint**, **charge**, **grievance**, **cause of action**, etc. The essence of a grievance bears most heavily on the person accused.

GRIEVANCE An allegation that something imposes an illegal obligation or burden, or denies some equitable or legal right, or causes injustice.

It is most commonly used to describe a complaint by an employer or employee that a term of a **collective bargaining agreement** is being breached. Most collective agreements establish a grievance procedure to be followed pursuant to such an allegation.

GRIEVOUS BODILY HARM Referred to in the *Criminal Code,* R.S.C. 1985, c. C–46, ss. 34 and 35,"'grievous bodily harm,' within the meaning of ss. 34 and 35 of the *Criminal Code*, is not limited to harm or injury that is permanent or life-threatening. In ordinary usage, 'grievous' bodily harm means harm or injury that is 'very severe or serious.'" *R. v. Paice*, 2005 SCC 22.

GROSS NEGLIGENCE 1. "[C]onduct in which...there is a very marked departure from the standards by which responsible and competent people in charge of motor vehicles habitually govern themselves." *McCulloch v. Murray*, [1942] S.C.R. 141. at 145. **2.** "[A] high or serious degree of **negligence**." *British Columbia Telephone Co. v. Quality*

Industries Ltd. (1984) 59 B.C.L.R. 68 at 71(C.A.). See **negligence**.

GROUND RENT An **estate of inheritance** in the **rent** of lands, an inheritable **interest** in and right to the rent collected through the **leasing** of certain lands. It is a **freehold estate**, and as such is subject to **encumbrance** by **mortgage** or **judgment (lien, attachment**, etc.). An incorporeal **hereditament**, the ground rent is an interest distinct from that held by the owner of the property whose estate is in the land itself and is therefore corporeal.

GROUNDS In the context of the **equality rights** provision in the **Canadian Charter of Rights and Freedoms**, personal characteristics that are the basis for discrimination and act as jurisprudential markers for suspect distinctions in equality claims, such as age, sex, or race. To raise a **Charter** challenge under s. 15, there must be a distinction based on an enumerated ground—a ground specifically protected and listed in the legislation—or an analogous ground. See *R. v. S. (S.)*, [1990] 2 S.C.R. 254.; *Vriend v. Alberta*, [1998] 1 S.C.R. 493.

GROW-OP Short for grow-operation. A building, frequently a **dwelling house**, all or some portion of which is converted to the large scale cultivation of marijuana. Police sometimes detect the presence of a grow-op through unusually high rates of electrical usage, which has led to a rise in **theft of electricity**. Other investigative techniques include the use of a **FLIR** to detect the amount of heat escaping from a building, or the use of a **digital recording ammeter** to determine the amount of electricity entering a building, whether it is measured by the electrical meter or not.

GUARANTEE 1. The person in whose favour the **guarantor** binds himself or herself. **2.** To agree or promise to be responsible for the **debt, default**, or miscarriage of another. **3.** [also **guaranty**] A **contract collateral** to the **principal** contract by which a person engages to answer for the **debt**, default, or miscarriage of another, *Campbell v. McIsaac* (1985), 9 N.S.R. (2d) 287 (N.S.S.C.). The contract of guaranty is dependent on the unchanged continu-

ance of the primary obligation, and any substantial alteration of the principal agreement (i.e., extension of time, partial release of security) renders the guaranty unenforceable. *Western Dominion Investment Co. Ltd. v. MacMillan,* [1925] 1 W.W.R. 852 (Man.K.B.).

GUARANTOR A **surety**. One who binds himself or herself by a **contract** of guaranty and agrees to pay the **debt** of another should the other **default**.

GUARANTY See **guarantee** (sense 3).

GUARDIAN A person appointed to take care of another person, his or her affairs and property. A person who has in law or in fact the **custody** or control of any child and is under a legal duty to provide necessaries for such child. Guardian "includes a head of a family and any other person who has in law or in fact the custody or care of a child." *Maintenance and Custody Act,* R.S.N.S. 1989, c. 160, s. 2(e), See also, e.g., *Stoakley v. Stoakley* (1976), 20 N.S.R. (2d) 675 (N.S.S.C.). See also **next friend**.

GUARDIAN AD LITEM A guardian appointed by the court for the purpose of defending or bringing an action on behalf of a minor. J. Walker & L. Sossin, *Civil Litigation* 62 (2010). See **guardian; next friend**.

GUARDIANSHIP Generally regarded as "the full bundle of rights and duties voluntarily assumed by an adult regarding an infant akin to those naturally arising from parenthood... [I]mplies the voluntary assumption of a duty to maintain, protect and educate the **ward**. It includes the power to correct, to grant or withhold consent to marriages and, if the **guardian** is also the parent, to delegate parental authority." *Anson v. Anson* (1987), 10 B.C.L.R. (2d) 357 at 361 (Co.Ct.) quoted in *N.P. v. LDS Adoption Services*, 2006 ABQB 78.

ADULT GUARDIANSHIP The appointment of a person by a court to serve as a guardian for an adult who is, by reason of age, physical or mental disability, or some other reason, unable to care for himself or herself, or to make decisions affecting his or her own affairs. See, e.g., *Adult Guardianship Act*, R.S.B.C. 1996, c. 6; *Adult Guardianship and Co-decision-making Act*, S.S. 2000, c. A–5.3.

GUEST One to whom hospitality is extended, often in the form of entertainment, lodging, and refreshment and usually in return for monetary compensation. The keeper of guests is at common law only required to inform his or her guests of any concealed danger of which he or she has knowledge.

Formerly, at common law, an innkeeper was **prima facie** liable for the loss of the guests' goods. This has generally been amended by provincial statute so that the innkeeper will only be liable where the loss is a result of the innkeeper's willful act, **default**, or **negligence**. See *Tourist Accommodations Act,* S.N.S. 1994–95, C–9 s. 11. See **social host liability**.

GUEST PASSENGER [GRATUITOUS PASSENGER] A passenger who has not paid to be transported in a motor vehicle. At one point, a guest passenger was not entitled to sue the driver in the case of an accident. Now, however, the driver of a vehicle may be liable to a guest passenger where he or she has been negligent, the degree of negligence required depending on provincial statutes. See e.g., *Motor Vehicle Act,* R.S.N.S. 1989, c. 293, s. 248(2).

GUILTY 1. The condition of having been found by the court to have committed the **crime** with which one was **charged** or some lesser **indictable offence. 2.** Also, the commission of a **civil** wrong or **tort**, but seldom used in this context. **3.** The word used by a prisoner to **confess** his or her crime when **pleading** to an **indictment**.

HABEAS CORPUS (*hā'-bē-ŭs kôr'-pŭs*) Lat.: you have the body. Known as the "GREAT WRIT," *habeas corpus* is a **prerogative writ** with a varied use in criminal and civil contexts. It is basically a procedure for obtaining a judicial determination of the legality of an individual's **custody**. *May v. Ferndale Institution*, 2005 SCC 82. In the criminal law context, it is used to bring the **petitioner** before the court to inquire into the legality of his or her confinement. In the civil context, the **writ** is used to challenge the validity of child custody and deportations. *In re Fred Storgoff* [1945] S.C.R. 526. *Habeas corpus* is a safeguard of the liberty of the subject. As a procedural writ, it is not a new **suit** different from the one dealt with at trial nor is it a means of appealing. It is a writ to which any person detained in prison is entitled and which is granted for the sole purpose of having a **superior court** determine whether the detention is legal. The judge's only **jurisdiction** under the writ is whether to order the release of the accused. *Habeas corpus* cannot be used to **nullify** the administration of criminal law. The right of *habeas corpus* is now recognized in the **Canadian Charter of Rights and Freedoms**, s. 10(*c*).

HABENDUM (*hā-běn'-dŭm*) Lat.: to have. The clause in a **deed** that determines what **estate** or **interest** is granted by the deed. *Re Gold and Rowe,* [1913], 4 O.W.N. 642 at 643 (H.C.). It begins with the words "to have and to hold." The *habendum* may reduce, enlarge, explain, or qualify, but not contradict or be repugnant to the estate granted. It is not essential to the deed. *Dunlap v. Dunlap* (1883), 6 O.R. 141 (Ch.). In modern **conveyancing**, the inclusion of the *habendum* clause has become somewhat redundant, since its function is normally performed by the granting clause in a conveyance. The deed's validity is not affected by the absence of the *habendum*.

HABITUAL CRIMINAL A term used in older versions of the **Criminal Code** to describe a person who was subject, "by reason of his criminal habits and mode of life," to be detained in a prison for an indeterminate period, where doing so was expedient for the protection of the public. The legislation was not limited to a criminal record for any particular type of crime, such as crimes of violence, though the nature of the person's criminal record could be relevant to whether their detention was expedient. See, e.g., *R. v. Poole*, [1968] S.C.R. 381. The term is no longer used, though a similar but more limited role is played now by **dangerous offender** or **long-term offender** designations.

HANSARD The official verbatim report of debates in **Parliament** and the **Legislatures**.

HARASSMENT 1. "[E]ngaging in a course of vexatious comment or conduct that is known or ought reasonably to be known to be unwelcome." *Human Rights Code*, R.S.O. 1990, c. H.19, s. 10 (1). **2.** A single piece of vexatious behaviour can, in some instances, be sufficient to constitute harassment. "[P]sychological harassment contains four elements. Firstly, it is a vexatious behaviour in the form of hostile or unwanted conduct, verbal comments, actions, or gestures. Such conduct, verbal comments, actions, or gestures must be repeated unless it meets the requirement of a single vexatious behaviour. The vexatious behaviour must affect the employee's dignity or psychological or physical integrity and, lastly, results in a harmful work environment." *Association du personnel de soutien du Collège A v. Collège d'enseignement général et professionnel A*, 2012 QCCA 441. See **criminal harassment**; **sexual harassment**.

HARD BARGAINING "It is the adoption of a tough position in the hope and expectation of being able to force the other side to agree to one's terms. [It] is not a violation of the duty [to bargain in good faith] because there is a genuine intention to continue collective bargaining and to reach an agreement." *Canadian Union of Public Employees v. The Labour Relations Board (N.S.) et al.*, [1983] 2 S.C.R. 311 at 341. Contrast **surface bargaining**. See **good faith bargaining**.

HARD CASES Cases that, in order to meet the exigencies presented by the extreme hardship of one **party**, produce decisions that may deviate from the true principles of law.

It is sometimes said that "hard cases make bad law" because logic is often deemphasized in a hard case, and later attempts to justify the new law thus created often compound the original inadequacy of reasoning.

HARD ENTRY See **knock and announce rule**.

HARMLESS ERROR See **curative proviso**.

HARM PRINCIPLE The idea that the law should only prohibit behaviour that causes harm to non-consenting third parties, rather than behaviour that exclusively affects the actor (or actors). Under this view, the actor's "own good, either physical or moral, is not a sufficient warrant" to regulate his or her conduct. J.S. Mill, *On Liberty* 14 (1998). The Supreme Court of Canada has held that the harm principle is not among the **principles of fundamental justice** recognized under s. 7 of the *Canadian Charter of Rights and Freedoms*. *R. v. Malmo–Levine*, 2003 SCC 74.

HATE PROPAGANDA Defined in the *Criminal Code*, R.S.C. 1985, c. C–46, ss. 318 and 319 as anything which advocates or promotes genocide or any communication by a person which promotes or incites hatred against an identifiable group where doing so would likely lead to a breach of the peace.

HEADNOTE A summary of the relevant facts of a case and a concise synopsis of the points of law decided therein. Placed at the beginning of a case report, the headnote is not an official portion of the reported **judgment** but is compiled by a commercial writer who extracts from the judgment the salient points in the areas of facts, issues, and decision. Despite the non-official status of headnotes, modern judges have been known to quote them in their judgments.

HEALTH CARE DIRECTIVE See **living will**.

HEARING A **proceeding** held by a judicial, quasi-judicial (see **quasi**) or **administrative tribunal** to determine **questions of law** and **questions of fact**. See also **fair hearing**.

Originally applied to **chancery** proceedings, where a judge sat without a **jury**, it is now loosely applied to any **common-law** trial whether **civil** or **criminal**. *R. v. McKenzie*, [1929] 1 W.W.R. 249 (Man.K.B.).

FINAL HEARING The final **arbitration** of a decision on the facts. Determination of a **suit** on its **merits** as distinguished from a hearing of preliminary questions. Compare **preliminary hearing**.

HEARING DE NOVO A new hearing. In **administrative law**, a Board may have a second hearing to cure the defects of the first. This is a hearing **de novo**, not an **appeal**.

In criminal law, TRIAL DE NOVO (see **trial**) is a method of appeal for **summary [conviction] offences** where the judge adjudicates on both the facts and the law. This is distinguished from an appeal by way of stated case. See **trial [trial de novo]**. *Criminal Code*, R.S.C. 1985, c. C–46, s. 822.

HEARSAY RULE "Hearsay" is a statement made by a **witness** reporting what another person has said, introduced to prove the truth of what that other person said. "The essential defining features of hearsay are therefore the following: (1) the fact that the statement is adduced to prove the truth of its contents and (2) the absence of a contemporaneous opportunity to **cross-examine** the **declarant**." *R. v. Khelawon*, 2006 SCC 57. The hearsay rule states that hearsay evidence is presumptively inadmissible, but it is subject to many exceptions, the most important of which is the **principled exception**. Traditional exceptions include circumstances where it is presumed that the circumstances give a sufficient guarantee that the statement is true, such as business records, dying declarations, spontaneous utterances, and statements against pecuniary interest. See **co-conspirator's exception**.

A statement is not hearsay if it is admitted not for the truth of its contents, but rather for some other purpose, such as to establish that the statement was made. For example, a witness might testify to hearing **slanderous** words spoken; the purpose would not be to show that the defamatory statements were true, but to show that the defamation had occurred. See **narrative**.

HEIR APPARENT That person who, should he or she survive his or her ancestor, will become the ancestor's heir. He or she does not become heir until the death of the ancestor, as no living person can have **heirs** (*nemo est haeres viventis*). The concept of heir apparent is also a reference to the heir to a throne.

HEIRS Strictly, those who would be designated by statute to inherit an **estate**, or portion of an estate, of an ancestor who dies without a **will** (i.e., **intestate**); in the law of wills, "heirs" in a **bequest** mean **devisees** and **legatees**. *Re Bolton,* [1918], 14 O.W.N. 87 (S.C.). The term may be used to refer to **issue** of the **testator**, next of kin, devisees or legatees by will, **heirs of the body**, or persons who take on intestacy.

An heir is (at **common law**) one appointed by law to succeed to an estate in an intestacy situation, or the person set out by **statute** to succeed, or in popular terms, a successor by will. See **intestate succession**.

HEIRS OF THE BODY Natural heirs; **lineal** descendants of the deceased, excluding, therefore, the spouse, adopted children, in-laws, etc.; used in **conveyances** to create an **estate** in **fee tail**, a concept abolished in Canada; **words of limitation** used by a **grantor** when attempting to keep the land granted within the family for succeeding generations.

HENRY VIII CLAUSE A provision in a **statute** that authorizes the creation of **regulations** that take priority over the enacting statute itself. "This breath-

taking power, to amend by regulation the very statute [that] authorizes the regulation, is known to legal historians as a "King Henry VIII" clause because that monarch gave himself power to legislate by proclamation, a power associated since the 16th century with executive autocracy." *Ontario Public School Boards' Assn. v. Ontario (Attorney-General)* (1997), 151 DLR (4th) 346 (Ont. S.C.). See *Reference re Broadcasting Regulatory Policy CRTC 2010–167 and Broadcasting Order CRTC 2010–168,* 2012 SCC 68.

HENSON TRUST See **trust**.

HEREDITAMENTS Anything that can be inherited. It is not just **property** a person has by **descent** from an ancestor, but also that which he or she has by purchase, and which his or her **heirs** can inherit from him or her. The term applies to both **real property** and **personal property**. There are two kinds of hereditaments: CORPOREAL and INCORPOREAL. The former generally are tangible things, such as land or houses. The latter are less tangible rights growing out of or connected to land, such as an **easement**, right to **rent** or **profit à prendre**.

HEREDITARY SUCCESSION The passing of **title** according to the laws of **descent**; the acquisition of title to an **estate** by a person by **operation of law** upon the death of an ancestor without a valid **will** affecting the property inherited. See **inheritance**. Compare **devise**.

HER MAJESTY [HIS MAJESTY] 1. The Crown in right of the provinces and in right of Canada. **2.** Also refers to the Sovereign of the United Kingdom, Canada and Her other Realms and Territories, and Head of the Commonwealth. See **Crown**.

HERMENEUTICS, LEGAL The study of the rules and principles governing the construction and interpretation of legal documents.

HE WHO SEEKS EQUITY MUST DO EQUITY A phrase describing an equitable principle which "means nothing more than that he who seeks the assistance of a Court of Equity must in the matter in which he so asks assistance do what is just as a term of receiving such assistance." *Richard v. Collins* (1912) 27 O.L.R. 390 at 398 (Div.Ct.) See **equity**.

HIGH COURT OF JUSTICE A superior **court of record** in England created by the *Judicature Acts of 1875*. In itself it performs no judicial function. The high court was a consolidation of both law and **equity jurisdictions** and presently consists of three divisions: Chancery division, Queen's Bench division, and the Family division.

HIGHWAY TRAFFIC ACTS See **Motor Vehicle Acts**.

HIGH SEAS See **UNCLOS III**.

HIMALAYA CLAUSE A term used to denote an exemption clause between a shipper of goods and a carrier that is extended to protect the carrier's agents, servants and independent contractors from liability for any damage to the goods even though they were not parties to the original contract. *Cami Automotive, Inc. v. Westwood Shipping Lines Inc.*, 2009 FC 664.

HOLDER A person in possession of a document of **title** or an **instrument** or an investment **security** drawn, issued, or **devised** to him or her or to his or her **order** or to bearer or in blank. See *Bills of Exchange Act,* R.S.C. 1985, c. B–4, s. 2, governing the law of **negotiable instruments**. "Holder" means the payee or endorsee of a **bill of exchange** or **promissory note** who is in possession of it, or the bearer thereof, (*Id.* s. 2). See **holder in due course**.

HOLDER IN DUE COURSE A **holder**, who has taken a **bill of exchange**; a holder free of most defences of prior parties to the **negotiable instrument** and free of conflicting title **claims** to the instrument itself. Under the *Bills of Exchange Act,* R.S.C. 1985, c. B–4, s. 55(1), a holder is one "who has taken a bill, complete and regular on the face of it, under the following conditions . . . (*a*) that he became the holder of it before it was overdue and without notice that it had been previously dishonoured, if such was the fact; and (*b*) that he took the bill

in **good faith** and for value, and that at the time the bill was negotiated to him he had no notice of any defect in title of the person who negotiated it."

HOLDING 1. In commercial and property law, **property** in which one has legal **title** and of which one is in **possession**; the term may be used to refer specifically to ownership of stocks or **shares** of **corporations**. **2.** In **procedure**, any ruling of the court, including rulings upon the **admissibility** of **evidence** or other questions presented during trial. Compare **obiter dictum**.

HOLDING COMPANY 1. A **corporation** that owns or controls other corporations through its majority **interest**; **2.** a corporation organized to hold the **stock** of other companies; **3.** a corporation that can influence the management of other companies by ownership of **securities** in the latter.

HOLDOVER TENANCY See **tenancy** [TENANCY AT SUFFERANCE].

HOLOGRAPHIC WILL A **will** wholly in the handwriting of and dated and signed by the **testator** requiring none of the other formalities essential for the validity of a conventional will. In particular, witnesses are not required. Most Canadian provinces recognize holographic wills. See, e.g., *Wills Act, 1996,* S.S. 1996, c. W–14.1, s. 8.

HOMAGE During the **feudal** period, the ceremony "wherein the vassal knelt before the lord, acknowledged himself to be his man, and swore **fealty** to him. It was frequently accompanied by a **grant** of land from the lord to the vassal, the land to be held of the lord by the vassal as **tenant**." C. Moynihan, *Introduction to the Law of Real Property* 3 (2d ed. 1988). As a consequence, any attempt by the vassal to **convey** more than the **estate** granted him was not only **tortious** conduct with regard to the lord, but was also **treasonous**.

HOMESTEAD LEGISLATION Legislation in some provinces giving one spouse (married or unmarried) certain rights in property that is or has been occupied by both of them as the family home.

Specifically, where one spouse is the owner of the homestead, that spouse is unable to sell, **devise**, **lease**, **mortgage**, or make any other **disposition** of the homestead unless the non-owning spouse consents in writing or other conditions are met. Compare **dower**; **family property**; **matrimonial home**.

HOMICIDE The killing of a human being by another, directly or indirectly, by any means. It is either **culpable** (a **crime**) or non-culpable. If the former, it is classed as either **murder**, **manslaughter** or **infanticide**. *Criminal Code*, R.S.C. 1985, c. C–46, ss. 222 (1), (2), (4).

JUSTIFIABLE HOMICIDE The common law distinguished between justifiable homicide and excusable homicide as instances of killing in self-defence. If the accused had acted entirely in self-defence it was a justifiable homicide, but if the accused bore some share of the blame, such as through provoking the attack, it was only an excusable homicide. Neither "justifiable homicide" nor "excusable homicide" is a term of art in **criminal** law, but the *Criminal Code* did until recently treat self-defence claims differently depending on whether the accused was or was not the initial aggressor and might still. See *Criminal Code,* R.S.C 1985, c. C–46, s. 34(2)(c).

HONOUR CLAUSE See **gentlemen's agreement**.

HONOUR OF THE CROWN A constitutional principle with its genesis in the *Royal Proclamation* of 1763, requiring governments to act in a **fiduciary** manner and with **good faith** toward Aboriginal peoples. The honour of the Crown exists as a source of obligation independently of treaties, and the **duty to consult** and **duty to accommodate** arise from the honour of the Crown. See *Beckman v. Little Salmon/Carmacks First Nation*, 2010 SCC 53.

HORNBOOK An older American term used to describe a treatise or book that summarizes the fundamental principles of a particular area of law; generally used by law students as a study aid.

HORS (*ôr'*) Fr.: outside of, besides, other than [sometimes *dehors* (dĕ-ôr')].

HOSTILE POSSESSION See **adverse possession**. See also **notorious possession**.

HOSTILE WITNESS See **witness**.

HOTCHPOT A type of clause in a **will** used when a parent does not wish to rely on the **presumption** against double portions with respect to his or her children to whom he or she has conferred benefits under a will. He or she then provides specifically in the will that benefits conferred in his or her lifetime on the **beneficiary** under the will are to be brought into the **estate** and accounted for accordingly. *In re Arbuthnot,* [1915] 1 Ch. 422; *Wood v. Barrett*, 2003 ABQB 986.

HOT PURSUIT "[C]ontinuous pursuit conducted with reasonable diligence, so that pursuit and capture along with the commission of the offence may be considered as forming part of a single transaction." *R. v. Macooh*, [1993] 2 S.C.R. 802, quoting R. Salhany, *Canadian Criminal Procedure* (5th ed. 1989). Also referred to as "fresh pursuit." Hot pursuit can justify a **peace officer** in entering a person's home or crossing into another jurisdiction in order to effect an **arrest**.

HOUSE ARREST An informal term sometimes used to describe a **conditional sentence** of imprisonment, or **bail** conditions so restrictive that the **accused** is in essence confined to his or her home.

HOUSE OF COMMONS The Canadian legislative lower house elected on the basis of universal adult suffrage. It is headed by the Prime Minister, who with his or her **Cabinet** operates solely through support of a majority of the members. That support is normally forthcoming from the party in power by virtue of party solidarity. See P.W. Hogg, *Constitutional Law of Canada* 9–15–17 (5th ed. 2007).

HOUSE OF LORDS The assembly of lords spiritual and temporal, forming the second branch of the British Parliament. It is the Supreme Court of Appeal from the Court of Appeal in England and the Superior Courts of Scotland and Northern Ireland.

HUMANITARIAN INTERVENTION The use of military force against a sovereign state in order to end human rights violations taking place within its borders. The doctrine of humanitarian intervention recognizes that there are limits to state sovereignty insofar as the treatment of people within state borders is concerned. Even so, international law demands that military actions justified on the basis of humanitarian intervention be authorized in advance by the United Nations Security Council. M. Freeman & G. Van Ert, *International Human Rights Law* 411 (2004).

HUMAN RIGHTS [LEGISLATION] Antidiscrimination law. Legislation "intended to give rise, amongst other things, to individual rights of vital importance, rights capable of enforcement…in a court of law." *Action Travail des Femmes v. Canadian National Railway Co.,* [1987] 1 S.C.R. 1114 at 1134. This type of legislation "is of a special nature and declares public policy regarding matters of general concern. It is not constitutional in nature in the sense that it may not be altered, amended or repealed by the Legislature. It is, however, of such nature that it may not be altered, amended, or repealed, nor may exceptions be created to its provisions, save by clear legislative pronouncement." *Winnipeg School Division No. 1 v. Craton,* [1985] 2 S.C.R. 150 at 156.

In Canada, human rights legislation is embodied in the federal **Canadian Human Rights Act** and various provincial and territorial antidiscrimination

statutes. These human rights statutes complement the **Canadian Charter of Rights and Freedoms** providing protection from discrimination to individuals in private activity, whereas the *Charter* protects individuals from discrimination in the area of governmental activity. *Retail, Wholesale & Department Union, Local 580 v. Dolphin Delivery Ltd.,* [1986] 2 S.C.R. 573. See **civil rights**.

HUNG JURY A colloquialism describing a jury that cannot reach a **verdict** by the degree of agreement required of the members. The jury is then dismissed, a new one is impanelled and the case is tried again **de novo**.

HYBRID OFFENCE An offence "drafted so that [it] can be prosecuted either as an indictable offence or as an offence punishable upon summary conviction." M. Manning & P. Sankoff, *Criminal Law* 44 (4th ed. 2009). See e.g., *Criminal Code,* R.S.C. 1985, c. C–46, s. 140 (public mischief); s. 266 (assault); s. 437 (false alarm of fire).

HYPOTHEC A type of **security interest** in property established by the *Civil Code of Québec,* under which a debtor's interest in property is subject to "the fulfillment of an obligation, in virtue of which the creditor may cause such property to be sold." L. Sarna & A Neudorfer, *The Law of Immoveable Hypothecs in Québec* 1 (2006). Hypothecs may be created with respect to both moveable and immoveable property, with moveable property being analogous to **personal property** at common law, and immoveable property being analogous to **real property**. See *Civil Code of Québec,* L.R.Q., c. C–1991, a. 2660–2802.

IBID. (*ĭb'-ĭd*) Lat.: in the same place; abbreviation of *ibidem.* Used to mean "in the same book" or "on the same page." It avoids repetition of source data in the reference immediately preceding.

ICC See **International Criminal Court.**

ID. (*ĭd*) Lat.: the same; abbreviation of *idem.* Used in citations to avoid repetition of the author's name and the title when a reference to an item immediately follows another to the same item.

ID CERTUM EST QUOD CERTUM REDDI POTEST (*ĭd sêr'-tŭm ĕst kwŏd sêr'-tŭm rĕd'-ē pō'-tĕst*) Lat.: that is certain which can be made certain.

IDENTIFIABLE GROUP Within the meaning of ss. 318–319 of the *Criminal Code*, R.S.C. 1985, c. C–46, it is "any section of the public distinguished by colour, race, religion, ethnic origin, or sexual orientation." See **genocide**; **hate propaganda**.

IDENTIFICATION PARADE A procedure in which a suspect is placed in a line-up with other persons in order for a witness to try to identify the accused from among those present. The same process is sometimes conducted through use of photographs of the suspect and various **foils**; this is referred to as a photo line-up.

IDENTITY THEFT Acquiring another person's signature, bank account number, Social Insurance Number, passport number, or other personal information for the purpose of committing one or more of a number of offences, such as **fraud** or forgery. *Criminal Code*, R.S.C. 1985, c. C–46, s. 402.2.

ID EST (*ĭd ĕst*) Lat.: that is, that is to say. Abbreviated **i.e.**

I.E. Abbreviation of **id est**.

IGNORANTIA LEGIS NON EXCUSAT (*ĭg-nō-rän'-shē-à lä'-gĭs nŏn ĕks-kū'-zät*) Lat.: ignorance of the law is no excuse; i.e., the fact that a **defendant** did not think his or her act was against the law does not prevent the law from punishing him or her for the prohibited act. "Ignorance of the law by a person who commits an offence is not an excuse for committing that offence." *Criminal Code,* R.S.C. 1985, c. C–46, s. 19. However, if a law or regulation has not been published in the **Canada Gazette**, an individual may not be convicted, as it is impossible to comply with a law of which the public has no notice. *R v. Molis* (1980), 55 C.C.C. (2d) 558 (S.C.C.). See also *Statutory Instruments Act*, R.S.C. 1985, c. S–22, s. 11(2). But ignorance of fact may prove to be a **defence**, as where lack of knowledge of the automatic suspension of a driver's licence constituted a defence to a charge of driving with a suspended license. In addition, lack of knowledge may constitute a defence to an offence where it is necessary for the Crown to prove the existence of **mens rea**. See *R. v. Prue; R. v. Baril* (1979), 46 C.C.C. (2d) 257 (S.C.C.). See also *R. v. Jorgensen*, [1995] 4 S.C.R. 55. See **colour of right**; **officially induced error**.

ILLEGALITY A term that describes any act or omission that is contrary to law. See **ex turpi causa non oritur actio**.

ILLEGAL WORK STOPPAGE A **strike** or **lockout** that is not authorized under the provisions of the governing labour relations statute (for example, a strike or lockout that occurs during the lifetime of a collective agreement). See, e.g., *Trade Union Act*, R.S.N.S. c. 475, s. 50.

ILLEGITIMATE Illegal or improper; applied to children, it means born out of wedlock, **bastards**.

ILLICIT In general, a term used to describe an act or conduct that is considered improper or immoral and/or not permitted by law.

IMAGINARY CRIME An action taken by a person who mistakenly believes it constitutes an offence. For example, a person who imports sugar into Canada under the mistaken belief that the importation of sugar is illegal commits an imaginary crime. Imaginary crimes are not considered **attempts** under s. 24 of the *Criminal Code*, R.S.C. 1985, c. C–46. As such, they are not culpable under Canadian criminal law. *United States of America v. Dynar*, [1997] 2 S.C.R. 462.

IMMIGRANT Popularly, a person who is born elsewhere and becomes a **Canadian citizen**. The term no longer has a technical legal meaning and is not used in the *Immigration and Refugee Protection Act*, S.C. 2001, c. 27.

IMMIGRATION The movement of persons into a foreign country for the purpose of permanently residing in that country. The *Immigration and Refugee Protection Act*, S.C. 2001, c. 27, and its regulations, outline, inter alia, the process and requirements for immigrating to Canada and obtaining **permanent resident** status. The provinces, by virtue of s. 95 of the **British North America Act, 1867** (now the **Constitution Act, 1867**) have concurrent jurisdiction to legislate with respect to immigration matters as long as the legislation is not repugnant to that of the federal **Parliament**. Most provinces have programmes which encourage settlement in their province. The Province of Quebec, however, has developed an immigration process that, in significant ways, is autonomous and distinct from that generally applicable in Canada.

IMMIGRATION MARRIAGE A marriage between a Canadian **citizen** or **permanent resident** and a **foreign national** that is based not on an authentic relationship between the parties, but is aimed instead at allowing the latter party to immigrate to Canada. These "marriages of convenience" are prompted as a result of the ability of citizens and permanent residents to sponsor their foreign spouses to stay in Canada as permanent residents, under s. 13 of the *Immigration and Refugee Protection Act*, S.C. 2001, c. 27. Spousal relationships are invalid under the Act if they are entered into purely for this purpose. *Immigration and Refugee Protection Regulations*, SOR/2002–227, s. 4(1).

IMMORAL CONDUCT Conduct inconsistent with the standards considered acceptable by the community as a whole. Immoral conduct may provide the basis for suspension or dismissal from certain professions, such as law, medicine, teaching, etc.

IMMUNITY A right of exemption from a **duty** or penalty; a favour or benefit granted in exception to the general rule.
DIPLOMATIC IMMUNITY Immunity from **suit** and legal process, accorded to an envoy or other public minister of a foreign sovereign power, or to the family or official or domestic staff of such an envoy or minister or to the families of such staff. "[T]he function of the diplomatic agent can be effectively exercised and ... he can accomplish the delicate mission with which he is charged, only if he enjoys complete liberty in the foreign State, [or] only if he is free from all subjection to the State in which he temporarily resides. And the sovereignty of the State which he represents would suffer a certain dependence if its diplomatic envoys did not remain subjects of the sovereign whom they were called upon to represent and serve. It is upon this necessity that the principle of the privilege of diplomatic immunity is founded ...." *Rose v. The King*, [1947] 3 D.L.R. 618 at 640 (Que.K.B., Appeal Side).
JUDICIAL IMMUNITY The doctrine that a judge should be shielded from actions against him or her for words, acts, or omissions in the discharge of the judicial function. "Each should be protected from liability to damages when he is acting judicially. Each should be able to do his work in complete independence and free from fear. He should not have to turn the pages of his books with trembling fingers, asking himself: 'If I do this, shall I be liable in damages?'" *R. v. Lippé*, [1991] 2 S.C.R. 114, quoting *Sirros v. Moore*, [1975] 1 Q.B. 118. Judicial immunity is not absolute. "In some cases, however, the actions and expressions of an individual judge trigger concerns about the integrity of the judicial function itself. When

a disciplinary process is launched to look at the conduct of an individual judge, it is alleged that an abuse of judicial independence by a judge has threatened the integrity of the judiciary as a whole." *Moreau-Bérubé v. New Brunswick (Judicial Council),* 2002 SCC 11.

SOVEREIGN IMMUNITY See **sovereign immunity**.

See *Foreign Missions and International Organizations Act,* S.C. 1991, c. 41.

IMPAIRED [DRIVING] Under section 253 (i)(a) of the *Criminal Code,* R.S.C. 1985, c. C–46, it is an offence to operate or have care and control of a motor vehicle, vessel, aircraft, or railway equipment while impaired by alcohol or a drug. Section 253(1)(b) of the *Criminal Code* creates the companion offence of operating or having care and control of a motor vehicle while having consumed alcohol in such a quantity that the concentration in the person's blood exceeds eighty milligrams of alcohol in one hundred millilitres of blood. The former offence is based on actual impairment, even if the concentration of alcohol in the person's blood is below the legal limit, while the latter offence is based on exceeding that legal limit, whether actually impaired or not. See **breathalyzer**; **intoxication**.

IMPANELLING See **empanelling**.

IMPARTIAL The state of being fair and neutral; lacking any and all **bias** and/or prejudice. A judge or a decision maker is expected to adopt an impartial manner with respect to the parties and issues that come before him or her in a given matter. *R. v. Valente,* [1985] 2 S.C.R. 673. Contrast **bias**.

IMPEACHMENT 1. Used most often in the law of **evidence** to indicate a process whereby evidence is adduced in order to question a **witness's** credibility. The **discovery** of witnesses permits counsel to solicit or adduce evidence that may later be used at trial to impeach the witness's veracity by pointing out discrepancies in the **testimony**. **2.** Also, a solemn **accusation** of great public offence, especially against a minister of

the **Crown**. In Canada, impeachment is practically obsolete, though it is still used extensively in the United States to indicate the procedure taken after an accusation of grave import has been made against a public officer.

"The object of prosecutions of impeachment [in England and the United States] is to reach high potent offenders, such as might be presumed to escape punishment in the ordinary tribunals, either from their own extraordinary influence, or from the imperfect organization and powers of those tribunals. These prosecutions are, therefore, conducted by the representatives of the nation, in their public capacity in the face of the nation, and upon a responsibility which is at once felt and reverenced by the whole community." J. Story, *Commentaries on the Constitution of the United States* 250 (1833).

IMPLICATION Intention, meaning; that which is inferred; though not expressly stated, a state of mind or facts that is deduced.

NECESSARY IMPLICATION In **statutory interpretation**, the doctrine that matters can be read as part of a statute despite not being explicitly stated, if they arise as a matter of necessity from its operating requirements. For example, courts can apply a "doctrine of jurisdiction by necessary implication" when determining the powers of a statutory tribunal . . . the powers conferred by an enabling statute are construed to include not only those expressly granted but also, by implication, all powers [that] are practically necessary for the accomplishment of the object intended to be secured by the statutory regime . . . ." (*ATCO Gas and Pipelines Ltd. v. Alberta (Energy and Utilities Board),* 2006 SCC 4, [2006] 1 S.C.R. 140, at para. 51). *R. v. Cunningham,* 2010 SCC 10. See also *R. v. Orbanski; R. v. Elias,* 2005 SCC 37.

IMPLIED The antithesis of express; not explicitly written or stated; referring, e.g., to a condition, consent, power, warranty, state of mind, or fact that is determined by deduction or **inference** from known facts and circumstances.

IMPLIED ASSERTION Reported behaviour or statements on the part of another person that imply a belief on the part of that person. For example, a ship captain choosing to sail on a vessel might imply a belief by that captain that the vessel is seaworthy. Also sometimes called "hearsay by conduct." See *R. v. Baldree*, 2012 ONCA 138.

IMPOSSIBILITY A defence of nonperformance of **contract** that arises when **performance** is impossible because of the destruction of the subject matter of the contract (as, for example, by fire) or the death of a person necessary for its performance; performance is then excused and the contract **duty** terminated. At common law, impossibility did not reach the cases where performance simply became expensive or difficult, and it has no application at all if the promise has been made expressly unconditional even as against unforeseen difficulties. The modern impossibility defence, however, "may excuse a party from performing obligations under a contract when that party will suffer extreme, unreasonable, and unforeseeable hardship due to an unavoidable event or occurrence." 30 R.A. Lord, *Williston on Contracts* (4th ed. 2004), s. 77:1, p. 279. The plea can only avail as an excuse for non-performance where the event that causes the impossibility cannot reasonably be supposed to have been in the contemplation of the parties when the contract was made; where the event was or might have been guarded against in the contract, **relief** will not be granted on account of it. J.D. McCamus, *The Law of Contracts* 573–74 (2005).

See **frustration**. See **attempt (impossible attempt)**.

IMPROVEMENT The act or process by which the quality and hence the value of a thing is increased. Any development of land or buildings through the expenditure of money or labour that is designed to do more than merely repair, replace, or restore to the original condition. Generally, "improvements" refer to structures of a permanent nature that

are attached and by concomitant necessity become part of **realty**.

IMPUTE To assign to a person or other entity the legal responsibility for the act of another, because of the relationship between the person so made liable and the actor, rather than because of actual participation in or knowledge of the act. See **vicarious liability**.

INADMISSIBLE EVIDENCE See **evidence**.

IN CAMERA (*ĭn kă'-mĕ-rà*) Lat.: in private; heard in a judge's chambers or a courtroom from which all spectators have been excluded. In general, court matters are of public record and are therefore open to the public; however, some matters—e.g., in family court—are *in camera,* and permission of the court and the **parties** is essential for attendance by others.

Section 486 of the *Criminal Code,* R.S.C. 1985, c. C–46 provides for in camera proceedings where it is ruled to be in the interest of public morals, the maintenance of order, the proper administration of justice, or if an open court could hurt international relations or affect national security or defence.

INCAPACITY Lack of ability; the quality or state of being incapable; the lack of legal, physical, or intellectual power; inability. See **incompetency**; minor; **non compos mentis**. Compare **insanity**.

INCARCERATION Confinement in a jail, prison, or penitentiary.

INCENDIARY 1. Arsonist; one who, under various conditions, intentionally or recklessly sets property on fire. **Arson** is an **indictable offence** under the *Criminal Code,* R.S.C. 1985, c. C–46, ss. 433–436.1. 2. An object capable of starting and sustaining a fire; an incendiary device.

INCEST An **indictable offence** involving sexual intercourse between persons related to each other where the tables of **affinity** and consanguinity would forbid marriage, e.g., parent and child, brother and sister, half-brother and sister, grandparent and grandchild. It is immaterial whether the relationship is traced through lawful wedlock, but the

accused must know of the relationship. *R. v. Schmidt* (1948), 90 C.C.C. 297 (Ont.C.A.). See *Criminal Code,* R.S.C. 1985, c. C–46, s. 155(1).

INCHOATE Describes something that has just begun; that which is still in a rudimentary stage. For example, inchoate offences are attempted crimes; a crime that has been started but not completed. A person can still be held liable for an attempted crime even if they have not carried the offence through to its completion. *Criminal Code*, R.S.C. 1985, c. C–46, s. 24.

INCHOATE DOWER See **dower**.

INCIDENTAL BENEFICIARY See **beneficiary**.

INCIDENTAL DAMAGES See **damages**.

INCIDENTAL EFFECT In a **division of powers** analysis, the doctrine that if a law is in **pith and substance** within the enacting level of government's jurisdiction, it is permitted to have an ancillary effect on matters outside that jurisdiction.

INCIDENTS In **feudal** England, obligations owed by **tenants** to feudal lords by virtue of their occupancy of the land. "[I]ncidents... varied depending on the type of tenure involved. The main ones were as follows: oaths of allegiance given by the tenant to the lord (**homage** and **fealty**); a right of the lord to call for financial contributions in certain circumstances (aids); transfer taxes (fines); death duties payable on the descent of land to an **heir** (relief and primer **seisin**); the power to recover the land when the tenurial term had expired or was forfeited (**escheat** and **forfeiture**); control over both (*a*) lands held by a minor, and (*b*) the marriage of the heir of the estate (wardship and marriage); and other local tax-like levies (customary dues)." B. Ziff, *Principles of Property Law* 62 (5th ed. 2010). The only one of these incidents with relevance to modern Canadian property law is the escheat. *Id.*

INCLOSURE See **enclosure**.

INCLUDED OFFENCE An **offence**, the elements of which constitute part of a different and more serious offence. "[W]here the commission of the offence charged, as described in the enactment creating it or as charged in the count, includes the commission of another offence, whether punishable by indictment or on summary conviction, the accused may be convicted . . . of an offence so included that is proved, notwithstanding that the whole offence that is charged is not proved." *Criminal Code*, R.S.C. 1985, c. C–46, s. 662(1). See *R. v. Sarrazin*, 2011 SCC 54.

INCOMPETENCY Lack of ability, qualification, fitness, or capacity to perform certain duties. The term may also be applied where one lacks the legal, physical, or intellectual fitness to discharge a particular duty or function.

When a person is adjudicated incompetent, a **guardian** may be appointed to manage the incompetent's affairs. An adjudicated incompetent lacks capacity to contract, and his or her contracts are **void**. In the case of one not formally declared incompetent, a contract may be **voidable** only. See S.M. Waddams, *The Law of Contracts* (6th ed. 2010), c. 19.

See **incapacity**; **minor**; **non compos mentis**. Compare **competent**.

INCORPORATE To combine together or unite to form a whole. To form a **corporation**; to organize and be granted status as a corporation by following procedures prescribed by law. See **association, memorandum of**.

INCORPORATION BY REFERENCE See **referential incorporation**.

INCORPOREAL Intangible, not material in nature. Incorporeal **property** or **chattels** cannot be seen or touched—they are rights only. **Copyrights** and **patent** rights are incorporeal, or CHOSES IN ACTION (see **chose**) enforceable only by an action. Compare **corporeal**.

INCORPOREAL HEREDITAMENT See **hereditaments**.

INCORPOREAL RIGHT A right issuing out of and annexed to or exercised with corporeal **inheritances**, as, e.g., **annuities** and rights of way.

INCORRIGIBLE Uncorrectable; a person, usually a juvenile, whose behaviour cannot be made to conform to standards dictated by law. Incorrigibility was formerly a basis upon which a child could be declared a **juvenile delinquent**. See also **dangerous offender, recidivist**.

INCREMENT An amount of increase in number, amount, or value. As to salaries, increments are the periodic, consecutive additions or increases that do not become part of salary until they accrue under the rule making such provision.

INCRIMINATE 1. To hold another, or oneself, responsible for **criminal** misconduct. **2.** To involve someone, or oneself, in an **accusation** of a crime.

INCULPATORY That which tends to **incriminate** or bring about a criminal conviction. Compare **exculpatory**.

INCUMBRANCE See **encumbrance**.

INDECENCY Behaviour that creates a significant risk of harm to others that is grounded in norms that society has formally recognized in the **Constitution** or similar fundamental laws, and that, in its degree, is incompatible with the proper functioning of society. "Three types of harm have thus far emerged from the jurisprudence as being capable of supporting a finding of indecency: (1) harm to those whose autonomy and liberty may be restricted by being confronted with inappropriate conduct; (2) harm to society by predisposing others to anti-social conduct; and (3) harm to individuals participating in the conduct." *R. v. Labaye*, 2005 SCC 80. The *Criminal Code*, R.S.C. 1985, c. C–46 incorporates indecency into a number of offences, for example, wilfully doing an indecent act in a public place (s. 173(1)(a)); presenting an indecent performance (s. 167); making an indecent telephone call (s. 372(2)); or keeping a **common bawdy house** (s. 210), which is a place kept for the purpose of the practice of acts of indecency (s. 197).

INDEFEASIBLE Incapable of being defeated or altered. "A **gift** that is subject to being defeated or terminated on an event such as remarriage is **defeasible**." *The Estate of Paul Dontigny v. The Queen*, [1974] 1 F.C. 418 at 420 (C.A.). In **real property**, indefeasible implies an **estate** in **fee simple**, or a perfect **title**.

IN DELICTO (*ĭn dĕ-lĭk′-tō*) Lat.: In fault, though not in equal fault. Compare **in part delicto**.

INDEMNIFY 1. To secure against loss or **damage** that may occur in the future; to **insure**. **2.** To provide compensation for loss or damage already suffered.

INDEMNITY 1. The obligation resting on one to make good any loss another person has incurred or may incur by acting at the former's request or for his benefit. **2.** The right that the person suffering the loss or damage is entitled to claim. Refers to a total shifting of economic loss onto the party chiefly or primarily responsible for that loss. Compare **contribution**.

INDENTURE A **deed** between two parties **conveying real estate** by which both **parties** assume obligations; implies a **sealed instrument**. Historically, it referred to a crease or wavy cut made in duplicates of the deed so their authenticity could be verified later.

INDEPENDENT CONTRACTOR See **contractor**.

INDIAN BAND COUNCIL See **band council**.

INDIAN See **status Indian; Aboriginal peoples**.

INDIAN BAND For purposes of the *Indian Act*, RSC 1985, c. I–5, a body of Indians " (a) for whose use and benefit in common, lands, the legal title to which is vested in Her Majesty, have been set apart before, on, or after September 4, 1951; (b) for whose use and benefit in common, moneys are held by Her Majesty; or (c) declared by the Governor in Council to be a band for the purposes of this Act." See **status Indian**.

INDIAN RESIDENTIAL SCHOOLS Federally funded and church-run schools to which **Aboriginal** children were sent after being removed from their homes. Approximately 150,000 Aboriginal children were sent to the 130 schools across Canada from the 1870s until 1996. Students were generally forbidden from speaking their Aboriginal language or from engaging in their own cultural practices; in addition, many students were physically or sexually abused. In 2008 the **Prime Minister** apologized to former students and their families for the federal government's role in operating the schools. A class action lawsuit over the matter was resolved by the **Indian Residential Schools Settlement Agreement**.

INDIAN RESIDENTIAL SCHOOLS SETTLE-MENT AGREEMENT A comprehensive settlement agreement resolving **class action** claims by former residents of Indian Residential Schools. Under the agreement, compensation was available to all former residents simply by reason of them having been residents, and further compensation was available to those who had suffered physical or sexual abuse. In addition, the settlement agreement provided for establishing a **Truth and Reconciliation Commission** to investigate and document the experiences of former residents.

INDIAN TITLE See **Aboriginal title**.

INDICIA (*in-dĭ'-shē- à*) Lat.: indications, signs. For example, that a statement was given under oath is taken to be an *indicia* of reliability, and slurred speech is taken to be an *indicia* of impairment by alcohol.

INDICTABLE OFFENCE Generally, a more serious criminal **charge** as distinguished from a **summary [conviction] offence**. However, in Canada, the distinction between indictable offences and summary conviction offences is blurred by the existence of **hybrid offences**, in which the **Crown prosecutor** can elect whether to proceed summarily or by indictment. An offence is considered to be an indictable one if proceeding by indictment is an option, and so hybrid offences qualify as indictable offences, for example, for purposes of powers of **arrest**. *Interpretation Act*, R.S.C. 1985, c. I–21, s. 34. Originally, indictable offences were tried only by the higher courts. This is still the case with

reference to particularly serious offences such as **murder** and **treason** under s. 469 of the *Criminal Code*, R.S.C. 1985, c. C–46. However, "in most cases, the accused has the option to be tried before a provincial court without a preliminary inquiry or a jury, or tried in a superior court with a preliminary inquiry and/or a jury." K. Roach, *Criminal Law* 520 (5th edition, 2012). See **crime**. Compare **misdemeanor**.

INDICTMENT An **accusation** in writing of a serious, i.e., **indictable offence**. It sets out the **charges** against the **accused**, and each **count** therein must be comprised of only one transaction or offence. It includes "(*a*) information or a count therein, (*b*), a **plea**, replication or other **pleading**, and (*c*) any record." *Criminal Code*, R.S.C. 1985, c. C–46, s. 2. By s. 673, it includes "an information or charge in respect of which a person has been tried for an indictable offence under Part XIX."

INDIGENT PERSON A person who has such small means or resources that he or she is in a general state of financial need (the working poor). "Even a person with regular employment can be considered indigent." *Mahmoodi v. Irankhah*, 2008 BCCA 512.

INDIRECT TAXATION See **direct taxation**.

INDISPENSABLE PARTY See **necessary party**.

INDIVIDUAL A **person**, but typically a natural person as opposed to an artificial person such as a **corporation**. See, e.g., *Income Tax Act*, R.S.C. 1985, c. 1 (5th Supp.), s. 248(1).

Section 15(1) of the **Canadian Charter of Rights and Freedoms** provides that "Every individual is equal before and under the law...." It has been ruled that *Charter* equality rights extend only to natural persons. *Canada (Attorney-General) v. Hislop*, 2007 SCC 10.

INDORSE See **endorse**.

INDUCING BREACH OF CONTRACT An economic **tort** that occurs when the defendant causes another party to break his or her contract with the plaintiff, thereby causing a loss. The tort can be committed either directly or indirectly. It occurs directly when the defendant performs an act that is intended to cause a breach of the plaintiff's contract and actually does so. It occurs indirectly when the defendant commits an unlawful act that causes a breach of the plaintiff's contract, even if this effect was unintended. The requirement that the act be unlawful prevents the tort from applying to legal practices, such as a lawful strike that causes an employer to breach its contract with another party. See P.H. Osborne, *The Law of Torts* 330–35 (4th ed. 2011).

INEVITABLE ACCIDENT Originally, a term in admiralty law for "that which a party charged with an offence could not possibly prevent by exercise of ordinary care, caution and maritime skill." *The Bolina* (1844), 3 Notes of Cases, 208; later applicable to motor vehicle accidents such that a person relying on the defence must satisfy a two-step test: (1) that the alleged cause of the accident could not have been prevented by the exercise of reasonable care, and (2) that, assuming such cause operated without **negligence** on the defendant's part, he or she could not, by the exercise of reasonable care, have avoided the accident. *Rintoul v. X-ray and Radium Industries Ltd.*, [1956] S.C.R. 674 at 678.

"Today, defendants in negligence cases normally do not need to avail themselves of the plea of inevitable accident; all they have to do is deny that they were negligent." A. Linden & B. Feldthusen, *Canadian Tort Law* 283–84 (9th ed. 2011). See **duty** [DUTY OF CARE].

IN EXTREMIS (*ĭn ĕks-trē'-mĭs*) Lat.: in the last stages (especially of illness); in contemplation of death. See **gift mortis causa** [DONATIO MORTIS CAUSA].

INFANT One not having reached the age of legal **majority**; a **minor**; a child. An infant's contracts are generally voidable, at the option of the infant. However, the law has held that an infant can validly contract for necessities (see, e.g., the various *Sale of Goods* statutes)

and contracts made while an infant can be ratified after reaching the **age of majority**. See S.M. Waddams, *The Law of Contracts* (6th ed. 2010), c. 18.

An infant is **liable** for his or her own **torts** although special rules relating to the capacity of a very young actor to form the necessary **intent** may protect him or her to some extent. For example, while a child of tender years is not normally charged with CONTRIBUTORY NEGLIGENCE (see **negligence**), mere age is not in itself the test, but rather the capacity of the infant to understand and appreciate danger; "it is a question for the jury in each case whether the infant exercised the care to be expected from a child of like age, intelligence and experience." *McEllistrum v. Etches,* [1956] S.C.R. 787 at 793. See A. Linden & B. Feldthusen, *Canadian Tort Law* 38–40, 155–56 (9th ed. 2011).

The *Criminal Code,* R.S.C. 1985, c. C–46, s. 13, prohibits **conviction** of anyone for an offence committed while under the age of twelve years. Provincial child welfare legislation may apply to children who are under the age of twelve and commit criminal offences. E. Greenspan, M. Rosenberg & M. Henein, *Martin's Annual Criminal Code, 2012* 52–53 (2011).

INFANTICIDE A form of culpable **homicide**; the killing of a child under one year of age by its mother. "A female person commits infanticide when by a wilful act or omission she causes the death of her newly-born child, if at the time of the act or omission she is not fully recovered from the effects of giving birth to the child and by reason thereof or of the effect of lactation consequent on the birth of the child her mind is then disturbed." *Criminal Code*, R.S.C. 1985, c. C–46, s. 233.

IN FEE [IN FEE SIMPLE] Absolute ownership of an **estate** in land. It is not used to describe a quality of a title to an **easement**, or other appurtenance or incorporeal interest.

INFERENCE A deduction from the **evidence** presented that, if reasonable, may have the validity of legal **proof**. *McLaren v. C.P.R.,* [1938] 4 D.L.R. 620

at 625 (Sask.C.A.). A deduction of an ultimate fact from other proved facts, which proved facts, by virtue of the common experience of man, will support but not compel such a deduction. Compare **presumption**.

INFERIOR COURT See **provincial courts**.

INFIRM Sickly, weak. In particular circumstances, the **testimony** of an infirm person can be obtained in a manner that differs from regular procedure to prevent its loss through his or her death. See **de bene esse**; **commission evidence**. Similarly, if a person has given evidence in some preliminary manner but has since become infirm, that prior evidence might be used at trial. See, e.g., *Nova Scotia Civil Procedure Rules*, Rule 18.20(5)(b) or *Criminal Code*, R.S.C. 1985, c. C–46, s. 715.

IN FLAGRANTE DELICTO (*ĭn-flă-grānt'-ē dĕ-lĭk'-tō*) Lat.: in the very act of committing a crime; "red-handed."

IN FORMA PAUPERIS (*ĭn fôr'-mà paw-pĕr'-ĭs*) Lat.: in the manner of a pauper. In **pleadings**, *in forma pauperis* historically granted a party the right to sue without assuming the burden of **costs** or the formalities of pleading, such as the page size and number of copies required. Many courts now have rules that make provision for the same situation. See, e.g., *Nova Scotia Civil Procedure Rules*, Rule 77.04. In the absence of such written provisions, it is possible that a court can still apply the historical *in forma pauperis* rules. See *Polewsky v. Home Hardware Stores Ltd.* (2003), 229 D.L.R. (4th) 308 (Ont. S.C.J.).

INFORMATION A statement by which a magistrate is informed of the **offence** for which a **summons** or **warrant** is required. In general, any person may lay an information, unless there is a statutory rule to the contrary. An information will suffice if it merely describes the alleged offence in ordinary, non-technical language. It is usually in writing and may be substantiated on oath. See *Criminal Code*, R.S.C. 1985, c. C–46, s. 789(1).

INFORMATION TO OBTAIN A sworn statement submitted in support of an application for a **warrant** or **authorization**.

INFORMATION AND BELIEF Verification of information to a degree of certainty that may fall short of actual knowledge, but is based on reasonable, good faith efforts to determine its truth or falsity. The term is used with reference to documents requiring verification, such as **affidavits**. See, e.g., *Alves v. First Choice Canada Inc.*, 2011 SKCA 118.

INFORMED CONSENT Consent given only after full disclosure of what is being agreed to. A phrase used in **tort** law with respect to the requirement that a patient be apprised of the nature and risks of a medical procedure before the physician can validly claim exception from **liability** for **battery** or from responsibility for medical complications. See *Reibl v. Hughes*, [1980] 2 S.C.R. 880, where a duty of disclosure, under negligence law, is imposed on doctors. Doctors must tell patients all material risks and any special risks that would be of concern to the reasonable person in the patient's position.

INFORMER PRIVILEGE A form of **privilege** protecting the identity of those who provide information confidentially to the police with regard to an **offence**. "The privilege arises where a police officer, in the course of an investigation, guarantees protection and confidentiality to a prospective informer in exchange for useful information that would otherwise be difficult or impossible to obtain." *R. v. Basi*, 2009 SCC 52. The guarantee can be made explicitly or implicitly. Informer privilege overrides the Crown's obligation of **disclosure** to an accused but is subject to the **innocence at stake exception**.

INFRA (*ĭn'-frà*) Lat.: below, beneath. In text, *infra* refers to a discussion or a citation appearing subsequently; the opposite of **supra** ["above"].

INFRINGEMENT An encroachment; interference with or violation of the right of another. For example, a person might infringe the **copyright** held by another by publishing that person's work without permission. A likely **remedy** in such a case would be an **injunction** to prevent future infringements, accompanied by an order for **damages** to compensate for the past infringement. The term is also used in talking about rights guaranteed under the **Constitution**. For example, an **investigative detention** carried out without **reasonable grounds to suspect** that the person was connected to a crime would infringe the right in s. 9 of the **Canadian Charter of Rights and Freedoms** to be free from **arbitrary** detention. Similarly, actions by government that are inconsistent with the exercise of an **Aboriginal right** would be said to infringe that right. See **Sparrow test**.

INFRINGEMENT OF PATENT See **patent** [PATENT INFRINGEMENT].

IN FUTURO (*ĭn fu-tū'-rō*) Lat.: in the future; at a later date. Compare **in praesenti**.

IN GENERE (*ĭn gĕ-nĕ'-rā*) Lat.: in kind; in the same class or species. Articles or things in the same genus are *in genere;* expresses any class relationship. Laws in the same subject are likewise said to be *in genere.* However, an *in genere* relationship between two **statutes** does not mean they are identical. Thus, laws in one area, though broadly designed to regulate one general field, may be aimed at different portions of that field and still be *in genere.* The term imports singleness in general but permits diversity of individual purposes.

INGRESS AND EGRESS 1. The entering upon and departure from; **2.** the means of entering and leaving; **3.** the right of a **lessee** to enter and leave the **leasehold**. See **easement**.

Ingress to and from the road is "the right of going from the **close** on to the road, or the right of going from the road on to the close." Egress from the road is "going out from the road—going forth from the road." *Somerset v. The Great Western Ry. Co.* (1882), 46 L.T. 893 at 884 (Q.B.).

INHERIT 1. Technically, to take as an **heir** at law solely by **descent**, rather than by **devise**; "in its strictly legal meaning, [the term] is used in contradistinction to acquiring by **will**, but in popular use this distinction is often disregarded" **2.** it also includes acquiring by will. *Perry v. Perry* (1918), 40 D.L.R. 628 (Man.C.A.).

INHERITANCE 1. Real property or **personal property** that is inherited by **heirs** according to the laws of **descent** and distribution. **2.** Popular use of the word includes property passed **by will**.

IN HOC (*ĭn hŏk*) Lat.: in this; in reference to this.

INJUNCTION A judicial **remedy** awarded for the purpose of requiring a party to refrain from doing a particular act or thing. Injunctions were first used by the **courts of equity** to restrain parties from conduct contrary to **equity** and good conscience. Today, with the merger of law and equity, they are also used in general courts of law, whereas law courts formerly were constrained to use the writ of **mandamus**.

A preventive measure, an injunction guards against future **injuries** rather than affording a remedy for past injuries. The court must be satisfied that there is a serious question to be tried and that on the facts the **plaintiff** is probably entitled to **relief**. Types of injunctions include:

INTERIM INJUNCTION Usually **ex parte**, one that restrains the defendant until some specified date.

INTERLOCUTORY INJUNCTIONS One that preserves the **status quo** until the case can be tried; the party applying for this injunction must give an undertaking in damages [covenant to reimburse the defendant] in case he or she is found in the wrong.

MANDATORY INJUNCTION See **mandatory injunction**.

PERMANENT INJUNCTION One that may be issued upon completion of a trial in which the injunction has been actively sought by a party.

See generally J. Martin, *Modern Equity* (18th ed. 2009) c. 25.

INJURIA ABSQUE DAMNO (*ĭn-jû'-rē-à äb'-skwā däm'-nō*) Lat.: wrong or insult without damage. "Injuria" refers to a tortious act. Where a **cause of action** requires that **damages** be **pleaded** as an element, this maxim expresses the rule that a wrong that causes no legally recognized damage cannot give rise to a cause of action. Although this is true in a **negligence** suit, it is not true in any cause of action in which NOMINAL DAMAGES (see damages) can be recovered, e.g., in intentional **torts** and actions for **breach of contract**. Compare **damnum absque injuria**.

INJURIA NON EXCUSAT INJURIAM (*ĭn-jû́-rē-à nŏn ĕks-kū́-zät ĭn-jû́-rē-äm*) Lat.: one wrong does not justify another.

INJURIOUS AFFECTION Reduction in market value of land or personal and business damages caused to a landowner by the construction of a public work (such as a highway). Injurious affection can be caused either to the remaining property of a landowner, part of whose property has been **expropriated**, or by any other landowner. In the latter case, three requirements must be met: (*a*) The damage must result from an act rendered lawful by statutory powers of the person performing such act; (*b*) The damage must be such as would be actionable under the common law, but for the statutory powers; and (*c*) The damage must be occasioned by the construction of the public work, not its use." *Antrim Truck Centre Ltd. v. Ontario* (*Minister of Transportation*), 2011 ONCA 419.

INJURY Any wrong or damage done to another, either to his person, rights, reputation, or **property**.
    "Injuries" means and includes "bodily injuries." *C.P.R. v. Robinson* (1891), 19 S.C.R. 292. However, unlike the ordinary meaning of injury, a LEGAL INJURY is any **damage** resulting from a violation of a legal right that gives rise to an **action** at law. See **damnum absque injuria**; **irreparable injury**.

IN KIND 1. Of the same or similar type or quality, though not necessarily the identical article; 2. in the same or similar manner.

IN LIMINE (*ĭn lĭm-ĕn-ē*) Lat.: in the beginning; means at the beginning or in the preliminary stages. For example,

a motion *in limine* is a preliminary motion brought before the beginning of a trial. L.S. Abrams & K.P. McGuinness, *Canadian Civil Procedure Law* 804 (2nd ed. 2010).

IN LOCO PARENTIS (*ĭn lṓ-kō pä-rĕń-tis*) Lat.: in the place of a parent. The term is used in many **statutes**, but the commonly accepted definition comes from the **common law**: "A person *in loco parentis* to a child is one who has acted so as to evidence his intention of placing himself towards the child in the situation which is ordinarily occupied by the father for the provision of the child's pecuniary wants." *Shtitz v. C.N.R.,* [1927] 1 W.W.R. 193 at 201 (Sask.C.A.).

INNOCENCE AT STAKE EXCEPTION An exception to **solicitor-client privilege** and **informer privilege**. The innocence at stake exception allows privilege to be breached where an **accused** establishes that the information sought from the communication is not available from any other source and that he or she is otherwise unable to raise a **reasonable doubt**. The applicant must demonstrate an evidentiary basis to conclude that a communication exists that could raise a reasonable doubt as to his or her guilt in order to have the trial **judge** examine the communication to determine whether it is, in fact, likely to raise a reasonable doubt. If so, the trial judge can order a **redacted** version of the document to be **disclosed**.

INNOCENT POSSESSION A **defence** to a **charge** of **possession** of some item of contraband, such as narcotics or child pornography. Possession is innocent when an **accused** asserts no more control over the object than is necessary to, for example, destroy it or deliver it to the authorities. See *R. v. Chalk*, 2007 ONCA 815.

INNUENDO 1. Originally, the part of a **pleading** in an **action** for **libel** that explains words spoken or written that are the basis of the action, thereby attaching to those words their proper meaning; 2. the meaning given to the alleged libelous words. Innuendo cannot enlarge the meaning of the words complained of. See *Merling v. Southam Inc.*, [2001] O.T.C. 792 (Ont. S.C.J.).

Since the purpose of innuendo is to explain the application of words used, words that are not libelous in themselves cannot be made so by innuendo. See, e.g., *Lysko v. Braley* (2006), 79 O.R. (3d) 721 (Ont. C.A.): "In their plain and ordinary meaning, the words are not reasonably capable of having a defamatory meaning. Since the appellant has not pleaded a legal innuendo nor the facts that would support a legal innuendo, this paragraph must be struck out."

IN OMNIBUS (*ĭn ŏm'-nĭ-būs*) Lat.: in all things; in all the world; in all nature; in all respects.

IN PAIS (*ĭn pā'-es*) Fr.: in the country. Applies to a transaction handled outside the court or without a legal **proceeding**.

IN PARI DELICTO (*ĭn pä'-rē dĕ-lĭk'-tō*) Lat.: in equal fault. Used with reference to an exception to the general rule that illegal transactions or **contracts** are not legally enforceable; thus, where the parties to an illegal agreement are not *in pari delicto,* the agreement may nevertheless be enforceable at **equity** by the less guilty party.

"The true test for determining whether or not the **plaintiff** and **defendant** were *in pari delicto,* is by considering whether the plaintiff could make out his case otherwise than through the medium of the illegal transaction to which he was himself a party." *Clark v. Hagar* (1894), 22 S.C.R. 510 at 524, citing *Taylor v. Chester* (1869), L.R. 4 Q.B. 309.

The term may also be used with reference to **liability** in **tort**, where the party most **negligent** may be required to bear the entire burden of the loss or **injury**. See also **clean hands**; **duress**. Compare **in delicto**.

IN PARI MATERIA (*ĭn pä'-rē mä-tĕr'-ē-à*) Lat.: on like subject matter. **Statutes** *in pari materia* are those that relate to the same **person** or things. In the **construction** of a particular statute or in the interpretation of any of the provisions, all acts relating to the same subject or having the same general purpose should be read in connection with it, as together constituting one law.

IN PERPETUITY Existing **forever**.

IN PERSONAM (*ĭn pĕr-sō'-näm*) Lat.: against the person. In **pleading**, an **action** against a person or persons, founded on personal **liability**, and requiring **jurisdiction** by the court over the **defendant**; an action whereby the plaintiff either seeks to subject defendant's general **assets** to **execution** in order to satisfy a money **judgment** or to obtain a judgment directing defendant to do an act or refrain from doing an act under sanction of the court's contempt power. Distinguished from an action **in rem**, where a valid judgment may be obtained, so far as it affects the **res**, without personal **service** of **process**. In an action to recover a judgment *in personam,* process must usually be personally served or there must be compliance with the substituted service specifically provided by some **statutes**. A judgment *in rem* is conclusive upon all who may have or claim any **interest** in the subject matter of the litigation.

IN PRAESENTI (*ĭn prā-zĕn'-tē*) Lat.: in the present. For example, when a grant of land is made *in praesenti,* it imports the transfer, subject to the limitations mentioned, of a present **interest** in the lands designated. Compare **in futuro**.

IN QUANTUM MERUIT See **quantum meruit**.

INQUEST A formal inquiry into the death of a person, overseen by a **coroner**. An inquest has limited jurisdiction. "Although an inquest has some of the trappings of a royal commission, it retains its essential quality of an investigation conducted by a medical man (or woman) into the death of individual members of the community. It must never be forgotten by the parties at every inquest that the central core of every inquest is an inquiry into how and by what means a member of the community came to [his or] her death. Notwithstanding the emerging public interest in the jury recommendations in the modern Ontario inquest, an inquest is not a trial; an inquest is not a royal commission; an inquest is not a public platform; an inquest is not a campaign or a lobby; an inquest is not a crusade." *Canadian Union of Public Employees (Toronto Civic Employees Union), Local 416 v. Lauwers*, 2011 ONSC 1317, quoting *Black Action Defence Committee v. Huxter, Coroner* (1992), 11 O.R. (3d) (Div. Ct.).

INQUISITORIAL SYSTEM See **adversary system**.

IN RE (*ĭn rā*) Lat.: in the matter of. Usually signifies a legal proceeding where there is no opponent, but rather some judicial disposition of a thing, or **res**, such as the **estate** of a **decedent**.

IN REM (*ĭn rĕm*) Lat.: against the thing. Signifies an action that is against the **res**, or thing, rather than against the person. A proceeding taken *in rem* is one taken against **property** and has for its object the disposition of the property, without reference to the **title** of individual **claimants**. See, e.g., *Hansen v. Trinity (The)*, 2007 BCSC 225. Compare **in personam**.

INSANITY A term previously used in the *Criminal Code,* R.S.C. 1985, c. C–46, s. 12, to mean a "disease of the mind." Under new provisions in 1992, it was replaced by the term **mental disorder**. These new provisions "are effectively identical to the previous s. 16 except for terminology which replaces the concept of insanity with the phraseology mental disorder. The new terminology still codifies the common law test of insanity, now termed mental disorder." E. Greenspan, M. Rosenberg & M. Henein, *Martin's Annual Criminal Code, 2012* 55–56 (2011).

IN SE (*ĭn sā*) Lat.: in and of itself. For example, **malum in se** refers to that which is evil in and of itself.

INSIDER 1. Generally, one **privy** to ordinarily nondisclosed information. **2.** In law, one with confidential information or access thereto, often relating to corporate acts to be carried out that will likely affect the market value of the **securities** of the **corporation**.

See, e.g., the *Canada Business Corporations Act*, R.S.C. 1985, c. C–44, s. 131.

INSIDER TRADING The dealing in **securities** of a corporation by someone who, by reason of being an **insider**, has knowledge of confidential information that might reasonably be expected to materially affect the value of those securities. A person engaging in insider trading is liable to compensate the seller or purchaser of the security for any damages suffered by the seller or purchaser as a result of the purchase or sale "unless the insider establishes that (*a*) the insider reasonably believed that the information had been generally disclosed; (*b*) the information was known, or ought reasonably to have been known, by the seller or purchaser; or (*c*) the purchase or sale of the security took place in the prescribed circumstances." *Canada Business Corporations Act*, RSC 1985, c. C–44, s. 131(4). In addition, insider trading is a **criminal** offence carrying a maximum penalty of ten years imprisonment. *Criminal Code*, R.S.C. 1985, c. C–46, s. 382.1.

INSOLVENCY 1. Inability to meet financial **obligations** as they mature in the ordinary course of business; **2.** excess of **liabilities** over **assets** at any given time.

The federal government has jurisdiction for the administrative control of **bankruptcy** and insolvency under s. 91 of the *Constitution Act, 1867.* The *Bankruptcy and Insolvency Act,* R.S.C. 1985, c. B–3, s. 2, defines an "insolvent person" as "a person who is not bankrupt and who resides, carries on business, or has property in Canada, whose liabilities to **creditors** provable as **claims** under this Act amount to one thousand dollars, and

(*a*) who is for any reason unable to meet his obligations as they generally become due, or

(*b*) who has ceased paying his current obligations in the ordinary course of business as they generally become due, or

(*c*) the aggregate of whose **property** is not, at a fair valuation, sufficient, or, if disposed of at a fairly conducted sale under legal process, would not be sufficient to enable payment of all his obligations, due and accruing due."

INSOLVENCY PROCEEDINGS See **bankruptcy**.

IN SPECIE (*ĭn spē'-shē*) Lat.: in kind; in like form. For example, to repay a loan *in specie* is to return the same kind of goods to the lender as were borrowed.

INSPECTION OF DOCUMENTS The right of a **party** to view and copy documents in the possession of the court or of the adverse party essential to the adverse party's **cause of action**. This is done as part of the **discovery** process before trial; but, apart from the production for pretrial inspection, a party may by the use of a SUBPOENA DUCES TECUM (see **subpoena**) require the production of documents at the time of trial for the purpose of introducing them into **evidence**. See, e.g., r. 30, *Ontario Rules of Civil Procedure,* R.R.O. 1990, Reg. 194.

Inspection of documents in criminal matters is governed by the *Criminal Code,* R.S.C. 1985, c. C–46, s. 603; inspection, testing, and examinations of exhibits comes under ss. 490(15) and 605.

INSTALMENT A portion of a **debt**; a part or portion of the total sum or quantity due. When a debt is divided into two or more parts, payable at different times, each part is called an instalment, and the debt is said to be payable by instalments.

IN STATU QUO (*ĭn stă'-tū kwō*) Lat.: in the former situation or condition. For example, in a **contract**, "in statu quo [ante]" means being placed in the same position in which a **party** was at the time of the inception of the contract sought to be **rescinded**.

INSTRUCTION Directions given by the judge to the **jury** prior to its deliberations, informing them of the law applicable to the facts of the **case** before them, to guide them in reaching a correct verdict according to law and the **evidence**; the **charge** to the jury by the judge.

INSTRUMENT 1. Generally, a formal legal document whereby rights are created or facts are recorded. The precise meaning varies by context. See, e.g., *Personal Property Security Act,* R.S.Y. 2002, c. 169, s. 1(1): "In this Act, 'instrument' means a bill of exchange, note, or cheque within the meaning of the Bills of Exchange Act (Canada), or any other writing that evidences a right to the payment of money and is of a type that, in the ordinary course of business, is transferred by delivery with any necessary endorsement or assignment, but does not include (*a*) a writing that is chattel paper, (*b*) a document of title, or (*c*) a security other than a security that is a bill of exchange or note within the meaning of the Bills of Exchange Act (Canada)." Alternatively, see *Real Property Act,* C.C.S.M. c. R30, s. 1: "In this Act, and in instruments purporting to be made or registered under this Act, unless the context otherwise requires, 'instrument' means a certificate of title, title, certificate of search or charge, book, record, plan, or data stored in the data storage system, relating to a dealing with land, or creating a mortgage, encumbrance, or lien thereon, or evidencing title thereto, and includes any duplicate of the instrument." **2.** An item or piece of equipment that can be used to perform some function, for example, as in possession of a break-in instrument (*Criminal Code,* R.S.C. 1985, c. C–46, s. 351) or an approved instrument for taking a breath sample (*Criminal Code,* s. 254, otherwise known as a **breathalyzer**.)

INSURABLE INTEREST The pecuniary relationship that a person has in the subject matter of an insurance policy, which is necessary to support the issuance of the policy.

INSURANCE "[A]n undertaking [by] one [party] to **indemnify** another [party] for an agreed **consideration**, from loss or liability in respect of an event, the happening of which is uncertain." *Re Bendix Automotive Ltd. & U.A.W.* (1971), 20 D.L.R. (3d) 151 at 157 (Ont.H.C.). Prior to the Supreme Court's judgment in *Kosmopoulos v. Constitution Insurance Co. of Canada,* [1987] 1 S.C.R. 2, it was trite law that an **insured** could only have an insurable interest in **property** in which he or she had legal or equitable **title**. In *Kosmopoulos*, the Court held that an insured can have an insurable interest in anything whose continued existence he or she benefits from, or if he or she would suffer a detriment if it were lost. See *id.*

INSURED One who obtains **insurance** on **property** or upon whose life insurance is obtained. Includes one who claims or may later claim to be an insured even though such claim may already have been contested by the **insurer**. *Winfield v. Walker* (1968), 65 W.W.R. (N.S.) 176 (B.C.C.A.).

INSURER The underwriter or insurance company that issues the policy of **insurance** for valuable **consideration**.

"The person who undertakes or agrees or offers to undertake a contract" of insurance. *The Insurance Act,* R.S.O. 1990, c. I. 8, s. 1.

INTANGIBLE PROPERTY Property that has no physical form. "'Intangible' would include an interest created by statute having the characteristics of a licence, coupled with an interest at common law, as in the case of a **profit à prendre**." *Saulnier v. Royal Bank of Canada*, 2008 SCC 58. Intangible property is sometimes characterized by what it is not. See, e.g., *Personal Property Security Act*, S.N.S. 1995–96, c. 13, s. 2(w): "'intangible' means personal property that is not goods, a document of title, chattel paper, a security, an instrument, or money."

INTEGRATION 1. The process by which the parties to an agreement adopt a writing or writings as the full and final expression of their agreement; **2.** the writing or writings so adopted. Thus where the parties to a contract have agreed to it as an integration, **parol evidence** is not **admissible** to supplement or vary its terms.

INTELLECTUAL PROPERTY (IP) Intangible property, such as creative works or inventions, that can be protected by **copyright**, **trademark**, **patent**, or other legal regimes. "Not all rights associated with IP can technically be called 'prop-

erty.' That is true of the right to trade freely or be free from IP claims, unfair competition, and misstatements about one's goods or business, and often one's rights as a licensee." D. Vaver, *Intellectual Property Law* 9 (2nd ed., 2011).

INTENT "[T]he exercise of the free will to use particular means to produce a particular result." *R v. Lewis* (1979), 47 C.C.C. (2d) 24, at 33 (S.C.C.). In the criminal context, intent is "the highest level of mens rea…which requires the accused to act with the…purpose to achieve the prohibited result…. Knowledge that something is very certain to occur, however, may be equated with an intent or purpose." K. Roach, *Criminal Law* 182 (5th edition, 2012). Where no mental element is mentioned in the definition of a crime, the general mens rea required is either the "intentional or reckless bringing about of the result." *R. v. Buzzanga and Durocher* (1979), 49 C.C.C. (2d) 369 (O.C.A.).

Two general classes of intent exist in the criminal law: GENERAL INTENT, which must exist in all crimes, and SPECIFIC INTENT, which is essential to certain crimes and which, as an essential element of the crime, must be proved **beyond a reasonable doubt**.

A general intent is simply the conscious decision to perform the action, while specific intent is the motivation behind performing the action, for example, the "specific intent to enhance the abilities of a terrorist group to facilitate or carry out a terrorist activity" necessary to a conviction under s. 83.18 of the *Criminal Code*, R.S.C. 1985, c. C–46. *R. v. Khawaja*, 2012 SCC 69. See **animo**; **mens rea**; **scienter**.

INTENTION IN COMMON See **common intention**.

INTER ALIA (*ĭn'-tĕr ä'-lē-à*) Lat.: among other things.

INTERDELEGATION The transfer of legislative authority over a matter given to one level of government under the **Constitution Act, 1867**, by that level of government to the other. Interdelegation is not permitted in Canadian constitutional law, even with the consent of both levels of government. However, governments can incorporate by reference the legislation of another level of government, or delegate powers to an administrative body appointed by that other level of government.

INTEREST 1. In commercial law, **consideration** or **compensation** paid for the use of money loaned or forbearance in demanding it when due. "[A] s a class of subject within exclusive Federal competence under s. 91(19) of the *B.N.A. Act* [interest] is a precise and unambiguous term, and in the absence of any contrary indication should be expounded in its natural and ordinary sense. It is not restricted to compensation determinable by application of a rate *per centum* to the principal amount of a loan, but covers compensation for the use of money by way of a fixed sum whether denominated a bonus, discount or premium, provided it is referable to principal money or to an obligation." *Re Unconscionable Transactions Relief Act, etc.,* [1962], O.R. 1103 (Ont. C.A.) per headnote. See *Interest Act,* R.S.C. 1985, c. I–15. **2.** In legal practice, the term connotes concern for the advantage or disadvantage of a party to the cause of action. Interest is a factor affecting the credibility of **witnesses**. Having such a concern is a requirement for the intervention of a third party in a lawsuit; it is also a ground for disqualifying a judge or juror. **3.** "The relation of being objectively concerned in something, by having a right or **title** to, a claim upon, or a share in a legal concern in a thing; especially right or title to **property**...." *Re Canequip Exports Ltd. and Smith* (1972), 8 C.C.C. (2d) 360 at 362 (Man.Q.B.).

BENEFICIAL INTEREST The benefit resulting from an interest in an estate that is less than legal ownership or control; the interest of the beneficiary as opposed to the interest of the **trustee** who holds legal **title**; the EQUITABLE INTEREST (see following) in property held in **trust** that the **beneficiary** may enforce against the trustee according to the terms of the trust. In a trust, the beneficial equitable interest must be distinct from the legal interest, or a **merger** will occur and the effort

by the creator of the trust (**settlor**) to create separate legal and equitable interests in particular property will be ineffective. See *Re Rispin* (1912), 25 O.L.R. 633 (C.A.); *Elgin Loan & Savings Co. v. National Trust Co.* (1903), 7 O.L.R. 1, affirmed (1905), 10 O.L.R. 41 (C.A.).

EQUITABLE INTEREST See **equity**.

EXECUTED INTEREST An interest in property presently enjoyed and possessed by a party.

EXECUTORY INTEREST One that may become actual at some future date or upon the happening of some contingency.

PROPRIETARY INTEREST Interest as an owner; a legal right or **title**. *Reid v. Morwick* (1918), 42 O.L.R. 224 at 237 (C.A.). Any right in relation to a **chattel** that enables one to retain its **possession** indefinitely or for a period of time.

SHIFTING INTEREST An interest created by cutting short one **freehold estate** in favor of another (not the **grantor**) as may occur in estates subject to a **condition** subsequent if certain events occur. Such shifts were illegal at common law. See further A.M. Sinclair & M.E. McCallum, *An Introduction to Real Property Law* 76–77 (6th ed. 2012).

SPRINGING INTEREST "[O]ne that comes from a grantor in the future (as it must where the **remainder** is **contingent** freehold and not preceded by a freehold in another **grantee**)." *Id.* at 73. Such springs were illegal at common law.

SUBSTANTIAL INTEREST In commercial law, a "large quantity" or "considerable amount of **shares**"; need not be a controlling interest. *Manning Timber Products Ltd. v. Min. of Nat. Revenue,* [1952] 2 S.C.R. 481.

VESTED INTEREST One in which there is a present fixed right of present or future **enjoyment** that carries with it a right of **alienation**, even though the right to possession or enjoyment may be postponed to some uncertain time in the future.

INTERIM Connotes a definite period of time with a fixed beginning and ending;

not strictly interchangeable with **interlocutory**.

INTERIM ORDER A temporary order, made until another or FINAL ORDER (see **order**) takes its place or a specific event occurs. See also **interlocutory**.

INTERJURISDICTIONAL IMMUNITY "[T]he idea that there is a 'basic, minimum, and unassailable content' to the heads of powers in ss. 91 and 92 of the **Constitution Act, 1867**, that must be protected from impairment by the other level of government... In cases where interjurisdictional immunity is found to apply, the law enacted by the other level of government remains valid but has no application with regard to the identified 'core.'" *Canada (Attorney-General) v. PHS Community Services Society*, 2011 SCC 44.

INTERLOCUTORY Not final. An order or judgment is interlocutory if it does not determine the **issues** at trial but directs some further **proceeding** preliminary to a final order or **decree**. Such order or judgment is subject to change by the court during the pendency of the action to meet the exigencies of the case.

INTERLOCUTORY DECREE See **decree**.

INTERLOCUTORY ORDER Any order made before the final disposition of the case.

INTERMITTENT SENTENCE A **sentence** of imprisonment of less than 90 days in which the days are not served consecutively.

INTERNATIONAL CRIMINAL COURT An international organization established under the *Rome Statute*, 2187 U.N.T.S. 3, with jurisdiction over four core crimes of **genocide**, **crimes against humanity**, **war crimes**, and **aggression**. The court consists of the Presidency (three judges who serve administrative roles as president and vice presidents of the court), the Chambers (eighteen judges, including those who work in the presidency), the Office of the Prosecutor (which investigates and conducts prosecutions), and the Registry (which provides administrative support). The court is located in The Hague.

INTERNATIONAL LAW The system of law that governs relations between states; also known as "the law of nations" or "public international law." Article 38(1) of the *Statute of the International Court of Justice* provides:

The Court, whose function is to decide in accordance with international law such disputes as are submitted to it, shall apply:

(*a*) international conventions, whether general or particular, establishing rules expressly recognized by the contesting states;

(*b*) international custom, as evidence of a general practice accepted as law;

(*c*) the general principles of law recognized by civilized nations;

(*d*) ...judicial decisions and the teachings of the most highly qualified publicists of the various nations, as subsidiary means for the determination of rules of law.

S. Rosenne, *Documents on the International Court of Justice* 61–89 (3d ed. 1991).

This is frequently regarded as the main statement of the sources of international law. See also J.H. Currie, *Public International Law* (2nd ed. 2008), c. 3.

INTERNET A global network of computer systems capable of electronically connecting individuals, corporations, and organizations around the world.

INTER PARES (*ĭn'-tĕr pär'-ās*) Lat.: among peers; among those of equal rank.

INTER PARTES (*ĭn'-tĕr pär'-tās*) Lat.: between the parties.

INTERPLEADER An equitable **action** in which a **debtor**, not knowing to whom among his or her **creditors** a certain debt is owed, and having no **claim** or stake in the property in dispute other than its proper disposition, will petition a court to require that creditors litigate the claim among themselves. It is used to avoid double or multiple **liability** on the part of the debtor. Interpleader is often used by insurance carriers, who deposit the proceeds of a policy in a court where several **persons** with conflicting rights have made claims.

Similarly, where goods, etc., taken in execution by a sheriff are claimed by a third person, the sheriff may apply for interpleader relief. Compare **joinder**.

INTERPROVINCIAL TRADE AND COMMERCE 1. Intercourse and traffic between citizens or inhabitants of different provinces. **2.** A federal head of power under the **Constitution Act, 1867**, s. 91 (2).

INTERROGATION An informal term used to describe the process by which suspects are rigorously questioned by police.

INTERROGATORIES In **civil actions** in some provinces, a pre-trial **discovery** tool in which written questions are propounded by a **party** to the action and served on another **person**, who must give written replies under oath. See, e.g., *Nova Scotia Civil Procedure Rules*, Rule 19.

IN TERROREM (*ĭn tĕr-rôr-ĕm*) Lat.: in fear. A term describing a legal document intended to frighten another party in the hope of compelling him or her to act in a certain way, without the need to commence a formal lawsuit.

INTERVENER A person or organization other than one of the parties to an **action** who is permitted to make submissions to the court.

INTERVENING CAUSE See **cause**.

INTER VIVOS (*ĭn'-tĕr vē'-vōs*) Lat.: between the living. Transactions *inter vivos* are those made while the **parties** are living, and not upon death (as in the case of **inheritance)** or upon contemplation of death **(causa mortis)**. A **deed**, therefore, is an **instrument** that conveys *inter vivos* a present **interest** in land or that conveys the **corpus** of a **trust** to the **trustees** [a DEED OF TRUST]. GIFT INTER VIVOS See **gift** [GIFT INTER VIVOS].

INTESTATE [INTESTACY] The condition of having died without leaving a valid **will**. Intestate property (i.e., undevised **property)** is that which a **testator** has failed to dispose of by will. Thus, an intestate estate is that left upon the death of a devisee to whom a testator willed

a **life estate** without providing for the **remainder**.

INTESTATE SUCCESSION The disposition of property according to the laws of descent and distribution upon the death of a person who has left no **will** or who has left a portion of his or her **estate** unaccounted for. See **heirs**; **intestate**. See e.g., *Succession Law Reform Act*, R.S.O. 1990, c. 46, Part II.

IN THE EXECUTION OF DUTY In referring to a police officer, that the officer is exercising a power, as opposed to merely being "on duty." "A police officer will be found to be in execution of his or her duty if acting in accordance with statutory or common law authority." *R. v. Backhouse* (2005), 194 C.C.C. (3d) 1, 28 C.R. (6th) 31 (Ont. C.A.).

IN TOTO (*ĭn tō'-tō*) Lat.: in entirety; e.g., to repay a debt *in toto*.

INTOXICATION State of impairment from alcohol or drugs. In the criminal law, voluntary intoxication is no **defence** against crimes of **general intent**, but may refute the existence of **mens rea** necessary for crimes of **specific intent**. *R. v. George*, [1960] S.C.R. 871. However, in order to comply with the **Charter**, a state of extreme intoxication akin to **automatism** was held in *R. v. Daviault*, [1994] 3 S.C.R. 63 to be a defence to general intent offences. In 1995, Parliament enacted s. 33.1 of the *Criminal Code*, R.S.C. 1985 c. C–46, which effectively overturned *Daviault* by providing that self-induced intoxication is not a defence to offences involving "an assault or any other interference or threat of interference by a person with the bodily integrity of another person." See K. Roach, *Criminal Law* 261–72 (5th ed. 2012). Compare **incompetency**. Intoxication may also be a mitigating factor reducing the punishment meted out for certain crimes. See **impaired [driving]**.

INTRA VIRES (*ĭn'-trà vī'-rāz*) Lat.: within the powers. See **ultra vires**.

INTRINSIC FRAUD See **fraud**.

INUIT Under s. 35 of the Constitution Act, 1982, one of the three **Aboriginal**

peoples of Canada, along with **Indians** and **Métis**. The Inuit occupy Arctic regions of Canada and other countries, and the word "inuit" means "the people" in Inuktitut, the language of most Canadian Inuit.

INURE To take effect, to operate; to serve to the use, benefit, or advantage of someone, in **property**, to **vest**.

INVEST To place **capital** with a view to securing income or profit.

There are two connotations in which the word *investing* can be used: the purchase of articles or property (1) for the income that can be obtained from them and (2) with the view to their resale. *First Torland Investments Ltd. v. M.N.R.,* [1969] C.T.C. 134 at 151–52 (Ex.).

INVESTIGATIVE DETENTION The ability of a police officer to briefly detain a person based on **reasonable grounds to suspect** that there is a clear nexus between the individual to be detained and a recent or ongoing **criminal** offence. "The overall reasonableness of the decision to detain, however, must further be assessed against all of the circumstances, most notably the extent to which the interference with individual liberty is necessary to perform the officer's duty, the liberty interfered with, and the nature and extent of that interference." *R. v. Mann,* 2004 SCC 52.

INVITATION TO SEXUAL TOUCHING A **hybrid offence** under s. 152 of the *Criminal Code,* R.S.C. 1985, c. C–46 that occurs when an accused, acting with a sexual purpose, "invites, counsels, or incites a person under the age of sixteen years to touch, directly or indirectly ... the body of any person, including the body of the person who so invites, counsels, or incites, and the body of the person under the age of sixteen years." See also **sexual exploitation**.

INVITATION TO TREAT A preliminary stage in the formation of a **contract** involving a solicitation to another party to commence negotiations. It is distinct from an **offer** insofar as an "offer communicates a willingness to be bound upon the next communication of the offeree," while a party who makes an invitation to treat does not yet intend to enter into contractual relations. J.D. McCamus, *The Law of Contracts* 34 (2005).

INVITEE One who comes upon another's land by the latter's express or implied invitation. The term "is reserved for those who are invited into the premises by the owner or occupier for some purpose of business or of material interest." *McLean v. Y.M.C.A.,* [1918] 3 W.W.R. 522 at 526 (Alta.C.A.). In **tort** law, the owner is not an insurer of the safety of invitees, but he or she owes a **duty** to them to exercise reasonable care for protection against latent defects in the premises that might cause injury. Compare **licensee**; **trespass**. See provincial *Occupiers Liability Acts*.

INVOLUNTARY [INVOLUNTARINESS] The status of physical actions performed by a person which are not a product of that person's conscious will. A reflex action will not be voluntary, nor will actions performed while the accused is in a state of **automatism**. If conduct is involuntary, it will not be considered to be the accused's act, and therefore cannot constitute the **actus reus** of an **offence**: "No one can be found criminally responsible for an involuntary act." *R. v. Bouchard–Lebrun,* 2011 SCC 58. See **voluntary**; **moral involuntariness**.

INVOLUNTARY BAILMENT See **bailment**.

I.O.U. A common abbreviation for "I owe you." It is a written acknowledgment of a debt signed by the debtor stating the amount owed and the person to whom it is payable.

IP ADDRESS Internet Protocol address. A unique number identifying a device that has connected to the **Internet** using the Internet Protocol.

IPSE DIXIT (*ĭp'-sā dĭks'-ĭt*) Lat.: he himself said it. An assertion the sole authority for which is that the speaker himself has said it.

IPSO FACTO (*ĭp'-sō făk'-tō*) Lat.: by the fact itself; in and of itself. "The sale of property should *ipso facto* end any interest the former owner may have in it."

IPSO JURE (*ĭp'-sō jū'-rā*) Lat.: by the law itself; merely by the law.

IRREPARABLE HARM A criterion used in determining whether particular forms of relief, such as an interlocutory injunction or a stay of a decision pending appeal, should be granted. Generally speaking, whether there will be irreparable harm is largely dependent on the question of whether any such harm could be adequately compensated for by **damages**. See *Edward Jones v. Voldeng*, 2012 BCCA 295. Sometimes also referred to as irreparable injury.

ISSUE 1. As a verb, to put into circulation; to send out, as to a buyer.

2. In the law of wills and real property, *issue* means descendants—all persons **descended** from a common ancestor may be regarded as issue. Some jurisdictions restrict issue to only "lawful, lineal defendants..." See, e.g., *Wills Act*, R.S.N.S. 1989, c. 505. It became a matter of judicial interpretation whether a reference to "issue" or "child" could refer to an **illegitimate** child. See, e.g., *Re Brand* (1957), 7 D.L.R. (2d) 579 (Ont.H.C.). New rights are being accorded to the illegitimate child with respect to both wills and **intestacy** situations. See, e.g., the *Intestate Succession Act*, R.S.N.S. 1989, c. 236, s. 16: "An illegitimate child shall be treated as if the child were the legitimate child of the child's mother or father." See also *Surette v. Harris* (1989), 91 N.S.R. (2d) 419, where s. 15 of the *Intestate Succession Act,* R.S.N.S. 1967, c. 153, was found unconstitutional because it discriminated against illegitimate children in intestacy situations.

3. In legal practice, an issue is a single certain point of fact or law disputed (or AT ISSUE) between **parties** to a **litiga-**tion, generally composed of an affirmative assertion by one side and a denial by the other.

ISSUED CAPITAL "The **shares** of [a] **corporation** that have been issued by the directors to the shareholders." J.A. VanDuzer, *The Law of Partnerships and Corporations* 597 (3rd ed. 2009). See **capital**. See also *Business Corporations Act,* R.S.O. 1990, c. B. 16, s. 23.

ISSUE ESTOPPEL A doctrine preventing the relitigation of a matter that has already been decided. The prerequisites for issue estoppel to apply are: "(1) that the same question has been decided; (2) that the judicial decision [that] is said to create the estoppel was final; and, (3) that the parties to the judicial decision or their privies were the same persons as the parties to the proceedings in which the estoppel is raised or their privies." *Danyluk v. Ainsworth Technologies Inc.*, 2001 SCC 44. In **criminal** law, issue estoppel applies narrowly to preclude the Crown from leading evidence that is inconsistent with findings made in the accused's favour in a previous proceeding. *R. v. Mahalingan*, 2008 SCC 63. Rather, the Crown is precluded from relitigating only those issues that were *decided in favour of the accused* at the earlier trial (paras. 22, 31, and 33). Moreover, the resolution of an issue in favour of the accused must be "a necessary inference from the trial judge's findings or from the fact of the acquittal" (para. 52). Issue estoppel does not apply where it is merely true that "the general circumstances of the case tend to indicate that the jury resolved the issue in favour of the accused." *R. v. Punko*, 2012 SCC 39.

ITO See **information**.

J. Justice; title given to judges of a provincial supreme court; the Federal Court of Canada, and the Supreme Court of Canada; (**C.J.** Chief Justice; **C.J.C.** Chief Justice of Canada [Chief Justice of the Supreme Court of Canada]).

JD Juris doctor. An undergraduate law degree conferred by American law faculties. Most Canadian law schools are now conferring a JD as an undergraduate law degree instead of the traditionally awarded **LL.B.** degree.

J.P. See **Justice of the Peace**.

JETSAM Goods that are voluntarily thrown or jettisoned from a ship on the verge of sinking in the hope of saving the ship. See **flotsam**.

JOBBER A middleman in the **sale** of goods; one who sells to anyone at a fraction above the market price and buys off anyone at a fraction below market. *Canada v. BASF Coatings & Inks Canada Ltd.* (1998), 235 N.R. 153 (F.C.A.). Jobbing "possibly means something more than selling by retail and less than selling by wholesale." *Cook v. Shaw* (1895), 25 O.R. 124 at 126 (Ch.D.). As distinguished from a **broker** or **agent**, who sells goods on another's behalf, a jobber actually purchases the goods himself or herself and then resells them. Compare **wholesaler**.

JOINDER 1. Uniting of two or more **causes of action** or **parties** in a single **suit**; 2. joining another party in a legal step or proceeding. See **class action**; **interpleader**; **real party in interest**. Compare **misjoinder**.

COMPULSORY JOINDER The mandatory joining of a **person** who must be made a party with others in an action under certain circumstances because his or her participation is necessary for a just adjudication of the **controversy**. See J. Walker & L. Sossin, *Civil Litigation* 133 (2010). A party must join all of his or her related claims against another or face the possibility of being barred from litigating them separately on the grounds that such action constitutes **multiplicity of suits**. If he or she is the defendant, a party must raise related claims as compulsory **counterclaims** in an analogous situation.

JOINDER OF CAUSES OF ACTION The joining of several **causes of action** in one without leave where the plaintiff claims and defendant is **alleged** to be **liable** in the same capacity in respect of all causes of action *or* if plaintiff claims and defendant is alleged to be liable in the capacity of **executor** or **administrator** of an **estate** in respect of one or more causes of action and in his or her personal capacity with reference to the same estate in respect of others.

JOINDER OF PARTIES The joining of all persons in one action as plaintiffs or defendants where the claim is in respect of the same transaction or series of transactions and where common questions of law or fact arise. See *Id* at 134–37.

PERMISSIVE JOINDER The joining of persons under certain circumstances, as plaintiff or defendants, in an action until such persons can sue or be sued separately. The interests of judicial economy encourage a party to raise as many unrelated claims in a single lawsuit as he may have against another party, with the court "severing" those that ought not to be tried together. See *Id* at 133–34.

Also, *see Criminal Code,* R.S.C. 1985, c. C–46, s. 593, referring to joinder of **accused** in certain criminal cases.

JOINT United, combined; a common as opposed to an individual interest or liability.

JOINT ACCOUNT A bank account in two or more names, consisting of funds held in **joint tenancy**; an account upon which cheques can be drawn or withdrawals made by both parties or either of them. *Duval v. Canada (Attorney-General)*, 2012 FC 480.

JOINT AND SEVERAL The condition in which rights and **liabilities** are shared among a group of persons collectively and also individually. Thus, if **defendants** in a **negligence suit** are jointly and severally liable, all may be sued together or any one may be sued for full **satisfaction** to the injured party. Compare **severally**.

See **contribution**; **indemnity**.

JOINT CUSTODY See **custody**.

JOINT LIABILITY Shared liability that results in the right of any one party sued to insist that others be sued with him or her; e.g., see *Tortfeasors Act,* R.S.N.S. 1989, c. 471, s. 5.

JOINT STOCK COMPANY An older term suggesting a company of association, usually unincorporated, that has the capital of its members pooled in a common fund; the capital stock is divided into **shares** and distributed to represent ownership **interest** in the company. A form of partnership that is distinguished from a partnership in the ordinary sense in that the membership of a joint stock company is changeable, its shares are transferable, its members can be many and not necessarily known to each other and its members cannot act or speak for the company.

JOINT TENANCY See **tenancy**.

JOINT TORTFEASORS Two or more persons who owe to another person the same **duty** and whose **negligence** results in injury to such other person, thus rendering the tortfeasors both **jointly and severally** (individually) **liable** for the injury; the parties must either act in concert or by independent acts unite in causing a single injury. See *Tortfeasors Act,* R.S.N.S. 1989, c. 471; *Negligence Act,* R.S.O. 1990, c. N. 1. See also **concerted action**; **contribution**. Compare **conspiracy**.

JOINTURE An **estate** or **property** secured to a prospective wife as a marriage settlement, to be enjoyed by her after her husband's decease. The estate existed under the **common law** as a means of protecting the wife's future, upon her husband's death, in lieu of **dower**. Compare **curtesy**.

JOINT VENTURE A business undertaking by two or more parties in which profits, losses and control are shared. Though the term is often considered synonymous with **partnership**, a joint venture may connote an enterprise of a more limited scope and duration, though there is the same sort of mutual **liability**. Compare **corporation**.

JOY-RIDING A common term used to describe the offence of taking a motor vehicle without the consent of the owner, "with intent to drive, use, navigate or operate it or cause it to be driven, used, navigated or operated." *Criminal Code*, R.S.C. 1985, c. C–46, s. 335.

JSD Doctor of Laws degree.

JUDGE-MADE LAW Law made in the **common-law** tradition; law arrived at by judicial **precedent** rather than by **statute**. See **stare decisis**; **common law**.

JUDGE SHOPPING Manipulating the timing of the laying of a **charge** in order to affect which **judge** will hear the matter. "[J]udge shopping is unacceptable both because of its unfairness to the accused, and because it tarnishes the reputation of the justice system." *R. v. Regan*, 2002 SCC 12. The term is also applied to efforts by an accused, through the use of an **election** or otherwise, to select or avoid a particular judge.

JUDGMENT The determination of a court of competent **jurisdiction** upon matters submitted to it.

DEFAULT JUDGMENT [JUDGMENT BY DEFAULT] A judgment automatically granted to a **plaintiff** in civil proceedings where the "defendant fails to respond to the plaintiff's proceedings within the required time." J. Walker & L. Sossin, *Civil Litigation* 222 (2010). If this occurs, the defendant "is deemed to admit the truth of all allegations" put forward in the plaintiff's **statement of claim**. *Id.* "However, a plaintiff is not entitled to judgment merely because the facts are deemed to be admitted, and the statement of facts must otherwise entitle the plaintiff to the judgment." *Id* at 223. See, e.g., *Nova Scotia Civil Procedure Rules*, Rule 8. A defendant may make a motion to have a default judgment set aside, but it will be successful only when the defendant shows that there is a "serious argument on the merits" against the plaintiff's allegations, and when there is a "reasonable excuse for delay" in responding to the plaintiff. *Temple v. Riley*, 2001 NSCA 36. Compare **ex parte**.

FINAL JUDGMENT One that fully determines any action or judicial proceeding so that all that remains to be done is **execute** the judgment. *Spelman v. Spelman*, [1943] 3 W.W.R. 181 (B.C.C.A.). As defined in the *Supreme Court Act*, R.S.C. 1985, c. S–26, s. 2(1), a final judgment is a decision that determines in whole or in part any substantive right of parties to a dispute in a judicial proceeding.

A final judgment is conclusive against the plaintiff if awarded for the defendant, and vice versa; however, it does not mean that any other legal recourse is precluded. If a superior court exists, the matter may be taken up on **appeal**. See also *Wolverton & Co. Ltd. v. Hooper* (1972), 24 D.L.R. (3d) 567 (B.C.C.A.).

JUDGMENT IN REM An adjudication pronounced upon the status of some particular subject matter [as distinguished from one pronounced upon persons] by a tribunal having competent authority for that purpose. *Monteiro (Re)* (2004), 12 E.T.R. (3d) 50 (Ont. S.C.J.).

JUDGMENT N.O.V. [NON OBSTANTE VEREDICTO] (*nŏn ŏb-stăn'-tā vĕ-rĕ-dĭk'-tō*) Lat.: notwithstanding the verdict. A judgment reversing the determination of the jury that is granted when it is obvious that the jury verdict had no reasonable support in fact or was contrary to law—i.e., the jury verdict was perverse based on the evidence before it. The motion for a judgment n.o.v. provides a second chance for the trial court to render what is, in effect, a **directed verdict** for the moving party. This power exists in Canada, but Canadian courts do not tend to use

the term "judgment n.o.v." to describe it. See, e.g., *Salter et al. v. Hirst el al.*, 2010 ONSC 3440.

SUMMARY JUDGMENT A **motion** put forward by a party to civil litigation for the purpose of disposing, without a trial, "claims and defences that are factually unsupported." J. Walker & L. Sossin, *Civil Litigation* 210 (2010). A "motion for summary judgment… permits the judge to examine not only the pleadings but affidavits, cross-examination of deponents, examinations for discovery, admissions, and other evidence." *Id.*

JUDGMENT CREDITOR A **creditor** who has obtained **judgment** against a **debtor** by which he or she can enforce **execution**.

JUDGMENT DEBTOR A **debtor** who has had a **judgment** entered against him or her by a **creditor** and who is liable to enforcement of the judgment by an order of **execution**.

JUDICATURE The judiciary; the area of government that was intended to interpret and administer the law.

JUDICATURE ACTS Statutes that organize the system of courts and delineate the **jurisdiction** thereof. The English *Supreme Court of Judicature Act, 1873* amalgamated the then existing superior courts into the Supreme Court of Judicature, consisting of the Court of Appeal and High Court of Justice. It also provided for the merger of the jurisdiction of the courts of law and equity. See the provincial *Judicature Acts*.

JUDICIAL COMMITTEE OF THE PRIVY COUNCIL [J.C.P.C.] A committee of judges chosen from among the members of the English Privy Council. It is a body constituted to hear appeals in both civil and criminal matters from the courts of the British dominions and colonies. The Judicial Committee of the Privy Council was the final court of appeal for Canada until 1949, when appeals from the Supreme Court of Canada were abolished. See **privy council**.

JUDICIAL COUNCIL Independent bodies of **jurists** that exist at national and provincial levels to investigate complaints about **judicial misconduct**. The Canadian Judicial Council operates under the *Judges Act,* R.S.C. 1985, J–1, and consists of the Chief Justice of the **Supreme Court of Canada**, serving as chair, and the Chief Justices and Associate Chief Justices of all the federally appointed courts in Canada.

All investigations are conducted by panels of the Council. The Council has discretion in pursuing complaints, but it must formally pursue any complaint if requested to do so by the federal Minister of Justice (Attorney-General) or the Attorney-General of a province under s. 63(1) of the *Judges Act*. If the Inquiry Committee recommends the removal of a judge, the matter then goes to the Judicial Council as a whole. After its investigation has been concluded the Council reports its findings to the Minister of Justice.

The Council has no authority to act on its own, but it can recommend the removal of the judge under s. 65(2) of the *Judges Act* if it concludes that the judge has become incapacitated or disabled from the execution of the office of judge by reason of (a) age or infirmity, (b) having been guilty of misconduct, (c) having failed in the due execution of that office, or (d) having been placed in a position incompatible with the due execution of that office.

JUDICIAL DECISION See **decision**.

JUDICIAL DISCRETION See **discretion**.

JUDICIAL ERROR A judgment erroneous in some aspect; an act performed by the court that is in error. Some mistake in the foundation, proceeding, **judgment**, execution of an **action** in a court of record requiring correction either by the court in which it occurred (error of fact) or by a superior court **(error of law)**.

JUDICIAL IMMUNITY See **immunity**.

JUDICIAL INDEPENDENCE The principle that the judiciary must be free to act without interference from any other entity. The principle is explicitly reflected in various constitutional documents but is broader than that and is "one of the pillars upon which our constitutional democracy rests." *Ell v. Alberta*, 2003 SCC 35.

JUDICIAL INTERIM RELEASE The procedures in the *Criminal Code*, R.S.C. 1985, c. C–46, ss. 515–523 governing when and whether a person charged with an **offence** will be released from **custody** pending **trial**. This is sometimes popularly referred to as **bail**, but that term is not used in any provision of the **Criminal Code**. The system starts from the assumption that all persons will be released on an **undertaking** without conditions, and the **Crown prosecutor** is required to prove otherwise. The language in the *Criminal Code* requires that the Crown must show cause why the accused should be detained, and so the process is sometimes referred to as a "show cause hearing." A **reverse onus** applies in some cases, such as offences committed for the benefit of a **criminal organization** (s. 515(6)(a)(ii)) or murder (s. 522(2)).

If an accused is not released on an undertaking without conditions, then more restrictive options are possible short of detention in custody. An accused can be released: (*a*) on an undertaking with conditions; (*b*) on a **recognizance** without **sureties** and without deposit of money; (*c*) on a recognizance with sureties but without deposit of money or other valuable security, or; (*d*) on a recognizance without sureties but with the deposit of money, with the consent of the prosecutor. As a result, the deposit of money or other valuable security as a means of securing release is not the most common option. Unless there is a reverse onus, the Crown is required to demonstrate that each more intrusive step is necessary and that release on the less restrictive basis is not appropriate.

The detention of an accused pending trial can be justified only on one or more of three grounds: that the detention is necessary to ensure the accused's attendance in court; that the detention is necessary for the protection or safety of the public; or that the detention is necessary to maintain confidence in the administration of justice having regard to all the circumstances, including a number of listed factors. These are often referred to as the primary, secondary, and tertiary grounds. A prior version of the tertiary ground was found to violate section 11(e) of the **Canadian Charter of Rights and Freedoms** (which guarantees everyone charged with an offence the right not to be denied reasonable bail without just cause) on the basis that the "public interest" was too vague and imprecise a term to give guidance to courts. *R. v. Morales*, [1992] 3 S.C.R. 711. The current version of the tertiary, which lists a number of specific factors to consider, has been upheld. *R. v. Hall*, 2002 SCC 64.

JUDICIAL MISCONDUCT Conduct of a judge that is "so manifestly and profoundly destructive of the concept of the impartiality, integrity and independence of the judicial role, that public confidence would be sufficiently undermined to render the judge incapable of executing the judicial office." *Report to the Canadian Judicial Council of the Enquiry Commission Established Pursuant to Subsection 63(1) of the Judges Act at the Request of the Attorney-General of Nova Scotia* (August 1990). See **Judicial Council**.

JUDICIAL NOTICE The court's recognition of certain facts that can be confirmed by consulting sources of indisputable accuracy, thereby relieving one party of the burden of producing **evidence** to prove these facts. A court can use this doctrine to admit as "proved" such facts that are common knowledge to a judicial professional or to an average, well-informed citizen—e.g., that the mail is not delivered New Year's Day.

"A court may accept without the requirement of proof facts that are either '(1) so notorious or generally accepted as not to be the subject of debate among reasonable persons; or (2) capable of immediate and accurate demonstration by resort to readily accessible sources of indisputable accuracy' ... The dictionary meaning of words may fall within the latter category." *R. v. Krymowski*, 2005 SCC 7.

JUDICIAL REVIEW 1. A superior court's examination of the conduct of an inferior court, board, committee, or **tribu-**nal, to ensure the conduct was proper in law (distinct from **appeal**). "By virtue of the **rule of law** principle, all exercises of public authority must find their source in law. All decision-making powers have legal limits, derived from the enabling statute itself, the **common** or **civil law,** or the **Constitution**. Judicial review is the means by which the courts supervise those who exercise statutory powers, to ensure that they do not over-step their legal authority. The function of judicial review is therefore to ensure the legality, the reasonableness, and the fairness of the administrative process and its outcomes." *Dunsmuir v. New Brunswick*, 2008 SCC 9.

Courts review the decisions of other bodies based on one of two standards: correctness and reasonableness. When applying the correctness standard, a court substitutes its own view of the proper decision for that of the decision-maker, while the reasonableness standard accords a measure of deference to the other decision-maker. Questions of law regarding **division of powers** are assessed on a correctness standard, while questions of fact, discretion, or policy are assessed based on reasonableness. What standard to use in any given situation "is dependent on the application of a number of relevant factors, including: (1) the presence or absence of a privative clause; (2) the purpose of the tribunal as determined by interpretation of enabling legislation; (3) the nature of the question at issue; and (4) the expertise of the tribunal." *Id.* **2.** A term referring to the judicial determination of the constitutional validity of legislation, usually with reference to Canada's constitutional **division of powers** or the **Canadian Charter of Rights and Freedoms**. The legal legitimacy of judicial review of legislation is confirmed by s. 52(1) of the *Constitution Act, 1982*, which declares that the "Constitution of Canada is the supreme law of Canada, and any law that is inconsistent with the provisions of the Constitution is, to the extent of the inconsistency, of no force or effect."

JUDICIAL SALE See **sheriff's sale**.

JUMP BAIL A colloquial expression meaning to leave the **jurisdiction** or to avoid **appearance** as a **defendant** in a **criminal** trial after **bail** has been posted, thus causing a forfeiture of bail; to **abscond** after the posting of bail.

JUMP PRINCIPLE "[I]nvolves the proposition that successive sentences to an offender should be increased gradually rather than by "jumps." *R. v. M. (A.)* (1996), 30 O.R. (3d) 313 at 314 (Ont.C.A.).

JURAT (*jŭr'-ät*) Lat.: has been sworn. The clause at the end of an **affidavit** or other legal document stating when, where and by whom it was sworn.

JURISDICTION 1. The geographical area that a legislative body is entitled to govern, or the subject matters about which that body is entitled to create rules. See **division of powers** (and, specifically, **Appendix III**); **intra vires**; **ultra vires**. **2.** To have this power, a court must have **territorial** jurisdiction (the action must have some connection to the geographical area over which the court has authority), subject matter jurisdiction (e.g., the **Federal Court** has jurisdiction to hear patent cases but not criminal cases), jurisdiction over the person (through, for example, proper notice alerting the person to the existence of the court proceedings), and temporal jurisdiction (an action must have been brought within any relevant **limitation period**). See **real and substantial connection**; **territorial principle**; **forum non conveniens**; **forum shopping**; **action in personam**; **action in rem**.

APELLATE JURISDICTION The power vested in a superior **tribunal** to correct legal errors an inferior tribunal and to revise their **judgments** accordingly.

CONCURRENT JURISDICTION Equal jurisdiction; that jurisdiction exercised by different courts at the same time, over the same subject matter and within the same territory, and wherein litigants may, in the first instance, resort to either court indifferently. The phrase is also used in constitutional law to refer to the situation where both provincial and federal governments have power to legislate in a given area.

JURIS IGNORANTIA EST CUM JUS NOSTRAM IGNORAMUS (*jŭ'-rĭs ĭg-nō-rän'-shē-à ĕst kūm jūs nōs'-träm ĭg-nō-rā'-mŭs*) Lat.: it is ignorance of the law when we are unfamiliar with our own rights.

JURISPRUDENCE 1. The science of law; the philosophy of law; the study of the structure of legal systems, i.e., of form, as distinguished from content. **2.** A term denoting the collective course of judicial decisions; **3.** incorrectly used as a synonym for "law." See R. Pound, 1 *Jurisprudence* 7–9 (1959).

JURIST 1. A legal scholar; one versed in law, particularly the **civil law** or the law of nations. **2.** A judge.

JUROR A person sworn as a member of a **jury**. **2.** A person selected for jury duty, but not yet chosen for a particular case.

JURY A group of people, composed of a cross-section of the community, summoned and sworn to decide on the facts at **issue** in a trial.

GRAND JURY As originally established in England in 1164, the grand jury was a body of local inhabitants required to report all suspected criminals in their district. Introduced into Canada (except Saskatchewan and Alberta) with English law, the grand jury is now abolished in England and Canada.

PETIT [PETTY] JURY An ordinary trial jury, as opposed to a grand jury. Its function is to determine issues of fact in civil and criminal cases and to reach a **verdict** in conjunction with those **findings**. Petit juries have been composed traditionally of twelve members, whose verdict was required to be unanimous. However, today the composition varies, and in some **jurisdictions** a jury hearing a civil matter may consist of six members.

s. 11(*f*) of the **Canadian Charter of Rights and Freedoms** guarantees an accused to a trial by jury for an offence with a punishment of imprisonment for five years or more, except in the case of an offence under military law. See *R. v. Krieger*, 2006 SCC 47.

See also *Criminal Code*, R.S.C. 1985, c. C–46, ss. 632–642 (challenge to jury); **hung jury**.

JURY NULLIFICATION A situation in which "a jury knowingly chooses not to apply the law and acquits a defendant regardless of the strength of the evidence against him. Jury nullification is an unusual concept within the criminal law, since it effectively acknowledges it may occur that the jury elects in the rarest of cases not to apply the law." *R. v. Latimer*, 2001 SCC 1. Although jury nullification can, as a matter of fact, occur, it is improper for a lawyer in a jury trial to point out this possibility to a jury. See *R. v. Morgentaler*, [1988] 1 S.C.R. 30.

JURY PANEL The group of potential jurors called to court, from whom the jurors for a trial will be selected. Sometimes also referred to as the array. See *Criminal Code*, R.S.C. 1985, c. C–46, ss. 629–631.

JUS ACCRESCENDI (*jŭs ăk-rĕs-ĕndī*) Lat.: the right of that which must accrue; right of **survivorship** by joint **tenancy**. In a joint tenancy situation, if one of the tenants dies, his or her interest automatically accrues to the surviving tenants, thereby increasing their interest. E.H. Burn, *Modern Law of Real Property* 243 (16th ed. 2000).

JUS COGENS (*yŭs kō'-gĕnz*) Lat.: compelling law. A fundamental rule of international law that overrides other rules, including **customary international law** and **treaties**; also referred to as a peremptory norm. See *Suresh v. Canada (Minister of Citizenship and Immigration)*, 2002 SCC 1.

JUS GENTIUM (*jŭs gĕn-tī-ŭm*) Lat.: the law of nations. Refers to the law which has been traditionally accepted and used by all nations.

JUST CAUSE Such reasons as would justify a particular course of action. In an employment context, it refers to those reasons which would entitle an employer to dismiss an employee. Whether just cause exists is a contextual inquiry, but it can include such things as incompetence, chronic absenteeism, or dishonesty. In the latter case, "just cause for dismissal exists where the dishonesty violates an essential condition of the employment contract, breaches the faith inherent to the work relationship, or is fundamentally or directly inconsistent with the employee's obligations to his or her employer." *McKinley v. BC Tel.*, 2001 SCC 38.

JUST COMPENSATION Full **indemnity** or remuneration for the loss or damage sustained by the owner of property taken or injured under the power of **eminent domain**. It comprises a settlement that leaves the owner no poorer and no richer than he or she was before the property was taken. The measure generally used is the fair **market value** of the property at the time of taking. Just compensation need not take account of anticipated or possible future profitability, or of sentimental or other nonobjective values, but is to be based on the property's value to a willing seller and a willing buyer.

JUS TERTII (*jūs tĕr'-shē-ī*) Lat.: the right of a third **party**; the legal right of a third. The term often appears in the context of **actions** involving claims of **title** to **real property**, wherein it is said that, because a possessor's title is good against all the world except those with a better title, one seeking to **oust** a possessor must do so on the strength of his or her own title and may not rely on a *jus tertii*, or the better title held by a third party. Third party rights are also considered as part of **contract** law. See **third-party beneficiary**.

JUSTICE OF THE PEACE A judicial officer appointed by a provincial **lieutenant-governor** or a federally appointed territorial Commissioner to carry out certain judicial or **quasi-judicial** functions depending upon the person's training and specific legal authorization. The authority of the Justice of the Peace is determined by federal, provincial, or territorial **legislation**. Depending upon the jurisdiction, the functions of Justices of the Peace may include issuing **summonses** and **warrants**, administering

oaths, receiving **pleas**, performing civil marriages as well as a wide variety of court-related duties. Some Justices of the Peace have the authority to preside over courts that deal with a wide range of matters such as bail hearings, traffic violations, child-protection cases, and matters pertaining to domestic violence, to name a few. Legal training may not be a prerequisite to become a Justice of the Peace, and in some jurisdictions, lawyers may be prohibited from performing some (e.g., presiding as a court) or all of the duties of a Justice of the Peace. See, e.g., *Justices of the Peace Act,* R.S.O. 1990, c. J. 4; *Justices of the Peace Act,* R.S.N.S. 1989, c. 244. See *Ell v. Alberta,* 2003 SCC 35.

JUSTICIABILITY "[A] set of judge-made rules, norms, and principles delineating the scope of judicial intervention in social, political, and economic life. In short, if a subject matter is held to be suitable for judicial determination, it is said to be justiciable; if a subject matter is held not to be suitable for judicial determination, it is said to be non-justiciable." *Bruker v. Marcovitz,* 2007 SCC 54, quoting Lorne Sossin, *Boundaries of Judicial Review: The Law of Justiciability in Canada.* Justiciability is a question of whether it is appropriate for a court to decide a dispute, not simply whether it has jurisdiction to do so. A matter that is one relating only to the doctrines of a particular religion might not be justiciable: "While the courts may not intervene in strictly doctrinal or spiritual matters, they will when civil or property rights are engaged." *Id.*

JUSTIFIABLE HOMICIDE See **homicide**.

JUSTIFICATION A category of **defence** to a criminal **charge** in which the accused is commended for his or her behaviour rather than merely forgiven for it; compare **excuse**. "A 'justification' challenges the wrongfulness of an action [that] technically constitutes

a crime. The police officer who shoots the hostage-taker, the innocent object of an assault who uses force to defend himself against his assailant, the Good Samaritan who commandeers a car and breaks the speed laws to rush an accident victim to the hospital, these are all actors whose actions we consider *rightful,* not wrongful. For such actions people are often praised, as motivated by some great or noble object." *Perka v. The Queen,* [1984] 2 S.C.R. 232. Compare **necessity**, **defence of**.

In actions for **defamation**, justification is a plea that the words complained of are "true in substance and in fact," which may provide a complete defence to an action in **libel** or **slander**. The defendant must prove that the facts were truly stated and that the **innuendo** is true. He or she must justify every injurious imputation. *Lougheed Estate v. Wilson,* 2012 BCSC 169.

JUVENILE COURT See **youth justice court**.

JUVENILE DELINQUENT The term used under the former *Juvenile Delinquents Act* to describe those between the ages of seven and sixteen who were dealt with under that act. The *Juvenile Delinquents Act* focused not on whether the young person had committed a particular offence under **criminal** law, but instead on whether the child was "misdirected and misguided." Criminal activity could lead to a finding that a child was a juvenile delinquent, but so could truancy or sexual immorality. The focus of the act was on **rehabilitation** rather than **punishment**, but the effect was that there was great unevenness and arbitrariness in the way different young persons were treated. The *Juvenile Delinquents Act* was eventually replaced with the *Young Offenders Act,* which aimed at holding young persons accountable according to their degree of responsibility for committing a criminal offence.

K.B. [Q.B.] See **Queen's [King's] Bench**.

K.C. [Q.C.] See **Queen's [King's] Counsel**.

KEEPER "[I]ncludes a person who (a) is an owner or occupier of a place, (b) assists or acts on behalf of an owner or occupier of a place, (c) appears to be, or to assist or act on behalf of an owner or occupier of a place, (d) has the care or management of a place, or (e) uses a place permanently or temporarily, with or without the consent of the owner or occupier." *Criminal Code,* R.S.C. 1985, c. C–46, s. 197(1). The term is used in the context of one who keeps a **common-bawdy house, common betting house** or **common gaming house**.

KETTLING The police tactic of using large numbers of officers to corral a crowd, closing off all exits or permitting only a single route of escape. The tactic was used by police in Toronto during G20 protests in 2010 and was the subject of much criticism, since it is generally only effective in dealing with peaceful protestors, can result in very long periods of detention, and captures everyone in an area whether they were part of the protest or not. Toronto police publicly announced following the G20 summit that they would not use the tactic again. Kettling was used by police in Montreal in 2012 in dealing with student protests over tuition fees. Kettling has been found by the European Court of Human Rights not to violate Article 5 of the Convention for the Protection of Human Rights and Fundamental Freedoms. See *Austin and Others v. The United Kingdom,* [2012] E.C.H.R. 459.

K.G.B. STATEMENT A **prior inconsistent statement** by a **witness** admitted for the truth of its contents (as an exception to the **hearsay** rule) rather than merely to **impeach** the witness. In *R. v. B. (K.G.),* [1993] 1 S.C.R. 740, the Supreme Court required that to be **admissible** for the truth of its contents, the statement had to have been made under **oath** or similar solemn declaration following an explicit warning to the witness as to the existence of severe **criminal** sanctions for the making of a false statement; it had to have been videotaped in its entirety; and the opposing party had to have a full opportunity to cross-examine the witness at trial respecting the statement. Subsequent cases have not insisted on strict compliance with all of these requirements.

KIDNAP To unlawfully take and carry away a person against his or her will. Kidnapping is **false imprisonment** with the extra element of movement of the person from one place to another. "[I]t is the element of movement that differentiated kidnapping from the lesser included offence of false imprisonment and made kidnapping an aggravated form of false imprisonment. The underlying concern was that by carrying the victim away, the kidnappers would be taking him or her beyond the protection of the country's laws." The abduction must be "against the victim's will, which can be accomplished either by force or by fraud." *R. v. Vu,* 2012 SCC 40. See *Criminal Code,* R.S.C. 1985, c. C–46, s. 279.

The original common-law offence was characterized by the requirement that the victim be taken out of the country, hence the reference in the *Criminal Code,* s. 279, to "transported out of Canada against the person's will." However, the ambit of the offence has been widened considerably. Kidnapping was only a **misdemeanour** at common law but is an **indictable offence** in Canada. Compare **abduction**.

KIENAPPLE PRINCIPLE The rule against multiple convictions derived from the decision of the Supreme Court of Canada in *R. v. Kienapple,* [1975] 1 S.C.R. 729. It holds that "an individual should not be subjected to more than one conviction arising out of the same 'cause or matter' or same 'delict' consisting of a single criminal act committed in circumstances where the offences alleged are comprised of the same facts and elements." *R. v. Barnes* (1991), 3 C.R. (4th) 1 at 16

(S.C.C.). The rule from *Kienapple* has now been entrenched in s. 11(*h*) of the *Charter*. Compare **issue estoppel**.

KIN [KINDRED] 1. person or persons related by blood **2.** family connection. See **consanguinity**.

KING CAN DO NO WRONG "It is a general and fundamental principle that the king cannot sanction any act forbidden by law. It is in this sense that the king is under and not above the laws, and is bound by them equally with his subjects. Therefore the laws relating to contracts as well as other laws are binding on the sovereign." *R. v. McLeod* (1882), 8 S.C.R. 1 at 32. See also *Arishenkoff v. British Columbia*, 2005 BCCA 481. See **rule of law**.

KING'S [QUEEN'S] BENCH See **Queen's [King's] Bench**.

KING'S [QUEEN'S] COUNSEL [K.C.] See **Queen's [King's] Counsel**.

KITING A term used to describe an illegal practice in which "a cheque is issued from a bank account whose balance is insufficient to cover it. To create confusion, money is recorded in more than one bank account at one moment in time. In most cases, the money is in transit or quite simply fictitious. The circulation of cheques between various accounts is jointly controlled… Thus, cheques and registered funds are circulated from one bank to another and from one account to another, in a manner that maintains fictitious bank balances in some accounts while depositing the very same amounts in other accounts." *Location Bristar Idealease Inc. (Trustee of)*, 2012 QCCS 211.

KLEPTOMANIA A medical term that describes a condition wherein the person inflicted has an uncontrollable desire to steal.

KNIGHT'S SERVICE Under the English system of tenures, military service provided by persons holding property directly from the Crown. Each of the tenants-in-chief was required to supply the King with a specific number of armed knights for forty days each year. The practice was abolished with the Tenures Abolition Act of 1660. See E.H. Burn, *Modern Law of Real Property* 16–18 (16th ed. 2000).

KNOCK AND ANNOUNCE RULE The rule requiring police officers not to enter a dwelling house by force in most situations. "Except in exigent circumstances, police officers must make an announcement before forcing entry into a dwelling house. In the ordinary case, they should give: '(i) notice of presence by knocking or ringing the door bell, (ii) notice of authority by identifying themselves as law enforcement officers, and (iii) notice of purpose by stating a lawful reason for entry.'" *R. v. Cornell*, 2010 SCC 31. Where exigent circumstances do exist, such as a reasonable belief that there are weapons in the premises and officer safety is at risk, or that easily disposed of evidence such as drugs will be found, police may use force to enter; this is referred to as a HARD ENTRY or DYNAMIC ENTRY. Police may not use a hard entry as part of a general policy, for example, to always enter forcibly when drugs are involved, but rather must justify the decision on the particular facts of any given situation. *Id.*

KNOWLEDGE In **criminal** law, one of the basic **fault elements** corresponding to the **external elements**, and which must generally be proven to find an accused guilty of an offence. An accused must be proven to have knowledge of any relevant circumstances, whether the provision creating the offence mentions the knowledge requirement or not. *Beaver v. The Queen*, [1957] S.C.R. 119. For example, to be proven guilty of assaulting a **peace officer**, it must be shown that the accused knew that the victim of the assault was a peace officer, or the offence will merely be **common assault**. To be guilty of **aiding and abetting** another person, the accused must be shown to have known of that other person's intention to commit the offence. *R. v. Briscoe*, 2010 SCC 13. Unless the requirement is changed by a particular provision, the Crown must prove actual **subjective** knowledge on the part of the accused. It is not sufficient to show that the accused ought to have known the fact. *R. v. Lucas*, [1998] 1 S.C.R.

439. Some *Criminal Code* provisions do modify the knowledge requirement; for example, a person can be guilty of **counselling** an offence if the accused "knew or ought to have known" that the offence was likely to be committed as a result. *Criminal Code*, R.S.C. 1985, c. C–46, s. 22(2). Similarly, an accused charged with **sexual assault** cannot argue lack of knowledge of the absence of consent if "the accused did not take reasonable steps, in the circumstances known to the accused at the time, to ascertain that the complainant was consenting." *Criminal Code*, s. 273.2(b). The Supreme Court has held that in the case of high stigma or high **punishment** offences, it will violate section 7 of the **Charter** if the *Criminal Code* specifies a lesser requirement than subjective fault, and therefore, that subjective fault is guaranteed for those offences. *R. v. Martineau*, [1990] 2 S.C.R. 633.

LABOUR DISPUTE Defined in the *Courts of Justice Act,* R.S.O. 1990, c. C–43, s. 102(1) as, "a dispute or difference concerning terms, tenure or conditions of employment or concerning the association or representation of persons in negotiating, fixing, maintaining, changing or seeking to arrange terms or conditions of employment, regardless of whether the disputants stand in the proximate relation of employer and employee."

LABOUR LAW That area of law dealing with employment in a unionized setting, including labour-management relations, union **certification**, **collective bargaining**, the union duty of fair representation, and so on. See **employment law**.

LABOUR STANDARDS Legislative requirements of employers and rights of employees relating to matters of the workplace. A few examples of labour standards imposed by **legislation** are hours of work, vacation time, statutory holidays, and minimum wages.

LABOUR UNION See **trade union**.

LACHES An equitable **defence** to an **action** based on the plaintiff's delay in bringing proceedings. "A good discussion of the rule and of laches in general is found in Meagher, Gummow and Lehane, *supra*, at 755–65, where the authors distill the doctrine in this manner, at 755:

> It is a defence [that] requires that a defendant can successfully resist an equitable (although not a legal) claim made against him if he can demonstrate that the plaintiff, by delaying the institution or prosecution of his case, has either (*a*) acquiesced in the defendant's conduct, or (*b*) caused the defendant to alter his position in reasonable reliance on the plaintiff's acceptance of the status quo, or other-

wise permitted a situation to arise [that] it would be unjust to disturb. . . .

Thus, there are two distinct branches to the laches doctrine, and either will suffice as a defence to a claim in equity. What is immediately obvious from all of the authorities is that mere delay is insufficient to trigger laches under either of its two branches. Rather, the doctrine considers whether the delay of the plaintiff constitutes acquiescence or results in circumstances that make the prosecution of the action unreasonable. Ultimately, laches must be resolved as a matter of justice as between the parties, as is the case with any equitable doctrine." *M.(K.) v. M.(H.)*, [1992] 3 S.C.R. 6.

LAND 1. Broadly, any ground, soil, earth, or terrain. **2.** More specifically, **real estate** or **real property**, including the soil and anything permanently affixed thereto. See *Reid's Heritage Homes Ltd. v. Canada*, [2002] T.C.J. No. 643. See **fixtures**.

LAND SALE A term used in the petroleum industry to refer to a lease of oil and gas rights on a parcel of land.

LANDED IMMIGRANT A term used in the predecessor to the *Immigration and Refugee Protection Act*, S.C. 2001, c. 27 that no longer has any technical meaning. See **permanent resident**.

LANDLORD One who **leases real property** to another. The person who is entitled to exact payment of the **rent**. See also statutory definitions; e.g., *Residential Tenancies Act, 2006,* S.O. 2006, c. 17, s. 2(1): "(a) the owner of a rental unit or any other person who permits occupancy of a rental unit, other than a tenant who occupies a rental unit in a residential complex and who permits another person to also occupy the unit or any part of the unit, (b) the heirs, assigns, personal representatives and successors in title of a person referred to in clause (a), and (c) a person, other than a tenant occupying a rental unit in a residential complex, who is entitled to possession of the residential complex and who attempts to enforce any of the rights of a landlord under a tenancy agreement or this Act, including the right to collect rent."

LANGUAGE RIGHTS See **fundamental freedoms**.

LAPSE The termination of a right, privilege, or option through neglect to exercise same within a specified time limit or by failure of a contingency.

When the person to whom property has been **devised** or **bequeathed** dies before the **testator**, the devise or **bequest** fails or lapses, and **property** falls into the residue, except that a lapsed share of residue does not fall into residue but devolves upon **intestacy**.

Proceedings lapse in event of the death of a **defendant** in criminal matters or where no step is taken in an **action** within appropriate time.

LARCENY The common-law crime of stealing, at one time distinguished as grand or petty larceny according to the value of that which was taken. The term **larceny** has been replaced by **theft** and does not appear in the *Criminal Code, R.S.C.* 1985, c. C–46.

LAST ANTECEDENT DOCTRINE In statutory **construction**, the doctrine under which relative or modifying phrases are to be applied only to words immediately preceding them, and are not to be construed as extending to more remote phrases, unless this is clearly required by the context of the statute or the reading of it as a whole.

LAST CHANCE [LAST CLEAR CHANCE] The doctrine that the person with the last clear chance to avoid the accident, damage, or injury to another is **liable**. A defendant may be liable in **negligence**, notwithstanding the plaintiffs contributory negligence, if he or she was aware of the plaintiff's negligence and did not exercise **due care** in avoiding it. See *Morris v. Hamilton Radial Electric Ry.* (1923), 54 O.L.R. 208 (A.D.); *Dowser v. C.N.R.,* [1929] 4 D.L.R. 233 (Alta.S.C.). The last clear chance doctrine became largely redundant when apportionment of liability became possible by statute (*Morin v. Blais*, [1977] 1 S.C.R. 570) and has been abolished in some jurisdictions. See, e.g., *Lawrence v. Prince Rupert* (*City*), 2005 BCCA 567.

LAST WILL AND TESTAMENT See **will**.

LATENT AMBIGUITY An ambiguity that is only apparent when one tries to apply the terms of a legal **document** to the facts. Extrinsic **evidence** is always admissible to show the intention of the parties in the case of a latent ambiguity, but might not be in the case of a **patent** ambiguity.

LATENT DEFECT A defect that is hidden from knowledge as well as from sight and one that would not be discovered even by the exercise of due diligence or of ordinary and reasonable care. *Temple v. Thomas*, 2007 ABQB 316. "A home inspection should reveal any patent defects and, if disclosed to the buyer, allow for a more thorough investigation into any latent defect in order to determine the nature of the defect. A home inspection is not intended to find latent defects." *Krawchuk v. Scherbak*, 2011 ONCA 352 quoting *Lyle v. Burdess*, 2008 YKSM 5. See also **warranty** [WARRANTY OF HABITABILITY].

LAW A "**statute** or long-settled principles." *Re Ashley,* [1934] O.R. 421 at 428 (C.A.). "[A] general term which includes not only statutes but also Orders and Regulations made under statutes." *Cooperative Committee on Japanese Canadians v. Attorney-General for Canada,* [1947] 1 D.L.R. 577 at 580 (P.C.). "[The] law should be regarded as the core matter which those persons and those institutions in any legal system utilize in order to effect an ongoing process in regulating the affairs and conduct of persons in society." G. Gall, *The Canadian Legal System* 19 (5th ed. 2004). "'Law' is a word and words have varying uses. Their meanings are to be discovered in the light of their uses ... they must not be plucked from their contexts ... Even the differences between speaking of 'law,' speaking of 'the law,' and speaking of 'a law' may be vital ... The following are paraphrases of some of the definitions of law which have been advanced from time to time over many thousands of years. (1) Law is the will of God expressed in His commands revealed to man through His chosen instruments. Obedience to God's will is the supreme command. (2) Law is in two great parts: Divine law, and human law.

They may conflict. Differing theories were developed to explain a person's duty if faced with a conflict between the dictates of the two. (3) Law is the product of humanity's capacity to reason, and it consists of all those principles and rules which, by the use of reason, can be seen to be necessary for, or which can be seen to promote, humanity's peaceful and happy life in a society of human beings. (4) Law is in two great parts: natural law and positive law. Natural law is the product of reason (as in (3) above) whereas positive law is made up of all the rules in force in actual legal systems. The two may sometimes conflict. Differing theories have been developed to explain a person's duty when faced with a conflict between the two. (5) Law is the command of the sovereign. The sovereign is that person, or group of persons, in any independent human society who, owing no obedience to any outside body or person, enjoys the habitual obedience of all persons in that society. (6) Law is the instrument humanity uses in its attempt to achieve justice in society. (7) Law is an instrument of social engineering. (8) Law is an instrument by which capitalist society ensures the suppression of the proletariat. With the establishment of communism law will wither away: (9) Law is what the courts declare to be the law." D. Derham, F. Maher & P. Waller, *An Introduction to Law* 177–78 (6th ed. 1991). See S. Waddams, *Introduction to the Study of Law* 1–15 (6th ed. 2004).

LAW AND ECONOMICS The application of the concepts and methodology of neo-classical economics to the study of law. Law and economics has both descriptive and normative branches. The descriptive branch seeks to "explain legal rules and outcomes as they are" through the lens of economic analysis. The normative branch, conversely, advocates that the legal system ought to maximize economic efficiency as one of its fundamental objectives. R. A. Posner, *Economic Analysis of Law* (8th ed. 2011).

LAWFUL EXCUSE A general term which includes "all of the defences which the common law considers sufficient reason to excuse a person from criminal liability. It can also include excuses specific to particular offences." *R. v. Holmes*, [1988] 1 S.C.R. 914.

LAW MERCHANT A body of commercial law governing merchants in England, with similar rules existing in other European states. These laws were first enforced by special English mercantile courts and later enforced in **common-law** courts of **law** and **equity**. The law merchant is particularly noted for its contributions to the law of negotiable instruments. The law merchant was the common law's recognition of usages and procedures that had developed over a long period among merchants in England and other European countries. As part of the common law of England, it was incorporated into Canadian law but has been largely supplanted by common-law evolution and statutory enactment.

LAW OF ADMIRALTY See **maritime law**.

LAW OF THE LAND A phrase first used in the Magna Carta referring to the then established law of the Kingdom as distinguished from Roman or **civil law**. **2**. Today the fundamental principles of justice commensurate with **due process of law**, i.e., those rights that the **legislature** or **Parliament** of Canada cannot abolish or significantly limit because they are fundamental to our system of liberty and justice. **3**. The law as developed by the courts or in **statutes** in pursuance of those basic principles or rights. The **Canadian Charter of Rights and Freedoms** guarantees the rights and freedoms set out in it "subject only to such reasonable limits prescribed by law as can be demonstrably justified in a free and democratic society."

LAW REFORM COMMISSION(S) Independent agencies created under federal law, and some provincial statutes, to review, make recommendations, and advise governments, concerning amendments and other changes to the laws of the particular jurisdiction. Examples are the Manitoba Law Reform Commission and the Law Reform Commission of Nova Scotia. The Law Reform Commission of Canada was created by the federal government in 1971 but was abolished in 1993. The Law Commission of Canada was then created in 1997, but it also was shut down in 2006.

LAW SOCIETY The body in each of the Canadian provinces and territories responsible for governing and regulating the legal profession in the interests of the public and the members of the profession. Amongst the societies' main purposes are supervising the admission of members to the profession, disciplining members, and generally advancing and maintaining the standard of legal practice in the Province or Territory. The following are the governing bodies of the legal profession in Canada: Barreau de Québec, Law Society of Alberta; Law Society of British Columbia; Law Society of Manitoba; Law Society of Newfoundland and Labrador; Law Society of Nunavut; Law Society of Saskatchewan; Law Society of the Northwest Territories; Law Society of Upper Canada; Law Society of Yukon; Nova Scotia Barristers' Society; Law Society of New Brunswick/Barreau de Nouveau– Brunswick; Law Society of Prince Edward Island. See, e.g., *Law Society Act*, R.S.O. 1990, c. L.8. See **bar**; **bar admission**.

LAWSUIT See **suit**.

LAWYER'S FEES 1. In general, the charge made by the lawyer for his or her services in representing a client; **2.** also, the charge made by other professionals for services they have rendered in the course of preparing and trying a case. See C.B.A. *Code of Professional Conduct* (2006) c. XI.

CONTINGENCY FEE A charge made by a lawyer under an agreement with the client that the lawyer will take a percentage of the **damages** awarded, instead of an hourly rate. Contingency fee agreements are subject to provincial regulations. See, e.g., *Solicitors Act*, R.S.O. 1990, c. S.15, s. 28.1. See *Lee (Guardian ad litem of) v. Richmond Hospital Society (c.o.b. Richmond Hospital)*, 2005 BCCA 107. In Canada, a **barrister** or **solicitor** may sue his or her client for unpaid fees and may exercise a possessory lien on the client's property in his or her posses-

sion to encourage payment (SOLICITOR'S LIEN). See **disbursements**.

LAY-OFF A term used to describe the temporary or permanent termination of employment due to a shortage or slow down in work and/or a change in the employer's staffing requirements.

LEADING QUESTION In the law of evidence, a question that directly or indirectly suggests the answer the **witness** is to give (especially "yes" or "no" answers). It is permitted in cross-examination but not normally in direct examination. *Maves v. Grand Trunk Pacific Ry. Co.* (1913), 5 W.W.R. 212 (Alta.-C.A.).

Leading questions may be asked of a witness who is **hostile** to the party examining. Other exceptions are recognized, including matters not in dispute. The trial judge has an overriding discretion to permit leading questions in the interests of justice. See D.M. Paciocco & L. Stuesser, *The Law of Evidence* 419–20 (6th ed. 2011).

LEARNED HAND FORMULA An American test for reasonableness or reasonable care.

LEARNED INTERMEDIARY RULE In **tort** law, a rule where the manufacturer's continuing duty to warn the ultimate consumer of risks associated with a product is met if they have warned a learned intermediary (e.g., a doctor) and his or her knowledge approximates that of the company. *Hollis v. Dow Corning Corp.* (1995), 129 D.L.R. 609 (S.C.C.).

LEASE An agreement whereby one party, the **landlord**, relinquishes his or her right to immediate possession of **property** while retaining ultimate legal ownership (**title**). "A conveyance by which a person having an estate in **hereditaments** transfers a portion of his interest therein to another, usually in consideration for a certain periodical **rent** or other recompense, and it imports that exclusive possession is given to the premises **conveyed**." *Garland Mfg. Co. v. Northumberland Paper etc. Co.* (1899), 31 O.R. 40 at 52 (Div.Ct.). The **interest** in the property remaining in the landlord is called the **reversion**. B. Ziff,

Principles of Property Law 288–89 (5th ed. 2010).

The difference between a lease and a **licence** is that the latter does not create any right or interest in the **land** itself and does not confer a right to exclusive possession of the party. See **PPSA**.

LEASEHOLD The **estate** in **real property** of a **lessee**, created by a **lease**. A **lessee** is granted exclusive right to possession for a certain term, while the **lessor** retains a reversionary interest. See, e.g., *Canadian Glassine Co. Ltd. v. Min. of Nat. Revenue,* [1974] C.T.C. 63 (Fed. Ct.). A leasehold interest is **personalty** and not **real property**.

It generally refers to an estate whose duration is fixed but may also be used to describe a **tenancy** at will, periodic tenancy, etc.

LEASEHOLDER One who possesses property.

LEGACY A disposition in a **testamentary instrument** of **personal property**. See *Re Tyhurst,* [1932] S.C.R. 713. Generally viewed as synonymous with **bequest**, it is properly distinguished from **devise**, which connotes a disposition of **real property**.

SPECIFY LEGACY A bequest of a thing or interest which can be identified separately from the rest of the **testator's** personal estate. A specific legacy is subject to **ademption** if the property named is no longer part of the testator's estate at the time of death.

GENERAL LEGACY A bequest which bears no direct relationship to the testator's property and which must be given to the **beneficiary** by the executor. "Accordingly, a gift of 'my grandfather's gold watch' or of 'the shares of XYZ, Ltd., now standing in my name' is a specific one, but a gift of 'a gold watch' or of '$10,000 worth of shares of XYZ, Ltd.' is likely to be a general one which must be paid out of the testator's personal estate if he or she does not own a gold watch or such shares at the date of death." *Wood Estate v. Arlotti, Wood,* 2004 BCCA 556.

DEMONSTRATIVE LEGACY "A general legacy, usually pecuniary, directed to be satisfied primarily (but not solely) out of a specified fund or a specified part of the testator's property." *Id.* Like a general legacy, a demonstrative legacy is not subject to ademption.

LEGAL AID The provision of publicly funded legal services to persons demonstrating financial need. In Canada, legal aid is administered provincially so the qualifications and range of services provided vary from province to province. There are three basic models for providing legal aid services in Canada: (1) The staff-lawyer model, which delivers legal aid to qualified applicants through a network of offices with salaried lawyers. This model is used in Newfoundland and Labrador and Saskatchewan. (2) The judicare model, where qualified recipients are given legal aid certificates entitling the bearer to an allotted amount of legal service. The person then takes the certificate to a lawyer in private practice, who in turn bills the legal aid fund for his or her services. Alberta and Ontario use the judicare model. The last model is a mixed one combining the staff-lawyer and judicare models. Lawyers on staff will take on clients, but there is also the ability to provide clients with certificates so they can obtain a lawyer in private practice. The majority of provinces and territories in Canada use this model (Nova Scotia, New Brunswick, Prince Edward Island, Quebec, Manitoba, British Columbia, Yukon, Northwest Territories, Nunavut). See **Rowbotham application**; **Fisher application**.

LEGAL BURDEN See **burden of proof**.

LEGAL CONSIDERATION See **consideration**.

LEGAL DUTY An obligation imposed by **law** to perform or refrain from an act, as the duty of **due care** in **negligence** law. Depending on the context, may arise by virtue of either **statute** or **common law**. *R. v. Coyne* (1958), 124 C.C.C. 176 (N.B.S.C.A.D.). **Breach** of a legal duty owed another is an element of negligence and is the essence of most actions in **tort**. Legal duties not otherwise imposed may be created by a **contract** or by one's entering into some other relationship (**landlord-tenant**, host-**invitee**, etc.). See **duty**.

LEGALESE A highly technical, wordy, and archaic form of legal writing. Legalese is characterized by long sentences, formalisms, jargon, and redundant phrasing. As such, it is discouraged by modern legal writing texts, which emphasize clarity and concision in drafting. See, e.g., T. Tjaden, *Legal Research and Writing* 341–44 (3rd ed. 2010).

LEGAL ETHICS See **professional responsibility**.

LEGAL RIGHTS See **Canadian Charter of Rights and Freedoms**.

LEGATEE One who takes a **legacy**; one beneficially entitled under the **will** to either **realty** or **personalty**. *Re Hord,* [1916], 10 O.W.N. 278 (H.C.).

LEGISLATE 1. To make or enact laws, rules, etc.; **2.** to exercise the power and function of making laws binding on those for whom they are made.

LEGISLATION Acts or **statutes** passed by a governing authority. Statutes and **instruments** of **Parliament** are referred to as federal legislation. Likewise, enactments of the provincial **legislatures** are referred to as provincial legislation. Rules made by an inferior body by virtue of the power vested in it by **Parliament** or a provincial legislature are referred to as **subordinate [delegated] legislation**.

LEGISLATIVE FACTS Non-adjudicative facts relating to legislation or judicial policy. See *R. v. Spence*, 2005 SCC 71.

LEGISLATIVE PRIVILEGE See **parliamentary privilege**.

LEGISLATURE A body of persons (**Parliament** or a provincial legislature) vested with constitutional power to pass **legislation** to govern the nation or province.

LESSEE One who holds an **estate** by virtue of a **lease** whether the original grantee of the lease or an assignee; the **tenant** of a **landlord**.

LESSER INCLUDED OFFENCE See **included offence**.

LESSOR One who grants a **lease** of **property** to another; **landlord**.

LET To **lease**, **demise** or **rent**.

LETTERS OF CREDIT "[A] specialized form of commercial credit, designed by their very nature to be free and clear of the inequities between the parties to the underlying transaction which they are issued to secure. They constitute an independent contract between the issuer ... and the beneficiary of the underlying transaction." *885676 Ontario Ltd. (Trustee of) v. Frasernet Holdings Ltd.* (1993), 99 D.L.R. (4th) 1 at 7 (Ont. Ct.Gen.Div.)

LETTERS ROGATORY A request to a foreign court to take **evidence** from a **witness** residing in that jurisdiction and remit it to the court making the request.

LEVY 1. To raise or collect. **2.** To assess, as to levy a tax. **3.** To seize land or **property** or rights through lawful **process** (see, e.g., *Execution Act,* R.S.O. 1990, c. E. 24, ss. 18, 19) or by force. See **writ** [WRIT OF EXECUTION] **4.** To wage or carry on (war). To levy war against Canada is to commit the criminal offence of high **treason**. *Criminal Code,* R.S.C. 1985, c. C–46, s. 46. **5.** An amount levied.

LEX FERENDA (*lĕks fĕ-rĕn-dă*) Lat.: the law that will be. International law rules that are emerging and might or might not crystallize into customary international law. Sometimes referred to as "soft" law, and generally used to mean "the law that should be."

LEX LOCI CONTRACTUS (*lĕks lō'-kē kŏn-trăk'-tŭs*) Lat.: the law of the place where the **contract** is made; the law by which the rights and obligations of the parties to the contract are to be governed (the proper law of the contract). See **conflict of laws**.

LEX LOCI DELICTI (*lĕks lō'-kē dĕ lĭk'-tī*) Lat.: the law of the place where the wrong or **offence** is committed. See **conflict of laws**; **choice of law**.

LEX LOCI DOMICILII (*lĕks lō'-kē dō-mĭ-sĭ'-lē-ī*) Lat.: the law of the place of a person's **domicile**.

LIABILITY 1. An obligation to do or refrain from doing something; **2.** a duty that eventually must be performed; **3.** an obligation to pay money; **4.** money owed, as opposed to an **asset**; **5.** responsibility for one's conduct, such as contractual liability, tort liability, or criminal liability. See **strict liability**; **vicarious [responsibility] liability**.

LIABLE Responsible for; obligated in law. See **liability**.

LIBEL Defamation in a printed or permanent form (e.g., printing, writing, signs or pictures) that tends to expose a person to public scorn, hatred, contempt or ridicule. Spoken defamation is called **slander**. The **tort** of libel is frequently deemed by statute to include "defamatory words in a newspaper or a broadcast"; see, e.g., *Libel and Slander Act,* R.S.O. 1990, c. L.12. s. 2. The truth of the published statement constitutes a total **defence** (justification) to an **action** for libel.

The *Criminal Code,* R.S.C. 1985, c. C–46, identifies blasphemous libel (s. 296), defamatory libel (ss. 300, 301) and seditious libel (s. 61) as offences.

Certain types of publications—e.g., fair and accurate reports of judicial or parliamentary proceedings—are accorded ABSOLUTE PRIVILEGE, i.e., freedom from liability for libels they may contain; see, e.g., *Libel and Slander Act,* R.S.O. 1990, c. L. 12, s. 3, and *Criminal Code,* s. 307. In addition, qualified **privilege** arises in relation to statements made in the discharge of a social, legal, or moral duty, or between persons having a "common interest" (e.g., references written by former employers). See *Hebert v. Jackson,* [1950] O.R. 799 (C.A.) and *Criminal Code,* s. 309. See also **fair comment**.

LIBEL TOURISM Choosing the most favourable **jurisdiction** in which to launch a defamation action, given that defamatory statements made on the **Internet** are likely to have been seen in many jurisdictions. See **forum shopping**.

LIBERTY One of the interests protected by s. 7 of the **Canadian Charter of Rights and Freedoms**. Liberty is infringed when a person is imprisoned, but also when his or her free movement in society is restricted, such as by a prohibition on attending certain public places. See *R. v. Heywood,* [1994] 3 S.C.R. 761.

LICENCE "Consent, permission, or clearance (all interchangeable terms) given by a right holder (the licensor) to someone (the licensee) to exercise a right held by the licensor. The licence can be oral or written. An exclusive licence gives the licensee alone the right of exercise, to the exclusion of even the licensor (this licence usually has to be written). A sole licence is the same, except the licensor can compete with the licensee. A non-exclusive licence allows the licensor to appoint other licensees in the same area to exercise the right." D. Vaver, *Intellectual Property Law,* 698 (2nd ed., 2011). The grant by a **licenser** to a **licensee** may give permission to carry on a trade, to enter premises or to do some other particular thing. Licences may be granted by private persons or by government authority, such as in the case of a driver's licence, liquor licence, etc. See **franchise**; **monopoly**.

In the law of **property**, a license is a personal **privilege** or permission with respect to some use of the land and is revocable at the will of the landowner. The privilege attaches only to the party holding it and not to the land itself since, unlike an **easement**, a licence does not represent an **estate** or **interest** in land. Compare **lease**.

LICENSEE One to whom a **licence** has been granted; in **property**, "a person whom the proprietor has not in any way invited—he has no **interest** in his being there—but he has either expressly permitted him to use his lands or knowledge of his presence more or less habitual having been brought home to him, he has then either accorded permission or shown no practical anxiety to stop his further frequenting the lands." *Robert Addie and Sons v. Dumbreck,* [1929] A.C. 358 at 371 (H.L.). In **tort** law, one's status as a licensee may affect the duty of care owed to him or her. See **due care**; **occupiers' liability**. Compare **invitee**.

LICENSER [LICENSOR] One who grants a **licence**.

LIEN The right to hold the **property** of another as **security** for the performance of an obligation. A **common-law** lien lasts only as long as possession is retained but is assertable for that time against all other interests. An equitable lien exists independently of possession but may not be asserted against the purchaser of a legal estate for value without notice of the lien.

LIEN NOTE A sales-financing document for goods that is primarily used in western Canada and is comprised of two parts, a **promissory note** and a document reserving title in the goods to the seller to the amount of the purchase price or balance outstanding. See *Lucka v. Cirka* (1955), 63 Man.R. 308 (Q.B.). The counterpart in eastern Canada is the **conditional sales** agreement, under which the buyer may take possession, but the property in the goods does not vest in him or her until the price is paid. See **PPSA**.

MARITIME LIEN A privileged claim (i.e., taking priority over **mortgages**, etc.) upon maritime property for service done to it or injury caused by it accruing from the moment the claim attaches, travelling with the property unconditionally, and enforced by means of an **action in rem**. E. Gold, A. Chircop, and H. Kindred, *Maritime Law* 265–75 (2003).

MECHANICS' LIEN A statutory claim to secure priority of payment for services rendered or performed or materials furnished by a mechanic or workman in the construction or repair of buildings and other structures on the land. Sometimes called GARAGEMAN'S LIEN. The **lien** attaches upon the **estate** or **interest** of the owner in the land, building, or structure. The law of mechanics' liens is entirely statutory. "Speaking generally, the object of the Mechanics' Lien Act is to prevent owners of land getting the benefit of buildings erected and work done at their instance on their land without paying for them." *Hickey v. Stalker*, [1924] 1 D.L.R. 440 at 441 (Ont.S.C.A.D.). See *Earl F. Wakefield Co. v. Oil City Petroleums*

(Leduc) Ltd., [1958] S.C.R. 361 at 364; *Re Shields (Trustee of Estate of Harris Construction Co. Ltd.) & City of Winnipeg* (1964), 47 D.L.R. (2d) 346 at 357 (Man.Q.B.). Also called a construction lien or a builder's lien. For an example of mechanics' lien legislation, see also *Mechanics' Lien Act*, R.S.N.S. 1989, c. 277; *Repair and Storage Liens Act*, R.S.O. 1990, c. R. 25; *The Builders' Liens Act*, C.C.S.M., c. B91. *Construction Lien Act*, R.S.O. 1990, c. C.30; *Builders' Lien Act*.

SOLICITOR'S LIEN See **lawyer's fees**.

VENDOR'S LIEN The right of an unpaid seller to retain property until the purchase price is paid. See, e.g., *Sale of Goods Act*, R.S.O. 1990, c. S. 1, s. 38.

LIEN JURISDICTIONS Jurisdictions in which **title** to **mortgaged premises** remains with the mortgagor pending payment of the mortgage price. See **mortgage**.

LIEUTENANT GOVERNOR Traditionally, the Queen's representative in the various provinces (the **Governor General of Canada** is the federal counterpart). The authority of the **executive** is vested at the provincial level in the Lieutenant-Governor. However, by convention the Lieutenant Governor only acts upon the advice of the provincial **Cabinet**. One of the Lieutenant Governor's most important functions is the granting of ROYAL ASSENT to **bills** approved by the **legislature**. Legally, this formal approval by the Lieutenant Governor is a prerequisite to a bill becoming a **statute**. See further G. Gall, *The Canadian Legal System* 48–49, 62 (5th ed. 2004). The office of the Commissioner plays the equivalent purpose in each of the three Territories.

LIEUTENANT GOVERNOR IN COUNCIL The provincial **Cabinet**. The Cabinet of the federal government is referred to as the **Governor in Council**.

LIFE ESTATE An estate whose duration is limited to or measured by the life of the person holding it or that of some other person [**per autre vie**]. Life tenants have the right to possession and to enjoy the profit of the estate, but lack the power to make significant alterations to property subject to the tort of

waste and to completely alienate full title, as the grantor retains the fee simple in **reversion**. No special terminology is needed to create a life estate, and it is construed from the words and intentions of the **testator**. See *Hurst v. Soucoup*, 2010 NBQB 216.

LIFE [LIVES] IN BEING In order for a future **interest** to be valid it must vest within the **perpetuity period** which consists of the duration of all the lives in being plus twenty-one years. The lives in being are all those persons who are alive at the time the instrument granting the interest takes effect. The number of lives in being can be narrowed to specific persons, such as a member of the Royal Family, etc., who generally are referred to as the "identified lives in being." See **rule against perpetuities**.

LIFTING THE CORPORATE VEIL See **piercing the corporate veil**.

LIMITATION PERIOD See **statute of limitations**.

LIMITED PARTNERSHIP See **partnership**.

LINEAL Refers to **descent** by a direct line of **succession** in ancestry.

LINE-UP See **identification parade**.

LIQUIDATE To settle; to determine the amount due and to whom due, and, having done so, to **extinguish** the indebtedness.

LIQUIDATE A BUSINESS To dissolve or **wind up** a limited company by having a **liquidator** convert all **assets** of a business into money, collect and pay all debts owed and owing, and distribute the balance among **shareholders** or owners. See *Canada Business Corporations Act*, R.S.C. 1985, c. C–44, ss. 207–228.

LIQUIDATE A CLAIM To determine by agreement or **litigation** the amount of a **claim**.

LIQUIDATED DAMAGES See **damages**.

LIQUIDATION DIVIDEND See **dividend**.

LIQUIDATOR The person charged by a court to **liquidate** a business upon its dissolution. See *Canada Business*

Corporations Act, R.S.C. 1985, c. C–44, ss. 217–228, as amended by S.C. 1992, c. 1, s. 57. See **receiver**.

LIS PENDENS (*lēs pĕn'-dĕns*) Lat.: a pending lawsuit. Legally, the term is equivalent to the maxim that, pending the suit, nothing should be changed. The doctrine of *lis pendens* is that one who has acquired an **interest** in **property** from a party to litigation respecting such property takes that interest subject to the **decree** or **judgment** in such litigation and is bound by it. See *Infini–T Holdings Ltd. v. Bell Aliant Regional Communications Inc.*, 2010 NLTD(G) 205. See also **pendente lite**.

CERTIFICATE OF LIS PENDENS A document registrable in land titles registries to warn persons (such as prospective purchasers) of the pending lawsuit. The certificate is, however, only an allegation of the fact that an action is pending and not a confirmation of it. *Granby Consolidated Mining, Smelting and Power Ltd. v. Esquimalt and Nanaimo Ry. Co.* (1919), 3 W.W.R. 331 (P.C.).

LITE PENDENTE See **pendente lite**.

LITERAL RULE A general rule of statutory interpretation that holds that the words of a statute are to be strictly and narrowly interpreted according to their literal or ordinary meaning. See **statutory interpretation**.

LITIGANTS The **parties** involved in a lawsuit; those involved in **litigation**; refers to all parties whether **plaintiffs** or **defendants**. The term is usually limited to those actively involved in the suit.

LITIGATION A controversy in a court; a judicial contest through which legal rights are sought to be determined and enforced. The term refers to **civil actions**. See also **action**; **case**; **suit**.

LITIGIOUS Having a propensity to engage in **litigation**. Thus, a citizen who repeatedly sues his or her neighbour over various issues would be called litigious. Compare **malicious prosecution**. See also **vexatious litigation**.

LIVERY OF SEISIN A ceremony in feudal times signifying an **alienation** of land by **feoffment**. Either **title** or the right of immediate **possession** could be transferred by livery of seisin. The ceremony was necessary at **common law** to grant any **freehold** estate. The grantee was said to be **seised** of the legal estate in the land. A.M. Sinclair & M.E. McCallum, *An Introduction to Real Property Law* 20–23 (6th ed. 2012).

LIVING TREE DOCTRINE A fundamental principle of Canadian constitutional interpretation stating that the courts should interpret its provisions in a broad and progressive manner so that the Constitution will be able to adapt to changing circumstances and social norms. The metaphor of the Constitution as a "living tree" was first formulated in *Edwards v. Canada (Attorney-General)*, [1930] A.C. 124 (P.C.) (the **"Persons Case"**), in which Lord Sankey L.C. warned against "[cutting] down the provisions of the [Constitution] by a narrow and technical construction" and suggested instead affording it a "large and liberal interpretation, so that the Dominion, to a great extent, but within certain fixed limits, may be mistress in her own house." *Id.* The doctrine does not "liberate the courts from the normal constraints of interpretation," and the original understanding of the text remains pertinent. The living tree doctrine simply provides that the text's original meaning is not necessarily binding. P.W. Hogg, *Constitutional Law of Canada* (5th ed. 2007). See *Canada (Attorney-General) v. Hislop*, 2007 SCC 10; *Reference Re Same-Sex Marriage*, 2004 SCC 79; *Re B.C. Motor Vehicle Act*, [1985] 2 S.C.R. 486.

LIVING WILL An informal term for a document setting out a person's wishes with regard to medical treatment should he or she become incapacitated and unable to express those wishes. Most commonly, it is meant to be a method by which a person can indicate that he or she does not wish to have life-prolonging treatment in certain circumstances. In the absence of legislation permitting them, such documents have no clear legal force but might well affect the behaviour of health care providers. Some provinces have created legislation dealing with living wills, which

are more commonly referred to as an ADVANCE DIRECTIVE, ADVANCE HEALTH CARE DIRECTIVE, or some similar term. In some provinces legislation also permits the advance appointment of a third person to make such health care decisions on a person's behalf, or to make decisions about that person's personal care. See, e.g., *Health Care Directives and Substitute Health Care Decision Makers Act*, S.S. 1997, c. H–0.001, or *Advance Health Care Directives Act*, S.N.L. 1995, c. A–4.1. In addition, some provinces have legislation allowing for the advance appointment of a third person to make decisions about a person's personal care. See *Personal Directives Act*, S.N.S. 2008, c. 8; L.E. Rozovsky, *The Canadian Law of Consent to Treatment* 131–34 (3rd ed. 2003).

LL.B. Bachelor of Laws degree; the LL.B. was traditionally awarded by Canadian law faculties as an undergraduate law degree. In recent years, most Canadian law schools have replaced it with the **JD** degree.

LL.D. Doctor of Laws degree conferred *honoris causa tantum*. An honourary degree given by Canadian universities for significant contribution to society.

LL.M. Master of Laws Degree.

LOBBYIST One engaged in the business of persuading persons involved in the legislative process to enact, defeat, or amend legislation to suit the interests of the lobbyist or the lobbyist's clients. Lobbyists are required to register as such. See, e.g., *Lobbyists Act*, S.A. 2007, c. L–20.5, or *Lobbyist Registration Act*, S.N.L. 2004, c. L–24.1.

LOCKOUT The closing of a place of employment, the suspension of work, or the refusal by an employer to continue to employ a number of his employees, for the purpose of exerting pressure upon the employees of a **trade union** in connection with their employment or **collective bargaining agreement**, in order to compel employees to agree to conditions of employment or to refrain from exercising existing rights and privileges. See provincial trade union statutes, e.g., *Labour Relations Act,* 1995, S.O. 1995, c. 1, Sched. A.

LOCO PARENTIS See **in loco parentis**.

LOCUS (*lō'-kŭs*) Lat.: the place.

LOCUS IN QUO (*lō'-kŭs ĭn kwō*) Lat.: the place where or in which; refers to the locale where an **offence** was committed or a **cause of action** arose.

LOCUS STANDI (*lō'-kŭs stăn'-dī*) Lat.: a place of standing. The right of a **party** to an action to appear and be heard on the question before any tribunal.

LOITER To hang idly about a place. A person who has a purpose for being present, such as waiting for a spouse, is not loitering. Loitering does not require any sort of malevolent intent. *R. v. Heywood*, [1994] 3 S.C.R. 761.

    Criminal prohibitions against loitering include doing so in a public place and obstructing others in a public place (*Criminal Code,* R.S.C. 1985, c. C–46, s. 175(1)(*c*)); loitering upon the property of another person, near a **dwelling house** at night (*id.* s. 177).

LONG ARM STATUTE A term used to describe a statute or rule that allows for the service of a writ on a defendant outside the jurisdiction of the court issuing the grant.

LONG-TERM OFFENDER Under s. 753.1 of the *Criminal Code*, R.S.C. 1985, c. C–46, a person who has been found guilty of a serious personal injury offence (which includes sexual offences or offences involving violence and carrying a potential sentence of ten years or more) and is to be sentenced to imprisonment for two years or more, for whom there is a substantial risk that he or she will reoffend, but for whom there is a reasonable possibility of eventual control of the risk in the community. See **dangerous offender**; **habitual criminal**.

LOSS OF CHANCE THEORY A claim in medical **negligence** cases based on the premise that the **defendant's** negligent actions deprived the **plaintiff** of the chance to avoid his or her injury. This approach was rejected by the Supreme Court of Canada in *Laferiere v. Lawson*

(1991), 78 D.L.R. (4th) 609 (SCC). In that case, the defendant brought an action against the plaintiff doctor for his failure to advise her that she had cancer. The defendant claimed that this deprived her of the chance to obtain treatment and a possible cure. The Court rejected the plaintiff's claim based on a lack of causation but awarded her damages on other grounds.

LOST MODERN GRANT, DOCTRINE OF A method of acquiring an **easement** through **prescription**. The doctrine of lost modern grant is based on the legal "fiction"; where a person who has enjoyed continuous use of another's land for a period of twenty years or more, the courts will operate on the basis that a grant of easement was made in the past but has since been lost.

LOST PROPERTY Property with which the owner has involuntarily parted through neglect, carelessness, or inadvertence. **Mislaid property**, on the other hand, is property the owner intentionally placed where he or she could again resort to it, but then forgot where he or she placed it. Compare **abandonment**.

LSAT Law School Admission Test. A standardized written examination administered to candidates for law school in Canada and the United States. The LSAT is designed to test reasoning abilities necessary for the study of law.

LURING A CHILD An **inchoate** offence involving the use of a computer or other telecommunications device to communicate with a person under the age of eighteen for the purpose of facilitating the commission of one or more designated sexual offences against that person. *Criminal Code*, R.S.C. 1985, c. C–46, s. 172.1. To "facilitate" the commission of an offence means to render it "easier" or "more probable." Someone may commit the offence, then, even when he or she did not yet form an intention to meet the young person in order to carry out one of the secondary offences set out in the section. *R. v. Legare*, 2009 SCC 56.

MAGISTRATE A judicial officer appointed under provincial legislation who exercises summary **jurisdiction** in matters of a **criminal** nature. The term *magistrate* commonly refers to a **justice of the peace** or a stipendiary magistrate. STIPENDIARY MAGISTRATES are appointed to act in certain populous places such as a town or county and are entitled to receive a salary for their services.

MAIL BOX RULE [POSTAL ACCEPTANCE RULE] In the law of contract, a rule that where an **offer** is sent through the mail or is in some other way communicated to the offeree and where the method of communication of **acceptance** is not prescribed by the offeror, when the offeree responds by mailing the acceptance, the **contract** is said to be effective at the time the acceptance is mailed even though it may not have been received by the offeror. Thus the offer cannot be revoked by a purported **revocation** sent by the offeror through the mail before the offeror receives the letter of acceptance mailed prior to the notice of revocation. See G.H.L. Fridman, *The Law of Contract in Canada* 69–71 (6th ed. 2011).

MAINTENANCE 1. The act of keeping in good repair, in efficient working order, in an efficient state. **2.** An agreement to finance or in any way assist in the **litigation** of another person in **consideration** of having a share in the fruits of litigation giving rise to an **action** in **tort**. Also called CHAMPERTY. *Kroeker v. Harkema Express Lines Ltd.* (1974), 2 O.R. (2d) 210 (H.C.); *Newswander v. Giegerich* (1907), 39 S.C.R. 354 at 358–60; *Craig v. Thompson* (1907), 42 N.S.R. 150 at 155–57 (S.C.). **3.** The supply of the necessaries of life for a person, such as food, shelter, and clothing.

Under various provincial **statutes**, maintenance may be sought from a parent for children in the custody of an agency (see, e.g., *Children and Family*

Services Act, S.N.S. 1990, c. 5, s. 52 as amended by S.N.S. 1994–95, c. 7, s. 13, or for the support of one spouse by the other, as well as maintenance for dependent children and parents (see, e.g., *Maintenance and Custody Act,* R.S.N.S. 1989, c. 160; *Family Relations Act,* R.S.B.C. 1996, c. 128, ss. 88, 89, 90). Such orders are also often referred to as support orders. See, e.g., *Divorce Act*, R.S.C. 1985, c. 3 (2nd Supp).

MAJORITY, AGE OF See **age of majority**.

MAJORITY OPINION [MAJORITY RULE] The **opinion** or rule of the greatest number; rule by the majority of those who actually vote rather than those entitled to vote. Majority rule is a basic premise of corporate law. The courts will not interfere with the internal management of a company where the majority of **shareholders** have assented to its actions. Thus, in general, a **resolution** concerning a matter within the competence of the corporation to determine and supported by a majority of shareholders is binding on the minority and hence upon the corporation as a whole. Compare **oppression**.

MAKER One who signs **(endorses)** a **promissory note**. By making the promissory note, the maker promises unconditionally to pay the note according to its tenor, i.e., the exact words of the **document**. See *Bills of Exchange Act,* R.S.C. 1985, c. B–4, ss. 176(1), 185.

MALA FIDE (*mă'-l à fīd*) Lat.: in bad faith. See **bona fide**.

MALFEASANCE The commission of an act that is positively wrong and unlawful, e.g., **trespassing**; wrongful conduct; an improper act. Compare **misfeasance**; **nonfeasance**.

MALICE 1. Generally in criminal law, malice means willfully, intentionally, and in the absence of legal excuse. "Malice in law does not necessarily mean any ill-will against any person but is established by a wrongful act done intentionally without just **cause** or excuse." *Manning v. Nickerson,* [1927] 3 D.L.R. 728 at 737 (B.C.C.A.), affirmed (*sub nom.*

Nickerson v. Manning), [1928] S.C.R. 91. "Malice is not limited to spite or ill will, although these are its most obvious instances. Malice includes any indirect motive or ulterior purpose, and will be established if the plaintiff can prove that the defendant was not acting honestly when he published the comment." *Cherneskey v. Armadale Publishers Ltd.,* [1979] 1 S.C.R. 1067 at 1099. If one acts maliciously, one intended to do the unlawful act with which one is charged. See also **malice aforethought**.

2. In the law of defamation, malice operates to defeat a claim of **qualified privilege** or **fair comment**. "Malice is commonly understood, in the popular sense, as spite or ill-will. However, it also includes ... 'any indirect motive or ulterior purpose' that conflicts with the sense of duty or the mutual interest [that] the occasion created ... Malice may also be established by showing that the defendant spoke dishonestly, or in knowing or reckless disregard for the truth." *Hill v. Church of Scientology of Toronto*, [1995] 2 S.C.R. 1130.

3. Malice is also an element of the **tort** of **malicious prosecution**, which is the malicious institution of a criminal **prosecution** without **reasonable and probable cause**. It requires an improper motive which is an abuse of the criminal justice system for ends it was not designed to serve. *Miazga v. Kvello Estate*, 2009 SCC 51.

MALICE AFORETHOUGHT Historically, in criminal law, the **intention** to commit **murder**. Malice aforethought may be either express or implied. Express malice exists where the accused deliberately deprives another of life or inflicts grievous bodily harm. Malice aforethought is implied by law where the accused intends to do an act that is likely to kill and from which death results. "Malice aforethought is a common name for all the following states of mind: (*a*) An intent preceding the act to kill or to do serious bodily injury to the person killed, or to any other person. (*b*) Knowledge that the act done is likely to produce such consequences, whether coupled with an intention to produce them or not. (*c*) An intent to commit any felony. (*d*) An intent to resist an officer of justice in the execution of his duty." *R. v. Graves* (1912), 9 D.L.R. 30 at 44 (N.S.S.C.), quoting from the Draft Code of England. "The expression 'malice aforethought' was subsequently adopted to distinguish murder from manslaughter, which denoted all culpable homicides other than murder. Malice aforethought was not limited to its natural and obvious sense of premeditation, but would be implied whenever the killing was intentional or reckless. In these instances, the malice was present and it is the premeditation which was implied by law." *R. v. Vaillancourt,* [1987] 2 S.C.R. 636 at para. 16.

In Canada, the term *malice aforethought* is not commonly used, being comprehended under the term **mens rea**. *Mens rea* is the mental element in most criminal offences and in relation to murder is the intentional killing of another or the intentional infliction of bodily harm that is likely to cause death whether by accident or mistake or where a person, for an unlawful object, does anything that he knows or ought to know is likely to cause death, and death results even though he or she may have sought to effect his or her object without causing death or bodily harm to any human being. See *Criminal Code*, R.S.C. 1985, c. C–46, s. 232. *R. v. Henry and Benzanson* (1974), 30 C.R. (N.S.) 15 (N.S.S.C.A.D.). *R. v. Tennant and Naccarato* (1975), 23 C.C.C. (2d) 80 at 89–96 (Ont. C.A.).

Compare **manslaughter**; **premeditation**.

MALICIOUS ARREST The arresting of a person on a criminal **charge** without **probable cause** or with knowledge that the person did not commit the offence charged. See *Croft v. Dunphy,* [1932] 1 D.L.R. 749 at 751 (N.S.S.C.); *Delancey v. Dale S. Co. Ltd.* (1959), 20 D.L.R. (2d) 12 (N.S.S.C.). Compare **false arrest**.

MALICIOUS PROSECUTION In the law of **torts**, the **abuse of legal process** by the malicious institution of a groundless **criminal** prosecution without reasonable and probable cause. "To succeed in an action for malicious prosecution, a plaintiff must prove that the prosecution was: (1) initiated by the defendant; (2) terminated in favour of the plaintiff; (3) undertaken without reasonable and probable cause; and (4) motivated by malice or a primary purpose other than that of carrying the law into effect." *Miazga v. Kvello Estate*, 2009 SCC 51. "In the context of a case against a Crown prosecutor, malice does not include recklessness, gross negligence, or poor judgment. It is only where the conduct of the prosecutor constitutes an "abuse of prosecutorial power" or the perpetuation of a "fraud on the process of criminal justice" that malice can be said to exist." *Id.*

MALPRACTICE 1. Improper or unskillful conduct on the part of a medical practitioner that results in injury to the patient. **2.** Generally, describes professional misconduct or **negligence** on the part of a person delivering professional services.

MALUM IN SE (*mă'-lŭm ĭn sā*) Lat.: evil in itself. Inherently evil, immoral; contrary to natural and moral law. For example, **murder** is *malum in se* because even without a specific criminal prohibition a civilized community would think it to be an evil and wrongful **act**. Compare **malum prohibitum**.

MALUM PROHIBITUM (*mă'-lŭm prō-hĭ' bĭ-tŭm*) Lat.: wrong because it is prohibited. Made unlawful by **statute** for the public welfare, but not inherently evil and not involving **moral turpitude**. The term refers to an act that is wrong only because it is made so by statute. It is contradistinguished from **malum in se**. For example, speeding along the highway is *malum prohibitum* because it has been so designated by statute as a result of a legislative determination that it is dangerous to the community though it may not be inherently dangerous, whereas reckless driving would be regarded as *malum in se*. See **regulatory offence**.

MANDAMUS (*măn-dā'-mŭs*) Lat.: we command. A discretionary **prerogative writ** issued by a **superior court** and used to compel public authorities to perform their duties, to ensure the proper exercise of **discretion**, or to compel observance of the rules of **natural justice** where a duty to observe those rules is required by **statute** or can be implied. The Supreme Court of Canada in *Apotex Inc. v. Canada (Attorney General)*, [1994] 1 F.C. 742 set out an eight-step test in regards to mandamus: 1) there must be a public legal duty to act, 2) the duty must be owed to the applicant, 3) there is a clear right to performance of that duty, 4) where the duty sought to be enforced is discretionary, certain rules apply, 5) no other adequate remedy is available to the applicant, 6) the order sought will be of some practical value or effect, 7) the Court in the exercise of its discretion finds no equitable bar to the relief sought, and 8) on a "balance of convenience" an order in the nature of mandamus should (or should not) issue.

A mandamus order is available in both **civil** and **criminal proceedings**. See the various provincial rules of court, e.g., *British Columbia Supreme Court Civil Rules*, B.C. Reg. 168/2009, Rule 21–3; *Nova Scotia Civil Procedure Rules*, Rule 64.

MANDATE A direction, request, or authoritative command; e.g., a cheque is a mandate by the **drawer** to his or her banker to pay the amount to the **holder** of the cheque. The term "mandate" (or mandatum) also refers to the **bailment** of money or goods to one who is to carry them from place to place or to do something about them without reward. See *Harris v. Sheffield* (1875), 10 N.S.R. 1 (S.C.). *Wills v. Brown*, [1912] 3 O.W.N. 580 at 581–82 (Co. Ct.), affirmed, [1912] 3 O.W.N. 583 (Div.Ct.); *Remme v. Wall* (1978), 29 N.S.R. (2d) 39 (S.C.).

MANDATORY An adjective describing procedural provisions, compliance with which is compulsory; compare **directory**.

MANDATORY INJUNCTION An **injunction** that requires the performance of a positive act rather than restraint from doing a particular act.

MANDATORY MINIMUM SENTENCE The lowest possible **sentence** that may be given upon **conviction** for an **offence**, as prescribed by statute. See, e.g., *Criminal Code*, R.S.C. 1985, c. C–46, ss. 172.1(2), 235. Mandatory minimum sentences are comparably rare in Canada, with most criminal and regulatory statutes merely prescribing the maximum possible sentence that may be given for an offence. Historically, it was possible for courts to evade mandatory minimum sentence provisions by granting a **constitutional exemption**. It remains possible for courts to strike down mandatory minimum sentences altogether under s. 12 of the **Canadian Charter of Rights and Freedoms**, on the basis that the minimum sentence would constitute **cruel and unusual punishment**. See, e.g., *R. v. Smickle*, 2012 ONSC 602.

MANDATORY ORDER A judicial order that compels a person to perform a particular act.

MANIFESTATION THEORY In insurance law, the theory that the injury or damage is said to occur only when it becomes apparent or ought to have become apparent. "On this theory, damage only occurs when it becomes known (on one formulation, to the insured, and on another, to the third party whose property is affected). Therefore, coverage is triggered when the insured or third party first becomes or could have become aware of the damage. Again, the result is that only the insurance policy in effect on the date of manifestation of the damage is triggered to respond to the loss." *Alie v. Bertrand & Frere Construction Co.* (2002), 62 O.R. (3d) 345 (Ont. C.A.)

MANIFEST UNFAIRNESS A consideration sometimes relevant to whether a law violates the **principles of fundamental justice**. In *R. v. Morgentaler*, [1988] 1 S.C.R. 30, a concurring opinion relied on the idea that the law against abortion was manifestly unfair as a basis for finding that it violated s. 7 of the **Canadian Charter of Rights and Freedoms**. That was not the majority opinion, and the concept, although sometimes related to **arbitrariness**, has not been fully developed. "*Morgentaler* applied

a 'manifest unfairness' test, which has never been adopted by the Court outside the criminal law, and certainly not in the context of the design of social programs." *Chaoulli v. Quebec (Attorney-General)*, 2005 SCC 35.

MANSLAUGHTER Under the *Criminal Code*, R.S.C. 1945, c. C–46, s. 234, culpable **homicide** that is neither **murder** nor **infanticide**. Manslaughter consists of causing the death of a human being, most frequently by means of an unlawful act or criminal negligence (ss. 222(5)(a) and (b)). If the accused intended to cause death, the offence would normally be murder; manslaughter only requires that a risk of bodily harm be reasonably foreseeable. *R. v. Creighton*, [1993] 3 S.C.R. 3. However, murder can be reduced to manslaughter if there was **provocation**.

MAREVA INJUNCTION An **injunction** preventing a **defendant** in a civil action from removing his or her **assets** from the jurisdiction prior to the court delivering its **judgment**. Such an injunction will only be granted if the applicant can persuade the court that there is a real risk that the assets will otherwise disappear. See *Tracy v. Instaloans Financial Solutions Centres (B.C.) Ltd.*, 2007 BCCA 481. See *Mareva Compania Naviera SA v. International Bulkcarriers SA* (1975), 2 Lloyd's Rep. 509 (C.A.).

MARIJUANA GROW-OP See **grow-op**.

MARITAL DEDUCTION [SPOUSAL DEDUCTION] In income tax law, the amount prescribed by the Act and regulations that a taxpayer is permitted to deduct for a dependent spouse. See *Income Tax Act*, R.S.C. 1985, c. 1, s. 118(1)(a).

MARITAL HOME The term used in legislation in New Brunswick to describe the **matrimonial home**. See, e.g., *Marital Property Act*, S.N.B. 1980, c. M–1.1.

MARITAL PROPERTY See **family property**.

MARITAL STATUS 1. "The status of being married, single, widowed, divorced or separated and includes the status of living with a person in a conjugal relationship outside marriage." *Human Rights*

Code, R.S.O. 1990, c. H.19, s. 10. **2.** The term is not defined in the **Canadian Human Rights Act**, R.S.C. 1989, c. H–6, s. 3, but has been interpreted to mean, "the status of a person in relation to marriage, namely, whether that person is single, married, divorced or widowed..." *Schapp v. Canada (Armed Forces)* (1990), 12 C.H.R.R. D/451 at D/456 (Fed.C.A.). See **marriage**; **spouse**.

MARITAL UNITY The now-abandoned common law rule that a husband and wife become one person for legal purposes upon marriage, and that the legal existence of the woman is suspended. See **coverture**; **married women's property acts**.

MARITIME LAW The traditional body of rules and practices particularly relating to commerce and navigation—to business transacted at sea or relating to navigation, ships, seamen, harbours, and general maritime affairs. See **admiralty and maritime jurisdiction**.

MARKETABLE TITLE A **title** that is free from plausible or reasonable objections and from material defects, called defects in title; a title permitting **quiet enjoyment**; a title acceptable to a reasonably well-informed and prudent **purchaser** or MORTGAGEE (see **mortgage**). *Penney v. Hartling* (1999), 177 N.S.R. (2d) 378 (N.S.S.C). The term *marketable title* is generally synonymous with **good title**.

MARKET OVERT An "open, public and legally constituted market," created by statute or established by long continual use where goods are exposed for sale by the owner. By statute, the law in England once provided that when goods were sold in market overt, a buyer acquired good **title** if they were bought in good faith and without notice of a defect in the seller's title. That statute was repealed in the 1990s.

MARKET VALUE The price that goods or **property** would bring in a market of willing buyers and willing sellers, in the ordinary course of trade; the price an asset would bring in a fair and open market. See *Nixon v. Trace*, 2012 BCCA 48.

Market value is generally established on the basis of sales of similar goods or property in the same locality, but where there have been no such prior sales, there is no single measure of value, and other evidence of value must be looked to. Market value is generally regarded as synonymous with ACTUAL VALUE, CASH VALUE, and FAIR MARKET VALUE.

MARRIAGE The Government of Canada presently recognizes the legal concept of marriage as the following: "Marriage, for civil purposes, is the lawful union of two persons to the exclusion of all others." *Civil Marriage Act*, S.C. 2005, c. 33 at s. 2. Formerly, the federal government did not recognize unions between those of the same sex; however, a series of cases from several provinces and one territory in the early 2000s proclaimed that it was unconstitutional to deny same-sex marriages. See, for example, *Halpern v. Attorney General of Canada*, [2002] O.J. No. 271 (S.C.). The federal government drafted a bill that would change the definition of marriage to include persons of the same sex, and referred the bill along with four questions to the Supreme Court of Canada in 2004; the Court found that the federal government had the authority to amend the definition of marriage to include persons of the same sex. The Court also stated that, based on freedom of religion under the **Charter**, it was unlikely that religious officials could be compelled by law to perform marriage ceremonies for same-sex couples. See **Reference re Same-Sex Marriage**, [2004] 3 S.C.R. 698. In the **Civil Marriage Act**, s. 3 states that "officials of religious groups are free to refuse to perform marriages that are not in accordance with their religious beliefs." In Canada, the federal Parliament has authority over the legal capacity to marry (i.e., who can marry whom). The provincial and territorial legislatures have the authority over solemnization of marriage, which includes requirements for such things as licences, determining who can conduct the ceremony and how, and registration. See **spouse, domestic partner**.

MARRIAGE CONTRACT [DOMESTIC CONTRACT] A written contract providing for the rights and obligations of **spouses** during marriage, and on separation, which usually provides for financial arrangements and division of property. *Webster v. Webster* (1986), 4 R.F.L. (3d) 225, at 227 (annotation). The term "domestic contract" is used more commonly in reference to cohabitation.

Most provincial **matrimonial property** statutes make provision for the effect of marriage contracts, i.e., *Family Property Act*, C.C.S.M. c. F–25: *Matrimonial Property Act*, R.S.N.S. 1989, c. 275, ss. 23–30; *Family Law Act*, R.S.O. 1990, c. F. 3, ss. 51–60.

MARRIED WOMEN'S PROPERTY ACTS General term describing provincial **statutes** (except those of Quebec) commonly referred to as Married Women's Property Acts, whereby married women are recognized in law as being capable of acquiring, holding, and disposing of **real** and **personal property** as separate from that of their husbands, and such property therefore may not be seized to extinguish the husband's debts. In Quebec, legislation of this type is covered by the Civil Code. See, e.g., *Married Women's Act*, R.S.A. 2000, c. M–6. See **marital unity**.

In addition, several provinces in Canada have enacted matrimonial property legislation governing the equitable division of family property between spouses upon termination of the marriage. Such legislation generally affects any **assets** acquired by either spouse before or during the marriage. See, e.g., *The Matrimonial Property Act,* R.S.A. 2000, c. M–8; *The Family Law Act,* R.S.O. 1990, c. F. 3; *Matrimonial Property Act,* R.S.N.S. 1989, c. 275.

MARSHALLING [MARSHALING] Arranging or ranking in order. The equitable doctrine of marshalling applies where there are two **creditors** (*A* and *B*) of the same **debtor** and two funds (*X* and *Y*) out of which payment must be claimed, and where the first creditor (*A*) can resort to both funds (*X,Y*) for the satisfaction of his debt but the other creditor (*B*) can resort to only one fund (*Y*). In this instance, equity will intervene and, in order to prevent the first creditor *A* from depriving the other creditor (*B*) of his or her **security**, order *A* to be paid out of the *X* fund to which *B* is not entitled, resorting to the *Y* fund only in case of deficiency, while allowing *B* to be paid out of the *Y* fund. If *A* has already paid himself or herself from the *Y* fund, the doctrine will apply to allow *B* to stand in *A*'s shoes and resort to the *X* fund to the extent to which the *Y* fund has been exhausted by *A*. See *Vysek v. Nova Gas International Ltd.*, [2002] A.J. No. 502 (Alta. Q.B.).

MARSHALLING ASSETS In the administration of the estate of a deceased person, arranging the assets so as to give effect to the priority of **debts**. In the distribution of an estate, ranking the assets in such a way as to achieve an equitable distribution of them among as many claims as possible according to the equities of the different parties. See generally *Re Steacy* (1917), 39 O.L.R. 548 at 550 (S.C.).

MARSHALLING LIENS The ranking or ordering of several parcels of land in order to satisfy a **judgment** or **mortgage** to which they are liable even though the **estates** were successively sold by the debtor. For example, in relation to mortgages, where a mortgage covers several lots and the owner sells the lots at different times to different purchasers who have no notice of the mortgage, the lots are liable to the charge of the mortgage debt in reverse order to which they were sold, i.e., the lot last sold is charged first under the mortgage. See generally *Collins v. Cunningham* (1892), 21 S.C.R. 139 at 150; *Ernst Bros. Co. v. Canada Permanent Mortgage Corp.* (1920), 47 O.L.R. 362 at 367–68 (S.C.).

MARTIAL LAW System of law, arbitrary in character, implemented in time of actual war by which officers of the Crown or military authorities exercise control over civilians in domestic territory in order to maintain public order and security.

In England, when a state of actual war, riot, insurrection or rebellion exists, the Crown by proclamation, or the military authorities by notice, may supersede the ordinary law and government of the country or parts of the country by using force to restore order. This use of force is sometimes termed martial law. During the time of actual war, military tribunals are given jurisdiction to try and to punish certain offenses, and civil courts have no authority to review the actions of military authorities. However, the powers of military authorities cease and those of civil courts are restored once the state of war ends. See generally *Ex parte Marais,* [1902] A.C. 109 at 114–16 (P.C.) (Cape of Good Hope).

The so-called military courts established under martial law are not really courts; and "[i]t is by this time a very familiar observation that what is called 'martial law' is no law at all. The notion that 'martial law' exists by reason of the proclamation ... is an entire delusion. The right to administer force against force in actual war does not depend upon the proclamation of martial law at all. It depends upon the question whether there is war or not. If there is war, there is the right to repel force by force, but it is found convenient and decorous, from time to time to authorize what are called 'courts' to administer punishments, and to restrain by acts of repression the violence that is committed in time of war ... But to attempt to make these proceedings of so-called 'courts-martial,' administering summary justice under the supervision of a military commander, analogous to the regular proceedings of Courts of justice is quite illusory." *Tilonko v. The Attorney-General of the Colony of Natal,* [1907] A.C. 93 at 94–95 (P.C.).

In Canada the term *martial law* is not used. However, under the *Emergencies Act,* R.S.C. 1985 (4th Supp.), c. 22, the issue of a proclamation by the **Governor-in-Council**, in the belief based on reasonable grounds, that a public welfare emergency (ss. 5–15), public order emergency (ss. 16–26), international emergency (ss. 27–36), or war emergency (ss. 37–45) exists in respect of Canada gives the Governor-in-Council sweeping powers. Depending on the class of emergency, orders and regulations may be issued to: regulate and control the distribution and availability of essential goods, services, and resources; prohibit public assembly and travel; control public utilities, industry and use of property; authorize the entry and search of any dwelling house or conveyance; deport persons; as well as arrest those in contravention of such orders and regulations made under the *Act.* The powers of the Governor-in-Council under this Act in time of a national emergency may broadly conform to what is generally described as martial law. See **military courts**.

MASTER [MASTER IN CHANCERY] In England, a senior official of the Court of Chancery who assisted the Chancellor in dealing with petitions, issuing original writs and hearing witnesses. Judicial functions were in time delegated to the Master, who would hear and report on cases to the Chancellor. The Master of the Rolls was chief among all the Masters in Chancery and, from the sixteenth century, was the chief assistant and deputy of the Chancellor. The offices of the Masters in Chancery were abolished in 1852 and were replaced by eight appointed Chief Clerks who, since 1897, have been called Masters of the Supreme Court.

In Ontario, a Master is a provincially appointed judicial officer exercising jurisdiction over **interlocutory** matters either as a Master of the Supreme Court of Ontario or as a County Court judge sitting in the capacity as a Local Judge or Local Master. See generally *Ontario Rules of Civil Procedure,* R.R.O. 1990, Reg. 194, rr. 37.02. 37.11–37.14.

MATERIAL Important, necessary; relating to a given matter.

MATERIAL ALTERATION Any alteration in a written **instrument** that changes its tenor or effect. Important alterations that materially or substantially change the legal nature of the instrument. See *Toronto-Dominion Bank v. Duffett,* 2004 NLSCTD 30. *Bills of Exchange Act,* R.S.C. 1985, c. B–4, s. 144, 145.

MATERIAL CHANGE IN CIRCUMSTANCES "[A] change, such that, if known at the time, would likely have resulted in different terms [in a **maintenance** order]. The corollary to this is that if the matter which relied on as constituting a change was known at the relevant time, it cannot be relied on as the basis for variation." *Willick v. Willick* (1994), 6 R.F.L. (4th) 161 at 179–80 (S.C.C.)

MATERIAL FACTS In pleadings, the facts upon which the party pleading relies but not the evidence by which they are to be proved; facts that are relevant to or have a bearing upon the issues in question. Material facts are those that the party to an action must plead and prove in order to obtain a judgment in his or her favour. "Parties are not required to plead the evidence by which material facts will be proved. The fact that material facts, supported by particulars, are not further supported by additional particulars does not mean that the allegations are merely assumptions or speculation." *Miguna v. Toronto (City) Police Services Board,* 2008 ONCA 799. See *Canadian Indemnity Co. v. Canadian Johns-Manville Co.,* [1990] 2 S.C.R. 549; *Sagi v. Cosburn, Griffiths & Brandham Insurance Brokers Ltd.,* 2009 ONCA 388.

In the law of insurance, a material fact is one that, if disclosed to a reasonable insurer, would influence him or her either to decline the risk altogether or not to accept it unless a higher premium is paid. See *Ontario Metal Products Co. Ltd. v. Mutual Life Insurance Co. of New York,* [1925] 1 W.W.R. 362 at 368 (P.C.) (Ont.); *McCammon v. Alliance Assurance Co. Ltd.,* [1931] 2 W.W.R. 621 at 626–27 (Sask.C.A.); *Melvin v. The British American Assurance Co. Ltd.* (1933), 6 M.P.R. 438 at 444 (N.S.S.C. in banco).

With regard to commercial transactions, material facts are those that could reasonably be expected to affect the price of something, and which a seller therefore has an obligation to disclose. See, e.g., *Real Estate Marketing and Development Act,* S.B.C. 2004, c. 41, s. 16(3) or *Securities Act,* R.S.A. 2000, c. S–4, s. l(gg).

MATRIMONIAL HOME The residence(s) occupied by married **spouses** as their family home. Legislation in each province gives each spouse certain rights in the matrimonial home, such as an equal right to possess it, or the ability to prevent a sale or granting of an interest in the home. See, e.g., *Family Law Act,* R.S.N.L. 1990, c. F–2, ss. 6–17; *Family Law Act,* R.S.O. 1990, c. F.3, ss. 17–28. See **homestead legislation**.

MATRIMONIAL PROPERTY See **family property**.

MATTER OF FACT See **question of fact**.

MATTER OF LAW See **question of law**.

MATURITY The date at which legal rights in an entity ripen; e.g., in relation to **negotiable instruments** it is the time when a **bill of exchange** or **promissory note** becomes due.

MAXIMS OF EQUITY See **equitable maxims**.

MAY A word used in statutes to permit a person or body to do something. See, e.g., *Human Rights Code,* R.S.B.C. 1996, c. 210, s. 27(1). The word is used to grant powers that are either discretionary or obligatory. Where a power is discretionary, "the person or body on whom it is conferred must decide whether to exercise it and may choose not to." R. Sullivan, *Statutory Interpretation* 73 (2nd ed. 2007). See, e.g., *Alberta (Minister of Justice and Attorney-General) v. Sykes,* 2011 ABCA 191. Conversely, where the power granted by the word "may" is coupled with a duty, or "where failure to exercise the power would tend to defeat the purpose of the legislation, undermine the legislative scheme, create a contextual anomaly, or otherwise produce unacceptable consequences," the power will usually be interpreted as obligatory. *Id,* 73–74. See for example *Bates v. Bates* (2000), 49 O.R. (3d) 1 (Ont. C.A.). See also **shall**.

McNEIL DISCLOSURE A process intended to bridge the gap between **disclosure** and **production**. When the **Crown prosecutor** becomes aware of potentially **relevant documents** in the hands of a third party, in some instances the

Crown has an obligation to obtain those records and disclose them, rather than require the **accused** to pursue a formal application for production. *R. v. McNeil*, 2009 SCC 3.

MECHANICS' LIEN See **lien**.

MED-ARB "Mediation arbitration, or med-arb, is an increasingly popular alternative dispute resolution mechanism in which the disputing parties and a third-party neutral attempt to reach a voluntary agreement through mediation, and then move to arbitration by the same third party if they are unsuccessful." Megan Telford, *Med-Arb: A Viable Dispute Resolution Alternative* (IRC Press, 2000).

MEDIATE DATA Facts from which ultimate facts may be inferred for purposes of **collateral estoppel**.

MEDIATELY Indirectly; deduced from proven facts.

MEDIATION An informal process of settling disputes through the intervention of a neutral third party, referred to as a "mediator." A mediator has no legal authority to impose a settlement on the disputing parties; he or she can only advise or assist the parties in reconciling their differences. See **med-arb**.

MEDIATOR See **mediation**.

MEECH LAKE ACCORD, THE The *Constitution Amendment, 1987* (commonly known as "The Meech Lake Accord") was signed by the Prime Minister of Canada and the ten provincial premiers on April 30, 1987. The central purpose of the Accord was to bring about the full and active participation of Quebec in Canada's constitutional evolution. To that end, the **Constitution** of Canada was to be interpreted in a manner consistent with "the recognition that Quebec constitutes within Canada a distinct society" (s. 1). Other provisions related to the appointment of senators (s. 2); provincial control over immigration matters (s. 3); changes in the appointment of judges to the **Supreme Court of Canada** (s. 6); changes in the administration of cost-shared programs between federal and provincial govern-

ments (s. 7); and future amendments to the Constitution of Canada (s. 9).

It was commonly understood that the Accord would not take effect unless ratified by the **Parliament** of Canada, and the ten provincial **legislatures**, by June 23, 1990 (three years after the first legislative approval by Quebec on June 23, 1987). Neither Manitoba nor Newfoundland met the June 23 deadline for ratification. On June 23, 1990, then Prime Minister Brian Mulroney confirmed the demise of the Accord.

MEETING OF MINDS See **consensus ad idem**.

MEGA-TRIAL A "trial that, because of the number of accused or the complex legal points to be dealt with, is exceptionally long." *Auclair v. R.*, 2011 QCCS 2661. Parliament has recently amended the *Criminal Code* to add new procedures aimed at accommodating the special institutional demands posed by mega-trials. See, e.g., *Criminal Code*, R.S.C. 1985, c. C–46, ss. 551.1–551.2.

MEIORIN TEST See **Bona Fide Occupational Requirement (BFOR)**.

MEMORANDUM An informal record; a note of the particulars of any transaction or matter. An agreement set down in writing with a particular purpose, e.g., memorandum of association of a company. Some written evidence of a contract or deed sufficient to satisfy the Statute of Frauds. See *Adam v. General Paper Co. Ltd.* (1978), 19 O.R. (2d) 574 (H.C.).

A legal memorandum is an informal note discussing the law in relation to a given factual problem, usually written by a law clerk or junior partner for the benefit of a senior partner of a law firm.

In a marine insurance policy, the memorandum is a clause inserted to prevent the underwriters from being liable for injury or minor damage to goods of a peculiarly perishable nature.

See also **association, memorandum of**.

MENS REA (*mĕnz rē'-à*) Lat.: guilty mind. A culpable state of mind. Also referred to as the "fault elements." Mens rea indicates the mental element or intent required for the commission of a criminal act. *Mens rea* encompasses several criminal states of mind: e.g., intention, knowledge, recklessness, willful blindness. In some statutory offences the mens rea may be described as a general intent or a specific intent. A crime of GENERAL INTENT—e.g., **sexual assault**—requires proof of the intention to do the prohibited act, whereas a SPECIFIC INTENT offence—e.g., theft—requires proof of a special mental element (in the case of theft, the taking of something with the intent to deprive, temporarily or absolutely, the owner or other person who has a special property or interest in it of the thing, or of his or her property or interest in it). See *Criminal Code* R.S.C. 1985, c. C–46, s. 322. The particular *mens rea* for an offence might be specified in the **Criminal Code** provision that creates that offence, but crimes are presumed to require the proof of *mens rea* whether it is specified or not. *Beaver v. R.*, [1957] S.C.R. 531. Compare **strict liability**. In a criminal prosecution, the Crown must prove beyond a reasonable doubt that the required mental state (mens rea) coexisted with the doing of the proscribed act (**actus reus**). The defences of **mental disorder**, drunkenness, or **mistake** may, in some cases, be raised to rebut the existence of mens rea.

MENTAL ANGUISH [MENTAL SUFFERING]

Compensable **injury** embracing all forms of mental pain, as distinguished from mere physical pain, including deep grief, distress, anxiety, and fright. See generally *Fidler v. Sun Life Assurance Co. of Canada*, 2006 SCC 30. The **tort** of intentional infliction of mental suffering is not actionable without proof of "recognizable physical or psychopathological harm." *Frame v. Smith,* [1987] 2 S.C.R. 99 at 128. A tort of negligent (as opposed to intentional) infliction of mental suffering has been argued for, but to date, without success. See, e.g., *Piresferreira v. Ayotte*, 2010 ONCA 384, or *Jones v. Kemball*, 2012 FC 27: "The Plaintiff claims damages for 'negligent infliction of mental suffering.' No such independent tort exists. In any event, in order to establish liability for psychiatric

injury, the injury must satisfy the legal concept of nervous shock. This does not include emotional upset, mental distress, grief, sorrow, anxiety, worry, or other transient and more minor psychiatric injury." Compare **nervous shock**; **pain and suffering**.

MENTAL CRUELTY

A course of behaviour of one spouse that endangers the other spouse's mental or physical well-being to such an extent that it renders intolerable the continued marriage relationship. Under the *Divorce Act,* mental cruelty constitutes grounds for **divorce**. See *Divorce Act,* R.S.C. 1985, c. 3, (2nd Supp.), s. 8(2)(b)(ii). Because divorce is available based on one year's separation, mental cruelty has become less significant as a concept than it was in the past.

MENTAL DISORDER

A disease of the mind or mental illness; used as a **defence** to criminal **charges**. Under s. 16(1) of the *Criminal Code,* R.S.C. 1985, c. C–46, no one "is criminally responsible for an act committed or an omission made while suffering from a mental disorder that rendered the person incapable of appreciating the nature and quality of the act or omission or of knowing that it was wrong."

The term "disease of the mind" is broadly interpreted. It "embraces any illness, disorder or abnormal condition which impairs the human mind and its functioning, excluding, however, self-induced states caused by alcohol or drugs, as well as transitory mental states such as hysteria or concussion. Thus, personality disorders may constitute disease of the mind. The word *appreciates* imports a requirement beyond mere knowledge of the physical quality of the act and requires a capacity to apprehend the nature of the act and its consequences." E. Greenspan, M. Rosenberg & M. Henein, *Martin's Annual Criminal Code, 2012* 55–56 (2011). See also *Cooper v. The Queen* (1980), 51 C.C.C. (2d) 129 (S.C.C.).

Previous to 1992, the term **insanity** was used in the *Code.* Now, it has been removed and the provisions dealing with insanity and fitness to stand trial have been consolidated under Part XX.I of the *Code* with the heading "Mental Disorder." See R. Salhany, *Canadian Criminal Procedure* 6–144ff. (6th ed. 1994).

See **competent**; **not criminally responsible by reason of mental disorder**; **M'Naghten Rule**. Compare **incompetency**; **non compos mentis**.

MENTAL HEALTH COURT A specialized **court** established by numerous provinces for the purpose of diverting **accused** persons with mental illnesses away from the mainstream **criminal** justice system, emphasizing treatment and **rehabilitation** rather than **punishment**. "Entry into [a] mental health court requires a diagnosis of one or more of a group of specific mental illnesses and a nexus between the illness and the offence." *R. v. Edmunds*, 2012 NLCA 26. Compare with **drug treatment court**.

MERCANTILE AGENT A person "having, in the customary course of business as an agent, authority either to sell goods or to consign goods for the purpose of sale, or to buy goods, or to raise money on the security of goods." *Factors Act*, R.S.O. 1990, F. 1, s. 1.

MERCANTILE LAW The branch of law (often called commercial law) that deals with the rules and institutions of commercial transactions. It is derived from the **law merchant**. See *Pearse & Edworthy Bros. v. Rur. Mun. Bjorkdale*, [1929] 2 D.L.R. 537 at 539 (Sask.C.A.).

MERCHANTABLE Saleable and fit for the market. "[W]hatever else merchantable may mean, it does mean that the article sold, if only meant for one particular use in ordinary course, is fit for that use; merchantable does not mean that the thing is saleable in the market simply because it looks all right." *Grant v. Australian Knitting Mills Ltd.*, [1936] A.C. 85 at 99–100 (P.C.) (Austl.). See also *Porter v. Dead River Ltd.* (1951), 29 M.P.R. 40 at 50 (N.B.S.C.A.D.).

MERCHANTABLE QUALITY The various provincial *Sale of Goods Acts* provide that where goods are bought by description from a seller who deals in goods of that description, whether or not he or she is the manufacturer,

there is an **implied condition** that the goods shall be of merchantable quality. Merchantable quality means "that the article is of such quality and in such condition that a reasonable man acting reasonably would after a full examination accept it under the circumstances of the case in performance of his offer to buy that article whether he buys for his own use or to sell again." *Bristol Tramways Carriage Co. Ltd. v. Fiat Motors Ltd.*, [1910] 2 K.B. 831 at 841 (C.A.). See also *Int'l Business Machines Co. Ltd. v. Shcherban*, [1925] 1 D.L.R. 864 at 868 (Sask.C.A.); *Farmer v. Canada Packers Ltd.*, [1956] O.R. 657 at 670 (H.C.).

MERCY KILLING See **euthanasia**.

MERE PUFF "A statement inducing a **contract** may be a 'mere puff' if the court considers that it was not seriously meant and that this should have been obvious to the person to whom it was made." H.G. Beale, ed., 1 *Chitty on Contracts* 238 (30th ed. 2008). Representations made as "mere puff" will not become part of the resulting contract and may not be relied upon in subsequent litigation. See, e.g., *Reinzuch v. Carey*, [1983] B.C.J. No. 1027 (B.C.S.C.).

MERGED SOVEREIGNTY The view that Aboriginal societies were not wholly subordinated to non-Aboriginal sovereignty but instead over time became merger partners. "If the principle of 'merged sovereignty' articulated by the **Royal Commission** is to have any true meaning, it must include at least the idea that Aboriginal and non-Aboriginal Canadians *together* form a sovereign entity with a measure of common purpose and united effort. It is this new entity, as inheritor of the historical attributes of sovereignty, with which existing **Aboriginal** and **treaty rights** must be reconciled." The view is put forward in the dissenting opinion in *Mitchell v. M.N.R.*, 2001 SCC 33, but has not been adopted by a majority of the Supreme Court.

MERGER The amalgamation of one thing into another; a consolidation.

1. In the law of **corporations**, the terms *merger* and *amalgamation* are often used interchangeably, although only the latter term has a specific legal meaning. AMALGAMATION is the fusion of two or more corporations and their continuance as one corporation. Such an amalgamation, or, popularly, a merger, is accomplished in several ways: (1) A sale of the assets of one (or more than one) corporation to an existing corporation in consideration of the issuance of paid-up shares or securities of the latter. The vendor corporation will then pay its liabilities and distribute its assets among its own shareholders and surrender its charter or in some other manner be dissolved; (2) a lease of the whole or a substantial part of the assets and business of one or more corporations to another corporation. In this case the **lessor** corporation remains in existence and distributes, by way of dividends among its shareholders, the rentals paid by the **lessee** corporation; (3) acquisition of shares of two or more corporations by a new corporation or by an existing corporation; (4) amalgamation by agreement between the corporations pursuant to special statutory provisions. This last-named method of effecting amalgamations is governed by both federal and provincial companies legislation. See, e.g., *Canada Business Corporations Act,* R.S.C. 1985, c. C–44, ss. 181, 182: *Companies Act,* R.S.N.S. 1989, c. 81, s. 134; *The Corporations Act,* R.S.O. 1990, c. C. 38, s. 113; *The Business Corporations Act,* R.S.O. 1990, c. B. 16, s. 174. See also *R. v. Black & Decker Manufacturing Co. Ltd.* (1974), 43 D.L.R. (3d) 393 at 399–400 (S.C.C.); *Attorney-General for Ontario v. Electrical Development Co. Ltd.* (1919), 45 O.L.R. 186 at 190 (H.C.).

2. In the law **of real property**, it is a general rule that where two estates in land become vested in one person and there is no intervening estate in another person, the lesser estate is merged, extinguished or drowned, by operation of law, in the greater estate. For example, if A becomes vested of a TENANCY FOR YEARS (see **tenancy**) and subsequently acquires, either by purchase or by inheritance, a **reversion** in **fee sim-**ple, then the tenancy for years, being the lesser estate, is merged in the fee simple and therefore no longer exists. See *Doe Dem. McPherson v. Hunter* (1848), 4 U.C.Q.B. 449; *Wigle v. Merrick* (1858), 8 U.C.C.P. 307; *Dalye v. Robertson* (1860), 19 U.C.Q.B. 411. In **equity**, the merger of a lesser **estate** in a greater, or the merger of a charge in the land, is a question of the intention, actual or presumed, of the person in whom the interest in the estates are united. Thus the lesser estate is not merged in the greater if there is an express or presumed intention that it shall be kept alive. Similarly, if a person acquires a charge upon land to which he or she is entitled and expresses his or her intention that the charge shall not merge, it remains alive. However, if there is an express or presumed intention in favour of merger, the charge will be extinguished. See *Henry v. Low* (1862), 9 Gr. 265.

3. Generally, in the law of **contracts**, where a **creditor** takes from his or her **debtor** a **security** of a higher nature than that already owing him or her— e.g., if he or she takes a bond or recovers **judgment** in respect of a simple contract debt—then his or her remedies on the lower security are merged, by operation of law, in the higher remedy and are thereby extinguished. The merger of the lower security in the higher only occurs with respect to the same debt and must involve the same parties. See *Gore Bank v. McWhirter* (1868), 18 U.C.C.P. 293; *Shenkman v. Steinbook* (1915), 7 W.W.R. 1051 at 1052 (Alta.Dist.Ct.). The term *merger* is also used in relation to an agreement that requires the execution of a deed—e.g., an agreement for the sale of land—where it is said that the agreement is superseded by the deed, or "merged" in it. See *Knight Sugar Co. v. Alberta Ry. & Irrigation Co.,* [1938] 1 D.L.R. 321 at 324 (P.C.).

MERITS The various elements that enter into or qualify the plaintiff's right to the **relief** sought or the defendant's right to prevail in his defence; the real matters in question rather than technicalities; the substance of a **litigant's** claim or refutation of a claim; the totality of the elements of a party's claim that tend to establish or refute the validity or credibility of his or her cause; the grounds of an action or defence. A person may be said to have a good cause of action or defence **on the merits**.

MESNE (*mēn*) Intermediate; between two extremes, especially in rank or time.

MESNE LORD In English feudal law a mesne lord was one who held lands under the authority of the King and who stood between the King and the tenants who occupied the land, known as tenants in demesne, thereby becoming a lord to the tenants.

MESNE PROFITS Rents and profits obtained from the land by one who is in unlawful possession of the land and who holds it against the true owner. See *Vivian v. Tizard,* [1918] 2 W.W.R. 765 at 766 (Sask.S.C.).

METES AND BOUNDS The limits or boundaries of property as marked by natural features or man-made structures. A method of describing the territorial limits of property by means of measuring distances and angles from designated landmarks and in relation to adjoining properties.

MÉTIS One of the three groups making up the **Aboriginal Peoples of Canada**, along with Indians and Inuit. The term "Métis" derives from the French word "métissage" (miscegenation), and the first Métis were the mixed-race children of Indians and Europeans. However, "[t]he term 'Métis' in s. 35 does not encompass all individuals with mixed Indian and European heritage; rather, it refers to distinctive peoples who, in addition to their mixed ancestry, developed their own customs, way of life, and recognizable group identity separate from their Indian or Inuit and European forebears." *R. v. Powley,* 2003 SCC 43. The matter is not authoritatively settled, but it has been held that Métis are Indians for **division of powers** purposes under s. 91(24) of the **Constitution Act, 1867**. See *Daniels v. Canada,* 2013 FC 6.

MILITARY COURTS Courts established under the *National Defence Act,* R.S.C. 1985, c. N–5, to deal with **service offences**. Some less serious offences can be tried by way of summary trial by a commanding officer or superior commanding officer; see ss. 163–164.1. Others will be tried by a court martial; see ss. 165–196.1. Military judges are appointed by the **Governor in Council** and must be barristers or advocates of at least ten years' standing at the bar of a province. *Id.,* s. 165.21.

MILITARY LAW "All laws, regulations or orders relating to the Canadian Forces." *Criminal Code,* R.S.C. 1985, c. C–46, s. 2. See **court martial**.

MINIMAL IMPAIRMENT A step in the **Oakes test** for determining whether a law or measure that violates the **Canadian Charter of Rights and Freedoms** can be saved as a **reasonable limit in a free and democratic society**. If a law does violate a *Charter* right and that violation is rationally connected to a sufficiently important objective, nonetheless, the law must be carefully tailored so that the right is impaired no more than necessary.

MINISTERIAL ACT [MINISTERIAL FUNCTION] The performance of acts, the making of decisions or the issuance of orders by a public servant or official, in which there is little or no element of discretion or independent judgment. The performance of a ministerial act, as required by statute or otherwise, may be enforced through an order of **mandamus**. The term is to be distinguished from **judicial** or **legislative acts** and **executive** or **administrative** acts, which involve the exercise of a substantial amount of **discretion** and individual judgment. See *M. Gordon & Son Ltd. v. Debly* (1956), 3 D.L.R. (2d) 1 at 5 (S.C.C.); *McDonald v. Attorney-General for Alberta* (1968), 66 W.W.R. (N.S.) 111 (Alta.S.C.A.D.); *Canadian Financial Co. v. O'Neill* (1977), 26 N.B.R. (2d) 221 at 223 (Co.Ct.).

MINOR A person not of full legal capacity; one under the **age of majority**; an infant.

MINORITY LANGUAGE EDUCATION RIGHTS See **Canadian Charter of Rights and Freedoms**.

MISAPPLICATION [MISAPPROPRIATION] OF PROPERTY
Generally, the use of funds or property for a wrongful purpose. The term is commonly used in relation to persons who, while acting in a **fiduciary** capacity—e.g., as a banker, trustee, director of a corporation, etc.—misapply funds intended for another purpose or who convert another's funds for their own benefit. "Misappropriation does not necessarily mean **peculation**, though it may mean that." *Hanna v. DeBlaquiere* (1853), 11 U.C.Q.B. 310 at 314.

In Canada, the misappropriation of money or valuable security by one under direction to apply such money or security to a particular purpose or to pay it to a person specified in the direction is treated as theft under s. 332(1) of the *Criminal Code,* R.S.C. 1985, c. C–46. See also s. 336. See, e.g., *R. v. Legare* (1977), 36 C.C.C. (2d) 463 (S.C.C.). See **larceny**.

MISAPPROPRIATION OF PERSONALITY
A **tort** that occurs when a defendant uses a plaintiff's "name, likeness, or other recognizable aspect of [his or] her personality" in order to promote his or her own economic interests. P.H. Osborne, *The Law of Torts* 323 (4th ed. 2011). The tort is intended to protect the plaintiff's right to control the use of his or her own personality for commercial reasons. It does not, however, prevent his or her likeness from being used in works of a "journalistic, biographical, or informational" nature. *Id.* See, e.g., *Gould Estate v. Stoddart Publishing Co.* (1996), 30 O.R. (3d) 520 (Ont. C.J.).

MISCARRIAGE OF JUSTICE
An unfairness in a criminal trial that justifies an appellate court in overturning an accused's conviction. Section 686(1) of the *Criminal Code*, R.S.C. 1985, c. C–46 sets out the bases upon which an appeal from conviction can be granted: (*a*) an unreasonable verdict; (*b*) an error of law that is not harmless (see **curative proviso**); or (*c*) a miscarriage of justice. "While s. 686(1)(*a*) provides three distinct bases upon which [an appellate court] may quash a conviction, each shares the same underlying rationale. A conviction that is the product of a mis-carriage of justice cannot stand. Section 686(1)(a)(i) is concerned with the most obvious example of a miscarriage of justice, a conviction that no reasonable trier of fact properly instructed could have returned on the evidence adduced at trial. Section 686(1)(a)(ii) read along with s. 686(1)(b)(iii) presumes that an error in law produces a miscarriage of justice unless the Crown can demonstrate the contrary with the requisite degree of certainty. Section 686(1)(a) (iii) addresses all other miscarriages of justice not caught by the two preceding subsections." Justice Charron in *R. v. Sinclair*, 2011 SCC 40, quoting *R. v. Morrissey* (1995), 97 C.C.C. (3d) 193 (Ont. C.A.)

MISCHIEF RULE
One of the basic rules of **statutory interpretation**, which holds that where statutory language is ambiguous, the court should look at the particular defect or "mischief" in the common-law that the statute was designed to correct remedy in order to ensure that its interpretation reinforces rather than undermines it.

MISDEMEANOUR
At common law, all crimes were divided into felonies, misdemeanours, and **treason**. Generally, misdemeanours were less serious offences than felonies and were sanctioned by less severe penalties. In Canada, the distinction between felonies and misdemeanours was abolished by the *Criminal Code,* S.C. 1892, c. 29, being replaced by **indictable offences** and offences punishable upon **summary conviction**. Indictable offences are generally understood to be more serious crimes (e.g., **murder, aggravated sexual assault, manslaughter**), whereas summary conviction offences are less serious (e.g., common **assault**, operation of a vessel while impaired by alcohol or a drug, willful destruction or damage of property not exceeding fifty dollars). The distinction between felonies and misdemeanours remains important in the United States.

MISFEASANCE
The doing of an act in a wrongful or injurious manner; the improper performance of a lawful act; "[a]n act or the failure to act which cre-

ates a risk of harm to another person." P.H. Osborne, *The Law of Torts* 464 (4th ed. 2011). Compare **malfeasance**; **nonfeasance**.

MISJOINDER Improper joining of plaintiffs or defendants in a single action, i.e., where persons are made parties who ought not to be. Compare **joinder**.

MISLAID PROPERTY Property that the owner has intentionally placed where he or she can resort to it, but which place is then forgotten. The finder of mislaid property acquires no **interest** or right to **possession**, and thus the proprietor of the place in which the mislaid object is found is the only one entitled to retain possession pending the search for the true owner. Compare **abandonment**; **lost property**.

MISNOMER A misnaming; a term applied to a mistake in the word or combination of words constituting a person's name and distinguishing him or her from other individuals. The giving of a wrong name to a person in pleadings.

MISREPRESENTATION Words or conduct that convey a false or misleading impression. A misrepresentation may be fraudulent, innocent, or negligent. A FRAUDULENT MISREPRESENTATION is one made with the knowledge it is false and with the intent to deceive the party to whom it is made. A fraudulent misrepresentation is actionable as a **tort** when it is made with the knowledge that the plaintiff will rely on the misrepresentation, as he or she in fact did, to his or her detriment. An INNOCENT MISREPRESENTATION is an untrue statement of fact made in the honest belief that it is true. A NEGLIGENT MISREPRESENTATION is one made carelessly and with no reasonable grounds for believing it to be true. Such a misrepresentation may give rise to a **tort** action. The tort has five criteria: "(1) there must be a duty of care based on a 'special relationship' between the representor and the representee; (2) the representation in question must be untrue, inaccurate, or misleading; (3) the representor must have acted negligently in making said misrepresentation; (4) the representee

must have relied, in a reasonable manner, on said negligent misrepresentation; and (5) the reliance must have been detrimental to the representee in the sense that damages resulted." *Queen v. Cognos Inc.*, [1993] 1 S.C.R. 87.

MISTAKE An unintentional act involving misapprehension or error in the existence of a thing, arising either from ignorance or from a false belief on the point. Mere forgetfulness is not a mistake against which the court will grant relief. *Walsh v. Quoddy Holdings Ltd.*, 2006 NBQB 356.

A distinction is often drawn between unilateral mistake, common mistake, and mutual mistake in the law of contract.

COMMON MISTAKE A mistake made when both parties are contracting under an error and share the same mistaken belief. "Each knows the intention of the other and accepts it, but each is mistaken about some underlying and fundamental fact." M.P. Furmston, *Cheshire, Fifoot and Furmston's Law of Contract* 284 (15th ed. 2007). For example, in contracting for the sale of a cow, A and B both believe the cow to be a breeder, when in fact it is barren.

MUTUAL MISTAKE A mistake made when "the [contracting] parties misunderstand each other and are at cross purposes. A, for example, intends to offer his Ford Sierra car for sale, but B believes that the offer relates to the Ford Granada [car] also owned by A." *Id.* at 236.

UNILATERAL MISTAKE A mistake by only one of the parties to the contract as to its terms or object. **Rectification** or alteration of the contract is available as a remedy for this type of mistake only if it can be shown that the other party was aware of the mistake and that his taking advantage of it would amount to **fraud** or constitute misrepresentation amounting to fraud. The contract may, however, be **rescinded** if the mistake is of a fundamental character. See *Sykes v. The King*, [1939] Ex.C.R. 77 at 85; *McMillen v. Chapman and S. S. Kresge Company Ltd.*, [1953] O.R. 399 at 405–06 (C.A.); *McMaster*

University v. Wilchar Construction Ltd., [1971] 3 O.R. 801 (H.C.); *Pacific Petroleums Ltd. v. Concordia Propane Gas Marketers Ltd.* (1977), 5 A.R. 421 (Alta.S.C.).

A further distinction is drawn between a mistake of law and a mistake of fact. In the law of **contract**, a MISTAKE OF FACT is "a mistake not caused by the neglect of legal duty on the part of the person making the mistake, and consisting in an unconscientiousness, ignorance, or forgetfulness of a fact past or present material to the transaction; or in the belief in the present existence of a thing material to the transaction which does not exist, or in the past existence of a thing which has not existed." *Black v. The Bank of Nova Scotia* (1889), 21 N.S.R. 448 at 460–61 (C.A.) quoted in *Gammon v. Seaside Chev–Olds Ltd.* (1997), 69 A.C.W.S. (3d) 1048 (N.B.Q.B.). A mistake of fact will justify **rescission** of the contract if the mistake is material to the nature of the transaction. However, a MISTAKE OF LAW—which consists of one's ignorance of the legal consequences of his conduct, though he or she is fully cognizant of the facts and substance of that conduct—is not generally regarded as sufficient to justify rescission or reformation of a contract, unless the mistake is a mutual one concerning the parties' relative and respective legal rights under the contract. See *U.S.A. v. Motor Trucks Ltd.* (1922), 52 O.L.R. 262 at 271–72 (S.C.A.D.); *Thompson v. Crawford,* [1932] O.R. 281, affirmed [1932] 41 O.W.N. 231 (C.A.). Compare **ignorantia legis non excusat**.

The criminal law has traditionally recognized the same dichotomy, allowing a mistake of fact in some cases to constitute a valid defence to a criminal prosecution, but relying on the maxim "Ignorance of the law is no excuse" with regard to mistakes of law. This maxim is now incorporated in s. 19 of the *Criminal Code,* R.S.C. 1985, c. C–46. Generally, only a mistake of fact is, in Canada, a valid defence since it negates one of the essential elements of those offences requiring a culpable state of mind, i.e., **mens rea**. However, although a mistake of law is no defence, a mistake of fact may arise from a misinterpretation of the law and may operate as a valid defence to a criminal prosecution. M. Manning & P. Sankoff, *Criminal Law* (4th ed. 2009), c. 9. See **officially induced error**.

MISTRIAL An erroneous or **nugatory trial**. A trial that is ended because of lack of **jurisdiction**, error in **procedure** or disregard of some other fundamental process before or during the trial. It does not result in a **judgment** for any party, but merely indicates a failure of the trial.

MITIGATING CIRCUMSTANCES Factors that tend to make an offence less serious and that can be taken into account to reduce the sentence that would otherwise be imposed on the offender. For example, that the offender is young can be a mitigating factor. Compare **aggravating circumstances**.

MITIGATION OF DAMAGES A requirement that one who seeks to recover damages by reason of a **breach of contract** or another's **tort** exercise reasonable diligence and care to avoid aggravating the injury or increasing the **damages**. The duty to mitigate damages, though not a duty in the sense that its breach will give rise to a **cause of action** against the person who violates it, expresses the general rule that one who was wronged must act reasonably to avoid or limit losses and cannot recover damages that could reasonably have been avoided. See generally *Southcott Estates Inc. v. Toronto Catholic District School Board*, 2012 SCC 51.

M'NAGHTEN RULE The **common-law** rule or test that was applied in establishing a defence of **mental disorder** as announced by the House of Lords in *M'Naghten's Case* (1843), 10 Cl. & Fin. 200; 8 E.R. 718 (H.L.). Under this rule an accused person was not criminally responsible if, at the time of committing the act, he or she was suffering from such mental disease or defect that he or she was unable to understand what he or she was doing or that it was wrong or if he or she committed an offence while laboring under a partial delusion (but is not in other respects insane) that, if true, would have provided a good defence. The test of mental disorder as a defence for purposes of Canadian criminal law is now covered by s. 16 of the *Criminal Code,* R.S.C. 1985, c. C–46.

MOBILITY RIGHTS See **Canadian Charter of Rights and Freedoms**.

MODIFIED OBJECTIVE TEST A form of the **objective** test that takes into account personal attributes of the accused such as age, experience, and education in order to make the standard of care higher or lower. It is contrasted with a uniform objective test, which holds all accused to the same standard whatever their personal characteristics. A modified objective test is not to be used in assessing whether the **mens rea** for an objective fault crime has been made out but is to be used in assessing the objective elements of a **defence**. *R. v. Hibbert*, [1995] 2 S.C.R. 973.

The Supreme Court of Canada has also used the term "modified objective" to describe requiring a marked departure from the **standard of care** of a reasonable person, rather than the mere departure which would satisfy the ordinary objective test, and to describe taking the surrounding circumstances into account. *R. v. Beatty*, 2008 SCC 5.

MODUS OPERANDI (*mō'-dŭs ŏp-ĕr-än'-dē*) Lat.: the manner of operation. The means of accomplishing an act; the mode or manner in which the offence was committed. Sometimes popularly referred to as the "M.O."

MOIETY A term used generally to denote the half part in contrast to *entirety,* which denotes the whole. To hold a moiety is to hold a half part. See *In re Angus' Will Trusts,* [1960] 1 W.L.R. 1296 at 1300 (Ch.D.).

MOLLITER MANUS IMPOSUIT (*mŏ'-lĭ-tĕr mä'-nŭs ĭm-pō'-zū-ĭt*) Lat.: the gentle laying of hands upon. At common law, a plea in defence to an action for **battery** whereby the defendant claimed that the battery was lawful and that he or she "laid hands upon the plaintiff gently," thereby using no more force than was necessary. Compare **self-defence**.

MONOPOLY The exclusive power vested in an individual, a combination of indi-

viduals, or a company to control a particular business or trade or the sale of a given commodity so as to prevent competition, restrict trade, and create exclusive control over prices.

The investigation and control of monopolies in Canada is governed by the *Competition Act,* R.S.C. 1985, c. C–34, as amended by R.S.C. 1985, c. 19, (2nd Supp.), which now uses the terms "abuse of dominant position" and "anti-competitive acts" when referring to the regulation of monopolies under the *Act.* See *Canada (Director of Investigation and Research) v. NutraSweet Co.* (1990), 32 C.P.R. (3d) 1 (Comp. Trib.). See **combines**.

MOOT CASE A case that seeks the determination of an abstract question not arising from currently existing facts or rights; an unsettled case presenting a topic for dispute.

MOOT COURT A court established for the purpose of arguing a **moot case**. Law students are usually required to argue fictional cases before such courts as part of their legal education.

MOOTNESS DOCTRINE "[A]n aspect of a general policy or practice that a court may decline a case which raises a merely hypothetical or abstract question. The general principal applies when the decision of the Court will not have the effect of resolving some controversy which affects or may affect the rights of the parties. If the decision of the court will have no practical effect on such rights it will decline to decide the case." *Borowski v. Canada (A.G.)*, [1989] 1 S.C.R. 342 at 353.

MORAL CONSIDERATION See **consideration**.

MORAL INVOLUNTARINESS [NORMATIVE INVOLUNTARINESS] The condition of being forced to take particular actions through overwhelming circumstances that deprive a person of any realistic choice. Although the actions are not literally **involuntary**, where circumstances are so extreme as to overwhelm normal human instincts, the behaviour is analogous to physically involuntary behaviour. As a result, it is a **principle**

of fundamental justice that a person cannot be convicted of an **offence** if his or her behaviour was morally involuntary. Moral involuntariness is the foundation of **defences** such as **necessity** or **duress**. "[I]t is a violation of s. 7 of the *Charter* to convict a person who has no realistic choice and whose behaviour is, therefore, morally involuntary." *R. v. Ryan*, 2013 SCC 3. See **involuntary**; **voluntary**.

MORAL RIGHTS Rights held by the creator of a work, which include the right to the integrity of the work and the right to be associated with the work as its creator by name or under a pseudonym, and the right to remain anonymous. In Canada, the right to the integrity of the work includes the right to prevent modifications of the work that are prejudicial to the author's honour or reputation. Moral rights remain with the creator of a work even if the work itself or copyright in it has been sold or assigned. See *Copyright Act*, R.S.C. 1985, c. C–42, s. 14.1, 14.2, 28.1, and 28.2. Planned amendments to the *Copyright Act* extend moral rights protection to performers.

MORAL TURPITUDE Baseness, corruptness, vileness, or dishonesty of a high degree. The term cuts across many areas of law and is a general disapproval of conduct. It does not necessarily connote a term of art.

MORTGAGE A conditional **conveyance** of a legal **estate** or **interest** in land or other **property** as **security** for the payment of a **debt**. The debt usually takes the form of a loan of money representing the purchase price (or a part thereof) of the property so conveyed. The party who conveys the property as security is called the MORTGAGOR whereas the party who receives the interest in such property is called the MORTGAGEE. The mortgage operates so as to rest legal ownership of the property in the mortgagee while equitable **title** remains vested in the mortgagor. Once the mortgagor has repaid the debt to the mortgagee, the mortgagor is entitled to have the security redeemed, i.e., to have the legal interest in the property transferred back to the mortgagor. This right in the mortgagor to have the legal interest in the property revert to him or her upon repayment of the debt to the mortgagee is known as the **equity of redemption**.

In several provincial jurisdictions, most notably in western Canada, a mortgage under the Land Titles or Torrens system operates as a form of security, creating a charge on land, and does not vest in the mortgagee any legal estate, registered title remaining vested in the mortgagor. See, e.g., *The Real Property Act*, C.C.S.M. 1988, c. R30, s. 1; *The Land Titles Act*, R.S.A, 2000, c. L–4, s. 1(o); *The Land Titles Act*, R.S.O. 1990, c. L. 5, uses the term *charge*, but this term is not defined. See also *Smith v. National Trust Co.* (1912), 1 D.L.R. 698 at 711–13 (S.C.C.).

CHATTEL MORTGAGE Conveyance of a present interest in **personal property**, also generally made as security for the payment of money, such as the purchase price of the property, or for the performance of some other act. The mortgage operates as a transfer of a property interest in the **chattels** to the mortgagee subject to the mortgagor's right to retain possession of the chattels. Chattel mortgages are governed by provincial Bills of Sale Acts. See, e.g., *The Personal Property Security Act*, R.S.O. 1990, c. P. 10; *Personal Property Security Act*, R.S.A. 2000, c. P–7.

EQUITABLE MORTGAGE A contract that creates an equitable charge on the property but does not transfer the legal estate to the mortgagee. Such a mortgage is enforceable under the equitable jurisdiction of the court. An equitable mortgage may be created (1) where only an equitable interest is mortgaged, (2) where the instrument executed by the mortgagor is not sufficient to transfer a legal estate or interest in the property, or (3) by a deposit of title deeds. B. Ziff, *Principles of Property Law* 434–35 (5th ed. 2010).

MORTGAGEE/MORTGAGOR See **mortgage**.

MORTIS CAUSA (*môr'-tĭs kaw'-z à*) Lat.: by reason of death. In contemplation of death. See **gift** [GIFT MORTIS CAUSA].

MORTMAIN Literally, dead hand; applies to all **property** that, from the nature of the purposes to which it is devoted, or the character of the **ownership** to which it is subjected, is for every practical purpose in a dead or unserving hand (not freely alienable). In England, *Mortmain Acts,* restricting any **alienation** of property that would limit its free circulation by means of **possession** or control by one **corporation** perpetually, constituted a response to such possession and control over lands by the Church and other ecclesiastical bodies; but the concept has been used with reference to any corporation that may hold property in perpetuity, and thus with a "dead hand."

MOTION An application to a court or judge for a direction or **order** that something be done that is for the benefit of the applicant. Generally, a motion is made by oral request of counsel in open court.

MOTIVE Ulterior intention; defined by the courts as that "which precedes and induces the exercise of the will." *R. v. Lewis,* [1979] 2 S.C.R. 821. In criminal law, proof of motive for a particular crime can be relevant but is not necessary for a conviction. The Crown is only required to prove the necessary mental element **(mens rea)** of the offence, which is distinct from motive. However, it is possible for Parliament to specify that a particular motive is necessary as part of the *mens rea* of an offence. See *R. v. Khawaja,* 2012 SCC 69. See **specific intent**.

MOTOR VEHICLE ACTS Various provincial acts that regulate the operation of motor vehicles on public highways and impose civil and quasi-**criminal** duties and liabilities on persons associated with the operation, ownership, and use of motor vehicles. Also called Highway Traffic Acts in some provinces. See, e.g., *Motor Vehicle Act,* R.S.N.S. 1989, c. 293; *Traffic Safety Act,* R.S.A. 2000, c. T–6.

MOVANT The moving party; the applicant for an **order** by way of **motion** before a court.

MOVE To make a **motion**; to make application to a court or other tribunal for a ruling, **order**, or particular **relief**.

MR. BIG STING A technique developed by the **Royal Canadian Mounted Police** for the investigation of criminal homicides. The sting involves the use of undercover police officers posing as members of a fictitious **criminal organization**, who elicit a suspect's cooperation in a number of illusory crimes in order to secure his or her trust and confidence. Eventually, they will use this relationship to induce a **confession** to the crime he or she is suspected of committing, usually as some kind of condition of entry into the organization. The name of the sting refers to the generic title of the leader of the fictional organization.

MULTIFARIOUS Characterized by **misjoinder** of parties or **causes of action** in a proceeding; the joining of wholly distinct and unconnected matters in the same action against one or more **defendants**. Modern practice favours the joining of several causes of action in the same proceeding in the interests of economy and the avoidance of a multiplicity of actions. *Nova Scotia Civil Procedure Rules,* Rule 35.

MULTIPARTITE Consisting of two or more parts or parties, as where several nations join in a treaty.

MULTIPLICITY OF SUITS [OR ACTIONS] The bringing of several different legal suits or actions against the same defendant on the same issue.

MUNICIPAL COURT An inferior court of limited **jurisdiction** established in towns or cities in some provinces, generally having jurisdiction in matters arising under municipal by-laws and over certain **civil** matters.

MUNICIPALITY A local government body established under provincial legislation, with powers delegated to it by the province. These powers include the collection of municipal taxes; local land-use regulation; and the administration of public transportation, utilities, and other local services. As creatures of statute, municipalities are subject to **judicial review** in the exercise of their powers. See, e.g., *Catalyst Paper Corp. v. North Cowichan (District)*, 2012 SCC 2.Various types of municipal governments exist in Canada, including cities, towns, townships, regional municipalities, and counties. See S.M. Mackuch, N. Craik & S.B. Leisk, *Canadian Municipal and Planning Law* (2nd ed. 2004).

MURDER At common law, the unlawful killing of another human being with **malice aforethought**. *R. v. Elnick, R. v. Clements, R. v. Burdie*, [1920] 2 W.W.R. 606 at 614–15 (Man.C.A.).

In Canada, if a person, directly or indirectly, by any means, causes the death of a human being, he or she has committed a **homicide**. *Criminal Code*, R.S.C. 1985, c. C–46, s. 222(1). Homicide is either culpable or not culpable, and only **culpable** homicide is an **offence**. To amount to murder, culpable homicide must fall within the terms of s. 229 of the *Criminal Code*, R.S.C. 1985, c. C–46. That section sets out various ways that the **mens rea** for murder can be satisfied, but all of those ways require **subjective** foresight of the death on the part of the **accused**; the provisions that had allowed **constructive murder** have been found to violate the **Canadian Charter of Rights and Freedoms**.

Murder in the first degree may be defined as an unlawful killing that is planned and deliberate or the victim of which is a police officer, prison employee, or other person employed for the preservation and maintenance of the public peace, while he or she was acting in the course of his duties. There are several other factors that, combined with the requirement for subjective fault, cause murder to be classified as first-degree murder; see ss. 231(2)–(6.2).

All murder that does not come within the definition of first degree murder is second degree murder. *Id.,* s. 231(7).

Both first and second degree murder are **indictable offences** punishable by a mandatory sentence of life imprisonment. A person convicted of first degree murder must serve at least twenty-five years' imprisonment before being eligible for parole, while a person convicted of second degree murder is subject to a minimum term of ten years' imprisonment without eligibility for parole, or such longer period, up to twenty-five years, as the trial judge, in his or her discretion, may impose. See *id.,* s. 745 and s. 745.4.

The attempt to commit murder is also an indictable offence, and everyone who so attempts, by any means, to commit murder is liable to imprisonment for life. *Id.,* s. 239.

Culpable homicide that otherwise would be murder may be reduced to **manslaughter** if the person who committed it did so in the heat of passion caused by sudden **provocation**. *Id.,* s. 232(1).

MUTATIS MUTANDIS (*mū tă-tĭs mū tăn-dĭs*) Lat.: *Earl Jowitt's Dictionary of Law* defines *mutatis mutandis* as "with necessary changes in points of detail" and *Black's Law Dictionary*, 9th ed., "with the necessary changes." See *Re Kipnes and A.G. Alta. et al.* (1966), 4 C.C.C. 387 (Alta.C.A.).

Also, in *Re Pinetree Development Co. Ltd. and Ministry of Housing for the Province of Ontario* (1976), 14 O.R. (2d) 687, 692 (Div. Ct.) *mutatis mutandis* is stated to mean "having changed those things which ought to be changed."

MUTUALITY OF OBLIGATION The responsibilities imposed on each of the parties to a **contract**, requiring each to do something in **consideration** of the other party's act or promise. Neither party to the contract is bound unless both are bound. See *Romfo v. 1216393 Ontario Inc.*, 2008 BCCA 179.

MUTUAL LEGAL ASSISTANCE TREATY A **treaty** entered into between Canada and another **state** under the *Mutual Legal Assistance in Criminal Matters Act*, R.S.C., 1985, c. 30 (4th Supp.), whereby either state can call upon the other for assistance in the investigation and prosecution of offences.

MUTUAL MISTAKE See **mistake**.

NAFTA North American Free Trade Agreement. NAFTA is an agreement between Canada, the United States, and Mexico to eliminate tariffs on goods and services traded between the three countries and to provide for a dispute settlement mechanism. Canada and the United States had previously entered into a bilateral free trade agreement in 1988; NAFTA, which came into force in 1994, superseded it.

NARRATIVE Evidence that is introduced not to prove a live issue or to support the **prosecution's** case, but merely to complete the narrative. It is used as a tool to make the evidence comprehensible, by filling in what would otherwise be obvious gaps in the story. For example, a police officer testifying about a call to attend at an address because of an assault is merely explaining how he or she came to be at the scene; the **testimony** is not introduced to prove that an assault was taking place. Narrative evidence is sometimes spoken of as an exception to the **hearsay** rule, but this is not correct; although the evidence would be inadmissible hearsay if it were introduced for the truth of its contents, it is not hearsay because that is not the purpose. Narrative evidence can also sometimes be introduced, although the evidence would otherwise be inadmissible as a **prior consistent statement**. In that context, narrative can be introduced for the limited purpose of helping the **trier of fact** to understand how a complainant's story was initially disclosed. The evidence cannot be used directly to confirm the truthfulness of the sworn allegation, but it can be used to show the fact and timing of a complaint, which might assist the trier of fact in assessing truthfulness or credibility. See *R. v. Dinardo*, 2008 SCC 24.

NATIONAL CONCERN DOCTRINE The notion that legislative subject matters that are provincial or local in scope under the Constitution can acquire dimensions of national interest or concern thereby requiring Parliament to pass legislation in relation to it under its PEACE ORDER AND GOOD GOVERNMENT POWER (P.O.G.G.). *R. v. Crown Zellerbach Canada Ltd.* [1988] 1 S.C.R. 401.

NATIONAL EMERGENCY DOCTRINE The notion that Parliament can legislate on matters normally of local or provincial jurisdiction under its PEACE ORDER AND GOOD GOVERNMENT POWER, in times of national emergency, such as war. *Reference re Anti-Inflation Act*, [1976] 2 S.C.R. 373. P.W. Hogg, *Constitutional Law of Canada* 17–19–32 (5th ed. 2007). See generally, *Emergencies Act*, R.S.C. 1985, c. 22 (4th Supp.).

NATIONALITY PRINCIPLE A principle of international law that "allows the assertion of jurisdiction by the state of which the accused person is a national, without regard to where the offence took place." R. Currie, *International & Transnational Criminal Law* 66 (2010). See **passive personality principle**; **protective principle**; **territorial principle**; **universal jurisdiction**.

NATIVE PEOPLES See **Aboriginal peoples**.

NATIVE RIGHTS See **Aboriginal rights**.

NATURAL DEATH ACT [STATUTE] See **living will**.

NATURALIZATION 1. Process of conferring citizenship on persons born outside the country. **2.** "...the power of enacting...what shall be the rights and privileges pertaining to residents in Canada after they have been naturalized." *Union Colliery Co. of British Columbia v. Bryden,* [1899] A.C. 580 at 58 (B.C.P.C.). See also *Black v. Law Society (Alberta)*, [1989] 1 S.C.R. 591. See generally *Citizenship Act*, R.S.C. 1985, c. C–29, though "naturalization" is not a term of art in that statute.

NATURAL JUSTICE "[A] duty of procedural fairness to persons in the course of lawful interference with various of their interests, including interests in property." *Walters v. Essex County Board* *of Education* (1973), 38 D.L.R. (3d) 693 at 697 (S.C.C.). The term is generally understood to apply to statutory **tribunals** charged with adjudicating disputes between others where legal rights and **interests** may be affected. These bodies must adhere to and apply the principles of natural justice—that is, give persons specially affected by the decision a reasonable opportunity of presenting their case, listen fairly to both sides (*audi alteram partem*) and reach a decision untainted by bias. See *Wiswell v. The Metropolitan Corp. of Greater Winnipeg,* [1965] S.C.R. 512. *The Queen (Ex parte Municipal Spraying & Contracting Ltd.) v. Labour Relations Board (Nova Scotia),* [1955] 2 D.L.R. 681 at 688 (N.S.S.C.). *Nicholson v. Haldimand-Norfolk Regional Board of Commissioners of Police,* [1979] 1 S.C.R. 311.

Although the matter remains unsettled, it is generally understood that the principles of natural justice apply to statutory boards exercising only **judicial** or quasi-judicial functions, while the duty of fairness (which may be something less than natural justice) applies to those bodies exercising administrative functions. See *Calgary Power Ltd. v. Copithorne,* [1959] S.C.R. 24. *Coopers & Lybrand v. Minister of National Revenue* (1978), 24 N.R. 163 (S.C.C.). *Nicholson v. Haldimand-Norfolk Regional Board of Commissioners of Police,* [1979] 1 S.C.R. 311 at 324–28. The level of procedural fairness owed by an administrative body varies in the circumstances. *Baker v. Canada (Ministry of Citizenship and Immigration),* [1999] 2 S.C.R. 817. See **administrative fairness**.

NATURAL LAW The law of nature. Under natural law theory, this law, which is different from man-made law, is said to be set forth by God through human reason to conform human nature, meaning the whole mental, moral, and physical constitution. Knowledge of natural laws may be attained merely by the light of reason, from the facts of their essential agreeableness with the constitution of human nature. Natural law is argued to exist regardless of whether it is enacted as **positive law**.

NATURAL LAW THEORY In jurisprudence, the view that the nature and value of any legal order is best understood by studying how the **positive law** of that legal order agrees or contrasts with **natural law**.

NATURAL PERSON A human being, as opposed to an **artificial person** such as a **corporation**. Particularly in the context of **tax** law, some persons have tried without success to draw a distinction between a natural person and a person to whom laws apply. See, e.g., *R. v. Klundert* (2008), 93 O.R. (3d) 81 (Ont. C.A.).

NCRMD See **not criminally responsible by reason of mental disorder**.

NECESSARIES OF LIFE A relative term that varies according to the social status and circumstances of the parties involved. It is not restricted to the basic things generally required to preserve life, such as food, shelter, clothing, and medical attention (necessities of life) but covers those things "necessary to maintain the person in the station of life in which he finds himself." *Consumer Gas Co. v. Stewart* (1980), 31 O.R. (2d) 559 at 561 (H.C.J.(Div.Ct.)).

Section 215 of the *Criminal Code,* R.S.C. 1985, c. C–46, imposes a legal duty on persons to provide the necessaries of life in certain situations: a parent, foster parent, guardian, or head of a family has a duty to provide for a child under sixteen years of age; a married person has a duty to provide necessaries of life for his or her spouse or common-law partner; a person has a duty to provide necessaries of life to a person under his or her charge who is unable to remove himself or herself from that person's charge or provide these necessaries of life on his or her own.

NECESSARY INFERENCE The only inevitable inference that can be deduced from a proposition. It is not a "necessary inference" if one can deduce another reasonable inference. Compare **presumption**.

NECESSARY PARTY A person whose **joinder** to an action is necessary in order that complete relief may be obtained by the **party** (either plaintiff or defendant) who is joining them. "[T]hen the court in its discretion may allow him to be added as a party....It enables all matters in dispute 'to be effectually and completely determined and adjudicated upon' between all those directly concerned in the outcome." *Gurtner v. Circuit,* [1968] 1 All E.R. 328 at 332 (C.A.).

NECESSITY, DEFENCE OF In **criminal** law, excusing the defendant of **guilt** for an **offence** that was committed in circumstances of "imminent peril or danger" where there "was no reasonable legal alternative to the course of action he or she undertook." There must also be "proportionality between the harm inflicted and the harm avoided." *R. v. Latimer,* [2001] 1 S.C.R. 3. See also *Perka et al. v. R.* (1984), 42 C.R. (3d) 113 (S.C.C.).

In **tort** law, there are two types of necessity—public and private. PUBLIC NECESSITY involves the interference with private rights for the safety and convenience of the public. The individual who suffers loss receives no compensation. PRIVATE NECESSITY exists when the defendant acts to protect his or her own interest, whether to preserve his or her own life, health or property, as long as no damage occurs to another's property. When damage does occur to another's property as the result of a claim of private necessity, there is a conflict of authority. One line of authority holds that you may cause property damage in order to save lives or property of greater value. *Bell Canada v. The Ship "Mar-Tirenno"* (1974), 52 D.L.R. (3d) 702 (F.C.). The other line of authority recognizes an incomplete **privilege**. The intrusion on another's property under claim of private necessity is protected as long as it is a technical tort and no damage is committed. Once damage occurs, the party who incurs the damage must be compensated by the party who received the benefit of the intrusion. *Read v. Smith* (1836), 2 N.B.R. 173 (S.C.).

Compare **justification**.

NEGATIVE PREGNANT In **pleading**, a **denial** that implies an affirmation of a substantial fact and hence is beneficial to opponent. Thus, when only a qualification or modification is denied while the fact itself remains undenied, the denial is pregnant with the affirmation of that fact.

NEGLIGENCE "The word 'negligence' has two meanings, one restricted and one broad. In its narrow sense, it refers to an act or omission [that] falls below the standard required by society. In this context, negligence connotes more than a mere state of mind. It refers to an evaluation of a particular course of action, comparing the state of mind of the actor to that of a **reasonable person**. The second and wider meaning of negligence makes reference to a *cause of action for negligence*. Negligence in the first sense is only one fragment of this expanded meaning." A. Linden & B. Feldthusen, *Canadian Tort Law* 114 (9th ed. 2011). An action for negligence has several elements that must be proven by the **plaintiff**. First, the **defendant** must have owed a **duty of care** to the plaintiff. Second, the defendant must have breached the **standard of care** required of a **reasonable person** in the circumstances. Third, the plaintiff must have suffered a loss of a type the law will recognise. Finally, the defendant's breach of the standard of care must have caused the plaintiff's loss in both fact and law. For the defendant to have caused the plaintiff's loss *in fact* means that the loss would not have occurred but for his or her breach of the standard of care. For the defendant to have caused the plaintiff's loss *in law* means that the loss was not too "remote" from the breach. *Mustapha v. Culligan of Canada Ltd.,* 2008 SCC 27. See **malfeasance; misfeasance; nonfeasance**.

CONTRIBUTORY NEGLIGENCE Conduct on the part of plaintiff that falls below the standard of care to which he or she should conform for his or her own protection and that, when combined with defendant's negligence, was a legally contributing cause bringing about the plaintiff's harm or injury. At common law the defendant can raise contributory negligence as a defence to a negligence action brought by the plaintiff against him or her, thereby alleging that the plaintiff's own negligence directly caused or contributed to his or her own injuries. As a defence, the **burden of proof** is on the defendant. Contributory negligence legislation has been enacted in all the common-law provinces. See, e.g., *The Negligence Act,* R.S.O. 1990, c. N. 1. Generally, the legislation apportions damages to reflect the degree of fault of each party, and if the degree of fault cannot be determined decisively, fault and damages will be split equally. A. Linden & B. Feldthusen, *Canadian Tort Law* 503 (9th ed. 2011). Compare **assumption of the risk.**

CRIMINAL [CULPABLE] NEGLIGENCE Such negligence as is necessary to incur criminal liability. "(1) Every one is criminally negligent who (a) in doing anything, or (b) in omitting to do anything that it is his duty to do, shows wanton or reckless disregard for the lives or safety of other persons. (2) For the purposes of this section, 'duty' means a duty imposed by law." *Criminal Code,* R.S.C., 1985, c. C–46, s. 219. In the context of criminal negligence where there is a duty to provide necessaries, the Crown must prove that the "omission represented *a marked and substantial departure* (as opposed to a *marked departure*) from the conduct of a reasonably prudent parent in circumstances where the accused either recognized and ran an obvious and serious risk to the life of his child or, alternatively, gave no thought to that risk." *R. v. J.F.,* 2008 SCC 60.

NEGLIGENCE PER SE Negligence as a matter of law. Frequently used in relation to a breach of a safety **statute** where violation would be regarded as statutory negligence." Fleming, J.G. *The Law of Torts,* 566 (9th ed. 1998). The terms *negligence per se* and *statutory negligence* are sometimes used interchangeably. *Ritchie and Colvin v. Ptaff,* [1954] O.W.N. 865 (C.A.); *The Lionel v. The Manchester Merchant,* [1970] S.C.R. 538.

NEGLIGENT INVESTIGATION A **tort** action requiring a police officer to meet the **standard of care** of a reasonable police officer in similar circumstances in investigating an alleged **offence.**

NEGOTIATE In reference to a **bill of exchange,** to transfer for value by **delivery** or **endorsement** for a valuable **consideration.** In **contract** law, the process preceding contract formation in a bilateral relationship. Negotiation ends when one or both parties terminate the interaction short of contract formation or when a contract is formed.

NEGOTIABLE INSTRUMENT An instrument that passes by delivery giving the **bona fide** holder for value a good **title.** A bona fide holder of the instrument for value is known as a **holder in due course,** and he or she holds it free from any claims, defects, or equities affecting the title of the transferor. A negotiable instrument usually contains an obligation or unconditional **promise** by the **maker** to pay a certain sum of money at a definite time to the holder or bearer of the instrument. A transfer of the instrument may operate as a complete legal transfer of the document and obligation which is enforceable by the transferee. **Bills of exchange, cheques,** and **promissory notes** are the most important kind of negotiable instruments. "A negotiable instrument is an unconditional promise to pay on demand or at a particular time." *Bank Leu AG v. Gaming Lottery Corp.* (2003), 175 O.A.C. 143.

NEIGHBOUR PRINCIPLE Basic rule in the law of negligence for determining whether there is a sufficient relationship of proximity between the defendant and the plaintiff to create a duty of care. It is based on the idea that every person has a duty of care to his or her neighbour, defined as "persons who are so closely and directly affected by my act that I ought reasonably to have them in contemplation when I am directing my mind to the acts or omissions which are called into question." *M'Alister (or Donoghue) v. Stevenson,* [1932] A.C. 562.

NEMO DAT QUOD NON HABET [NEMO DAT RULE] (*nā-mō dăt qwŏd nŏn hăbĕt*) Lat.: one cannot give that which one does not have. Commonly referred to as the NEMO DAT RULE, it means that a seller cannot transfer a better title than he or she actually possesses. Under this rule, the buyer of the property takes on the risk that the seller can in fact give good title. Some exceptions to *nemo dat* do exist for **bona fide purchasers** for value without notice where the transaction involves currency, **negotiable instruments**, voidable title, **factors**, or special statutory regulations. B. Ziff, *Principles of Property Law*, 458–59 (5th ed. 2010). See **equity's darling**.

NEMO EST SUPRA LEGIS (*nā'-mō ĕst sū'-prá lā'-gĭs*) Lat.: nobody is above the law.

NEMO JUDEX IN CAUSA SUA DEBET ESSE (*nā'-mō jū'-dĕks ĭn kaw'-zá sū'-à dĕ'-bĕt ĕ'-sĕ*) Lat.: no one ought to be a judge in one's own cause. Usually referred to as the second limb of the principles of **natural justice**, the rules against bias do not require the courts to look for proof of actual bias. To determine whether there was a **reasonable apprehension of bias**, the courts ask what would the reasonable and rightminded person conclude, having "a certain amount of knowledge about the relevant process and the adjudicator under scrutiny." D. Mullan, *Administrative Law* 327 (2001). See S. Blake, *Administrative Law in Canada* 105–21 (5th ed. 2011).

NERVOUS SHOCK Psychiatric damage caused by severe emotional upset that leads to an identifiable illness and gives a **cause of action** in **tort** law. Grief and sorrow are not included under this tort, and it is not meant to compensate for unusual injuries suffered by those who are particularly vulnerable to mental injury: "The question is what a person of ordinary fortitude would suffer." *Mustapha v. Culligan of Canada Ltd.*, 2008 SCC 27. Liability depends not only on the type of damage, but also on whether "'psychiatric damage' suffered was a reasonably foreseeable consequence of the negligent conduct." A. Linden & B. Feldthusen, *Canadian Tort Law* 432 (9th ed. 2011). See *Alcock v. Chief Constable of South Yorkshire*

Police, [1991] 4 All E.R. 907 (H.L.); *Page v. Smith*, [1995] 2 All E.R. 736 (H.L.); A. Linden & B. Feldthusen, *Canadian Tort Law* (9th ed. 2011), c. 11.

NET ESTATE The total value of a person's estate after liabilities have been deducted from assets. The concept is relevant to **succession**. See, e.g., *Succession Law Reform Act*, R.S.O. 1990, c. S.26, s. 72.

NET INCOME Gross income after all deductions and exemptions. See *Oryx Realty Corp. v. M.N.R.*, [1974] C.T.C. 430 (F.C.A.).

NEWLY BORN CHILD refers to a person under one year of age. *Criminal Code*, R.S.C. 1985, c. C–46, s. 2.

NEW MATTER In pleading, issues raised by the **defendant**, which are more than denials of the **plaintiff's** allegations, encompassing new issues and new facts to be proven. New matter implies that the alleged **cause of action** never did exist and that the essential allegations are not the truth.

NEXT FRIEND "[I]n all cases where a party cannot sue for himself, the court employs a prochein amy as its officer to conduct the suit for him...." *Morgan v. Thorne* (1841), 7 M. & W. 400 at 409; 151 E.R. 821 at 825 (Ex.). This officer of the court, originally known as a "prochein amy," was later named by the Chancery Division *next friend*, and the term became applied universally. Generally, persons under legal disability, such as infants, could only bring an action by their next friend. See, e.g., *Weir v. Weir*, [1939] 1 D.L.R. 57 (Man.K.B.) The term *next friend* is not used often in Canada, being replaced in many jurisdictions by GUARDIAN AD LITEM. The **guardian** *ad litem* performs the same functions as the next friend; i.e., he or she commences or defends proceedings on behalf of a minor or a mentally incompetent person. See *Nova Scotia Civil Procedure Rules*, Rule 36.

NEXT OF KIN Refers to the nearest in blood, "... and not to the statutory next of kin, unless the testator has in some way referred to the statutory as distinct from common law kinship." *Re Young*

(1928), 62 O.L.R. 275 at 278 (Ont.S.C.). See also *Fasken v. Fasken*, [1953] 2 S.C.R. 10 at 14-15; *Re Jardin Estate, Re Carey Estate, Royal Trust Company v. Jardine* (1956), 18 W.W.R. (N.S.) 445 at 449–50 (Alta.S.C.A.D.).

NGO Non-governmental organization. An NGO is typically legally constituted, for example, by registration as a society, and it operates independently of government and will have a focus on some particular area or activity. Many NGOs are devoted to social, economic, or environmental concerns. Examples of NGOs operating in Canada include Médecins Sans Frontières, the Sierra Club Canada, the Canadian Centre for Ethics in Sport, and Habitat for Humanity.

NIHIL (*nī'-hĭl*) Lat.: nothing, not at all, in no respect. Nil is an often used form to express the noun.

NIL See **nihil**.

NISI PRIUS (*nī'-sī prē'-ŭs*) Lat.: unless before. A trial at *nisi prius* was a jury trial before a single judge as opposed to actions tried at the bar, that is, before the full court, which consisted of several judges. Trial at nisi prius followed after the sheriff was commanded to bring the jurors from the county where the cause of action arose to the court at Westminster "unless before" that day [*nisi prius*] the justices of assize came to that county.

NO FORCE AND EFFECT Under s. 52 of the *Constitution Act, 1982,* any law which is inconsistent with the provisions of the *Constitution Act, 1982* (which includes the **Canadian Charter of Rights and Freedoms**) is, to the extent of the inconsistency, of no force and effect. Laws and provisions which are of no force and effect are commonly referred to as being "struck down." See *R. v. Wholesale Travel Group Inc.* (1991), 8 C.R. (4th) 145 (S.C.C.). See **notwithstanding clause**.

NOLLE PROSEQUI (*nŏl'- à prŏs'-ē-kwē*) Lat.: unwilling to proceed. The authority conferred by the *Criminal Code,* R.S.C. 1985, c. C–46, s. 579(1), upon the **Attorney-General** to grant a stay of

proceedings upon an indictment termed under the common law "entering a *nolle prosequi."* This proceeding does not operate as an acquittal but merely suspends the proceedings. *R. v. Imperial Tobacco Co. of Canada, Ltd.,* [1942] 1 W.W.R. 363 at 368–69 (Alta.S.C.A.D.) *R. v. Spence* (1919), 31 C.C.C. 365 (Ont. S.C.A.D.). Any proceedings stayed may be recommenced without laying a new charge or preferring a new indictment by the Crown giving notice to the clerk of the court in which the stay of proceedings was entered. However, notice must be given within one year after the entry of the stay; otherwise the proceedings shall be deemed never to have been commenced. *Criminal Code,* R.S.C. 1985, c. C–46, a. 579(2). See **stay**.

NOLO CONTENDERE (*nō'–lō kŏn-těn'-dě-rā*) Lat.: I do not wish to contend. A plea whereby the accused does not contest the facts alleged and accepts a finding of guilt, but at the same time does not admit that the facts are true. The plea is not permitted in Canada: *Criminal Code*, R.S.C. 1985, c. C–46, s. 606.

NOMINAL DAMAGES See **damages**.

NOMINAL PARTY See **party**.

NON COMPOS MENTIS (*nŏn kŏm'-pōs měn'-tĭs*) Lat.: of unsound mind; insane. *Ex parte Barnsley* (1744), 3 Atk. 168 at 171; 26 E.R. 899 at 900 (Ch.); *Re Kelly* (1875), 6 P.R. 220 (Ch.Cham.).

NON-CONFORMING USE A **use** of land or buildings that lawfully existed prior to the enactment of a **zoning** by-law and that does not conform to the by-law enacted but may continue to exist as a non-conforming use. *Re M M Project Management Services Inc.,* 2012 BCSC 47. Many provinces have enacted planning acts or similar legislation that gives protection to a non-conforming use of land or buildings. See, e.g., *The Planning Act,* R.S.O. 1990, c. P. 13. Compare **variance**.

NON-CUSTODIAL SENTENCE See **probation**.

NON-DISCLOSURE In insurance law, the failure of the assured to bring to the notice of the insurers a material fact he or she is under a duty to reveal. Non-disclosure can result in the insurer being entitled to void the insurance contract. *Sagl v. Cosburn, Griffiths & Brandham Insurance Brokers Ltd.*, 2009 ONCA 388.

NON EST FACTUM (*nŏn ĕst făk'-tŭm*) Lat.: it is not his deed. The old common-law defence that allows a person who has signed a written document in ignorance of its character to plead that, notwithstanding his or her signature, "it is not his deed." See *Farrell Estates Ltd. v. Win-Up Restaurant Ltd.*, 2010 BCSC 1752. *Marvco Color Research v. Harris,* [1982] 2 S.C.R. 774.

NON-EXCULPATORY DEFENCES "Defences" that afford an accused with the means to avoid conviction for reasons unrelated to his or her guilt; i.e. **officially induced error, abuse of process**.

NONFEASANCE The neglect or failure to do some act that ought to be done; e.g., failing to clear a sidewalk of ice and snow. See *Childs v. Desormeaux*, 2006 SCC 18. It differs from **misfeasance**, which is the improper performance of an act one may lawfully do.

NON OBSTANTE VEREDICTO [N.O.V.] (*nŏn ŏb-stän'-tā vĕr-ĕ-dĭk'-tō*) Lat.: notwithstanding the verdict. See **judgment** [JUDGMENT N.O.V.].

NON-PERFORMANCE Generally, the failure to keep the terms of a **contract** rendering the party failing to do so liable to the innocent party in damages for breach of contract.

NON-PROFIT ORGANIZATION Under the *Income Tax Act*, R.S.C. 1985, c. 1, s. 1, a club, society, or association that is not a charity but is organized and operated exclusively for social welfare, civic improvement, pleasure, or recreation, or for any other purpose except profit, and no part of the income of which is payable to any proprietor, member, or shareholder of the organization.

NON-REBUTTABLE PRESUMPTION See **presumption** [CONCLUSIVE PRESUMPTION].

NON-REPAIR The failure to keep a bridge or roadway in a fit state of repair. In some provinces, a municipality is not liable at common law for injury caused by non-repair, but can be liable by statute. See, e.g., *Municipal Act*, R.S.O. 1990, c. M.45, s. 284. See, e.g., *Cartner v. Burlington*, 2010 ONCA 407.

NONRESIDENCE, NONRESIDENT Nonresident is the condition applied to a person who is not ordinarily resident in Canada. Nonresident means not resident in Canada. *Income Tax Act*, R.S.C. 1985, c. 1 (5th Supp.), s. 248(1) as amended; *Erikson v. M.N.R.,* [1980] C.T.C. 2117 (T.R.B.). Residence sometimes represents one of the qualifications of a director of a corporation. See *Canadian Business Corporations Act*, R.S.C. 1985, c. C–44, s. 105(3).

NON SEQUITUR (*nŏn sĕ'-kwĭ-tūr*) Lat.: it does not follow; often abbreviated non seq. When an action or decree is non sequitur, it is unrelated to the preceding events. A non sequitur is something that has no logical or temporal purpose for its place in the progression of events; it is logically, temporally, and spatially incoherent.

NON SUI JURIS (*nŏn sū'-ē jū'-rĭs*) Lat.: not by his own authority or legal right. This maxim refers to those who are not legally **competent** to manage their own affairs as regards **contracts** and other causes in which this **incompetency** restricts their granting **power of attorney** or otherwise exercising self-judgment. Compare **non compos mentis**.

NONSUIT A **judgment** rendered against a plaintiff, dismissing his or her action on the basis that the evidence presented by the plaintiff is not sufficient to make out a **prima facie case**. The term is generally used in **civil** proceedings; compare **directed verdict**, which applies to **criminal** matters. The word "nonsuit" was once a term of art, referring before 1883 to the abandonment of a case at the trial before the jury gave their verdict. The **civil procedure** rules of the various provinces and territories do not use the term "nonsuit" in describing such an application to dismiss an action, but the term is commonly used in judgments. In assessing a nonsuit application, the trial judge assumes the evidence presented is true and gives the most favourable meaning to evidence capable of giving rise to competing inferences. If, on that basis, the plaintiff has put forward some evidence on all elements of its claim, the judge must dismiss the motion; if not, the motion is granted. See *Johansson v. General Motors of Canada Ltd.*, 2012 NSCA 120. See SUMMARY JUDGMENT (**judgment**).

NON-STATUS INDIANS A term used to describe those Indians who are not entitled to be registered under the *Indian Act*, R.S.C. 1985, c. I–5 and are therefore not accorded the same rights and responsibilities as those who are. See **non-treaty Indians**.

NON-TREATY INDIANS A term used in previous versions of the *Indian Act*, R.S.C. 1985, c. I–5. For example, the *Indian Act, 1876,* S.C. 1876, c. 18 defined a non-treaty Indian as "any person of Indian blood who is reputed to belong to an irregular band, or who follows the Indian mode of life, even though such person be only a temporary resident in Canada." The term no longer has a technical meaning. See **Aboriginal rights**; **treaty Indian**.

NONUSER A person who may lose a right acquired by use. The term is mainly used with reference to **easements**, **profits à prendre** (the right to take the production of another's land), and similar rights. Such rights may be extinguished by the nonuser for a certain number of years, but not fewer than twenty years. The nonuser must show an intention to cease to exercise a right or must neglect to use it.

NORTH AMERICAN FREE TRADE AGREEMENT See **NAFTA**.

NORWICH ORDER An equitable remedy allowing for discovery against a third party before an action is commenced. "[A]n action for discovery may be allowed against an 'involved' third party who has information that the claimant alleges would allow it to identify a wrongdoer, so as to enable the claimant

to bring an action against the wrongdoer where the claimant would otherwise not be able to do so." *GEA Group AG v. Flex-N-Gate Corporation*, 2009 ONCA 619. Such an order was first granted in *Norwich Pharmacal Co. v. Comrs. of Customs and Excise,* [1974] A.C. 133 (H.L.).

NOSCITUR A SOCIIS (*nō'-sĭ-tūr à sō'-sē-ĭs*) Lat.: The meaning of a word can be understood by its companions. One can get the meaning of a word from its accompanying words or by reference to the meaning of words or phrases associated with it. "English words derive colour from those which surround them." *Borne v. Norwich Crematorium Ltd.,* [1967] 2 All E.R. 576 at 578 Ch.). The maxim is generally applied as an aid to interpretation of statutory language. "When two or more words susceptible of analogous meaning, are coupled together, *noscitur a sociis;* they are understood to be used in their cognate sense. They take, as it were, their colour from each other; that is the more general is restricted to a sense analogous to the less general." *Fraser v. Pere Marquette R.W. Co.* (1908), 18 O.L.R. 589 at 602 (C.A.); *The Queen v. France* (1898), 1 C.C.C. 321 at 331–32 (Que.Q.B.).

NOTA BENE (*nō'-tà bā'-nā*) Lat.: note or mark well. Usually written *N.B.,* it is used to call attention to something important in a text.

NOTARY PUBLIC A person authorized to administer oaths, take affidavits, and execute, authenticate or certify documents or copies of documents. In most provincial jurisdictions private persons may receive permission to act as notaries or may be appointed by the provincial Lieutenant-Governor. In some provinces a lawyer admitted to practice within the jurisdiction can act as a notary public. See, e.g., *Notaries and Commissioners Act,* R.S.N.S. 1989, c. 312, s. 11. For variations in appointment of notaries compare *Notaries and Commissioners Act,* R.S.N.S. 1989, c. 312; *Notaries Public Act,* R.S.A. 2000, c. N–6; *Notaries Public Act,* R.S.S. 1978, c. N–8; *Notaries Act,* R.S.B.C. 1996, c. 334.

NOT CRIMINALLY RESPONSIBLE

NOT CRIMINALLY RESPONSIBLE BY REASON OF MENTAL DISORDER A verdict in the *Criminal Code*, R.S.C. 1985, c. C–46, whereby a person who could otherwise be convicted of an offence is found, by reason of a mental disorder, to be not criminally responsible. A person found not criminally responsible is sent to a **review board**, which decides whether to release the person unconditionally, to release the person on conditions, or to detain the person in custody in a hospital. See **mental disorder**.

NOT GUILTY As a plea, the alternative to pleading guilty. The plea does not assert that the accused is **factually innocent**, but merely puts the **Crown** to the proof of all of the elements of the offence. A not guilty plea raises all grounds of **defence**. *Criminal Code*, R.S.C. 1985, c. C–46, s. 613. Other than the **special pleas** of **autrefois acquit**, **autrefois convict**, and **pardon**, not guilty is the only plea other than guilty.

As a **verdict**, a finding of not guilty is the only alternative to a conviction. "The criminal trial is to determine whether the Crown has proven its case beyond a reasonable doubt. If so, the accused is guilty. If not, the accused is found not guilty. There is no finding of factual innocence since it would not fall within the ambit or purpose of criminal law." *R. v. Mullins-Johnson*, 2007 ONCA 720, quoting *The Lamer Commission of Inquiry Pertaining to the Cases of: Ronald Dalton, Gregory Parsons, Randy Druken*.

NOTICE 1. Information or knowledge regarding a fact actually brought to a person's attention; **2.** also, the **service** of a document on a **defendant** in an action that has been commenced against him or her.

Notice may be *actual (express), constructive,* or *implied.* Actual notice is express notice when any fact is conveyed to a person either in writing or by oral communication.

ACTUAL NOTICE "[A]ctual notice [is] knowledge, not presumed as in the case of constructive notice, but shown to be actually brought home to the party charged with it, either by proof of his own admission or by the evidence of witnesses who are able to establish that the very fact, of which notice is to be established, not something which would have led to the discovery of the fact if an enquiry had been pursued, was brought to his knowledge." *Coventry Homes Inc. v. Beaumont (Town) Subdivision and Development Appeal Board*, 2001 ABCA 49, quoting *Rose v. Peterkin* (1885), 13 S.C.R. 677 at 694.

CONSTRUCTIVE NOTICE Knowledge of a fact imputed by law to a person, even though he or she may not have actual knowledge of it, since the circumstances should have put him or her on inquiry. In addition, in some provinces, registration of a **conveyance** of an **interest** in land is deemed to give notice of that interest to all persons who later receive an interest in that land. See, e.g., *The Registry Act*, R.S.O. 1990, c. R.20, s. 74; *The Registry Act*, C.C.S.M. c. R.50, s. 53. However, the same is not necessarily true of registration of personal property. "A first-to-register rule rests on a notion that registration constitutes 'notice to all,' a concept [that] has been abolished under the **PPSA**. As Jackson J.A. explained (para. 31):

> Registration, in the context of the PPSA, does not serve this purpose. While its incidental purpose is to permit prospective creditors to search debtor names, and certain types of personal property by virtue of serial numbers, the fundamental effect of registration is to establish priorities by virtue of the time of registration, and for the purposes of the PPSA only. Registration no longer constitutes actual or constructive notice in the context of the PPSA. Section 47 of the PPSA abolishes that concept."

Bank of Montreal v. Innovation Credit Union, 2010 SCC 47.

IMPLIED NOTICE A variety of actual notice that arises where the existence of a fact is within the knowledge of a party so that he or she is put upon inquiry and can discover the true facts by making reasonable inquiry. For example, in the law of **agency**, notice can be implied or imputed by law to the **principal** when notice of any issue or matter is given to an **agent** when the matter is within the scope of his or her agency. The principal cannot deny notice except to charge that the agent is in collusion with the party claiming such notice. See generally *Cave v. Cave* (1880), 15 Ch.D. 639 at 643–44; *Berwick & Co. v. Price,* [1905] 1 Ch. 632 at 639.

JUDICIAL NOTICE See **judicial notice**.

NOTICE OF APPEAL A written notice that follows the Rules of Practice of the appropriate appellate court, given by a **litigant** to the other party and listing the grounds of his or her appeal from a court's verdict.

NOTICE OF ASSESSMENT A notice from a taxing authority—for example, the Minister of Revenue under the *Income Tax Act* or, in a municipal corporation, the clerk in regard to real property situated within the boundaries of the municipal unit—whereby a taxpayer is informed of the tax assessment owed by him or her. See *Income Tax Act,* R.S.C. 1985, c. 1 (5th Supp.), s. 152(2)

NOTICE OF DISHONOUR In regard to **bills of exchange**, a notice given by the payee or endorsee thereof, to all concerned other than the acceptor that the bill was not honoured at presentment. Notice of dishonour is required in order that parties to the bill can protect themselves by taking up the bill and commencing action against the party ultimately responsible upon it. See *Bills of Exchange Act,* R.S.C. 1985, c. B–4, s. 101.

NOTICE OF MOTION In an action, a written notice that one party wishing to undertake an **interlocutory** proceeding serves on other interested parties to the litigation instructing the others of the relief that is sought from the court, and including the time, date, and location where the motion is to be heard. The form and particulars of such notice are regulated by the Rules of Practice of the appropriate courts. See, e.g., *Ontario Rules of Civil Procedure,* R.R.O. 1990, Reg. 194, r. 37.06; *Rules of Court, New Brunswick,* N.B. Reg. 82–73, r. 37. Not all provincial rules make use of this term. See, e.g., *Supreme Court Civil Rules*, B.C. Reg. 168/2009.

NOTICE TO QUIT A notice of the termination of a tenancy given by either a landlord or a tenant. The form and particulars of such notices are regulated by the relevant provincial statutes relating to landlords and tenants. See, e.g., *Residential Tenancies Act,* R.S.N.S. 1989, c. 401, s. 10; *Landlord and Tenant Act,* R.S.N.B. 1973, c. L–1, s. 19; *Landlord and Tenant Act,* R.S.P.E.I. 1988, c. L–4, s. 77. In some provincial jurisdictions the term *notice of termination* is used. See *Residential Tenancies Act, 2004,* S.A. 2004, c. R–17.1.

NOTORIOUS POSSESSION Occupation of **real property** in an open undisguised and conspicuous manner, so that such possession is well known and recognized. The term is one of the elements in defining or determining a claim of **adverse possession** that involves an assertion of a right to property not by legal **title** but by possession and occupation for a period of time governed by statute (at least twenty years under provincial Statutes of Limitations). The possession is required to be actual, continuous and notorious so that the titleholder without actual **notice** of such possession may be presumed in law to have received notice. See, e.g., *Spicer v. Bowater Mersey Paper Co.*, 2004 NSCA 39.

Where an **interest** in an **easement** is claimed to have been acquired by **prescription** (having acquired an interest through continuous use for a period of twenty years rather than by legal right or title), it must be shown, in addition to use for the required period, that use of the easement was such that it could be said to be *nec vi, nec clam, nec precario*—i.e., not by violence, not secretly but by open and notorious use, and not by request or permission of the owner of the land over which the claim is being asserted. See *Kaminskas v. Storm et al.,* 2009 ONCA 318.

NOTWITHSTANDING CLAUSE Section 33 of the **Canadian Charter of Rights and Freedoms** permits **Parliament** or a **provincial** legislature to "expressly declare in an Act of Parliament or of the legislature, as the case may be, that the Act or a provision thereof shall operate notwithstanding a provision included in section 2 or sections 7 to 15 of this Charter." Section 2 sets out the **fundamental freedoms**, while ss. 7 to 15 guarantee **legal rights** and **equality** rights. Any such declaration ceases to have effect after five years unless it is re-enacted.

The government of Quebec used the notwithstanding clause (also called the override clause) to require French-only business signs in that province, thus overriding the *Charter* guarantee of **freedom of expression**. See *Ford v. Quebec (A.G.)*, [1988] 2 S.C.R. 712. Generally, the notwithstanding clause is very infrequently invoked.

N.O.V. See **judgment** [JUDGMENT N.O.V.].

NOVATION Agreement of one **party** to a **contract** to the substitution of a new party to replace one of the original parties to the contract. The result is a new contract on the same terms as the old, but with a new party. A common example is where a creditor at the request of the debtor agrees to the substitution of another party as debtor in place of the original debtor. "A novation is a trilateral agreement by which an existing contract is extinguished and a new contract brought into being in its place. Indeed, for an agreement to effect a valid novation, the appropriate consideration is the discharge of the original debt in return for a promise to perform some obligation. The assent of the beneficiary (the creditor or mortgagee) of those obligations to the discharge and substitution is crucial. This is because the effect of novation is that the creditor may no longer look to the original party if the obligations under the substituted contract are not subsequently met as promised." *National Trust Co. v. Mead*, [1990] 2 S.C.R. 410. Novation requires that three conditions are met: (1) the new debtor assumes the complete liability; (2) the creditor accepts the new debtor as the principal debtor, not merely as an agent or guarantor; and (3) the creditor accepts the new contract

in full satisfaction and substitution for the old contract.

NOVELTY "[A] common sense and logical principle that if a jurisdiction concerning a subject matter did not exist in 1867, then it is not a jurisdiction that our case law requires be exercised by an s. 96 superior court judge." *Reference re Amendments to the Residential Tenancies Act (N.S.)*, [1996] 1 S.C.R. 186.

NOVUS ACTUS INTERVENIENS See **cause** [SUPERSEDING CAUSE].

NUDUM PACTUM (*nu'-dum päk'-tŭm*) Lat.: a nude **contract**. A bare agreement; a bare **promise** made without **consideration**. A bare contract is not enforceable unless made under **seal**. See, e.g., *Baker v. British Columbia Insurance Co.*, 76 B.C.L.R. (2d) 367 (B.C.C.A.).

NUGATORY Void; of no effect; invalid. For example, **judicial proceedings** in a court that lacks **jurisdiction** are sometimes considered nugatory. Compare **voidable**.

NUISANCE An act or omission, causing injury to a person's health, comfort, or convenience, or impairing the **use** and enjoyment of one's property and giving rise to an action for damages. Unlike **negligence**, where the damage must be shown to have been caused by some want of care, in nuisance it is the injury itself that gives rise to an action for damages.

There are two kinds of nuisance, public and private. A PUBLIC NUISANCE is an act that interferes with a right enjoyed by all members of the community. A PRIVATE NUISANCE is an interference with the use or enjoyment of a person's land or of rights in the land. "Private nuisance is the unreasonable interference with an occupier's use and enjoyment of his or her land. In *St. Lawrence Cement Inc. v. Barrette*, 2008 SCC 64, [2008] 3 S.C.R. 392, at para. 77 the Supreme Court summarized the description of the tort by several well-known academics:

At common law, nuisance is a field of liability that focuses on the harm suffered rather than on prohibited conduct (A. M. Linden and B. Feldthusen,

Canadian Tort Law (8th ed. 2006), at p. 559; L. N. Klar, *Tort Law* (2nd ed. 1996), at p. 535). Nuisance is defined as unreasonable interference with the use of land (Linden and Feldthusen, at p. 559; Klar, at p. 535). Whether the interference results from intentional, negligent, or non-faulty conduct is of no consequence provided that the harm can be characterized as a nuisance (Linden and Feldthusen, at p. 559). The interference must be intolerable to an ordinary person (p. 568). This is assessed by considering factors such as the nature, severity, and duration of the interference; the character of the neighbourhood; the sensitivity of the plaintiff's use; and the utility of the activity (p. 569). The interference must be substantial, which means that compensation will not be awarded for trivial annoyances (Linden and Feldthusen, at p. 569; Klar, at p. 536).

Public nuisance is the unreasonable interference with the use and enjoyment of a public right. *In Ryan v. Victoria (City)*, [1999] 1 S.C.R. 201, 168 D.L.R. (4th) 513, at para. 52, the Court described it in these terms:

[52] The doctrine of public nuisance appears as a poorly understood area of the law. 'A public nuisance has been defined as any activity [that] unreasonably interferes with the public's interest in questions of health, safety, morality, comfort, or convenience': see Klar, *supra*, at p. 525. Essentially, '[t]he conduct complained of must amount to . . . an attack upon the rights of the public generally to live their lives unaffected by inconvenience, discomfort, or other forms of interference': See G. H. L. Fridman, *The Law of Torts in Canada*, Vol. I (1989), at p. 168. An individual may bring a private action in public nuisance by pleading and proving special damage. See, e.g., *Chessie v. J. D. Irving Ltd.* (1982), 22 C.C.L.T. 89 (N.B.C.A.). Such actions commonly involve allegations of unreasonable interference with a public right of way, such as a street or highway. See *ibid.*, at p. 94.

The same conduct may constitute both a public nuisance and a private nuisance. Ordinarily, an action in public nuisance must be brought in the name of the Attorney-General. Individuals may, however, bring an action in public nuisance if they can prove special damage unique to them. Compare **right to farm legislation**.

A COMMON NUISANCE occurs where one commits "an unlawful act or fails to discharge a legal duty and thereby (a) endangers the lives, safety, health, property, or comfort of the public or (b) obstructs the public in the exercise or enjoyment of any right that is common to all the subjects of Her Majesty in Canada." *Criminal Code*, R.S.C. 1985, c. C–46, s. 180(2). Under s. 180(1), everyone who commits a common nuisance and thereby endangers the lives, safety, or health of the public or causes physical injury to any person is guilty of an **indictable offence** and is liable to two years' imprisonment. See also **abatable nuisance**.

NULLA POENA SINE LEGE (*nŭl-ă pē-nă sī-nă lēj*) Lat.: no punishment without a law (also sometimes *nullum crimen sine lege* (*nŭl'-ŭm krē'-měn sī'-nā lēj*), "no crime without a law"). In Canada, the criminal system operates on the principle that a person cannot be punished except in accordance with fixed, predetermined law. Under s. 9 of the *Criminal Code*, R.S.C. 1985, c. C–46, no person can be convicted for an offence at common law, except contempt of court. K. Roach, *Criminal Law* 82–83 (5th edition, 2012).

NULLITY Of no legal force or effect; invalid. Where **criminal** proceedings are found to be a nullity due to some procedural irregularity, there is no bar to the **Crown** commencing new proceedings. *R. v. Dudley*, 2009 SCC 58.

NULLIUS FILIUS (*nŭl-ē-ŭs fĭl-ē-ŭs*) Lat.: son of no one; means an illegitimate child. See **bastard**.

NUMBERED TREATIES A series of eleven **treaties** signed between **Aboriginal peoples** in Manitoba, Saskatchewan, Alberta, British Columbia, and the Northwest Territories and the government of Canada between 1871 and 1921. Under these treaties, Aboriginal people ceded their claim to land in exchange for **reserve** lands, hunting and fishing rights, annual payments, and other promised benefits.

NUNAVUT COURT OF JUSTICE A court that, in its structure, is unique to the territory of Nunavut. Other provinces and territories have a separate **superior court** and **inferior court**, but in Nunavut the two courts have been combined into one, which has jurisdiction over all matters that would come before either. See **Outline of Canada's Court System, Appendix I**. Because most communities in Nunavut are small and isolated, the court travels to them on circuit.

NUNC PRO TUNC (*nŭnk prō tŭnk*) Lat.: now for then. A judgment *nunc pro tunc* is entered when the court directs a proceeding to be dated as of an earlier date than that on which it was actually taken. A **judgment** that was delayed by act of the court can be antedated, or if the plaintiff has died between the hearing and date when the judgment was given, a judgment *nunc pro tunc* may be entered. See, e.g., *Murphy v. Stefaniak*, 2007 ONCA 819.

OAKES TEST A standard inquiry articulated by the Supreme Court of Canada in *R. v. Oakes,* [1986] 1 S.C.R. 103 for the interpretation of s. 1 of The **Canadian Charter of Rights and Freedoms**, which guarantees the Charter rights and freedoms "subject only to such reasonable limits prescribed by law as can be demonstrably justified in a free and democratic society." If it is determined that a *Charter* violation has been prescribed by law, the *Oakes* test applies to perform the balance of the s. 1 analysis.

"To establish that a limit is reasonable and demonstrably justified, two central criteria must be satisfied. First, the objective which the measures responsible for a limit on a Charter right or freedom are designed to serve, must be 'of sufficient importance' to warrant overriding a constitutionally protected right or freedom...

"Second, once a sufficiently significant objective is recognized, then the party invoking s. 1 must show that the means chosen are reasonable and demonstrably justified...First, the measures adopted must be carefully designed to achieve the objective in question... Second, the means, even if rationally connected to the objective in this first sense, should impair 'as little as possible' the right or freedom in question...Third, there must be a proportionality between the effects of the measures which are responsible for limiting the Charter right or freedom, and the objective which has been identified as of 'sufficient importance'..."

OATH An affirmation of the truth of a statement that, if made by a person who knows it to be false, may subject him or her to prosecution for **perjury** or other legal proceeding. See *Criminal Code,* R.S.C. 1985, c. C–46, ss. 131, 132. Traditionally, the purpose of an oath was to invoke in the mind of a witness the apprehension of punishment by a supreme being in the event of falsehood, though this is no longer seen as its exclusive meaning. "[W]hile the underlying purpose of an oath as a pledge under possible retribution by one's God or other Supreme Being may no longer be in vogue for many people in our society today, an oath still imports a sense of moral obligation to state the truth." *Monaghan v. Joyce,* 2004 NLSCTD 42. A witness can choose to make a **solemn affirmation** rather than swear an oath. Writings (e.g., **affidavits)** as well as oral **testimony** may be made "under oath."

OATH-HELPING The presentation of evidence by a party with the sole purpose of bolstering the credibility of one of that party's own witnesses. Oath-helping is not permitted. See *R. v. Beland,* [1987] 2 S.C.R. 398.

OBITER DICTUM (*ō'-bĭ-têr dĭk'-tŭm*) Lat.: a saying by the way; a passing or incidental statement. A statement made or decision reached in a court **opinion** that is not essential for disposition of the case. *Obiter dicta* (or simply "*obiter*") are generally contrasted with the **ratio decidendi** of a decision. At one point the view was that a *ratio decidendi* was binding on lower courts, while *obiter dicta* were not. At other times it has been suggested that even *obiter* of the Supreme Court of Canada was binding on lower courts. Neither of those views is now seen as correct. "All *obiter* do not have, and are not intended to have, the same weight. The weight decreases as one moves from the dispositive *ratio decidendi* to a wider circle of analysis, which is obviously intended for guidance and which should be accepted as authoritative. Beyond that, there will be commentary, examples, or exposition that are intended to be helpful and may be found to be persuasive, but are certainly not 'binding' in the sense the *Sellars* principle, in its most exaggerated form, would have it." *R. v. Henry,* 2005 SCC 76.

OBJECTIVE As matters would appear to a reasonable person. A **criminal** offence that depends on whether the **accused** met the standard of a reasonable person (for example, dangerous driving) is referred to as an objective fault crime. See **modified objective test; subjective**.

OBLIGATION A legal duty. **1.** It "refers to something in the nature of a contract, such as a **covenant, bond** or **agreement**." *Stokes v. Leavens* (1918), 40 D.L.R. 23 at 24 (Man.C.A.). **2.** In the law of **tort** it refers to the bond created as a result of the special relationship existing between two or more persons, giving rise, e.g., to a duty to exercise **due care**.

OBLIGATION OF A CONTRACT The civil obligation, binding efficacy, coercive power, or legal duty of performing a contract. Thus the term refers not to any duty that arises out of the contract itself, but to the legal requirements that bind the contracting parties to the performance of their undertaking. But except where **specific performance** is available as a remedy, one cannot be compelled to actually perform a contract obligation; rather, he or she merely subjects himself or herself to liability in **damages** if he or she fails to honor the obligation of a contract.

OBSCENE PUBLICATION "Any publication a dominant characteristic of which is the undue exploitation of sex, or of sex and any one or more of the following subjects, namely crime, horror, cruelty, and violence." *Criminal Code*, R.S.C. 1985, c. C–46, s. 163(8). Determining whether material is obscene requires consideration of the risk of harm it creates. "The courts must determine as best they can what the community would tolerate others being exposed to on the basis of the degree of harm that may flow from such exposure. Harm in this context means that it predisposes persons to act in an anti-social manner as, for example, the physical or mental mistreatment of women by men, or, what is perhaps debatable, the reverse. Anti-social conduct for this purpose is conduct [that] society formally recognizes as incompatible with its proper functioning. The stronger the inference of a risk of harm, the lesser the likelihood of tolerance." *R. v. Butler*, [1992] 1 S.C.R. 452. "[N]ot all sexually explicit erotica depicting adults engaged in conduct [that] is considered to be degrad-

ing or dehumanizing is obscene. The material must also create a substantial risk of harm [that] exceeds the community's tolerance." *Little Sisters Book and Art Emporium v. Canada (Minister of Justice)*, 2000 SCC 69.

Section 163(8) does not violate section 2(b) (freedom of expression) of the **Canadian Charter of Rights and Freedoms,** and is not so vague as to violate s. 7 of the Charter. *R. v. Red Hot Video Ltd.* (1985), 18 C.C.C. (3d) 1 (B.C.C.A.).

OBSCENITY See **obscene publication**.

OBSOLESCENCE A term that describes, "[t]he decrease in the functional value of a building, caused by changing utility conditions and is due to one or both of the following factors: 1. Internal obsolescence or obsolescence resulting from the decrease in the ability of a building to serve the purpose for which it was constructed... 2. External obsolescence or obsolescence resulting from the changes of the character of the surrounding district." Prouty and Collin's Appraiser's Manual quoted in *Dominion Textile Co. Ltd. v. City of Montreal*, [1946] Rev. Leg. 257 at 264. (Q.S.C.).

OBSTRUCTION OF JUSTICE Acting to "obstruct, pervert or defeat the course of justice"; it is a criminal offence. Among acts that constitute an obstruction of justice are dissuading a person by threats from giving evidence; influencing a person in his or her capacity as a **juror**; or, being a person who may give evidence or act as a juror, accepting bribes or threats in connection with those duties. *Criminal Code*, R.S.C. 1985, c. C–46, s. 139. See **embracery**.

"[T]he *actus reus* of the offence will be established only if the act tended to defeat or obstruct the course of justice... With respect to *mens rea*, it is not in dispute that this is a specific intent offence... The prosecution must prove, beyond a reasonable doubt, that the accused did in fact intend to act in a way tending to obstruct, pervert, or defeat the course of justice. A simple error of judgment will not be enough. An accused who acted in good faith, but whose conduct cannot be characterized as a legitimate exercise of the discretion, has not committed the criminal offence of obstructing justice." *R. v. Beaudry*, 2007 SCC 5. See generally *R. v. Barros*, 2011 SCC 51.

OCCUPANT One who takes **possession**; one who has the actual use or possession of a thing; one who holds possession and exercises control over a thing. The person with actual possession, such as a **tenant**, as distinguished from **landlord**, who retains the legal **ownership**.

OCCUPATIONAL DISEASE [INDUSTRIAL DISEASE] A disease peculiar to or characteristic of a particular industrial process, trade, or occupation; "a condition that results from exposure in a workplace to a physical, chemical or biological agent to the extent that the normal physiological mechanisms are affected and the health of the worker is impaired thereby." *Occupational Health and Safety Act,* R.S.O. 1990, c. O.1, s. 1. It usually arises after long and continued exposure to conditions of employment that are more dangerous than those found in employment and living conditions in general and frequently includes such diseases as silicosis, coal miners' pneumonoconiosis, lead poisoning, and frost-bite, among others. *Workers' Compensation Act,* S.N.S. 1994–95, c. 10. Where an employee suffers from a disease or injury as a result of his work, there arises, subject to statutory conditions, an entitlement to compensation. See, e.g., *Workplace Safety and Insurance Act,* S.O. 1997, c. 16, Sch. A. See also **workmen's compensation acts**, **labour standards**.

OCCUPATIONAL HAZARD A risk that is peculiar to a particular type of employment or work place and that arises as a natural incident of such employment or of employment in such a place.

OCCUPIERS' LIABILITY Common law rules holding the occupier of land or other premises responsible for injuries to visitors, which varied depending on whether the visitor was an **invitee**, a **licensee**, or a **trespasser**. Most jurisdictions have altered the common law rules. See, e.g., *Occupiers' Liability Act*, R.S.A. 2000, c. O–4; *Occupiers' Liabil-*

ity Act, R.S.O. 1990, c. O.2; *Occupiers Liability Act*, R.S.B.C. 1996, c. 337.

OCCUPYING THE FIELD See **paramountcy**; **preemption**.

OFFENCE Behaviour that is by **statute** made unlawful. Broadly speaking, offences can be divided into **crimes** (which deal with morally blameworthy behaviour) and **regulatory offences** (which make behaviour illegal not because it is inherently blameworthy, but to achieve some goal in the ordering of society, for example, by prohibiting hunting except during specified periods). The distinction matters for two primary reasons. Most importantly, different presumptions are made about the **fault elements** of the two types of offences; crimes are presumed to have **subjective** fault such as **knowledge** or **intent**, but regulatory offences are presumed to be **strict liability**. Secondly, investigative powers that are created for the regulatory (or "administrative") context cannot be used for criminal law purposes. "Where a lower constitutional standard is applicable in an administrative context, as in this case, the police cannot invoke that standard to evade the prior judicial authorization that is normally required for searches or seizures in the context of criminal investigations." *R. v. Cole*, 2012 SCC 53. See **malum in se**; **malum prohibitum**.

OFFENCE-RELATED PROPERTY Property by means or in respect of which an **indictable offence** is committed, that is used in connection with the commission of such an offence, or that is intended to be used for committing such an offence. *Criminal Code*, R.S.C. 1985, c. C–46, s. 2.

OFFENDER A person who has been found guilty of a criminal offence. Defined under s. 2 of the *Criminal Code,* R.S.C. 1985, c. C–46, as " a person who has been determined by a court to be guilty of an offence, whether on acceptance of a plea of guilty or on a finding of guilt."

OFFENSIVE WEAPON A class of weapon divided by the *Criminal Code,* R.S.C. 1985, c. C–46, s. 84(1), into prohibited and restricted weapons, including firearms, notwithstanding the exceptions listed in s. 84(1) of the *Criminal Code*.

"[P]rohibited weapon means (a) a knife that has a blade that opens automatically by gravity or centrifugal force or by hand pressure applied to a button, spring or other device in or attached to the handle of the knife, or (b) any weapon, other than a firearm, that is prescribed to be a prohibited weapon."

"[R]estricted weapon means any weapon, other than a firearm, that is prescribed to be a restricted weapon."

"[P]rohibited firearm means (a) a handgun that (i) has a barrel equal to or less than 105 mm in length, or (ii) is designed or adapted to discharge a 25 or 32 calibre cartridge, but does not include any such handgun that is prescribed, where the handgun is for use in international sporting competitions governed by the rules of the International Shooting Union, (b) a firearm that is adapted from a rifle or shotgun, whether by sawing, cutting or any other alteration, and that, as so adapted, (i) is less than 660 mm in length, or (ii) is 660 mm or greater in length and has a barrel less than 457 mm in length, (c) an automatic firearm, whether or not it has been altered to discharge only one projectile with one pressure of the trigger, or (d) any firearm that is prescribed to be a prohibited firearm."

"[R]estricted firearm means (a) a handgun that is not a prohibited firearm, (b) a firearm that (i) is not a prohibited firearm, (ii) has a barrel less than 470 mm in length, and (iii) is capable of discharging centre-fire ammunition in a semi-automatic manner, (c) a firearm that is designed or adapted to be fired when reduced to a length of less than 660 mm by folding, telescoping or otherwise, or (d) a firearm of any other kind that is prescribed to be a restricted firearm." See **firearm**; **weapon**.

OFFER "[A] manifestation of willingness to be bound by one party [to a contract] that has a certain legal result, namely, that of giving the other party the power to conclude a binding contract by acceptance." S.M. Waddams, *The Law of Contracts* 21 (6th ed. 2010).

A communication addressed to numerous persons will not generally be an offer but will rather be considered an invitation for offers (which may then become **contracts** through acceptance). This is the case in most mail-order settings and in newspaper advertisements.

To constitute an offer there must be "language of promise" (i.e., "I may" or "I want" is not as likely to be construed as an offer as is a communication using the language "I will") and a sufficiently definite statement of terms so that an acceptance may be made without suggesting new terms.

OFFEREE In **contract** law, the **party** to whom an **offer** is addressed and who may be bound upon **acceptance** of the offer.

OFFEROR In **contract** law, the **party** who makes the **offer** and indicates a willingness to enter into legal relations.

OFFICER 1. A person invested with the authority of a particular position or office. The term embraces the idea of **tenure**, duration, **emoluments** and duties, the last-named being continuing and permanent and not occasional or temporary. An officer may be either public or private in that the office he or she occupies may or may not be invested with a public trust. **2.** Corporate personnel appointed by the directors and charged with the duty of managing the day-to-day affairs of the **corporation**. J. A. VanDuzer, *The Law of Partnerships and Corporations*, 15, 280–84 (3rd ed. 2009). See **peace officer**; **public officer**.

OFFICIAL Defined in s. 118 of the *Criminal Code*, R.S.C. 1985, c. C–46 as a "person who (*a*) holds an office, or (*b*) is appointed or elected to discharge a public duty." The Supreme Court of Canada has held that a Minister of the Crown, a Lieutenant-Governor, and members of the civil service come within this definition because they fulfill a government function. *Sommers v. R.*, [1959] S.C.R. 678.

OFFICIAL IMMUNITY See **immunity**.

OFFICIAL LANGUAGES Refers to the languages used by government in communication with the general public. French and English are the official languages of Canada and have equal status in terms of the operation and activities of **Parliament** and the federal government. New Brunswick also has official languages legislation authorizing the use of both the French and English languages within the province. See *Official Languages Act*, S.N.B. 2002, c. O–05.

The status of English and French as the official languages of Canada and New Brunswick has been entrenched in ss. 16–22 of the **Canadian Charter of Rights and Freedoms**. See P.W. Hogg, *Constitutional Law of Canada* (5th ed. 2007), c. 56.

OFFICIALLY INDUCED ERROR A common law exception to the rule in s. 19 of the *Criminal Code*, R.S.C. 1985, c. C–46, that ignorance of the law is no excuse, which applies when a person has acted on inaccurate advice about the law from an authorized representative of the state. For the defence to be made out, "the accused must prove six elements: (1) that an error of law or of mixed law and fact was made; (2) that the person who committed the act considered the legal consequences of his or her actions; (3) that the advice obtained came from an appropriate official; (4) that the advice was reasonable; (5) that the advice was erroneous; and (6) that the person relied on the advice in committing the act." *Lévis (City) v. Tétreault*, 2006 SCC 12.

OFFICIOUS BYSTANDER TEST A basis for reading an implied term into a contract. A term will be presumed to have been the intention of the parties based on the "officious bystander" test if it is "a term [that] the parties would say, if questioned, that they had obviously assumed." *M.J.B. Enterprises Ltd. v. Defence Construction (1951)*, [1999] 1 S.C.R. 619.

OFFICIOUS INTERMEDDLER One who performs an act that confers a benefit upon another, although he or she had neither a contractual duty nor a legally recognized interest in performing the act, and who may nevertheless expect payment or **restitution** for the benefit conferred.

OFFSET See **setoff**.

OLIGOPOLY An industry in which a few large sellers of substantially identical products dominate the market, e.g., the automobile industry. An oligopolistic industry is more concentrated than a competitive one but is less concentrated than a **monopoly**.

OMBUDSMAN A government official appointed to receive, investigate, and report on grievances of the public against the government's acts, omissions, decisions, and recommendations. The term ombudsperson is increasingly used.

OMISSION A neglect or failure to do something; that which is left undone. The neglect will not give rise to liability unless there is a **duty** to act. Thus, since a parent owes a duty of protection to a child, if the parent fails to do what is required to protect the child, the parent may face criminal liability; a nurse who neglects a patient may face **tort** and/or **criminal** liability. Thus, an omission, though it consists of a failure to act, will constitute the **actus reus** that is a component of criminal liability. See also *Criminal Code,* R.S.C. 1985, c. C–46, ss. 217, 219.

OMNE TESTAMENTUM MORTE CONSUMATUM EST (*ōm-nē tē-stă-měn-tŭm mŏr-tē kōn-sŭ-măt-ŭm ēst*) Lat.: every **will** is brought to completion by death. A will has no legal effect until the death of the testator/testatrix.

ON DEMAND When requested. For example, a note payable on demand is payable when the sum is requested. Such a note is called a **demand note** if no due date is stated in the obligation.

A demand note includes a bill in which no time for payment is expressed. *Bills of Exchange Act,* R.S.C. 1985, c. B–4, s. 22(1).

ON THE MERITS A decision based on the essential facts of a case, rather than one based on a technical rule of practice such as a failure of **service** or lack of **jurisdiction**. In the criminal context, the phrase also refers to a decision based on whether the elements of the **offence** can be proven, rather than one resulting from the **exclusion of evidence** for a violation of a **Charter** right or from a defence such as **entrapment**. It is not necessary that a previous trial be on the merits for the accused to be able to invoke the **double jeopardy** rule. "There is no basis, in the Code or in the common law, for any super-added requirement that there must be a trial 'on the merits.' That phrase merely serves to emphasize the general requirement that the previous dismissal must have been made by a court of competent jurisdiction, whose proceedings were free from jurisdictional error and which rendered judgment on the charge." *R. v. Riddle*, [1980] 1 S.C.R. 380.

ONUS PROBANDI (*ō'-nŭs prō-băn'-dē*) Lat.: the onus or **burden of proof.** "The strict meaning of the term *onus probandi* is this, that if no evidence is given by the party on which the burden is cast, the issue must be found against him." *Barry v. Butlin* (1838), 2 Moo. P.C. 480, quoted in *Harmes v. Hinkson,* [1946] 2 W.W.R. 433 at 447 (Can.P.C.).

OPEN COURT A court or place that the public knows is a court and to which they may resort and have free access. Most legal proceedings take place in open court except where confidentiality is a recognized interest (e.g., in **divorce** or **juvenile delinquency** proceedings).

OPEN COURT PRINCIPLE The concept that the public is presumptively entitled to access to the courts to observe proceedings. The open court principle is described as a hallmark of a democratic society and a cornerstone of the common law. "It is integral to public confidence in the justice system and the public's understanding of the administration of justice. Moreover, openness is a principal component of the legitimacy of the judicial process and why the parties and the public at large abide by the decisions of courts." *Vancouver Sun* (*Re*), 2004 SCC 43.

OPEN POSSESSION See **notorious possession**.

OPERATION OF LAW By or through law; refers to the determination of rights and obligations through the automatic effects of the law and not by any direct act of the party affected. Thus, when one dies **intestate**, one's **heirs** take according to the provincial statute of **descent** and **distribution**, "by operation of law." So, too, in certain instances the law will impose a constructive **trust** upon a transaction "by operation of law" to protect certain classes of persons.

OPINIO JURIS Short for *opinio juris sive necessitatis* (*ō-pĭn'-ē-ō yŭ'-rĭs sē'-vā nĕ-sĕs'-ĭ-tă-tŭs*) Lat.: "opinion that an act is necessary by rule of law." The belief on a part of a state that a practice is required by law, as opposed to by some other cause. See **customary international law**.

OPINION The reason given for a court's **judgment**, **finding** or conclusion, as distinguished from the decision, which is the judgment itself. An opinion of a court implies its adoption by a "carrying vote" of the judges. Opinions are usually written by a single judge, and if there were more than one judge deciding the matter, other judges will join in the opinion. If a majority of a multi-judge tribunal joins in the opinion, it is a **majority opinion**. On some occasions there will be a majority result but no majority opinion, where different cohorts of judges reach the same conclusion by different routes. For example, four of nine judges might conclude that there was no **prima facie** violation of an accused's **Charter** rights, while two others conclude that those rights were violated but the violation was saved under s. 1. The majority result would be that there was no **Charter** breach, but there would be no majority opinion. In such circumstances the opinion attracting the most support is sometimes referred to as the PLURALITY OPINION. A plurality opinion does not necessarily create a binding result for lower courts. For example, in *R. v. Gomboc*, 2010 SCC 55, the plurality opinion of four judges held that a person never had a **reasonable expectation of privacy** in a particular type of information. The other five judges specifically disagreed with that conclusion, though three of the five sided with the plurality about the ultimate result in the case.

CONCURRING OPINION (also minority opinion) A judgment that arrives at the same conclusion as that reached by the majority, but that is subscribed to by a minority of judges.

DISSENTING OPINION A view that disagrees with the disposition made of the case by the court, with the facts or law on the basis of which the court arrived at its decision and/or with the principles of law announced by the court in deciding the case. Opinions may also be written expressing a dissent "in part."

PER CURIAM OPINION An opinion "by the court" that expresses its decision in the case without identifying the author.

"Opinion" also refers to the conclusions reached by a witness that are drawn from his or her observations of the facts. See **expert witness**; **opinion evidence**.

OPINION EVIDENCE Testimony that draws a conclusion about facts, rather than merely reporting the facts themselves. "As a general rule, a **witness** may not give opinion evidence but may testify only to facts within her or his knowledge, observation, and experience. It is the province of the **trier of fact** to draw inferences from the proven facts. A qualified **expert witness**, however, may provide the trier of fact with a 'ready-made inference,' which the **jury** is unable to draw due to the technical nature of the subject matter." Bryant *et al.*, *The Law of Evidence in Canada* (3d ed., 2009), §12.2. A non-expert witness will be permitted to give an opinion on matters that do not require special knowledge and where the inference from the facts and the facts themselves cannot really be separated (for example, "he was drunk").

OPPRESSION To manage the affairs of a corporation in a manner that unfairly disregards the interests of any security holder, creditor, director, or officer. The behaviour must involve a lack of probity and fair dealing but need not be unlawful. See *Mahood v. High Country Holdings Inc.*, 2000 BCSC 1755.

OPTION TO PURCHASE The right to buy something at a fixed price within a specified period of time.

ORAL CONTRACT See **contract**.

ORDER 1. A direction of the court on some matter incidental to the main proceeding that adjudicates a preliminary point or directs some step in the proceeding.

2. In commercial law, an order "for particular goods given either under a contract previously made or sent in the form of a request for a specific quantity of named" goods. *White v. National Paper Co.*, [1914] 6 O.W.N. 521 at 522 (C.A.).

3. "'Orders' and **'Regulations'** are merely the terms used to designate the mode of exercising the powers conferred on the **Governor-in-Council**." *Re George Edwin Gra*y (1918), 57 S.C.R. 150 at 155.

"'Order' is a proper term for describing an act of the Governor-in-Council by which he exercises a law-making power, whether the power exist as part of the prerogative or devolve upon him by statute." *Id.* at 167.

Order is generally understood as comprising subordinate legislation issued for a particular situation, as distinct from regulation, which is generally taken to comprise subordinate legislation of general and substantive effect.

A FINAL ORDER is one that finally disposes of the rights of the parties.

See **interlocutory order**; **restraining order**.

ORDER PAPER The list of **bills** awaiting a vote by Parliament or a legislature in order to become **statutes**. Upon prorogation, a bill is said to "die on the order paper" unless the government has specifically announced in advance that it will carry over to the next session.

ORDINANCE A local law that applies to persons and things subject to the local **jurisdiction**. "The word 'ordinance' has no technical significations; it means no more than an instrument embodying an order or direction." *R. v. Markin* (1969), 2 D.L.R. (3d) 606 at 607 (B.C.S.C.) quoting *Metcalfe v. Cox,* [1895] A.C. 328 it 338.

Usually the word is used in its municipal law context to mean an act of a city council or similar body that has the same force and effect as a statute when it is duly enacted. It is a form of subordinate legislation differing from laws **(statutes)** enacted by the federal or provincial **legislatures**. Ordinances are enacted to regulate **zoning**, highway speed, parking, refuse disposal and other matters typically and traditionally of local concern.

ORDINARY PERSON Most often, the **reasonable person**. However, the defence of **provocation** applies when an ordinary person is provoked to lose self-control and kills as a result. "While I believe that the two fictional entities share the same attributes, at first blush some may question this as a logical inconsistency, given that a 'reasonable' person would not commit culpable homicide in the first place. Indeed, 'reasonableness' often defines the standard of conduct [that] is expected at law, and conduct [that] meets this standard, as a general rule, does not attract legal liability. The inconsistency is resolved when it is recalled that the defence is only a partial one, and that the defendant, even if successful, will still be guilty of manslaughter. The use of the term 'ordinary person' therefore reflects the normative dimensions of the defence; that is, behaviour [that] comports with contemporary society's norms and values will attract the law's compassion." *R. v. Tran*, 2010 SCC 58.

ORIGINAL In **copyright** a work, the production of which involved intellectual effort rather than being the product of a mere mechanical exercise. The work need not be creative in the sense that it is novel or unique, but it must have involved the exercise of skill and judgment. Originality requires the use of knowledge, developed aptitude, or practised ability in producing the work, and a capacity for discernment or ability to form an opinion or evaluation by comparing different possible options in producing the work. *CCH Canadian Ltd. v. Law Society of Upper Canada*, 2004 SCC 13.

ORPHAN WELLS Oil or gas wells for which the license operators have become insolvent or cannot be found.

OSTENSIBLE AUTHORITY See **apparent authority**.

OUSTER The wrongful dispossession or exclusion of a person from property, usually associated with the acts of a co-tenant that exclude other co-tenants from their legal right to share **possession**. The ouster of co-tenants with **proper notice** will commence the running of the **statute of limitations** for purposes of **adverse possession**.

OUTLAW In the medieval period, a person who was literally placed outside the law, and therefore could not call upon its protections. In its usage today it refers colloquially to a person with little respect for the law (for example, an outlaw motorcycle gang). It is also used as a verb, meaning to make something illegal.

OVERBREADTH Under s. 7 of the **Canadian Charter of Rights and Freedoms**, the **principle of fundamental justice** that in pursuing a legitimate objective, the State cannot use means that are broader than is necessary to accomplish that objective. *R. v. Heywood*, [1994] 3 S.C.R. 761.

OVERDRAFT A term used to denote a negative balance in a person's bank account.

OVERHOLDING TENANT A tenant who does not vacate the rented premises after a tenancy has expired or been terminated. See, e.g., *Residential Tenancies Act*, SA 2004, c. R–17.1, s. 1 or *Residential Tenancy Act*, SBC 2002, c. 78, s. 57(1).

OVERREACHING In commercial law, the taking of unfair advantage over another through cunning, cheating, or generally fraudulent practices; synonymous with **fraud**. Contracts that are the product of overreaching in an unequal bargaining context may be unenforceable under modern concepts of fraud or the **unconscionability** doctrine.

OVERRIDE CLAUSE See **notwithstanding clause**.

OVERRIDING ROYALTY An unencumbered share or fractional interest of the gross value of the production of minerals, oil, or gas, granted by a person who has the right under a lease to extract those minerals, oil, or gas. An overriding royalty is granted to a third party in exchange for consideration such as money or services. *Bank of Montreal v. Dynex Petroleum Ltd.*, 2002 SCC 7.

OVERRULE 1. To overturn or make **void** the **holding** (decision) of a prior **case**; generally accomplished by a court in a different and subsequent case, when it makes a decision on a point of law exactly opposite to that made in the prior case. A decision can be overruled only by the same court or a higher court within the same **jurisdiction**. The overruling of a decision generally destroys its value as **precedent**. The term should be distinguished from **reverse**, which applies to a higher court's overturning of a lower court's decision in the same case, though sometimes the distinction is not made. **2.** To deny a position, objection, or other point raised to the court, such as in "overruling a motion for a new trial" or "objection overruled."

OVERT ACT Open, non-secretive act. An overt act is required to find criminal liability for **treason**. See *Criminal Code, R.S.C. 1985, c. C–46, s. 46(4).*

OWNERSHIP "[T]he right of enjoying and disposing of things in the most absolute manner, provided that no use be made of them which is prohibited by law or by regulations." *Johnston v. Minister & Trustees of St. Andrew's Church, Montreal* (1877), 1 S.C.R. 235 at 317.

The term has been given a wide range of meanings but is often said to comprehend both the concept of **possession** and, further, that of **title**, and thus to be broader than either.

ALLODIAL OWNERSHIP Free ownership, not subject to the restrictions or obligations associated with **feudal tenures**.

TENURIAL OWNERSHIP The holding of land subject to specific **services** or obligations owed to another.

OYER AND TERMINER Special tribunals empowered to hear and determine cases within their criminal **jurisdiction**, commissioned by the Crown when the delay involved in ordinary prosecution could not be tolerated, as in the case of sudden insurrection.

PACTUM (*päk'-tŭm*) Lat.: pact, **contract**, agreement. An agreement that is unenforceable because it lacks **consideration** is said to be **nudum pactum**, meaning a naked or bare agreement.

PAIN AND SUFFERING One of the basic heads of **damages** in **contract** and **tort**. Now a term of art describing a single head of damage, not distinguishing between pain on the one hand and suffering on the other. As the term is used in **judgments** and **statutes**, no physical pain is necessarily implied. See, e.g., *Canada (Canadian Human Rights Commission) v. Canada (Attorney-General)*, 2011 SCC 53.

PAR Equal to the established value; denotes the face amount or stated value of a **negotiable instrument**, stock or bond, not the actual value it would receive on the open market. **Bills of exchange**, **stocks** and the like are AT PAR when they sell at their nominal value, above or below par when they sell for more or less.

PARALEGAL A non-lawyer who works independently, performing certain types of legal services before a board, **tribunal**, or some **courts** for a fee. See P. Cory, *Framework for Regulating Paralegal Practice in Ontario* (2000), p. 1. An issue that arises is whether paralegals are, in certain circumstances, engaged in the unauthorized practice of law; see, e.g., *Law Society of British Columbia v. Mangat*, 2001 SCC 67. The term is sometimes also used to describe non-lawyers who work in a lawyer's office under the supervision of a lawyer and assist with legal services, but this practice is less controversial. In some provinces, paralegals are governed by legislation; see, e.g., *Law Society Act*, R.S.O. 1990, c. L.8, ss. 25.1–26.3.

PARAMOUNTCY The condition of being superior to all others; supreme. "The rule which has been adopted by the courts is the doctrine of 'federal paramountcy': where there are inconsistent (or conflicting) federal and provincial laws, it is the federal law which prevails. A similar rule has been adopted in the United States and Australia, and apparently by all modern federal constitutions. The doctrine of paramountcy applies where there is a federal law and a provincial law which are (1) each valid, and (2) inconsistent....Validity depends on ... [whether] the 'matter' (or pith and substance) of the law [comes] within the classes of subjects or heads of power allocated to the enacting Parliament or Legislature...It is only if each law independently passes the test of validity that it is necessary to determine if the laws are inconsistent." P.W. Hogg, *Constitutional Law of Canada* 16–3 (5th ed. 2007).

PARAMOUNT TITLE A **title** that will prevail over another asserted against it. It signifies an immediate right of **possession** and is generally referred to as the basis for **eviction** of a **tenant** by one with a right of possession superior to that of the tenant.

PARAMOUR One's lover; one who stands in the place of a spouse, but without the legal rights attached to the marital relationship.

PARCENER One who holds an **estate** jointly with others, usually by virtue of **descent** or **inheritance**. The term is no longer widely used, since it is now said to be indistinguishable from TENANCY IN COMMON (see **tenancy**).

PARDON An exercise of mercy through the sovereign's prerogative. "The effect of a pardon under the great seal is to clear the person from all infamy and from all consequences of the offence for which it is granted, and from all statutory or other disqualifications following upon conviction." *8 Halsbury's Laws of England* (4th ed.), para. 952.

In Canada, the *Criminal Code, R.S.C. 1985, c. C–46*, authorizes the **Governor-in-Council** to reduce a sentence of imprisonment by granting a free pardon or a conditional pardon or to remit, in whole or in part, any pecuniary penalty, fine or forfeiture (ss. 748 and

748.1). See also **record suspension**; **Royal Prerogative of Mercy**.

PARENS PATRIAE (*pā'-rĕnz pā'-trē-ī*) Lat.: "parent of the country." Originally the duty of the English sovereign to protect his or her subjects. At present, it is the power of the superior court to deal with matters involving persons under disability, particularly children; in some provinces, this power is preserved by the *Judicature Act* (e.g., R.S.N.S. 1989, c. 240, s. 43(10) & (11)). See *Beson v. Director of Child Welfare*, [1982] 2 S.C.R. 716 (S.C.C.).

PARENT 1. A person's legal father, mother, or **guardian. 2.** Defined in the *Fatal Accidents Act*, R.S.N.B. 1973, c. F–7, s. 1, as "a father, mother, grandfather, grandmother, step-father, step-mother and adoptive parent and a person who stood *in loco parentis* to the deceased." **3.** Under the *Youth Criminal Justice Act*, S.C. 2002, c. 1, s. 2, includes "any person who is under a legal duty to provide for the young person or any person who has, in law or in fact, the custody or control of the young person, but does not include a person who has the custody or control of the young person by reason only of proceedings under this Act."

PARENT CORPORATION A company owning over 50 percent of the voting shares in another company, called the **subsidiary**. The term also refers to a large organization that subdivides itself internally into a number of departments each of which is technically a separate organization.

PARI DELICTO See **in pari delicto**.

PARLIAMENT The federal legislature of Canada consisting of the **Queen**, the **Senate** and the **House of Commons**. Previously, its life was fixed for five years, divided into sessions (one or more each year), with the ruling government being able to set an election date anytime within that five-year period. In May, 2007, the *Canada Elections Act*, S.C. 2000, c. 9 was amended to state that federal elections in Canada will be set on a fixed date every four years, except if a vote of non-confidence has passed against the government: "56.1 (1) Nothing in this section affects the powers of the Governor General, including the power to dissolve Parliament at the Governor General's discretion, (2) Subject to subsection (1), each general election must be held on the third Monday of October in the fourth calendar year following polling day for the last general election, with the first general election after this section comes into force being held on Monday, October 19, 2009."

PARLIAMENTARY PRIVILEGE "[T]he sum of the privileges, immunities, and powers enjoyed by the Senate, the House of Commons, and provincial legislative assemblies, and by each member individually, without which they could not discharge their functions." *Canada (House of Commons) v. Vaid*, 2005 SCC 30. Parliamentary privilege gives immunity from the law for Members of Parliament and the legislatures to the extent that is necessary to allow them to do their legislative work.

PARLIAMENTARY SOVEREIGNTY The principle that, within their **jurisdiction**, **Parliament** and the **legislatures** have the ability to make, amend, or repeal any law, including overriding the effect of court decisions. The **Canadian Charter of Rights and Freedoms** imposes some limits on the options available to governments, but even portions of that are subject to the **notwithstanding clause**.

PAROL Fr.: oral; expressed verbally. See **parol contract**; **parol evidence**.

PAROL CONTRACT An oral contract; a contract that is communicated orally and not written. See **parol evidence**; **parol evidence rule**.

PAROLE 1. Conditional release from imprisonment or other confinement after actually serving part of the **sentence**. In Canada, there is a distinction between day parole and full parole. Under s. 99(1) of the *Corrections and Conditional Release Act*, S.C. 1992, c. 20, day parole is the authority granted an offender to be at large during his or her term of imprisonment in preparation for full parole or statutory release upon the condition that the offender "return to a penitentiary, community-based residential facility, provincial correctional facility, or other location each night." Full parole allows the offender to be at large during the term of imprisonment. See *Frankie v. Commissioner of Corrections (Can.)* (1993), 61 F.T.R. 274 (Fed. T.D.). Compare **probation**.

2. In **international law** a promise given by prisoners of war, when they have leave to depart from custody, that unless discharged, they will return at the appointed time and will not take up arms against the government whose forces captured them.

PAROL EVIDENCE Evidence that is oral rather than written; the ordinary kind of evidence given by a witness in court. Such evidence usually becomes an issue when relating to a transaction contained in a written **instrument** such as a **will**, **deed**, or **contract**.

PAROL EVIDENCE RULE A rule of **substantive law** that operates to prevent parties to a **contract** from altering, contradicting or varying the terms of a written document considered to be the final expression of their agreement. However, parol evidence is admissible to prove **fraud**, **duress**, **mistake**, **misrepresentation**, lack of capacity, the existence of a separate oral agreement that modifies or rescinds the main contract, the existence of a separate oral agreement to a matter on which the document is silent and which is not inconsistent with its terms, or to prove that the parties did not intend the document to be a complete and final statement of the entire transaction. See further S.M. Waddams, *The Law of Contracts*, 227–30 (6th ed. 2010).

PARTIAL See **bias**.

PARTIALLY DISCLOSED PRINCIPAL See **principal**.

PARTICEPS CRIMINIS (*păr-tĭ-cĕps crĭ-mĭ-nĭs*) Lat.: criminal participant. A person who participates in a crime; the term includes **accessory after the fact**.

PARTICULARS, BILL OF See **bill of particulars**.

PARTITION Judicial division of property interests jointly held, usually land; "the division of lands, **tenements**, and **hereditament** belonging to co-owners, and the allotment among them of the parts, so as to put an end to community of ownership between some or all of them." 32 *Halsbury's Laws of England* (3d ed.), para. 539.

PARTNERSHIP The "relation that subsists between persons carrying on a business in common with a view to profit." *Partnerships Act*, R.S.O. 1990, c. P.5. See also *Backman v. Canada*, 2001 SCC 10.

Each partner is authorized by his or her fellow-partners to bind the members of the partnership for acts done in the normal course of carrying on business. A partner is jointly and severally liable for the extent of any loss unless he or she is a member of a publicly registered limited liability partnership.

LIMITED PARTNERSHIP (LP) A form of business organization in the nature of a partnership involving two or more persons in which one or more of the partners have limited their liability for debts to the amount they have agreed to invest in the business by registering a prescribed form. See *Limited Partnerships Act,* R.S.O. 1990, c. L. 16. An LP has two types of partners: limited partners and general partners. General partners are the same as the partners in a partnership at common law, while limited partners enjoy limited liability but cannot take part in managing the partnership. Not all provinces provide for limited partnerships.

LIMITED LIABILITY PARTNERSHIP (LLP) A special form of partnership created by statute for use by certain professions (in particular law and accounting). In an LLP, all partners have the same status (unlike an LP), but each partner is not jointly and severally liable with other partners (unlike a common law partnership). See, e.g., *Partnership Act*, R.S.N.S. 1989, c. 334, ss. 48–71; *Partnerships Act*, R.S.O. 1990, c. P.5, ss. 10, 44.1–44.4.

PART PERFORMANCE A doctrine that the **statute of frauds** does not apply where there has been performance or part performance of an oral contract or where otherwise the result would be a **fraud** against or injustice to the other party. See, e.g., *Neighbourhoods of Cornell Inc. v. 1440106 Ontario Inc.* (2003), 11 R.P.R. (4th) 294 (Ont. Sup. Ct. J.), aff'd (2004), 22 R.P.R. (4th) 176 (Ont. C.A.).

PARTY A participant who is directly interested in any affair, **contract**, or **conveyance**, or who is actively concerned in the **prosecution** and **defence** of any legal proceeding as **plaintiff** or **defendant**.

NECESSARY PARTY See **necessary party**.

NOMINAL PARTY A party appearing on the **record** not because he or she has any real interest in the case, but because technical rules of **pleading** require his or her presence in the record.

PARTIES TO A CRIME See **abet**; **aid and abet**; **common intention**; **counselling**.

THIRD PARTY A procedural method whereby a **defendant** in an **action** may join additional parties to the action.

PARTY WALL A wall erected on a property boundary as common support to structures on both sides that are under different ownerships. See, e.g., *Parkinson v. Reid*, [1966] S.C.R. 162.

PASSING-OFF A tort action in which the defendant has represented his or her goods in such a way as to make others believe that they were the plaintiff's goods. "The gist of the concept of passing-off is that the goods are in effect telling a falsehood about themselves which is calculated to mislead. The law on this matter is designed to protect traders against that form of unfair competition which consists in acquiring for oneself, by means of false or misleading devices, the benefit of the reputation already achieved by rival traders." *Salmond on Torts* 400–01 (17th ed. 1977) quoted in *Consumers Distributing Co. v. Seiko Time Canada Ltd.* (1984), 1 C.P.R. (3) 1 at 13. The tort of passing off is also reflected in the *Trade-marks Act*, RSC 1985, c. T–13, s. 7(b),(c). See **goodwill**.

PASSIVE PERSONALITY PRINCIPLE A principle of international law under which "a state may assert jurisdiction over an extraterritorial criminal offence where *the victim* was one of its nationals." R. Currie, *International & Transnational Criminal Law*, 68 (2010). See **nationality principle**; **protective principle**; **territorial principle**; **universal jurisdiction**.

PASSPORT An identification document issued by or under the authority of the Minister of Foreign Affairs. It identifies the holder as a Canadian citizen and is required in order to enter and travel in most foreign countries.

PATENT 1. Apparent on the face of an instrument. **2.** By **statute**, "letters patent" for an invention. Patents are **monopolies**, a limited exclusive privilege the law allows a patentee in his or her own invention as a natural right arising from production and differs from **ownership** in that the owner is required to hand it over to the public after a seventeen-year period; if, however, the patent application was filed after October 1, 1989, the term of the patent is twenty years. *Patent Act,* R.S.C. 1985, c. P–4. A patent may be granted for invention of any new and useful art, process, machine, manufacture, or composition of matter or any new and useful improvements in any art, process machine, manufacture or composition of matter. No patent can be obtained for a scientific principle or abstract theorem. The inventor must apply for a **grant** of a patent and, upon application, there is a presumption of novelty that may be disproved by an opposing party attacking the grant by showing prior common general knowledge of the subject matter of the patent. The design of the patent law is to reward those who make substantial discovery or invention that adds to our knowledge and advances the useful arts. Patents are not available for higher life forms in Canadian patent law because they do not qualify as an "invention." See *Harvard College v. Canada (Commissioner of Patents)*, 2002 SCC 76.

PATENT INFRINGEMENT The act of a person who, without license from the patentee, either directly or indirectly makes, uses, or puts into practice the invention or any part of it that is embraced by the claims. It includes doing one of the things that, by terms of the grant, a person is not entitled to do, or colourably imitating the invention in any way or taking its substance. Infringement is determined by the state of the prior art at the time the patent was issued. See *Consolidated Car Heating Co. v. Came,* [1903] A.C. 509 (P.C.).

PATENT PENDING A phrase that describes the state of a patent that has been applied for but has not yet been granted.

PATENT DEFECT A defect that could be recognized upon reasonably careful inspection or through ordinary diligence and care. Compare **latent defect**.

PATERNITY SUIT An action to prove the father of an illegitimate child and to provide **maintenance** for the child. Proof of paternity is usually accomplished by oral evidence and a blood test on the possible father. The suspect father does not necessarily always have to be proved the father but must be one of the possible **putative** fathers.

PATERNITY TEST A term used to describe the Human Leukocyte Antigen Tissue Typing Test, which is used in resolving paternity disputes. It is administered by taking and comparing blood samples from the mother, child, and alleged father. The test can determine paternity with a high degree of probability and can determine conclusively whether a man is *not* the father.

PAT. PEND. [PATENT PENDING] See **patent**.

PATRIATION Although there is no exact definition of "patriation," the term is commonly used in the context of the "bringing home" of the **Constitution** to Canada. As its final legislative act for Canada, the British Parliament passed the *Canada Act, 1982* (U.K.), c. 11, with the *Constitution Act, 1982* appended as Schedule B., ensuring Canada a certain autonomy from the United Kingdom. See *Patriation Reference,* [1982] 2 S.C.R. 793; P.W. Hogg, *Constitutional Law of Canada,* 3–9–15 (5th ed. 2007).

PATRICIDE The killing of one's own father.

PAWN To give **personal property** to another as **security** for a loan; property deposited with another as security for payment of a **debt**.

PAWNBROKER A commercial lender; a person who grants a loan on **security** of personal property left in his or her custody. The lender retains the goods until the **debt** is repaid.

PAY EQUITY An employment policy which requires the payment of equal pay for work of equal value to men and women. In Canada, the federal government and some provinces have passed pay equity legislation, which establishes pay equity commissions and outlines the administration of pay equity programs for employers within their jurisdiction.

Pay equity legislation extends previous policies of equal pay for equal work, i.e., where female clerks must be paid the same as their male counterparts. Pay equity considers skill, effort, responsibility, and working conditions in evaluating which different job categories should be paid on the same level. See *Pay Equity Act,* R.S.N.S. 1989, c. 337; *Pay Equity Act,* R.S.O. 1990, c. P.7.

PAYABLE TO BEARER See **bearer instrument**.

PEACEABLE POSSESSION Possession that is continuous and not interrupted by adverse **suits** or other hostile action intended to oust the possessor from the land. The term often refers to parties in **adverse possession** of land, and thus has nothing to do with actual **ownership**. The existence of adverse claims is not precluded, so long as no actual attempt to dispossess is made. An action to **quiet title** generally requires a showing of peaceable possession by the one bringing the action.

PEACE BOND A **recognizance** entered into before a **justice** by which a person promises to keep the peace and be of good behaviour. A peace bond is prompted by a person laying an information stating a fear, on reasonable grounds, that another person will cause personal injury to him or her or to his or her **spouse** or **common-law partner** or child, or will damage his or her property.

If the justice is satisfied that the fears are reasonable, a peace bond will be ordered. A peace bond is akin to a **civil** remedy and does not result in a criminal record and is focused on prevention rather than **punishment**. See *Criminal Code*, R.S.C. 1985, c. C–46, s. 810.

PEACEFUL ENJOYMENT See **quiet enjoyment**.

PEACE OFFICER A person employed for the preservation and maintenance of the public peace or for the service or execution of civil process; under the *Criminal Code*, R.S.C. 1985, c. C–46, s. 2, the term includes mayors, wardens, reeves, sheriffs, deputy sheriffs, sheriffs officers, justice of the peace, prison officials, police officers, customs officials, fisheries officers, pilots in command of aircraft and members of the armed forces under certain conditions.

A peace officer is limited territorially by the jurisdiction of the authority that appoints him or her.

PECULATION The fraudulent **misappropriation** to one's own use of money or goods entrusted to his or her care. See **embezzlement**; **larceny**.

PECUNIARY Relating to money and monetary affairs; consisting of money or that which can be valued in money. Many fatal injury statutes limit recovery to PECUNIARY LOSS, i.e., a loss of money or of something that can be translated into an economic loss. The loss of affection that a parent suffers by the **negligent** death of a child is not such a loss, whereas the loss of actual or anticipated financial support by the deemed child is pecuniary loss.

PENAL INSTITUTION A place of confinement for **convicted** criminals. Penal institutions include local and county jails and workhouses, reformatories, penitentiaries, prison camps and farms, as well as the modern CORRECTIONAL INSTITUTIONS (nomenclature now used to describe many penal institutions previously called prisons). The **Constitution Act**, **1867**, distinguishes between penitentiaries, which are under federal jurisdiction, and public and reforma-

tory prisons, which are under provincial jurisdiction.

PENAL LAW A law enacted to preserve the public order, which defines an offence against the public and inflicts a penalty for its violation. **Statutes** that grant a private **[civil] action** against a wrongdoer are not considered penal, but remedial in nature.

PENALTY 1. A punishment, particularly a monetary payment. The *Criminal Code*, R.S.C. 1985 c. C–46, s. 734.8(1), defines penalty as being all the sums of money, including **fines**, in default of payment of when a term of imprisonment is imposed. In the non-criminal context, such punishments are typically called an administrative monetary penalty. See, e.g., *Agriculture and Agri-Food Administrative Monetary Penalties Act*, S.C. 1995, c. 40.

2. The nominal sum specified payable by a party in breach of a contract. "'The essence of liquidated damages is a genuine covenanted pre-estimate of the damages' likely to accrue; while the 'essence of a penalty is a payment of money stipulated as in terrorem of the offending party.' ... Whether the sum stipulated to be paid is a penalty or **liquidated damages** is to be decided upon [the construction of] the terms of the contract, the circumstances under which it was entered into, [the] nature of the undertaking, and the loss which at the time the contract was made the parties might have considered as flowing from its breach." *Sask. Co-op Wheat Producers Ltd. v. Zurowski*, [1926] 3 D.L.R. 810 at 819 (Sask.C.A.). Cited in *Don West Construction Ltd. v. Port Stanley (Village)* (1983), 21 A.C.W.S. (2d) 442 (Ont. Cty. Ct.).

As **equity** will afford **relief** against a penalty, only a sum representing the actual loss incurred can be recovered. Compare also **damages** [EXEMPLARY DAMAGES].

PENDENTE LITE [LITE PENDENTE] (*pĕn-dĕn'-tā lē'-tā*) Lat.: pending the **suit**; contingent upon the determination of a pending lawsuit. Thus, funds may be deposited with the clerk of the court *pendente lite*—i.e., so that those funds can be used to make payment to the opposing party if the depositing party loses the lawsuit. See also **lis pendens**.

PENITENTIARY An institution or facility that houses persons who have been convicted of an **offence** and sentenced to two or more years imprisonment. Parliament has jurisdiction over penitentiaries under s. 91(28) of the **Constitution Act, 1867**. Contrast with **prison**.

PEOPLE A group sharing a number of characteristics, such as a common language and a common culture. A "people" might include only a portion of the population of a **state**. See *Reference Re Secession of Quebec*, [1998] 2 S.C.R. 217.

PER ANNUM (*pĕr ăn'-ŭm*) Lat.: through the course of a year; annually. Anything (e.g., interest, wages, rent) calculated per annum is calculated on the basis of a year in time. See **year**.

PER [PUR] AUTRE VIE (*pĕr [pûr] ō'-tr vē*) Fr.: for another's life. A life **estate** that terminates on the death of another person or persons who may be the **grantor** or a third party called the CESTUI QUE VIE. An estate *per autre vie* may be created by express limitation by **deed** or **will** or by the **assignment** of an existing life estate.

PER CAPITA (*pĕr kăp'-ĭ-tà*) Lat.: through the head, top, summit. Through the leader or capital (of a country); defined by the heads or polls according to the number of individuals, share and share alike. Anything figured per capita is calculated by the number of individuals (heads) involved and is divided equally among all. Compare **per stirpes**.

PER CURIAM (*pĕr kyū'-rē-ăm*) Lat.: by the court. Used to distinguish an opinion of the whole court from an opinion written by one judge. See **opinion**.

PER DIEM (*pĕr dē'-ĕm*) Lat.: by the day. Used in connection with a means of calculating compensation or expenses.

PEREMPTORY Absolute, conclusive, positive, not admitting of question or appeal. A peremptory trial date may be established by the court on its own **motion** or at the request of a **party** to insure timely disposition of the case. In the selection of a jury, each side has a right to a fixed number of peremptory **challenges** to the seating of potential jurors.

PEREMPTORY WRIT At common law, an original writ requiring the presence of the defendant in **civil actions** for certain cases including **trespass**.

PEREMPTORY CHALLENGE The right to dismiss a prospective **juror** during the selection process without any specified reasons. Both the **Crown** and the defence are entitled to a certain number of peremptory challenges in a **criminal** trial. See *Criminal Code*, R.S.C. 1985, c. C–46, s. 634

PEREMPTORY PLEA See **dilatory plea**.

PERFECTED Completed, executed, enforceable, merchantable; refers especially to the status ascribed to **security interests** after certain events have occurred. The necessary events in order to achieve PERFECTION can be broken down into two categories

Certain security interests are perfected by no more than the creation of the security interest itself. An example of such an automatic perfected security interest is a purchase money security interest in consumer goods.

Other security interests require the creditor to take certain steps to perfect, including taking possession of the collateral, or filing.

There are many consequences that flow from perfection. The most important is that a perfected security interest has **priority** over an unperfected interest. The date of perfection is also the time from which courts judge priority contests with other perfected creditors.

PERFORMANCE The fulfillment of an obligation or a promise; especially, completion of one's obligation under a **contract**. See **specific performance**; **substantial performance**.

PERIODIC TENANCY See **tenancy**.

PERJURY Section 131 of the *Criminal Code*, R.S.C. 1985, c. C–46, defines the act of perjury as a false statement by a person, with an intent to mislead, knowing that the statement is false whether or not such a statement is made in a judicial **proceeding**. The **burden of proof** is on the Crown to prove the statement false. It is no defence that the accused's statements are true if he or she knew and intended that they would be taken in another sense. *Farris v. The Queen,* [1965] 3 C.C.C. 245 (Ont.C.A.). See also **subornation of perjury**.

PERMANENT FIXTURE See **fixtures**.

PERMANENT INJUNCTION See **injunction**.

PERMANENT RESIDENT "A person who has acquired permanent resident status and has not subsequently lost that status under section 46." *Immigration and Refugee Protection Act,* S.C. 2001, c. 27, s. 2.(1). To become a permanent resident, a person must have been issued a visa or other required document issued by the federal government and, in some cases, have met the selection criteria of the province in which he or she will reside, and must have come to Canada in order to establish permanent residence. The person must also comply with the minimum residency period every five years, which is set out in s. 28 of the Act. Under section 46 of the Act a person loses permanent resident status, *inter alia,* by becoming a Canadian citizen, by a final determination made outside Canada that he or she has failed to comply with the Act's residency requirements, when a removal order made against him or her comes into force, or on a final determination to vacate a decision to allow a claim or application.

PERMISSIVE WASTE See **waste**.

PER MY ET PER TOUT (*pĕr mē ā pĕr tū*) Law Fr.: by half and by whole. In **joint tenancy**, each tenant's share is the whole, for purposes of **tenure** and **survivorship [tout]**, and each share is an **aliquot** portion for purposes of **alienation [my]**.

PERPETUITIES, RULE AGAINST See **rule against perpetuities**.

PERPETUITY See **in perpetuity**.

PER QUOD (*pĕr kwŏd*) Lat.: through which; by which; whereby. False imputations may be **actionable per se**—in themselves—or *per quod*—on allegation and proof of special **damage**. In a **libel** or **slander** action, words used that are not on their face, in their usual and natural usage, injurious, but that become so as a consequence of extrinsic facts and that require an **innuendo**, are actionable *per quod.*

PER SE (*pĕr sā*) Lat.: through itself, by means of itself. Not requiring extraneous evidence or support to establish its existence. For example, **negligence** *per se* refers to acts that are inherently negligent, i.e., that implicitly involve a **breach** of duty, obviating the need to expressly allege the existence of the duty.

PERSON In law, an individual or incorporated group having certain legal rights and responsibilities. This has been held to include foreign and domestic **corporations**. Compare **artificial person**; **natural person**.

PERSONAL ACTION An action brought by an injured party for the recovery of **property** or for **damages** done to his or her person or property.

PERSONAL CARE DIRECTIVE See **living will**.

PERSONAL INFORMATION Material that reveals information about an identifiable individual. "Personal information" is defined, and is in general exempted from public disclosure, under various statutes; see, e.g., the *Privacy Act*, R.S.C., 1985, c. P–21, or the *Access to Information Act*, R.S.C., 1985, c. A–1. Depending on the context and the particular statute, personal information can include what hours a person was at work, personal opinions, and medical history, and it might or might not include the person's name.

PERSONAL JUDGMENT Judgment imposed on a defendant requiring sums to be advanced from whatever assets he or she has within the **jurisdiction** of the issuing court, as distinguished from a judgment directed against particular property (called an **in rem** judgment) or a judgment against a **corporate** entity.

PERSONAL PROPERTY See **personalty**.

PERSONAL REMEDY An order granted to an applicant under s. 24 of the **Canadian Charter of Rights and Freedoms** for a violation of his or her *Charter* rights. Under s. 24(1), a **court** of competent jurisdiction can grant "such remedy as the court considers appropriate and just in the circumstances," which is an open-ended remedial power. The most extreme remedy under this section is a **stay** of proceedings, which halts all further action against a person charged with an **offence** with regard to that conduct. A stay of proceedings can only be granted in the clearest of cases. *R. v. Regan*, 2002 SCC 12. Other remedies might include an adjournment when an **accused** has not received **disclosure** in a timely fashion, **damages** in certain circumstances, or a reduction in sentence. See *R. v. Bjelland*, 2009 SCC 38; *Vancouver (City) v. Ward*, 2010 SCC 27; *R. v. Nasogaluak*, 2010 SCC 6. Under s. 24(2), evidence that has been obtained by means of a Charter violation can be excluded "if it is established that, having regard to all the circumstances, the admission of it in the proceedings would bring the administration of justice into disrepute." See **Grant test**.

PERSONAL SERVICE See **service**.

PERSONALTY The class of property that deals with the right in **chattels**. Chattels are property of a temporary character and can be easily moved about; also, they can be handled, transferred, altered and destroyed without much difficulty. The distinguishing feature from **real property** is that the forms of action lie **in personam** in the form of **conversion**, **detinue** and **replevin**. B. Ziff, *Principles of Property Law* (5th ed. 2010).

PERSON IN AUTHORITY A person with some measure of control over an **accused** and the proceedings against him or her. The "person in authority" requirement distinguishes a **confession** from an **admission**; both are incrimin-

ating statements by an accused, but if the statement was made to a person in authority, it is a confession and must be proven **voluntary** at a **voir dire** in order to be **admissible evidence**. Police officers, prison guards, and others engaged in the arrest or detention of an accused are presumptively persons in authority. Other persons, such as a parent, a victim, or an employer, might be found to be a person in authority on the facts of a particular case. The test is whether the accused person **subjectively** believes that the person could influence the course of the prosecution, and whether that is an **objectively** reasonable belief. The subjective portion of the test means that an undercover police officer is not a person in authority.

PERSON IN NEED OF PROTECTION A person in need of protection is a person in Canada whose removal to his or her country or countries of nationality or, if he or she does not have a country of nationality, his or her country of former habitual residence, would subject him or her personally

(a) to a danger, believed on substantial grounds to exist, of torture within the meaning of Article 1 of the Convention Against Torture; or

(b) to a risk to his or her life or to a risk of cruel and unusual treatment or punishment if

(i) the person is unable or, because of that risk, unwilling to avail himself or herself of the protection of that country,

(ii) the risk would be faced by the person in every part of that country and is not faced generally by other individuals in or from that country,

(iii) the risk is not inherent or incidental to lawful sanctions, unless imposed in disregard of accepted international standards, and

(iv) the risk is not caused by the inability of that country to provide adequate health or medical care.

Immigration and Refugee Protection Act, S.C. 2001, c. 27, s. 97(1). See also **refugee**; **Convention Refugee**; **deportation**.

PERSONS CASE In the case of *Henrietta Muir Edwards et al. v. Attorney-General* *for Canada* (the "Persons Case"), [1930] A.C. 124 the Judicial Committee of the Privy Council held that women were "persons" as designated in s. 24 of the **Constitution Act, 1867** [B.N.A. Act] and could therefore be summoned to and become members of the Senate of Canada.

PER STIRPES (*pĕr stûr'-pāz*) Lat.: or stock; by family stock representation. Denotes how an **estate**, or portion of an estate, should be distributed on an **intestacy**. The essential characteristic of an intestate's estate *per stirpes* is that each distributee inherits in a representative capacity and stands in the place of a deceased ancestor. Thus each beneficiary receives a share in the property to be distributed, not necessarily equal, but the proper fraction of the fraction to which the person through whom he or she claims from the ancestor would have been entitled. It is distinguished from a distribution **per capita**, which is a provision for equal division among the beneficiaries, each receiving the same share as the others without reference to the intermediate course of descent from the ancestor. See *Dice v. Dice Estate*, 2012 ONCA 468.

PER TOUT ET NON PER MY (*pĕr tū ā nōn pĕr mē*) Law Fr.: by the whole and not by half. A term applied to a tenancy by the entirety or a joint tenancy (see **tenancy**); e.g., joint tenants or spouses who own property by the entirety own an **undivided interest** in the whole of the property but not an individual interest in half the property.

PETITION A prayer (formal request) from a person or group to a power or person for the exercise of his authority in the redress of some wrong. In old English law, a petition was addressed to the King and later to the Chancellor in a situation where a case was beyond the ordinary **writ** system.

PETITIONER One who presents a petition to a court or other body in order to either institute an **equity** proceeding or take an **appeal** from a **judgment**. The adverse party is called the **respondent**.

PETIT JURY See **jury**.

PHISHING Attempting to obtain information such as credit card details or usernames and passwords through the use of an electronic communication that falsely appears to be from a trusted source.

PICKETING The practice, often used in labour disputes, of patrolling, usually with placards, to publicize a dispute or to secure support for a cause.

PIERCING THE CORPORATE VEIL The process of disregarding the corporate entity and imposing liability on a person or entity other than the offending **corporation** itself.

Generally the corporate form isolates both individuals and **parent corporations** [see **subsidiary**] from liability for corporate misdeeds. However, there are times (such as when incorporation itself was accomplished to perpetrate a **fraud)** when the court will ignore the corporate entity and strip the organizers and managers of the corporation of the limited liability they usually enjoy. See, e.g., *642947 Ontario Limited v. Fleischer et al.* (2001), 56 O.R. (3d) 417 (Ont. C.A.); *Nisker v. Canada*, 2008 FCA 37.

PIRACY 1. In the context of commercial **tort**, the **misappropriation** or theft of a trade secret or an idea (under certain circumstances), or of a **trademark. 2.** Also, the illicit representing or reproduction of a copyrighted writing or article as a sound recording or work of art. See **copyright; infringement. 3.** Considered a crime under **international law** and under the *Criminal Code,* R.S.C. 1985, c. C–46, s. 74. In the criminal context, piracy is an **indictable offence** involving, inter alia, theft of a Canadian ship or its cargo, or a mutinous act on board a Canadian ship.

PITH AND SUBSTANCE The dominant matter with which a law is concerned; its real character. Used in the **division of powers** analysis to help determine whether a law passed by one level of government is **intra vires** or **ultra vires**. See, e.g., *Reference re Assisted Human Reproduction Act*, 2010 SCC 61. See **double aspect doctrine**.

PLAGIARISM Appropriation of the literary composition of another and passing off as one's own the product of the mind and language of another.

PLAINTIFF The one who initially brings the **suit**; a person who brings an **action**. Also, a **defendant** who brings a **counterclaim** will be considered a plaintiff as relating to his or her counterclaim. See **complainant**.

PLAIN VIEW DOCTRINE The rule that **evidence** that is discovered by a police officer with a prior justification for being present in a location is admissible if it is discovered inadvertently. The evidence must be readily apparent to the ordinary use of senses.

PLANNED AND DELIBERATE One of several potential criteria turning second degree murder into first degree murder; see *Criminal Code*, R.S.C. 1985, c. C–46, s. 231(2). "It has been held that 'planned' means that the scheme was conceived and carefully thought out before it was carried out, and 'deliberate' means considered, not impulsive." *R. v. Nygaard*, [1989] 2 S.C.R. 1074.

PLEA 1. In **equity**, a special answer showing or relying upon one or more things as a cause why the **suit** should be dismissed, delayed or barred. **2.** At **law**, broadly, any one of the common-law **pleadings**. **3.** Technically, the defendant's answer by matter of fact to the plaintiff's **declaration**, as distinguished from a **demurrer**, which is an answer by a matter of law. In criminal procedure, at his or her **arraignment**, the defendant will enter a plea of not guilty, guilty or a special plea, e.g., AUTREFOIS ACQUIT (see **double jeopardy**).

PLEA BARGAINING [PLEA AGREEMENT] An informal practice where the **accused** uses his or her right both to plead not guilty and to demand a full trial in order to bargain for a benefit that is usually related to a **charge** or the **sentence**. A plea bargain usually consists of an agreement with the **Crown prosecutor** to make a joint submission to the judge as to sentence. The Crown prosecutor is expected to abide by that agreement, and repudiating it could be, but is not necessarily, an **abuse of process**. "The repudiation of a plea agreement is not just a bare allegation. It is evidence that the Crown has gone back on its word. As everyone agrees, it is of crucial importance to the proper and fair administration of criminal justice that plea agreements be honoured. The repudiation of a plea agreement is a rare and exceptional event. In my view, evidence that a plea agreement was entered into with the Crown, and subsequently reneged by the Crown, provides the requisite evidentiary threshold to embark on a review of the decision for abuse of process." *R. v. Nixon*, 2011 SCC 34. The judge is not bound by the joint submission (*Criminal Code*, R.S.C 1985, c. C–46, s. 606(1.1)(b)(iii)), but there is an expectation that the recommendation will not be departed from without sound reasons. *R. v. Taylor*, 2008 CMAC 1.

PLEAD 1. To make a **pleading**; **2.** to answer **plaintiff's common-law declaration**; **3.** in criminal law, to answer to the **charge**, either by admitting or by denying guilt.

PLEADINGS Statements in writing served by each party alternatively to his or her opponent, stating the facts relied on to support his or her case and giving all details his or her opponent needs to know in order to prepare his or her case in answer. The usual pleadings in an action are the **statement of claim**, the **defence**, any **counterclaim**, a reply to the counterclaim, and any demands for further and better particulars.

PLEA IN ABATEMENT See **dilatory plea**.

PLEBISCITE The means of securing an expression of popular view from the common people on particular issues, usually by a yes/no response. The plebiscite has been used widely in many Canadian provinces in seeking local views, particularly concerning the sale of liquor. See **referendum**.

PLEDGE Property given to secure repayment of a debt. See *Caisse Populaire Desjardins de Val-Brillant v. Blouin*, 2003 SCC 31. Compare **PPSA**.

PLENARY Full; complete; absolute; perfect; unqualified. In judicial proceedings, the term denotes a complete, formally **pleaded** suit wherein a **bill** or **petition** or **complaint** is filed by one or more persons against one or more other persons who file an **answer** or a response. Compare **summary proceeding**.

POLICE BAIL An informal term referring to the provisions in the *Criminal Code*, R.S.C. 1985, c. C–46, ss. 503(2),(2.1) permitting police officers to release a detained person on conditions, rather than requiring that person to attend a **judicial interim release** hearing before a justice. *R. v. Oliveira*, 2009 ONCA 219.

POLITICAL ASYLUM See **asylum**.

POLITICAL QUESTION A question that is not properly subject to judicial determination because resolution of it is committed exclusively to the jurisdiction of another branch of government. The political question doctrine is not part of Canadian law. "The notion that there are inherently 'political' questions beyond the courts' jurisdiction was emphatically rejected in *Operation Dismantle Inc. v. The Queen*, [1985] 1 S.C.R. 441." *Newfoundland (Treasury Board) v. N.A.P.E.*, 2004 SCC 66.

POLL TAX An equal tax or a tax of a fixed amount upon all persons, or all persons of a particular category, without reference to property or lack of it.

POLYANDRY A form of polygamy in which a woman has more than one husband at the same time. See **polygamy**.

POLYGAMY The offence, under s. 293 of the *Criminal Code*, R.S.C. 1985, c. C–46, of having more than one spouse at one time. The constitutionality of the polygamy provisions has been questioned. *Reference re: Criminal Code of Canada (B.C.)*, 2011 BCSC 1588.

POSITIVE LAW Law enacted and adopted by proper authority for the government of an organized jural society; "law set by political superiors to political inferiors." J. Austin, *The Province of*

Jurisprudence Determined 9 (2d ed. 1954).

POSITIVISM In **jurisprudence**, the view that any legal system is best studied by concentrating on the **positive law** of that system; formed in reaction to **natural law** theory that claims that some principles or rules of human conduct are discoverable by reason alone and that there is a necessary connection between law and morals.

POSSE COMITATUS (*pŏ'-sā kŏm'-ĭ-tä'-tŭs*) Lat.: power or force of a country. The authority of the sheriff to assemble all able-bodied male inhabitants above the age of fifteen, except peers and clergymen, to defend the country against enemies of the Crown, to keep the peace, to pursue felons, or to enforce the royal writ. The term has become obsolete since the establishment of police forces.

POSSESSION The right to **custody**, dominion and control of **property**. The basic elements of possession are (1) intent to control (*animus possidendi*) and (2) sufficient physical control (*factum possidendi*). See *The "Tubantia"* [1924] P. 78 (H.C.J.).
ACTUAL POSSESSION occurs when a person has direct physical control over the thing at a given time. CONSTRUCTIVE POSSESSION occurs when a person, although not in actual possession, knowingly has both the power and the intention at a given time to exercise control over the thing, either directly or through another person.
In criminal law, by s. 4(3) of the *Criminal Code,* R.S.C. 1985, c. C–46, a person has custody when he or she has anything in his or her possession or knowingly in the actual possession or custody of another person or has it in any place, whether or not that place belongs to or is occupied by him or her, for use or benefit of himself or herself or another person. To constitute possession within the criminal law there must be knowledge of what the thing is and some act of control. See *R. v. Morelli*, 2010 SCC 8.

POSSESSORY ACTION A lawsuit brought for the purpose of obtaining or maintaining possession of **real property**. In a common instance, a landlord will bring a possessory action to evict holdover tenants (see **tenancy** [TENANCY AT SUFFERANCE]), praying that the court will issue a writ of possession against the holdover tenants.

POSSESSORY INTEREST A right to exert control over certain land to the exclusion of others, coupled with an intent to exercise that right. It is this privilege of exclusive occupation that distinguishes possessory from non-possessory interests. One holding a non-possessory interest is subject to specific restrictions with respect to the use he or she may make of land, but the holder of a possessory interest is limited only by the rights of others (including co-owners, neighbours or **remaindermen)**. Examples of non-possessory interests include **easements**, **remainders**, and the rights retained by the grantor of a **life estate**. See **adverse possession**.

POSSIBILITY OF A REVERTER The possibility of the return of an **estate** to the **grantor**, should a specified event occur or a particular act be performed in the future. The **interest** that remains in a grantor or **testator** after the **conveyance** or devise of a fee simple determinable (see **determinable fee)** and that permits the grantor to be revested automatically of his **estate** on, for example, **breach** of a condition. *Re Tilbury West Public School Board and Hastie,* [1966] 2 O.R. 20 (H.C.). Compare **re-entry [right of]**.

POSTAL ACCEPTANCE RULE See **mail box rule**.

POST FACTO See **ex post facto**.

POSTHUMOUS CHILD A child that is born after the death of his or her father.

POST MORTEM (*pōst môr'-těm*) Lat.: after death. An autopsy or examination of a dead body to ascertain the cause of death.

POST-OFFENCE CONDUCT A type of **circumstantial evidence** that looks to the behaviour of the accused person after an event as a way of making inferences about his or her state of mind at the time of the event. "Under certain circumstances, the conduct of an accused after a crime has been committed may provide circumstantial evidence of the accused's culpability for that crime. For example, an inference of guilt may be drawn from the fact that the accused fled from the scene of the crime or the jurisdiction in which it was committed, attempted to resist arrest, or failed to appear at trial. Such an inference may also arise from acts of concealment, for instance, where the accused has lied, assumed a false name, changed his or her appearance, or attempted to hide or dispose of incriminating evidence." *R. v. White,* [1998] 2 S.C.R. 72. Also referred to as "after-the-fact conduct." Previously referred to as "consciousness of guilt," but that language was discarded as too limited and as undermining the **presumption of innocence**.

POWER OF APPOINTMENT The legal authority given by a **grantor** (the **donor** of the power) to the **donee** of the power (also called the APPOINTOR) to appoint **property**, or an **interest** therein, to some person (the APPOINTEE). The power may be created by **deed** or **will**. A power may be (1) GENERAL, where the appointor may appoint anyone including himself or herself, (2) SPECIAL, where the choice of appointees is restricted by the terms of the power, or (3) HYBRID, where the appointor is given power to appoint anyone except certain people or groups of people. A power of appointment is distinguished from a trust power in that a power of appointment is discretionary whereas a trust power is obligatory upon the appointor. A bare power is usually coupled with a **gift over** in default of appointment.

POWER OF ATTORNEY An instrument in writing authorizing another to act as one's **agent** or attorney. It confers upon the agent the authority to perform certain specified acts or kinds of acts on behalf of his or her **principal**. Its primary purpose is to evidence the authority of the agent to third parties with whom the agent deals.

The traditional power of attorney ceases to be effective if the principal becomes incapacitated. Legislation has been enacted in some jurisdictions to provide for an **enduring** or **durable power of attorney**. In such cases, the enduring power of attorney authorizes the management of the estate of the **donor**, and is not terminated by reason of the donor's legal incapacity. See, e.g., *Powers of Attorney Act,* R.S.N.S. 1989, c. 352.

POWER OF SALE A provision in a **mortgage** which gives the mortgagee the authority to sell the mortgaged **property** on default of payment by the mortgagor in satisfaction of the **debt**.

PPSA (PERSONAL PROPERTY SECURITY ACT) Provincial or territorial **legislation** governing virtually all **security interests** in **personal property**, as opposed to **real property**. Every common law province and every territory has a PPSA; in Quebec, the **Civil Code** accomplishes similar goals. The PPSA regime is intended to replace prior **common law** or statutory approaches to granting a security. See, e.g., *Personal Property Security Act,* R.S.P.E.I. 1988, c. P–3.1, s. 3: "...Subject to section 4, this Act applies to (a) every transaction that in substance creates a security interest, without regard to its form and without regard to the person who has title to the **collateral**; and (b) without limiting the generality of clause (a), a **chattel mortgage, conditional sale contract, fixed charge, floating charge, pledge**, trust indenture, trust receipt, **assignment, consignment, lease, trust,** or transfer of **chattel** paper where it secures payment or performance of an obligation."

PRAYER FOR RELIEF That part of the **pleading** where the type of **relief** and **remedies** sought are enumerated (money **damages, injunction,** etc.) It is common to add a general request for "such other and further relief as to the court may seem just and proper" to enable the court to grant whatever relief it feels is appropriate.

PREAMBLE A preliminary clause in a **treaty, constitution, statute,** or other legal **instrument** that states the intent, purpose or spirit of the instrument. The preamble may be looked at to ascertain the intention of the legislation, but the enacting clauses are the ones that ultimately govern interpretation of the Act. "[A] preamble may afford useful light as to what a statute intends to reach, and ... if an enactment is itself clear and unambiguous, no preamble can clarify or cut down the enactment." *Powell v. The Kempton Park Racecourse Co. Ltd.,* [1899] A.C. 143 (H.L.). Compare **purview**. See **recitals**.

PRECATORY Advisory; in the nature of a prayer, request, recommendation or entreaty; conveying or embodying a recommendation or advice or the expression of a wish, but not a positive command or direction. The term is applied to language, usually in a **trust** or a **will**, by which the **settlor** or **testator** expresses a wish or a desire to benefit another but does not impose an enforceable obligation upon any party to carry out his or her wish.

PRECATORY TRUST See **trust**.

PRECAUTIONARY PRINCIPLE A principle at **international law** aimed at anticipating and preventing causes of environmental degradation. "Where there are threats of serious or irreversible damage, lack of full scientific certainty should not be used as a reason for postponing measures to prevent environmental degradation." *114957 Canada Ltée (Spraytech, Société d'arrosage) v. Hudson (Town),* 2001 SCC 40.

PRECEDENT 1. The doctrine [of judicial precedent] whereby a previously decided case is recognized as authority for the disposition of future cases. In the **common law**, precedents are regarded as a major source of law. A precedent may involve a novel question of common law or it may involve the interpretation of a **statute**. In either event, to the extent that future cases rely upon the precedent or distinguish it from themselves without disproving of it, the case will serve as a precedent for future cases under the doctrine of **stare decisis**. See further G. Gall, *The Canadian Legal System* (5th ed. 2004), c. 11. See **stare decisis; obiter dictum; ratio decidendi. 2.** The term is also used to denote a copy of an **instrument** used as a guide in preparing another instrument of similar description.

PRECEDENT CONDITION See **condition precedent**.

PRECEDING ESTATE A prior **estate** upon which a **future interest** is limited. Thus, a **remainder** is said to **vest** upon the termination of a preceding estate, such as a **life estate**.

PREDISPOSITION REPORT Under the former *Young Offenders Act,* R.S.C. 1985, c. Y–1, it was a report on the personal and family history and present environment of a young person. The *Young Offenders Act* has been repealed and replaced by the *Youth Criminal Justice Act,* S.C. 2002, c. 1; predisposition report is not used in the new act. See **Pre-Sentence Report**.

PREEMPTION 1. At common law, the term expressed the King's right to buy provisions and other necessities for the use of his household in preference to others. **2.** The contractual right of a buyer of property to purchase it prior to third parties, if he or she chooses to do so, when the owner of the property decides to sell it. A right of preemption is distinct from an **option to purchase** insofar as "an option gives the optionee the unilateral right to exercise the option and thereby require the optionor to sell the subject-matter of the option upon prearranged terms. A right of preemption, or right of first refusal, does not give the grantee the unilateral power to compel the grantor to sell the property in question. Instead, the grantor has the sole power to decide whether to make an offer. It is only at that point that the grantee... is given the opportunity of purchasing the property." *Mitsui & Co. (Canada) Ltd. v. Royal Bank of Canada,* [1995] 2 S.C.R. 187. **3.** Formerly at international law, it expressed the right of a nation to detain goods of a stranger in transit so as to afford its subjects a preference of purchase.

PREFERENCE A priority of payment given by an **insolvent** person to one creditor or to a certain class of his creditors over others. Under the *Bankruptcy and Insolvency Act,* R.S.C. 1985, c. B–3, s. 95, a FRAUDULENT PREFERENCE is not permitted. If the payment is made within three months of bankruptcy, the debtor was insolvent at the date of the payment, and, as a result of the payment, the creditor receives a preference over other creditors, then the payment is presumed to be a fraudulent preference. "However, it is a rebuttable presumption. In that regard, the courts have interpreted the above-quoted phrase as placing an onus on the creditor to establish that the debtor's dominant intent was not to prefer that creditor... it is settled law that the creditor's knowledge of the debtor's insolvency at the time of the payment is an irrelevant consideration. On the other hand, it is relevant that the corporate debtor knew of its insolvency at the date of the payment. If the debtor is related to the creditor, the payment will be scrutinized with greater care and suspicion. However, it is no defence to an allegation of fraudulent preference that the creditor exerted pressure on the insolvent debtor to secure the payment." *St. Anne Nackawic Pulp Co. (Trustee of) v. Logistec Stevedoring (Atlantic) Inc.,* 2005 NBCA 55.

PREFERRED DIVIDEND See **dividend**.

PREFERRED INDICTMENT A term sometimes used to describe a **direct indictment**.

PREFERRED SHARES Shares that confer on the holders some preference over other classes of shares in respect of either dividend or repayment of capital or both. P. Davies, *Gower and Davies' Principles of Modern Company Law* 821–23 (8th ed. 2008).

PREFERRED STOCK A class of stock entailing certain rights beyond those attached to common stock; corporate stock having preference rights. It represents a contribution to the capital of the corporation and is in no sense a loan of money. By general definition, preferred stock is stock entitled to a preference over other kinds of stock in the payment of **dividends**. The dividends come out of earnings [income] and not out of **capital**. Unless there are net earnings, there is no right to dividends.

PREJUDGMENT INTEREST Interest owing to a successful litigant for the period between the date of loss and the date the judgment is paid. Prejudgment interest is not to be used to punish either the successful or unsuccessful litigant, but is merely a reflection of the fact that one party has had the benefit of money owing to the other for a period of time.

PREJUDICE 1. Bias, preconceived opinion. For example, a bias based on race might constitute prejudice, which could disqualify a person from serving as a juror. See *R. v. Spence*, 2005 SCC 71. **2.** Deprivation of some legal right without just cause. For example, in considering an accused's right under the **Canadian Charter of Rights and Freedoms** to a trial within a reasonable time, "prejudice...is concerned with the three interests of the accused that s. 11(b) protects: liberty, as regards to pre-trial custody or bail conditions; security of the person, in the sense of being free from the stress and cloud of suspicion that accompanies a criminal charge; and the right to make full answer and defence, insofar as delay can prejudice the ability of the defendant to lead evidence, cross-examine witnesses, or otherwise to raise a defence." *R. v. Godin*, 2009 SCC 26. Similarly, in determining whether **evidence** is **admissible**, courts weigh the probative value of the evidence against its **prejudicial effect**; in this context, prejudice requires that there be something unfair about the admission of the evidence. "Just because a piece of evidence operates unfortunately for an accused does not of itself render the evidence inadmissible or the trial unfair." *R. v. Jesse*, 2012 SCC 21.

PREJUDICIAL EFFECT The risk of an unfocused **trial** and a wrongful conviction. The mere fact that **evidence** operates unfortunately toward an **accused** or increases the likelihood of conviction does not mean that the evidence is prejudicial. It will only be prejudicial if it operates unfairly, for example, by creating the possibility that a **jury** will convict the accused because it sees the accused as a bad person rather than because of proof of guilt for the particular offence. Prejudicial effect can also include undue consumption of time at the trial or potential confusion of the issues in the mind of the jury. Evidence

will be excluded if its prejudicial effect outweighs its **probative** value.

PREJUDICIAL ERROR An error that affects or presumptively affects the final results of the trial; an error substantively affecting the parties' legal rights and obligations. See **reversible error**.

PRELIMINARY HEARING A term sometimes used to describe what the *Criminal Code*, R.S.C. 1985, c. C–46 refers to as a **preliminary inquiry**.

PRELIMINARY INQUIRY "A hearing conducted in accordance with Part XVIII of the *Criminal Code*, before an accused is placed on trial for an indictable offence. An accused either can be committed for trial or discharged at the end of the preliminary inquiry. Originally, a preliminary inquiry was presumptively required in the case of all indictable offences, although it could be waived, but in its current form the preliminary inquiry is held on request and might be restricted to particular issues." S. Coughlan, *Criminal Procedure* 429 (2nd ed. 2012).

PREMEDITATION 1. Forethought; the act of meditating in advance, considering and contemplating prior to acting. It is a prior determination to do an act, but such determination need not exist for any particular period before it is carried out. **2.** In criminal law, the existence of premeditation in addition to the intent to cause death turns murder into first degree murder. "Murder is first degree murder when it is planned and deliberate." *Criminal Code*, R.S.C. 1985, c. C–46, s. 231(2).

PREMISES A term of inconsistent usage relating to real property. Some older authority holds that the term refers to the grounds immediately surrounding a house. *Martin v. Martin* (1904), 8 O.L.R. 462 (Ont. C.A.). More commonly courts use the term to refer to both land and the building on it, or even to only a part of that building: e.g., "the facts about the nature of the premises related only to the structure of the building." *Halifax (Regional Municipality) v. Nova Scotia (Human Rights Commission)*, 2012 SCC 10. Many statutes define the term to include not only buildings but other structures on the land, such as scaffolding, electrical poles, and railway cars: see, e.g., *Occupiers' Liability Act*, R.S.A. 2000, c. O–4, s. 1(d). See generally *R. v. Le*, 2011 MBCA 83.

PRENATAL NEGLIGENCE A **tort** action where the child sues a third party for harms done before it was born. *Duval v. Seguin* (1973), 40 D.L.R. (3d) 666 (Ont. C.A.). However, in *Dobson v. Dobson*, [1999] 2 S.C.R. 753, the Supreme Court of Canada held that the tort of prenatal negligence did not exist and that no legal duty of care could be imposed on a pregnant woman toward her foetus or subsequently born child. See **wrongful birth**.

PREPONDERANCE OF THE EVIDENCE The evidence with the most weight; the standard of proof used in most **civil** cases. It refers to the proof that leads the trier of fact (see **fact finder**) to find that the existence of the fact in issue is more probable than not. The general rule in civil cases is that the party having the **burden of proof** must produce a preponderance of evidence or that such evidence (when weighed with that opposed to it) has more convincing force, from which results the greater probability in favour of the party upon whom the burden rests. See **balance of probabilities**.

PREROGATIVE WRIT A class of writs granted by a court in its discretion if the matter so merits. Generally, the writs are a method by which the courts can exercise control over **administrative tribunals**, even in the absence of a specific right of appeal. The most common of these "extraordinary remedies" are the **writ of prohibition**, **mandamus**, **quo warranto**, **habeas corpus**, or **certiorari**.

PRESCRIPTION A term that signifies a manner of acquiring a **property** right as a result of the use or enjoyment of land openly and peacefully, and without interruption, for a prescribed period of time. At **common law** such a right was said to be acquired if enjoyed from "time immemorial." The time limit for acquiring a prescriptive right is commonly set by provincial **statutes**. In real estate law, prescription is one of the

principal means of creating or acquiring an **easement**. See further, B. Ziff, *Principles of Property Law* 386–89 (5th ed. 2010).

PRESCRIPTIVE JURISDICTION The ability of a state to pass domestic laws that govern the conduct of individuals or affect their rights or property. "Prescriptive jurisdiction (also called legislative or substantive jurisdiction) is the power to make rules, issue commands, or grant authorizations that are binding upon persons and entities." *R. v. Hape*, 2007 SCC 26. See **enforcement jurisdiction**.

PRE-SENTENCE REPORT Under the *Youth Criminal Justice Act*, S.C. 2002, c. 1., ss. 2 and 40, it is a report on the personal and family history and present environment of a young person found guilty of an offence under the Act. It is used to assist the court in determining the appropriate sentence for the young person given the circumstances.

PRESENTMENT 1. In criminal law, formerly a written accusation of **crime** made and returned by the **grand jury** upon its own initiative in the exercise of its lawful inquisitorial powers. Grand juries no longer exist in Canada.
2. In commercial law, the presenting of a **bill of exchange** or **promissory note** to the party on whom is **drawn**, for his or her acceptance, or to the person bound to pay, for payment. Where the instrument has been **executed** and the parties bound thereby, presentment means presentment for payment, as distinguished from presentment for **acceptance**, which is made before the instrument is due.

PRESUMPTION An assumption arising from a given set of facts that has sufficient evidentiary weight to require the production of further **evidence** to overcome the assumption thereby established. A presumption may be one of law or of fact.
A PRESUMPTION OF LAW is one that must be made, either because of some statutory provision or a common law rule (such as the **presumption of advancement**).

A PRESUMPTION OF FACT is one that relates to the particular evidence in a case. For example, on proof of an injury to the plaintiff in a **class action** suit, "the court can draw from the evidence a presumption of fact that the members of the group have suffered a similar injury." *St. Lawrence Cement Inc. v. Barrette*, 2008 SCC 64.

CONCLUSIVE [NON-REBUTTABLE] PRESUMPTION One that no evidence, however strong, no argument, or consideration will be permitted to overcome.

REBUTTABLE PRESUMPTION An ordinary presumption that must, as a matter of law, be made once certain facts have been proved, and that is thus said to establish a certain conclusion **prima facie** once those facts have been adduced; but it is one that may be rebutted. If it is not overcome through introduction of contrary evidence, it becomes conclusive. See *R. v. Oakes*, [1986] 1 S.C.R. 103.

PRESUMPTION OF ADVANCEMENT See **advancement**.

PRESUMPTION OF CONSTITUTIONALITY
A rule of construction providing that statutes are presumed to be constitutional unless proven otherwise. The main legal implication of the presumption of constitutionality is that where a statutory provision is capable of supporting both constitutional and unconstitutional interpretations, each of which is plausible, a court should adopt the interpretation that upholds the law, rather than striking it down. P.W. Hogg, *Constitutional Law of Canada*, 15–23 (5th ed. 2007).

PRESUMPTION OF DEATH At common law, a person was presumed dead if he or she had not been heard from or of for seven years. The common law presumption has been replaced by a statute that allows a court, upon application, to make an order declaring that a person is presumed dead. For example, *The Presumption of Death Act*, C.C.S.M. c. P120, s. 2(1) permits such an order to be made when "(a) a person has been absent and not heard of or from by the applicant, or to the knowledge of the applicant by any other person, since a day named; (b) the applicant has no reason to believe that the person is living; and (c) reasonable grounds exist for supposing that the person is dead."

PRESUMPTION OF INNOCENCE In the **Canadian Charter of Rights and Freedoms**, section 11(d) provides that anyone charged with an offence has the right "to be presumed innocent until proven guilty according to law in a fair and public hearing by an independent and impartial tribunal." Speaking of the right enumerated in s. 11(d), in *R. v. Oakes,* [1986] 1 S.C.R. 103, the Supreme Court stated that the right was "crucial." "It ensures that until the State proves an accused's guilt beyond all reasonable doubt, he or she is innocent. This is essential in a society committed to fairness and social justice. The presumption of innocence confirms our faith in humankind; it reflects our belief that individuals are decent and law-abiding members of the community until proven otherwise."

The presumption of innocence existed at common law. See *Woolmington v. Director of Public Prosecutions,* [1935] A.C. 462 (H.L.). See also *R. v. Lifchus*, [1997] 3 S.C.R. 320.

PRESUMPTION OF RESULTING TRUST See **advancement**.

PRESUMPTION OF SURVIVORSHIP A **common law** rule in matters relating to **wills** and **estates**, that in situations where two people die together and it is impossible to determine which of the two died first, the younger of the two is presumed to have survived the older. Some provinces have legislation that adopts a different approach. For example, the *Survivorship Act*, S.N.B. 1991, c. S–20 provides that when two or more persons die within ten days of one another or in circumstances where the order of death cannot be determined, they are deemed to have died at the same time. In such circumstances, the property of each person "shall be disposed of as if that person had survived the other or others."

PRESUMPTIVE EVIDENCE Evidence that is indirect or **circumstantial**; **prima facie** evidence; evidence that is not

conclusive and admits of explanation or contradiction; evidence that must be treated as true and sufficient until and unless rebutted by other evidence, i.e., evidence that a statute deems to be presumptive of another fact unless rebutted. See, e.g., s. 348(2), *Criminal Code,* R.S.C. 1985, C–46. See **presumption**.

PRICE FIXING The cooperative setting of price levels or ranges by competing firms; an illegal trade practice involving a **conspiracy** or agreement among sellers to raise, depress, fix, peg, or stabilize prices. See *Competition Act,* R.S.C. 1985, c. C–34 , s. 45(1).

PRIMA FACIE (*prī'-mà fā'-shà*) Lat.: at first sight; on the face of it. A fact presumed to be true unless disproved by contrary evidence. See *Craig v. McKay* (1906), 12 O.L.R. 121 (C.A.).

PRIMA FACIE CASE The presentation of **evidence** that, if believed, would establish each of the elements necessary for the action to succeed. In assessing whether a *prima facie* case is made out, a judge does not decide whether evidence is, in fact, likely to be believed, but merely whether it would establish the necessary things if it were believed. The term is used in many contexts, including **civil** proceedings and **criminal** cases, among others. "A *prima facie* case...is one [that] covers the allegations made and which, if they are believed, is complete and sufficient to justify a verdict in the complainant's favour in the absence of an answer." *New Brunswick (Human Rights Commission) v. Potash Corporation of Saskatchewan Inc.,* 2008 SCC 45, quoting *Ontario Human Rights Commission v. Simpsons–Sears Ltd.,* [1985] 2 S.C.R. 536. Compare **nonsuit**.

PRIMA FACIE EVIDENCE "Prima facie evidence is evidence which, if accepted by the tribunal, establishes a fact in the absence of acceptable evidence to the contrary." 15 *Halsbury's Laws of England,* (3d ed.), para. 506.

PRIME MINISTER The head of the Canadian federal government. By unwritten constitutional convention, the **Governor General of Canada** is tasked with selecting a person as Prime Minister who is most likely to command the "confidence" of the **House of Commons**. In modern times, this person has invariably been the leader of the political party that holds a majority or plurality of seats in the House of Commons after an election. The Prime Minister is responsible for "advising" the Governor General on matters like the selection of other ministers, the enactment of **legislation**, judicial appointments, and the summoning, **prorogation**, and dissolution of **Parliament**. For all practical purposes, however, the Governor General will always follow the Prime Minister's advice. The "Prime Minister... effectively controls the executive branch of government through his control over ministerial appointments and over the cabinet. But... the Prime Minister effectively controls the legislative branch as well. In the normal situation of majority government (and assuming a compliant **Senate**), the Prime Minister's leadership of the majority party in the House of Commons, reinforced by strict party discipline, and sanctioned by his power to dissolve the House for an election, enables him to determine what legislation will be enacted." P.W. Hogg, *Constitutional Law of Canada,* 9–12 (5th ed. 2007). See also P.J. Monahan, *Constitutional Law,* 64–77 (3rd ed. 2006).

PRIMOGENITURE Ancient **common law** of **descent** in which the eldest son takes all property of his decedent father. The opposite of primogeniture, BOROUGH ENGLISH, where the youngest son inherited on the death of the father, existed under local custom in at least one jurisdiction even while primogeniture prevailed elsewhere in England. Under the local custom of GAVELKIND, all sons took equally. In the event all **issue** of the **decedent** were daughters, they took equal shares in **coparceny**. See generally J.H. Baker, *An Introduction to English Legal History* 303–07 (3rd ed. 1990).

PRINCIPAL Most important; primary; highest in rank, authority, character, degree or importance.

 1. In criminal law, the person who actually committed the **offence**. The **common law** distinguished between a principal in the first degree (the actual perpetrator) and a principal in the second degree (someone who **aided or abetted**). That distinction is now described in the case law as the difference between a principal and a party. See, e.g., *R. v. Ruzic*, 2001 SCC 24. However, for some purposes, the definition of a party to an offence includes the person who actually committed it. *Criminal Code*, R.S.C. 1985, c. C–46, s. 21(1)(a).

2. In agency law, a person who authorizes an **agent** to act on his or her behalf. Principals may be "disclosed" or "undisclosed." "Disclosed principals are those whose existences are revealed to the third party by the agent with whom the third party is transacting." G. Fridman, *Canadian Agency Law* 138 (2009). "Where a principal is undisclosed," however, "neither the identity of the principal nor the fact that the agent is acting on behalf of someone else is revealed to the third party." *Id.* See also F.M.B. Reynolds, *Bowstead and Reynolds on Agency* (18th ed. 2006), c. 1.

3. In commercial law, the amount that is received in the case of a loan, or the amount upon which interest is charged.

PRINCIPLED EXCEPTION A basis for admitting **evidence** that would otherwise be inadmissible because it violates the hearsay rule. Under the principled exception, hearsay is admissible if it meets the two criteria of necessity and reliability. "Necessity" refers to whether it is necessary to admit the hearsay in order to have the particular testimony: the criterion is met if the **declarant** is deceased, but also if the declarant has **recanted** from a previous statement. "Reliability" is divided into "threshold reliability" and "ultimate reliability." Ultimate reliability concerns the weight that will actually be attached to the evidence by the **trier of fact** and is not the issue in assessing whether to admit evidence under the principled exception. Threshold reliability asks whether there is sufficient reliability to allow the evidence to be put before the trier of fact. Threshold reliability can be met in two distinct ways. First, the circumstances in which the statement came about can be such that there is no real concern about

whether the statement is true or not; for example, a statement by a child about a type of sexual activity of which he or she is unlikely to have any independent knowledge will meet threshold reliability in that way. Second, a statement can meet threshold reliability because, in the circumstances, its truth and accuracy can nonetheless be sufficiently tested; for example, a statement that was made under oath, subjected to cross-examination, and admitted as testimony at a former proceeding will meet threshold reliability in that way. See *R. v. Khelawon*, 2006 SCC 57.

In deciding whether to admit hearsay, a judge should first consider the traditional exceptions and then look at the principled exception. The traditional exceptions are presumptively valid, but they are subject to modification in light of the principled analysis of necessity and reliability. See *R. v. Starr*, 2000 SCC 40. See **K.G.B. statement**.

PRINCIPLES OF FUNDAMENTAL JUSTICE The basic tenets and principles of the legal system. Under s. 7 of the **Canadian Charter of Rights and Freedoms**, any measure that violates life, liberty, or security of the person must accord with the principles of fundamental justice. The principles of fundamental justice are not limited to procedural guarantees, and whether a particular principle is a principle of fundamental justice rests on the essential role of that principle within the legal system. To be a principle of fundamental justice: "(1) It must be a legal principle; (2) There must be a consensus that the rule or principle is fundamental to the way in which the legal system ought fairly to operate; and (3) It must be identified with sufficient precision to yield a manageable standard against which to measure deprivations of life, liberty, or security of the person." *R. v. D.B.*, 2008 SCC 25.

PRIOR CONSISTENT STATEMENT An earlier statement by a witness that is to the same effect as the testimony at trial. The general rule is that such a statement is not **admissible**, both because it violates the rule against **hearsay** and because it is **oath-helping**: "Repetition does not, and should not be seen to, enhance the value or truth of testimony." *R. v. Ellard,* 2009 SCC 27. That general rule is subject to long-established exceptions, for example, that a prior consistent statement is admissible to rebut an allegation of **recent fabrication** or to show the witness's state of mind at the time the statement was made. It has been proposed that an approach similar to the principled exception to the hearsay rule ought to be adopted with regard to prior consistent statements, but to date the only impact of that argument has been to create a further exception to the rule against admissibility, allowing the admission of spontaneous exculpatory statements made by an accused person upon or shortly after arrest for the purpose of showing the reaction of the accused when first confronted with the accusation, provided the accused testifies and thereby exposes himself or herself to cross-examination. See *R. v. Edgar,* 2010 ONCA 529; and *R. v. Dinardo,* 2008 SCC 24.

PRIOR INCONSISTENT STATEMENT A previous statement by a **witness** to a different effect than the testimony of that witness in court. The traditional rule was that a prior inconsistent statement is admissible only to **impeach** the **credibility** of a **witness**, but not as evidence of the truth of its contents. That rule is now subject to exception where the prior inconsistent statement qualifies for admission, as an exception to the **hearsay** rule, as a **K.G.B. statement**.

PRIORITY Preference; the condition of coming before, or of coming first; e.g., in a **bankruptcy** proceeding, the right to be paid before other **creditors** out of the assets of the bankrupt party. The term may also be used with reference to a **prior lien**, prior **mortgage**, etc.

PRIOR LIEN A first or superior **lien**, though not necessarily one antecedent to others.

PRISON Technically, a provincial institution or facility to which persons who are convicted of a criminal offence and sentenced to less than two years are confined for the duration of their sentence. It includes a penitentiary, common jail, public or reformatory prison, lock-up, guardroom or other place in which persons who are charged with or convicted of offences are usually kept in custody. *Criminal Code,* R.S.C. 1985, c. C–46, s. 2. The provinces have jurisdiction over prisons under s. 92(6) of the **Constitution Act, 1867**. See **penitentiary**.

PRIVACY A person's interest in being left alone, primarily but not exclusively by the state. Privacy consists of at least three interests: personal privacy, territorial privacy, and informational privacy. See **reasonable expectation of privacy**. Also, provisions in federal and some provincial legislation "relate to an individual's access to and use of personal information in government data banks concerning himself...." G. Gall, *The Canadian Legal System* 573–74 (5th ed. 2004). See, e.g., *Privacy Act,* R.S.C. 1985, c. P–21; *Privacy Act,* R.S.N.L. 1990, c. P–22. Compare **freedom of information**.

PRIVATE COMMUNICATION Defined in s. 183 of the *Criminal Code,* R.S.C., c. C–46, as "any oral communication, or any telecommunication, that is made by an originator who is in Canada or is intended by the originator to be received by a person who is in Canada and that is made under circumstances in which it is reasonable for the originator to expect that it will not be intercepted by any person other than the person intended by the originator to receive it, and includes any radio-based telephone communication that is treated electronically or otherwise for the purpose of preventing intelligible reception by any person other than the person intended by the originator to receive it." *R. v. Cheung* (1995), 100 C.C.C. (3d) 441 (B.C.S.C.).

PRIVATE INTERNATIONAL LAW See **conflict of laws**.

PRIVATE LAW Those areas of law dealing with the relationships between individuals, such as claims for damages in **tort** or under a **contract**. Contrast **public law**.

PRIVATE PROSECUTION A prosecution commenced by a private individual, rather than by an agent of the **attorney-**

general of a province. Private prosecutors are bound by the same obligations and liabilities as public prosecutors. Indeed, a private prosecution should not be confused with a "private action between the parties." A private prosecutor is merely permitted "under criminal law to prosecute in the place of the attorney-general." S. Coughlan, *Criminal Procedure* 46 (2nd ed. 2012).

PRIVATIVE CLAUSE "A statutory provision which attempts to eliminate or restrict the scope of **judicial review**. Sometimes called a "preclusive" or "no certiorari" clause." D.J. Mullan, *Administrative Law* (2001), at 545. A privative clause cannot prevent a court from reviewing a decision for an excess of **jurisdiction**. *Dunsmuir v. New Brunswick*, 2008 SCC 9.

PRIVILEGE 1. A basis for keeping otherwise **relevant** and **admissible evidence** from a **trier of fact** in order to protect a particular relationship that depends on **confidentiality**. Privileges are divided into "class privilege" and "case-by-case privilege." In a class privilege, all communications that fall into the category automatically qualify for privilege; communications between **spouses** are one example of a class privilege, as is **solicitor-client privilege** and **informer privilege**. Whether communications between other categories of people, such as priests and penitents or journalists and informants, should be regarded as privileged is decided on a case-by-case basis using the **Wigmore test**. See A.W. Bryant, S.N. Lederman, & M.K. Fuerst, *The Law of Evidence in Canada* (3rd ed. 2009), c. 14.

2. A particular advantage or benefit enjoyed by a person, company or class, beyond the common advantages of other citizens; "an advantage conferred over and above ordinary law." *Re Turner* (1922), 65 D.L.R. 130 (Sask.K.B.). Examples include the personal privilege of an ambassador from arrest, exemption from jury duty among certain professionals, and special immunities and advantages given to persons within special relationships such as attorney/client, doctor/patient, etc.

3. In the law of **libel** and **slander**, a **defence** that impliedly admits the defamatory nature of the words complained of but seeks to defend it on the grounds that the words were published on a privileged occasion exempting the defendant from liability. Privilege may be absolute, like that enjoyed by judges, juries, the parties, and their counsel in judicial proceedings. See, e.g., *Comeau v. Pole*, 2005 NBCA 113. It may also be qualified, as in a defence of **fair comment**. "The defamatory statement ... is only protected when it is fairly warranted by some reasonable occasion or exigency, and when it is fairly made in discharge of some public or private duty or in the conduct of the defendant's own affairs in matters in which his interests are concerned." *Halls v. Mitchell*, [1928] S.C.R. 125 at 133 quoted in *Home Equity Development Inc. v. Crow*, 2004 BCSC 124. See also the various provincial **defamation** or libel and slander statutes.

PRIVILEGED [CONFIDENTIAL] COMMUNICATIONS Communications that occur between spouses and in certain other relationships usually of a professional nature, e.g., solicitor and client, priest and penitent. Designating a communication as privileged allows the speaker to resist legal pressure to disclose its contents.

PRIVITY A relationship between parties arising out of a mutuality of interest.

PRIVITY OF CONTRACT The doctrine whereby one can enforce contractual rights against another only if one was a party to the contract. Under the general doctrine of privity of contract, no one who is not an original party to a contract is entitled to seek to enforce the terms of the contract or is bound by any of its provisions. *Great Northern Ry. Co. v. Cole Agencies Ltd.* (1964), 49 W.W.R. (N.S.) 153 at 159 (Sask.Q.B.). The general doctrine has been relaxed in a few notable decisions of the Supreme Court of Canada. See, e.g., *London Drugs* case referred to in **Third Party Beneficiary** entry. See also *Fraser River Pile & Dredge Ltd. v. Can-Dive Services Ltd.*, [1999] 3 S.C.R. 108.

PRIVITY OF ESTATE The relationship between persons who have property interest in the same estate, such as **lessor** and **lessee** or **joint tenants**.

PRIVY Persons who have an interest in some matter, action or thing, and the relation is other than that of actual **contract**.

PRIVY COUNCIL, CANADA According to s. 11 of the *Constitution Act, 1867,* "There shall be a Council to aid and advise in the Government of Canada, to be styled the Queen's Privy Council for Canada; and the Persons who are to be Members of that Council shall be from Time to Time chosen and summoned by the **Governor General** and sworn in as Privy Councillors, and Members thereof may be from Time to Time removed by the Governor General." In Canada the Privy Council is by convention the federal **cabinet**, and its advice to the Governor-General is tantamount to a direction. P.W. Hogg, *Constitutional Law of Canada* 9–10–9–11 (5th ed. 2007). The cabinet ministers are all appointed to the Queen's Privy Council for Canada. Appointments are for life, so that its membership also includes ministers of past governments as well as some honourary appointments for persons of distinction. The cabinet, however, constitutes the only active part of the Privy Council, and it exercises all the powers of that body except certain powers reserved specifically unto the Governor-General or the Prime Minister.

PRIZE FIGHT "[A]n encounter or fight with fists or hands between two persons who have met for that purpose by previous arrangement made by or for them" but excluding boxing matches in which the participants "wear boxing gloves of not less than one hundred and forty grams each in mass," and events held by an athletic body established by a provincial legislature. *Criminal Code*, R.S.C. 1985, c. C–46, s. 64. Participating in, promoting, or being present at a prize fight "as an aid, second, surgeon, umpire, backer, or reporter" is a **summary offence** under the *Criminal Code*. *Id.*

PROBABLE CAUSE See **reasonable grounds to believe**.

PROBATE The procedure for determining the validity of a **will** and for the proper distribution of an **estate**. The surrogate or probate court of the province has jurisdiction to issue certificates of probate to acknowledging that the will has been proved and registered and that the **administration** of the estate will be **executed**.

PROBATION In criminal law, a non-custodial sentence; the release of an accused into the community under the supervision of a probation officer. The release is conditional on the accused acting in a manner stipulated by his special officer. Compare **parole**.

PROBATIVE Tending to prove or proving facts, evidence and issues.

PRO BONO (*prō bō'-nō*) Lat.: for the good of; i.e., pro bono publico: for the public good or welfare. This term is often used in reference to legal services offered pro bono by a lawyer; legal services that are donated by the lawyer.

PROCEDURAL FAIRNESS See **natural justice**.

PROCEDURE The mode of proceeding by which a legal right is enforced, including the whole law of evidence, the enforcement of a right, rules of limitation, methods of execution and formal steps in an action. The rules of procedure do not extend to the substantive right. See **substantive law**.

PROCEEDING "[T]he form in which actions are brought and defended, the manner of intervening in suits and of conducting them." *Eddy v. Stewart,* [1932] 3 W.W.R. 71 at 74 (Sask.C.A.). The term is usually broader in meaning than **action** and is also applied to any step in an action. In its derivative sense, the term means the action of going onward, advancing.

PROCEEDS OF CRIME Any **property**, benefit, or advantage obtained or derived directly or indirectly as a result of the commission, in Canada or elsewhere, of an **indictable offence** or a **conspiracy** to commit an indictable offence. *Criminal Code*, R.S.C. 1985, c. C–46, s. 462.3.

PROCESS 1. A formal writing **(writ)** used by the court to exercise **jurisdiction** over a person; usually refers to the method used to compel attendance of a **defendant** in court in a **civil** suit. See **service**; **service of process**. **2.** Also, the **proceeding** in any action from beginning to end. **3.** In patent law, the method by which certain subject matter is transformed into a different state of thing. Patent law protects not only the thing produced but also the process of producing the same. *The Commissioner of Patents v. CIBA Ltd.*, [1959] S.C.R. 378; *McKay v. Weatherford Canada Ltd.*, 2008 FCA 369.

PROCLAIM [PROCLAMATION] In the case of **legislation**, to declare to be in force. A proclamation will be published by **Parliament** or the **legislature** in the appropriate **gazette**.

PROCTOR 1. One who manages another's affairs, acting as that person's **agent**. **2.** Also, a lawyer who **probates** an **estate** on behalf of the **executor** of a **will**. Compare **administrator**.

PRODUCTION The release to an **accused** person of records that are in the hands of a third party rather than the **Crown prosecutor**. Because there might be third party privacy interests competing with the accused's interest in receiving **evidence**, a more stringent test must be met for production of third party documents than for **disclosure** of material in the hands of the Crown. *R. v. O'Connor*, [1995] 4 S.C.R. 411. The production of third party records in the prosecution of certain offences (primarily sexual offences) is governed by a statutory scheme; see *Criminal Code*, R.S.C. 1985, c. C–46, ss. 278.1–278.91.

PRODUCTS LIABILITY A concept in the law of **torts** regarding the circumstances in which a manufacturer who designs and puts a product on the market is liable to the ultimate consumer to ensure that the goods so marketed are free from defects arising from **negligence** or lack of care on the part of the manufacturer. See, e.g., *Tabrizi v. Whallon Machine*

Inc., 29 C.C.L.T. (2d) 176; *Hanke v. Resurfice Corp.*, 2003 ABQB 616, aff'd by *Resurfice Corp. v. Hanke*, 2007 SCC 7 *Andersen v. St. Jude Medical Inc.*, 2012 ONSC 3660. See **warranty**.

PROFESSIONAL CONDUCT See **professional responsibility**.

PROFESSIONAL RESPONSIBILITY "The essence of professional responsibility is that the **lawyer** must act at all times *uberrimae fidei*, with utmost good faith to the court, to the client, to other lawyers, and to members of the public." *Canadian Bar Association Code of Professional Conduct (C.B.A. Code)* (2009). All Canadian jurisdictions refer to the *C.B.A. Code* to a greater or lesser extent when dealing with ethical principles and professional standards of conduct which should be observed by members of the legal profession. Some jurisdictions, such as, Newfoundland and Labrador, Prince Edward Island, Northwest Territories, Nunavat and the Yukon adopted the *Code* with some modifications. Other jurisdictions, such as Nova Scotia, use the *C.B.A. Code* as a model, with changes to emphasize and to provide greater clarity which better reflects the practice of lawyers in the jurisdiction. See, e.g., Nova Scotia Barristers' Society *Code of Professional Conduct* (2012).

PROFIT À PRENDRE "[A] right to enter the land of another to harvest specific natural produce of the land, such as timber, crops, minerals, turf, peat, sand, soil, fish, or animals. The thing taken must be part of the land—minerals or crops, for example—or wild animals existing on the land. Rights to take water may be granted as easements, but not as *profits à prendre*." A.M. Sinclair & M.E. McCallum, *An Introduction to Real Property Law* 58–59 (6th ed. 2012). An oil and gas lease is generally considered to be a *profit à prendre. Berkheiser v. Berkheiser and Glaister*, [1957] S.C.R. 387.

PRO FORMA (*prō fôr'-mà*) Lat.: for the sake of form. As a matter of form. In an appealable **decree** or **judgment**, the term usually means that the decision was rendered, not upon intellectual conviction that the decree was right, but merely to facilitate further proceedings.

PROGRESSIVE DISCIPLINE In **labour** and **employment** law, the concept that less severe penalties should initially be employed in the case of an employee who is in breach of the rules, giving him or her a chance to mend the behaviour or face increasing sanctions.

PROHIBITED MARK A mark that is not permitted to be adopted as a **trade-mark**. See *Trade-marks Act*, R.S.C., 1985, c. T–13, s. 9.

PROHIBITION See **writ** [WRIT OF PROHIBITION].

PROMISE A declaration that binds the person who makes it, either in honour, conscience or law, to do or forbear a certain specific act, and that gives the person to whom it is made a right to expect or claim performance of the thing promised. It is an essential element of an **offer** in **contract**. See also **covenant**.

PROMISEE A person who receives a **promise** or undertaking relating to some event.

PROMISOR One who makes a **promise** or gives an undertaking relating to some event.

PROMISSORY ESTOPPEL See **estoppel**.

PROMISSORY NOTE 1. A kind of **negotiable instrument** wherein the maker agrees (promises) to pay a specific sum at a definite time. **2.** "[A]n unconditional promise in writing made by one person to another person, signed by the maker, engaging to pay, on demand or at a fixed or determinable future time, a sum certain in money to, or to the order of, a specified person or to bearer." *Bills of Exchange Act*, R.S.C. 1985, c. B–4, s. 176.

PROPORTIONALITY The fundamental principle of sentencing. Proportionality requires that a sentence reflects the gravity of the offence, and also that the sentence does not exceed what is appropriate, given the moral blameworthiness of the offender. *R. v. Ipeelee*, 2012 SCC 13.

PROPOSAL A contract between a **debtor** and the **creditors** for an **arrangement** that becomes binding on the parties by **statute**; a contemplation of some arrangement between a debtor and creditors whereby the debtor's assets will be wrested or controlled by the trustee in bankruptcy while the arrangement is being carried out. See *Bankruptcy and Insolvency Act*, R.S.C. 1985, c. B–3, ss. 50–66.4.

PROOF The quantity or quality of **evidence** that tends to establish the existence of a fact in issue; the persuasion of the **trier of fact** (see **fact finder**) by the production of evidence of the truth of a fact alleged. It includes the **burden of proof** borne by a party, who will lose on the issue if after reviewing all the evidence the judge or jury entertains the appropriate degree of doubt. See also **inference**; **preponderance of the evidence**; **presumption**; **reasonable doubt**.

PROOF BEYOND A REASONABLE DOUBT See **reasonable doubt**.

PROPERTY That which belongs exclusively to a person; in a legal sense, the aggregate of rights or **interests** that are subject to **ownership**. The term may denote the thing or object to which the rights or interests apply or the legal relation that exists with respect to those rights. Property may be an object having physical existence or it may be an intangible thing such as a **patent** right or **domain name**. Property is usually divided into two classes, real and personal. Compare **possession**. See **real property**; **personalty**.

COMMON PROPERTY That which belongs to the citizenry as a whole; property owned by TENANTS IN COMMON (see **tenancy)**, or in some jurisdictions, where designated by statute, that owned by spouses.

PROPRIETARY INTEREST See **interest**.

PRO RATA (*prō ra'-ta*) Lat.: according to the rate, i.e., in proportion; according to a measure that fixes proportions. It has no meaning unless referable to some rule or standard. Thus, a lease terminated by agreement before the expiration of the full term may call for payment of rent on a *pro rata* basis for the expired term of the lease; an adjudicated bankrupt, after establishing **insolvency**, is relieved of liability to all tested creditors after engaging in a *pro rata* distribution of his or her assets among those creditors.

PROROGATION The bringing of a session of **Parliament** (or a provincial legislature) to an end. This, like dissolution that brings Parliament to an end, can be done only by an exercise of the royal prerogative. Adjournment to a future hour on the same day, or to a future day, can be effected by Parliament's own motion; all business lapses upon prorogation and must be reintroduced in the new session or the new Parliament.

PRO SE (*prō sā*) Lat.: for himself or herself; in one's own behalf. For example, one represents himself or herself *pro se* in a legal **action** when he or she does so without aid of **counsel**. Such a person would more commonly be referred to as a **self-represented litigant**.

PROSECUTION The act of pursuing a criminal **trial** by the Crown.

PROSECUTOR A public official who prepares and conducts the prosecution of persons accused of crime. The provincial prosecutors are usually called **Crown prosecutors**. The basic role of the prosecutor is to seek justice and not convictions. The office is charged with the duty to see that the laws of the jurisdiction are faithfully executed and enforced. In the enforcement of laws, the prosecutor has the responsibility of making a decision of who and when to prosecute, a decision with respect to which the prosecution has broad directions. See **Crown Prosecutor**; see also **Director of Public Prosecutions**.

PROSECUTORIAL DISCRETION The **constitutional** principle that the Attorney-General is entitled to act independently when supervising prosecutorial decisions and that decisions made as part of that discretion are not reviewable by courts, short of an abuse of process. "'Prosecutorial discretion' is a term of art. It does not simply refer to

any discretionary decision made by a Crown prosecutor. Prosecutorial discretion refers to the use of those powers that constitute the core of the Attorney-General's office and [which] are protected from the influence of improper political and other vitiating factors by the principle of independence.

Without being exhaustive, we believe the core elements of prosecutorial discretion encompass the following: (a) the discretion whether to bring the prosecution of a charge laid by police; (b) the discretion to enter a stay of proceedings in either a private or public prosecution, as codified in the *Criminal Code*, R.S.C. 1985, c. C–46, ss. 579 and 579.1; (c) the discretion to accept a guilty plea to a lesser charge; (d) the discretion to withdraw from criminal proceedings altogether...; and (e) the discretion to take control of a **private prosecution**... While there are other discretionary decisions, these are the core of the delegated sovereign authority peculiar to the office of the Attorney-General.

Significantly, what is common to the various elements of prosecutorial discretion is that they involve the ultimate decisions as to *whether* a prosecution should be brought, continued, or ceased, and *what* the prosecution ought to be for." *Krieger v. Law Society of Alberta*, 2002 SCC 65.

PROSECUTRIX A term formerly used to describe a female victim in a sexual assault case. It was rooted in the fact that historically, it was up to the victim in sexual assault cases to initiate proceedings against an accused. See **complainant**.

PROSPER WARNING The requirement that a person who (1) has been **arrested** and has expressed a desire to exercise the right to **counsel** under the **Canadian Charter of Rights and Freedoms**; (2) has been unsuccessful in doing so; and (3) has expressed a desire to waive the right to counsel be advised that the police have a duty to hold off from investigating until that person has had a reasonable opportunity to consult with counsel. See *R. v. Prosper*, [1994] 3 S.C.R. 236.

PROSTITUTE 1. "A person of either sex who engages in prostitution." *Criminal Code*, R.S.C. 1985, c. C–46, s. 197(1). **2.** "[T]he selling of a talent or capacity for an unworthy purpose." *R. v. Patterson* (1972), 9 C.C.C. (2d) 364 at 366 (Ont.Co.Ct.).

PROSTITUTION The act or practice of offering one's body to another for sexual purposes in exchange for payment. Prostitution is not itself a crime, but much activity associated with it is, such as being found in a **common bawdy house** or communicating in public for the purpose of prostitution.

PRO TANTO (*prō tän'-tō*) Lat.: to such extent; for so much; as far as it goes.

PROTECTIVE PRINCIPLE A principle of international law holding that "states are justified in acting to protect or prevent harm to their vital national interests, and thus in limited circumstances they may assert jurisdiction over extra-territorial acts [that] threaten or subvert these interests." R. Currie, *International & Transnational Criminal Law* 69–70 (2010). See **nationality principle; passive personality principle; territorial principle; universal jurisdiction**.

PROVINCIAL COURTS [INFERIOR COURTS] According to s. 92(14) of the **Constitution Act, 1867**, each provincial legislature may make laws in relation to "Administration of Justice in the Province, including the Constitution, Maintenance, and Organization of Provincial Courts, both of Civil and of Criminal Jurisdiction, and including Procedure in Civil Matters in those Courts."

Each province and territory has a provincial court, and these courts hear cases involving either federal or provincial **laws**. The names and divisions of these courts may vary from place to place, but their role is the same. Provincial courts deal with most **criminal** offences, **family law matters** (except **divorce**), **young persons** (from 12 to 17 years old), traffic violations, provincial **regulatory offences**, and claims involving money, up to a certain amount (set by the province in question). Private disputes involving limited sums of money may also be dealt with in most provinces at this level in Small Claims courts. In addition, all **preliminary inquiries**—hearings to determine whether there is enough evidence to justify a full trial in serious criminal cases—take place before the provincial courts.

A number of courts at the provincial level are dedicated exclusively to particular types of offences or groups of offenders. See **drug treatment court; mental health court; youth justice court**.

PROVINCIAL SUPERIOR COURT See **superior court**.

PROVISO A condition or stipulation. Its general function is to except something from the basic provision, to qualify or restrain its general scope, or to prevent misinterpretation.

PROVOCATION "[A] partial **defence** that reduces **murder** to **manslaughter**. It is available when the **accused** is faced with a sudden act or insult that would make an ordinary person lose self-control, and which caused the accused to act suddenly and before his or her passions had cooled." K. Roach, *Criminal Law* 521 (5th edition, 2012). See *Criminal Code*, R.S.C. 1985, c. C–46, s. 232. See also *R. v. Tran*, 2010 SCC 58.

PROXIMATE CAUSE See **cause**. See further A. Linden & B. Feldthusen, *Canadian Tort Law* (9th ed. 2011), c. 10.

PROXIMITY Part of the test for determining whether a person is liable to another for the tort of **negligence**. "The proximity inquiry asks whether the case discloses factors [that] show that the relationship between the **plaintiff** and the **defendant** was sufficiently close to give rise to a legal **duty of care**. The focus is on the relationship between alleged wrongdoer and victim: Is the relationship one where the imposition of legal liability for the wrongdoer's actions is appropriate?" No single unifying characteristic determines whether the proximity test is met, but "factors such as expectations, representations, reliance, and property or other interests involved" are among the usual considerations. *Hill v. Hamilton–*

Wentworth Regional Police Services Board, 2007 SCC 41.

PROXY A term used to describe both the agent and the instrument appointing him or her that enables an individual to vote in the place of another at a company's shareholders' meeting. A two-way proxy enables members to direct the proxy to vote for or against a resolution. Usually the **articles of incorporation** of the company provide for proxy votes. See *Montreal Trust Co. v. The Oxford Pipe Line Co. Ltd.,* [1942] O.R. 490 (C.A.).

PSYCHOLOGICAL DETENTION The forms of **detention** under ss. 9 and 10 of the **Canadian Charter of Rights and Freedoms** in which there is no physical restraint. "Psychological detention is established either where the individual has a legal obligation to comply with the restrictive request or demand, or a reasonable person would conclude by reason of the state conduct that he or she had no choice but to comply." *R. v. Grant,* 2009 SCC 32.

PUBLICATION The act of rendering information known to the public; making information available to persons other than one's self. In a defamation action, the communication of a defamatory statement to a third party, i.e., some one other than the person being defamed. See **defamation**.

PUBLICATION BAN An order from a **judge** preventing **publication** of the details of a proceeding in a **court**. A publication ban does not prevent the public from attending court and viewing the proceedings, but it does prevent publication of any of those proceedings while the ban is in place. Some publication bans are mandatory, such as the prohibition on the publication of details at a **bail** hearing in the *Criminal Code,* R.S.C. 1985, c. C–46, s. 517. Other publication bans are discretionary. Discretionary publication bans are governed by the **Dagenais/Mentuck test**.

PUBLIC DOMAIN 1. Lands owned by the government, e.g., Indian reserves and national parks. **2.** Information that is generally available to the public because it cannot be **copyrighted**, or copyright has expired or been forfeited, is said to be in the public domain.

PUBLIC EASEMENT A public right of way. A right exercisable by anyone, whether he or she owns land or not, merely by nature of the general law— e.g., the public right of way over a highway or a footpath.

PUBLIC INTEREST STANDING A basis upon which a private individual or organization can challenge the constitutionality of a law. One seeking public interest standing to have legislation declared invalid must show that there is a serious issue as to its invalidity, that he or she is affected by it directly or that he or she has a genuine interest as a citizen in the validity of the legislation, and that there is no other reasonable and effective manner in which the issue may be brought before the Court. These three considerations are not to be treated as hard and fast requirements, each of which must be independently satisfied: "They should be assessed and weighed cumulatively, in light of the underlying purposes of limiting standing and applied in a flexible and generous manner that best serves those underlying purposes." *Canada (Attorney-General) v. Downtown Eastside Sex Workers United Against Violence Society,* 2012 SCC 45. See **standing**.

PUBLIC LAW Those areas of law dealing with the ways in which the state governs an individual's role in society, such as **criminal** law or **human rights legislation**.

PUBLIC MISCHIEF The act of causing a peace officer to enter on or continue an investigation by (1) falsely accusing someone of an offence; (2) causing someone to be suspected of having committed an offence that the person has not committed; (3) falsely reporting an offence; (4) falsely reporting a death. *Criminal Code,* R.S.C. 1985, c. C–46, s. 140(1).

PUBLIC NUISANCE See **nuisance**.

PUBLIC OFFICER 1. A position created to fulfil a public function or duty. **2.**

An officer of a joint stock company or corporation.

The *Interpretation Act,* R.S.C. 1985, c. I–21, s. 2, states: A "'public officer' includes any person in the federal public administration who is authorized by or under an enactment to do or enforce the doing of an act or thing or to exercise a power, or on whom a duty is imposed by or under an enactment."

PUBLIC POLICY Prevailing ideas about the conditions necessary to preserve the well-being of a community, which can act to limit or override what would otherwise be the result dictated by a contract or legislative scheme. "Unless modified by statute, public policy operates independently of the rules of contract. For example, courts will not permit a husband who kills his spouse to obtain her life insurance proceeds, regardless of the manner in which the life insurance contract was worded... public policy 'applies regardless of the policy wording—it is imposed because of the courts' view of social values.'" *Oldfield v. Transamerica Life Insurance Co. of Canada,* 2002 SCC 22.

PUBLIC PROPERTY Property dedicated to the use of the public, and over which the government (municipal, provincial or federal) has dominion and control. Thus the term may be used either to describe the use to which the property is put or to describe the character of its ownership. See also **public domain**.

PUBLIC SALE See **sale**.

PUBLIC WELFARE OFFENCE See **regulatory offence**.

PUISNE JUDGE Of lower rank. A judge other than the chief judge of a court.

PUNISHMENT "The arsenal of sanctions to which an accused may be liable upon **conviction** for a particular **offence**," without necessarily including "every potential consequence" that follows from conviction. *R. v. Rodgers,* 2006 SCC 15. A state action against a convicted **offender** constitutes "punishment" where it is "imposed in

furtherance of the purposes and principles of sentencing," or where it is "punitive" in nature or constitutes a "true penal consequence." *Id*; *R. v. Wigglesworth,* [1987] 2 S.C.R. 541. Thus, the collection of DNA samples from some offenders, compulsory registration in a **sex offender registry**, and compulsory participation in an alcohol ignition interlock program have all been held not to constitute punishment. See *R. v. Rogers,* 2006 SCC 15; *R. v. Dyck,* 2008 ONCA 309; *R. v. Wilson,* 2011 ONSC 89.

PURCHASER One who acquires goods or lands in exchange for money. One to whom land is expressly transferred other than by **descent**, e.g., by the act of the parties, by **conveyance** on **sale**, by **will** or by **gift**. A purchaser for value is one who obtains a property for a valuable, as distinguished from a merely good, **consideration**.

PURE ECONOMIC LOSS Losses that are not causally connected to physical injury to a plaintiff's person or physical damage to his or her property. Five categories of negligence claims for which a **duty of care** has been found with respect to pure economic losses have been articulated: (1) The Independent Liability of Statutory Public Authorities; (2) Negligent Misrepresentation; (3) Negligent Performance of a Service; (4) Negligent Supply of Shoddy Goods or Structures; and, (5) Relational Economic Loss. See *Design Services Ltd. v. Canada,* 2008 SCC 22.

PURLOIN To steal; to commit theft.

PURVIEW The enacting part or body of a **statute** as distinguished from other parts of it, such as the **preamble**. Conduct is said to be WITHIN THE PURVIEW of a statute when such conduct properly comes within the statute's purpose, operation or effect. See **recitals**.

PUTATIVE Alleged; supposed; commonly used in family law. Thus, a putative father is a person declared to be the father of an illegitimate child in an **affiliation** proceeding.

Q.B. **[K.B.]** See **Queen's** **[King's] Bench**

Q.C. **[K.C.]** See **Queen's** **[King's] Counsel**

QUAERE (*kwē'-rē*) See **query**.

QUALIFYING PERIOD Under the *Employment Insurance Act*, S.C. 1996, c. 23, s. 8, it is generally the 52 weeks immediately prior to a claimant becoming unemployed. The claimant's unemployment benefits under the Act are determined based on the number of hours in which he or she was employed in insurable employment during those 52 weeks.

QUALIFIED PRIVILEGE A term used to describe an occasion where a person is entitled to make statements containing defamatory matter and not be held liable to the person(s) being defamed. Such an occasion only exists where the person making the statement can prove that he or she had an interest or a duty to make it known to the person to whom it was made, and that the person to whom it was made has a corresponding duty or interest to receive it. The defence of qualified privilege in a **defamation** action can be defeated by the **plaintiff** showing that the **defendant** published the statement with **malice** or that the limits of the duty or interest have been exceeded. *Hill v. Church of Scientology of Toronto*, [1995] 2 S.C.R. 1130. "[Q]ualified privilege has traditionally been grounded in special relationships characterized by a 'duty' to communicate the information and a reciprocal 'interest' in receiving it." *Grant v. Torstar Corp.*, 2009 SCC 61. See **malice**; **privilege**.

QUALIFIED TRUSTEE "[W]here the owner of real property agrees to sell it to a purchaser, he becomes a "qualified trustee" for the purchaser, with the result that if the owner later wrongfully sells the property to a second purchaser

and receives the price from him, he is accountable to the first purchaser for the price as trust property to be transferred to the first purchaser upon his completing his obligations under the first contract." H.G. Beale, ed., 1 *Chitty on Contracts* 1936 (30th ed. 2008).

QUANTUM MERUIT (*kwän'-tŭm mĕ'-rū-ĭt*) Lat.: wherefore; on what account. As much as he or she has earned. Where one renders service or performs work for another, under a **contract**, express or implied, and the party gaining the benefit of such service or work fails to pay for such benefit, the other party is said to be entitled to recover a reasonable price for services on the basis of quantum meruit—as much as he or she deserves. Quantum meruit is based on an implied promise to pay where one party has performed work for another, in whole or in part, without remuneration, and the other party has thereby unjustly gained the benefit of the services rendered. See *Stevenson v. Katz*, 2008 BCSC 565; *D.A. Browning & Associates Inc. v. Tweedy*, 2009 PESC 31.

The principle of quantum meruit is generally subsumed in the law of **restitution** or **unjust enrichment** that permits a **plaintiff** to recover where the defendant has been unjustly enriched by the receipt of a benefit at the plaintiff's expense. See *Kerr v. Baranow*, 2011 SCC 10.

QUANTUM VALEBAT [VALEBANT] (*kwän'-tŭm vălĕ-băt*) Lat.: as much as it was worth. A pleading in an action for payment for goods, in which the plaintiff claims the defendant promised to pay the market value of the goods sold and delivered.

QUARE CLAUSUM FREGIT (*kwä'-rā kl äu'-zŭm frä'-gĭt*) Lat.: wherefore he broke the close. An early form of **trespass** designed to obtain **damages** for unlawful entry upon another's **land**. The **form of action** was called trespass quare clausum fregit or trespass qu. cl. fr. **Breaking a close** was the technical **common-law** expression for unlawful entry upon land. Even without an actual fence the **complainant** would **plead** that the "defendant with force and arms broke and entered the close of the **plain-**

tiff," since in the eyes of the common law, every unauthorized entry upon the soil of another was trespass.

QUARANTINE 1. The right of a **widow** to remain in the marital home and be maintained at the expense of the heir for forty days following her husband's death, at the end of which time her dower would be assigned to her. **2.** The confinement of persons, ships, or animals suspected of having or carrying a communicable disease for a given period of time.

QUASH To annul, set aside, discharge or vacate by judicial decision. For example, a wrongful **conviction** on a criminal charge in an inferior court may be quashed by an appellate court.

QUASI (*kwā′-zī*) Lat.: as it were; so to speak; about, nearly, almost, like.

QUASI-CONTRACTS The class of **contracts** where the law imposes an obligation on one who has retained money that belongs to another or who has gained some benefit from another without reward, to return to the other party the monies lawfully belonging to him or her or to properly pay such party for the benefit gained. Thus, for example, an action for money had and received or for recovery of money paid under mistake of fact was said to be based on implied or quasi-contract. See *Dominion Distillery Products Co. Ltd. v. The King,* [1937] Ex.C.R. 145 at 163–65; *Re Grand River Motors Ltd.,* [1932] O.R. 712 at 721–22 (C.A.). The more modern and widely accepted view in Canada is that these are cases of **unjust enrichment** for which an action will lie in **quantum meruit** or **restitution**.

QUASI-CRIMINAL Describes a **proceeding** that although not actually a criminal **prosecution** is sufficiently similar in terms of the "grievous loss" (civil fine, loss of employment, loss of license, suspension from school, etc.) or the stigma to be attached to warrant some of the special procedural safeguards of a criminal proceeding. See *R. v. Bonnick* (2003), 45 M.V.R. (4th) 129 (Ont. C.J.).

QUASI-EASEMENT If a person owns land that is essentially two separate and abutting properties, any rights exercised by the owner over one of the properties, such as a right of way, is not an easement but a quasi-easement. Under the rule in *Wheeldon v. Burrows*, if the lands are later severed and sold, the quasi-easement would develop into a full easement, provided it was reasonably necessary for the enjoyment of the property and that it was in use at the time of grant. *Wheeldon v. Burrows* (1879), 12 Ch.D. 31, [1874–80] All E.R. Rep. 669, 41 L.T. 329 (C.A.). B. Ziff, *Principles of Property Law* 383–84 (5th ed. 2010). See **easement**.

QUASI-JUDICIAL A term used to describe the acts of persons, bodies, or tribunals that are not strictly judicial, in the sense of performing the functions of courts or judges, but are similar in that they have authority or discretion to decide important issues affecting the rights and obligations of opposing parties, and whose decisions have the effect of imposing serious sanctions or consequences on the parties directly or indirectly affected thereby. Generally, quasi-judicial boards and tribunals are under a duty to act in accordance with the rules of **natural justice**. See *Nicholson v. Haldimand-Norfolk Regional Board of Commissioners of Police,* [1979] 1 S.C.R. 311 at 324–28; *Coopers & Lybrand v. Minister of National Revenue* (1978), 24 N.R. 163 at 172–73 (S.C.C.); *Re Abel and Director, Penetanguishene Mental Health Centre; Re Abel and Advisory Review Board* (1979), 46 C.C.C. (2d) 342 at 357–59 (Ont.H.C.).

QUEBEC ACT 1774 A statute of the British Parliament that enlarged the territory of Quebec, provided for a governor and appointed councillors, took steps to protect the religious freedom of Roman Catholics, and restored the use of French **civil law**, which had been removed by the **Royal Proclamation of 1763**.

QUEEN In Canada, Queen Elizabeth II (or the present reigning British monarch) is the formal head of state. Section 9 of the **Constitutional Act, 1867** states: "The Executive Government and Authority of and over Canada is hereby declared to continue and be vested in the Queen." In reality, however, the Queen is only the nominal head of state. The powers vested in her are delegated at the federal level to the **Governor General** of Canada and at the provincial level to the **Lieutenant-Governor** of the province. See further P.W. Hogg, *Constitutional Law of Canada* 9–2 (5th ed. 2007). See **Crown**.

QUEEN'S [KING'S] BENCH Court of Queen's Bench or Court of King's Bench (depending on the reigning monarch); the English **common-law** court, both civil and criminal, so called because the Queen or King formerly presided. In Canada, the provinces of Manitoba, Saskatchewan, Alberta, and New Brunswick have a Court of Queen's Bench.

QUEEN'S [KING'S] COUNSEL [Q.C., K.C.] In England, near the end of the sixteenth century, one or two senior **barristers** were appointed King's or Queen's Counsel (depending upon the sex of the monarch). They were required to give services to the **Crown** when requested. By the nineteenth century they had become more numerous, and their duties to the Crown merely nominal. The title today is basically one of distinction conferred on prominent barristers. See L. Curzon, *English Legal History* (2d ed. 1979). See also J.H. Baker, *An Introduction to English Legal History* 187–89 (3rd ed. 1990). In Canada the title "is awarded to solicitors who have never argued a case in court, to law teachers, and even to politicians who have no more than nominal membership in the legal profession. Certain formal privileges survive, such as the right to wear a silk gown and to argue cases from within the Bar in court (that is, from a position closer to the judge). But by and large, in Canada it has become a mere honourary appendage, indicating little more than a certain degree of seniority and a certain degree of acceptability to the government that has awarded the title." S.M. Waddams, *Introduction to the Study of Law* 114 (6th ed. 2004).

QUE ESTATE Fr.: whose estate; refers to a right in land in the form of an easement or **profit a prendre** that has been obtained through prescription. E.H. Burn, *Cheshire and Burn's Modern Law of Real Property* 624 (16th ed. 2000).

QUERY Question; indicates that the proposition or rule it introduces is unsettled or is open to some question.

QUESTION OF FACT Disputed factual contention that is traditionally left for the **jury** to decide. For example, in a **battery** case, a question of fact would be whether A touched B. The legal significance of the touching of B by A is left for the judge to decide since it amounts to a **question of law**.

QUESTION OF LAW Disputed legal contentions that are traditionally left for the judge to decide. The occurrence or nonoccurrence of an event is a **question of fact**; its legal significance is a question of law. Questions of law are generally determined by considering legal authorities and arguments.

It is often difficult to decide whether a question is one of fact or of law. In some cases, questions of mixed fact and law arise. For example, deciding whether a particular condition an **accused** claims to suffer from meets the definition of a **disease of the mind** involves an assessment of the particular evidence in the case, not just a general principle of law, and is a question of mixed law and fact. The question of whether the accused actually suffers from that condition is a question of fact. *R. v. Bouchard-Lebrun*, 2011 SCC 58. Generally, an **appeal** must be based on a question of law, though both questions of fact and questions of law might arise in the appeal. Different standards of review apply depending on whether the question is one of law, fact, or mixed law and fact. *Housen v. Nikolaisen*, [2002] 2 S.C.R. 235, 2002 SCC 33.

QUIA TIMET (*kwē'-ă tē'-mĕt*) Lat.: because he fears. An injunction *quia timet* is one that seeks to prevent damage that has not yet occurred but is about to occur.

QUICKLAW A computerized Canadian legal research system formerly provided by QL Systems Ltd, now provided by LexisNexis Canada. It has a wide variety of legal data bases, including the most recent Supreme Court of Canada decisions, Canadian and international news, and federal and provincial statutes and regulations.

QUID PRO QUO (*kwĭd prō kwō*) Lat.: what for what; something for something; in some legal contexts, synonymous with **consideration**; sometimes referred to simply as the "quid" and always indicating that which a party receives or is promised in return for something he or she promises, gives or does.

QUID PRO QUO SEXUAL HARASSMENT A form of **sexual harassment** where a person must perform sexual acts in exchange for job benefits and/or job security. The person being harassed is made aware, either directly or indirectly, that a failure to comply with the demand for sexual acts will result in dismissal, failure to obtain promotions, or some form of disciplinary action. *Foisy v. Bell Canada* (1984), 18 D.L.R. (4th) 222 (Q.S.C.). See also, **sexual harassment**; **quid pro quo**.

QUIET ENJOYMENT The right to unimpaired use and enjoyment of **property leased** or **conveyed**. As to leased premises a guarantee of quiet enjoyment is usually expressed by a **covenant** of quiet enjoyment in a written lease, but such a covenant may be implied from the landlord-tenant relationship where it is not so expressed. This covenant is violated if the tenant's enjoyment of the premises is substantially disturbed either by wrongful acts or omissions of the landlord or by or persons claiming a **paramount title** to the landlord. The covenant may be and often is included in a **deed** conveying title to property, but in this context it does not arise by implication. See B. Ziff, *Principles of Property Law*, 301–3 (5th ed. 2010).

QUIET[ING] TITLE An equitable **action** to determine all adverse claims to the property in question; a **suit** in **equity** brought to obtain a final determination as to the **title** of a specific piece of **property**; such a suit is usually the result of various individuals asserting

contradictory rights to the same parcel of land. An action can be brought under statute in some provinces to have title to the property judicially investigated and to determine any adverse claims to such property. See, e.g., *Quieting Titles Act,* R.S.N.S. 1989, c. 382; *Quieting of Titles Act,* R.S.N.B. 1973, c. Q–4; *Quieting Titles Act,* R.S.P.E.I. 1988, c. Q–2.

QUISTCLOSE TRUST A type of **constructive trust** that arises when funds are advanced for a particular purpose but cannot be used for that purpose. In *Barclays Bank Ltd. v Quistclose Investments Ltd.*, [1970] A.C. 567 (H.L.), Quistclose had advanced funds to a borrower in order for it to pay a dividend; when the borrower became insolvent before paying that dividend, Quistclose was able to recover the funds as money held in trust for it, rather than those funds being used to pay the borrower's other debts. See *Carevest Capital Inc. v. Leduc (County)*, 2012 ABCA 161.

QUITCLAIM DEED A **deed** that conveys only that right, **title**, or **interest** that the **grantor** has or may have, and that does not require that the grantor thereby pass a **good title**. The grantor of a quitclaim deed does not represent that he or she has any interest in the property for which he or she gives the deed—merely that whatever interest he or she may have he or she **conveys** to the **grantee**. Compare **warranty** [WARRANTY DEED].

QUORUM The minimum number of members of a body who must necessarily be present in order to transact the business of that body. Usually, but not neccesarily, a quorum requires a majority.

A quorum is generally required to render legitimate any actions voted on or taken, for example, by directors or shareholders of limited companies or **corporations**. While a quorum is usually a majority of either the total membership or the members present, this general principle can be altered by the body to require or permit that more or less than a majority of the body is necessary to transact business. See, e.g., *Canada Business Corporations Act,* R.S.C. 1985, c. C–44, s. 114(2); 139(1).

QUOTA In a supply-management agricultural market, a maximum quantity that can be sold. "The federal Agency was given authority to set overall provincial quotas and to impose levies or charges on the marketing of eggs by egg producers, to be collected on its behalf by the provincial egg marketing boards. In Ontario, the Ontario Farm Products Marketing Board was the provincial board setting individual egg production quotas for its producers based on the province's assigned quota. The Ontario legislation also prohibited egg production by anyone who did not have a quota." *Fédération des producteurs de volailles du Québec v. Pelland*, 2005 SCC 20. Under governing legislation, quota can only be bought and sold on the terms allowed by regulation, which can include price caps. *Taylor v. Dairy Farmers of Nova Scotia*, 2012 NSCA 1.

QUOTATION 1. In commercial usage, a statement of the price of an item; also the price stated in response to an inquiry; **2.** more generally, the word-for-word repetition of a statement from some authority, case or law.

QUO WARRANTO (*kwō wä'-r àn-tō*) Lat.: by what right or authority. A prerogative remedy, now falling into disuse in most provincial jurisdictions, by which one seeks to inquire or establish by what authority a person holds public office. The remedy is available against persons who hold public office created by royal charter, royal prerogative or by statute, and its purpose is to remove those who have usurped their office. A person could be found to have usurped his or her office by acting without statutory qualifications to hold the particular office or appointment or by losing the required qualifications during the term of office. There must be a purported exercise of the allegedly usurped office before this remedy will be issued, and the court may, in its discretion, refuse to grant this form of relief where other more appropriate remedies are available. In British Columbia, the *Judicial Review Procedure Act,* R.S.B.C. 1996, c. 241, s. 18, abolishes quo warranto and replaces it with injunctive relief.

R

R. Abbreviation used in case citation for Rex (lat.: king) or Regina, (lat.: queen), depending on the reigning monarch at the time.

RACIAL PROFILING Attributing criminal activity to an identified group on the basis of race or colour and therefore targeting individual members of that group. See *Peart v. Peel Regional Police Services Board* (2006), 43 C.R. (6th) 175 (Ont. C.A.).

RANDOM VIRTUE TESTING Providing a person with an opportunity to commit an offence without acting on a reasonable suspicion that this person is already engaged in criminal activity or pursuant to a *bona fide* inquiry. Random virtue testing is a form of **entrapment**. *R. v. Mack*, [1988] 2 S.C.R. 903.

RAPE The predecessor offence to what is now referred to as **sexual assault**. The former offence of rape required proof of penetration and was limited to acts of sexual intercourse between people not married to one another. The offence of sexual assault, which has neither of those limitations, is seen "not only as a crime associated with emotional and physical harm to the victim, but as the wrongful exploitation of another human being." *R. v. Mabior*, 2012 SCC 47.

RAPE SHIELD LAW A reference to ss. 276 and 277 of the *Criminal Code*, R.S.C. 1985, c. C–46, which limit the type of evidence admissible in **sexual assault** trials concerning the complainant's past sexual history. In effect, the provisions "shield" the complainant from cross-examination at trial. In *R. v. Seaboyer* (1991), 66 C.C.C. (3d) 321 (S.C.C.), the Supreme Court of Canada held that these sections of the *Criminal Code* were unconstitutional. The Supreme Court stated that they violated an accused's right to a fair trial as guaranteed under ss. 7 & 11(d) of the **Canadian Charter of Rights and Freedoms**, by depriving him of the defence of a full cross-examination of the **complainant**. After *Seaboyer,* the government changed the sections, which now "essentially codifies the decision in *Seaboyer* and provides a mechanism for the trial judge to determine the admissibility of evidence of prior sexual activity," *R. v. Darrach,* [2002] 2 S.C.R. 443 at para. 1.

RATIFICATION The act or process of formally ratifying, adopting or confirming a **contract**, treaty or other transaction by the parties, which they were not legally bound by originally.

1. In **contract**, the adoption by a person of a contract entered into on his or her behalf by someone who acted without authority as that person's agent. "Ratification must be based on knowledge of all of the material facts and may be express or implied." *Hunt v. TD Securities Inc.* (2003), 66 O.R. (3d) 481 (Ont. C.A.).

Infants can ratify their contracts themselves after reaching the age of majority. The ratification is binding without new **consideration**. Ratification is presumed unless the infant disaffirms a long-standing contract within a reasonable time after reaching his or her **majority**. *Blackwell v. Farrow,* [1948] O.W.N. 7 (H.C.).

2. In **international law**, after a **treaty** has been signed, normally it is not binding until it is ratified. Ratification is a formal ceremony where the parties exchange solemn confirmations, adopting the treaty by their own internal law.

RATIO DECIDENDI (*ră'-shē-ō dā-sĭ-dĕn'-dē*) Lat.: the reason for the decision. The principle that the case establishes. At one point, the view was that a clear line could be drawn between the *ratio decidendi* (or "ratio") of a decision and **obiter dicta** in that decision, but the notion of such a clear distinction has been dismissed. "[T]he submissions of the attorneys general presuppose a strict and tidy demarcation between the narrow *ratio decidendi* of a case, which is binding, and *obiter*, which they say may safely be ignored. I believe that this supposed dichotomy is an oversimplification of how the common law develops." *R. v. Henry*, 2005 SCC 76.

RATIO LEGIS (*rǎ'-shē-ō lě'-gǐs*) Lat.: legal reason or ground. The underlying principle; the theory, doctrine or science of law. Thus, the *ratio legis* of a loitering by-law is to allow law enforcement officers more latitude in attempting to prevent crime rather than to rely solely on apprehension and sentencing as a deterrent.

RATIONAL CONNECTION A step in the **Oakes test** for determining whether a law or measure that violates the **Canadian Charter of Rights and Freedoms** can be saved as a **reasonable limit in a free and democratic society**. If a law does violate a *Charter* right, the objective of doing so must be sufficiently important to warrant overriding a *Charter* right. To be rationally connected, the *Charter* violation must actually be capable of helping to achieve that sufficiently important objective.

R.C.M.P. See **Royal Canadian Mounted Police**.

READ(ING) DOWN Interpreting a **statute** which is capable of two meanings in a way which will not violate the **Canadian Charter of Rights and Freedoms**.

READ(ING) IN A court's ability, when granting a **remedy** for a violation of the **Canadian Charter of Rights and Freedoms**, to add words to a statute in order to cure a constitutional defect. For example, in *Schachter v. Canada*, [1992] 2 S.C.R. 679, the Supreme Court of Canada read in words to the then *Unemployment Insurance Act, 1971*, S.C. 1970–71–72, c. 48 in order to extend benefits to a group which was not given to them under the legislation.

READING THE RIOT ACT Colloquially, to speak firmly to an uncooperative person. Strictly, under s. 67 of the *Criminal Code*, R.S.C. 1985, c. C–46, it is when a justice, mayor, sheriff, warden, or the head of a penitentiary proclaims to "twelve or more persons [who] are unlawfully and riotously assembled together" words to the effect of "Her Majesty the Queen charges and commands all persons being assembled immediately to disperse and peaceably to depart to their habitations or to their lawful business on the pain of being guilty of an offence for which, on conviction, they may be sentenced to imprisonment for life. God save the Queen."

REAL ACTION Any type of legal proceeding involving lands, tenements, and **herditaments**. See **real property**.

REAL AND SUBSTANTIAL CONNECTION A basis upon which jurisdiction can be claimed by courts over a **criminal law** or **civil law** issue even if the events did not take place entirely within the territory over which the court has jurisdiction. Jurisdiction based on a real and substantial connection is an exercise of the **territorial principle**. See *R. v. Libman*, [1985] 2 S.C.R. 178; *Club Resorts Ltd. v. Van Breda*, 2012 SCC 17.

REAL ESTATE Every possible **interest** in land, except for a mere **chattel** interest; every estate, interest and right—legal and equitable—in **lands, tenements**, and **hereditaments**.

REAL PARTY IN INTEREST The individual entitled to the benefits of a successful **action**; one who is essentially, fundamentally and truly interested in the subject matter, in contrast to a party who has only a small, formal or unimportant interest in or relation with the action.

REAL PROPERTY Lands, **tenements**, and **hereditaments**; in other words, land and buildings erected upon it. Generally, all interests in land are real property, except for **leaseholds** for a term of years, which are **personalty** or **chattels**.

The difference between real property and **personal property** is that real property (immovable property) can always be recovered by a real **action (action in rem)** and personal property (movable property, e.g., chattels) can be recovered by an **action in personam**, i.e., **conversion, detinue, replevin**.

To be classified as a real property, a movable must be sufficiently incorporated into the construction or buildings in which it is installed to form an integral part. It will not become unmovable by nature merely by reason of it forming part of a system. *City of St. Laurent v. Quebec Hydro-Electric Commission,* [1978] 2 S.C.R. 529.

Real property comprises two distinct classes called CORPOREAL and INCORPOREAL HEREDITAMENTS (see **hereditaments**). Corporeal hereditaments are physical matters such as land, over which ownership is exercised; incorporeal hereditaments are not things but rights, such as **easements**.

REALTY An **estate** in land; another word for **real property**.

REASONABLE AND PROBABLE GROUNDS
See **reasonable grounds to believe**.

REASONABLE APPREHENSION OF BIAS TEST
A test used for determining whether a judge should be disqualified from hearing a case due to **bias**. The test is whether a **reasonable person** with knowledge of all the facts and looking at the situation objectively would have a reasonable apprehension that the judge would not act in an impartial manner. *Chrétien v. Canada (Commission of Inquiry into the Sponsorship Program and Advertising Activities)*, 2008 FC 802, aff'd 2010 FCA 283. See **bias**.

REASONABLE DOUBT
Refers to the level of certainty needed by a juror to form a legally sound determination of the guilt of the **accused**. In the **instructions** to the jury at a criminal trial, these words signify that there is a **presumption** of innocence unless guilt is so manifestly proven that the jury can have no reasonable doubt of the guilt of the criminal **defendant**. Reasonable doubt is not just a mere presence in the mind, but neither does the notion require that the evidence be so certain that no chance of error can be present. It means that the evidence must be so complete and convincing that any reasonable doubts of the facts are erased from the minds of the jurors. The Supreme Court has said that the concept of reasonable doubt can be explained to a jury in the following terms: "A reasonable doubt is not an imaginary or frivolous doubt. It must not be based upon sympathy or prejudice. Rather, it is based on reason and common sense. It is logically derived from the evidence or absence of evidence. Even if you believe the accused is probably guilty or likely guilty, that is not sufficient. In those circumstances you must give the benefit of the doubt to the accused and acquit because the Crown has failed to satisfy you of the guilt of the accused beyond a reasonable doubt. On the other hand you must remember that it is virtually impossible to prove anything to an absolute certainty, and the Crown is not required to do so. Such a standard of proof is impossibly high. In short, if, based upon the evidence before the court, you are sure that the accused committed the offence, you should convict since this demonstrates that you are satisfied of his guilt beyond a reasonable doubt." *R. v. Lifchus*, [1997] 3 S.C.R. 320.

REASONABLE EXPECTATION OF PRIVACY
The interest protected by s. 8 of the **Canadian Charter of Rights and Freedoms**, that gives everyone the right to be free from unreasonable search and seizure. A reasonable expectation of privacy is judged by the normative question of the level of privacy a person is entitled to expect, rather than an analysis of the actual risk to a person's privacy in any particular situation. It includes at least three types of privacy interests: personal privacy, territorial privacy, and informational privacy. Whether an accused has a reasonable expectation of privacy in any given situation depends on an application of the "totality of the circumstances" test. "The 'totality of the circumstances' test is one of substance, not of form. Four lines of inquiry guide the application of the test: (1) an examination of the subject matter of the alleged search; (2) a determination as to whether the claimant had a direct interest in the subject matter; (3) an inquiry into whether the claimant had a subjective expectation of privacy in the subject matter; and (4) an assessment as to whether this subjective expectation of privacy was objectively reasonable, having regard to the totality of the circumstances." *R. v. Cole*, 2012 SCC 53.

REASONABLE GROUNDS TO BELIEVE [REASONABLE BELIEF]
The standard required to authorize many police powers, such as obtaining a **search warrant** or **arresting**

a person without a warrant. Reasonable grounds as a standard to arrest requires that the arresting officer **subjectively** believe that the suspect has committed the **offence** and that, **objectively**, a reasonable person would reach the same conclusion. Reasonable grounds do not require as much evidence as a **prima facie case** but do require that the thing that is believed is more likely than not. See *R. v. Storrey*, [1990] 1 S.C.R. 241. Various *Criminal Code* provisions used to refer to "reasonable and probable" grounds. Although the words "and probable" have been removed, the standard still requires that the belief be more likely than not. *R. v. Loewen*, 2011 SCC 21.

REASONABLE GROUNDS TO SUSPECT [REASONABLE SUSPICION] A standard authorizing some police investigative techniques, such as an **investigative detention**. Reasonable grounds to suspect is a lower standard than **reasonable grounds to believe** but must be more than a mere hunch. See, e.g., *R. v. Mann*, 2004 SCC 52.

REASONABLE LIMITS IN A FREE AND DEMOCRATIC SOCIETY The major factor under s. 1 of the **Canadian Charter of Rights and Freedoms** determining whether a limitation on a right or **fundamental freedom** can be justified. Section 1 requires that any such limitation must be prescribed by law, which requires that it be explicit or implicit in a **statute**, a regulation, or the **common law**. If it is, the limitation will be justified if it is a reasonable one in a free and democratic society. That question is answered by applying the **Oakes Test**.

REASONABLE MAN See **reasonable person**.

REASONABLE PERSON An imaginary person who possesses and uses the qualities of carefulness, intelligence and judgment that society requires of its members for the protection of their own interest and the interests of others.

In *Arland v. Taylor,* [1955] O.R. 131 (C.A.) Mr. Justice Laidlaw noted at p. 142: "[The reasonable person is] a mythical creature of the law whose conduct is the standard by which the Courts measure the conduct of all other persons and find it to be proper or improper in particular circumstances as they may exist from time to time. He is not an extraordinary or unusual creature; he is not superhuman; he is not required to display the highest skill of which anyone is capable; he is not a genius who can perform uncommon feats, nor is he possessed of unusual powers of foresight. He is a person of normal intelligence who makes prudence a guide to his conduct. He does nothing that a prudent man would not do and does not omit to do anything a prudent man would do. He acts in accord with general and approved practice. His conduct is guided by considerations which ordinarily regulate the conduct of human affairs. His conduct is the standard, adopted in the community by persons of ordinary intelligence and prudence." The reasonable person test implies different standards for different activities—"A reasonable person will not show the same anxious care when handling an umbrella as when handling a loaded gun"—but does not vary according to the characteristics of the accused. Thus, there is a uniform standard of the reasonable person, which does not vary depending on the experience, age, or other characteristics of the person. *R. v. Creighton*, [1993] 3 S.C.R. 3. Compare **modified objective test**.

REASONABLE SUSPICION See **REASONABLE GROUNDS TO SUSPECT**.

REBUTTAL EVIDENCE Evidence introduced by one **party** in an **action** to justify, repulse, counteract or dispose of the evidence given by the other party or a **witness**. Rebuttal evidence can also be employed to contradict other evidence or to rebut a **presumption**.

REBUTTER In **common law**, a **pleading** that was an answer of fact given by a **defendant** to the **plaintiff's** response to the defendant's **surrejoinder**. This form of pleading is seldom used, and many provincial **jurisdictions** have abandoned it with a reform to their Civil Procedure Rules.

RECANT To deny that a prior statement is true.

RECEIVER An impartial person appointed by the court on an **interlocutory** application to collect and receive the benefits **(rents**, issues, and profits of land or personal **estate)**, which it does not seem reasonable to the court that either party should collect or receive, or to enable the same to be distributed among the persons entitled. The reason for the appointment of a receiver is to safeguard the **property** until the rights of the **parties** have been determined. For example, in a proceeding to extinguish a **partnership** a receiver is frequently engaged to sell off the company assets.

Receivers have very broad powers in relation to the disputed property and may take possession of the subject matter and do all such acts of **ownership**—in relation to the receipts of rents, compelling payment of them, management, letting lands and houses, and otherwise making the property productive—for the parties ultimately declared to be entitled thereto.

During **bankruptcy**, the official receiver can be appointed INTERIM RECEIVER at any time after the presentation of the **petition** into the court. If so appointed, the receiver has the duty to act until a **trustee** is appointed. A mortgagee can engage a receiver of the mortgaged property when the **mortgage** becomes payable.

By way of equitable **execution**, a receiver can be appointed by the court to allow a **judgment creditor** to obtain payment of the debt, when the possession of property is in the hand of the debtor or the ordinary process of execution cannot be used to get at an interest in land.

RECEIVERSHIP 1. An equitable **remedy** whereby **property** is by court **order**, for the benefit of the affected parties, placed under the supervision and control of a **receiver**. Because of **action** by creditors, a failing business may be placed in receivership, but the business is often continued, subject to the power of the receiver. Receivership is usually not the main **relief** sought in an action but is ancillary to the main purpose of the action. Usually a receivership order is used to protect property during

litigation concerning entitlement to the property. **2.** Receivership is also used to describe property affected by the remedy; for example, property is said to be IN RECEIVERSHIP. Compare **bankruptcy**.

RECENT FABRICATION An allegation that a witness has made a statement or is giving testimony that is false and has been created in response to the circumstances of the case. "To be 'recent,' the fabrication need only have been made after the event testified about ... A mere contradiction in the evidence is not enough to engage the recent fabrication exception. However, a 'fabrication' can include being influenced by outside sources." *R. v. Ellard*, 2009 SCC 27. An allegation of recent fabrication can be rebutted by the admission of a **prior consistent statement**, but that statement must date from a time before the motive to fabricate arose. "Admission on the basis of this exception does not require that an allegation of recent fabrication be expressly made—it is sufficient that the circumstances of the case reveal that the 'apparent position of the opposing party is that there has been a prior contrivance.'" *R. v. Stirling*, 2008 SCC 10.

RECENT POSSESSION "[T]he doctrine of recent possession may be succinctly stated in the following terms. Upon proof of the unexplained possession of recently stolen property, the **trier of fact** may—but not must—draw an inference of guilt of theft or of offences incidental thereto. Where the circumstances are such that a question could arise as to whether the **accused** was a thief or merely a possessor, it will be for the trier of fact upon a consideration of all the circumstances to decide which, if either, **inference** should be drawn. In all recent possession cases, the inference of guilt is permissive, not mandatory, and when an explanation is offered which might reasonably be true, even though the trier of fact is not satisfied of its truth, the doctrine will not apply." *R. v. Kowlyk*, [1988] 2 S.C.R. 59.

RECEPTION, DOCTRINE OF The adoption of English law in the colonies. The method by which English law was acquired in a colony depended on whether the colony was settled or conquered. If settled, the inhabitants brought the system of law with them. Generally, the date of reception in settled colonies is the date the legislature was established.

RECESS 1. A temporary adjournment in the course of a **trial** or **hearing**. The adjournment can vary in length from minutes to days. **2.** Also, the time between sittings of the same legislative body at its usual or adjourned session, but not the time between the final adjournment of one body and the convening of another at the next regular session. Compare **sine die**.

RECIDIVIST A person who, after having been convicted of an offence and serving his or her sentence or being pardoned, commits another offence.

RECIPROCITY A practice carried on between persons, **corporations**, provinces, or countries whereby courtesies or privileges given by one are reciprocated by the other. For example, if State X allows workers from State Y to work there, State Y in permitting workers from State X to work in Y would be participating in reciprocity. Other examples include **maintenance orders**, **custody** orders. Compare **comity**.

RECITALS Introductory paragraphs preceding the formal part of a **contract**, **statute**, or other legal document that explain the purpose behind the document, set out facts that the parties take to be true, or otherwise provide context to assist in understanding the document. For example, recitals in the **preamble** to the **Constitution Act, 1867**, include "whereas the Provinces of Canada, Nova Scotia, and New Brunswick have expressed their Desire to be federally united into One Dominion under the Crown of the United Kingdom of Great Britain and Ireland, with a Constitution similar in Principle to that of the United Kingdom" and "whereas it is expedient that Provision be made for the eventual Admission into the Union of other Parts of British North America." Recitals are sometimes referred to as "whereas clauses."

RECKLESSNESS "Knowledge of a danger or risk and persistence in a course of conduct [that] creates a risk that the prohibited result will occur...The culpability in recklessness is justified by consciousness of the risk and by proceeding in the face of it." *R. v. Briscoe*, 2010 SCC 13, quoting *Sansregret v. The Queen*, [1985] 1 S.C.R. 570. Recklessness requires **subjective** fault on the part of a person and is an alternative **mens rea** to **intention** for most **criminal offences**.

RECOGNIZANCE A written acknowledgment of a monetary debt not exceeding $500.00, given by an accused person in order to be released from custody, and that can be enforced if that person fails to attend court as required within the recognizance. Entering into a recognizance is one possible method of obtaining **judicial interim release**. See *Criminal Code*, R.S.C. 1985, c. C–46, Form 11.

RECORD 1. To maintain in written or printed form or by any alternate means such as tape, film or video. **2.** The precise chronicle of a trial (action) from its beginning to its termination, including the **conclusions of law** recorded by the proper officer of the court for the purpose of preserving the exact state of facts.

During an appeal, the **appellant** cannot go outside the RECORD OF APPEAL—that is, the items introduced in **evidence** in the lower court—in making his or her case.

Certiorari is an available remedy to **quash** a decision, on the ground that there is an error "on the face of the record." The record must contain at least the documents, the **pleadings**, if any, and the **adjudication**, but not the evidence nor the reasons for a decision, unless the **tribunal** chooses to incorporate them. *Id.*

RECORD SUSPENSION An order by the National **Parole** Board under the *Criminal Records Act*, R.S.C. 1985, c. C–47 which requires that the judicial record of a person's conviction be kept separate and apart from other criminal records. The effect of a record suspension is, for all but a few purposes, to remove any disqualification or obligation to which the person was subject under any Act of **Parliament** because of that conviction. The time before which an application for a record suspension varies and is five years for the least serious offences, ten years for most other offences, or not at all in the case of a list of offences, most of which are sexual offences. The criteria for granting a record suspension are (a) that the applicant has been of good conduct and has not been convicted of another offence, and (b) that ordering the record suspension would provide a measurable benefit to the applicant, would sustain his or her rehabilitation in society as a law-abiding citizen, and would not bring the administration of justice into disrepute.

RECOUPMENT The right of a **defendant** to have the **plaintiff's** award of **damages** against the defendant reduced; a right of deduction from the amount of the plaintiff's claim by reason of either a payment thereon or some loss sustained by the defendant because of the plaintiff's wrongful or defective **performance** of the **contract**, out of which his **claim** originated. It has been defined to be a keeping back of something that is due, because there is an equitable reason for withholding it. The word is nearly synonymous with discount, deduction or reduction. See also **counterclaim**; **setoff**.

RECOVERY 1. An individual's repossession of something wrongfully taken or detained from him or her, to which he or she is otherwise entitled. **2.** The result of a **judgment** of the court that leads to the establishment of a right. The successful **party** in a **suit** to obtain a judgment recovers those things that the **tribunal** believes him or her to have been deprived of, although recovery does not necessarily mean restoration of the whole. **3.** Also, the amount collected and the amount of the judgment. **4.** In the context of criminal law, recovery pertains to the recovery by an accused from **mental disorder**, s. 16 of the *Criminal Code*, R.S.C. 1985, c. C–46. See also ss. 672.5(10)(b) (ii), 672.51(3), 672.86.

RECTIFICATION   [REFORMATION] The rewording or rewriting of a **contract**

in cases where the written form of the agreement does not express what was actually agreed upon. It is an equitable doctrine based on the notion of **unjust enrichment**. Because of this, rectification is only allowed upon the clear and satisfactory showing of a mutual **mistake**. See *Pepper v. Prudential Trust Co. Ltd.,* [1965] S.C.R. 417. It is an exception to the **parol evidence rule**. See *Alampi v. Swartz* (1964), 43 D.L.R. (2d) 11 (Ont.C.A.). It is important to distinguish cases of mistaken assumption where rectification does not apply. "In order to get rectification it is necessary to show that the parties were in complete agreement on the terms of their contract, but by an error wrote them down wrongly; and in this regard, in order to ascertain the terms of their contract, you do not look into the inner minds of the parties—into their intentions.... You look at their outward acts, that is, at what they said or wrote to one another in coming to their agreement, and then compare it with the document which they have signed. If you can predicate with certainty what their contract was, and that it is by a common mistake, wrongly expressed in the document, then you can rectify the document; but nothing less will suffice." *Rose (London) Ltd. v. Pim Jnr. & Co. Ltd.,* [1953] 2 Q.B. 450 (C.A.).
   Compare **rescission**.

REDACT To remove confidential or **privileged** information from a **document**.

REDEMPTION A right possessed by the mortgagor upon payment of the **mortgage** to regain legal **title** to the **property**. "This equity of redemption is an estate in land and the person entitled to it is in **equity** the owner of the land." *Fletcher v. Rodden* (1882), 1 O.R. 155 at 160 (Ch.D.).

REDUCTIO AD ABSURDUM (*rā-dŭk'-tē-ō ăd ăb-sûr'-dŭm*) Lat.: reduction to the absurd. The process whereby a legal argument is reduced to the absurd by showing that the argument ultimately follows to a preposterous position or contradiction.

RE-ENTRY [RIGHT OF] The resumption of **possession** pursuant to a right reserved when the former possession was surrendered. It was a remedy given by feudal law for nonpayment of rent and also refers to a right reserved in the **conveyance** of a **fee** that is subject to a **condition** subsequent. See **conditional fee**. See, e.g., *Ratepayers of Calgary (City) v. Canada*, 2000 ABQB 43. Under **common law**, the right of re-entry was usually available to the **grantor** through self-help. Recent judicial decisions have for the most part denied this right even if reserved in the **deed** or **instrument** of conveyance. A **suit** to **quiet title** is the preferred course.

Landlord-tenant legislation in Canada generally allows the landlord to elect to terminate the **lease** when there has been default in payment of **rent**, and this may be done by peaceable 're-entry' without previous judicial **proceedings**, in the exercise of self-help.

REFEREE An **arbitrator**. A person appointed by a court; a quasi-judicial officer to whom the court refers a matter. The referee may take **testimony**, arbitrate a dispute between parties and report his or her findings to the court, upon which the court can base a judgment. See **Master**.

REFERENCE CASE A case sent to a **referee** or court for a decision or recommendation on a point of law. "Each Canadian jurisdiction has conferred non-judicial functions on its courts, by enacting a statute which enables the government to refer a question of law to the courts for an **advisory opinion**." P.W. Hogg, *Constitutional Law of Canada* 8–16 (5th ed. 2007). "The *Supreme Court Act* [R.S.C. 1985, c. S–26] imposes on the Court the function of giving advisory opinions on questions referred to the Court by the federal government.... A provincial government has no power to direct a reference to the Supreme Court of Canada. However, each of the ten provinces has enacted legislation permitting the provincial government to direct a reference to the provincial court of appeal.... When the provincial court of appeal has rendered an opinion on a reference . . . there is an appeal as of right to the Supreme Court of Canada." *Id.* at 8–15–16

REFERENCE RE SAME-SEX MARRIAGE, [2004] 3 S.C.R. 698. The federal government asked the Supreme Court of Canada a series of questions regarding same-sex marriages in Canada. On December 9, 2004, the Supreme Court found that (a) the federal government had the right to change the definition of marriage, (b) changing the definition of marriage to include same-sex couples would not infringe the *Charter,* and (c) religious officials cannot be forced to marry same-sex couples if doing so is contrary to their religious beliefs. After the Reference, the *Civil Marriage Act,* S.C. 2005, c. 33 was passed, s. 2 of which states that "[m]arriage, for civil purposes, is the lawful union of two persons to the exclusion of all others." See also **marriage, Civil Marriage Act, spouse.**

REFERENDUM 1. Like the **plebiscite**, a method used for obtaining the community view on a particular issue. **2.** In western Canada, the referendum has also been used as a vehicle to permit voters to participate directly in lawmaking. In the latter sense the referendum is more than advisory in nature and might require that, on petition of a certain percentage of voters, certain provincial laws be suspended until the whole electorate has voted on them. Such provincial attempts at direct democracy have included the *Initiative and Referendum Act,* S.M. 1916, c. 59, which was found to be **ultra vires** the powers of the province in that it interfered with the office of the **Lieutenant-Governor** (Re *Initiative and Referendum Act,* [1919] A.C. 935 (P.C.)), and invested the primary powers of legislation in a body other than the Legislature (*Re Initiative and Referendum Act* (1916), 27 Man.R. 1 (C.A.)). See P.W. Hogg, *Constitutional Law of Canada* 14–10–16 (5th ed. 2007).

REFERENTIAL INCORPORATION A practice whereby a legislative body adopts ("incorporates") a law passed by another legislative body. Referential incorporation is consistent with Canada's constitutional **division of powers**. *Ontario (Attorney-General) v. Scott* [1956] 1 S.C.R. 137. It is used especially when a government desires to "enact the law of another jurisdiction" instead of "repeating in full the desired rules." P.W. Hogg, *Constitutional Law of Canada* 14–22 (5th ed. 2007).

REFORMATION See **rectification**.

REFUGEE Under the *Convention on the Status of Refugees* (1951), 189 U.N.T.S. 138 (in force April 22, 1954) the term "shall apply to any person who:... (2) ... owing to well-founded fear of being persecuted for reasons of race, religion, nationality, membership of a particular social group or political opinion, is outside the country of his nationality and is unable or, owing to such fear, is unwilling to avail himself of the protection of that country; or who, not having a nationality and being outside the country of his former habitual residence as a result of such events, is unable or, owing to such fear, is unwilling to return to it...." Canada is a party to the Convention, and refugees have a right to remain in Canada subject to the provisions of the *Immigration and Refugee Protection Act,* S.C. 2001, c. 27, and its *Regulations.* See **Convention Refugee**; **Person in Need of Protection**. See further M. Jones and S. Baglay, *Refugee Law* (2007).

REGISTER 1. To record formally and exactly; to enroll; to enter precisely in a list or the like. **2.** A public record to establish matters of fact such as births, deaths, and marriages. **3.** Also, the books of a company incorporated under one of the various Companies Acts requiring certain matters of disclosure, e.g., the manner in which shares are held by directors of the company.

REGISTERED CHARITY An organization registered as having charitable status under the *Income Tax Act*, R.S.C. 1985, c. 1, and therefore able to give tax-creditable receipts to those who make donations.

REGISTRY ACTS Legislation in each of the provinces of Canada providing for the registration of instruments affecting **real property (deeds, mortgages,** etc.) and for the effect of such registration. Such a statute affords a means of giving public notice of the nature of an interest in land that is claimed, and establishes priorities between claimants to enable the determination of the rights of all parties claiming an interest in a property and the exact limits of the property. In Canada, two systems of land registration are in existence, the registry office system and the land titles system, and reference must be made to the appropriate provincial legislation.

LAND TITLES SYSTEM A record system based upon the Torrens system of registration in Australia, which provides protection for a **bona fide purchaser** from a "registered" owner to the extent that the purchaser does not have to go behind the **register** and search the **vendor's title** in order to satisfy himself or herself as to its validity. When land is transferred under this system, the transferee becomes the registered owner and earlier links in the **chain of title** are immaterial. See further B. Ziff, *Principles of Property Law* 469–74 (5th ed. 2010). See also the various provincial statutes, e.g., *Land Title Act*, R.S.B.C. 1996, c. 250. *Land Titles Act,* 2000, S.S. 2000, c. L–51; *Land Titles Act,* R.S.O., 1990, c. L.–5.

REGISTRY SYSTEM A record system that differs from the land titles system in that it is a "system of deed, not title, recordation. This means that the system attempts to compel registration of all interests in the land. If an interest is not registered it is liable to be defeated by a subsequent interest... Under the registry system practically any instrument may be registered. The registrar is not concerned with the intrinsic worth of the instrument but records it for what it is worth. It is also inevitable under a deed registration system that there be a continual lengthening of the title which must be searched by successive purchasers. Thus, not only does the search become more difficult, the risk of error increases." A.H. Oosterhoff & W.B. Rayner, *Anger and Honsberger: Law of Real Property* 1621, 1628–29 (2nd ed. 1985).

REGINA Lat.: Queen

REGISTRY [OF DEEDS] A system or delegated public office that serves to give notice to third parties of **inter alia** changes in the ownership of **real property** effected by **conveyance** of that property. See **registry acts**.

REGNAL YEAR The year of the reign of the monarch. Sessions of the federal **Parliament** and of most provincial legislatures have traditionally been designated by the regnal year or years of the monarch during which sessions were held. For example, instead of using the calendar year 1967, the designation 15 & 16 Eliz. II might be used. The regnal year method was also the traditional method for the **citation** of **statutes**. It is no longer a common method of citation for Canadian statutes. However, the regnal year must still be used in citing British statutes prior to 1963.

REGULATIONS A form of SUBORDINATE LEGISLATION (see **legislation**). It is a normal practice for most modern **statutes** to confer lawmaking powers upon the **Governor General in Council** or **Lieutenant Governor in Council** for the further carrying out of the purposes of the statute in question. Such practice enables the government (federal or provincial) to act expeditiously and provide additional regulations without the necessity of enacting new statutes. The power to enact regulations may also be conferred upon a Minister or government official (e.g., a Registrar of Motor Vehicles), an administrative board, etc. The various provincial *Regulation Acts* and the federal *Statutory Instruments Act*, R.S.C. 1985, c. S–22, contain definitions of regulations and information concerning requirement of publication, etc. See further S.M. Waddams, *Introduction to the Study of Law* 88–89 (6th ed. 2004).

REGULATORY CAPTURE An informal term describing the situation when a regulated industry is able to exert an undue measure of influence over the agency that is meant to regulate it, so that it ceases to be appropriately monitored.

REGULATORY OFFENCE Behaviour that is made unlawful not because it is morally blameworthy but in order to achieve some goal in the regulation of society; also referred to as a "public welfare offence" or an "administrative offence." "[S]ome conduct is prohibited, not because it is inherently wrongful, but because unregulated activity would result in dangerous conditions being imposed upon members of society, especially those who are particularly vulnerable. The objective of regulatory legislation is to protect the public or broad segments of the public (such as employees, consumers, and motorists, to name but a few) from the potentially adverse effects of otherwise lawful activity. Regulatory legislation involves a shift of emphasis from the protection of individual interests and the deterrence and **punishment** of acts involving moral fault to the protection of public and societal interests. While criminal offences are usually designed to condemn and punish past, inherently wrongful conduct, regulatory measures are generally directed to the prevention of future harm through the enforcement of minimum standards of conduct and care." *R. v. Wholesale Travel Group Inc.*, [1991] 3 S.C.R. 154. See **malum in se**; **malum prohibitum**.

REGULATORY TAKING The term used in Australia and the United States for what in Canada is more usually referred to as a **de facto expropriation**.

REHABILITATION A goal of sentencing recognized under s. 718 of the *Criminal Code*, R.S.C. 1985, c. C–46, which focuses on the need to reform offenders and reintegrate them into society, so they will not re-offend once their sentences are complete. Compare **denunciation**; **deterrence**; **retributive justice**; **separation**.

REHEARING A retrial or reconsideration of the issues by the same court or body in which the suit or matter was originally heard, and upon the **pleadings** and **depositions** already in the case.

REID INTERROGATION TECHNIQUE A method of inducing confessions from suspects used by North American law enforcement agencies. The technique has nine steps, which are generally aimed at psychologically manipulating suspects by convincing them that the police are certain of their guilt and that making a confession is congruent with their self-interest. For example, an interrogating officer will often present a suspect with a choice of alternative explanations of what happened, each of which is dispositive of the suspect's guilt, but one of which is better than the others. See F.E. Inbau et al., *Criminal Interrogation and Confessions* (5th ed. 2013); T. Nadon, *The Reid Interrogation Technique* (2012), 91 C.R. (6th) 359. Some courts have thrown doubt on the accuracy of the technique and its potential of inducing false confessions. See, e.g., *R. v. M.J.S.*, 2000 ABPC 44.

REJOINDER In **pleadings**, at **common law**, an answer to **plaintiff's** replication by some matter of fact, in an **action at law**. This largely historical procedural device was prevalent prior to procedural reforms of the nineteenth century. See, e.g., *London Life Insurance Co. v. Wright*, [1881] 5 S.C.R. 466.

RELATION BACK The principle by which an act done at a later time might be deemed by law to have occurred at a prior time.

RELATOR ACTION OR PROCEEDING "**Judicial review** proceedings to which the **Attorney-General** has lent her or his support in a situation where the individual carrying the proceedings may lack **standing** to maintain those proceedings in her or his own right." D. Mullan, *Administrative Law* 546 (2001). Compare **public interest standing**.

RELEASE The act or writing by which some **claim**, right, or **interest** is given up to the person against whom the claim, right or interest could have been enforced. For example, a person may sign a release that ends his or her right to sue someone for an injury caused by that person.

In the law of property, the holder of a **fee simple** may convey to another a term of years and then subsequently release his or her **reversionary** interest (LEASE AND RELEASE) to the possessor of the term of years; conversely, should the possessor of the term of years quit the premises before the end of the term, he or she may be said to have surren-

dered the remainder of the term to the **grantor**.

RELEASE ON RECOGNIZANCE See **recognizance**.

RELEVANT Applying to the matter in question; affording something to the purpose. **Evidence** must be relevant to be admissible in a judicial proceeding. "To be logically relevant, an item of evidence does not have to firmly establish, on any standard, the truth or falsity of a fact in issue. The evidence must simply tend to 'increase or diminish the probability of the existence of a fact in issue.' See Sir Richard Eggleston, *Evidence, Proof, and Probability* (2nd ed. 1978), at p. 83. As a consequence, there is no minimum probative value required for evidence to be relevant." *R. v. Arp*, [1998] 3 S.C.R. 339. See **admissible evidence**.

RELIABILITY How accurate a **witness's** testimony should be regarded to be. "Accuracy engages consideration of the witness's ability to accurately (i.) observe; (ii.) recall; and (iii.) recount events in issue." *R. v. H.C.*, 2009 ONCA 56. See **credibility**; *R. v. H.P.S.*, 2012 ONCA 117.

RELIANCE Dependence, trust in what is deemed sufficient support or authority.
DETRIMENTAL RELIANCE Reliance by one party on the acts, representations or promises of another that causes the first party to allow a worsening of his or her position; an important element in many legal contexts. If such a detrimental change of position is established, and if the reliance appears to have been justified under the circumstances, it may preclude **revocation** of an offer of waiver, may support a promise as a **contract** even without **consideration** (see **estoppel** [PROMISSORY ESTOPPEL]), and is a necessary ingredient in an action to recover upon a claim of **fraud**. See further S.M. Waddams, *The Law of Contracts* 138–57 (6th ed. 2010).

RELICTION The gradual and imperceptible withdrawal of water from land that it covers by the lowering of its surface level from any cause. If the retreat of the waters is permanent—i.e., not merely seasonal—the owner of the contiguous property acquires ownership of the dry land thus created. Compare **dereliction**. See also **accretion**; **avulsion**.

RELIEF 1. The redress or assistance awarded to a **complainant**, by the court, especially a **court of equity**, including such remedies as **specific performance**, **injunction**, **rescission** of a contract, etc.; but the term may also comprehend an award of money **damages**. The term AFFIRMATIVE RELIEF is often used to indicate that the gist of relief is protection from future harm rather than compensation for past injury.

2. In feudal property law, a payment made by the **heir** of a deceased **tenant** to the lord in order to step into his ancestor's shoes and keep the family home and land intact. A.M. Sinclair & M.E. McCallum, *An Introduction to Real Property Law* 3 (6th ed. 2012). Thus, it operated as a kind of inheritance tax. Because inheritance was a privilege to be paid for, the lord possessed unlimited discretion in fixing the price payable by the tenant. Abuse of this prerogative led to the charging of exorbitant reliefs, which effectively disinherited the tenant's descendant and therefore inspired many ingenius efforts to avoid them. Inheritance later became a matter of right, but the payment of relief to the lord continued.

3. More generally, the assistance that society gives to those in need, usually that which is administered by a branch of the government. Relief in this sense is often called public assistance or welfare.

REMAINDER That part of an **estate** in land that is left upon the termination of the immediately preceding estate and that does not amount to a **reversion** to the grantor or his heirs. The legal conditions for a remainder are that there must be a precedent particular estate, whose regular termination the remainder must await; the remainder must be created by the same **conveyance**, and at the same time, as a particular estate; the remainder must **vest** in right during the continuance of the particular estate; and no remainder can be limited after a **fee simple**. Thus, if A, being the owner

of land [in fee simple] gives it by deed or will to B for life, and after the death of B, to C in fee, the estate given to C is called a remainder, because it is the remnant or remainder of the estate or title which is left after taking out the lesser estate [life estate] given to B.

See further A.M. Sinclair & M.E. McCallum, *An Introduction to Real Property Law* (6th ed. 2012), c. 8.

CONTINGENT [EXECUTORY] REMAINDER "[A]ny remainder which is created in favor of an ascertained person but is subject to a **condition** precedent; is created in favor of an unborn person; or is created in favor of an existing but unascertained person. It was not, according to the older **common law** definition, an estate, but merely the possibility of an estate.... A contingent remainder becomes a **vested** remainder if any condition precedent is fulfilled and if the **remainderman** is ascertained before the termination of the preceding estate. Thus, A conveys to B for life, then to C and his heirs if C marries. At the time of the conveyance C is unmarried. The state of the title at that time is: life estate in B, contingent remainder in fee simple in C, reversion in fee simple in A. C marries while B is yet living. C's remainder becomes vested immediately on his marriage and all of the characteristics of a vested remainder attach thereto. The vesting of C's remainder operates to divest the **reversion** in A." C. Moynihan, *Introduction to the Law of Real Property* 129 (2d ed. 1988).

EXECUTED REMAINDER A remainder interest that is **vested** as of the present, though the enjoyment of it may be withheld until a future date.

VESTED REMAINDER A **remainder** that is limited to an ascertained person in being, whose right to the **estate** is fixed and certain, and that does not depend upon the happening of any future event, but whose **enjoyment** of the estate is postponed to some future time. See **remainder** [CONTINGENT REMAINDER].

"Remainders are either vested or contingent according to whether they are or are not, respectively, presently ready to take effect in possession upon the determination of the preceding estate or estates.

"A remainder is vested if the person entitled to it will obtain possession of the land upon the happening of no other contingency than the natural expiration of the prior estate (*Lundy v. Maloney* (1861), 11 U.C.C.P. 143 ...).

"In other words, a remainder limited to take effect automatically upon the expiration of the prior particular estate is a vested remainder because a present estate is conferred although it is not to be enjoyed until that future time. The estate granted by way of remainder does not depend for its existence upon any contingency, even though the time when it will come into possession may be uncertain when the estate is created. The remainder may actually end or be divested before the preceding estate ends and thus never come into possession, but that possibility does not prevent it from being vested. On the other hand, a contingent remainder is one limited to depend for its existence upon the happening of some event or the performance of some condition, which may never happen, or be performed, or may not happen or be performed until after the preceding estate ends." A.H. Oosterhoff & W.B. Rayner, *Anger and Honsberger: Law of Real Property* 395 (2d ed. 1985). See also B. Ziff, *Principles of Property Law* 242 (5th ed. 2010).

REMAINDERMAN One who has an interest in land **in futuro**; one who has an interest in an estate that becomes possessory at some point in the future after the termination, by whatever reason, of a present possessory interest. Remainderman usually refers to one who holds an interest in a **remainder**, whether **vested** or **contingent**. It may also refer to one who holds an interest in an executory limitation. Sometimes referred to as a remainder person.

REMAND To order or send back; a judicial order sending a prisoner back to **custody**. Remand is dealt with in various sections of the *Criminal Code,* R.S.C. 1985, c. C–46. For example, under s. 672.11, a court that has rea-

sonable grounds to believe evidence is necessary to determine the mental condition of an accused found guilty of an offence may remand the accused for assessment to determine whether the accused should be detained in a treatment facility.

REMEDY The means employed to enforce or redress an injury. The most common remedy at law consists of money **damages**. The courts of **chancery** developed a number of equitable remedies where none could be had at **common law**. The remedies of **specific performance**, **injunction** and **recission** are important examples. Today a court will not normally employ an equitable remedy unless the evidence clearly indicates that such a remedy is necessary to preserve the rights of a party.

CHARTER REMEDY A remedy granted for a violation of a right or freedom guaranteed under the **Canadian Charter of Rights and Freedoms**. The remedy might be granted under s. 52 of the **Constitution Act, 1982**, and address the legislation itself by means of **reading in, reading down**, or a **declaration of invalidity**. Alternatively, the remedy might be a **personal remedy** under s. 24, which could include exclusion of evidence, a stay or proceedings, or some other order having an impact only in the immediate case.

PREROGATIVE [EXTRAORDINARY] REMEDY A remedy available in the area of **administrative law** where a **tribunal** has exceeded its **jurisdiction** or breached a rule of natural justice. These remedies in the form of **writs** (known as PREROGATIVE WRITS) are granted by the courts and may have the effect of **quashing** a decision or prohibiting an administrative tribunal from hearing a particular matter. Examples include **certiorari, mandamus, prohibition**, etc. See further G. Gall, *The Canadian Legal System* 557–58 (5th ed. 2004).

REMITTER The act by which a person, who has **good title** to land, and enters upon the land with less than his or her original title, is restored to his or her original good title. The doctrine whereby the law will relate back from a defective title to an earlier valid title.

REMITTITUR (*rē-mĭ'-tĭ-tūr*) Lat.: reduction. The **procedural** process by which the **verdict** of a **jury** is diminished by subtraction; generally, any reduction made by the court without the consent of the jury. The theory of ADDITUR is a corollary to that of *remittitur:* the former increases an inadequate verdict; the latter decreases an excessive verdict. It is a universal rule that a *remittitur* may not be granted by a court in lieu of a new trial unless consented to by the party unfavourably affected thereby.

REMOTENESS A judicial concept used to limit the extent of potential **liability** that may stem from a single act; a point in the continuum of events between the **defendant's** act and the **plaintiff's** injury beyond which the law will not allow **recovery**. Remoteness may be assessed by determining what was a reasonably foreseeable consequence of the defendant's **wrongful act**.

REMOTENESS OF DAMAGE In the law of **tort**, the notion that one's **liability** is limited to results PROXIMATELY CAUSED (see **cause)** by one's conduct or omission. "[N]egligent defendants who owe a general duty are not liable unless their conduct is the 'proximate cause' of the plaintiffs' losses. Causation alone is not enough; it must be demonstrated that the conduct was the *proximate* cause of the damage." A. Linden & B. Feldthusen, *Canadian Tort Law* 361 (9th ed. 2011); *Overseas Tankship v. Morts Dock (Wagon Mound No. 1)*, [1961] A.C. 388 (P.C.). See also *Mustapha v. Culligan of Canada Ltd.*, 2008 SCC 27.

REMOVAL A change in place or position, as the removal of a **proceeding** to another court.

RENDITION To surrender a person to another jurisdiction. The term "rendition" was used in the *Fugitive Offenders Act*, R.S.C. 1985, c. F–32, which applied between Commonwealth countries; that Act was repealed and replaced by the *Extradition Act*, S.C. 1999, c. 18, which instead refers to "surrender."

RENT Periodic payment by a **tenant** of land or of other corporeal **hereditament**. Payment is usually in money but may be a non-monetary compensation, e.g., in the form of goods or labour.

RENUNCIATION 1. In **contract** law, a party who by words or conduct refuses to perform, or who disables himself or herself from performing a contract, is said to have broken or breached the contract by renunciation. See *Hochster v. de la Tour* (1853), 3 E. & B. 678; 118 E.R. 922. See further S.M. Waddams, *The Law of Contracts* 438–40 (6th ed. 2010).

2. Also, a disclaimer or refusal by a person to perform a legal function, e.g., to act as the **executor** or **administrator** of an **estate**.

RENVOI The rule in **conflict of laws** (or PRIVATE INTERNATIONAL LAW) that in some jurisdictions the capacity of a nonresident to sue upon a cause arising locally may be determined by the court looking to the law of his or her **domicile** rather than to the local law. An application of the renvoi doctrine occurs when the whole law of a foreign state, including its conflict of laws rules, is looked to for a solution. If reference is to the whole law, and not merely the internal law of the other state, then use of the renvoi concept is involved. Take, for example, the case of a citizen of Canada permanently residing in Germany who dies leaving personal property in Ontario. Assuming the Ontario conflict of laws rule to be that the law of the **decedent's** domicile will govern the matter, the Ontario **forum** would look to the "law" of Germany. If the forum should merely look to the law applicable to a German dying in Germany leaving personal property there, the court would be rejecting use of the renvoi. If, however, the forum looks to the whole law, i.e., including the German conflicts rule, this is making use of the renvoi. See further J. Walker, *Canadian Conflict of Laws* (6th ed. 2005), c. 5.

REORGANIZATION The transfer of substantially all the assets of an old **corporation** to a newly formed corporation, in which the **shareholders** own the same proportion of **stock** as in the old corporation.

REPATRIATION The term sometimes used to describe the process by which the **British North America Act**, an Act of the British Parliament, became the **Constitution Act, 1867**, and is subject to amendment exclusively within Canada. See **patriation**.

REPEAL 1. To abolish, rescind, annul by legislative act. **2.** The abrogation or annulling of a previously existing law by the enactment of a subsequent statute, which either declares that the former law shall be revoked and abrogated or contains provisions so contrary to or irreconcilable with those of the earlier law that only one of the two can stand in force. The latter is the IMPLIED REPEAL; the former, the EXPRESS REPEAL.

REPLACEMENT WORKER A person who works for an **employer** during an ongoing **strike** or **lockout**. The use of replacement workers is an **unfair labour practice** in British Columbia and Québec. *Labour Relations Code*, R.S.B.C. 1996, c. 244, ss. 6(3), 68; *Labour Code*, R.S.Q., c. 27, s. 109.1. Most jurisdictions that do not ban replacement workers impose restrictions on their use. For example, s. 94(2.1) of the *Canada Labour Code*, R.S.C. 1985, c. L–2 provides that replacement workers may not be hired "for the demonstrated purpose of undermining a trade union's representative capacity." Replacement workers are invariably temporary because Canadian labour legislation guarantees unionized employees the right to return to their jobs upon the conclusion of a lawful strike or lockout. See, e.g., *Trade Union Act*, R.S.N.S. 1989, c. 475, s. 53(3)(a); *Labour Relations Act*, C.C.S.M. c. L10, s. 12(1).

Some provincial labour relations statutes draw a distinction between "replacement workers" and "strikebreakers," with strikebreakers being hired by the employer in order to "interfere with, obstruct, prevent, restrain, or disrupt the exercise of any right before or during a lawful strike." *Labour Relations Act*, C.C.S.M. c. L10, s. 1. While hiring replacement workers is generally permissible, hiring strikebreakers is not. See, e.g., *Labour Relations Act, 1995*, S.O. 1995, c. 1, Sch. A, s. 78; *Labour Relations Code*, R.S.A. 2000, c. L–1, s. 154.

REPLEVIN An **action** that lies for the recovery of the thing taken, rather than for the value of that thing; a possessory remedy; a legal form of action ordinarily employed only to recover **possession** or the value of specific **personal property** unlawfully withheld from the plaintiff plus **damages** for its detention. Replevin is primarily a possessory action in which the issues ordinarily are limited to the plaintiff's title or right to possession of the goods. Compare **trespass**; **trover**.

REPLEVY To deliver to the owner; to redeliver goods that have been kept from the rightful owner. See **replevin**.

REPLY In **pleadings** the **plaintiff's** answer if the **defendant**, instead of merely resting his or her **defence** on a denial of the plaintiff's allegations, has raised an affirmative defence, i.e., pleaded in **confession and avoidance**. See, e.g., *Federal Courts Rules*, SOR/98–106, s. 171.

REPRESENTATION A statement made before or at the time of the entering into a **contract**. A representation may become a term of a contract **(condition** or **warranty)** if so intended by the parties. However, even if not a term of the contract, a representation will, if it is false and if it induced the making of the contract, give a right to the party deceived by it to **rescind** the contract. See further S.M. Waddams, *The Law of Contracts* (6th ed. 2010), c. 13. See **misrepresentation.**

REPUDIATION A term used to describe the conduct of one of the parties to a **contract** which demonstrates to the other that it will not fulfill the terms of the contract. It entitles the other party not to perform its obligations under the contract and claim **damages**. Also described as a **breach** that goes "to the root of the contract." See further,

S.M. Waddams, *The Law of Contracts* 438–40 (6th ed. 2010).

RES (*rās*) Lat.: thing. The subject matter of **actions** that are primarily **in rem**, i.e., actions that establish rights in relation to an object, as opposed to a person, or **in personam**. For example, in an action that resolves a conflict over **title** to **real property**, the land in question is the *res*. Tangible **personal property** can also be a *res,* as in the corpus of a trust. In a **quasi** *in rem* **proceeding**, land or **chattels** that are seized and **attached** at the beginning of the action, in order that they may later be used to satisfy a personal **claim**, are the *res* of such suits. The term refers as well to the status of individuals. Thus, in a divorce suit, the marital status is the *res*. The purpose of a *res* is to establish a court's **jurisdiction**; if the property lies within the state where the action is brought, or an individual in a divorce action is a **domiciliary** of the state, then jurisdiction is established.

RESCIND To **abrogate** a **contract**, release the parties from further obligation to each other and restore the parties to the positions they would have occupied if the contract had never been made. For instance, in rescinding a sales contract, any monies paid or goods received would usually be returned to their original holders, though the parties could agree otherwise.

RESCISSION "An **equitable** remedy that annuls or avoids a **contract**. Rescission is a **remedy** granted to a plaintiff in the case of fraud, or an innocent misrepresentation, or because of some other action on the defendant's behalf that amounts to **undue influence, unconscionability**, or makes the bargain questionable on some other equitable grounds. Rescission in equity operates to roll the contract back to the position the parties were in prior to contracting ... It is also important for the plaintiff to be able to effect **restitutio in integrum**. That requires both parties to be restored to their pre-contractual positions. The degree of complete restoration will vary depending on the particular underlying cause of action. In the case of fraud, a court will be less particular with giving complete restoration, whereas for an innocent **misrepresentation**, anything less than complete restoration will bar rescission." J. Berryman, *The Law of Equitable Remedies* 341 (2000).

RESCUE DOCTRINE Tort rule that holds a **tortfeasor** liable to his or her victim's rescuer, should the latter injure himself or herself during a reasonable rescue attempt. The doctrine derives from the fact that "the wrong that imperils life is a wrong to the imperilled victim; it is a wrong also to the rescuer." *Wagner v. International R.R. Co.,* 133 N.E. 437, quoted in *Joudrey v. Swissair Transport Company,* 2004 NSSC 130. See also A. Linden & B. Feldthusen, *Canadian Tort Law* 393–95 (9th ed. 2011).

RESERVATION 1. A clause in any **instrument** of **conveyance**, such as a **deed**, that creates a lesser **estate**, or some right, interest or profit in the estate granted to be retained by the **grantor**. An example might be a conveyance of land wherein the grantor reserves the right to mines and minerals.
　　2. In practice, the term refers to the act of a court or other body in delaying a decision on a point of law. The court may reserve decision and proceed with the matter, or may adjourn the proceedings pending its decision. When the court "takes the matter under advisement," it in effect reserves decision, often so that it may render a written decision.

RESERVATION, POWER OF Under s. 55 of the *Constitution Act, 1867,* the **Governor-General** of Canada has the power to give assent to **bills** passed by Parliament or to reserve such assent for "signification of the Queen's pleasure." Similarly, under s. 90 of the **Constitution Act, 1867,** the **Lieutenant-Governor** of a province has the power to reserve bills for consideration of the federal government, which could then give or refuse assent to the bill. The power of reservation has become politically inoperative.

RESERVE "A tract of land, the legal title of which is vested in Her Majesty, that has been set apart by Her Majesty for the use and benefit of [an Indian] band." *Indian Act*, R.S.C. 1985, c. I–5, s. 2.

RES EXTINCTA (*rās ĕk-stĭnk'-tă*) Lat.: the thing did not exist. A term that describes the **common-law** principle that if the subject matter of a **contract** is proven not to exist, the contract will be **void**. *Romank v. Achtem*, 2009 BCSC 1757. See **mistake; res sua**.

RES GESTAE (*răs gĕs'-tī*) Lat.: the thing done. Declarations that are subject to the **hearsay rule** may be admissible if they qualify as *res gestae,* i.e., if they constitute a part of the thing done, under a recognized exception to the hearsay rule. "There are three basic situations in which the courts have properly invoked the *res gestae* doctrine to admit utterances offered for their truth. They may be categorized as: (1) declarations of bodily and mental findings and conditions; (2) declarations accompanying and explaining relevant acts; and (3) spontaneous exclamations." Bryant *et al., The Law of Evidence in Canada* (3d ed., 2009), §6.301. The statement "I am in pain" might be admitted as *res gestae* under the first category to prove that the **declarant** was in pain if the statement was made reasonably contemporaneously with the sensation. A declarant's statement "I am giving this as a loan" made while handing money to another person might be admitted as *res gestae* under the second category, to explain the nature of the act performed. The statement "He stabbed me" might be admitted as a spontaneous exclamation, provided it was made so contemporaneously with the event that there was no danger of concoction or distortion.

RESIDENCE "Generally, residence means a person's permanent place of abode and not his temporary place of abode.... The mere physical presence of a person in a place does not constitute his residence there but in addition he must have the present intention of remaining there for some time but not necessarily for all time." *Re Fulford and Townshend,* [1970] 3 O.R. 493 at 500 (Surr.Ct.) quoted in *Cruz v. Royal & SunAlliance Insurance Co. of Canada,* [2001] O.F.S.C.I.D. No. 87.

"There is a difference between residence and **domicile**. The latter is more permanent and is the jurisdiction which a person regards or intends to make his permanent home for all time unless some unforeseen circumstances in future change that intention." *Id.* at 501. Compare **domicile**.

RESIDENT ALIEN See **residence; alien**.

RESIDUARY BEQUEST See **bequest; residuary legacy**.

RESIDUARY CLAUSE A clause in a **will** that conveys to the beneficiary of a **residuary legacy** everything in a **testator's estate** not **devised** to a specific **legatee**. It will include **legacies** that were originally **void** either because the disposition was illegal or because for any other reason it was impossible that it should take effect. It operates to transfer to the residuary legatee such portion of the property as the testator has not perfectly disposed of.

RESIDUARY ESTATE The part of a **testator's** estate that remains undisposed of after all of the **estate** has been discharged through the satisfaction of all claims and specific legacies with the exception of the dispositions authorized by the **residuary clause**; the portion of the estate that remains after payment of debts and other classes of legacies.

RESIDUARY LEGACY A general **legacy** into which all the assets of the estate fall after the satisfaction of other legacies and payment of all debts of the estate and all costs of administration. However, the words *residuary legatee* by themselves **prima facie** do not apply to real estate, though their application might be extended so as to do so when the context requires. See *Re Wightman,* [1945] 4 D.L.R. 754 (Alta.S.C.).

RESIDUE The **remainder** of a **testator's estate** after payment of **debts** and **legacies**.

RES IPSA LOQUITUR (*rās ĭp'-sà lō'-kwĭ-tûr*) Lat.: the thing speaks for itself. A circumstantial rule of **evidence** based on the concept that, when an accident occurs under circumstances where it is so improbable that it could have happened without the negligence of the **defendant**, the mere happening of the accident gives rise to an inference that the defendant was **negligent**. When a **plaintiff** has established a **prima facie** case against a defendant through the doctrine of *res ipsa loquitur,* the evidentiary obligation on the defendant is to put forward an explanation of the accident that is consistent with the facts and shows no negligence on his or her part. The doctrine expired in Canada in *Fontaine v. British Columbia (Official Administrator)*, [1998] 1 S.C.R. 424. Now, circumstantial evidence will be weighed by the trier of fact to determine if there is a *prima facie* case of negligence. See A. Linden & B. Feldthusen, *Canadian Tort Law* 254–55 (9th ed. 2011).

RESISTING ARREST Assaulting a person with intent to resist or prevent a lawful **arrest**, whether of oneself or another person. *Criminal Code*, R.S.C. 1985, c. C–46, s. 270(1)(b).

RES JUDICATA (*rās jū-dǐ-kä'-tà*) Lat.: a thing decided. If the thing actually and directly in dispute has been already adjudicated upon, it cannot be litigated again. "The plea of *res judicata* applies, except in special cases, not only to points upon which the Court was actually required by the parties to form an **opinion** and **pronounce** a judgment, but to every point which properly belonged to the subject of litigation, and which the parties, exercising reasonable diligence, might have brought forward at the time." *Henderson v. Henderson*, [1843–60] All E.R. Rep. 378, quoted in *Furlong v. Avalon Bookkeeping Services Ltd.*, 2004 NLCA 46.

RES NULLA (*rās nŭl-ă*) Lat.: A thing of no one. A term that describes items that have not previously been the subject of **ownership**.

RESOLUTION An expression of opinion or intention passed at a meeting, often used in company management. See **by-laws**; **resolved**.

RESPITE 1. A delay, postponement or **forbearance** of a **sentence**, not comprehending a permanent suspension of execution of the judgment; a respite of execution. **2.** Also, a delay in repayment granted to a debtor by the creditor. See **grace period**.

RESPONDEAT SUPERIOR (*rā-spŏn'-dā-ät sū-pěr'-ē-ôr*) Lat.: let the superior reply. A maxim in **contract** law where one who expects to derive an advantage from an act done by another person for him or her must answer for any injury that a third person may sustain from it. See **scope of employment**. Compare **vicarious liability**.

RESPONDENT A person against whom a petition is presented, a summons is issued or an **appeal** is brought.

RESPONSIBLE GOVERNMENT A system of government in which the **executive** branch is dependent on the support of ("responsible to") the elected **legislature**. Responsible government was initially introduced to Canadian colonial legislatures starting in the 1840s. It is now one of the foundational **unwritten constitutional principles** of Canada's constitutional framework.

RESPONSIBLE COMMUNICATION ON MATTERS OF PUBLIC INTEREST A defence to a claim of **defamation** available to journalists and others who publish matters of public interest in any medium. The defence will apply where "A. The publication is on a matter of public interest, and B. The publisher was diligent in trying to verify the allegation, having regard to: (a) the seriousness of the allegation; (b) the public importance of the matter; (c) the urgency of the matter; (d) the status and reliability of the source; (e) whether the plaintiff's side of the story was sought and accurately reported; (f) whether the inclusion of the defamatory statement was justifiable; (g) whether the defamatory statement's public interest lay in the fact that it was made rather than its truth ("reportage"); and (h) any other relevant circumstances." *Grant v. Torstar Corp.*, 2009 SCC 61.

RES SUA (*rās sū'-à*) Lat.: one's own thing. A term that describes the common law principle that a contract will be void if the party purchasing under the contract already owned that which he or she sought to purchase. *Romank v. Achtem*, 2009 BCSC 1757. See **mistake**; **res extincta**.

RESTITUTIO IN INTEGRUM (*rĕs-tĭ-tū'-tē-ō ĭn ĭn-tĕg'-rŭm*) Lat.: restoration to the whole. To restore a person to the position he or she was in before a breach of contract or tort.

RESTITUTION Act of making good, or of giving the equivalent for, any loss, damage, or injury; **indemnification**. The term commonly used today to describe a **remedy** available to prevent **unjust enrichment**.

RESTORATIVE JUSTICE A model of justice that seeks "to hold the **offender** accountable in a more meaningful way, repairing the harm caused by the **offence**, reintegrating [the offender] into the community and achieving a sense of healing for both the **victim** and the community." This model views **crime** as a harm done to victims and communities, not just the state. Both the victim and the community have a greater role in defining the harm and how it might be repaired. The format is often a face-to-face meeting where the victim, the offender and members of the community discuss their concerns and feelings about the crime and develop a way for the offender to make reparations. *A Program for Nova Scotia: Restorative Justice*, Executive Summary, Nova Scotia Department of Justice, 1998.

RESTRAINING ORDER An order granted without notice or hearing, demanding the preservation of the **status quo** until a hearing can be had to determine the propriety of **injunctive relief**, temporary or permanent. The restraining order is issued upon application of a plaintiff requesting the court to forbid an action or a threatened action of the defendant; the form of request will generally be upon an order to show cause why the injunctive relief the plaintiff seeks ought not be granted. After a hearing, a preliminary or permanent injunction may issue. Compare **injunction**.

RESTRAINT OF TRADE [UNREASONABLE] Contractual interference with free competition in business and commercial transactions that tends to restrict production, affect prices or otherwise control the market to the detriment of purchasers or consumers of goods and services. Ordinarily reasonable restraints of trade are made unreasonable if they are contrary to public policy.

RESTRAINT ON ALIENATION Restriction on the ability to **convey real property** interests, any attempt at which is in **derogation** of the **common-law** policy in favour of free alienability; interests thus created are **void** or **voidable** as unlawful restraints on alienation.

Although fees on condition subsequent and fee simple determinables are, in general, permissible **estates**, a condition that states, "but if any attempt is made to alienate the land, the **grantor** and his **heirs** reserve the right to re-enter and declare the estate forfeit," would be against the policy. As a consequence, a rule exists requiring that there be a person capable of transferring absolute interest in possession within a certain period of time. See **alienation**; **rule against perpetuities**. However, in estates created by short-term **leases** such restraints are permissible. The determination of validity is based upon the nature and quality (duration) of the restraint, the type of estate in question and the penalty imposed for violation of the restraint.

RESTRICTIVE COVENANT A promise existing as part of an agreement, restricting the use of **real property** or the kind of buildings that may be erected thereupon; the promise is usually expressed by the creation of an express **covenant**, **reservation** or exception in a **deed**. In order for a grantor to enforce the covenant against REMOTE GRANTEES, i.e., subsequent owners who take title from the first grantee, the covenant must **run with the land**. In **equity**, negative or restrictive covenants run with the land, except against a **bona fide purchaser** for value without notice. Positive covenants do not run with the land. See *Durham Condominium Corporation No. 123 v. Amberwood Investments Limited et al.* (2002), 58 O.R. (3d) 481 (Ont.

C.A.); *Lohse v. Fleming*, 2008 ONCA 307.

RESTRICTIVE ENDORSEMENT An endorsement on a **bill of exchange** that prohibits or inhibits further endorsement of the bill. See **endorse**.

RESULTING TRUST See **trust**.

RESULTING USE See **use**.

RETAINER 1. The appointment of a barrister or solicitor to take or defend proceedings, or to counsel or otherwise act for the client. **2.** The document by which such employment is evidenced. **3.** A preliminary fee paid to a lawyer for work to be done. See *Paoletti v. Gibson*, 2009 ONCA 71.

RETIRE 1. In reference to **bills of exchange**, to recover, redeem, regain by the payment of a sum of money; to withdraw from circulation or from the market.

2. Also, to withdraw voluntarily from office, a public station, business or other employment.

3. A **jury** is retired at the point when the judge has submitted the case to it for its consideration and **verdict**.

RETRACTION Withdrawal of a **renunciation**, declaration, **accusation**, premise, etc. As to a **defamation**, a retraction can be effective only if it is complete, unequivocal and without lurking insinuations or hesitant withdrawals. It must, in short, be an honest endeavour to repair all the wrong done by the defamatory imputation.

RETRIBUTIVE JUSTICE A theory of justice holding that the **punishment** of offenders is justifiable purely on the grounds that, having committed crimes, they deserve to be punished. It is distinct from vengeance insofar as it "represents an objective, reasoned, and measured determination of an appropriate punishment [that] properly reflects the moral culpability of the offender" and "incorporates a principle of restraint," requiring "the imposition of a just and appropriate punishment, and nothing more." *R. v. C.A.M.*, [1996] 1 S.C.R. 500. It is also distinct from **deterrence** or **rehabilitation**, since

it is unconcerned with whether others are dissuaded from offending, or with reintegrating the offender into society. Instead, its goal is to inflict suffering on the offender in response to the offence. Numerous moral and legal philosophers have advocated retributive justice as a legitimate goal of criminal law. See, e.g., M. Moore, *Placing Blame: A Theory of the Criminal Law* (1997); R.A. Duff, "Retrieving Retribution," *Retributivism: Essays in Theory and Policy* (2011). See **separation**.

RETROACTIVE Refers to a rule of law, whether legislative or judicial, that relates to things already decided in the past. A RETROSPECTIVE law is one that relates back to a previous transaction and gives it some different legal effect from that which it had under the law when it occurred. Similarly, in respect to **ex post facto** laws, retroactivity refers to the imposition of **criminal** liability on behaviour that took place prior to the enactment of the statute. It should be noted, however, that judicially created law (common law) is often retroactive in its effects, the court's decision being made on the basis of a previously existent fact pattern wherein the actors could not possibly have predicted at the time of their actions the court's eventual interpretation of the law but are nevertheless held accountable to it. Substantive law is presumed not to apply retrospectively, but "procedural provisions are an exception to the presumption against retrospectivity." *Application under s. 83.28 of the Criminal Code (Re)*, 2004 SCC 42.

RETROSPECTIVE See **retroactive**.

RETURN 1. A report from an official, such as a sheriff, stating what he or she has done in respect to a command from the court, or why he or she has failed to do what was requested. A FALSE RETURN is a false or incorrect statement by an official that acts to the detriment of an interested party.

2. A report from an individual or **corporation** as to its earnings, etc., for tax or other governmental purposes.

REVERSAL As used in **opinions**, **judgments** and **mandates**, the setting aside, annulling, **vacating** or changing to the contrary the decision of a lower court or other body. Compare **overrule**; **quash**; **remand**. See also **affirm**.

REVERSE ONUS A statutory provision requiring the **accused** in a **criminal** matter to bear some **burden of proof** with regard to an element of the **offence**. A legal burden requires the accused to prove, on **balance of probabilities**, some fact relating to an element of the offence. For example, a person whose ability to drive is impaired by alcohol and who is found in the driver's seat of a vehicle will be deemed to have care and control of it, unless that person establishes that he or she did not occupy that seat for the purpose of setting the vehicle in motion: *Criminal Code*, R.S.C. 1985, c. C–46, s. 258(1)(a). An evidentiary burden merely requires the accused to show the existence of some doubt about an element. For example, a person who has broken and entered into a place will be presumed to have intended to commit an indictable offence "in the absence of evidence to the contrary": *Criminal Code*, s. 348(2)(a). A reverse onus will violate the **presumption of innocence** guaranteed by s. 11(d) of the **Canadian Charter of Rights and Freedoms** but in some cases can be saved under s. 1 of the Charter as a **reasonable limit in a free and democratic society**.

REVERSE STING An undercover operation in which police officers pose as the **vendors** rather than as the **purchasers** of illegal narcotics. *R. v. Campbell*, [1999] 1 S.C.R. 565.

REVERSIBLE ERROR Error substantially affecting an **appellant's** legal rights and obligations that, if uncorrected, would result in a miscarriage of justice and that justifies reversing a **judgment** in the inferior court; synonymous with **prejudicial error**. Compare **harmless error**.

REVERSION "[T]he returning of the land to the **grantor** or his heirs after the grant is determined.... Where the residue of the **estate** always continues in him who made the particular estate. The idea of a reversion is founded on the principle that where a person has not parted with his whole estate and interest in a piece

of land, all that which he has not given away remains in him, and the possession of it reverts or returns to him upon the determination of the preceding estate." *Mercer v. Attorney-General for Ontario* (1881), 5 S.C.R. 538 at 626–27. Compare **remainder**.

REVERTER See **reversion**. See also **possibility of a reverter**.

REVIEW Judicial reexamination of the proceedings of a court or other body; a reconsideration of its former decision; often used to express what an **appellate court** does when it examines the **record** of a lower court or agency's determination that is on **appeal** before the court.

REVIEW BOARD In criminal law, a board established under s. 672.38 of the *Criminal Code*, R.S.C. 1985, c. C–46, p. 254, to make dispositions with regard to a person found **not criminally responsible by reason of mental disorder**. It must have at least five members, the chairperson must be a judge (or a person qualified for or retired from that office), and the board must contain at least one member qualified to practise psychiatry and at least one other member qualified to practise psychiatry or to have training in mental health and be qualified to practise medicine or psychology. Although created by the *Criminal Code*, a review board is treated as having been established under the laws of the province in which it sits, and members are appointed by the Lieutenant Governor in council. A review board makes a disposition with regard to the person found not criminally responsible within 45 days of that finding, and is also required to conduct an annual review of the status of each such person. At any such hearing, the board can release the person unconditionally, release the person on conditions, or detain the person in custody in a hospital. See also **mental disorder**; **not criminally responsible by reason of mental disorder**.

REVISED STATUTES A publication by government authority of unrepealed public general statutes. Every ten or fifteen years, most Canadian jurisdictions revise and consolidate their public general acts in order to eliminate errors, consolidate amendments and generally tidy things up. When the revision is completed, the revised statutes are proclaimed in force and the former versions are repealed. See, e.g., *Legislation Revision and Consolidation Act*, R.S.C. 1985, c. S–20.

REVOCATION 1. The recall of a power or authority conferred; **2.** the cancellation of an **instrument** previously made; **3.** the cancellation of an **offer** by the offeror, which, if effective, terminates the offeree's power of **acceptance**. Synonymous with cancellation.

REVOCATION OF PAROLE Cancellation of **parole**.

REVOCATION OF PROBATION Cancellation of **probation**.

REVOKE To annul, repeal, rescind, cancel privileges.

REX Lat.: King

RIGHT IN GROSS A right that exists on its own, independent of all other rights; a right not appendant to or otherwise annexed to land. See **à prendre**.

RIGHT OF ACTION See **cause of action**.

RIGHT OF REDEMPTION See **redemption**.

RIGHT OF RE-ENTRY See **re-entry, right of**.

RIGHT OF WAY The right to pass over another's land. A public right of way can be created by statute or by **dedication** and **acceptance**.

RIGHT TO FARM LEGISLATION Laws giving farms immunity from nuisance claims or other similar actions if they are operated in accordance with normal agricultural practices. See, e.g., *The Agricultural Operations Act*, S.S. 1995, c. A–12.1 or *Farm Practices Protection (Right to Farm) Act*, R.S.B.C. 1996, c. 131.

RIGOR MORTIS (*rĭ'-gôr môr'-tĭs*) Lat.: stiffness of death; medical terminology depicting the rigidity of the muscles after death. Medical authorities agree that it is not possible to fix the time of death from the onset of rigor mortis.

RIOT "[A]n **unlawful assembly** that has begun to disturb the peace tumultuously." *Criminal Code*, R.S.C. 1985, c. C–46, s. 64.

RIOT ACT A historical Act of the British Parliament allowing authorities to go to a place where twelve or more people were "unlawfully, riotously, and tumultuously assembled together," and to make a proclamation in the king's name ordering its members to disperse on threat of criminal sanction. *Riot Act* (UK), 1 Geo. I, c. 5. Parts of the *Riot Act* have been incorporated into Canada's *Criminal Code*, R.S.C. 1985, c. C–46. See **reading the riot act**.

RIPARIAN RIGHTS Rights that accrue to owners of land on the banks of water ways, such as the use of such water, ownership of soil under the water, etc.; "rights which a riparian owner (one whose lands run to and are bounded by water) may have in respect to water may be divided into those rights which are natural rights of user ... and those rights which are acquired by **prescription**." 2 A.H. Oosterhoff & W.B. Rayner, *Anger and Honsberger: Law of Real Property* 962 (2d ed. 1985). See also *Hoyt v. Loew*, 2008 NSSC 29.

ROBBERY Forcible stealing; as defined in the *Criminal Code*, R.S.C. 1985, c. C–46, s. 343, "Every one commits robbery who (*a*) steals, and for the purpose of extorting whatever is stolen or to prevent or overcome resistance to the stealing, uses violence or threats of violence to a person or property; (*b*) steals from any person and, at the time he steals or immediately before or immediately thereafter, wounds, beats, strikes or uses any personal violence to that person; (*c*) assaults any person with intent to steal from him; or (*d*) steals from any person while armed with an offensive weapon or imitation thereof." Compare **burglary**.

ROME STATUTE An international treaty that came into force in 2002, creating a permanent **international criminal court**. *Rome Statute*, 2187 U.N.T.S. 3.

ROWBOTHAM APPLICATION An application to a **trial court** for a conditional

stay of proceedings until state-funded counsel is provided. In order to succeed, an applicant must show that **legal aid** is not available to him or her, that he or she lacks the means to employ **counsel**, and that counsel is necessary to ensure a fair trial, which is a right under ss. 7 and 11(d) of the **Canadian Charter of Rights and Freedoms**. *R. v. Rowbotham* (1988), 63 CR (3d) 113 (Ont. C.A.). See **Fisher application**.

ROYAL ASSENT The term used to describe the act of agreement by the **Governor General** or **Lieutenant Governor** that transforms a **bill** that has been passed by **Parliament** or a provincial **legislature** into a **law**. Depending on what is specified in the statute, the law will take effect on Royal Assent, on a date specified in the **Act**, or on a date to be **proclaimed** by the **Governor General in Council** or the **Lieutenant Governor in Council**.

ROYAL CANADIAN MOUNTED POLICE [R.C.M.P.] The national police force of Canada, now governed by the *Royal Canadian Mounted Police Act*, S.C. 1986, c. 11. It is "responsible for an unusually large breadth of duties, from policing in isolated rural towns, the far north, and urban areas; providing protection services (among them the **Queen**, the **Governor General**, the **Prime Minister**, and other ministers of the **Crown**; the justices of the **Supreme Court of Canada**; and visiting dignitaries or diplomatic missions); enforcing federal laws (including wire fraud, counterfeiting, drug trafficking, and other related matters); providing counterterrorism and domestic security; and participating in various international policing efforts." A.R. Nadeau, *Federal Police Law 2010* xiv (2009). Officers of the force are appointed and have the status of a **peace officer** in every part of Canada.

ROYAL COMMISSION See **commission of inquiry**.

ROYAL PREROGATIVE The "residue of discretionary or arbitrary authority, which at any given time is legally left in the hands of the **Crown**": *Canada (Prime Minister) v. Khadr*, 2010 SCC

3, quoting A. V. Dicey, *Introduction to the Study of the Law of the Constitution* (8th ed. 1915), at p. 420. The **executive** decides how to exercise its powers, but **courts** have the jurisdiction to determine whether a prerogative power asserted by the Crown in fact exists and whether the executive has infringed the *Charter* or other constitutional norms in exercising it.

ROYAL PREROGATIVE OF MERCY The ability of the **Crown**, through the **Governor General in Council**, to exempt a person in whole or in part from the consequences of being found guilty of an offence. "Where the courts are unable to provide an appropriate remedy in cases that the executive sees as unjust imprisonment, the executive is permitted to dispense 'mercy' and order the release of the offender. The royal prerogative of mercy is the only potential remedy for persons who have exhausted their rights of appeal and are unable to show that their sentence fails to accord with the *Charter*." *R. v. Sarson*, [1996] 2 S.C.R. 223. The Royal Prerogative of Mercy is preserved in s. 749 of the *Criminal Code*, R.S.C. 1985, c. C–46, and the ability of the **executive** to grant a **pardon** under s. 748 is one aspect of it. What was formerly called a pardon but is now referred to as a **record suspension** is also available from the National **Parole** Board under the *Criminal Records Act*, R.S.C. 1985, c. C–47.

ROYAL PROCLAMATION OF 1763 A Proclamation by George III following the Seven Years War with regard to the territory in North America that then became British. It made a number of provisions for governance of the newly acquired territories, including preserving the use of the French language in Quebec but imposing English law; this latter measure was reversed in the **Quebec Act 1774**. The greatest continuing significance of the Royal Proclamation is in its influence on **Aboriginal rights**; it has been referred to as "the 'Magna Carta' of Indian rights in North America and Indian 'Bill of Rights.'" *R. v. Marshall; R. v. Bernard*, 2005 SCC 43. Section 25 of the **Canadian Charter of Rights and Freedoms** provides that it should not be interpreted in a way that would abrogate or derogate from any rights or freedoms that have been recognized by the Royal Proclamation.

The Royal Proclamation recognized **Aboriginal title** in lands that had not been ceded to the Crown and also proclaimed that land could not be obtained from the Aboriginal inhabitants by anyone except the Crown. It also reserved for **Indians** all land not falling within the new governments, as well as "all the Lands and Territories lying to the Westward of the Sources of the Rivers [that] fall into the Sea from the West and North West," and prohibited European settlement in those areas. The Royal Proclamation's "objective, so far as the Indians were concerned, was to provide a solution to the problems created by the greed [that] hitherto some of the English had all too often demonstrated in buying up Indian land at low prices." *R. v. Sioui*, [1990] 1 S.C.R. 1025.

ROYALTY 1. A share of profits paid to the producer of intellectual property such as music or a book. 2. In the oil and gas industry, a share of profits paid to the landowner by the person granted a license to exploit the resource. "Typically, in contractual arrangements between landowners and oil and gas producers, the owner grants the producer the right to drill for, produce, and take the resource, reserving a 'royalty interest' [which] entitles the owner to a portion of the oil or gas produced, payable in kind or in money or both." *Mobil Oil Canada, Ltd. v. Canada*, 2001 FCA 333.

RULE AGAINST MULTIPLE CONVICTIONS See **Kienapple principle**.

RULE AGAINST PERPETUITIES The rule in the law of **real property** that "a future interest is void unless it would vest in interest, if at all, only within a period measured by lives in being plus a further period of 21 years." A.M. Sinclair & M.E. McCallum, *An Introduction to Real Property Law* 102 (6th ed. 2012). See **life in being**. The purpose of the rule is to prevent the possibility of remoteness of vesting and the problems that would be created by long tie-ups of

property and unreasonable **restraints on alienation**. *Id.*

RULE IN SHELLEY'S CASE The rule is "where a grant of a life estate to A is followed in the same instrument (will or deed) by a grant mediately or immediately to A's heirs, or heirs of the body, the grant of the remainder is transformed into a remainder in fee simple to the first grantee. By the rule … a grant to A for life, and remainder to A's heirs must be interpreted to give A a life estate and also a fee simple in remainder, and the heirs nothing. Put another way, the Rule treats the words "and heirs" as being words of limitation defining the estate that A receives, not words of purchase identifying the heirs as grantees." A.M. Sinclair & M.E. McCallum, *An Introduction to Real Property Law* 18 (6th ed. 2012).

RULE IN WILD'S CASE In **real property** law, a rule of **construction** by which a **devise** to "B and his children," where B has no children at the time the gift **vests** in B, is read to mean a gift to B in **fee tail**, the words "and his children" thus being construed as **words of limitation** and not words of purchase. *Wild's Case* (1599), 6 Co. Rep. 16f; 77 E.R. 277. See further 1 A.H. Oosterhoff & W.B. Rayner, *Anger and Honsberger: Law of Real Property* 138–39 (2d ed. 1985).

RULE NISI A preliminary and conditional decision. "Rules fall into two categories, a rule absolute and a rule nisi. A rule absolute is one that is operative forthwith and constitutes an adjudication upon some point at some stage in an action or a proceeding; a rule nisi does not. It merely indicates that the Court is satisfied that a prima facie case has been made out to justify calling upon the other side to make answer at the time and place indicated to the contention upon which the rule was founded. If the party does not appear when called upon, or if he does not show good grounds for setting aside the rule, the rule becomes absolute and it then constitutes an adjudication upon the matters in dispute and then becomes appealable." *R. v. Gillespie*, 2000 MBCA 1, quoting *R. v. United Fishermen and Allied Workers'*

Union et al. (1967), 63 D.L.R. (2d) 356 (B.C.C.A.).

RULE OF CAPTURE The rule that where underground mineral reserves, such as pools of oil and gas, extend under more than one piece of land, landowner A has no claim against landowner B for reserves brought to the surface from B's land, even if the reserves originated under A's land. The rule has been modified by statute in most jurisdictions; see, e.g., *Oil and Gas Conservation Act*, R.S.A. 2000, c. O–6 and *Anderson v. Amoco Canada Oil and Gas*, 2004 SCC 49.

RULE OF LAW A foundational principle of the Canadian **constitution**, dictating that the law is supreme over any body of government or individual. The Preamble to the *Constitution Act 1982* states that Canada is founded upon principles that recognize the rule of law. "The rule of law embraces at least three principles. The first principle is that the 'law is supreme over officials of the government as well as private individuals, and thereby preclusive of the influence of arbitrary power': *Reference re Manitoba Language Rights*, at p. 748. The second principle 'requires the creation and maintenance of an actual order of positive laws [that] preserves and embodies the more general principle of normative order': *ibid.*, at p. 749. The third principle requires that 'the relationship between the state and the individual . . . be regulated by law': *Reference re Secession of Quebec*, at para. 71." *British Columbia (Attorney-General) v. Christie*, 2007 SCC 21.

RUN WITH THE LAND A phrase used with respect to **covenants** in the law of real property where the burden or benefit of the covenant passes to persons who succeed to the **estate** of the original contracting parties. For example, with respect to covenants made between a **lessor** and **lessee**, "[a] covenant is said to run ... with the land when either the liability to perform it, or the right to take advantage of it, passes to the assignee of the tenant." See further 1 A.H. Oosterhoff & W.B. Rayner, *Anger and Honsberger: Law of Real Property* 253ff. (2d ed. 1985).

S

SALE A **contract** by which **property**, real or personal, is transferred from the seller **(vendor)** to the buyer **(vendee)** for a fixed price in money, paid or agreed to be paid by the buyer. In Canada, a contract for the sale of goods must be distinguished from other contracts generally and from the law dealing with other kinds of sales (e.g., the sale of land). The distinction is important because contracts for the sale of goods are regulated by the *Sale of Goods* legislation in the common-law provinces and territories. See, e.g., *Sale of Goods Act,* R.S.O. 1990, c. S.1. Section 2(l) of this Ontario statute defines a contract for the sale of goods as "a contract whereby the seller transfers or agrees to transfer the property in the goods to the buyer for a money consideration called the price, and there may be a contract of sale between one part owner and another." See further G.H.L. Fridman, *Sale of Goods in Canada* (5th ed. 2004), c. 1.

ABSOLUTE SALE Generally, a sale wherein the property passes to the buyer upon completion of the agreement between the parties. However, contracts for the sale of goods may be regarded as absolute, i.e., effective from the time they are made "though such terms as relate to the passing of property ... or the time for payment of the price may not take effect until the time or event fixed by the contract." *Id.* at 24.

CONDITIONAL SALE A sale in which the buyer receives **possession** and the right of use of the goods sold, but the transfer of title is not effectuated until performance of some condition, usually the complete payment of the purchase price. Such contracts may be governed by special **legislation** such as that concerned with conditional sales agreements, CHATTEL MORTGAGES (see **mortgage**), and **secured transactions**, and need not necessarily be governed by the *Sale of Goods* legislation. Under the lat-

ter, conditional sales would seem to be "contracts which are intended to be binding on the parties (and to pass property in the goods which are sold) only on the occurrence of some stipulated event or circumstance." *Id.* at 26. See **PPSA**.

EXECUTED SALE Status when nothing remains to be done by either party to effect a complete transfer of the **title** to the **property** concerned.

EXECUTION SALE See **sheriff's sale**.

EXECUTORY SALE An agreement to sell where something more remains to be done before all the terms of the agreement are performed.

PUBLIC SALE A sale upon notice to the public and in which members of the public may bid.

SALE BY DESCRIPTION By the *Sale of Goods Acts,* "where there is a contract for the sale of goods by description, there is an implied **condition** that the goods will correspond with the description...." See, e.g., *Sale of Goods Act,* R.S.O. 1990, c. S.1, s. 14. There may be a sale by description, however, even if the buyer has actually seen the goods. See *Grant v. Australian Knitting Mills Ltd.,* [1936] A.C. 85 at 100 (P.C.) (Austl.).

SALE BY SAMPLE If the sale of goods "is by sample, as well as by description, it is not sufficient that the bulk of the goods corresponds with the sample if the goods do not also correspond with the description." See, e.g., *Sale of Goods Act,* R.S.O. 1990, c. S.1, s. 14.

SHERIFF'S SALE See **sheriff's sale**.

TAX SALE A sale of land for non-payment of taxes.

SALMOND TEST A test for determining **vicarious liability**. It holds "employers are vicariously liable for (1) employee acts authorized by the employer; or (2) unauthorized acts so connected with authorized acts that they may be regarded as modes (albeit improper modes) of doing an authorized act." *P.A.B. v. Curry,* [1991] 2 S.C.R. 534.

SALVAGE 1. A doctrine under **maritime law** allowing a party (the salvor) who successfully rescues a vessel in distress to claim compensation from its owner. The doctrine of salvage requires that the salvor's efforts be voluntary. Crew members serving on the vessel under contracts of employment are entitled to compensation for salvage only where their actions went beyond the terms of their contracts, or where their contracts have lapsed (for example, where their ship has been abandoned by order of its master). See E. Gold, A. Chircop, & H. Kindred, *Maritime Law* (2003), c. 15. **2.** A principle of insurance law whereby, in situations where an **insured** has suffered a **constructive** total loss of the insured property, the **insurer** is permitted to claim **title** to any remaining part of it. The policy justification underlying salvage is to prevent the insured from being over-indemnified for a loss by being able to claim insurance payments on the whole loss while also keeping whatever remains of the insured property. D. Boivin, *Insurance Law* 274–77 (2004).

SAME-SEX SPOUSE See **spouse**.

SANCTION A consequence or punishment for violation of accepted norms of social conduct, which may be of two kinds: those that redress **civil** injuries (civil sanctions) and those that punish **crimes** (penal sanctions).

SATISFACTION The ending of an obligation by performance, e.g., the payment of a debt; a release and discharge of an obligation.

An accord is an agreement whereby an earlier obligation between the parties is discharged; the **consideration** that makes the agreement operative is the satisfaction. See also **accord and satisfaction**.

SCIENTER (*sī'-ĕn-tûr*) Lat.: knowledge. Previous knowledge of an operative state of facts; a claim in **pleading** that a thing has been knowingly done by a **defendant** or **accused**; also the cognizance by an animal's owner of its disposition.

SCOPE OF EMPLOYMENT The range of activities encompassed by one's employment; generally the phrase is used to denote the area within which an employer will be liable for the **torts** of his or her employees. See, e.g., *British Columbia Ferry Corp. v. Invicta Security*

Service Corp. (1998), 167 D.L.R. (4th) 193 (B.C. C.A.). In *Bazely v. Curry*, [1999] 2 S.C.R. 534, the Supreme Court held that employers may be found **vicariously liable** for torts committed by their employees without reference to whether those torts were committed within the scope of their employment. Nonetheless, the old "scope of employment" test "continues to have application" in Canadian tort law. *T.W. v. Seo* (2005), 256 D.L.R. (4th) 1 (Ont. C.A.). See also **respondeat superior**.

SCRIP Land or money given to Métis as compensation for the loss of Aboriginal title to land, or in exchange for withdrawing from a **treaty** in the case of those Métis who fell into one. Scrip was a certificate that could be exchanged for land or its value in money, but frequently ended up being purchased by scrip buyers for a percentage of its worth. This practice was and remains controversial: "The history of scrip speculation and devaluation is a sorry chapter in our nation's history." *R. v. Blais*, 2003 SCC 44. See generally *Papaschase Indian Band No. 136 v. Canada (Attorney-General)*, 2004 ABQB 655, aff'd *Canada (Attorney-General) v. Lameman*, 2008 SCC 14.

SCRIVNER "A person who holds money put into his hands until he has an opportunity of investing. Even if the person is an attorney or a solicitor, his employment is not in consequence of his character as solicitor." *Fedak v. Monti* (1981) 16 C.C.L.T. 287 at 292 (Ont.H.C.).

SEAL 1. At common law, an impression on wax, wafer, or other tenacious substance of being impressed; **2.** a formal method of communicating assent to a written document.

Every corporation must have a COMMON SEAL, since such a body cannot exhibit its intention by acts or discourse of a personal nature, but acts and speaks through its common seal, except, e.g., in instances when it is represented by an officer, agent or attorney in the course of ordinary day-to-day business.

SEALED INSTRUMENT One that is signed and has the **seal** of the signer attached.

An **instrument** is sufficiently sealed if the party, with intent to seal, places a die or stick or his finger on sealing wax or on a wafer, or merely on the paper or parchment. It is not necessary that any mark or impression be made, provided there is an intention to seal.

A sealed contract, or CONTRACT UNDER SEAL, is a FORMAL CONTRACT (as distinguished from a contract without a seal— a SIMPLE CONTRACT) that did not require **consideration** at **common law**.

SEARCH AND SEIZURE A police practice whereby premises are searched and property is seized that may be pertinent in the investigation and prosecution of a crime. A search and seizure is constitutionally limited by s. 8 of the *Canadian Charter of Rights and Freedoms,* which provides that "everyone has the right to be secure against unreasonable search or seizure." A search is any investigative technique that infringes a person's **reasonable expectation of privacy**, and a search conducted without a warrant is **prima facie** an unreasonable one. See *Hunter v. Southam Inc.,* [1984] 2 S.C.R. 145. See further S. Coughlan, *Criminal Procedure* 63–130 (2nd ed. 2012).

SEARCH INCIDENT TO ARREST The power of a police officer to **search** a person who has been **arrested**. The arrest must have been lawful, and the search must be for some purpose related to that arrest and must be conducted reasonably. No separate reasonable grounds are necessary to conduct the search, which is justified if the arrest itself was lawful. The search can be conducted on the accused's person and the surrounding area, including a vehicle. See **search incident to investigative detention**.

SEARCH INCIDENT TO INVESTIGATIVE DETENTION The power of a police officer to **search** a person who is subject to an **investigative detention**. The term is a misnomer because the search is not an incident of the investigative detention; the power arises only when there are separate reasonable grounds to believe that the safety of the police officer or others is at risk. The search power is initially limited to a pat-down search. See *R.v.*

Mann, 2004 SCC 52. See **search incident to arrest**.

SEARCH WARRANT Under the *Criminal Code,* R.S.C. 1985, c. C–46, s. 487(1), an order issued by a justice that authorizes a **peace officer** (or person named in the warrant) to conduct a search of specified premises and to seize "(a) anything on or in respect of which any offence against this Act or any other Act of Parliament has been or is suspected to have been committed, (b) anything that there are reasonable grounds to believe will afford evidence with respect to the commission of an offence . . . against this Act or any other Act of Parliament, (c) anything that there are reasonable grounds to believe is intended to be used for the purpose of committing any offence against the person for which a person may be arrested without warrant, or (c.1) any offence-related property." See further S. Coughlan, *Criminal Procedure* 68–87 (2nd ed. 2012). See further, e.g., *R. v. Debot* (1986), 30 C.C.C. (3d) 207 (Ont.C.A., aff'd [1989] 2 S.C.R. 140.

SECESSION "[T]he effort of a group or section of a state to withdraw itself from the political and constitutional authority of that state, with a view to achieving statehood for a new territorial unit on the international plane." *Reference re Secession of Quebec*, [1998] 2 S.C.R. 217.

SECONDARY LIABILITY Being guilty of an offence not as the **principal**, but as a **party**.

SECONDARY PICKETING The picketing by striking employees of a third party who is not involved in the dispute that gave rise to the strike, but is somehow affiliated with employer. *Retail, Wholesale, and Department Store Union, Local 558 v. Pepsi-Cola Canada Beverages* (*West*) *Ltd.*, 2002 SCC 8.

SECUNDUM (*sĕ-kūn'-dŭm*) Lat.: immediately after; beside; next to. In law publishing, the second series of a treatise may be called *secundum,* as in Corpus Juris Secundum (C.J.S.).

SECURED CREDITOR "[A] person holding a **mortgage**, **hypothec**, **pledge**, charge or lien on or against the property of the debtor or any part of that property as security for a debt due or accruing due to the person from the debtor, or a person whose claim is based on, or secured by, a negotiable instrument held as collateral security and on which the debtor is only indirectly or secondarily liable." *Bankruptcy and Insolvency Act*, R.S.C. 1985, c. B–3, s. 2, as amended by S.C. 1992, c. 27.

SECURED TRANSACTIONS See **credit**.

SECURITIES Stock certificates, bonds or other **evidence** of a secured indebtedness or of a right created in the holder to participate in profits or **assets** distribution of a profit-making enterprise; more generally, written assurances for the return or payment of money; **instruments** giving to their legal holders right to money or other property. They are therefore instruments that have value and are used as such in regular channels of commerce. The issuing and trading of securities are regulated by provincial legislation. See, e.g., *Securities Act,* R.S.O. 1990, c. S. 5.

PUBLIC SECURITIES Those certificates and other **negotiable instruments** evidencing the debt of a governmental body.

SECURITY DEPOSIT Money that a **tenant** deposits with a **landlord** to ensure the landlord that the tenant will abide by the **lease** agreements; a fund from which the landlord may obtain payment for **damages** caused by the tenant during his or her occupancy.

SECURITY INTEREST An **interest** in **real** or **personal property** that secures the payment of an obligation. At common law, security interests either are consensual or arise by **operation of law**. Those arising by operation of law include judgment **liens** and statutory liens.

The clearest examples of security interests are the **mortgage**, the **pledge**, and the CONDITIONAL SALE (see **sale**). The mortgage involves the situation wherein the mortgagor gives the mortgagee a security interest in a specific asset, which is usually real property. The pledge deals with the situation wherein the creditor takes possession of the property. The conditional sale involves the situation wherein the seller gives credit and takes a security interest. See **PPSA**.

SECURITY OF THE PERSON One of the interests protected by s. 7 of the **Canadian Charter of Rights and Freedoms**. Security of the person protects a person's physical and mental integrity and includes "a notion of personal autonomy involving, at the very least, control over one's bodily integrity free from state interference and freedom from state-imposed psychological and emotional stress." *A.C. v. Manitoba (Director of Child and Family Services)*, 2009 SCC 30.

SEDITION Under the *Criminal Code,* R.S.C. 1985, c. C–46, ss. 59 and 61, it is an **indictable offence** to speak seditious words, i.e., words expressive of a seditious intention. A seditious intention is an intention to raise disaffection and discontent among Her Majesty's subjects or to promote public disorder. See *Rex v. Felton* (1916) 25 C.C.C. 207 (Alta. S.C.A.D.). See also **seditious libel**.

SEDITIOUS LIBEL A libel that expresses a seditious intention, viz., teaching or advocating, publishing or circulating any writing that advocates the use of force as a means of accomplishing a governmental change in Canada. *Criminal Code,* R.S.C. 1985, c. C–46, s. 59(2). Words constitute a seditious libel "if they are expressive of a seditious intention, and...are both calculated (likely) and intended to stir up and excite discontent and disaffection among His Majesty's subjects." *Rex v. Giesinger* (1916), 32 D.L.R. 325 at 330 (Sask.S.C.).

SEDONA CANADA PRINCIPLES The recommendations in a report produced by a working group of Canadian judges, lawyers, and technologists proposing principles to govern electronic **discovery**.

SEISED The condition of legally owning and possessing **realty**. A person seised of **real property** has a **freehold estate** with possession or a right to possession. The phrase imports legal **title** as opposed to a beneficial **interest**.

SEISIN A term that describes the **title** of a **freehold estate** with a right of immediate **possession**, the term really being synonymous with possession. "In feudal times the title or right of immediate possession of a freehold estate was transmissable by ... **livery of seisin** ... Now livery of seisin has been done away with by statute and replaced by transfer by deed." 2 A.H. Oosterhoff & W.B. Rayner, *Anger and Honsberger: Law of Real Property* 1259 (2d ed. 1985). Today, "seisin" is generally considered synonymous with ownership.

SEIZURE A forcible taking of possession, *Pacific Finance Co. v. Ireland,* [1931] 2 W.W.R. 593 (Alta.S.C.A.D.); the act of forcibly dispossessing an owner of property, under actual or apparent authority of law; the taking of property into the **custody** of the court in **satisfaction** of a **judgment**, or in consequence of a violation of public law. When a **writ** of seizure is executed by a sheriff, **chattels** in possession of a **debtor** are taken away. See also **search and seizure**.

SELF-DEALING A type of trading in which a party acts upon secret information obtained by his or her or another's special position in the corporation; synonymous with **insider trading**. It may involve sale or purchase of stock by the director, officers, and majority **shareholders** of a **corporation**.

SELF-DEFENCE The right that exists to protect one's person, or members of one's family, and, to a lesser extent, one's property, from harm by an aggressor. It may be a valid **defence** to a criminal **charge** or to **tort** liability. See generally *Criminal Code,* R.S.C. 1985, c. C–46, s. 34 (defence of person), s. 35 (defence of property). While one may use force to repel an attack, real or apprehended, such force must be reasonable. In *R. v. Lavallee,* in determining whether the accused's perceptions and actions are reasonable, the court held that the accused's situation and experiences should be taken into account, modifying the objective rea-

sonable person test; (1990), 76 C.R. (3d) (S.C.C.). See also *R. v. Pintar* (1996), 30 O.R. (3d) 483.

SELF-DETERMINATION The right of a **people** to freely determine their political status and freely pursue their economic, social, and cultural development. "[T]he right to self-determination of a people is normally fulfilled through internal self-determination—a people's pursuit of its political, economic, social, and cultural development within the framework of an existing state. A right to external self-determination (which, in this case, potentially takes the form of the assertion of a right to unilateral secession) arises in only the most extreme of cases and, even then, under carefully defined circumstances. External self-determination can be defined as in the following statement from the Declaration on Friendly Relations as:

> [t]he establishment of a sovereign and independent State, the free association or integration with an independent State, or the emergence into any other political status freely determined by a people constitute modes of implementing the right of self-determination by that people."

Reference Re Secession of Quebec, [1998] 2 S.C.R. 217.

SELF-EXECUTING Requiring no further steps to have legal effect. Most commonly used in referring to international **treaties**, which are not self-executing; the appropriate level of government must enact **legislation** before any enforceable right arises. The same is not true of **Aboriginal** treaties, which do give rise to rights immediately.

SELF-INCRIMINATION, PRIVILEGE AGAINST At common law, the rule that everyone was entitled to refuse to answer a question that might incriminate him or her. The common law rule has been replaced by s. 5 of the *Canada Evidence Act,* R.S.C. 1985, c. C–5, which removes the right to refuse to answer but provides that "when a witness 'objects to answer on the ground that his answer may tend to criminate him,' then 'the answer so given shall not be used or admissible in evidence against him'... in subsequent criminal proceedings, save in prosecutions for perjury or for the giving of contradictory evidence." *R. v. Noël,* 2002 SCC 67. In addition, s. 13 of the **Canadian Charter of Rights and Freedoms** provides that "A witness who testifies in any proceedings has the right not to have any incriminating evidence so given used to incriminate that witness in any other proceedings, except in a prosecution for perjury or for the giving of contradictory evidence." "[A] party seeking to invoke s. 13 must first establish that he or she gave 'incriminating evidence' under compulsion at the prior proceeding. If the party fails to meet these twin requirements, s. 13 is not engaged and that ends the matter." *R. v. Nedelcu,* 2012 SCC 59.

SELF-REPRESENTED LITIGANT A person who is not represented by **counsel** in **litigation**. Sometimes referred to as "unrepresented," but "self-represented" is the more common term. It is generally held that judges and the judicial system in general have an obligation to provide assistance to self-represented litigants to see to it that they are not unfairly prejudiced, while keeping within limits dictated by the **adversary system**. "Judges have a responsibility to inquire whether self-represented persons are aware of their procedural options, and to direct them to available information if they are not. Depending on the circumstances and nature of the case, judges may explain the relevant law in the case and its implications, before the self-represented person makes critical choices." *Statement of Principles on Self-represented Litigants and Accused Persons,* Canadian Judicial Council, September 2006.

SENATE Canada's upper legislative chamber. It is based on the principle of representation by population (24 Senators for each of the four historical regions of Canada—the three Maritime provinces, Quebec, Ontario, and the four Western provinces—and six Senators for Newfoundland and Labrador), and its members are appointed by the federal government rather than elected. The Senate has virtually the same powers as the **House of Commons**. However, because of its appointed nature it has generally been subordinate to the House of Commons.

SENILE DEMENTIA (*dĕ-mĕn'-shē-à*) Lat.: a state where mental faculties are enfeebled. Insanity that occurs as the result of old age and is progressive in character; an incurable form of fixed insanity resulting in a total collapse of mental faculties that, in its final state, necessarily deprives one of **testamentary** capacity because of loss of power to think, reason, or act sanely. See also **competent**; **incompetency**; **non compos mentis**.

SENTENCE The punishment ordered by a court to be inflicted upon a person convicted of a crime. See *Criminal Code,* R.S.C. 1985, c. C–46, s. 673, 785(l).

CONCURRENT SENTENCE A sentence that overlaps with another for a period of time as opposed to a consecutive sentence that runs by itself, beginning after or ending before the running of another sentence.

CONSECUTIVE SENTENCE A sentence that runs separately from and after one or more other sentences to be served by the same individual. Under the *Criminal Code,* R.S.C. 1985, c. C–46, s. 718.3(4), the court that convicts the accused may direct that terms of imprisonment be served one after the other in the circumstances described. It is within the trial judge's discretion to determine whether sentences are to be served consecutively or concurrently. See R. Salhany, *Canadian Criminal Procedure* 8–37–8–39 (6th ed. 1994).

INDETERMINATE SENTENCE A sentence imposed for an indeterminate period up to a certain maximum, in addition to any other sentence. "Prior to 1978, there were provisions under the *Prisons and Reformatories Act* [R.S.C. 1985, c. P–20] which permitted the courts in certain provinces, such as British Columbia and Ontario, to impose indeterminate sentences ... Those provisions were repealed by the Parliament of Canada in 1977." R. Salhany, *supra,* 8–46.1.

SUSPENDED SENTENCE A sentence whose imposition or execution has been withheld by the court on certain terms and conditions. Under s. 731 of the *Criminal Code,* the court may suspend the passing of sentence "having regard to the age and character of the offender, the nature of the offence and the circumstances surrounding its commission" and direct that the accused be released upon conditions prescribed in a **probation** order. See R. Salhany, *supra,* 8–48–8–54.7.

In 1996, the sentencing provisions of the Criminal Code were substantially revised to include express principles for sentencing and a new sanction, the conditional sentence, in the hopes of reducing the use of prison and expanding the use of **restorative justice** principles. See *Criminal Code,* R.S.C. 1985, c. C–46, s. 718 (for the purposes and principles of sentencing), s. 673 and s. 785(1). *R. v. Proulx,* [2000] 1 S.C.R. 61.

SENTENCING CIRCLE A procedure sometimes used in the sentencing of **Aboriginal** offenders, that has developed as a practice of the courts rather than from any statutory basis. A sentencing circle typically involves the offender, the victim, community elders, supporters for the parties, and others. The participants sit in a circle and discuss the offence, its causes, and the possibilities for reintegrating the offender into the community. A judge is not bound by any recommendations from the sentencing circle and has discretion as to whether to hold one at all. No single set of criteria has been developed, though factors such as the following tend to be considered: "(1) the willingness and suitability of the convicted person; (2) the willingness of the victim (freely given); (3) the willingness of a suitable community to participate in the circle and in implementing its recommendations; (4) whether the offence, in all the circumstances, is one that requires a term of imprisonment; and (5) such other relevant factors as may appear important to the Trial Judge, in the context of the case." *R. v. J.J.,* [2005] 1 C.N.L.R. 254.

SEPARATION 1. A goal of sentencing under s. 718 of the *Criminal Code,* R.S.C. 1985, c. C–46, emphasizing the need to isolate certain offenders from society for the sake of public safety. Compare **denunciation**; **deterrence**; **rehabilitation**; **retributive justice. 2.** A legal state of affairs that occurs when married or cohabiting spouses opt to live separate and apart. Separations are often governed by separation agreements between the parties, which may regulate issues such as division of property, **custody** of children, and spousal support. See further S.R. Fodden, *Family Law* (1999), c. 13.

SEQUESTER To separate from, as in to sequester assets or to sequester witnesses during a trial. See **sequestration**.

SEQUESTRATION 1. In equity, the act of seizing or taking possession of the property belonging to another until he or she complies with an **order** or **judgment**. In some cases it might direct a sheriff to go on the **real property** and receive **rents** and profits therefrom until the debt concerned has been paid; "a **writ** of sequestration is an extraordinary remedy, only to be employed as a last resort...." *Cudmore v. Cudmore* (1921), 50 O.L.R. 489 at 490 (H.C.).

2. The term also applies to the **common-law** practice whereby **juries** (e.g., in **capital offence** cases) might be sequestered, or kept together throughout the trial and deliberations and guarded from improper contact, until they were discharged. The common-law practice concerning sequestration has been replaced by the provisions of the *Criminal Code,* R.S.C. 1985, c. C–46, s. 647, in which **discretion** is given to the trial judge to permit jurors to separate before the jury retires to consider a verdict.

3. Sequestration of **witnesses** may be ordered by the court in order to ensure that in-court testimony of each witness not be coloured by what another witness said. The order of sequestration usually forbids the witnesses who have not yet testified from talking with witnesses who have testified.

SERIATIM (*sĕr-ē-ä'-tĭm*) Lat.: in due order, successively; in order, in succession; individually, one by one; separately; severally.

SERIOUS BODILY HARM "[A]ny hurt or injury, whether physical or psychological, that interferes in a substantial way with the physical or psychological integrity, health, or well-being of the complainant." *R. v. McCraw*, [1991] 3 S.C.R. 72. See **bodily harm**.

SERVANT One who works for, and is subject to, the control of his or her master; a person employed to "perform services in the affairs of another and who with respect to the physical conduct in the performance of the services is subject to the other's control or right to control.

"In determining whether one acting for another is a servant or an independent **contractor**, the following matters of fact, among others are considered: (a) the extent of control which, by the agreement, the master may exercise over the details of the work; (b) whether or not the one employed is engaged in a distinct occupation or business; (c) the kind of occupation, with reference to whether, in the locality, the work is usually done under the direction of the employer or by a specialist without supervision; (d) the skill required in the particular occupation; (e) whether the employer or the workman supplies the instrumentalities, tools, and the place of work for the person doing the work; (f) the length of time for which the person is employed; (g) the method of payment, whether by the time or by the job; (h) whether or not the work is a part of the regular business of the employer; (i) whether or not the parties believe they are creating the relation of master and servant; and (j) whether the principal is or is not in business." *Restatement of Agency* (2d) s. 220, at 485–87. A master is in many instances liable, under the theory of **respondeat superior**, for the torts of his or her servant, but not for those of an independent contractor. See also **agent**. See further G.H.L. Fridman, *Canadian Agency Law* 19–21 (2009).

See *T. B. Bright & Co. Ltd. v. Kerr,* [1939] S.C.R. 63; *Performing Right Society Ltd. v. Mitchell,* [1924] 1 K.B. 762.

SERVICE **Delivery** or communication of a **pleading**, **notice**, or other paper in a **suit** to the opposite party, so as to charge him or her with receipt of it and subject him or her to its legal effect; the bringing to notice, either actually or constructively.

PERSONAL SERVICE Actual delivery to the party to be served; "the essential ingredient ... is that the process delivered to the defendant must be so delivered under circumstances which enable the court to conclude that he knew, or reasonably should have known, what it was, or, ... that he knew the document was a writ, issued against him by the plaintiff, and knew, in addition, the general nature of the claim therein advanced." *Orazio v. Ciulla* (1966), 57 W.W.R. (N.S.) 641 at 646 (B.C.S.C.). See further G. Watson, *Civil Litigation* 357 (4th ed. 1991).

SUBSTITUTED SERVICE Service by a means other than on the defendant personally. Where a plaintiff is unable to effect prompt personal service, the court may order substituted service by a variety of methods, e.g., by mail at his last-known address; by leaving the writ with the defendant's spouse or other relative or his solicitor, etc. See further *id.* at 390ff.

SERVICE EX JURIS The service of a **writ** on a defendant outside the jurisdiction of the court that issues it.

SERVICE OFFENCE An offence that violates the provisions of the *National Defence Act*, R.S.C. 1985, c. N–5; the *Criminal Code*, R.S.C. 1985, c. C–46; or any other Act of Parliament, committed by a person who is subject to the Code of Service Discipline created under the *National Defence Act*.

SERVICE OF PROCESS The communication of the substance of the **process** to the defendant, either by actual delivery, or by other methods whereby defendant is furnished with reasonable notice of the proceedings against him or her to afford him or her opportunity to appear and be heard. For the types of service of process see **service**.

SERVICES At common law, the acts done by an English **feudal tenant** for the benefit of his lord, which formed the **consideration** for the property granted to him by his lord. Services were of several types, including knight's service, military service and the more varied kind of certain and determinate service called **socage**. See also **tenure**.

SERVIENT ESTATE [TENEMENT] In an **easement** situation, the estate that is subject to use in some way for the benefit of a **dominant estate**, the dominant estate being one to which certain rights or benefits are legally owed by the servient estate.

SERVITUDES A term which refers to rights of use over property belonging to another person. See, e.g., **covenants**; **easements**; **profit a prendre**.

SESSION "[T]he period of time during which members of the Legislature are called together for the dispatch of public business." *Re Sessional Allowances under the Ontario Legislative Assembly Act,* [1945] 2 D.L.R. 631 at 636 (Ont.C.A.). The term refers **inter alia** to the sittings of **Parliament**, the courts, etc.

SET ASIDE To annul or make **void**, as to set aside a **judgment**. When **proceedings** are irregular, they may be set aside on **motion** of the **party** whom they injuriously affect. See also **reversal**.

SETOFF In civil procedure, a method by which a **defendant** in an **action** can plead a claim against the **plaintiff** without commencing a separate action; in effect, similar to a **counterclaim** by the defendant against the plaintiff that diminishes the plaintiff's potential recovery. See, e.g., *Courts of Justice Act,* R.S.O. 1990, c. C. 43, s. 111, and similar provisions in other common-law provinces. "There is, however, another **equity** which has sometimes been called 'set-off,' but which does not in any way depend upon the statute, which arises when the claims are upon the same **contract** or are so interwoven by the dealings between the parties that the Court can find that there has been established a mutual credit, or an agreement, express

or implied, that the claims should be set one against the other." *Burman v. Rosin, Rosin v. Burman* (1915), 35 O.L.R. 134 at 136 (Ont.H.C.) quoted in *Caraberis and Bond v. Her Majesty the Queen* (1998), 98 DTC 1865 (Tax Ct.).

SETTLEMENT Generally, the conclusive fixing or resolving of a matter; the arrangement of a final disposition of it. A compromise achieved by the **adverse parties** in a **civil suit** before final **judgment** whereby they agree between themselves upon their respective rights and obligations, thus eliminating the necessity of judicial resolution of the controversy. Compare **plea bargaining** in the criminal context. See further L.S. Abrams and K.P. McGuinness, *Canadian Civil Procedure Law* 777–93 (2nd ed. 2010).

SETTLOR One who creates a **trust** by giving **real** or **personal property** "in trust" to another (the **trustee)** for the benefit of a third person (the **beneficiary)**. One who gives such money is said to "settle" it on, or bring **title** to rest with, the trustee, and is also called the **donor** or TRUSTOR.

SEVERABLE CONTRACT One that, in the event of a **breach** by one of the parties, may be justly considered as several independent agreements that have been expressed in a single **instrument**. Where a contract is deemed severable, a breach thereof may constitute a default as to only a part of the contract, saving the defaulting party from the necessity of responding in **damages** for a breach of the entire agreement. See further G.H.L. Fridman, *The Law of Contract in Canada* 545 (6th ed. 2011).

SEVERABLE STATUTE A statute the remainder of which remains valid when a portion has been declared invalid, because the statute is one whose parts are not wholly interdependent. After the invalid portion of the act has been stricken out, if that which remains is self-sustaining and capable of separate enforcement without regard to the portion of the statute that has been cast aside, the statute is said to be severable.

SEVERALLY Separate and apart from. **1.** In a **note**, each who severally promises to pay is responsible separately for the entire amount. **2.** In a **judgment** against more than one defendant, arising out of one **action**, each may be **liable** for the entire amount of the judgment, thereby permitting the successful plaintiff to recover the entire amount of the judgment from any defendant against whom he or she chooses to institute a suit. Compare **joint**; **joint and several**; **joint tortfeasors**.

SEVERALTY Refers to the holding of property solely, separately and individually. "A person who is sole owner of an **estate** is said to hold it in severalty because he holds it in his own right with no one having any interest **jointly** with him." 1 A.H. Oosterhoff & W.B. Rayner, *Anger and Honsberger: Law of Real Property* 787 (2d ed. 1985).

SEVERANCE 1. The act of separating; the state of being disjoined or separated. In **contract** law, when a contract contains several distinct promises or a promise which is by its terms divisible into distinct promises, some of which are illegal and others legal, the court may enforce those that are legal and refuse to enforce those that are illegal. This is known as severance or the "doctrine of severability of promises." See, e.g., *Attwood v. Lamont*, [1920] 3 K.B. 571 (C.A.). See further G.H.L. Fridman, *The Law of Contract in Canada* 410–13 (6th ed. 2011). **2.** In **criminal** law, a judicial decision to try two jointly charged **accused** in separate trials, or to hold separate trials for two charges laid against an accused in a single **information**.

SEXISM Discrimination or prejudice directed against a class of persons based on gender, usually women.

SEXIST LANGUAGE Any type of communication, oral or written, that reveals **discrimination** against persons based on their gender. Generally, any language that a **reasonable person** would regard as derogatory or demeaning to the gender of the persons to whom the comments are directed. See **gender neutral language**.

SEXSOMNIA A common term used to describe a condition that causes sufferers to engage in involuntary sexual activity while asleep. Sexsomnia has been recognized as a defence to **sexual assault** on the basis that involuntary actions are not culpable. Non-consensual sexual activity initiated while asleep, however, may give rise to an **NCRMD** verdict under s. 16 of the *Criminal Code*, R.S.C. 1985, c. C–46. See, e.g., *R. v. Luedecke*, 2008 ONCA 716.

SEXUAL ASSAULT *An Act to Amend the Criminal Code in Relation to Sexual Offences* S.C. 1980–81–82–83, c. 125 repealed the provisions in the *Criminal Code*, R.S.C. 1970, c. C–34, dealing with **rape**, and created new **offences** dealing with sexual assault and aggravated sexual assault.

In *R. v. Chase*, [1987] 2 S.C.R. 293, the Supreme Court of Canada defined sexual assault under s. 271 of the *Criminal Code*, R.S.C. 1985, c. C–46, as "assault within any one of the definitions of that concept in [s. 265(1)] of the *Criminal Code*, which is committed in circumstances of a sexual nature, such that the sexual integrity of the **victim** is violated." (Section 265(1) is the general assault provision of the *Code*)." Accordingly, sexual touching of any sort can constitute a sexual assault if it is done without consent or if the **consent** is **vitiated**, for example, by **fraud**. *R. v. Mabior*, 2012 SCC 47.

Under s. 271 of the *Code*, sexual assault is either an **indictable** or **summary offence**, with a maximum penalty on **indictment** of 10 years imprisonment. The former offence of rape required, at one time, that the accused and the complainant were not married, but s. 278 of the *Criminal* Code now specifies that a husband or wife can be charged with sexual assault against his or her spouse.

AGGRAVATED SEXUAL ASSAULT "Every one [*sic*] commits an aggravated sexual assault who, in committing a sexual assault, wounds, maims, disfigures, or endangers the life of the complainant." (s. 273(1)). Aggravated sexual assault is an indictable offence, with a maximum of life imprisonment.

Sexual assault is an offence of general **intent**.

SEXUAL EXPLOITATION An offence under s. 153 of the *Criminal Code*, R.S.C. 1985, c. C–46 that occurs when an accused commits the offences of **sexual interference** or **invitation to sexual touching** against a person between sixteen and eighteen years of age, in the context of a relationship of trust, authority, or dependency.

SEXUAL HARASSMENT Under s. 3(o) of the Nova Scotia *Human Rights Act,* R.S.N.S. 1989, c. 214, as amended by S.N.S. 1991, c. 12, sexual harassment means "(i) vexatious sexual conduct or a course of comment that is known or ought reasonably to be known as unwelcome, (ii) a sexual solicitation or advance made to an individual by another individual where the other individual is in a position to confer a benefit on, or deny a benefit to, the individual to whom the solicitation or advance is made, where the individual who makes the solicitation or advance knows or ought reasonably to know that it is unwelcome, or (iii) a reprisal or threat of reprisal against an individual for rejecting a sexual solicitation or advance." See *Janzen v. Platy Enterprises Ltd.,* [1989] 1 S.C.R. 1252.

SEXUAL INTERFERENCE Directly or indirectly touching a person under sixteen years of age for a sexual purpose, with a part of the body or an object. Sexual interference is a **hybrid offence** under s. 151 of the *Criminal Code,* R.S.C. 1985, c. C–46. See also **sexual exploitation**.

SEX OFFENDER REGISTRY A database of people convicted of sexual offences, containing identifying information such as their names, addresses, telephone numbers, and physical characteristics. Sex offender registries have been established at both the federal and provincial levels of government. See *Sex Offender Information Registration Act,* S.C. 2004, c. 10; *Christopher's Law (Sex Offender Registry), 2000,* S.O. 2000, c. 1. They have also survived numerous constitu-

tional challenges under ss. 7 and 11 of the **Canadian Charter of Rights and Freedoms**. See, e.g., *R. v. Dyck,* 2008 ONCA 309; *Morin v. R.,* 2009 QCCA 187; *R. v. Warren,* 2010 ABCA 133.

SEXUAL ORIENTATION One's sexual preference. A term that means "heterosexual, homosexual or bi-sexual and refers only to consenting adults acting within the law." *Human Rights Act,* R.S.Y. 2002, c. 116, s. 37. Sexual orientation is a prohibited ground of discrimination in many provincial human rights acts. See, e.g., Ontario *Human Rights Code,* R.S.O. 1990, c. H.19, s. 1; Nova Scotia *Human Rights Act,* R.S.N.S. 1989, c. 214, s. 5(n). It is also a prohibited ground of discrimination in the *Canadian Human Rights Act,* R.S.C. 1985, c. H–6, s. 3(1), as amended by S.C. 1996, c. 14, s. 2. Prior to its amendment, sexual orientation had been effectively **read into** the *Act.* See *Haig v. Canada* (199), 5 O.R. (3d) 495 at 508 (C.A.). See **spouse**.

SHALL A word used in statutes "to impose a duty on persons or to indicate the binding character of conditions or rules." R. Sullivan, *Statutory Interpretation* 78 (2nd ed. 2007). Unlike the word **may**, which is capable of granting powers that are either discretionary or obligatory, the word "shall" always connotes imperative duties. "The interpretation question that arises in connection with 'shall' is what… the consequences of breaching" a duty imposed by it are. In this respect, a distinction is drawn between duties that are **mandatory** and duties that are **directory**. If a mandatory duty is breached, actions taken under the statute in relation to the breach are invalid. If a directory duty is breached, however, no invalidity will result. See *Rehman v. Alberta College and Assn. of Respiratory Therapy,* 2001 ABQB 222; *Toronto (City) v. W.J. Holdings Ltd.,* 2010 ONSC 6067.

SHAM PLEADING One that is clearly and indisputably false and presents no real **issue** of fact to be determined; a **defence** wholly unsupported by the facts. Bad faith is not necessary. However, such a pleading may be resorted to for purposes of delay and annoyance.

SHARE A "bundle of rights against a **corporation**. Although a share is **personal property**, the claim it represents in the corporation is neither a property right in the corporation's assets nor a proportionate ownership interest in the corporation itself." J.A. VanDuzer, *The Law of Partnerships and Corporations* 225 (3rd ed. 2009). Shareholders in a corporation have three basic rights: (a) the right to dividends released by the corporation's **directors**, (b) the right to attend and vote at shareholder meetings, and (c) the right to a proportionate part of the assets of the corporation upon **winding up**. The directors may issue special classes of shares without one or more of these rights, but all three rights must somehow be distributed between the different classes of shares issued. See, e.g., the *Canada Business Corporations Act*, R.S.C. 1985, c. C–44, s. 24(4).

SHAREHOLDER One who is holder or proprietor of one or more **shares** of stock of a **corporation**. To be a shareholder of an incorporated company is to be possessed of the evidence, usually **stock certificates**, that the holder is the real owner of a certain individual portion of the property in actual or potential existence held by the company in its name as a unit for the common benefit of all the owners of the entire **capital** stock of the company.

SHELLEY'S CASE See **Rule in Shelley's Case**.

SHERIFF An official appointed by the **Crown** who has numerous duties, including the serving of legal documents such as WRITS OF SUMMONS (see **writ**) and **subpoenas**, the maintaining of good order in Her Majesty's courts and the **seizure** and sale under court order of the property of judgment debtors.

SHERIFF'S SALE A sale of **property** by the **sheriff** under authority of a court's **judgment** and WRIT OF EXECUTION (see **writ**) in order to satisfy an unpaid judgment, **mortgage**, **lien** or other **debt** of the owner (**judgment debtor**). An EXECUTION SALE of **real property** has

the same effect as a **conveyance** by **quitclaim deed**, in that only such **title** as the judgment debtor has at the time of the sale is passed. Any title or **interest** acquired after the time of sale is not conveyed.

SHIFTING INTEREST See **interest**.

SHIFTING USE See **use**. See also **interest** [EXECUTORY INTEREST].

SHOW CAUSE ORDER An **order**, made upon the **motion** of one party, requiring a party to appear and show cause [argue] why a certain thing should be permitted or not permitted. It requires the adverse party to meet the **prima facie case** made by the applicant's verified **complaint** or **affidavit**.

An order to show cause is an accelerated method of beginning a **litigation** by compelling the adverse party to respond in a much shorter period of time than he or she would normally have to respond to a **complaint**. The order may or may not contain temporary restraints [see **restraining orders**] but will generally be "returnable" in a few days, which means that the opposing party must prepare answering affidavits and persuade the court that an issue of a fact exists that requires a full, plenary trial proceeding or simply argue on the return date that even if the plaintiff's statements in his or her moving papers are true, they do not state a cause of action or justify the relief prayed for in the order to show cause.

Compare **summons**.

SHOW CAUSE HEARING See **judicial interim release**.

SIMILAR ACT EVIDENCE Evidence of prior discreditable acts by an **accused** that would normally be inadmissible as **character evidence**, except that the similarity of the acts in question is probative of an issue at trial. For example, where the identity of the offender is in doubt, evidence that the accused has behaved in the way in which the offender is known to have behaved might be admissible. Relevant factors in assessing whether the prior behaviour is similar enough to be admissible as similar act evidence include the extent to which the other acts are similar in detail to the charged conduct, the number of occurrences of the similar acts, the circumstances surrounding or relating to the similar acts, and any distinctive features unifying the incidents. Also called similar fact evidence. See *R. v. Handy*, 2002 SCC 56.

SIMILAR FACT EVIDENCE See **similar act evidence**.

SIMPLE CONTRACT See **sealed instrument**.

SIMULTANEITY The concept in **criminal** law that the **actus reus** and **mens rea** of an **offence** must occur at the same point in time.

SINE DIE (*sē'-nā dē'-ā*) Lat.: without day, without time. A legislative body adjourns *sine die* when it adjourns without appointing a day on which to appear or assemble again.

SINE QUA NON (*sē'-nā kwä nŏn*) Lat.: without which not; that without which the thing cannot be, i.e., the essence of something. For example, in **tort** law, the act of the defendant, without which there would not have been a tort. See **cause**.

SINKING FUND An accumulation, by a corporation or government body, of money invested for the purpose of repaying a **debt** or debts. In government bodies, a sinking fund is a fund arising from taxes, imposts or duties, which is appropriated toward the payment of interest due on a public loan and for the eventual payment of the **principal**.

SLANDER A defamatory statement. At common law, a distinction was drawn between **libel** and slander. "Originally the distinction turned on whether the communication was written (libel) or verbal (slander). Libel is viewed as the more serious form of defamation because of its permanence, the greater likelihood that it was premeditated, and its capacity for wider dissemination …. Slander is, in contrast, more likely to be transient and impromptu, and its publication is limited to those within hearing distance of the defendant." P.H. Osborne, *The Law of Torts* 412 (4th ed. 2011). The distinction between libel and slander has been

abolished in numerous provinces. See, e.g., *Defamation Act*, R.S.P.E.I. 1988, c. D–5; *Defamation Act*, R.S.A. 2000, c. D–7. In other provinces, the only residual practical difference between libel and slander has to do with "proof of damage." While a plaintiff in an action for slander must generally prove special damage, a plaintiff alleging libel does not. Osborne, *supra* at 412–13. "Special damage includes any material or financial loss" but not "embarrassment or emotional distress caused by the slanderous imputation." *Id.*

SLAPP Strategic Lawsuits Against Public Participation. Litigation commenced, often for **defamation** or interference with economic interest, against individuals objecting to development or other activities. The defining feature of a SLAPP suit is that it is not commenced with the expectation of success but rather as a means of intimidating and deterring the individuals who are the subjects of the action.

SMALL CLAIMS COURTS See **Provincial Courts**.

SOCAGE [SOCCAGE] In feudal England, a type of tenure founded upon certain and designated services performed by the vassal for his lord, other than military or knight's service. Where the services were considered honourable, it was called FREE SOCAGE and where the services were of a baser nature, it was called VILLEIN SOCAGE. By the statute 12 Car. 2, c. 24, almost all **tenures** by knight-servants were converted into FREE AND COMMON SOCAGE. See 2 Bl.Comm. 79–80. See also **homage**; **statute of tenures**.

SOCIAL FACTS Social science research used to construct a frame of reference or background context for deciding factual issues crucial to the resolution of a particular case, such as evidence about battered wife syndrome or the feminization of poverty. See *R. v. Spence*, 2005 SCC 71. Compare **legislative facts**; **adjudicative facts**.

SOCIAL HOST LIABILITY The now-rejected suggestion that a private person hosting a party at which alcohol is served owes a **duty of care** to people who might be injured by intoxicated party-goers as they drive home. "[A]s a general rule, a social host does not owe a duty of care to a person injured by a guest who has consumed alcohol." *Childs v. Desormeaux*, 2006 SCC 18.

SOCIETY A number of persons associated together by a common interest or purpose, which can be either **incorporated** or unincorporated.

SODOMY Anal intercourse. Originally only an ecclesiastical offence, in Canada it is a **hybrid offence** under the *Criminal Code*, R.S.C. 1985 c. C–46, s. 159. Under s. 159(2) of the *Criminal Code*, anal intercourse engaged in private between spouses or consenting adults over the age of 18 is not a crime. Various courts have found the provision to violate the guarantee of **equality rights** in the **Canadian Charter of Rights and Freedoms** because it sets a different age of consent for same-sex sexual activity than for opposite-sex sexual activity, or because it is limited to activity including two people. *R. v. C.M.* (1995), 23 OR (3d) 629 (C.A.); *R. v. Roth*, 2002 ABQB 145. See also **buggery**.

SOLEMN AFFIRMATION A secular alternative to an **oath** provided for by federal and provincial evidence statutes. Solemn affirmations, when properly delivered, have the same legal effect as oaths. See, e.g., *Canada Evidence* Act, R.S.C. 1985, c. C–5, s. 14; *Evidence Act*, R.S.N.S. 1989, c. 154, s. 62; *Alberta Evidence Act*, R.S.A. 2000, c. A–18, s. 17.

SOLE PROPRIETORSHIP A form of business organization that occurs when "an individual starts to carry on business for her own account without taking the steps necessary to use some other form of organization, such as a **corporation**." J.A. Van Duzer, *The Law of Partnerships and Corporations* 7 (3rd ed. 2009). Since there is no legal distinction between the business and the sole proprietor, all benefits and liabilities accrued by the business are those of the sole proprietor alone. A sole proprietor is responsible for performing all **contracts** entered into in the course of

running the business and, through the doctrine of **vicarious liability**, for all torts committed by employees. *Id.*, 7–8.

SOLICITATION An offence developed by the later common-law courts to reach conduct whereby one enticed, incited or opportuned another to commit a **felony** or certain **misdemeanours** injurious to the public welfare. See *R. v. Higgins* (1801), 102 E.R. 269. Under the *Criminal Code* R.S.C. 1985, c. C–46, s. 212, everyone who "procures, attempts to procure or solicits a person to have illicit sexual intercourse with another person" is guilty of an **indictable offence**. With regard to the former offence of soliciting for the purpose of prostitution, the Supreme Court of Canada held: "It must be noted...that the word 'solicit' is not defined in the *Criminal Code*, therefore, the Courts below have taken what I am of the opinion was a proper course and have turned to English dictionaries for the purpose of defining the word.... [In the] Shorter Oxford Dictionary... the definition is exact and I quote it. 'c. of women; to accost and importune (men) for immoral purposes.'" See *Hutt v. The Queen* (1978), 82 D.L.R. (3d) 95 at 100 (S.C.C.). That offence has now been replaced with communicating in public for the purpose of prostitution. *Criminal Code*, R.S.C. 1985, c. C–46, s. 213; *Reference re ss. 193 and 195.1(1) (c) of the Criminal Code (Man.)*, [1990] 1 S.C.R. 1123.

SOLICITOR See **barrister and solicitor**.

SOLICITOR-CLIENT COSTS A costs award that compensates the client for the amount actually spent on legal fees; a full indemnity award. Solicitor-client costs should not be awarded unless there is something in the behaviour of the losing party that takes the case outside the ordinary. *Winters v. Legal Services Society*, [1999] 3 S.C.R. 160. See **costs**.

SOLICITOR-CLIENT PRIVILEGE The rule that communications made in confidence between a **solicitor** and client cannot be compelled to be disclosed. The **privilege** has been described as a "cornerstone of our judicial system" and a **principle of fundamental justice**. *R. v. McClure*,

2001 SCC 14. The privilege rests with the **accused**, and a lawyer is not allowed to reveal the content of the communications without the consent of the client. An exception to solicitor-client privilege arises with the **innocence at stake exception**.

SOLICITOR GENERAL [OF CANADA OR OF A PROVINCE] Minister of the **Cabinet** responsible for reformatories, prisons, penetentiaries, parole, remission and statutory release, the **Royal Canadian Mounted Police**, and the Canadian Security Intelligence Service. *Department of the Solicitor General Act,* R.S.C. 1985, c. S–13, s. 4. The *Department of the Solicitor General Act* was repealed in 2005; the *Department of Public Safety and Emergency Preparedness Act,* S.C. 2005, c. 10, states that the Solicitor General in place at the time s. 7 of the Act comes into effect automatically becomes the Minister of Public Safety and Emergency Preparedness.

SOLVENCY The ability to pay all **debts** and just claims as they come due. "In considering the question of whether a debtor is solvent or insolvent, I do not think his position can be properly considered from a more favourable point of view than this—to inquire whether all his **property**, both **real** and **personal**, subject to **execution** be sufficient if realised upon at the present time to pay his debts in full, and in considering the question of how much can be realised out of his property, both the land and personal property must be estimated not at what he thinks the property is worth, nor at what others say the property is worth, but at what the property will bring on the market at a forced sale; for the debtor is not in a position to wait for favourable opportunities to sell." *Wagner v. Harrows,* [1923] 1 D.L.R. 186 at 190 (Sask.C.A.).

SOUNDS IN Has a connection or association with; is concerned with; thus, though a party to a lawsuit has **pleaded damages** in **tort**, it may be said that the **action** nevertheless "sounds in" **contract** if the elements of the offence charged appear to constitute a contract, rather than a tort, action. Whether the court will consider it a tort or a contract may influence the damage measure since, for example, punitive damages (see **damages** [EXEMPLARY DAMAGES]) are recoverable in tort but not in contract. See, e.g., *Dominion Chain Co. Ltd. v. Eastern Construction Co.* (1976), 68 D.L.R. (3d) 385 (Ont.C.A.), where the court considered whether an action against an architect, engineer or builder for negligent performance of contractual duties "sounds only in" contract.

SOVEREIGN IMMUNITY A doctrine precluding the institution of a **suit** against the Sovereign [government] without the Sovereign's consent when the Sovereign is engaged in a governmental function; originally based on the maxim "the King can do no wrong." Another rationale is that the Sovereign is exempt from suit, not because of any formal conception or obsolete theory, but on the logical and practical ground that there can be no legal right against the authority that makes the law on which the right depends, In Canada, Her Majesty the Queen is the head of state and head of the executive government. While modern common-law doctrine is that the Sovereign, as the representative of executive authority, can incur liabilities in the same way as other persons (i.e., that "the **Crown** is subject to the law of the land"), still the Crown enjoys certain special and peculiar privileges, such as immunity from statutory control. See, e.g., *Interpretation Act,* R.S.O. 1990, c. I.11, s. 11: "No Act affects the rights of Her Majesty, Her heirs or successors, unless it is expressly stated therein that Her Majesty is bound thereby." See further C. McNairn, *Governmental and Intergovernmental Immunity in Australia and Canada* 3 (1977).

In the area of **international law** there are "general principles ... according to which a sovereign State is held to be immune from the **jurisdiction** of another sovereign State. This is sometimes said to flow from international **comity** or courtesy, but may now more properly be regarded as a rule of international law, accepted among the community of nations. It is binding on the municipal Courts of this country in the sense and to the extent that it has been received and enforced by these Courts." *Compania Naviera Vascongado v. S.S. Cristina,* [1938] A.C. 485 at 502 (H.L.). See further J.H. Currie, *Public International Law* 364–411 (2nd ed. 2008).

SOVEREIGNTY "'Sovereignty' refers to the various powers, rights, and duties that accompany statehood under international law." *R. v. Hape,* 2007 SCC 26.

SOVEREIGNTY ASSOCIATION A term that has developed in Canadian constitutional law to describe a possible political, social and economic partnership between Canada and a sovereign Quebec, the details of which would presumably be worked out either immediately before or after Quebec's formal separation from the rest of Canada.

SPARROW TEST The framework for determining whether an **Aboriginal right** is protected under s. 35 of the *Constitution Act 1982,* Schedule B, to the *Canada Act 1982* (UK), 1982, c. 11. The Court in *R. v. Sparrow,* [1990] 1 S.C.R. 1075 asked whether there had been an Aboriginal right and if so, whether it had been extinguished, and if not, whether it had been infringed, and if so, whether the infringement was justified. The same framework has been adapted for use in determining the extent of constitutional protection for **Aboriginal peoples'** rights under **treaty** and under **statute**. See *R. v. Badger,* [1996] 1 S.C.R. 771.

SPECIAL DAMAGES See **damages** [CONSEQUENTIAL DAMAGES].

SPECIAL PLEA In criminal law, an alternative to the pleas of **guilty** and **not guilty**. The special pleas are **autrefois acquit** and **pardon**, and in the case of a charge of defamatory libel, justification. *Criminal Code,* R.S.C. 1985, c. C–40, ss. 607, 611.

SPECIAL TRAVERSE See **traverse**.

SPECIALTY A **contract** under seal. See **sealed instrument**.

SPECIE Money that has an intrinsic value, e.g., gold and silver coins. These are coins made of scarce metals that are usually minted in various denomina-

tions differentiated by weight and fineness. Most often these coins are stamped with government seals and insignias signifying their value as currency. See also **in specie**.

SPECIFIC BEQUEST [LEGACY] See **bequest** [SPECIFIC BEQUEST].

SPECIFIC DEVISE Generally, a **gift** by **will** of a particular piece of **real property**. Compare **specific bequest**.

SPECIFIC INTENT See **intent**; **mens rea**.

SPECIFIC PERFORMANCE An equitable **remedy** which consists of a requirement that the party guilty of a **breach of contract** undertake to perform his or her obligations under the contract rather than pay **damages** for non-performance.

One can obtain a decree of specific performance for the purchase of a unique chattel such as a rare painting. At one point all contracts for the sale of land were presumed to be enforceable through specific performance, but the presumption in the law that all parcels of land are unique has been weakened. *Raymond v Anderson,* 2011 SKCA 58.

There are cases in which the court of equity will not specifically enforce a contract even though the remedy at law is inadequate. Personal service contracts and construction contracts are common examples, due to the difficulty of the court's overseeing proper performance by the defaulting party. *Semelhago v. Paramadevan* (1996), 136 D.L.R. (4th) 1 (S.C.C.). See further S.M. Waddams, *The Law of Contracts* (6th ed. 2010), c. 20.

SPENDTHRIFT TRUST A **trust** created to provide a fund for maintenance of a **beneficiary** that is so restricted that it is secure against the beneficiary's improvidence and beyond the reach of his or her **creditors**.

SPLITTING A CAUSE OF ACTION Impermissible practice of bringing an **action** for only part of the **cause of action** in one **suit**, and initiating another suit for another part; consists in dividing a single or individual cause of action into several parts or claims and bringing several actions thereon. See, e.g.,

Cox v. Robert Simpson Co. Ltd. et al. (1973), 1 O.R. (2d) 333 (Ont. C.A.); *Athanassiades v. Lee,* [2010] O.J. No. 4605 (Ont. S.C.J.). Under the general policy against splitting the causes of action, the law mandatorily requires that all **damages** sustained or accruing to one as a result of a single **wrongful act** be claimed and recovered in one action or not at all. See also **multiplicity of suits**. Compare **joinder**; **misjoinder**.

SPOUSE Under the *Divorce Act,* R.S.C. 1985, c. 3, (2d Supp.), s. 2, a spouse "means either of two persons who are married to each other," making the Act applicable only to persons who were legally married at the time proscribed by **statute**. The exact same definition for spouse is found in the *Family Law Act,* R.S.O. 1990, c. F. 3, s. 2(1). Currently, spouses can be of the opposite sex or the same sex; however, this was not always the case. The federal government changed the definition of marriage in 2005 with the passing of the *Civil Marriage Act,* S.C. 2005, c. 33. Section 2 of that Act states that "[m]arriage, for civil purposes, is the lawful union of two persons to the exclusion of all others." This change to the definition of marriage came after judicial activity had resulted in many changes to law removing discriminatory distinctions between same-sex and opposite-sex couples. After the **Supreme Court of Canada** released its decision in *Reference re Same Sex Marriage,* [2004] 3 S.C.R. 698, the *Civil Marriage Act* was passed and couples of the same sex were legally allowed to marry. Some provincial and territorial statutes also recognize unmarried persons, both opposite sex and same sex, cohabiting in a common-law relationship as a "spouse" for the purpose of the particular statute. To qualify as a "common-law spouse" the parties must have been living together in a conjugal, or "marriage-like" relationship. Most statutes set a specific time limit for cohabitation—e.g., one to three years. See for example *Family Maintenance Act,* C.C.S.M. c. F20. Under certain federal legislation, for example the *Income Tax Act,* R.S.C. 1985, c. 1 (5th Supp.), some benefits may be extended to common-law spouses. See also **domestic partnership, marriage, Civil Marriage Act, Reference re Same Sex Marriage**.

SPRINGING INTEREST See **interest**.

SPRINGING USE See **use**. See also **interest** [EXECUTORY INTEREST].

STAKEHOLDER Originally, a third party chosen by two or more persons to hold **property** or money, the right or **possession** of which is in dispute, and to deliver that property or money to the person who establishes the right to it. See, e.g., *Walsh v. Trebilcock* (1894), 23 S.C.R. 695. More commonly today the term is used to refer to any person who has an interest in something. For example, "credits effectively balanced the interests of the 'three main stakeholders in the telecommunications markets,' namely customers, competitors, and carriers." *Bell Canada v. Bell Aliant Regional Communications*, 2009 SCC 40.

STALKING See **criminal harassment**.

STANDARD OF CARE Part of the test for whether a person is liable to another for the **tort** of **negligence**. If a person has a **duty of care** to another person, then he or she must behave in the manner of the ordinary, reasonable, prudent, and cautious person in those circumstances in order to meet the standard of care.

STANDARD OF PROOF See **burden of proof**.

STANDARD OF REVIEW Generally, the standard of review applicable in a case refers to the level of deference that a court will afford to the decision of a subordinate decision-maker when reviewing its decision. In the context of an appellate court reviewing the decision of a lower court, there are two standards of review. The standard of review applicable to the lower court's decisions on questions of law is "correctness," which means that the lower court's decision will be overturned unless the higher court determines that it has reached the right decision. For questions of fact, the applicable standard of review is whether the lower court made a "palpable and overriding error" in its assessment of the facts. *Housen v. Nikolaisen*, 2002 SCC 33. In the context of a court reviewing the decision of an **administrative tribunal** on **judicial review**, there are two standards of review: correctness and reasonableness. The standard of review applicable in a case depends on a multi-factor "standard of review analysis" set out in *Dunsmuir v. New Brunswick*, 2008 SCC 9.

STANDING The legal right of a person or group to challenge in a judicial forum the conduct of another especially with respect to government conduct. See **public interest standing**.

STANDING MUTE In a criminal trial, refusing to **plead**; today deemed to be a **plea** of **not guilty**. *Criminal Code*, R.S.C. 1985, c. C–46, s. 606(2).

STAR CHAMBER An ancient court of England that received its name because the ceiling was covered with stars; it sat with no **jury** and could administer any penalty but death. The Chamber was largely responsible for developing the offences of **forgery, conspiracy, perjury**, and **attempt** to commit crimes. It was abolished in 1641 because it did not adhere to the principle of **due process**, having been used by the Crown near its end to avoid potentially uncooperative juries when trying offences such as **treason**. Today, the Star Chamber is often used as a watchword for an unfair court, for example, "The right to stand silent before the accusations of the state has its historical roots in the general revulsion against the practices of the Star Chamber." *R. v. Henry*, [2005] 3 S.C.R. 609, 2005 SCC 76.

STARE DECISIS (*stä′-rä dĕ-sī′-sĭs*) Lat.: to stand by that which was decided. The rule by which lower courts are required to follow the decisions of a higher court in the same jurisdiction. *Stare decisis* also requires that courts generally follow their own precedents, though this is not an absolute rule. In *Stuart v. Bank of Montreal* (1909), 41 S.C.R. 516, the **Supreme Court of Canada** indicated that it felt bound by its own prior decisions. Since then the Court has made clear that it is willing to overturn its own precedents, but that this "is a step not to be lightly undertaken." *Ontario (Attorney-General) v. Fraser*, 2011 SCC 20. See G. Gall, *The Canadian Legal System* (5th ed. 2004), c. 11.

STATE A political entity with a permanent population, a defined territory, and a government, and that has the capacity to enter into relations with the other states.

STATE IMMUNITY The doctrine that a **state** is not subject to the jurisdiction of the courts of another state. Under the *State Immunity Act*, R.S.C. 1985, c. S–18, exceptions are made for, among other things, the commercial activity of other states for acts that cause damage to property or deaths in Canada, or in some cases, for terrorist activity.

STATELESS PERSON A person who is not considered as a national by any State under the operation of its law: *Convention Relating to the Status of Stateless Persons*, September 28, 1954.

STATEMENT OF CLAIM The written statement of a **plaintiff** in a **cause of action** the purpose of which is to "set out the remedy claimed from the **defendant**, e.g., **damages** or **specific performance**, and describe the events that took place which would justify the court awarding this remedy...." A part of the **pleadings** exchanged between plaintiff and defendant. See G. Watson, *Civil Litigation* 717 (4th ed. 1991).

STATEMENT OF DEFENCE In **pleading**, the **defendant's** reply to the **plaintiff's** **statement of claim**. See further G. Watson, *Civil Litigation* 718 (4th ed. 1991).

STATUS INDIAN A person registered as an **Indian** under the *Indian Act*, R.S.C. 1985, c. I–5, which provides certain benefits to those registered under it. Not all those people who self-identify as Indian or who would be perceived as such qualify for registration or have registered; such persons are often referred to as "non-status Indians."

STATUS OFFENCE A **crime** in which the fault is not a particular piece of behaviour by the accused but some characteristic of the person, such as being a **prostitute**. Status offences have largely or entirely disappeared from Canadian **criminal** law, and there is a question whether they would violate s. 7 of the **Canadian Charter of Rights and Freedoms**. See *R. v. Budreo* (2000), 142 C.C.C. (3d) 225, 32 C.R. (5th) 127 (Ont. C.A.).

STATUS QUO (*sta'-tus kwo*) Lat.: the postures, positions, conditions or situations that existed.

STATUTE An act of the legislature; in Canada an act of a provincial legislature or the Federal **Parliament** adopted pursuant to constitutional authority. Statutes constitute a primary source of law and are enacted, for example, to prescribe conduct, define crimes, create inferior government bodies, appropriate public monies, and in general promote the public good and welfare. In Canada, the **Constitution Act, 1867** divides legislative power between the provincial legislatures and the Parliament of Canada. See **constitution**. Compare **common law**; **ordinances**; **regulations**. See further G. Gall, *The Canadian Legal System* 40 (5th ed. 2004).

STATUTE OF FRAUDS The statutory requirement that certain **contracts** be in writing to be enforceable. Most such statutes are patterned after the English statute enacted in 1677. Contracts to answer for a **creditor** for the **debt** of another, contracts made in **consideration** of marriage, contracts for the sale of land or affecting any **interest** in land (except short-term **leases)**, and contracts not to be performed within one year from their making, must be evidenced by a written memorandum, and signed by the PARTY TO BE CHARGED, (i.e., by the defendant in an action for **breach)**. Under a separate section of the English statute and as enacted in provincial legislation, a contract for the sale of goods where the contract price exceeds a certain specified amount (e.g., forty dollars or more) must likewise be in writing. See, e.g., *Sale of Goods Act,* R.S.O. 1990, c. S.1.

There are several exceptions to the statute. For example, PART PERFOR-MANCE is an important exception and operates to take an oral contract "out of the statute," i.e., to render it enforceable. In the case of a sale of goods within the statute, acceptance of part or all of the goods by the buyer or payment of all or part of the purchase price by the buyer suffices as part performance as to that portion of the contract. See further, e.g., S.M. Waddams, *The Law of Contracts* (6th ed. 2010), c. 6.

STATUTE OF LIMITATIONS Any law that fixes the time within which **parties** must take judicial action to enforce rights or else be thereafter barred from enforcing them.

Most actions at law have a statutory time beyond which the action may not be brought. **Equity** proceedings are governed by an independent equity doctrine called **laches**. These limitations are also an essential element of **adverse possession**, prescribing the time at which the adverse possessor's interest in the property becomes unassailable. The policy behind the enactment of such laws consists of the belief that there is a point beyond which a prospective defendant should no longer need to worry about the possible commencement in the future of an action against him or her, that the law disfavors "stale evidence," and that no one should be able to "sit on" rights for an unreasonable amount of time without forfeiting his or her claims. See, e.g., *Limitations Act, 2002,* S.O. 2002, c. 24, Sch. B.

STATUTE OF QUIA EMPTORES (*kwē'-à ĕmp-tô'-rēz*) Lat.: because the buyers. An English statute passed in 1290 that abolished **subinfeudation**. The statute's practical effect on land transactions was that, after land was sold, the seller had no further connection to it. See B. Ziff, *Principles of Property Law* 65–66 (5th ed. 2010).

STATUTE OF TENURES An English statute (*The Tenures Abolition Act 1660*, 12 Car 2 c. 24) that abolished knight service as a method of holding title to land and replaced it with free and common **socage**. The important difference between the two was that knight's service was of a variable nature, while the obligations under socage were more fixed and certain. The Statute of Tenures also introduced duties on various items, such as beer and cider, as a means of compensating the monarch for the service lost.

STATUTE OF USES An English statute (27 Hen. VIII, C. 10) enacted in 1535, for the purpose of preventing the separation of legal and equitable **estates** in land, a separation that arose whenever a **use** was created at **common law**. The purpose was to unite all legal and equitable estates in the **beneficiary** (the holder of the equitable estates) and to strip the **trustee** (the holder of the legal **title**) of all interest. (See **use** for a discussion of the statute's application.)

STATUTE OF WESTMINSTER, 1931 A statute of the **Parliament** of the United Kingdom intended to give full legislative autonomy to Canada and the other self-governing dominions that were former British colonies. The Statute provided **inter alia** that "(1) the U.K. Parliament could only legislate for a Dominion at its request and with its consent, and (2) the Dominion could repeal any English Statute, imperial or otherwise." P. Fitzgerald & K. McShane, *Looking At Law* 26 (2d ed. 1982). The Statute of Westminster did not, however, give Canada authority to alter or repeal the **British North America Acts** because to that time no amending formula had been agreed upon between the provinces and the Parliament of Canada. Such an amending formula was not achieved until the British Parliament enacted the *Canada Act, 1982,* which incorporated the *Constitution Act, 1982.* The latter enactment provides in Part V a procedure for amending the Constitution of Canada.

STATUTE OF WILLS An early English statute prescribing the conditions necessary for a valid disposition through a **will**. Today, the term is used broadly to refer to the statutory provisions of a particular **jurisdiction** relating to the requirements for valid testamentary dispositions. See generally B. Ziff, *Principles of Property Law* 295 (5th ed. 2010). See further the various provincial wills statutes, e.g., *Wills Act,* R.S.N.S. 1989, c. 505.

STATUTORY DECLARATION In effect, an oath; a written statement of facts signed and solemnly declared to be true by the person making it (the declarant) before a person with authority to take such declarations, such as a Commissioner of Oaths.

STATUTORY HOLIDAY A day upon which, by law, all businesses are required to be closed so that all employees can have a vacation day. Exceptions are made for some types of businesses or employees. Each jurisdiction has its own separate list of statutory holidays. In the *Canada Labour Code,* R.S.C., 1985, c. L–2, nine dates are declared to be "general holidays": New Year's Day, Good Friday, Victoria Day, Canada Day, Labour Day, Thanksgiving Day, Remembrance Day, Christmas Day, and Boxing Day.

STATUTORY INSTRUMENT [STATUTORY ORDER] See **regulation**; see also **subordinate legislation**.

STATUTORY INTERPRETATION Rules governing how an **enactment** is to be understood. Many principles have been articulated and are applied as appropriate, such as the **absurdity principle**, the **ejusdem generis rule**, or **strict construction**. However, none is strictly a rule: "[T]oday there is only one principle or approach, namely, the words of an Act are to be read in their entire context and in their grammatical and ordinary sense harmoniously with the scheme of the Act, the object of the Act, and the intention of Parliament." *Bell ExpressVu Limited Partnership v. Rex,* 2002 SCC 42, quoting Driedger, *Construction of Statutes* (2nd ed. 1983). See **construction**; **golden rule**; **literal rule**.

STATUTORY RAPE An informal term used to describe the offence of sexual activity with a person below the age of consent, which is designated as sixteen years of age. *Criminal Code,* R.S.C. 1985, c. C–46, s. 150.1. It is "statutory" rape in the sense that even if the activity was nominally consensual and so would not constitute **sexual assault** (which has replaced the former offence of **rape** in the *Criminal Code*), the consent of the other person "is not a defence." There are "close in age" exceptions, so that a person who is less than two years older than a twelve- or thirteen-year-old **complainant** or less than five years older than a fourteen- or fifteen-year-old complainant can rely on consent. An accused can raise a mistaken belief in the age of the complainant as a defence, but only if he or she took all reasonable steps to ascertain the age of the complainant. *Id.*, s. 150(6).

STAY A halt in a judicial **proceeding** where, by its **order**, the court will not take further action until the occurrence of some event. Inherent **jurisdiction** rests with the court to stay all proceedings that are, for example, frivolous or vexatious or an abuse of the process of the court. A stay may be temporary or permanent. In **criminal** law, the **prosecutor** has the ability to stay proceedings against an **accused**; that stay becomes permanent if no new proceedings are commenced within one year. *Criminal Code*, R.S.C. 1985, c. C–46, s. 579. In addition, under the **Canadian Charter of Rights and Freedoms**, a **judge** can order a stay as a **remedy** for a breach of a right. This stay (sometimes called a judicial stay) is permanent and is only to be given as a remedy in the clearest of cases. Compare **adjournment**; **continuance**; **recess**.

STAY OF EXECUTION process whereby a **judgment** is precluded from being executed for a specific period of time.

STATUTORY OFFENCE See **regulatory offence**.

STIRPES See **per stirpes**.

STOCK CERTIFICATE A written **instrument** evidencing a **share** in the ownership of a **corporation**.

STOCK DIVIDEND See **dividend**.

STOCKHOLDER See **shareholder**.

STOCKHOLDER'S DERIVATIVE ACTION A **suit** whereby a **shareholder**, **director**, former director, or other person brings an action in the name of the **corporation**, in circumstances where the board of directors fails to do so. Such an action can only be brought where "(*a*) the **complainant** has given notice to the directors of the corporation or its subsidiary

of the complainant's intention to apply to the court under subsection (1) not less than fourteen days before bringing the application, or as otherwise ordered by the court, if the directors of the corporation or its subsidiary do not bring, diligently prosecute or defend, or discontinue the action; (*b*) the complainant is acting in good faith; and (*c*) it appears to be in the interests of the corporation or its subsidiary that the action be brought, prosecuted, defended, or discontinued." *Canada Business Corporations Act*, R.S.C. 1985, c. C–44, s. 239.

STOCK OPTION The granting to an individual of the right to purchase a corporate **stock** at some future date at a price specified at the time the option is given rather than at the time the stock is purchased. Such options involve no commitments on the part of the individual to purchase the stock, and the option is usually exercised only if the price of the stock has risen above the price specified at the time the option was given.

Stock options are a form of incentive compensation. They are usually given by a corporation in an attempt to motivate an employee or **officer** to continue with the corporation or to improve corporate productivity in a manner that will cause the price of the corporation's stock to rise and thereby increase the value of the option. See also **dividend** [STOCK DIVIDEND].

STRAW MAN 1. A colloquial expression designating arguments in **briefs** or **opinions** created solely for the purpose of debunking or "discovering" them. Arguments so created are like straw men because they are, by nature, insubstantial.

2. In commercial and property contexts, the term may be used when a transfer is made to a third party, the straw man, simply to re-transfer to the transferror in order to accomplish some purpose not otherwise permitted. Thus, if a **covenant running with the land** must be included in the deed in the jurisdiction, such a covenant can be established subsequently by conveying the property to a straw man and obtaining from him or her a new grant with the desired convenant now in the **deed**.

STREET RACING 1. "[O]perating a motor vehicle in a race with at least one other motor vehicle on a street, road, highway, or other public place." *Criminal Code*, R.S.C. 1985, c. C–46, s. 2. Street racing now fulfills the **actus reus** of numerous **crimes** involving dangerous operation of a motor vehicle and criminal negligence causing death or bodily harm. See, e.g., *id*, s. 249.2. **2.** A common term for Ontario's "stunt driving" offence under s. 172 of the *Highway Traffic Act*, R.S.O. 1990, c. H.8.

STRICT CONSTRUCTION A principle of statutory interpretation that "if a penal provision is reasonably capable of two interpretations, [the] interpretation [that] is the more favourable to the accused must be adopted." *R. v. Goulis* (1981), 20 C.R. (3d) 360 (Ont.C.A.). The rule can only be applied if a provision is genuinely ambiguous. As a general proposition, "[t]he applicable principle is not 'strict construction but s. 12 of the *Interpretation Act*, which provides that every enactment 'is deemed remedial and shall be given such fair, large, and liberal construction and interpretation as best ensures the attainment of its objects.'" *Canada 3000 Inc., Re; Inter-Canadian (1991) Inc. (Trustee of)*, 2006 SCC 24. See **statutory interpretation**.

STRICT LIABILITY In **tort** law, **liability** without a showing of fault. It is often the case in tort law that one who engages in an activity that has an inherent risk of injury, something classified, for example, as ultra-hazardous, is liable for all injuries **proximately caused** by his or her enterprise, even without a showing of **negligence**. Thus, one who uses explosives or who harbours wild animals is liable for resulting injuries even if he or she uses utmost care. See, e.g., G.H.L. Fridman, *The Law of Torts in Canada* 199–229 (6th ed. 2010). *Rylands v. Fletcher* (1868), 3 L.R. H.L. 330.

Strict liability is also one of the three types of **regulatory offences** established by the **Supreme Court of Canada** in *R. v. Sault Ste Marie*, [1978] 2 S.C.R. 1299. The Court held that regulatory offences could (a) have **mens rea**; (b) be strict liability; or (c) be **absolute liability**. Regulatory offences are presumed to be strict liability, which means that the Crown is required to prove the **actus reus** of the offence, after which the accused can avoid conviction by proving, on a balance of probabilities, that he or she was not negligent; this is also referred to as the defence of **due diligence**. See *R. v. Wholesale Travel Group Inc.*, [1991] 3 S.C.R. 154.

STRIKE "[I]ncludes a cessation of work or a refusal to work or to continue to work by employees, in combination, in concert or in accordance with a common understanding, and a slowdown of work or other concerted activity on the part of employees in relation to their work that is designed to restrict or limit output." *Canada Labour Code*, R.S.C. 1985, c. L–2, s. 3. A refusal by employees to cross a picket line has been held to constitute a strike. *Canadian Broadcasting Corp. v. Canadian Wire Service Guild, Local 213*, [1981] 2 Can. L.R.B.R. 462. See also the definition of strike in the various provincial labour relations acts.

STRIKEBREAKER See **replacement worker**.

STRIP SEARCH "[T]he removal or rearrangement of some or all of the clothing of a person so as to permit a visual inspection of a person's private areas, namely genitals, buttocks, breasts (in the case of a female), or undergarments." *R. v. Golden*, 2001 SCC 83. A strip search is seen as more intrusive than a pat-down search but less intrusive than a body cavity search. Extra requirements must be met before a strip search is allowed as a **search incident to arrest**.

STYLE OF CAUSE The parties to a lawsuit or case; the names of the parties involved in a court case; e.g. *Jones v. Smith; R. v. Norman.*

SUA SPONTE (*sū'- à spŏn'-tā*) Lat.: of itself or of one's self; without being prompted, as where the court moves to declare a mistrial *sua sponte,* through its own volition, without a **motion** being made by either of the parties.

SUBCONTRACTOR One to whom the principal contractor sublets part of, or all of, a contract; also refers to portions obtained from other subcontractors. One who takes a part of a contract for the principal [general] contractor or another subcontractor.

SUBINFEUDATION The process that developed under **feudal** law whereby the **grantee** of an **estate** in land from his lord granted a smaller estate in the same land to another. In 1066, William the Conqueror claimed all the land of England for the Crown. Subsequently, he granted land to barons for their use in exchange for **services**, but retained ultimate **ownership**, this grant process being call infeudation. Such barons held land IN CAPITE (by direct grant from the king). Subinfeudation was the process by which barons further divided the land by making grants to knights in return for knight services, and the term also includes all subsequent grants and subdivisions by knights and their grantees. Owners under subinfeudation held land "in service" to their grantor and owed nothing directly to the king.

Used by lords to evade numerous **incidents** owed to the crown, subinfeudation was made illegal by the Statute of **Quia Emptores**, 18 Edw. I.C.I., and was replaced by the modern concept of **alienation**. B. Ziff, *Principles of Property Law* 60–61, 65–66 (5th ed. 2010).

SUBJECTIVE Relating to the actual state of mind of the accused. Generally, liability for a **crime** depends on subjective fault rather than **objective** fault. For example, an **accused** will not be guilty of possession of stolen goods if he or she subjectively did not know the goods were stolen, even if a reasonable person would have recognized that fact.

SUBJECT MATTER The thing in dispute; the nature of the **cause of action**; the real **issue** of fact or law presented for **trial** as between **parties**; the object of a **contract**.

SUB JUDICE (*sŭb jū'-dĭ-sā*) Lat.: under a court; before a court or judge for consideration. Thus, the "instant matter" or the "case at bar" will be called the "matter (case) *sub judice*."

SUBLEASE A transaction whereby a **tenant** [one who has **leased premises** from the owner, or **landlord**] grants an **interest** in the leased premises less than his own, or reserves to himself or herself a **reversionary** interest in the term. See **assignment**, which connotes the **conveyance** of the whole term of a lease.

SUBLET To make a **sublease** accompanied by a surrender of the **premises** or at least a part thereof. See **let**. Compare **assignment**.

SUB MODO (*sŭb mō'-dō*) Lat.: under a qualification; subject to a **condition** or qualification.

SUB NOMINE [SUB NOM.] (*sŭb nō'-mē-nā*) Lat.: under the name. Used to indicate that the title of a case has been altered at a later stage in the proceedings; e.g., *A v. B, aff'd sub nom. C v. B.*

SUBORDINATE [DELEGATED] LEGISLATION Rules, **regulations**, by-laws, etc., made by persons or bodies under the authority given in a **statute**. There has been an ever-growing tendency in the twentieth century to enact **legislation** in general terms concerning many matters the detailed rules of which could not possibly be drawn up by the members of **Parliament** or a provincial legislature. The difficulty is surmounted by giving the power to make such rules to subordinate authorities such as boards or commissions, government departments, municipalities, etc. The power to make such laws is thus "delegated," and the rules that are made in this way are termed "delegated" or "subordinate" legislation. See further G. Gall, *The Canadian Legal System* 40–41 (5th ed. 2004).

SUBORNATION OF PERJURY "[T]he act of causing a witness to swear falsely in a judicial proceeding." *R. v. Picard* (1937), 68 C.C.C. 82 (Que.Mag.Ct.). Formerly, subornation of perjury was a specific offence in the *Criminal Code* and defined as "counselling or procuring a person to commit any perjury which is actually committed." *Id.* at 83. The offence would be included today under the *Code* provisions relating to obstructing justice. See *Criminal Code,*

R.S.C. 1985, c. C–46, s. 139. See further *R. v. Savinkoff,* [1963] 3 C.C.C. 163 (B.C.C.A.).

SUBPOENA (*sŭ-pē'-nà*) Lat.: under penalty. A **writ** issued under authority of a court to compel the **appearance** of a **witness** at a judicial proceeding, the disobedience of which may be punishable as a **contempt of court.**
SUBPOENA AD TESTIFICANDUM (*äd tĕs'tĭ-fĭ-kän'-dūm*) Subpoena to testify. It is a technical and descriptive name for the ordinary subpoena. Compare **summons.**
SUBPOENA DUCES TECUM (*dū'-chĕs tā'-kūm*) Under penalty you shall bring it with you. Type of subpoena issued by a court at the request of one of the parties to a **suit** which requires a witness having under his or her control documents or papers relevant to the controversy to bring such items to court during the trial.

SUBROGATION "Subrogation is, as the *Concise Oxford Dictionary* defines it, 'the substitution of one party for another as creditor, with the transfer of rights and duties.'" *Dwyer v. Liberty Insurance Co. of Canada,* 2002 NLCA 75.
    Subrogation typically arises when an insurance company pays its insured under a collision protection feature of an insurance policy; in that event the company is subrogated to the cause of action of its insured. So too, under **Workers' Compensation Acts** the board is subrogated to the injured worker's right (up to the amount of the board's payments) to sue the responsible party.

SUBROGEE One who, by **subrogation,** succeeds to the legal rights or claims of another.

SUBROGOR One whose legal rights or claims are acquired by another through **subrogation.**

SUBSIDIARY An inferior position or capacity; usually used in describing the relationship between **corporations.**
SUBSIDIARY CORPORATION One in which another corporation owns at least a majority of the shares and thus has control; it has all of the normal elements of a corporation **(charter, by-**laws, directors,** etc.) but its **stock** is controlled by another corporation known as the **parent corporation.** This relationship of parent and subsidiary often becomes important for tax purposes and for determining whether a court will ignore the corporate existence of the subsidiary and **pierce the corporate veil.**

SUB SILENTIO (*sŭb sĭ-lĕn'-shē-ō*) Lat.: under silence; silently. When a later opinion reaches a result contrary to what would appear to be controlling authority, it is said that the later case, by necessary implication, overrules *sub silentio* the prior holding.

SUBSTANTIAL PERFORMANCE [COMPLIANCE] The **performance** of all the essential terms of a contract so that the purpose of the contract is accomplished; however, unimportant omissions and defects may exist in the strict performance of the contract. *Hoenig v. Isaacs,* [1952] 2 All E.R. 176 (C.A.). Whether entire performance is a **condition** precedent to payment "depends on the **construction** of the contract." "When a contract provides for a specific sum to be paid on completion of specified work, the courts lean against a construction of the contract which would deprive the contractor of any payment at all simply because there are some defects or omissions. The promise to complete the work is ... construed as a term of the contract, but not as a condition. It is not every breach of that term which absolves the employer from his promise to pay the price, but only a breach which goes to the root of the contract, such as an abandonment of the work when it is only half done. Unless the breach does go to the root of the matter, the employer cannot resist payment of the price. He must pay it and bring a cross-claim for the defects and omissions, or, alternatively, set them up in diminution of the price." *Id.* at 180–81. See **breach of contract.**

SUBSTANTIVE EQUALITY The test under s. 15(2) of the **Canadian Charter of Rights and Freedoms** for deciding whether a law or measure is discriminatory. Substantive equality looks not to whether people are treated equally, but rather to whether that treatment has an equal impact on all people. "Substantive equality, unlike formal equality, rejects the mere presence or absence of difference as an answer to differential treatment. It insists on going behind the facade of similarities and differences. It asks not only what characteristics the different treatment is predicated upon, but also whether those characteristics are relevant considerations under the circumstances. The focus of the inquiry is on the actual impact of the impugned law, taking full account of social, political, economic, and historical factors concerning the group. The result may be to reveal differential treatment as discriminatory because of prejudicial impact or negative stereotyping. Or it may reveal that differential treatment is required in order to ameliorate the actual situation of the claimant group." *Withler v. Canada (Attorney-General)*, 2011 SCC 12.

SUBSTANTIVE LAW The **positive law** that creates, defines and regulates the rights and duties of the **parties** and that may give rise to a **cause of action**, as distinguished from adjective law, which pertains to and prescribes the practice and **procedure** or the legal machinery by which the substantive law is determined or made effective.

SUBSTITUTED SERVICE See **service [of process]**.

SUBTENANT One who **leases** all or part of rented **premises** from the original **lessee** for a term less than that held by the original lessee. The original lessee becomes the sublessor as to the subtenant. Most leases either prohibit subletting or require the lessor's permission in advance. The original lessee remains responsible for the subtenant's obligations to the lessor. Compare **assignment**.

SUCCESSION The process by which the property of a **decedent** is taken through **descent** or by **will**. It is a word that clearly excludes those who take by **deed**, **grant**, **gift**, or any form of purchase or **contract**. See **inheritance**; **intestate succession**.

SUE The act of bringing a civil action against another person. See **suit**.

SUE AND LABOUR CLAUSE A provision in an **insurance** contract obliging an **insured** to take reasonable steps to protect the insured property from further damage after a loss occurs. The **insurer** must compensate the insured for his or her preservation efforts. *Hartford Fire Insurance Co. v. Benson & Hedges*, [1978] 2 S.C.R. 1088.

SUICIDE The voluntary and intentional killing of oneself; the completed act was a **felony** at **common law**. Under the *Criminal Code*, R.S.C. 1985, c. C–46, s. 241, it is an **offence** to counsel or procure a person to commit suicide or to aid or abet a person to commit suicide. See *Rodriguez v. British Columbia (Attorney-General)*, [1993] 3 S.C.R. 519. Suicide by one in possession of his or her mental faculties is ordinarily excluded from insurance coverage, if it occurs within a specified period of time (normally two years) after the policy is taken out.

SUI GENERIS (*sū'-ē j'ĕn-ĕ-rĕs*) Lat.: of its own kind. General term used to denote a situation with a unique or unusual set of facts or circumstances. For example, **Aboriginal title** is said to be *sui generis* because, unlike other **proprietary interests** in land, it cannot be transferred, sold, or surrendered to anyone other than the **Crown**; it arises from occupation of land prior to British sovereignty; and it is held communally. *Delgamuukw v. British Columbia*, [1997] 3 SCR 1010.

SUI JURIS (*sū'-ē jūr'-ĭs*) Lat.: of his own right. Describes one who is no longer dependent, e.g., one who has reached the age of **majority** or has been removed from the care of a **guardian**; signifies one capable of caring for himself or herself. Compare **emancipation**; **incompetency**.

SUIT Any **proceeding** in a court of justice by which an individual seeks a decision of the court or pursues a **remedy** that the law affords.

SUMMARY [CONVICTION] OFFENCE In Canada all crimes are classified as

indictable offences or offences punishable on summary conviction. Generally speaking, summary offences, which may be federal or provincial, are those of a less serious nature and carry a lesser penalty. The procedure to try all summary conviction offences under the *Criminal Code* or other Act of **Parliament** is set out in Part XXVII of the *Criminal Code,* R.S.C. 1985, c. C–46. Under s.787(1), the maximum penalty for most summary convictions is a fine up to a maximum of $2000, and/or imprisonment up to six months. Summary offences are tried by justices or provincial court judges, and proceedings are generally quicker than, for example, in a trial by judge and jury. See further R. Salhany, *Canadian Criminal Procedures* (6th ed. 1994). See also S. Coughlan, *Criminal Procedure* 36–39 (2nd ed. 2012).

SUMMARY JUDGMENT See **judgment** [SUMMARY JUDGMENT].

SUMMONS A call to appear in court; an order requiring the **appearance** of a **defendant** in an action under penalty of having **judgment** entered against him for failure to do so; in **criminal** law, an order to an accused informing him or her of an alleged offence and requiring him or her to appear in court to answer the allegation. See **writ** [WRIT OF SUMMONS]; **process**; **service**. Compare **subpoena**.

SUNSET CLAUSE A term often used to describe a provision within a statute that stipulates a date or time that the statute will cease to have effect. Section 33(3) of the **Canadian Charter of Rights and Freedoms** is referred to as a sunset clause because it states that any legislative override enacted under s.33 will cease to have effect five years after the date it is enacted.

SUO NOMINE (*sū'-ō nō'-mē-nā*) Lat.: in his own name.

SUPERSEDING CAUSE See **cause**.

SUPERIOR COURT A federally appointed court that has jurisdiction only within a single province or territory and that is authorized by s. 96 of the **Constitution Act, 1867**. Every province and territory has a superior court, though the name of the court differs from province to province (such as "Supreme Court" in Nova Scotia or "Superior Court of Justice" in Ontario). Superior courts typically have jurisdiction over all types of disputes occurring in the jurisdiction and will conduct trials in some matters, but they also can hear appeals from lower-level courts or administrative bodies. In many provinces the superior courts have special divisions, such as a **unified family court**. Every province and territory also has a court of appeal, which is also federally appointed and which is also a superior court. See **Appendix I**, **Outline of Canada's Court System**.

SUPERNUMERARY The term applied to a judge who has retired from full-time service on the **bench** but who continues to sit on some matters. Some provinces have abolished the status of supernumerary judge; see *Mackin v. New Brunswick (Minister of Finance)*, 2002 SCC 13.

SUPERVENING CAUSE See **cause** [INTERVENING CAUSE].

SUPRA (*sū'-prà*) Lat.: above. In a written work, it refers the reader to a part preceding that which he is presently reading, as compared with the command **infra**, which directs the reader forward.

SUPREME COURT OF CANADA The highest court of appeal in Canada, created under the *Supreme Court Act*, R.S.C. 1985, c. S–26. It has jurisdiction over all matters arising in lower courts. The court consists of nine judges, and under the *Supreme Court Act,* three of those judges must come from Quebec. By tradition three of the other judges are appointed from Ontario, two from the western provinces, and one from the Atlantic provinces. Some **criminal** law matters reach the court by right, where a judge in a provincial court of appeal has dissented in the result on a **question of law**. In any other cases, matters are only heard by the Supreme Court if it decides to grant leave. In addition, the court also hears **reference cases**. See **Appendix I**, **Outline of Canada's Court System**.

SURETY 1. One who undertakes to pay money or perform other acts in the event that his or her **principal** fails therein; the surety is directly and immediately liable for the **debt**. Unlike an insurer, who might be found to pay a loss only on the happening of a defined **contingency**, a surety "became bound, it might be, unconditionally and without previous notice or demand, to pay the debt or make good the default which the principal was or should be liable to pay or make good, and the surety must see he did it." *Whalen v. Union Indemnity Co.,* [1932] 41 O.W.N. 208 (H.C.) **2.** In **criminal** law, "a third party who agrees to forfeit a sum of money if the person for whom she stands surety fails to appear in court in accordance with the terms of a recognizance." S. Coughlan, *Criminal Procedure* (2nd ed. 2012).

SURFACE BARGAINING The appearance of bargaining without any real intention to reach an agreement. "[A] term which describes a going through the motion, or a preserving of the surface indications of bargaining without the intent of concluding a collective agreement." *Toronto Typographical Union, No. 91 v. The Daily Times,* [1978] O.L.R.B. Rep. 604 at 610. Contrast with **good faith bargaining**.

SURREBUTTER In **common-law pleading**, a **plaintiff's** answer to the **defendants rebuttal (rebutter)**.

SURREJOINDER In **common-law pleading**, a **plaintiffs** answer to the **defendant's rejoinder**.

SURRENDERED LANDS "[A] **reserve** or part of a reserve or any interest therein, the legal title of which remains vested in Her Majesty, that has been released or surrendered by the [Indian] band for whose use and benefit it was set apart. *Indian Act,* R.S.C. 1985, c. I–5, s. 2.

SURROGATE A judicial officer of limited **jurisdiction**, who administers matters of **probate** and **intestate succession**.

SURROGATE COURT A provincial court of limited **jurisdiction** that is concerned with the **probate** of **wills** and the administration of **estates**. In some jurisdictions such a court may be known as the PROBATE COURT.

SURVIVAL STATUTE A statute that preserves for a **deceased's estate** or personal representatives a **cause of action** vested in the deceased. See, e.g., *Survival of Actions Act,* R.S.N.S. 1989, c. 453; *Fatal Injuries Act,* R.S.N.S. 1989, c. 163; *Family Law Act,* R.S.O. 1990, c. F.3. Part V.

SURVIVORSHIP A right whereby a person becomes entitled to property by reason of his or her having survived another person who had an interest in it. It is one of the elements of a **joint tenancy**. See also **survival statute**.

SUSPENDED SENTENCE See **sentence**.

T

TAIL, ESTATE IN See **fee tail**.

TAKING A VIEW The practice of a **trier of fact**, during a **trial**, visiting a relevant location in order to make observations.

TALESMAN A person summoned for **jury** selection when the ordinary process has not resulted in a complete jury. If all persons who had been summoned to attend for jury duty have been selected, excused, **challenged** for cause, or subject to a **peremptory challenge**, and a full jury has not yet been selected, the court may order the sheriff to summon by word of mouth other potential **jurors**; those persons are referred to as "talesmen." *Criminal Code*, R.S.C. 1985, c. C–46, s. 642.

TANGIBLE PROPERTY Property, either **real** or **personal**, capable of being **possessed** and of being perceived by the senses; accessible; identifiable. Tangible property is **corporeal**, as distinguished from **intangible property** or **incorporeal rights** in property, such as **franchises**, **copyrights**, **easements** and goodwill.

TARIFF 1. A tax or duty imposed on imported items. **2.** A list or schedule of imported items on which a tax or a duty is imposed, as well as the rate at which the item is taxed. **3.** A schedule of fees charged by a lawyer for standard legal services. The tariff system has largely been in Canada and most lawyers now charge according to the amount of time spent on a legal transaction. S.M. Waddams, *Introduction to the Study of Law* 115 (6th ed. 2004). **4.** A fee charged for the use of a **copyrighted** work.

TAX A rate or sum of money that people are compelled by a competent authority to pay for support of the government and that is commonly levied upon **assets** or **real property** (property tax), or income derived from office, employment, business or property (income tax), or upon the sale or purchase of **goods** (sales tax).

Taxes can be direct or indirect. By section 92(2) of the **Constitution Act, 1867**, provincial legislatures are empowered to impose only DIRECT TAXATION, i.e., upon the individual from whom the tax is to be exacted. An INDIRECT TAX is one exacted from an individual with the understanding that he or she will indemnify himself or herself at another's expense. *A.-G. for Manitoba v. A.-G. for Canada,* [1925] A.C. 561 (P.C.).

AD VALOREM TAX A tax on the value of the actual property subject to taxation laid as a percentage of that value, as opposed to a specific tax, which is applied as a fixed sum to all of a certain class of articles.

CAPITAL GAINS TAX See **capital** [CAPITAL GAIN].

ESTATE TAX A tax on the transfer of property, not on the property itself. Estate taxes are based on the power to transmit or the transmission from the dead to the living, while **inheritance** taxes are based on the right to receive the property and are thus applied to the recipients thereof.

EXCISE TAX See **excise**.

POLL TAX See **poll tax**.

TAX COURT OF CANADA The Tax Court of Canada gives individuals and companies an opportunity to settle disagreements with the federal government on matters arising under federal tax and revenue legislation. The Tax Court of Canada primarily hears disputes between the federal government and taxpayers after the taxpayer has gone through all other options provided for by the *Income Tax Act*. The Tax Court is independent of the Canada Customs and Revenue Agency and all other government departments. Its headquarters are in Ottawa, and it has regional offices in Montreal, Toronto, and Vancouver. See **federalism**. See Chart, **Appendix I**.

TAX SALE See **sale**.

TELEWARRANT A procedure authorized under s. 487.1 of the *Criminal Code*, R.S.C. 1985, c. C–46 permitting certain **warrants** to be issued by means of telecommunication where it is impracticable for the police officer to appear personally in front of a **justice of the peace**.

TEMPORARY RESIDENT A **foreign national** who seeks to enter or remain in Canada. To become a temporary resident such foreign national must establish that they hold a visa or other document required under the *Immigration and Refugee Protection Regulations*, and will leave Canada by the end of the period authorized for their stay. See *Immigration and Refugee Protection Act*, S.C. 2001, c. 27, ss.20.(1) and 20.(2). See **permanent resident**.

TEMPORE (*tĕm'-pô-rā*) Lat.: for the time of.

TENANCY 1. Generally, a **tenant's** right to possess an **estate**, whether by **lease** or by **title**. A tenancy cannot be created unless exclusive **possession** is conferred on the tenant.
2. In a more limited sense, a holding in subordination to another's title, as in the **landlord**-tenant relationship.
HOLDOVER TENANCY See TENANCY AT SUFFERANCE.
JOINT TENANCY A tenancy "created where the same interest in **real** or **personal property** is passed by the same conveyance to two or more persons in the same right or by **construction** or **operation of law** jointly, with a right of ownership, i.e., the right of the survivor or survivors to the whole property." *R. v. Uniacke*, [1944] 3 W.W.R. 323 at 327 (Sask.C.A.). To have a joint tenancy, the four **unities** of time, **title**, **interest** and **possession** must be present. See A.M. Sinclair & M.E. McCallum, *An Introduction to Real Property Law* 113–15 (6th ed. 2012).
PERIODIC TENANCY In landlord-tenant law, a tenancy for a particular period (a week, month, year, or number of years), plus the expectancy or possibility that the period will be repeated. In contrast to a TENANCY FOR YEARS [see following], a periodic tenancy must be terminated by due **notice** to quit by either the landlord or the tenant, unless one party has failed to perform some part of his or her obli-

gation. A periodic tenancy is considered a form of TENANCY AT WILL [see following] and is created either by express agreement or by implication from the manner in which rent is paid. For example, if A holds B's land with no express time limitation, and rent is paid yearly, it will be deemed a TENANCY FROM YEAR TO YEAR. Provincial statutes govern the time necessary for due notice to be given. See, e.g., *Residential Tenancies Act*, R.S.N.S. 1989, c. 401, s.10. Tenancies from year to year are **alienable**. See B. Ziff, *Principles of Property Law* 290 (5th ed. 2010).
TENANCY AT SUFFERANCE [HOLDOVER TENANCY] In landlord-tenant law, a tenancy that comes into existence when one at first lawfully possesses **land** as under a **lease** and subsequently holds over beyond the end of one term of such lease or occupies the land without such lawful authority. For example, if A has a TENANCY FOR YEARS [see following] for one month, at the end of that month, if A continues in **possession**, A becomes a tenant at sufferance [or holdover tenant]. Thus a tenancy at sufferance cannot arise from an agreement, which distinguishes it from a TENANCY AT WILL [see following]. A tenant at sufferance differs from a **trespasser** only in that he or she originally entered with the landlord's permission. The landlord has a right to establish a landlord-tenant relationship (i.e., extend the lease) of a tenant at sufferance. Reciprocally, a tenant cannot be sued for trepass as a tenant at sufferance before the landlord enters and demands possession. A tenant at sufferance cannot grant such an estate to a third person.
TENANCY AT WILL In landlord-tenant law, a leased **estate** that confers upon the tenant the right to **possession** for an indefinite period such as is agreed upon by both **parties**. A tenancy at will is characterized primarily by the uncertain term and the right of either party to terminate upon proper **notice**. A tenancy at will may arise out of an express **contract** or by **implication**. Because a tenancy at will is determin-

able at any time, the tenant cannot **assign** or **grant** his estate to another.

TENANCY BY THE ENTIRETY The ownership of property, real or personal, **tangible** or **intangible**, by a husband and wife together. In addition to the four unities of time, title, interest, and possession, there is a fifth unity, that of husband and wife. Neither is allowed to **alienate** any part of the property so held without consent of the other, and the survivor of the marriage is entitled to the whole property.

Upon the passage of statutes in all jurisdictions in Canada making a married woman, at law, a femme sole the doctrine has all but disappeared. See B. Ziff, *Principles of Property Law* 338–39 (5th ed. 2010).

TENANCY FOR YEARS An estate in land created by a lease and limited to endure for any specified and definite term, whether in weeks, months, or years. It is DETERMINABLE (i.e., it ends) upon expiration of that term and does not require **notice** or **re-entry** by the landlord nor notice to quit by the tenant. However, if the tenant stays on, the tenancy may be converted into a TENANCY AT SUFFERANCE [which see], TENANCY AT WILL [which see] or PERIODIC TENANCY [which see], determinable as tenancies of those kinds. A tenancy for years is **alienable**, subject to lease restrictions against **assignment** or **sublease**. See B. Ziff, *Principles of Property Law* 289 (5th ed. 2010).

TENANCY FROM MONTH TO MONTH See PERIODIC TENANCY.

TENANCY FROM YEAR TO YEAR See PERIODIC TENANCY.

TENANCY IN CAPITE (*ĭn kä'-pē-tā*) Lat.: in chief; tenancy-in-chief. In feudal law, the holding of land directly from the Crown.

TENANCY IN COMMON A form of tenancy that "arises when owners have community of possession but distinct and several **titles** to their **shares** which need not necessarily be equal: and there is no right of **survivorship** between owners in common." *R. v. Uniacke*, [1944] 3 W.W.R. 323 at 327 (Sask.C.A.).

See generally B. Ziff, *Principles of Property Law* 288–310, 336–49 (5th ed. 2010).

TENANT "[T]he person who, by reason of his **possession** or occupancy or his rights thereto, whether by **priority** of **contract** or **estate**, for the time being holds the premises under **title** immediately or mediately from the landlord or his predecessor in title, and by reason of his so holding is the person liable for the time being to pay the rent. Or, to put it still another way, during the course of the existence of a term of years, the persons who are respectively **landlord** and **tenant** may—one or both—change from time to time, and the enactment refers to the persons who, for the time being, stand in the relationship of landlord and tenant." *Re Calgary Brewing & Malting Co.* (1915), 9 W.W.R. 563 at 565 (Alta.S.C.) quoted in *Critical Control Solutions Corp. v. 954470 Alberta Ltd.*, 2005 ABQB 753.

The term may include "**sub-tenant** and the assigns of the tenant and any person in actual occupation of the premises under or with the assent of the tenant during the currency of the lease, or while the rent is due or in arrear, whether or not he has attorned to or become the tenant of the landlord." *Phalen v. Levitt,* [1923] 2 D.L.R. 600 at 602 (Alta.S.C.).

A tenant need not occupy the premises. *Anderson v. Scott* (1912), 8 D.L.R. 816 (Alta.S.C.A.D.).

LIFE TENANT A person who is entitled to the use and occupancy of premises for the duration of his or her life.

TENANT IN FEE SIMPLE A holder of an estate of **freehold**, the most extensive interest a person can have.

A tenant in fee simple has lands, tenements or **hereditaments** to hold to him or her and his or her heirs forever, generally, absolutely and simply, without mentioning what heirs, but leaving that to his or her own pleasure or to the disposition of the law. The word *fee* alone, without any qualifying words, serves to designate a **fee simple estate** and is not infrequently used in that sense.

Both a life tenant and a tenant in fee simple hold a **freehold estate**, not a **leasehold estate**. See also **tenancy**.

TENDER In contract law a tender is generally a formal bid to supply, for example, goods or services at a specific price to another in response to a request or "call for tenders." Traditionally, a call for tenders was not regarded as an **offer**, but merely an "invitation" to a group of competitive tenderers to ascertain whether the party making the call could obtain a favourable "offer" with respect to a contemplated sale or other project. In such circumstances the party making the tender could revoke its bid at any time before acceptance.

However, in some circumstances a call for tenders may be fairly specific, as where an expression such as "lowest bid will be accepted" is used. The courts might regard this as an indication that the party issuing the call is actually making an "offer" which can be turned into a contract by the party who submits the lowest bid. (See *Spencer v. Harding* (1870), 5 L.R. C.P. 561; *Murphy v. Alberton (Town)* (1993), 114 Nfld. & P.E.I.R. 34 (P.E.I. S.C.)). Today in Canada the case law on tenders must be read in light of *R. in Right of Ontario v. Ron Engineering & Construction (Eastern) Ltd.*, [1981] 1 S.C.R. 111 in which a contract arose automatically upon the submission of defendant's tender, imposing certain obligations, even before final selection of the successful tenderer. See also *M.J.B. Enterprises Ltd. v. Defence Construction (1951) Ltd.*, [1999] 1 S.C.R. 619.

The term may also apply in a **debtor-creditor** situation where a debtor makes an unconditional "tender" coupled with a manifested ability to carry out the offer and production of the subject matter (normally money), unless such production is waived by the creditor.

Tender is an offer of performance that, if unjustifiably refused, places the refusing party in default and permits the party making tender to exercise his or her remedy for **breach of contract**.

Finally, as a verb, to place material before a court, i.e., to tender evidence.

LEGAL TENDER An offer of payment in a form the creditor is obliged to accept, e.g., the currency of a country.

TENDER OFFER A public offer made to **shareholders** of a particular **corporation** to purchase a specific number of shares of **stock** at a specific price. The price quoted in such an **offer** is payable only if the offeror is able to obtain the total amount of stock specified in the offer, usually the number of shares sufficient to give the offeror control of the corporation.

TENDER YEARS DOCTRINE A historical presumption in **family law** that the **custody** of very young children ("children of tender years") should be granted to the mother over the father. See, e.g., *Re Orr*, [1933] O.R. 212 (Ont. C.A.); *Bell v. Bell*, [1955] O.W.N. 341 (Ont. C.A.). The doctrine has now been virtually abandoned by the courts as a factor in awarding custody. See, e.g., *Van de Perre v. Edwards*, 2001 SCC 60, or the reference to "formulaic solutions like 'the tender years doctrine'" in *A.C. v. Manitoba (Director of Child and Family Services)*, 2009 SCC 30. Today the predominant concern in legal decisions involving children is the **best interests of the child**.

TENEMENT 1. A technical word applicable to all real estate, including offices and dignities that concern land and profits issuing out of land. **2.** Strictly, property of a permanent and fixed nature including both **corporeal** and **incorporeal real property**. **3.** In modern usage, any house, building, or structure attached to land, and also any kind of human habitation or dwelling inhabited by a **tenant**.

A **servient tenement** is the estate or land over which an **easement** or some other service exists in favour of the **dominant tenement**.

TENURE Right to hold; manner of holding land or office. **1.** In real property law, since the monarch is absolute owner of land, the possessor is a mere **tenant** and the mode of possession is tenure while the extent of the interest is an **estate**.

2. Tenure refers also to a statutory or **contractual** right of certain public servants and teachers to retain their positions permanently, subject only to removal for adequate cause or economic necessity.

TERM OF COURT A definite time period prescribed by law for a court to administer its duties. Term and session are often used interchangeably, but, technically, term is the statutory time prescribed for judicial business and session is the time a court actually sits to hear cases. In general, terms of court no longer have any special significance, fixed periods of days having replaced the stated terms of court.

TERRA NULLIUS (*tĕ-rŭ' nŭl'-ē-ŭs*) Lat.: the land of no one; unclaimed land. *R. v. Marshall; R. v. Bernard*, 2005 SCC 43.

TERRITORIAL SUPERIOR COURT See **superior court**.

TERRORISM An "act intended to cause death or serious bodily injury to a civilian, or to any other person not taking an active part in the hostilities in a situation of armed conflict, when the purpose of such act, by its nature or context is to intimidate a population, or to compel a government or an international organization to do or to abstain from doing any act." *International Convention for the Suppression of Terrorist Bombings,* 37 I.L.M. 249, s. 2(1)(b), as quoted in *Suresh v. Canada (Minister of Citizenship and Immigration),* [2002] 1 S.C.R. 3., para. 98.

TERRORIST ACTIVITY Under the *Criminal Code*, R.S.C. 1985, c. C–46, s. 83.01, any of a number of listed offences included in various international agreements, or an offence involving serious violence, substantial property damage, or serious disruption of essential services, and that is committed in whole or in part for a political, religious, or ideological purpose, objective, or cause, with the intention of intimidating the public or compelling a person, government, or domestic or international organization to do or to refrain from doing any act. See *R. v. Khawaja*, 2010 ONCA 862.

TERRORIST GROUP "Means (a) an entity that has as one of its purposes or activities facilitating or carrying out any terrorist activity, or (b) a listed entity, and includes an association of such entities." *Criminal Code,* R.S.C. 1985, c. C–46, s. 83.01.

TESTACY The state or condition of leaving a valid **will** at one's death, as distinguished from **intestacy**, the condition of dying without leaving a will.

TESTAMENT Strictly, a testimonial or just statement of a person's wishes concerning the disposition of his or her **personal property** after death, in contrast to a **will**, which is strictly a **devise** of **real estate**. Commonly, however, will and testament are considered synonymous. The law of testaments is statutory. The word is rarely used today except in the formal heading of one's will, which reads "This is the last will and testament of ..."

TESTAMENTARY Relating to the grant and revocation of the **probate** of **wills** and of administration and incidental matters.

TESTAMENTARY DISPOSITION A **gift** of property that takes effect at the time of the death of the person making the disposition. It can be effected by **deed**, by an **inter vivos** transaction, or by will. All **instruments** used to make testamentary dispositions must comply with the requirements of the **statute of wills**. See **causa** [CAUSA MORTIS].

TESTAMENTARY INSTRUMENT "[A]ny will, codicil, or other testamentary writing or appointment, during the life of the testator whose testamentary disposition it purports to be and after his death, whether it relates to real or personal property or both." *Criminal Code,* R.S.C. 1985, c. C–46, s. 2.

TESTATOR [TESTATRIX] One who makes and executes a **testament** or **will**, testator applying to a man, testatrix to a woman. See also **intestate; testament; testamentary** [TESTAMENTARY DISPOSITION]. Compare **administrator; executor**.

TESTIMONIUM CLAUSE The part of a will or deed that states when and by whom it was witnessed and signed. Generally starts with the words, "In witness whereof..."

TESTIMONY A statement made by a **witness**, under oath, usually related to a legal **proceeding** or legislative hearing; **evidence** given by a competent witness, under oath or affirmation, as distinguished from evidence derived from writing and other sources. Evidence is the broader term and includes all testimony, which is one species of evidence. See **expert witness**.

TESTIS [TESTES] Lat.: witness[es].

THEFT A positive act of acquisition, without consent, by one without title, of another's **property** with an intent to deprive. The *Criminal Code,* R.S.C. 1985, c. C–46, s. 322, states that "[e]very one commits theft who fraudulently and without **colour of right** takes, or . . . converts to his use, or the use of another person, anything whether animate or inanimate, with intent to deprive, temporarily or absolutely, the owner of it or a person who has a special property or interest in it, of the thing or of his property or interest in it." See **larceny**.

THEFT OF ELECTRICITY The offence under s. 326 of the *Criminal Code*, R.S.C. 1985, c. C–46, of fraudulently using electricity. A **grow-op** uses unusually high amounts of electricity, and police are able to obtain power consumption records without a search warrant (*R. v. Plant*, [1993] 3 S.C.R. 281), which has led to a rise in the rate of the commission of this offence as those growing marijuana try to evade detection. Theft of electricity is sometimes detected through use of a **DRA**.

THIN SKULL RULE 1. A general rule in negligence law based on the principle that "you must take your victim as you find him or her." If a defendant has a preexisting condition or weakness that as a result of the plaintiff's actions makes him or her vulnerable to additional injury, the plaintiff is liable for all damage caused. *Hay (or Bournhill)*

v. Young, [1943] A.C. 92 at 109–10 (H.L.). Contrast with **crumbling skull**. **2.** In criminal law, if a person commits an unlawful act against another with a preexisting condition ("thin skull") that results in that person's death, he or she will be held to have caused the death even though it could not be foreseen. *R. v. Smithers* (1977), 34 C.C.C. (2d) 427 (S.C.C.).

THIRD PARTY See **party**.

THIRD-PARTY BENEFICIARY A person who is not a party to a **contract**, but who is able to enforce the contract where the contract was entered into for his or her own benefit, as an exception to the **privity** rule. Recent Canadian case law has permitted third parties to enforce some kinds of contracts. For example, the Supreme Court of Canada has permitted employees to obtain the benefit of a limitation of liability clause contained in a contract of storage made by their employer. *London Drugs Ltd. v. Kuehne & Nagel International Ltd.*, [1992] 3 S.C.R. 299.

TIDE-LAND Land over which the tide ebbs and flows; land covered and uncovered by ordinary tides. The limit of the tide-land is usually the mean high tide. See also **avulsion; reliction; foreshore**.

TITHE In old English law, a right of the clergy to extract for the use of the church one tenth of the produce of lands and personal industry of the people. Comparable to rent charges or **ground rents**.

TITLE Ownership. In property law, a term denoting the facts that, if proved, will enable a **plaintiff** to recover **possession** or a **defendant** to retain possession of a thing; the right to possess a thing, but entirely different from **property** in the thing. "The term title means on the one hand the right of ownership and on the other the instrument or evidence of such right." *Re Vancouver Improvement Co.* (1893), 3 B.C.R. 601 at 605 (B.C.S.C.). "Title is merely evidence of the formal right of ownership." *Mann v. Canada*, [1995] 2 C.T.C. 2049 (Tax Ct.).

ADVERSE TITLE A title asserted in opposition to another; one claimed to have been acquired by **adverse possession**.

CLEAR TITLE See **clear title**.

CLEAR TITLE OF RECORD A title that the **record** shows to be an **indefeasible** unencumbered **estate**. It differs from a CLEAR TITLE in that the latter can be demonstrated by **evidence** independent of the record.

COLOUR OF TITLE See **colour of title**.

DEFECTIVE TITLE See **defective title**.

EQUITABLE TITLE "[T]he right of the party to whom it belongs to have the legal title transferred to him." *Tennant v. Rhineland* (1918), 38 D.L.R. 271 at 279 per Cameron, J.A. dissenting (Man.C.A.).

Ownership that is recognized by **a court of equity** or founded upon equitable principles, as opposed to formal legal title. The purchaser of real property can specifically enforce his or her contract for purchase and as a result, prior to the actual **conveyance**, he or she has an enforceable equitable title, which can be terminated only by a **bona fide purchaser**. See **specific performance**.

GOOD TITLE See **good title**.

MARKETABLE TITLE See **marketable title**.

QUIET TITLE See **quiet title**.

TITLE SEARCH A search made through the records maintained in the **Registry of Deeds** to determine the state of a **title**, including all **liens**, **encumbrances**, **mortgages**, **future interests**, etc., affecting the property; the means by which a **chain of title** is ascertained.

TORRENS SYSTEM A system of land titles registration first developed in Australia in 1858 by Robert Torrens. The purpose of the system was to simplify the system of land registration through the creation of a government-authorized register. The register establishes all the interests in the land and provides the purchaser with a certificate of title, thereby eliminating the need to search public records for prior title. The central feature of this system is that once the land is registered and a certificate of title has been issued to the purchaser, the government guarantees it to be accurate. Any errors that occur are compensated under a central insurance fund. See **registry acts**.

TORT "[I]njury; wrong. The **breach** of a **duty** imposed by law, whereby some person acquires a right of action for damages." *Lawson v. Wellesley Hospital* (1976), 9 O.R. (2d) 677 at 681 (Ont.C.A.).

"Tort is not a noun which has both a popular meaning and a legal meaning. It only has a legal meaning and is not a word which is used in a popular sense." *Id.* at 681.

"In very general terms, a tort is a civil wrong, other than a breach of contract, which the law will redress by an award of damages." *Id.* at 682, quoting Fleming, *The Law of Torts,* 3d ed.

TORTFEASOR One who is held liable or admits liability for a **tort**.

JOINT TORTFEASORS See **joint tortfeasors**.

TORTIOUS Unlawful; an adjective describing conduct that subjects the actor(s) to **tort** liability.

TORTURE "[A]ny act or omission by which severe pain or suffering, whether physical or mental, is intentionally inflicted on a person (*a*) for a purpose including (*i*) obtaining from the person or from a third person information or a statement, (*ii*) punishing the person for an act that the person or a third person has committed or is suspected of having committed, and (*iii*) intimidating or coercing the person or a third person, or (*b*) for any reason based on discrimination of any kind." *Criminal Code,* R.S.C. 1985, c. C–46, s. 269.1(1).

TOTALITY PRINCIPLE In **criminal** law, the requirement that a **judge** who orders an offender to serve **consecutive sentences** for multiple **offences** ensures that the cumulative sentence rendered does not exceed the overall culpability of the offender. *R. v. M. (C.A.),* [1996] 1 S.C.R. 500.

TOWAGE A maritime service whereby one vessel (the "tug") moves another vessel (the "tow") from one place to another, where the tow requires the motive power of the tug. The service is usually based on a contract of towage between the vessels, "and thus the fundamental responsibilities of both [vessels] are governed by the terms, conditions, and exemptions" of the contract. E. Gold, A. Chircop & H. Kindred, *Maritime Law* 575 (2003).

TO WIT Namely; that is to say.

TRADE FIXTURE Property placed on or annexed to rented **real estate** by a **tenant** for the purpose of aiding himself or herself in the conduct of a trade or business.

Unlike other **fixtures**, which become part of the real property, trade fixtures remain the property of the tenant and will be taken by him or her provided they can be removed without causing material injury to the property. "Trade fixtures refer to things placed on and connected to the realty, but in a way that the connection can be severed, restoring their character as chattels." *Caledonia Service Station Inc. v. Cango Inc.*, 2011 ONCA 184.

TRADE-MARK "... (a) a mark that is used by a person for the purpose of distinguishing or so as to distinguish wares or services manufactured, sold, leased, hired or performed by him from those manufactured, sold, leased, hired or performed by others, (b) a certification mark, (c) a distinguishing guise, or (d) a proposed **trade-mark**." *Trade-marks Act*, R.S.C. 1985, c. T–13, s. 2.

TRADE SECRET A common law term that has been incorporated into various statutes and that describes knowledge that the possessor has an economic interest in keeping secret. In the *Access to Information Act*, R.S.C. 1985, c. A–1, it refers to a plan or process, tool, mechanism, or compound of which it is true that: the information is secret in an absolute or relative sense (i.e., known only by one or a relatively small number of persons); the possessor of the information has acted with the intention to treat the information as secret; the information is capable of industrial or commercial application; and the possessor has an interest worthy of legal protection.

Merck Frosst Canada Ltd. v. Canada (Health), 2012 SCC 3.

TRADE UNION "[A]n organization of employees formed for purposes that include the regulation of relations between employees and employers and includes a provincial, national, or international trade union, a certified council of trade unions and a designated or certified employee bargaining agency." *Labour Relations Act, 1995*, S.O. 1995, c. 1, Sch. A, s. 1(1). See similar provincial statutes and *Canada Labour Code*, R.S.C. 1985, c. L–2.

TRADING WITH THE ENEMY Entering into contractual relations with any person or company carrying on business in a hostile country. At common law, such contracts were considered void and unenforceable, even when they were "entered into prior to the commencement of hostilities." H.G. Beale, ed., 1 *Chitty on Contracts* 1104–5 (30th ed. 2008). See *The Bayer Company Limited v. Farbenfabriken vorm Fried. Bayer and Co. et al.*, [1944] O.R. 305 (Ont. H.C.J.).

TRAFFIC In criminal law, it means the sale and distribution of illegal material, notably narcotics. Under the *Controlled Drugs and Substances Act*, S.C. 1996, c. 19, s. 2(1), it "means, in respect of a substance included in any of Schedules I to IV, (a) to sell, administer, give, transfer, transport, send or deliver the substance, (b) to sell an authorization to obtain the substance, or (c) to offer to do anything mentioned in paragraph (a) or (b), otherwise than under the authority of the regulations."

TRANSCRIPT A copy or anything written from an original. It is most commonly used to refer to the official written record of the proceedings of a **court**, **administrative tribunal**, or pretrial procedure, such as **discovery**.

TRANSFER "The 'transfer of possession' is the act of the person who has the control or possession of the object and then tries to pass it on to another." *R. v. Daoust*, 2004 SCC 6.

"As a verb, [transfer] means 'to make over the legal **title** or ownership of to another.' As a noun, it means the making over of such title or ownership." *Re Gill Lumber Ltd. and United Bro. of Carpenters* (1973), 42 D.L.R. (3d) 271 at 274 (N.B.S.C.A.D.).

TRANSFEREE The person to whom something is **transferred**.

TRANSFEROR The person who **transfers**.

TRANSFERRED INTENT A concept in **tort** law that states that if defendant intends harm to A but harms B instead, the intent is said to be transferred to the harm befalling the actual victim, as far as defendant's liability to B in tort is concerned. This is only a "fiction," or a legal conclusion, created in order to accomplish the desired result in terms of liability.

TRAVERSE A **common-law pleading** that denies the opposing party's **allegations** of fact. See **denial**.

GENERAL TRAVERSE A blanket denial, stated in general terms, intended to cover all the allegations.

SPECIAL TRAVERSE A denial that is not absolute, but that seeks to establish a denial through the presentation of supplementary facts that, if accurate, would render the allegations untenable. See **absque hoc**; **confession and avoidance**.

TREASON An **indictable offence** against the Queen's authority or person punishable by fourteen years' imprisonment or, for high treason, by life imprisonment. See *Criminal Code,* R.S.C. 1985, c. C–46, ss. 46–48.

Treason includes acts such as (*a*) use of force against a government; (*b*) communication of prejudicial information to a foreign state; (*c*) conspiracy to commit high treason or (*a*) above; (*d*) forms and overtly manifests an intention to commit high treason or (*a*) or (*b*) above.

HIGH TREASON (*a*) Killing or harming or attempting to kill Her Majesty; (*b*) levying war against Canada or so preparing; or (*c*) assisting an enemy of Canada.

TREASURE TROVE A "treasure trove consists of cached gold and silver in coin, bullion, or manufactured form, the ownership of which is unknown." B. Ziff, *Principles of Property Law* 153 (5th ed. 2010). In England, when a treasure trove is discovered, ownership in it vests with the Crown. This is likely also the case in Canada at common law. *Id.* See *Ontario v. Mar-Dive Corp.* (1996) 141 D.L.R. (4th) 477 (Ont. Gen. Div.) at para. 42.

TREATY An agreement made between two or more independent states that intend to be bound at **international law** by its provisions. J.H. Currie, *Public International Law* 127–33 (2nd ed. 2008). Treaties "may take the form of reciprocal undertakings between as few as two states ('bilateral' treaties), or more generalized agreements adhered to by several or even, on occasion, most states in the world ('multilateral' treaties). Their subject matter ranges from very specific undertaking and performance agreements between states—akin to domestic law contracts, and therefore sometimes called 'treaty contracts'—to broad codifications or restatements of certain substantive areas of international law." *Id* at 123.

"Other words used as a synonym for treaties, or for particular types of treaty, are agreement, pact, protocol, charter, statute, act, covenant, declaration, engagement, arrangement, accord, regulations, [and] provisions. Some of these words have alternative meanings (that is, they can also mean something other than treaties), which makes the problem of terminology even more confusing." P. Malanczuk, *Akehurst's Modern Introduction to International Law* 36 (7th ed. 1997). See also Currie, *supra* at 125.

TREATY INDIAN Informally, a term used to describe a person who is registered as an Indian under the *Indian Act*, R.S.C. 1985, c. I–5. The term is not used in the *Indian Act*. See *Native Council of Nova Scotia v. Canada (Attorney-General),* 2011 FC 72.

TREBLE DAMAGES See **damages** [DOUBLE DAMAGES].

TRESPASS 1. A **form of action** instituted to recover **damages** for any unlawful injury to the plaintiff's person, property or rights, involving immediate force or violence. **2.** Also used to signify the act itself that causes such injury. **3.** In modern usage the term most often connotes a wrongful interference with or disturbance of the possession of another and is applied to **personalty** as well as to **realty**.

CONTINUING TRESPASS An invasion of another's rights that is of a more than temporary nature, e.g., the erection of a structure or dumping of rubbish on another's land.

TRESPASS ON THE CASE One of the two early English actions at common law dealing with **torts** (the other being simply trespass). Trespass on the case, or simply "case," afforded remedy against injury to person or property indirectly resulting from the conduct of the defendant. The action of trespass covered only directly resulting injury. "The classic illustration of the difference between trespass and case is that of a log thrown into the highway. A person struck by the log as it fell could maintain trespass against the thrower, since injury was direct; but one who was hurt by stumbling over it as it lay in the road could maintain, not trespass, but an action on the case." W.P. Keeton, *Prosser and Keeton on Torts* 29 (5th ed. 1984).

TRESPASS QUARE CLAUSUM FREGIT (*kwä'-rā klau'-zūm frā'-gĭt*) Lat.: wherefore he broke the **close**. An early form of trespass to **land**; "consists merely of personal entry by the defendant, or by some other person through his procurement, into land or buildings occupied by another, and is actionable **per se** without any proof of damage. *Sorlie v. McKee,* [1927] 1 D.L.R. 249 at 258 (Sask.C.A.).

TRESPASS VI ET ARMIS (*vē ĕt 'är'-mĭs*) **1.** Trespass with force and arms, or by an unlawful means; **2.** a remedy for injuries accompanied with force or violence, or where the act done is in itself an immediate injury to another person or property.

TRIAL "[T]he examination of a **cause**, civil or **criminal**, before a Judge who has jurisdiction over it, according to the laws of the land." *Dunlup v. Haney* (1899), 7

B.C.R. 300 at 302 (B.C. S.C.), quoted in *Dalby v. Rothon,* 2007 BCSC 310.

"A trial is where the Judge (with the assistance of a jury) has to decide which of two parties is entitled to succeed." *Dunlop v. Haney* (1899), 7 B.C.R. 300 at 302.

TRIAL DE NOVO (*dē nō'-vo*) "Strictly ... a new trial before another tribunal than that which held the first trial, as distinguished from a rehearing before the same tribunal." *R. v. Rice,* [1930] 3 D.L.R. 911 at 914 (N.S.S.C.).

TRIBUNAL An officer or body having authority to **adjudicate** judicial or **quasi-**judicial matters. See also **forum**.

TRIER OF FACT In a judicial or administrative proceeding, the person or persons responsible for determining the relevant facts. In a jury trial, the jury acts as the trier of fact while the judge is the TRIER OF LAW. In a trial by judge alone, the judge is the trier of both fact and law. In administrative proceedings, the official or officials conducting the hearing will play both roles.

TRIPS AGREEMENT The *Agreement on Trade-Related Aspects of Intellectual Property Rights, Including Trade in Counterfeit Goods,* administered by the World Trade Organization and requiring signatories to provide protection for **intellectual property** rights. Canada became a signatory to TRIPS on January 1, 1995.

TROVER An early common-law **tort action** to recover **damages** for a wrongful **conversion** of **personal property** or to recover actual **possession** of such property. Originally, the action was limited to cases in which lost property had been found and converted by the finder to his or her own use. Later the action was expanded to include property not actually lost and found, but only wrongfully converted. At first, a fiction was created (when the facts revealed otherwise) that such property had been lost and found, but since the distinction was later abandoned, the use of such a fiction became unnecessary. Compare **detinue**; **replevin**; **trespass**; **detainer**.

TRUST A right of **property** held by one party for the benefit of another. It implies two interests, one legal and the other **equitable**; the **trustee** holding the legal title or interest, and the CESTUI QUE TRUST, or **beneficiary**, holding the equitable title or interest. See **PPSA**.

"The one thing necessary to give validity to a declaration of trust [is] that the donor, or grantor ... should have absolutely parted with that interest which had been his up to the time of the declaration, having effectually changed his right in that respect and put the property out of his power, at least in the way of interest." *In re Garden Estate,* [1931] 2 W.W.R. 849 at 857 (Alta.S.C.).

ALTER EGO TRUST An **inter vivos** trust permitted as an estate planning tool under the *Income Tax Act*, R.S.C. 1985, c. 1 (5th Supp). "Provided the settlor is age 65 or older, he or she may 'roll' assets to a trust that is for his or her sole benefit during his or her lifetime and then for the benefit of his or her chosen beneficiaries." *Mawdsley v. Meshen*, 2012 BCCA 91.

CESTUI QUE TRUST (*sĕ'-tĭ kŭ*) Old Fr.: one for whose benefit the trust is created; a beneficiary.

CONSTRUCTIVE TRUST (REMEDIAL TRUST) A trust that is imposed upon parties, independent of any express agreement, in order to prevent one party from being **unjustly enriched** by the contributions of the other. "Imposed without reference to intention to create a trust, the constructive trust is a broad and flexible equitable tool used to determine beneficial entitlement to property...Where the plaintiff can demonstrate a link or causal connection between his or her contributions and the acquisition, preservation, maintenance, or improvement of the disputed property, a share of the property proportionate to the unjust enrichment can be impressed with a constructive trust in his or her favour." *Kerr v. Baranow*, 2011 SCC 10. Contrast RESULTING TRUST [following].

EXPRESS TRUST A trust created by the free and deliberate acts of the parties, including an affirmative intention of the **settlor** (the one granting the property) to set up the trust, usu-

ally evidenced by some writing, **deed** or **will**. Trusts are generally classified as either express or implied, the latter class including RESULTING TRUSTS and CONSTRUCTIVE TRUSTS. A valid express trust requires the cooperation of three parties: the settlor, the **trustee**, and the beneficiary.

HENSEN TRUST A trust in which the trustee has absolute discretion over whether and how the funds will be used on behalf of the beneficiary. Because the assets in the trust are not vested in the beneficiary, the beneficiary is not disqualified from government benefits programs that have a means test. A Henson Trust is typically used for the benefit of disabled persons. See *Ontario (Ministry of Community and Social Services, Income Maintenance Branch) v. Henson* (Ont. C.A.), [1989] O.J. No. 2093.

PRECATORY TRUST "[A] trust established by precatory words, such as expressions of confidence, request or desire that property will or shall be applied for the benefit of a definite person or object, where these words are construed in **equity** as imperatively constituting a trust." 38 *Halsbury's Laws of England* (3d ed.) para. 1372.

RESULTING TRUST A trust arising by implication of law when it appears from the nature of the transaction that it was the intention of the **parties** to create a trust. It is therefore to be distinguished from a constructive trust in that it arises automatically out of certain circumstances by **operation of law**, while a constructive trust is a **remedy** that **equity** applied in order to prevent injustice or in order to do justice. Thus a resulting trust involves the element of **intent**, which though implied, makes it more like an EXPRESS TRUST. A constructive trust, in contrast, is sometimes found contrary to the parties' intent, in order to work equity or frustrate **fraud**.

"A resulting trust arises when title to property is in one party's name, but that party, because he or she is a fiduciary or gave no value for the property, is under an obligation to return it to the original title owner." *Pecore v. Pecore*, 2007 SCC 17.

TRUSTEE DE SON TORT A person who is not a trustee but who comes into control of trust property and acts inconsistently with the terms of the trust, despite knowing of its existence. It is a form of **constructive trust** but is narrower, since not every constructive trust requires that the person have control over trust property.

TRUSTEE 1. One who holds legal **title** to **property** in **trust** for the benefit of another person, and who is required to carry out specific duties with regard to the property, or who has been given power affecting the disposition of property for another's benefit. **2.** Also used loosely as anyone who acts as a **guardian** or **fiduciary** in relationship to another, such as a **public officer** towards his constituents or a partner to his co-partner. See **use**. Compare **settlor**. Includes **executor** and **administrator**.

TRUSTEE IN BANKRUPTCY One appointed to hold in **trust** for a **bankrupt** in accordance with the *Bankruptcy and Insolvency Act,* R.S.C. 1985, c. B–3, ss. 13–41. He or she takes legal **title** to the property and/or money for equitable distributon among the bankrupt's **creditors**.

TRUST FUND Real or **personal property** held in **trust** for the benefit of another person; the corpus [**res**] of a trust.

TRUSTOR One who creates a **trust**; usually called the **settlor**.

TRUTH AND RECONCILIATION COMMISSION A commission established by the Federal government in 2008 to learn the truth about what happened in **Indian Residential Schools** and to inform all Canadians about those events. Under the terms of its mandate, "[T]here is an emerging and compelling desire to put the events of the past behind us so that we can work towards a stronger and healthier future. The truth telling and reconciliation process, as part of an overall holistic and comprehensive response to the Indian Residential School legacy, is a sincere indication and acknowledgement of the injustices and harms experienced by Aboriginal people and the need for continued healing. This is a profound commitment to establishing new relationships embedded in mutual recognition and respect that will forge a brighter future. The truth of our common experiences will help set our spirits free and pave the way to reconciliation." The Commission is holding hearings across the country to give survivors of the Indian Residential Schools the opportunity to tell their stories and is holding national events to provide education about the history of the Schools. Ultimately, the Commission will prepare a complete historical record concerning the residential schools, make recommendations, and establish a national research centre. See **Indian Residential Schools Settlement Agreement**.

TRY TITLE To submit to judicial scrutiny the legitimacy of **title** to property. See also **quiet title**.

TWO-HUNDRED-MILE LIMIT An exclusive fishing zone of 200 nautical miles that was declared by Canada in 1977 after multilateral negotiations and is aimed at preventing the decline of fish stocks off Canada's shores. Although at the time the claim of jurisdiction was an expansion beyond the traditionally recognized 12-mile limit, a 200-mile **exclusive economic zone** for coastal states that extends to more than just fishing rights has since been recognized generally; see **UNCLOS III**. The phrase is still sometimes used colloquially but inaccurately to refer to the exclusive economic zone.

TWO-ROW WAMPUM A representation of the first treaty made between the Haudenosaunee (Mohawk) peoples and the first Europeans in North America. The two-row wampum is a belt of white beads, with two rows of purple. The purple rows represent the Haudenosaunee and European peoples, travelling paths down the same river together but separately. The beads separating the purple rows represent peace, friendship, and respect. The wampum represents that each of the two people remain sovereigns of their own destiny. See *Mitchell v. M.N.R.*, 2001 SCC 33.

UBERRIMA FIDES (*ū-bûr-ē'-mā fē'-dāz*) Lat.: of the utmost good faith. A term used to describe a certain class of contract where the promisee is under a duty to make known to the promisor every fact that would affect his or her decision to enter into the contract. Insurance contracts fall into this class of contract; the person applying for insurance is under a duty to disclose all relevant information to the insurer.

ULTERIOR INTENTION See **motive**.

ULTRAHAZARDOUS ACTIVITY An uncommon activity giving rise to **strict liability**, which necessarily involves risk of serious harm to the person, land or **chattels** of others and which cannot be eliminated by the exercise of utmost care. For example, blasting is universally recognised as an ultrahazardous activity. It should be noted that strict liability in this context means the duty owed cannot be delegated; e.g., an owner of property who hires an independent **contractor** to perform blasting cannot escape **liability** for damage resulting from the blasting operation.

ULTRA VIRES (*ŭl'-tr à vī'-rāz*) Lat.: beyond, outside of, in excess of powers; that which is beyond the power authorized by law for an entity. The term applies, for example, to an action of a **corporation** that is beyond the powers conferred upon it by its charter, or by the **statute** under which it was created. See *Communities Economic Development Fund v. Canadian Pickles Corp.*, [1991] 3 S.C.R. 388.

The doctrine of *ultra vires* is also enshrined in the Canadian constitutional system. Under the doctrine, "the *B.N.A. Act* possessed a supremacy over all statutes enacted by the **Parliament** of Canada and by the legislatures of the ten provinces. The result of this was that any Act passed by Parliament or a legislature had to conform to the jurisdictional constraints set out in ss. 91 and 92 of the *B.N.A. Act.*" G. Gall, *The Canadian Legal System* 68 (5th ed. 2004). This doctrine continues in the **Constitution Act, 1867**. See **division of powers**.

In the field of **administrative law**, an administrative tribunal may only enact rules or make decisions within the bounds of the authority granted to it by its governing statute." Action taken outside of its legal jurisdiction could be declared *ultra vires* by a court of law. *Id.* at 358.

UMPIRE 1. A third party chosen to make a decision in a labour dispute when the **arbitrators** have failed to reach an agreement. **2.** The Supreme Court of Canada is often referred to as the *ultimate umpire* of the constitution in resolving disputes over the **division of powers** between the federal and provincial governments. See, e.g., *Québec (Procureure générale) v. Canada (Procureure générale)*, 2011 QCCA 591.

UNA VOCE (*un à vōkĕ*) Lat.: with one voice; unanimously.

UNANIMITY A state in which all parties involved in a matter are in agreement.

UNANIMOUS SHAREHOLDERS AGREEMENT An agreement between all the **shareholders** of a **corporation** "that restricts, in whole or in part, the powers of the **directors** to manage, or supervise the management of, the business and affairs of the corporation." *Canadian Business Corporations Act*, R.S.C. 1985, c. C–44, s. 146(1). Since unanimous shareholders agreements by definition require the consent of all of a company's shareholders, they are only practically feasible in small, closely held corporations.

UNCLEAN HANDS One of the equitable maxims embodying the principle that a party seeking equitable **relief** must not have done any dishonest or unethical act in the transaction upon which he or she maintains an action in **equity**; a court of conscience will not grant relief to one guilty of **unconscionable** conduct. Compare **clean hands**.

UNCLOS III The United Nations Convention on the Law of the Sea. Concluded in 1982, it arose from the third United Nations Conference discussing the Law of the Sea; the Convention came into force in 1994 once sixty countries had ratified it. Canada ratified the Convention in 2003. The Convention establishes six maritime zones, all of which are measured relative to the baseline, which approximately corresponds to the low water mark of a **state's** coastline. A state's internal waters consist of all waters landward of the baseline, and, subject to minor exceptions, states have full sovereignty over them. The Territorial Sea is the area out to 12 nautical miles from the baseline, and states have sovereignty over the airspace, seabed, and subsoil of that region. Other states enjoy the right of innocent passage through the Territorial Sea provided they respect conditions arising out of international norms. The contiguous zone is the area from 12 to 24 nautical miles; it is a buffer zone within which a state may act to prevent infringement of laws governing its territory or territorial sea, such as customs, immigration or environmental laws. The Exclusive Economic Zone (referred to as the EEZ) extends from 12 to 200 nautical miles; states have jurisdiction over exploration, scientific research, protection of the marine environment and economic exploitation of the resources in the water and in or below the seabed within their EEZ. However, other states have rights to navigate through or fly over an EEZ. The Continental Shelf presumptively extends from 12 to 200 nautical miles, but under a complex formula in article 76 of the Convention requiring scientific evidence about the thickness of sedimentary rocks in the area, a state can make a claim that the natural extension of its land territory to the outer edge of the continental margin extends further. Finally, the High Seas is the area beyond any state's EEZ, and the Convention specifically provides that no state can claim sovereignty over any of that area. These zones are generally regarded as now being part of **customary international law**, and, therefore, appropriate jurisdiction over them can be exercised even by states that are not signatories to the Convention. In addition, the Convention contains the "Arctic Clause," which gives Canada, among other nations, the ability to act to prevent, reduce, or control marine pollution from vessels in ice-covered areas within the EEZ.

UNCONSCIONABLE In **contract** law, terms so unreasonable to the interest of a contracting party as to render the contract unenforceable.

"However one articulates the test for unconscionability, I am satisfied that it involves more than a finding of inequality of bargaining power between the parties to a contract. Both the test adopted by the application judge in *Eckstein* and the test in *Harry* of the British Columbia Court of Appeal recognize that a determination of unconscionability involves a two-part analysis—a finding of inequality of bargaining power and a finding that the terms of an agreement have a high degree of unfairness." *Birch v. Union of Taxation Employees, Local 70030* (2008), 93 O.R. (3d) 1 (C.A.).

UNCONSTITUTIONAL Any law that violates or is inconsistent with the Constitution of Canada. Section 52 of the *Constitution Act, 1982*, states that, "the Constitution of Canada is the supreme law of Canada, and any law that is inconsistent with the provisions of the Constitution is, to the extent of the inconsistency, of no force or effect." See **ultra vires**.

UNDERLEASE See **sublease**.

UNDERTAKING 1. In **litigation**, a promise given by one party to another party to the lawsuit in exchange for obtaining something from that party. For example, one party discloses information to the other, in exchange for the undertaking that the information will not be used for any purpose but the litigation at hand. *Kitchenham v. Axa Insurance Canada*, 2008 ONCA 877. **2.** In **criminal** law, a written promise to appear in court and to comply with conditions until that time, given to a police officer or a judge as a condition of being released. *Criminal Code*, R.S.C. 1985, c. C–46, Forms 11.1, 12.

UNDERWRITE To ensure the satisfaction of an obligation, such as an **insurance** contract or the sale of **bonds**. To underwrite an insurance contract is to act as **insurer** for the life or property of another.

To underwrite a **stock** or bond issue is to ensure the sale of stocks or bonds by agreeing that if they are not all taken up by the public, the underwriter will take what remains. See *Montreal Trust Co. v. Richardson,* [1922] 1 W.W.R. 548 (S.C.C.).

UNDISCLOSED PRINCIPAL See **principal**.

UNDIVIDED INTEREST [UNDIVIDED RIGHTS] That interest or right in **property** owned by TENANTS IN COMMON (see **tenancy)** or **joint tenants** whereby each tenant has an equal right to make use of and enjoy the entire property.

An undivided interest derives from UNITY OF POSSESSION (see **unities)**, which is essential to the above tenancies. Undivided interests in property are to be distinguished from interests that have been **partitioned**, i.e., divided and distributed to the different owners for their use in **severalty**.

An undivided interest may be of only a fractional share, e.g., "an undivided one quarter interest," in which case the holder is entitled to one quarter of all profits and sale proceeds but has a right to possession of the whole.

UNDUE HARDSHIP The limiting point beyond which an employer no longer has a **duty to accommodate** difference in order to avoid **discrimination** under s. 15 of the **Charter** or **human rights legislation**. Relevant considerations include the financial cost of accommodation, the relative interchangeability of the workforce and facilities, and the prospect of substantial interference with the rights of other employees. *Central Alberta Dairy Pool v. Alberta (Human Rights Commission),* [1990] 2 S.C.R. 489. See **bona fide occupational requirement**.

UNDUE INFLUENCE 1. Influence of another that destroys the requisite free agency of a **testator** or **donor** and creates a ground for nullifying a **will** or invalidating an improvident **gift**. "To be undue influence in the eye of the law there must be ... coercion. It must not be a case in which a person has been induced by means such as I have suggested to you to come to a conclusion that he or she will make a will in a particular person's favour, because if the testator has only been persuaded or induced by considerations which you may condemn, really and truly to intend to give his property to another, though you may disapprove of the act, yet it is strictly legitimate in the sense of its being legal. It is only when the will of the person who becomes a testator is coerced into doing that which he or she does not desire to do, that it is undue influence." *Wingrove v. Wingrove* (1885), 11 P. 81 at 82. See also *Neyedley v. Neyedley,* 2004 SKQB 246; *Pollard Estate v. Falconer,* 2008 BCSC 516.

2. Also, influence of another that impedes, prevents or otherwise interferes with the free exercise of the franchise of any voter. *Re MacDonald Election* (1923), 23 Man.R. 542 (C.A.). Compare **duress**.

UNEQUIVOCALLY 1. Clearly; absolutely **2.** In criminal law, it means "beyond reasonable doubt." *R. v. Bolianatz* (1987), 20 B.C.L.R. (2d) 304 at 308 (C.A.).

UNEXECUTED USE See **use**.

UNFAIR ADVANTAGE See **undue influence**.

UNFAIR LABOUR PRACTICE Behaviour by an employer or a **trade union** that violates certain statutory obligations. For example, under the *Public Service Labour Relations Act,* S.C. 2003, c. 22, ss. 186–187, an employer cannot interfere with the formation of an employee organization, and an employee organization cannot act in bad faith in the representation of any employee in the **bargaining unit**.

UNFIT TO STAND TRIAL It "means unable on account of **mental disorder** to conduct a defence at any stage of the proceedings before a verdict is rendered or to instruct counsel to do so, and, in particular, unable on account of mental disorder to (*a*) understand the nature or object of the proceedings, (*b*) understand the possible consequences of the proceedings, or (c) communicate with counsel." *Criminal Code*, R.S.C. 1985, c. C–46, s. 2. See *id.*, ss. 672.22–33. See also **competent**.

UNFORESEEABLE PLAINTIFF A person to whom no **duty of care** is owed. In **negligence** law, a defendant does not owe a duty of care to those persons beyond the foreseeable range of danger. *Lamarche v. Grebenjak*, 2010 ONSC 2316.

See **proximity; neighbour principle**.

UNIFIED FAMILY COURTS Unified family courts, found in several provinces, permit all aspects of **family law** to be dealt with in a single court with specialized judges and services. The unified family courts consist of **superior court judges**, who hear matters of both provincial and federal jurisdiction. These courts encourage the use of constructive, non-adversarial techniques to resolve issues, and provide access to a range of support services, often through community organizations. These services differ from province to province but typically include such programs as parent-education sessions, mediation, and counselling.

UNIFORM LAW CONFERENCE OF CANADA An annual conference to which the federal government and participating provincial and territorial governments send delegates. The Criminal Section of the Conference makes recommendations to the Federal government for changes to the **criminal** law. The Civil Section aims at producing uniform statutes for areas of law within provincial jurisdiction, which are recommended for enactment by the relevant governments. Under its constitution, the mandate of the Conference is "to facilitate and promote the harmonization of laws throughout Canada by developing, at the request of the constituent jurisdictions, Uniform Acts, Model Acts, Statements of Legal Principles, and other documents deemed appropriate to meet the demands that are presented to it by the constituent jurisdictions from time to time."

UNILATERAL CONTRACT "A contract [that] results from an act made in response to an **offer**, as, for example, in the simplest terms, 'I will pay you a dollar if you will cut my lawn.' No obligation to cut the lawn exists in law, and the obligation to pay the dollar comes into being upon the performance of the invited act." *R. (Ont.) v. Ron Engineering*, [1981] 1 S.C.R. 111.

UNILATERAL MISTAKE See **mistake**.

UNION See **trade union**.

UNION SECURITY CLAUSE A provision in a **collective bargaining agreement** requiring membership in or payments to the **union** as a condition of employment. There are five basic types of union security clause, which range from more to less restrictive. A "closed shop" clause requires all prospective hirees to become union members as a prerequisite to employment. A "union shop" clause requires all current employees to join the union in order to keep their jobs. A "maintenance of membership" clause requires all employees hired after the negotiation of the agreement to join the union but allows other employees to opt out of joining the union. An "agency shop" clause (or "Rand formula") does not compel employees to join the union but requires regular payments to the union in lieu of union dues. Finally, a "voluntary check-off" clause does not require employees to join the union but allows them to opt-in to making payments to the union in lieu of union dues. Union security clauses are typically protected by federal and provincial labour legislation. See, e.g., *Canada Labour Code*, R.S.C. 1985, c. L–2, s. 68; *Trade Union Act*, R.S.N.S. 1989, c. 475, s. 59; *Labour Relations Code*, R.S.B.C. 1996, c. 244, s. 15(1). In addition, several types of union security clauses have survived constitutional challenges under ss. 2(*b*) and 2(*d*) of the *Charter*. See, e.g., *Lavigne v. Ontario Public Service Employees Union*, [1991] 2 S.C.R. 211; *R. v. Advance Cutting & Coring Ltd.*, 2001 SCC 70.

UNITIES The **common-law** requirements necessary to create a **joint tenancy**, or a TENANCY BY THE ENTIRETY (see **tenancy**). A joint tenancy requires the FOUR UNITIES of **interest, possession**, time, and title, and, in addition, a tenancy by the entirety requires unity of person. See A.M. Sinclair & M.E. McCallum, *An Introduction to Real Property Law* 113–15 (6th ed. 2012).

UNITY OF INTEREST The requirement that interests of the co-tenants in a joint tenancy be equal. An individual joint tenant cannot encumber his or her share by **mortgage** without destroying this unity; to preserve the joint tenancy the mortgage must be agreed to by all. Tenants in common are not subject to this unity of interest rule and may have unequal shares in the same property. See **tenancy** [TENANCY IN COMMON].

UNITY OF PERSON The common law requirement for the creation of a tenancy by the entirety that the co-tenants be husband and wife, based on the conception that marriage created a unity of person. "Upon the passage of statutes in all jurisdictions effectively making a married woman, at law, a *femme sole,* the doctrine of tenancy by the entirety had to disappear, for the fifth unity, from a property viewpoint, had gone. While there are one or two cases to the contrary outstanding in Canada, it would appear only correct to say that a conveyance in this country today to A and B will create a tenancy in common in them; whether A and B are husband and wife will be immaterial for this determination. Modern legislation concerning matrimonial property, referred to earlier, will have greater control in the future as well." *Id.* at 114.

UNITY OF POSSESSION The requirement that "each of the co-owners must have the same estate in land, each must have an equal share in that estate, and each must have the same quality of estate." *Id.* at 113. If a joint tenant encumbers his or her share with a mortgage, goes bankrupt or sells his or her share, the joint tenancy is considered severed as their estates are different, and they then hold as tenants in common.

Unity of possession is necessary for each of the types of co-tenancies. See **undivided interest**.

UNITY OF TIME The requirement that the interests of the co-tenants in a joint tenancy must commence (or **vest)** at the same moment in time.

UNITY OF TITLE The requirement that all tenants of a joint tenancy acquire their interests under the same **title**; thus such co-tenants cannot hold by different **deeds**.

UNIVERSAL AGENT One authorized to transact all the business of his or her **principal**. See **agent**.

UNIVERSAL JURISDICTION A principle of international law that "*any* state can expand its **prescriptive jurisdiction** to cover certain criminal acts, even without any **territorial, nationality**, or **protective**-type links between the state and the accused or her conduct." R. Currie, *International & Transnational Criminal Law* 71 (2010). See **nationality principle; passive personality principle; protective principle; territorial principle**.

UNIVERSAL LEGACY The whole of the testator's estate. "[I]n the use of [the term *universal legacy*] the testator was referring to the whole residue of his estate, real and personal, after payment of his debts and funeral expenses." *Yost, Re,* [1927] 1 W.W.R. 925 at 926 (Alta.C.A.).

UNJUST ENRICHMENT The modern designation for the older doctrine of QUASI-CONTRACTS (see **quasi**), which are not true contracts, but are obligations created by the law when money, **property** or services have been obtained by one person at the expense of another under such circumstances that in **equity** and good conscience he or she ought not to retain it. See *Kerr v. Baranow*, 2011 SCC 10.

See also **quantum meruit; restitution**.

UNLAWFUL ACT 1. An act that is not authorized or justified by law; illegal **2.** "There appear to be three categories of actions… which sometimes fall into the description 'unlawful' or 'illegal'… (*a*) offences against statutes prohibiting defined conduct; (*b*) actions which are without legal consequence in the sense of creating enforceable rights, such as gaming contracts; and (c) actions taken by statutory bodies outside the limits of authority granted or established in the statute." *Nepean Hydro Electric Commission v. Ontario Hydro*, [1982] 1 S.C.R. 347 at 406–407. In **criminal** law, the use of the term "unlawful" varies depending on whether one is speaking of a person accused of an offence or of an action by the state. "Absent a law to the contrary, individuals are free to do as they please. By contrast, the police (and more broadly, the state) may act only to the extent that they are empowered to do so by law." *R. v. Mann*, 2004 SCC 52. Accordingly, to say that a private person has acted unlawfully is to say that he or she has done something a law said he or she could not. To say that a state actor has acted unlawfully is to say that he or she has done something in the absence of a specific law authorizing him or her to do so.

UNLAWFUL ASSEMBLY Under s. 63(1) of the *Criminal Code*, R.S.C. 1985, c. C–46, "An unlawful assembly is an assembly of three or more persons who, with intent to carry out any common purpose, assemble in such a manner or so conduct themselves when they are assembled as to cause persons in the neighbourhood of the assembly to fear, on reasonable grounds, that they (a) will disturb the peace tumultuously, or (b) will by that assembly needlessly and without reasonable cause provoke other persons to disturb the peace tumultuously."

"The provision of the Code prohibiting unlawful assemblies is for the purpose of drawing the line between a lawful meeting and an assembly, either unlawful in its inception, or which is deemed to have become unlawful either by reason of the action of those assembled, or by reason of the improper action of others having no sympathy with the objects of the meeting." *Rex v. Patterson*, [1931] 3 D.L.R. 267 at 274 (Ont.A.D.).

"It will be seen that to constitute the offence there need be no intention on the part of any member of the assembly to commit an offence but it is the manner in which the assembly conducts itself that brings it within the purview of the section." *Rex v. Jones and Sheinin*, [1931] 3 W.W.R. 716 at 720 (Alta.S.C.A.D.).

UNLAWFUL DETAINER The act of holding **possession** without right, as in the case of a tenant whose lease has expired. See **forcible detainer**; **tenancy** [TENANCY AT SUFFERANCE].

UNNATURAL ACT [OFFENCE] See **crime against nature**.

UNREASONABLE VERDICT A verdict that a properly instructed **jury**, acting judicially, could not have rendered. This standard will be met in the case of a jury when the verdict cannot be supported on the evidence and also, in the case of a trial by judge alone, when the reasons are illogical or irrational, even if the verdict could be supported on the evidence. *R. v. Sinclair*, 2011 SCC 40.

UNREPORTED DECISION A **judgment** that is not published in any **case reporter**. Unreported decisions have gained more influence in recent years as a result of the increasing availability of electronic databases of judicial and administrative decisions, which often include cases that are not otherwise reported in print. See **Quicklaw**.

UNWRITTEN CONSTITUTIONAL PRINCIPLES Principles of Canada's constitutional order that are not codified in any constitutional document. Examples of unwritten constitutional principles include democracy, the **rule of law**, **federalism**, **responsible government**, and **judicial independence**. Unwritten constitutional principles have been treated as binding in numerous cases. See, e.g., *Reference re Remuneration of Judges*, [1997] 3 S.C.R. 3; *Reference re Secession of Quebec*, [1998] 25 S.C.R. 17. See further P.W. Hogg, *Constitutional Law of Canada* 15–51–15–56 (5th ed. 2007).

USAGE 1. A rule or practice that is usually observed by government but not regarded as obligatory. However, if the rule or practice is observed long enough it may stop being a usage and become a convention. P.W. Hogg, *Constitutional Law of Canada* 1–25–27 (5th ed. 2007).

2. A practice that is well known and universally accepted in a given trade, business, or profession. In some situations, a usage may be incorporated into the terms of a contract. See G.H.L. Fridman, *The Law of Contract in Canada* 512–13 (6th ed. 2011).

USE The right to enjoy the benefits flowing from **real** or **personal property**.

Uses, historically, have been created (1) by express provision in a valid **deed**; (2) by implication to the conveyor when **conveyance** is made without **consideration** (called a RESULTING USE); (3) by bargain and sale; (4) by covenant to stand **seised**. Under the **Statute of Uses**, the party in whom a use was created was deemed seised of a like **estate** as he had in the use; hence "A to B for the use of C for life" was operative under the statute to convey to C a life estate. It should be noted that not all uses were converted under the Statute to legal interests or estates. The Statute applied to PASSIVE USES, i.e., instances where the legal titleholder had no obligations with respect to the estate other than to hold title. Thus A to B for the use of C created a passive use that the Statute converted into a legal estate in C. Those not so converted, classified as UNEXECUTED USES, were a use raised on a non-**freehold estate**, i.e., a **tenancy**, "A to B for 10 years for the use of C"; a USE ON A USE, "A to B for the use of C for life, then to the use of D"; and ACTIVE USES, which constitute the modern **trusts**, i.e., where a person holds legal title but unlike in passive use the legal titleholder has duties and obligations to perform in connection with his or her holding. Thus A to B to invest for the benefit of C creates an active use, and legal title does not merge with C's use. See E.H. Burn, *Cheshire and Burn's Modern Law of Real Property* 49–54 (16th ed. 2000); B. Ziff, *Principles of Property Law* 217–24 (5th ed. 2010).

An important effect of the *Statute of Uses* was the validation of EXECUTORY INTERESTS (see **interest**), a species of **future interests** that had heretofore been recognized only in equity. Two kinds of executory interests so converted into legal estates were the springing and shifting uses. A SHIFTING USE is a use that arises in derogation of another, i.e., shifts from one beneficiary to another, depending on some future **contingency**. A SPRINGING USE is a use that arises upon the occurrence of a future event and that does not take effect in derogation of any interest other than that which results to the grantor, or remains to him or her in the meantime. Thus, A to B and his heirs to the use of C and his heirs beginning at some future date creates a legal estate in B, a resulting use for the interim period in A, and a springing use in C when his or her interest comes into effect. If A conveys property to B for the use of C unless a contingency occurs in which case D should have the use, C obtains an equitable estate but if the contingency occurs then the equitable estate shifts to D, who has a shifting use. "A shifting use is one which cuts short a prior use estate in a person other than the conveyor; a springing use is one which cuts short a use estate in the conveyor." *Id.* at 178.

The term *use* has frequently arisen in the matter of construction of **wills** where, for example, a **testator** gave his widow a **life estate** in his **residue** directing his trustees to "allow her to 'use' so much of it as she may wish during her lifetime."

USUFRUCT A right originating in the **civil law** to use and enjoy, independent of ownership, certain advantages, benefits or profits attached to land, produced by, or incidental to it. For example, "The proprietor of **riparian** lands has a right incident to the land, independent of the ownership of the solum of the stream or river, to the flow of water through or by his land in its natural state, and if the stream is polluted or otherwise interfered with, so as to affect this right, by an upper riparian proprietor, the lower riparian proprietor who has suffered damage in law, though not in fact, may maintain an action for an injunction unless the person causing the interference with his right has a prescriptive right to do so." *McKie v. The K.V.P. Co. Ltd.,* [1948] 3 D.L.R. 201 at 209 (Ont.H.C.). Other examples of usufructuary rights include such things as the right to light, air, and water. It has been suggested that **Aboriginal title** can be understood in part as a kind of usufructary right. See the reasons of LeBel J. in *R. v. Marshall; R. v. Bernard,* 2005 SCC 43.

USURY An unconscionable or exorbitant rate of **interest**; an excessive and illegal requirement of compensation for **forbearance** on a **debt**. Charging interest at a rate of over sixty percent per annum is a criminal **offence** punishable by up to five years imprisonment. *Criminal Code*, R.S.C. 1985, c. C–46, s. 347.

UTTER To put forth; to execute; to offer a forged instrument with representations by words or acts, directly or indirectly, that the instrument is valid; defined in the *Criminal Code,* R.S.C. 1985, c. C–46, s. 448, to include "sell, pay, tender and put off." To utter **counterfeit** money or a coin that is not current are indictable offences relating to currency under ss. 452 and 453 of the *Criminal Code, id.* "The element of deception or dishonesty which, in general, the word 'utter' imports is inherent in the sale of counterfeit money to be circulated as currency since the inevitable consequence is the defrauding of the public...." *Regina v. Kelly and Lauzon* (1980), 48 C.C.C. (2d) 560 at 566 (Ont.C.A.).

UXOR [UX.] (*ŭk-sōr*) Lat.: wife; commonly abbreviated *ux. Uxorcide* is a term used to denote the killing of a wife by her husband. See **et ux**.

VACATE 1. To render **void**; to **set aside**, as "to vacate a **judgment**." See **reversal**.

2. To move out; to render vacant as in "vacating **premises**." See *Fefferman v. McCargar*, [1947] 2 W.W.R. 742 (Alta.S.C.) where an order to vacate signified the termination of the relationship of **landlord** and **tenant**.

See **abandonment**.

VAGRANCY A general term for a class of minor offences such as idleness without employment, having no visible means of support; roaming or **loitering**; wandering from place to place without any lawful purpose. Vagrancy statutes developed following the breaking of the English feudal estates. The downfall of the feudal system led to labour shortages. The *Statutes of Laborers,* 23 Edw. 3, c. 1 (1349); 25 Edw. 3, c. 1. (1350) were enacted to stabilize the working force by prohibiting increases in wages and prohibiting the movement of workers in search of improved conditions. Later, the poor laws included vagrancy provisions to prevent the movement of "wild rogues" and the "notorious brotherhood of beggars." See *Ledwith v. Roberts,* [1937] 1 K.B. 232 at 271. The *Criminal Code*, R.S.C. 1985, c. C–46, s. 179 eventually reduced the definition of vagrancy to only two things: (a) supporting oneself in whole or in part by gaming or crime and (b) having been committed of certain specified offences, being found loitering in or near a school ground, playground, public park, or bathing area. However, the Supreme Court of Canada struck down the latter provision as a violation of the **Canadian Charter of Rights and Freedoms** on the basis that it was overbroad. See *R. v. Heywood*, [1994] 3 S.C.R. 761.

VAGUENESS DOCTRINE The general principle that a law will be held to be unconstitutional if it does not give fair notice to persons of the type of conduct that is prohibited or place limitations on law enforcement discretion. The doctrine is founded on the fundamental principle of justice under s. 7 of the **Canadian Charter of Rights and Freedoms** that a law cannot be so "vague" or devoid of content that it is impossible for citizens to ascertain its meaning. "It is essential in a free and democratic society that citizens are able, as far as possible, to foresee the consequences of their conduct in order that persons be given fair notice of what to avoid, and that the discretion of those entrusted with law enforcement is limited by clear and explicit legislative standards." *Reference re ss. 193 and 195(1)(c) of the Criminal Code* (*Man.*), [1990] 1 [S.C.R.] 1123 at 1152. See also, *Canada v. Pharmaceutical Society (Nova Scotia)* (1992), 74 C.C.C. (3d) 289 (S.C.C.).

VALUABLE CONSIDERATION See **consideration**.

VANDALISM The willful destruction or defacement of public or private property.

VARIANCE 1. A lack of concordance between **allegations** contained in the **pleadings** and facts sought to be proven at trial. The court has it in its discretion, according to the desirability of doing justice to the parties, to allow amendment of the pleadings to incorporate allegation of the new fact. J. Walker & L. Sossin, *Civil Litigation* 102 (2010). See *Sullivan v. Hoppmann Bros. Ltd.,* [1968] 2 O.R. 201 (H.C.).

2. In **zoning** law it is an exemption from the application of a zoning ordinance or **regulation** permitting a use that varies from that otherwise permitted under the zoning regulation. The exception is granted by the appropriate authority in special circumstances to protect against an undue hardship wrought by strict enforcement of the zoning regulations. See **non-conforming use**.

VEL NON (*vĕl nŏn*) Lat.: or not. "The question of his being guilty, *vel non*, is for the **jury** to determine."

VENDEE Buyer; **purchaser**, especially in a **contract** for the **sale** of **realty**.

VENDOR Seller; especially person who sells **real property**. The word seller is used more often to describe a **personal property** transaction. See *R. v. Thomas Equipment Ltd.* (1979), 10 Alta.L.R. (2d) 1 (S.C.C.); *Cairns Construction Ltd. v. Government of Saskatchewan* (1960), 24 D.L.R. (2d) 1 (S.C.C.).

VENIRE (*vĕ-nē'-rā*) Lat.: to come. Refers to the common-law process by which jurors are summoned to try a case. The process of jury selection is now governed by the *Criminal Code*, R.S.C. 1985, c. C–46, but the term "venire" is sometimes used informally to refer to the **jury panel**.

VENIRE DE NOVO (*dā nō'-vō*) Lat.: to come anew. "[A] **writ** issued by the Court of King's Bench when moved by a writ of error (i.e., alleging an error appearing on the face of the record of an inferior court), vacating the verdict and directing the sheriff to summon jurors anew (whence the name of the writ). Writ of error in **criminal** cases was abolished in England by the *Criminal Appeal Act* 1907, s. 20. *Venire de novo* was and still is available in some other circumstances ... its scope is highly technical." *D. P. P. of Jamaica v. White,* [1977] 3 All E.R. 1003 at 1007 (P.C.).

VENUE A neighbourbood, a neighbouring place; sometimes synonymous with place of trial. In general, it refers to a place or area where something is done or takes place. Venue may refer to the place of trial or the place where an alleged crime is said to have been committed, depending on the interpretation of relevant statutory provisions. *R. v. Garbera*, 2011 ONSC 4871. A trial will normally be held where the crime was committed, but it is possible for a court to order a change of venue to another location in the province if that is "expedient to the ends of justice." *Criminal Code*, R.S.C. 1985, c. C–46, s. 599.

VERDICT Historically, the decision of a **jury** in a **trial**, as distinct from the decision of a **judge**, which is a **judgment**. See *R. v. Murray and Fairbairn* (1913),

27 O.L.R. 382 (C.A.). The distinction is sometimes reflected in the language of the *Criminal Code*, R.S.C. 1985, c. C-46. See, e.g., s. 676, which permits the Crown to appeal "against a judgment or verdict of acquittal." However, other sections of the *Criminal Code* (e.g., s. 672.27) and many decisions of courts use the term "verdict" to refer to a decision by a judge alone, and so the distinction is not clearly drawn today.

DIRECTED VERDICT See **directed verdict**.

GENERAL VERDICT An ordinary verdict declaring simply which party prevails, or in a criminal case, a determination as to the guilt or innocence of the accused. "A verdict of acquittal is a general verdict, so that there are no findings on which the Court of Appeal can rely to decide what the verdict *would* have been but for the error in law." *Morgentaler v. The Queen*, [1976] 1 S.C.R. 616.

SPECIAL VERDICT One rendered on certain specific factual issues posed by the courts. "For example, on a trial for publishing a defamatory libel the judge may give to the jury a direction or opinion on the matter in issue and they may find a special verdict on the issue. Again, where it is found that the accused committed the act but was at the time suffering from mental disorder so as to be exempt from criminal responsibility by virtue of s. 16(l), the jury are required to state in their verdict that the accused "committed the act or made the omission but is not criminally responsible on account of mental disorder." [Citing *Criminal Code,* R.S.C. 1985, c. C–46, ss. 317, 672.34.] R. Salhany, *Canadian Criminal Procedure* 6–136.7 (6th ed. 1994).

VERIFICATION Confirmation of the correctness, truth, or authenticity of a **pleading** of other paper **affidavit**, oath, or **deposition**.

VESTED Fixed, accrued, or absolute; not contingent; generally used to describe any right or **title** to something that is not dependent upon the occurrence or failure to occur of some specified future event (**condition** precedent). Although sometimes used to refer to an immediate possessory **interest** in property, the more technically proper definition comprehends as well interests that will only become rights to actual **possession** of property at some later time **[in futuro]**. Originally applied in reference to estates in **real property**, it has come to be applied to other property interests, e.g., **personal property, trust**. Compare **contingent estate**. See also *Canada Permanent Trust Co. v. Lasby,* [1985] 1 W.W.R. 489.

VESTED ESTATE A property **interest** that will necessarily come into **possession** in the future merely upon the DETERMINATION (end) of the **preceding estate**. Thus for there to be a vested estate there must exist a known person who would have an immediate right to possession upon the expiration of the prior estate.

"When an estate commences or takes effect, it is said to be vested, the word vest being derived from the old French *vestir* and the Latin *vestire,* to clothe, that is, to clothe with a right. Therefore, a condition precedent is one to be performed before an estate can vest and a condition subsequent is one to be performed after it has vested. It is not necessary that the estate be in possession, for an interest can vest in right before it comes into possession and the event to which a condition subsequent refers need not be a **remainder** ..." (*Cunliffe v. Brancker* (1876), 3 Ch.D. 393, (C.A.); *White v. Summers,* [1908] 2 Ch. 256, (265)." 1 A.H. Oosterhoff & W.B. Rayner, *Anger and Honsberger: Law of Real Property* 301ff. (2d ed. 1985).

VESTED INTEREST See **interest**.

VESTED REMAINDER See **remainder**.

VESTED RIGHTS A right that has become so fixed that it is not subject to being divested without consent of the owner.

VETROVEC WARNING "[A] clear and sharp warning to attract the attention of the jurors to the risks of adopting, without more, the evidence of the witness." *Vetrovec v. The Queen,* [1982] 1 S.C.R. 811. A *Vetrovec* warning is to be delivered when there is **testimony** from an "unsavoury" **witness**, such as those who

have an amoral character, a criminal lifestyle, a past dishonesty, or an interest in the outcome of the trial. The warning does not require that there be corroboration for the testimony of an unsavoury witness, but warns the jury of the dangers of relying on that testimony in the absence of corroboration.

VEXATIOUS LITIGATION Civil action instituted for an ulterior motive other than to enforce a true legal claim or maliciously and without **probable cause**. *McMeekin v. Alberta (Attorney-General),* 2012 ABQB 625; *Dobson v. Green,* 2012 ONSC 4432. See **litigious**; **malicious prosecution**.

VICARIOUS LIABILITY The imputed responsibility of one person for the acts of another; occurs "when the law holds one person responsible for the misconduct of another, although he is himself free from personal blameworthiness or fault. It is therefore an instance of strict (no fault) liability." J. Fleming, *The Law of Torts* 409 (9th ed. 1998). See **Salmond test**.

In tort law, if an employee, EE, while in the **scope of his or her employment** for employer, ER, drives a delivery truck, and hits and injures P crossing the street, ER will be vicariously liable, under the doctrine of **respondeat superior**, for injuries sustained by P. In criminal law, while **prima facie** a principal is not criminally responsible for the acts of his or her servants, **Parliament** or a **legislature** may make a prohibition or duty absolute, in which case the **principal** is liable even if, in fact, the act is done by his or her servants. See, e.g., *Allen v. Whitehead,* [1930] 1 K.B. 211. Compare **strict liability**.

VICINAGE Neighbourhood; vicinity. Its contemporary meaning denotes a particular area where a crime was committed, where a **trial** is being held or from which **jurors** are called.

VICTIM The "person to whom harm was done or who suffered physical or emotional loss as a result of the commission of the offence." *Criminal Code,* R.S.C. 1985, c. C–46, s. 722(4)(*a*).

VICTIM IMPACT STATEMENT A written statement from the victim of an "**offence** describing the harm done to, or loss suffered by, the victim arising from the commission of the offence." The statement may be included as evidence for use in determining the sentence imposed on the convicted offender. *Criminal Code,* R.S.C. 1985, c. C–46, s. 722.

VIDELICET (*vĭ-dĕl'-ĭ-sĕt*) Lat.: that is to say. See **viz.**

VI ET ARMIS (*vē ĕt är'-mĭs*) Lat.: by force and by arms. See **trespass** [TRESPASS VI ET ARMIS].

VILLEIN SOCAGE See **socage.**

VILLENAGE A menial form of feudal **tenure** in which the **tenant** [the VILLEIN] was required to perform all **services** demanded by the lord of the manor.

VIOLENT OFFENCE One of four alternative prerequisites to be met before a **young person** can be committed to **custody** as a **sentence** under the *Youth Criminal Justice Act,* S.C. 2002, c. 1, s. 39. The test for whether an offence is harm-based rather than force-based, and the term refers to "an offence in the commission of which a young person causes, attempts to cause, or threatens to cause bodily harm." *R. v. C.D.; R. v. C.D.K.,* [2005] 3 S.C.R. 668.

VIS MAJOR (*vĭz mä-yôr'*) Lat.: a greater force, superior force. Used in civil law to mean an **act of God** and has reference to "every event which the prudence of man cannot foresee and which cannot be resisted when it is foreseen." See *Stachniak v. Thorhild (County No. 7),* 2001 ABPC 65. The term is synonymous with FORCE MAJEURE.

"The decisions make it clear that it is a **question of fact** whether an occurrence of nature is so phenomenal or of such a magnitude as not to be reasonably foreseen and guarded against, the capacity to foresee being based on previous experience and knowledge of nature's law." See *Low v. C.P.R.,* [1949] 2 W.W.R. 433 at 453 (Alta.S.C.) app'd in *Frache v. City of Lethbridge* (1954), 13 W.W.R. (N.S.) 609 at 615 (Alta.S.C.).

It is not necessary to sustain a plea of *vis major* that such an event should never have happened before. *Bénard v. Hingston* (1918), 39 D.L.R. 137 (S.C.C.).

VISITOR Under the former *Immigration Act,* R.S.C. 1985, c. I–2, a **visitor** was defined as " a person who is lawfully in Canada, or seeks to come into Canada, for a temporary purpose." A **visitor** was distinguished from a **Canadian citizen**, a **permanent resident**, a person in possession of a special permit allowing him or her to be in Canada, and an **immigrant** authorized to come into Canada—e.g., for an immigration interview. The new *Immigration and Refugee Protection Act,* S.C. 2001, c. 27, contains no such definition, although the status of visitor may possibly retain the same, or similar meaning. In the *Immigration and Refugee Protection Regulations,* SOR/2002–227, s. 191, under the new Act, a visitor is noted to be "a class of persons who may become **temporary residents**."

VITIATE To void; to render a nullity; to impair.

VIVA VOCE (*vē'-vă vō'-chā*) Lat.: with the living voice; orally.

VIZ. Abbreviated form of the Latin word **videlicet**, meaning *namely, that is to say*. A term used in pleadings to particularize or explain what goes before it.

VOID Empty, having no legal force, ineffectual, unenforceable, incapable of being ratified. For example, a person declared **incompetent** loses all power to deal with his or her property, and any **instrument** he or she makes is void. *In re Marshall, Marshall v. Whateley,* [1920] 1 Ch. 284. A **contract** that is void "will not qualify as valid." G.H.L. Fridman, *The Law of Contract in Canada* 338 (6th ed. 2011). Certain contracts made by **infants** may be void on the basis of illegality, on the basis of lack of capacity to contract, by reason of the operation of **mistake** in contracting, etc. G.H.L. Fridman, *The Law of Contract in Canada* 153 (6th ed. 2011). Compare **voidable**.

VOIDABLE Capable of being later annulled; a valid act that, though it may be avoided, may accomplish the thing sought to be accomplished until the fatal defect in the transaction has been effectively asserted or judiciously ascertained and declared. For example, "in contract, transactions executed by a person found to be mentally incompetent are voidable at the option of the mentally incapacitated party or their personal representative." *Lagoski v. Shano* (2007), 232 O.A.C. 21.

VOIR DIRE (*vwär dēr*) Fr.: to speak the truth. **1.** A VOIR DIRE EXAMINATION may refer to a preliminary examination of a witness by the court requiring him or her "to speak the truth" with respect to questions put to him or her. **2.** A *voir dire* examination during a trial refers to a **hearing** out of the presence of the **jury** by the court upon some issue of fact or law that requires an initial determination by the court or upon which the court must rule as a matter of law alone. For example, if the prosecution seeks to admit a **confession** of the **accused**, the court must conduct a *voir dire* examination to determine if the statements were obtained **voluntarily**. This determination must be made by the court before the jury is permitted to hear the confession.

VOLENTI NON FIT INJURIA (*vō-lĕn'-tē nŏn fēt ĭn-jū'-rē-à*) Lat.: the volunteer suffers no wrong; no legal wrong is done to him who consents. In **tort** law, a defence asserting that the plaintiff consented to the damage done or, in full knowledge of the nature and extent of the risk he or she was running, elected to take that risk. *Dube v. Labar,* [1986] 1 S.C.R. 649.

VOLUNTARY 1. With regard to a **confession**, not motivated by hope of advantage or fear of prejudice. A confession must be proven voluntary to be admissible, which requires that it was made by a person with an operating mind and not in an atmosphere of oppression. The accused must have made a meaningful choice whether to confess or not

for a statement to be voluntary. See *R. v. Oickle,* 2000 SCC 38. **2.** With regard to behaviour that might constitute the **actus reus** of an **offence**, behaviour that is "the product of a free will and controlled body, unhindered by external constraints." *R. v. Ruzic,* 2001 SCC 24. "It is a **principle of fundamental justice** that only voluntary conduct...should attract the penalty and stigma of criminal liability." *Id.* See *R. v. Bouchard-Lebrun,* 2011 SCC 58. See **involuntary**; **moral involuntariness**.

VOLUNTARY WASTE See **waste**.

VOTING TRUST The accumulation in a single hand, or in a few hands, of **shares** of corporate **stock** belonging to many owners in order thereby to control the business of the **company**.

"Under the voting trust agreement the parties gave up a **property** right— the right to vote their shares as they saw fit at meetings of shareholders of the Company—and placed that property under the control of the majority. The property right created by the agreement was the right of the majority to vote the shares at the meeting of shareholders of the Company.... Under the voting **trust agreement** the parties had an obligation to act in good faith and make their decision at a meeting." *Field v. Bachynski* (1977), 1 Alta.R. 491 at 508, 510 (Alta.S.C.A.D.).

VOYEURISM A **hybrid offence** under s. 162 of the *Criminal Code,* R.S.C. 1985, c. C–46, that "addresses those who observe or make recordings of another person for a sexual purpose while that other person has a reasonable expectation of privacy." M. Manning & P. Sankoff, *Criminal Law* 932 (4th ed. 2009). The observation or recording must be "surreptitious," and it may be done by mechanical or electronic means. "The offence thus covers the classic case of the 'peeping Tom' who looks through the blinds, and also the modern hightech version where webcams or other recording devices are used." *Id.*

WAGER 1. A bet; stake. **2.** "[A] contract entered into without color of fraud between two or more persons for a good consideration, and upon mutual promises to pay a stipulated sum of money, or to deliver some other thing to each other, according as some prefixed and equally uncertain contingency should happen within the terms upon which the contract was made." *Bank of Toronto v. McDougall* (1877), 28 U.C.C.P. 345 at 350–51 (Ont.). **3.** Also referred to as a "gaming contract." See G.H.L. Fridman, *The Law of Contract in Canada* 352–60 (6th ed. 2011).

WAGES 1. Broadly, any compensation given to a third party in consideration of his or her work or services. **2.** Payment paid by an employer to an employee for his or her labour, including vacation pay.

WAIVER The act of giving up a right, which can be done explicitly or in limited circumstances implicitly. Where a right is explicitly waived in writing, "waiver" refers to the document that records it. "Waiver occurs where one party to a contract or to proceedings takes steps [that] amount to foregoing reliance on some known right or defect in the performance of the other party ... Waiver will be found only where the evidence demonstrates that the party waiving had (1) a full knowledge of rights; and (2) an unequivocal and conscious intention to abandon them. The creation of such a stringent test is justified since no consideration moves from the party in whose favour a waiver operates." *Saskatchewan River Bungalows Ltd. v. Maritime Life Assurance Co.*, [1994] 2 SCR 490. It has been claimed that the "so called 'waiver'" is in reality a branch of **estoppel**. *Teasdall v. Sun Life Assurance Co. of Canada,* [1927] 2 D.L.R. 502 at 509 (Ont.S.C.A.D.). Contemporary Canadian law, however, recognizes that waiver and estoppel are distinct concepts and have

different elements. See, e.g., *Dunn v. Vicars*, 2009 BCCA 477.

WANT OF CONSIDERATION See **consideration**.

WANT OF PROSECUTION The failure to carry forward an **action** or an **appeal**. Where there has been inordinate delay by a party in pursuing the action or appeal, the other party can apply to have the matter dismissed for want of prosecution. See, e.g., *Azeri v. Esmati–Seifabad*, 2009 BCCA 133. Not all decision-makers have this authority. See *Premium Brands Operating GP Inc. v. Turner Distribution Systems Ltd.*, 2001 BCCA 75.

WANTON Grossly **negligent** or careless; extremely **reckless**. "'Wantonness' is perhaps a subclass of recklessness. It is a wild, mad or arrogant kind of recklessness and thus closely related to '**wilfulness.**'" *R. v. Walker* (1974), 8 N.S.R. (2d) 300 at 306 (S.C.A.D.). Also, "conduct which [indicates] reckless indifference of consequences." *Regina v. Moroz,* [1972] 2 W.W.R. 307 at 316 (Alta.S.C.A.D.). See *R. v. Tutton*, [1989] 1 S.C.R. 1392.

WAR CRIME "[M]eans an act or omission committed during an armed conflict that, at the time and in the place of its commission, constitutes a war crime according to customary international law or conventional international law applicable to armed conflicts, whether or not it constitutes a contravention of the law in force at the time and in the place of its commission." *Crimes Against Humanity and War Crimes Act,* S.C. 2000, c. 24, s. 4.

WARD 1. A person, usually a child, placed by the court under the care and supervision of a guardian. See **guardian**. **2.** An electoral division within a city or town. **3.** A separate area(s) in a hospital or prison designated for specific persons or activities—e.g., psychiatric ward.

WAR MEASURES ACT A federal statute that conferred special powers on the federal Cabinet to enact orders and regulations on matters of provincial jurisdiction in the event of a "war, invasion, or insurrection, real or apprehended." The *War Measures Act*, R.S.C. 1985, c. W–2, was enacted in 1904 and proclaimed into force for both World Wars. It was also invoked during the "October Crisis" of October 1970, in response to the increasing terrorist activities of the Front de' libération du Québec (F.L.Q.) ("apprehended insurrection"). It was repealed by the *Emergencies Act*, R.S.C. 1985, c. 22 (4th Supp.), which makes provisions for (1) public welfare emergencies; (2) public order emergencies; (3) international emergencies; (4) war. See **martial law**.

WARRANT A written **order** directing the **arrest** of a person or persons, issued by a court, body or official having authority to issue warrants of arrest (see also **bench warrant**); also a **writ** from a competent authority directing the doing of a certain act.

DNA WARRANT A type of warrant authorizing the police to take a bodily substance from a person when they have reasonable grounds to believe that a forensic DNA analysis of that substance will provide evidence about whether it matches the DNA of a bodily substance found on any person or at any place associated with an offence. *Criminal Code*, R.S.C. 1985, c. C–46, s. 487.05. DNA warrants may only be issued for the investigation of specific offences set out in s. 487.04 of the *Criminal Code*.

SEARCH WARRANT An order that certain premises or property be searched for particularized items that if found are to be seized and used as **evidence** in a criminal **trial** or destroyed as contraband. See **search warrant**.

WARRANT OF COMMMITAL Section 744 of the *Criminal Code*, R.S.C. 1985, c. C–46 provides: "A **peace officer** or other person to whom a warrant of committal authorized by this or any other Act of Parliament is directed shall arrest the person named or described therein, if it is necessary to do so in order to take that person into custody, convey that person to the prison mentioned in the warrant and deliver that person, together with the warrant, to the keeper of the prison..." See *Re Rombough's Detention* (1963), 43 W.W.R. (N.S.) 287 (Alta. S.C.).

The word *warrant* is also used in commercial and property law to refer to a particular kind of guarantee or assurance creating an express **warranty** as to the quality and validity of what is being conveyed. See **guarantee**; merchantable; **warranty**.

WARRANTY An assurance by one **party** to a **contract** of the existence of a fact upon which the other party may rely, intended precisely to relieve the **promisee** of any duty to ascertain the fact for himself or herself; amounts to a **promise** to **indemnify** the promisee for any loss if the fact warranted proves untrue. Such warranties are made either overtly (EXPRESS WARRANTIES) or by implication (IMPLIED WARRANTIES).

A warranty is term of a contract that is collateral to the main purpose of the contract, i.e., that is not so vital as to effect a discharge of the contract, if the circumstances are or become inconsistent with it. *Jorian Properties Ltd. v. Zellenrath et al.* (1984), 46 O.R. (2d) 775 (Ont. C.A.). Whether a term of a contract is a **condition** or a warranty depends upon the intention of the parties at the time of making the contract. *Liu v. Yuen*, 2007 BCSC 302. The distinction between a condition and a warranty has found statutory codifiction in the various provincial statutes dealing with the sale of goods. For example, the *Sale of Goods Act*, R.S.O. 1990, c. S.1, s. 12(2), states: "Whether a stipulation in a contract of sale is a condition the breach of which may give rise to a right to treat the contract as repudiated or a warranty the breach of which may give rise to a claim for damages but not to a right to reject the goods and treat the contract as repudiated depends in each case on the construction of the contract, and a stipulation may be a condition, though called a warranty in the contract."

See further G.H.L. Fridman, *The Law of Contract in Canada* 477–9, 485–6 (6th ed. 2011).

WARRANTY DEED The terms or clause in a deed that forms a **covenant running with the land**, insuring the continuing validity of **title**, the **breach** of which occurs at the time of **conveyance** and gives rise to an action by the last **vendee** against the first or any other warrantor. Compare **quitclaim deed**.

WARRANTY OF FITNESS A warranty that goods are suitable for the special purpose of the buyer. When goods are ordered for a particular purpose known to the vendor, the law implies a warranty by the vendor that they shall be fit for that purpose. *Wharton v. Tom Harris Chevrolet Oldsmobile Cadillac Ltd.*, 2002 BCCA 78.

WARRANTY OF HABITABILITY [More properly, an implied or express COVENANT OF HABITABILITY] A promise by a landlord that at the inception of the lease there are no **latent defects** in facilities vital to the use of premises for residential purposes, and that these facilities will remain in usable condition during the duration of the lease.

WARRANTY OF MERCHANTABILITY A warranty that the goods are reasonably fit for the general purposes for which they are sold.

WASTE Generally, an act, by one in rightful **possession** of land who has less than a **fee simple** interest in the land, which decreases the value of the land or the owner's **interest** or the interest of one who has an estate that may become possessory at some future time (such as a **remainderman, lessor, mortgagee, reversioner**).

AMELIORATING WASTE "[A]n act [that] results in an improvement to the property and is only actionable where the improvement results in an increased burden to the owner of the property." *British Columbia (Director of Civil Forfeiture) v. Onn*, 2009 BCCA 402. While a "life tenant will not be liable for this type of waste," he or she "cannot demand payment for the improvements." *Halsbury's Laws of Canada*, "Real Property" 181 (2012).

EQUITABLE WASTE The commission of "wanton or extravagant acts of destruction" to the estate by the life tenant. E.H. Burn, *Cheshire and Burn's Modern Law of Real Property* 298 (16th ed. 2000). "Examples of the application of this rule occur where the tenant dismantles a mansion or other house, cuts saplings at unreasonable times, or fells timber that has been planted for the ornament or shelter" of the estate. *Id.* The life tenant will be liable for this type of waste, even if the grant provides that the life tenant is "unimpeachable for waste." A.M. Sinclair & M.E. McCallum, *An Introduction to Real Property* 16 (6th ed. 2012).

PERMISSIVE WASTE Permissive waste occurs when "the tenant passively allows the property to fall into a state of disrepair, for example, where a house is allowed to fall into decay." *British Columbia (Director of Civil Forfeiture) v. Onn*, 2009 BCCA 402. In other words, it "arises from a mere act of omission, not of commission." E.H. Burn, *Cheshire and Burn's Modern Law of Real Property* 297 (16th ed. 2000).

VOLUNTARY WASTE "[A] wrong of omission consisting of a positive act of injury to the inheritance." E.H. Burn, *Cheshire and Burn's Modern Law of Real Property* 295–96 (16th ed. 2000). "The life tenant will be liable for this type of waste, but not if it results from the reasonable use of the land," such as "working an existing mine or cutting wood for personal use." *Halsbury's Laws of Canada*, "Real Property" 181 (2012).

WATCHING AND BESETTING See **criminal harassment**.

WATERFIELD TEST See **ancillary powers doctrine**.

WAYBILL A document detailing the persons and/or goods being transported by a carrier.

WEAPON "[A]ny thing used, designed to be used, or intended for use (a) in causing death or injury to any person or (b) for the purpose of threatening or intimidating any person and, without restricting the generality of the foregoing, includes a **firearm**." *Criminal Code*, R.S.C. 1985, c. C–46, s. 2. See also, **offensive weapon**.

WEIGHT OF THE EVIDENCE The relative value of the totality of **evidence** presented on one side of a judicial dispute, in light of the evidence presented on the other side; refers to the persuasiveness of the testimony of the **witnesses**. See **against the [manifest] [weight of the] evidence; burden of proof**.

WEIS [WAIS] Term used to denote abandoned goods.

WELL-FOUNDED FEAR OF PERSECUTION A requirement for obtaining **refugee** status under the *Immigration and Refugee Protection Act*, R.S.C. S.C. 2001, c. 27. The persecution must be based on race, religion, nationality, membership in a particular social group, or political opinion, and the fear must be both **subjectively** felt by the applicant and **objectively** justified.

WESTMINSTER, STATUTE OF See **Statute of Westminster**.

WHEREAS CLAUSE See **recitals**.

WHIPLASH INJURY Neck injury commonly associated with rear-end-type automobile collisions; caused by a sudden and unexpected forced forward movement of the body while the unsupported head of an automobile occupant attempts to remain stationary consistent with the law of physics, subjecting the neck to a severe strain while in a relaxed position. It is a frequent claim in **tort** actions arising from such collisions. See, e.g., *Wild v. Toth*, 2004 BCSC 1449.

WHISTLEBLOWER A person who reveals **confidential** information out of a concern for the public interest. Protection from liability on the part of whistleblowers is provided in some jurisdictions; see, e.g., *The Public Interest Disclosure (Whistleblower Protection) Act,* C.C.S.M. c. P217; *Personal Information Protection and Electronic Documents Act*, S.C. 2000, c. 5, s. 27. "Whistleblower laws create an exception to the usual duty of loyalty owed by employees to their employer. When applied in government, of course, the purpose is to avoid the waste of public funds or other abuse of state-conferred privileges or authority. In relation to the private sector (as here), the purpose still has a public interest focus because it aims to prevent wrongdoing 'that is or is likely to result in an offence.' (It is the 'offence' requirement that gives the whistleblower law a public aspect and filters out more general workplace complaints.) The underlying idea is to recruit employees to assist the state in the suppression of unlawful conduct. This is done by providing employees with a measure of immunity against employer retaliation." *Merk v. International Association of Bridge, Structural, Ornamental and Reinforcing Iron Workers, Local 771*, 2005 SCC 70.

WHOLESALER Middleman; a person who buys large quantities of goods and resells to other distributors rather than to ultimate consumers; one who deals with the trade who buy to sell again, while the retail trader deals direct with the consumer. Compare **jobber**.

WIDOW A woman whose spouse is deceased and who has not remarried. See **dower**.

WIDOWER A man whose spouse is deceased and who has not remarried. See **curtesy**.

WIGMORE TEST A set of four criteria used to determine case-by-case **privilege** as opposed to a class privilege. Where confidentiality is not guaranteed (as it is, for example, in the class privilege of **solicitor-client privilege**), it must be decided on a case-by-case basis whether confidentiality should be respected for a particular communication. The criteria are: (1) the relationship must originate in a confidence that the source's identity will not be disclosed; (2) anonymity must be essential to the relationship in which the communication arises; (3) the relationship must be one that should be sedulously fostered in the public interest; and (4) the public interest served by protecting the identity of the informant must outweigh the public interest in getting at the truth. See *R. v. National Post*, 2010 SCC 16.

WILD'S CASE, RULE IN See **Rule in Wild's Case**.

WILDCAT STRIKE A term used to describe a strike by unionized employees that has not been authorized by the union to which the striking employees are members.

WILL A person's declaration of how he or she desires his or her **property** to be disposed of after his or her death, which declaration is revocable during his or her lifetime, operative for no purpose until death, and applicable to the situation that exists at his or her death. A will may also contain other declarations of the **testator's** desires as to what is to be done after he or she dies but it must dispose of some property. See H.S. Black, *Wills and Estates: Cases, Text, and Materials* (2009).

The difference between a will and a **deed** is that, by means of a deed, a present **interest** passes on **delivery**, while a will takes effect only upon the death of the testator. Will is generally used as synonymous with **testament**, but the latter is technically confined to the disposition of **personal property**. LAST WILL AND TESTAMENT is an expression commonly used to refer to the most recent document directing the disposition of the real and personal property of the party. See **causa** [MORTIS CAUSA]; **codicil**; **living will**. Compare **gift**; **testamentary** [TESTAMENTARY DISPOSITION].

WILLFUL [WILFUL] "[A]s used in courts of law, [willful] implies ... that the person of whose action or default the expression is used, is a free agent, and that what has been done arises from the spontaneous action of his will." *In re Young and Hartson's Contract* (1886), 31 Ch.D. 168 at 174 (C.A.).

"Generally in penal statutes the word 'wilful' or 'wilfully' means something more than a voluntary or intentional act; it includes the idea of an action intentionally done with a bad motive or purpose, or as it is otherwise expressed 'with an evil intent.'" *Anderson and Eddy v. Canadian Northern Ry. Co.* (1917), 35 D.L.R. 473 at 480 (Sask.S.C.).

"The word 'wilfully' has not been uniformly interpreted and its meaning to some extent depends upon the context in which it is used. Its primary meaning is 'intentionally,' but it is also used to mean 'recklessly.'" *R. v. Buzzanga & Durocher* (1979), 49 C.C.C. (2d) 369 at 379 (Ont.C.A.). See also *R. v. Muma* (1989), 51 C.C.C. (3d) 85 (Ont.C.A.).

WILLFUL BLINDNESS [WILFUL BLINDNESS] A deliberate closing of one's mind to the possible consequences of one's actions. In criminal law, it describes a situation where a person becomes aware of the need to make some inquiries but omits to do so. Willfull blindness is deemed to be actual knowledge. See **knowledge**. Contrast with **recklessness**.

WINDING UP The process of **liquidating** a corporation. The **assets** of the enterprise are used to discharge liabilities, and the resulting net assets are distributed to the **shareholders** on a **pro rata** basis, according to preference.

The term *winding up* usually refers to the procedures carried out by a liquidator, but the courts have used it to describe discontinuance of a business as well. *Merritt v. M.N.R.,* [1940–41] C.T.C. 226 (Ex.Ct.); *Kennedy v. M.N.R.,* [1972] C.T.C. 429 (F.).

Liquidation procedures are usually prescribed and regulated by statute, e.g., the *Winding-up and Restructuring Act,* R.S.C. 1985, c. W–11.

WIPO The World Intellectual Property Organization. A United Nations organization located in Geneva and aimed at protecting intellectual property rights throughout the world by, among other things, administering various treaties.

WITHDRAW[AL] To remove; to take back. When a **charge** is withdrawn, the judicial process ceases to operate and the issue is removed from the **consideration** of the courts. Compare **stay**.

A provincial attorney-general, in withdrawing a charge, is exercising a judicial discretion in his or her capacity as chief law enforcement officer, with which discretion the courts are most reluctant to interfere. *R. v. Nixon*, 2011 SCC 34.

WITHOUT PREJUDICE A phrase that may have the effect of excluding from evidence the documents upon which it is written. "The claim of privilege for correspondence written without prejudice is applicable only to correspondence containing offers of compromise or respecting **bona fide** negotiations entered into for the settlement of disputes." *Sherren v. Boudreau* (1973), 6 N.B.R. (2d) 701 at 703 (N.B.S.C.A.D.).

"All communications expressed to be written without prejudice, and fairly made for the purposes of expressing the writer's view on the matter of litigation or dispute, as well as overtures for settlement or compromise, and which are not made with some other object in view and wrong motives are not admissible in evidence." *Pirie v. Wyld* (1886), 11 O.R. 422 at 429 (Common Pleas Div.) quoted in *Darwich v. Awde* (2006), 152 A.C.W.S. (3d) 396 (Ont. S.C.J.).

WITNESS One who gives evidence in a cause before a court and who **attests** or swears to facts or gives or bears **testimony** under oath. Witness is defined in s. 118 of the *Criminal Code,* R.S.C. 1985, c. C–46 as "a person who gives **evidence** orally under **oath** or by **affidavit** in a judicial **proceeding**, whether or not he is competent to be a witness, and includes a child of tender years who gives evidence but does not give it under oath, because, in the opinion of the person presiding, the child does not understand the nature of an oath." See also *Canada Evidence Act,* R.S.C. 1985, c. C–5, ss. 3–16.1 as amended.

ADVERSE WITNESS AND HOSTILE WITNESS "[A]n 'adverse' witness is one who is opposed in interest or unfavourable in the sense of opposite in position to the party calling that witness, whereas a 'hostile' witness is one who demonstrates an antagonistic attitude or hostile mind toward the party calling him or her." Under s. 9 of the *Canada Evidence Act*, a person calling a witness can seek a declaration that that person is adverse, and thereby be entitled to **impeach** that witness by calling evidence of prior statements inconsistent with the witness's current testimony. A declaration that a witness is hostile is made at **common law** and entitles the person calling the witness to cross-examine the witness in a more wide-ranging fashion. *R. v. Figliola*, 2011 ONCA 457.

WORDS OF ART Words that have a particular meaning in a particular area of study; e.g., in law, **last clear chance**, PROMISSORY ESTOPPEL (see **estoppel**), and **reliance** are all words of art, because they have either no meaning or different meanings outside a legal context. Also referred to as a "term of art."

WORDS OF LIMITATION Words used in an **instrument** conveying an **interest** in **property** that seem to indicate the party

to whom a **conveyance** is made, but that actually indicate the type of **estate** by the **grantee**; e.g., in a conveyance from A "to B and his heirs" "and his heirs" are words of limitation, in that they delimit the estate taken by B, namely, a **fee simple**; and since a fee simple vests in B an absolute power to **alienate** the fee, B is under no obligation to give his or her heirs anything.

"Following upon the Conveyancing and Law of Property Act, 1881, the several provinces passed statutes which generally provide that in a deed it is not necessary to use the word 'heirs' to convey a fee simple but the words 'in fee simple' may be used, or other words sufficiently indicating the intention, and, furthermore, if no words of limitation are used, a deed can pass all the estate or interest held by the grantor unless a contrary intention appears in the **deed** [Canadian provincial legislation cited]." 1 A.H. Oosterhoff & W.B. Rayner, *Anger and Honsberger: Law of Real Property* 102 (2d ed. 1985). See generally *id.,* chaps. 5 & 6. See *Trollup v. Patterson*, [1970] S.C.R. 317.

On the other hand, WORDS OF PURCHASE are those that indicate the grantees or persons who take, as they would seem to indicate; hence, in the preceding example, "to B" are words of purchase.

WORKERS' COMPENSATION ACTS (WORKMEN'S COMPENSATION) Statutes that in general establish the liability of an employer for injuries that arise out of and in the course of employment, e.g., the *Workplace Safety and Insurance Act, 1997,* S.O. 1997, c. 16, Sch. A. In Canada, agencies known as workers' compensation boards have been created in every jurisdiction.

"Workers' compensation boards are public bodies created by statute. Employers and employees governed by the scheme are required to participate. As the title suggests, workers' compensation is an activity-specific scheme which provides compensation for personal injuries that occur in the course of employment. Minor injuries are excluded from most schemes by a requirement that the employee must be disabled beyond the day of the accident in order to make a claim. In part, the Canadian schemes are 'pure' no-fault, because the legislation prohibits the employee from suing his employer in **tort**. The employee, however, has the option of either claiming from the fund or bringing a tort action against a person other than his employer. Nevertheless, the vast majority of work-related accident claims are dealt with by workers' compensation boards and not courts." R. Solomon, B. Feldthusen, & R. W. Kostal, *Cases and Materials on the Law of Torts* (4th ed. 1996), at 532.

"The **damages** payable under workers' compensation schemes differ significantly from those awarded in **negligence**. For example, there is no recovery for pain and suffering or loss of amenities." *Id.*

WORTHIER TITLE, DOCTRINE OF The rule that "in a grant or devise a life estate, followed, in the same instrument, by an attempted remainder to the heirs of the **grantor** or **testator**, the attempted **remainder** is void, and the grantor or estate of the testator gets a **reversion** in fee simple." A.M. Sinclair & M.E. McCallum, *An Introduction to Real Property Law* 20 (6th ed. 2012).

WRAP MORTGAGE [WRAPAROUND MORTGAGE] "[A]n instrument devised primarily to allow a mortgagor to retain current mortgages on his property at relatively low interest rates while allowing him to borrow additional funds at lower than current second or subsequent mortgage interest rates." *Olympic Enterprises Ltd. v. Dover Financial Corp.* (1995), 147 N.S.R. 121 at 122 (S.C.). See **mortgage**.

WRIT "[I]n law a written command, precept or formal order ... in the name of the sovereign." *McBrearty v. McBrearty,* [1941] 1 W.W.R. 590 at 591 (Sask.K.B.). It is a mandatory precept issued by the authority, and in the name of the sovereign or the state for the purpose of compelling a person to do something therein mentioned. Issued by a court or other competent tribunal, it is directed to the sheriff or other officer authorized to execute the same. In every case the writ itself contains directions as to what is required to be done. See **peremptory** [PEREMPTORY WRIT]; **prerogative writ**.

WRIT OF ASSISTANCE See **assistance, writ of**.

WRIT OF CORAM NOBIS [WRIT OF ERROR CORAM NOBIS; CORAM NOBIS] (*kôr'-am no'-bĭs*) Lat.: before us; in our presence, i.e., in our court. The purpose of the writ is to bring the attention of the court to, and obtain relief from, errors of fact, such as a valid **defence** existing in the facts of the case, that, without **negligence** on the part of the defendant, was not made, through either **duress, fraud** or excusable **mistake**; these facts not appearing on the face of the record and being such as, if known in season, would have prevented the rendition and entry of the **judgment** questioned. The writ does not correct errors of law. It is addressed to the court that rendered the judgment in which injustice was allegedly done, in contrast to **appeals** and review, which are directed to another court.

WRIT OF ERROR An early common-law **writ** issued by the **Appellate Court**, directing the trial judge to send up the **record** in the case. The one seeking the review, whether the **plaintiff** or **defendant** in the trial court, is termed the plaintiff in error, while his or her opponent is called the defendant in error. The Appellate Court review only alleged errors of law. A writ of error is similar to a writ of **certiorari**, but, unlike a writ of certiorari, it is a writ of right and lies only where **jurisdiction** is exercised according to the course of the **common law**.

WRIT OF EXECUTION A writ issued after the determination of an issue the object of which is to enforce the **judgment** of the Court. It authorizes the **sheriff** to **levy** on property belonging to the **judgment debtor** for the benefit of the plaintiff in whose favour the judgment has been granted. It "shall include writs of *fieri facias,* **sequestration** and **attachment** and all subsequent writs that may issue for giving effect thereto [to judgments]." *Ross v. Rogers and CNR,* [1927] 3 W.W.R. 169 at 171 (Sask.K.B.).

WRIT OF FIERI FACIAS (*fē-âr'-ē fǎ'-shǔs*) (Lat.: cause to be done) See WRIT OF EXECUTION.

WRIT OF PROHIBITION A **process** or writ issued by a superior court that prevents an inferior court or tribunal from exceeding its **jurisdiction** or usurping jurisdiction with which it has not been vested by law. It is an extraordinary writ because it issues only when the party seeking it is without other means of redress for the wrong about to be inflicted by the act of the inferior tribunal. It is a **prerogative writ**. In addition, as noted by McGillivray, J.A. in *Rex v. Fodor,* [1938] 2 D.L.R. 290 at 302 (Alta.S.C.A.D.): "[In my opinion] prohibition lies not only in cases of lack of jurisidiction over the subject matter or over the person but also in cases in which the inferior court proceeds in circumstances that show bias or self-interest or a perversion of the principles of natural justice."

WRIT OF SUMMONS A writ issued by a court in order to compel the defendant to appear if he or she wishes to reply to the charge made against him or her; a basic method for commencing court proceedings in civil matters. "In most provinces, the writ and the statement of claim have now been combined, and in some cases, the term 'writ' has been eliminated altogether, so that the plaintiff commences the claim by issuing the statement of claim itself." J. Walker & L. Sossin, *Civil Litigation* 106 (2010). See **summons**.

WRONGFUL ACT An act that, without necessarily being illegal, is contrary to moral or ethical standards and results in some harm being done to individuals or the community. The term is more comprehensive than the phrase *unlawful act,* but all unlawful acts are wrongs. See, e.g., *Honda Canada Inc. v. Keays,* 2008 SCC 39: "Punitive damages are restricted to advertent wrongful acts that are so malicious and outrageous that they are deserving of punishment on their own."

The defence of **provocation** requires that the accused acted in response to a "wrongful act or an insult that is of such a nature as to be sufficient to deprive an ordinary person of the power of self-control."

WRONGFUL BIRTH A **tort** action brought against physicians in connection with the birth of a child. "Actions for wrongful birth are brought by the parents (rather than by the child) who claim that their child would not have been conceived or born but for the doctor's negligence. In such claims, the parents seek damages associated with the birth and care of a child. Wrongful birth claims may arise from the birth of a healthy—but unplanned—child, as in cases where a doctor is alleged to have negligently performed a sterilization procedure. More commonly, wrongful birth claims involve the birth of a disabled child, as in cases where parents would have elected not to conceive a child had they received accurate genetic counseling about the likelihood that their child would be born with a disability, or to abort a child had they received advice regarding harm that can be caused *in utero* by such diseases as Rubella." *Paxton v. Ramji,* 2008 ONCA 697. Compare **wrongful life**.

WRONGFUL LIFE "A claim brought by a child against a doctor or other healthcare provider for allowing a child to be born with birth defects where, but for the wrongful act or omission of the doctor, the child would not have been born at all. In the words of the trial judge, liability in such cases is framed 'but for the negligence I would not have been born.'" *Paxton v. Ramji,* 2008 ONCA 697. Unlike **wrongful birth** actions, which are brought by the parents of the child, wrongful life actions have generally been found not to be recognized in Canada, though the matter is not entirely settled. *Id.*

WRONGFUL DISMISSAL 1. A breach of an employment contract by an employer. **2.** The unjustifiable termination of an employee's employment by an employer. In a wrongful dismissal suit the burden is on the defendant employer to show cause for the plaintiff's dismissal.

YEAR In federal statutes, refers to any period of twelve consecutive months, except that a reference to a 'calendar year' means a period of twelve consecutive months commencing on the first day of January and a reference by number to a Dominical year means the period of twelve consecutive months commencing on the first day of January of that year. *Interpretation Act,* R.S.C. 1985, c. I–21, s. 37.

FISCAL YEAR [FINANCIAL YEAR] In relation to money provided by **Parliament** or the Consolidated Revenue Fund, or the accounts, taxes or finances of Canada, the period beginning on and including the 1st day of April in one year and ending on and including the 31st day of March in the next year. *Id.*

TAXATION YEAR For the purpose of the *Income Tax Act,* R.S.C. 1985, c. 1 (5th Supp.), s. 249(1), "*(a)* in the case of a corporation or Canadian resident partnership, a fiscal period, and (*b*) in the case of an individual, a calendar year, and when a taxation year is referred to by reference to a calendar year the reference is to the taxation year or years coinciding with, or ending in, that year."

In **contract** law, the meaning of the term *year* is a matter of **construction** and may or may not mean the calendar year current at the date of the contract. *Ozias v. Reeves & Co.* (1911), 1 W.W.R. 517 (S.C.C.). In a life insurance policy, the term *yearly* was interpreted to mean "yearly from the time provided by law for payment of the first installment." *Gill v. Great West Life Assurance Co.,* [1911] 2 O.W.N. 777 at 778 (Div.Ct.).

YEAR-BOOKS The reports of cases in England covering the period 1289 to 1537. Though invaluable to the legal historian, the Year-Books are of little value to the modern lawyer. Written in Anglo-Norman, they are largely concerned with the form of **pleadings**, often

to the exclusion of the reasons for the decision.

YEAS AND NAYS Terms used to denote affirmative and negative oral votes in a legislative assembly.

YELLOW DOG CONTRACT A contract in which employees are required to promise not to join a union as a condition of their employment. *Reference re ss. 193 and 195(1)(c) of the Criminal Code (Man)* (1990), 56 C.C.C. (3d) 65 at 96 (S.C.C.).

YELLOW DOG UNION An employee association that is dominated or heavily influenced by an employer in its formation, management, or policy-making. Such associations may refer to themselves as **unions**, but Canadian labour legislation disallows them from gaining **certification** as **bargaining agents** for their employee members. See, e.g., *Trade Union Act,* R.S.N.S. 1989, v. 475, s. 25(15); *Labour Relations Act, 1995,* S.O. 1995, c. 1, Sch. A, s. 15; *Labour Relations Code,* R.S.B.C. 1996, c. 244, s. 31.

YIELD To give way to another; to give the "right of way." In motor vehicle cases it has been held that the effect of a yield sign is to "give [the] other party the right of going through the intersection first." *Hammond v. Smith* (1964), 45 D.L.R. (2d) 762 at 766 (N.S.Co.Ct.). However, it has also been stated that the effect of such a sign is to warn drivers of potential danger and that the sign itself does not necessarily alter existing rules of right of way. *Johnson v. Semple and Mills* (1962), 36 D.L.R. (2d) 319 (P.E.I.S.C.).

YOUNG OFFENDER The term used under the now-repealed *Young Offenders Act,* R.S.C. 1985, c. Y–1, to refer to a **young person** who was found guilty of an offence. The *Young Offenders Act* replaced **juvenile delinquent** legislation and was itself replaced by the *Youth Criminal Justice Act,* S.C. 2002, c. 1. In part, the change of name reflected that not everyone dealt with under such legislation is in fact an **offender**.

YOUNG PERSON "a person who is or, in the absence of evidence to the contrary, appears to be twelve years old or older, but less than eighteen years old and, if the context requires, includes any person who is charged under this Act with having committed an offence while he or she was a young person or who is found guilty of an offence under this Act." *Youth Criminal Justice Act,* S.C. 2002, c. 1, s. 2(1).

YOUTH CRIMINAL JUSTICE The body of rules dealing with the application of the **criminal** law to **young persons**, as set out in the *Youth Criminal Justice Act,* S.C. 2002, c. 1. Young persons are subject to the same prohibitions as any other member of society, but special rules normally prohibit the publication of the name of any young person charged with an offence, create **youth courts** where the trials will take place, provide for **extrajudicial measures** in some cases, and create separate **youth custody facilities** where sentences can be served.

YOUTH CUSTODY FACILITY "[M]eans a facility designated under subsection 85(2) for the placement of young persons and, if so designated, includes a facility for the secure restraint of young persons, a community residential centre, a group home, a child care institution and a forest or wilderness camp." *Youth Criminal Justice Act,* S.C. 2002, c. 1, s. 2(1).

YOUTH JUSTICE COURT [YOUTH COURT] Previously named youth court, a "youth justice court is any court that may be established or designated by or under an Act of the legislature of a province, or designated by the Governor in Council or the lieutenant governor in council of a province, as a youth justice court for the purposes of this Act." *Youth Criminal Justice Act,* S.C. 2002, c. 1, s. 13.

YOUTH JUSTICE COURT JUDGE [YOUTH COURT JUDGE] Formerly called a youth court judge, a "youth justice court judge is a person who may be appointed or designated as a judge of the youth justice court or a judge sitting in a court established or designated as a youth justice court." *Youth Criminal Justice Act,* S.C. 2002, c. 1, s. 13.

YOUTH WORKER "[M]eans any person appointed or designated, whether by title of youth worker or probation officer or by any other title, by or under an Act of the legislature of a province or by the lieutenant governor in council of a province or his or her delegate to perform in that province, either generally or in a specific case, any of the duties or functions of a youth worker under this Act." *Youth Criminal Justice Act,* S.C. 2002, c. 1, s. 2(1).

ZEALOT A term used to describe a fanatical person.

ZERO-RATE MORTGAGE A **mortgage** in which a large down payment is made and the balance [the remainder of the purchase price] is paid in equal installments with no interest charges.

ZONE A parcel or area of land that has been set aside for a particular purpose or activity—e.g., a commercial zone. See **zoning**.

ZONE OF EMPLOYMENT See **scope of employment**.

ZONING Legislative action, usually on the municipal level, that separates or divides municipalities into districts for the purpose of regulating, controlling or in some way limiting the use of private property and the construction and/or structural nature of buildings erected within the zones or districts established. Historically, land use regulation was primarily achieved using the common-law **restrictive covenant**. Zoning represents "an improvement on restrictive covenants" in at least two ways. First, unlike restrictive covenants, zoning "is comprehensive in scale and unaffected by land ownership. The technical requirements of ascertainable land, of benefits and burdens, and lack of notice are totally removed." Second, because zoning is "legislatively imposed … it divorces land use control decisions from private ownership and enables all interest groups in the political arena to have the potential of affecting land uses." S.M. Mackuch, N. Craik & S.B. Leisk, *Canadian Municipal and Planning Law* 193, 195–6 (2nd ed. 2004).

Zoning power is usually an aspect of DELEGATED LEGISLATION (see **legislation**). See, e.g., *Quebec (Attorney-General) v. Lacombe*, 2010 SCC 38.

ZYGOTES Human reproductive eggs that are fertilized in vitro (outside the body). Once the zygotes are implanted into a woman's womb, they are referred to as embryos. The growing area of reproductive technology has raised important questions about the legal status of human zygotes and whether they should be regarded as personal property. See *Proceed with Care: Final Report of the Royal Commission on New Reproductive Technologies*, 15 November 1993, Ch. 22. See *Reference re Assisted Human Reproduction Act*, 2010 SCC 61.

Appendix I

Outline of Canada's Court System

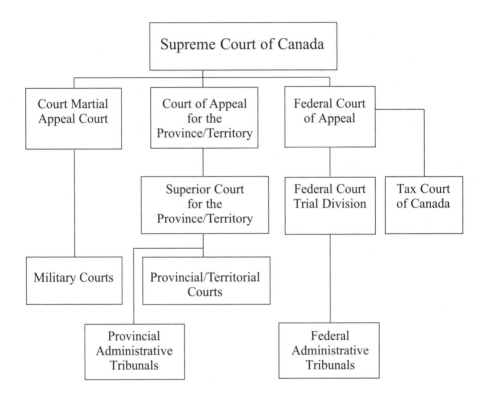

(This chart is adapted with permission from the Department of Justice publication *Canada's Court System*, *http://canada.justice.gc.ca*. Refer to the dictionary entries for each court for more information.)

The Structure of the Courts in Canada

There are, broadly speaking, four levels of courts in Canada. Both the federal and provincial governments have the ability to create courts and appoint judges to them. Some courts that have jurisdiction only in one province or territory are nonetheless courts to which judges are appointed by the federal government.

Every province and every territory (except Nunavut) has a trial-level court with jurisdiction solely in that territory, sometimes referred to as an inferior court. This level of court will have limited jurisdiction but normally includes, for example, criminal law, some aspects of family law, and some private law disputes. There is not generally a single trial-level court in a province or territory, and different courts might exist: small claims court, family court, youth court, and so on.

Every province and territory also has a superior court, which has jurisdiction only within that territory but to which judges are appointed by the federal government. Superior courts typically have jurisdiction over all types of disputes occurring in the jurisdiction and will conduct trials in some matters but also can hear appeals from lower-level courts or administrative bodies.

Every province and territory also has a court of appeal, which again has jurisdiction only within that territory but to which judges are appointed by the federal government. A court of appeal will hear only appeals, normally only from the superior court but in some rare instances directly from a provincial court or an administrative body.

The highest court in Canada, and final court of appeal, is the Supreme Court of Canada, which hears appeals from all provinces and territories. In most instances, a matter can only reach the Supreme Court of Canada after having been decided by a provincial or territorial court of appeal, but there are exceptions.

In addition, there are other federally appointed courts that run parallel to the provincial courts and that have jurisdiction over some particular areas of law, such as copyright or immigration, which are in federal jurisdiction according to the division of powers in ss. 91 and 92 of the *Constitution Act, 1867*. (See Appendix III for the text of those sections.) The Federal Court and the Tax Court have authority to conduct trials, and the decisions of each can be appealed to the Federal Court of Appeal, which in turn can be appealed to the Supreme Court of Canada.

Further, there are trial-level and appeal-level courts dealing with matters of military justice.

Finally, both the federal and provincial governments have the authority to create administrative tribunals that have jurisdiction to decide disputes in certain limited fields.

Appendix II

Canadian Charter of Rights and Freedoms

Whereas Canada is founded upon principles that recognize the supremacy of God and the rule of law.

Guarantee of Rights and Freedoms

1. The *Canadian Charter of Rights and Freedoms* guarantees the rights and freedoms set out in it subject only to such reasonable limits prescribed by law as can be demonstrably justified in a free and democratic society.

Fundamental Freedoms

2. Everyone has the following fundamental freedoms:

   (a) freedom of conscience and religion;

   (b) freedom of thought, belief, opinion and expression, including freedom of the press and other media of communication;

   (c) freedom of peaceful assembly; and

   (d) freedom of association.

Democratic Rights

3. Every citizen of Canada has the right to vote in an election of members of the House of Commons or of a legislative assembly and to be qualified for membership therein.

4. (1) No House of Commons and no legislative assembly shall continue for longer than five years from the date fixed for the return of the writs at a general election of its members.

(2) In time of real or apprehended war, invasion or insurrection, a House of Commons may be continued by Parliament and a legislative assembly may be continued by the legislature beyond five years if such continuation is not opposed by the votes of more than one-third of the members of the House of Commons or the legislative assembly, as the case may be.

5. There shall be a sitting of Parliament and of each legislature at least once every twelve months.

Mobility Rights

6. (1) Every citizen of Canada has the right to enter, remain in and leave Canada.

(2) Every citizen of Canada and every person who has the status of a permanent resident of Canada has the right

(a) to move to and take up residence in any province; and

(b) to pursue the gaining of a livelihood in any province.

(3) The rights specified in subsection (2) are subject to

(a) any laws or practices of general application in force in a province other than those that discriminate among persons primarily on the basis of province of present or previous residence; and

(b) any laws providing for reasonable residency requirements as a qualification of the receipt of publicly provided social services.

(4) Subsections (2) and (3) do not preclude any law, program or activity that has as its object the amelioration in a province of conditions of individuals in that province who are socially or economically disadvantaged if the rate of employment in that province is below the rate of employment in Canada.

Legal Rights

7. Everyone has the right to life, liberty and security of the person and the right not to be deprived thereof except in accordance with the principles of fundamental justice.

8. Everyone has the right to be secure against unreasonable search or seizure.

9. Everyone has the right not to be arbitrarily detained or imprisoned.

10. Everyone has the right on arrest or detention

(a) to be informed promptly of the reasons therefor;
(b) to retain and instruct counsel without delay and to be informed of that right; and
(c) to have the validity of the detention determined by way of *habeas corpus* and to be released if the detention is not lawful.

11. Any person charged with an offence has the right

(a) to be informed without unreasonable delay of the specific offence;

(b) to be tried within a reasonable time;

(c) not to be compelled to be a witness in proceedings against that person in respect of the offence;

(d) to be presumed innocent until proven guilty according to law in a fair and public hearing by an independent and impartial tribunal;

(e) not to be denied reasonable bail without just cause;

(f) except in the case of an offence under military law tried before a military tribunal, to the benefit of trial by jury where the maximum punishment for the offence is imprisonment for five years or a more severe punishment;

(g) not to be found guilty on account of any act or omission unless, at the time of the act or omission, it constituted an offence under Canadian or international law or was criminal according to the general principles of law recognized by the community of nations;

(h) if finally acquitted of the offence, not to be tried for it again and, if finally found guilty and punished for the offence, not to be tried or punished for it again; and

(i) if found guilty of the offence and if the punishment for the offence has been varied between the time of commission and the time of sentencing, to the benefit of the lesser punishment.

12. Everyone has the right not to be subjected to any cruel and unusual treatment or punishment.

13. A witness who testifies in any proceedings has the right not to have any incriminating evidence so given used to incriminate that witness in any other proceedings, except in a prosecution for perjury or for the giving of contradictory evidence.

14. A party or witness in any proceedings who does not understand or speak the language in which the proceedings are conducted or who is deaf has the right to the assistance of an interpreter.

Equality Rights

15. (1) Every individual is equal before and under the law and has the right to the equal protection and equal benefit of the law without discrimination and, in particular, without discrimination based on race, national or ethnic origin, colour, religion, sex, age or mental or physical disability.

(2) Subsection (1) does not preclude any law, program or activity that has as its object the amelioration of conditions of disadvantaged individuals or groups including those that are disadvantaged because of race, national or ethnic origin, colour, religion, sex, age or mental or physical disability.

Official Languages of Canada

16. (1) English and French are the official languages of Canada and have equality of status and equal rights and privileges as to their use in all institutions of the Parliament and government of Canada.

(2) English and French are the official languages of New Brunswick and have equality of status and equal rights and privileges as to their use in all institutions of the legislature and government of New Brunswick.

(3) Nothing in this Charter limits the authority of Parliament or a legislature to advance the equality of status or use of English and French.

16.1. (1) The English linguistic community and the French linguistic community in New Brunswick have equality of status and equal rights and privileges, including the right to distinct educational institutions and such distinct cultural institutions as are necessary for the preservation and promotion of those communities.

(2) The role of the legislature and government of New Brunswick to preserve and promote the status, rights and privileges referred to in subsection (1) is affirmed.

17. (1) Everyone has the right to use English or French in any debates and other proceedings of Parliament.

(2) Everyone has the right to use English or French in any debates and other proceedings of the legislature of New Brunswick.

18. (1) The statutes, records and journals of Parliament shall be printed and published in English and French and both language versions are equally authoritative.

(2) The statutes, records and journals of the legislature of New Brunswick shall be printed and published in English and French and both versions are equally authoritative.

19. (1) Either English or French may be used by any person in, or in any pleading in or process issuing from, any court established by Parliament.

(2) Either English or French may be used by any person in, or in any pleading in or process issuing from, any court of New Brunswick.

20. (1) Any member of the public in Canada has the right to communicate with, and to receive available services from, any head or central office of an institution of the Parliament or government of Canada in English or French, and has the same right with respect to any other office of any such institution where

(a) there is significant demand for communications with and services from that office in such language; or

(b) due to the nature of the office, it is reasonable that communications with and services from the office be available in both English and French.

(2) Any member of the public in New Brunswick has the right to communicate with, and to receive available services from, any office of an institution of the legislature or government of New Brunswick in English or French.

21. Nothing in sections 16 to 20 abrogates or derogates from any right, privilege or obligation with respect to the English and French languages, or either of them, that exists or is continued by virtue of any other provision of the Constitution of Canada.

22. Nothing in sections 16 to 20 abrogates or derogates from any legal or customary right or privilege acquired or enjoyed either before or after the coming into force of this Charter with respect to any language that is not English or French.

Minority Language Educational Rights

23. (1) Citizens of Canada

(a) whose first language learned and still understood is that of the English or French linguistic minority population of the province in which they reside, or

(b) who have received their primary school instruction in Canada in English or French and reside in a province where the language in which they received that instruction is the language of the English or French linguistic minority population of the province have the right to have their children receive primary and secondary school instruction in that language in that province.

(2) Citizens of Canada of whom any child has received or is receiving primary or secondary school instruction in English or French in Canada, have the right to have all their children receive primary and secondary school instruction in the same language.

(3) The right of citizens of Canada under subsections (1) and (2) to have their children receive primary and secondary school instruction in the language of the English or French linguistic minority population of a province

(a) applies wherever in the province the number of children of citizens who have such a right is sufficient to warrant the provision to them out of public funds of minority language instruction; and

(b) includes, where the number of those children so warrants, the right to have them receive that instruction in minority language educational facilities provided out of public funds.

Enforcement

24. (1) Anyone whose rights or freedoms, as guaranteed by this Charter, have been infringed or denied may apply to a court of competent jurisdiction to obtain such remedy as the court considers appropriate and just in the circumstances.

(2) Where, in proceedings under subsection (1), a court concludes that evidence was obtained in a manner that infringed or denied any rights or freedoms guaranteed by this Charter, the evidence shall be excluded if it is established that, having regard to all the circumstances, the admission of it in the proceedings would bring the administration of justice into disrepute.

General

25. The guarantee in this Charter of certain rights and freedoms shall not be construed so as to abrogate or derogate from any aboriginal, treaty or other rights or freedoms that pertain to the aboriginal peoples of Canada including

(a) any rights or freedoms that have been recognized by the Royal Proclamation of October 7, 1763; and

(b) any rights or freedoms that now exist by way of land claims agreements or may be so acquired.

26. The guarantee in this Charter of certain rights and freedoms shall not be construed as denying the existence of any other rights or freedoms that exist in Canada.

27. This Charter shall be interpreted in a manner consistent with the preservation and enhancement of the multicultural heritage of Canadians.

28. Notwithstanding anything in this Charter, the rights and freedoms referred to in it are guaranteed equally to male and female persons.

29. Nothing in this Charter abrogates or derogates from any rights or privileges guaranteed by or under the Constitution of Canada in respect of denominational, separate or dissentient schools.

30. A reference in this Charter to a province or to the legislative assembly or legislature of a province shall be deemed to include a reference to the Yukon Territory and the Northwest Territories, or to the appropriate legislative authority thereof, as the case may be.

31. Nothing in this Charter extends the legislative powers of any body or authority.

Application of Charter

32. (1) This Charter applies

(a) to the Parliament and government of Canada in respect of all matters within the authority of Parliament including all matters relating to the Yukon Territory and Northwest Territories; and

(b) to the legislature and government of each province in respect of all matters within the authority of the legislature of each province.

(2) Notwithstanding subsection (1), section 15 shall not have effect until three years after this section comes into force.

33. (1) Parliament or the legislature of a province may expressly declare in an Act of Parliament or of the legislature, as the case may be, that the Act or a provision thereof shall operate notwithstanding a provision included in section 2 or sections 7 to 15 of this Charter.

(2) An Act or a provision of an Act in respect of which a declaration made under this section is in effect shall have such operation as it would have but for the provision of this Charter referred to in the declaration.

(3) A declaration made under subsection (1) shall cease to have effect five years after it comes into force or on such earlier date as may be specified in the declaration.

(4) Parliament or a legislature of a province may re-enact a declaration made under subsection (1).

(5) Subsection (3) applies in respect of a re-enactment made under subsection (4).

Citation

34. This part may be cited as the *Canadian Charter of Rights and Freedoms.*

Appendix III

Division of Powers, *Constitution Act, 1867*

Legislative Authority of Parliament of Canada

91. It shall be lawful for the Queen, by and with the Advice and Consent of the Senate and House of Commons, to make Laws for the Peace, Order, and good Government of Canada, in relation to all Matters not coming within the Classes of Subjects by this Act assigned exclusively to the Legislatures of the Provinces; and for greater Certainty, but not so as to restrict the Generality of the foregoing Terms of this Section, it is hereby declared that (notwithstanding anything in this Act) the exclusive Legislative Authority of the Parliament of Canada extends to all Matters coming within the Classes of Subjects next hereinafter enumerated; that is to say,

1. Repealed.

1A. The Public Debt and Property.

2. The Regulation of Trade and Commerce.

2A. Unemployment insurance.

3. The raising of Money by any Mode or System of Taxation.

4. The borrowing of Money on the Public Credit.

5. Postal Service.

6. The Census and Statistics.

7. Militia, Military and Naval Service, and Defence.

8. The fixing of and providing for the Salaries and Allowances of Civil and other Officers of the Government of Canada.

9. Beacons, Buoys, Lighthouses, and Sable Island.

10. Navigation and Shipping.

11. Quarantine and the Establishment and Maintenance of Marine Hospitals.

12. Sea Coast and Inland Fisheries.

13. Ferries between a Province and any British or Foreign Country or between Two Provinces.

14. Currency and Coinage.

15. Banking, Incorporation of Banks, and the Issue of Paper Money.

16. Savings Banks.

17. Weights and Measures.

18. Bills of Exchange and Promissory Notes.

19. Interest.

20. Legal Tender.

21. Bankruptcy and Insolvency.

22. Patents of Invention and Discovery.

23. Copyrights.

24. Indians, and Lands reserved for the Indians.

25. Naturalization and Aliens.

26. Marriage and Divorce.

27. The Criminal Law, except the Constitution of Courts of Criminal Jurisdiction, but including the Procedure in Criminal Matters.

28. The Establishment, Maintenance, and Management of Penitentiaries.

29. Such Classes of Subjects as are expressly excepted in the Enumeration of the Classes of Subjects by this Act assigned exclusively to the Legislatures of the Provinces.

And any Matter coming within any of the Classes of Subjects enumerated in this Section shall not be deemed to come within the Class of Matters of a local or private Nature comprised in the Enumeration of the Classes of Subjects by this Act assigned exclusively to the Legislatures of the Provinces.

Exclusive Powers of Provincial Legislatures

92. In each Province the Legislature may exclusively make Laws in relation to Matters coming within the Classes of Subjects next hereinafter enumerated; that is to say,

1. Repealed.

2. Direct Taxation within the Province in order to the raising of a Revenue for Provincial Purposes.

3. The borrowing of Money on the sole Credit of the Province.

4. The Establishment and Tenure of Provincial Offices and the Appointment and Payment of Provincial Officers.

5. The Management and Sale of the Public Lands belonging to the Province and of the Timber and Wood thereon.

6. The Establishment, Maintenance, and Management of Public and Reformatory Prisons in and for the Province.

7. The Establishment, Maintenance, and Management of Hospitals, Asylums, Charities, and Eleemosynary Institutions in and for the Province, other than Marine Hospitals.

8. Municipal Institutions in the Province.

9. Shop, Saloon, Tavern, Auctioneer, and other Licences in order to the raising of a Revenue for Provincial, Local, or Municipal Purposes.

10. Local Works and Undertakings other than such as are of the following Classes:

   (*a*) Lines of Steam or other Ships, Railways, Canals, Telegraphs, and other Works and Undertakings connecting the Province with any other or others of the Provinces, or extending beyond the Limits of the Province;

   (*b*) Lines of Steam Ships between the Province and any British or Foreign Country;

   (*c*) Such Works as, although wholly situate within the Province, are before or after their Execution declared by the Parliament of Canada to be for the general Advantage of Canada or for the Advantage of Two or more of the Provinces.

11. The Incorporation of Companies with Provincial Objects.

12. The Solemnization of Marriage in the Province.

13. Property and Civil Rights in the Province.

14. The Administration of Justice in the Province, including the Constitution, Maintenance, and Organization of Provincial Courts, both of Civil and of Criminal Jurisdiction, and including Procedure in Civil Matters in those Courts.

15. The Imposition of Punishment by Fine, Penalty, or Imprisonment for enforcing any Law of the Province made in relation to any Matter coming within any of the Classes of Subjects enumerated in this Section.

16. Generally all Matters of a merely local or private Nature in the Province.

Bibliography

The following list includes references to books found to be valuable source materials in the preparation of this dictionary. The list does not purport to cover all the materials examined or cited in the text.

Abrams, Linda S., and Kevin P. McGuinness. *Canadian Civil Procedure Law*. Markham, Ont: LexisNexis, 2008.

Baker, J.H. *An Introduction to English Legal History*. 3rd ed. London: Butterworths, 1990.

Beale, Hugh G., ed. *Chitty on Contracts*. 30th ed. London: Sweet & Maxwell, 2008.

Beatson, Jack, Andrew Burrows, and John Cartwright. *Anson's Law of Contract*. 29th ed. Oxford: Oxford University Press, 2010.

Berryman, Jeffrey. *The Law of Equitable Remedies*. Toronto: Irwin Law, 2000.

Bissett-Johnson, Alastair, and Winifred Holland. *Matrimonial Property Law in Canada*. Agincourt: Burroughs, 1980.

Black, Howard S. *Wills and Estates: Cases, Text and Materials*. Toronto: Emond Montgomery, 2009.

Blake, Sara. *Administrative Law*. 5th ed. Markham, Ont.: LexisNexis Canada, 2011.

Boivin, Denis. *Insurance Law*. Toronto: Irwin Law, 2004.

Borrie, Gordon J. *Public Law*. 2d ed. London: Sweet & Maxwell, 1970.

Bouvier, John. *Bouvier's Law Dictionary*. 8th ed. by F. Rawles. St. Paul, Minn.: West Publishing Co., 1914.

Bryant, Alan W., Sidney N. Lederman, & Michelle K. Fuerst. *The Law of Evidence in Canada*. 3rd ed. Markham, Ont.: LexisNexis Canada, 2009.

Burn, E.H., *Cheshire and Burn's Modern Law of Real Property*. 16th ed. Oxford: Oxford University Press, 2000.

Castel, J.G. *Introduction to Conflict of Laws*, 4th ed. Markham, Ont.: LexisNexis Canada, 2002.

Coughlan, Steve. *Criminal Procedure*. 2nd ed. Toronto: Irwin Law, 2012.

Currie, John H. *Public International Law*. 2nd ed. Toronto: Irwin Law, 2008.

Currie, Robert J. *International and Transnational Criminal Law*. Toronto: Irwin Law 2010.

Curzon, L. B. *English Legal History*. 2d ed. Estover, Plymouth: MacDonald & Evans Ltd., 1979.

Davies, Paul L. *Gower and Davies' Principles of Modern Company Law*. 8th ed. London: Sweet & Maxwell, 2008.

Falconbridge, John Delatre. *The Law of Negotiable Instruments in Canada*. Toronto: Ryerson Press, 1964.

Fleming, J. *The Law of Torts*. 9th ed. Sydney: LBC Information Services, 1998.

Fodden, Simon R. *Family Law*. Toronto: Irwin Law, 1999.

Freeman, Mark, and Gibran Van Ert. *International Human Rights Law*. Toronto: Irwin Law, 2004.

Fridman, G.H.L. *Introduction to the Canadian Law of Torts*. Markham, Ont.: LexisNexis Canada, 2003.

_____. *Sale of Goods in Canada*. 5th ed. Toronto: Carswell, 2004.

_____. *Canadian Agency Law*. Markham, Ont.: LexisNexis Canada, 2009.

_____. *The Law of Torts in Canada*. 6th ed. Toronto: Carswell, 2010.

_____. *The Law of Contract in Canada*. 6th ed. Toronto: Carswell, 2011.

Furmston, M.P. *Cheshire, Fifoot and Furmston's Law of Contract*, 15th ed. Oxford: Oxford University Press, 2007.

Gall, Gerald L. *The Canadian Legal System*. 5th ed. Toronto: Carswell, 2004.

Gold, Edgar, Aldo Chircop, and Hugh Kindred. *Maritime Law*. Toronto: Irwin Law, 2003.

Green, L. C. *International Law Through the Cases*. 4th ed. London: Stevens & Sons. 1978.

Greenspan, Edward L., Marc Rosenberg, and Marie Henein. *Martin's Annual*

Criminal Code, 2012. Aurora, Ont.: Canada Law Book, 2011.

Harris, Edwin C. *Canadian Income Taxation.* 4th ed. Toronto: Butterworth & Co., 1986.

Hayton, David J. *Megarry's Manual of the Law of Real Property.* 6th ed. London: Stevens & Sons, 1982.

Hertz, Michael. *Introduction to Conflict of Laws.* Toronto: Carswell Co., 1978.

Heuston, R.F.V., & R.A. Buckley, *Salmond & Heuston on the Law of Torts.* 21st ed. London: Sweet & Maxwell, 1996.

Hogg, Peter W. *Constitutional Law of Canada.* 5th ed. Toronto: Carswell, 2007.

_____. *Canada Act 1982 Annotated.* Toronto: Carswell Co., 1982.

_____. *Meech Lake Constitutional Accord Annotated.* Toronto: Carswell Co., l988.

Hurtig, Mel. *The Canadian Encyclopedia.* 2d ed. Edmonton: Hurtig Publishers Co., 1988.

Inbau, Fred, et al. *Criminal Interrogation and Confessions.* 5th ed. Burlington, MA: Jones & Bartlett Learning, 2013.

Ivamy, E. R. Hardy. *General Principles of Insurance Law.* 5th ed. London: Butterworth & Co., 1986.

James, Fleming, Geoffrey C. Hazard, and John Leubsdorf. *Civil Procedure.* 4th ed. Toronto: Little, Brown & Co., 1992.

Jones, Martin, and Sasha Baglay. *Refugee Law.* Toronto: Irwin Law, 2007.

Kindred, Hugh M., et al. *International Law, Chiefly as Interpreted and Applied in Canada.* 7th ed. Toronto: Emond Montgomery, 2006.

Krishna, Vern. *Income Tax Law.* 2nd ed. Toronto: Irwin Law, 2012.

Linden, Allen M., and Bruce Feldthusen. *Canadian Tort Law.* 9th ed. Markham, Ont.: LexisNexis Canada, 2011.

Lord, Richard A. *Williston on Contracts.* 4th ed. Eagan, MN: West, 2004.

MacKenzie, James. *Feeney's Canadian Law of Wills.* 4th ed. Toronto: Butterworth & Co., 2000.

Makuch, Stanley M., Neil Craik and Signe B. Leisk. *Canadian Municipal and Planning Law.* 2nd ed. Toronto: Carswell, 2004.

Malanczuk, Peter. *Akehurst's Modern Introduction to International Law.* 7th rev. ed. London: Routledge, 1997.

Manning, Morris, and Peter Sankoff. *Criminal Law.* 4th ed. Markham, Ont.: LexisNexis Canada, 2009.

Marrocco, Frank N., and Henry M. Goslett. *The 2003 Annotated Immigration Act of Canada.* Toronto: Carswell-A Thompson Company, 2003.

Martin, Jill E. *Modern Equity.* 18th ed. London: Sweet & Maxwell, 2009.

McCamus, John D. *The Law of Contracts.* Toronto: Irwin Law, 2005.

McGregor, Harvey. *McGregor on Damages.* 18th ed. London: Sweet & Maxwell, 2009.

Meehan, Eugene, and John H. Currie. *The Law of Criminal Attempt.* 2nd ed. Toronto: Carswell, 2000.

Mill, John Stuart. *On Liberty and Other Essays.* Oxford: Oxford University Press, 1998.

Monahan, Patrick J. *Constitutional Law.* 3rd ed. Toronto: Irwin Law, 2006.

Mossman, Mary Jane. *Families and the Law: Cases and Commentary.* Toronto: Captus, 2012.

Mullan, D. *Administrative Law.* Toronto: Irwin Law, 2001.

Nadeau, Alain-Robert. *Federal Police Law 2010.* Toronto, Thomson Canada, 2009.

Oosterhoff, A. H., and W. B. Rayner. *Anger and Honsberger: Law of Real Property.* 2d ed. Aurora: Canada Law Book, 1985.

Osborne, P.H. *The Law of Torts.* 4th ed. Toronto: Irwin Law, 2011.

Paciocco, David M., and Lee Stuesser. *The Law of Evidence.* 6th ed. Toronto: Irwin Law, 2011.

Pollock, F., and F. W. Maitland. *History of English Law.* 2d ed. London: Cambridge Univ. Press, 1903.

Posner, Richard A. *Economic Analysis of Law.* 8th ed. New York: Aspen, 2011.

Price, Griffith. *The Law of Maritime Liens.* London: Sweet & Maxwell, 1940.

Reynolds, F.M.B. *Bowstead and Reynolds on Agency.* 18th ed. London: Sweet & Maxwell, 2006.

Roach, Kent. *Criminal Law*. 5th ed. Toronto: Irwin Law, 2012.

Rozovsky, Lorne E. *The Canadian Law of Consent to Treatment*. 3rd ed. Markham, Ont.: LexisNexis Canada, 2003.

Salhany, Roger E. *Canadian Criminal Procedure*. 6th ed. Toronto: Canada Law Book. 1994.

Schwartz, Victor E., Kathryn Kelly, and David F. Partlett. *Cases and Materials on Torts*. 11th ed. New York: Foundation Press, 2005.

Sharpe, Robert J., and Kent Roach. *The Canadian Charter of Rights and Freedoms*. 4th ed. Toronto: Irwin Law, 2009.

Sinclair, Alan M., & Margaret E. McCallum, *An Introduction to Real Property Law*. 6th ed. Markham, Ont.: LexisNexis Canada, 2012.

Stuart, Don. *Canadian Criminal Law: A Treatise*. Scarborough, Ont.: Carswell, 2011.

Sullivan, Ruth. *Statutory Interpretation*. 2nd ed. Toronto: Irwin Law, 2007.

Sutherland, H. *Fraser's Handbook on Canadian Company Law*. 8th ed. Toronto: Carswell Co., 1994.

Tapper, Colin. *Cross and Tapper on Evidence*. 12th ed. Oxford: Oxford University Press, 2010.

Traub, Walter M. *Falconbridge on Mortgages*. 5th ed. Aurora, Ont.: Canada Law Book, 2003.

VanDuzer, J. Anthony. *The Law of Partnerships and Corporations*. 3rd ed. Toronto: Irwin Law, 2009.

Vaver, David. *Intellectual Property Law*. 2nd ed. Toronto: Irwin Law, 2011.

Waddams, S.M. *The Law of Contracts*. 6th ed. Aurora, Ont.: Canada Law Book, 2010.

_____. *Introduction to the Study of Law*. 6th ed. Toronto: Carswell, 2004.

Walker, Janet. *Canadian Conflict of Laws*. 6th ed. Markham, Ont. LexisNexis Canada, 2005.

Walker, Janet, and Lorne Sossin. *Civil Litigation*. Toronto: Irwin Law, 2010.

Watson, Garry D., W. A. Bogart, Allan C. Hutchinson, and Robert J. Sharpe. *Canadian Civil Procedure*. 3d ed. Toronto: Emond Montgomery Publications Ltd., 1988.

Watson, Garry D., W. A. Bogart, Allan C. Hutchinson, Janet Mosher, and Kent Roach. *Civil Litigation*. 4th ed. Toronto: Emond Montgomery Publications Ltd., 1991.

Watts, Peter G. *Bowstead and Reynolds on Agency*. 19th ed. London: Sweet & Maxwell, 2010.

Williston, W. B., and R. J. Rolls. *The Law of Civil Procedure*. Toronto: Butterworth & Co., 1970.

Ziegel, J. S. *Studies in Canadian Company Law*. Toronto: Butterworth & Co., 1967.

Ziff, B., J. deBeer, D. Harris and M. McCallum. *A Property Law Reader* (2d ed. 2008).

Ziff, Bruce. *Principles of Property Law*. 5th ed. Toronto: Carswell, 2010.